Animals
and the Law

A Sourcebook

CONTEMPORARY LEGAL ⛪ ISSUES

Animals
and the Law

A Sourcebook

Jordan Curnutt

A B C 🍂 C L I O

Santa Barbara, California Denver, Colorado Oxford, England

Library of Congress Cataloging-in-Publication Data

Curnutt, Jordan.
Animals and the law : a sourcebook / Jordan Curnutt.
      p. cm. — (Contemporary legal issues)
   Includes bibliographical references and index.
   ISBN 1-57607-147-2 (hardcover : alk. paper); 1-57607-542-7 (e-book)
   1. Animal rights—United States. 2. Animal welfare—Law and legislation—United States. 3. Animals—Law and legislation—United States. I. Title. II. Series.
KF390.5.A5 C87 2001
344.73'049—dc21
2001004036

06 05 04 03 02 01   10 9 8 7 6 5 4 3 2 1

This book is also available on the World Wide Web as an e-book.
Visit abc-clio.com for details.

ABC-CLIO, Inc.
130 Cremona Drive, P.O. Box 1911
Santa Barbara, California 93116–1911

This book is printed on acid-free paper ∞.

Manufactured in the United States of America

For Gabriel

Contents

Preface

Animals and the Law is a survey of the most important federal and state laws, regulations, and court cases concerning nonhuman animals. Our focus is especially on laws establishing protections for these creatures, but we also consider many of the restrictions on keeping animals as property; some laws simultaneously regulate the use of animals as property *and* promote nonhuman well-being. Although this book is not the first one in the relatively new discipline of animal law, no other text has brought together as much legal and factual material ranging over the entire field of human practices involving animals. After an initial discussion on the nature of legal rights and their relevance to nonhumans, five successive chapters discuss not only the key legal rules and judicial decisions, but also sketch the activities with animals that the law seeks to govern.

We begin with companion animals—"pets." Here, we first outline anticruelty laws, followed by an examination of two cruelty-related issues, animal hoarding and human sexual contact with animals. After that, our attention turns to shelters and pounds, and then a concentration on laws impacting the two most highly prized companion animals, dogs and horses. The next chapter covers animal agriculture, with an emphasis on the slaughter of livestock for human consumption; along with transportation standards, this is the main area where legal restrictions on the use of farm animals are found. This chapter closes with sections on the other major forms of animal agriculture, fur farming and commercial trapping.

Our inquiry then takes us to the use of nonhumans for entertainment: circuses, zoos, dog races, horse races, rodeos, cockfighting, and dogfighting. The regulation of recreational hunting is included here as well since "sport" hunting is a manner of exploiting animals primarily for human amusement or play. A chapter on wildlife follows this one. Dominating our discussion of wild animals are legal protections for migratory birds and endangered animal species, bears and bald eagles, fur seals, dolphins, whales, and marine mammals generally. Finally, the chapter on laboratory animals highlights the federal Animal Welfare Act and its regulations, the preeminent source of legal standards for the care and treatment of the several species used as subjects for research and testing. Ancillary standards from the National Institutes of Health and the Public Health Service are also surveyed here. This chapter additionally features sections on primates as laboratory animals, the dissection of animal bodies in higher education, and legal protections for research facilities against vandals and saboteurs.

Animals and the Law is presented in accessible, ordinary English, defining or explaining all technical terms and legal jargon. Aiming at an audience that knows little or nothing about the law, I have written here principally for the general, college-educated reader with serious interests in human practices involving animals and in the legal rules that structure and guide those practices. Even so, I also presume that this book will be useful to legal professionals and law students, especially those studying and working in animal law. Thus, I have attempted to strike a balance between the ponderous, footnote- and citation-ridden legal prose characteristic of law reviews and a facile form of "pop" law that sacrifices rigor and depth for an easy appeal. It remains of course for readers to judge how well I have achieved that equilibrium.

Jordan Curnutt

Acknowledgments

A book of this scope cannot be the product of one person. The invaluable contributions of many people have made *Animals and the Law* far better than it otherwise would have been. I am most grateful to all these benefactors. Here at St. Cloud State University in Minnesota, special recognition must be given to Ann Lindstrom, my research assistant, whose determined and diligent searches saved me many hours of labor; Joan Discroll, librarian in the Inter-Library Loan office, whose patience and willingness to track down books and articles from all over the country transformed a teaching college into something resembling a research institution; and Connie Hoffman, Government Documents Librarian, who often guided me through the intricacies of these most obscure of catalogued items.

In addition, numerous individuals working around the country in the animal protection community, in the animal use community, in government, and in the private sector have given generously of their time and expertise. Among those especially deserving of commendation are Jonathan Balcombe (Associate Director for Education, Animal Research Issues), Erik Sakach (West Coast Regional Office Director), Ellen Buck (D.V.M., Director of Equine Protection), and Julie Shellenberger (Issues Specialist, Companion Animal Outreach), all from the Humane Society of the United States; Gary Guccione, Executive Director, National Greyhound Association; Linda Blythe, D.V.M. and Professor of Veterinary Medicine, Oregon State University; Jane Garrison, Elephant Specialist, People for the Ethical Treatment of Animals; Robin Duxbury, Investigations Director, Project Equus; John Kooney, The Jockey Club; Bob Adamcik and Doug Staller, both wildlife biologists for the United States Fish & Wildlife Service; Gene Bauston of Farm Sanctuary; Susan Netboy, Director, Greyhound Protection League; David Wolfson, attorney at Millbank, Hadley, McCloy & Tweed; Cindy Shoonholz and T. J. Walter, both of the Professional Rodeo Cowboys Association; Teresa Platt, Executive Director, Fur Commission USA; Camilla Fox, Wildlife Program Coordinator, Animal Protection Institute; Keith Roehr, D.V.M. and Pet Care Facilities Veterinarian, Colorado Department of Agriculture; Dorothy Woodland, Food Safety Inspection Service, United States Department of Agriculture; Kimberly Pacheco, Freedom of Information Act officer for the Animal and Plant Health Inspection Service, United States Department of Agriculture; Temple Grandin, Assistant Professor of Animal Science at Colorado State University and consultant and designer for Grandin Livestock Handling Systems Inc.; Ariana Huemer; and Dug Hanbicki.

I should also mention my editor at ABC-CLIO, Alicia Merritt, whose faith and flexibility have been indispensable for bringing this project to a successful conclusion.

Finally, my deepest debts, for this and so much more, are to my wife Rosemarie, for cheerfully and lovingly enduring life with a temperamental writer struggling with a boundless topic and limited talent.

Animals and the Law

A Sourcebook

1. Introduction

WHAT IS ANIMAL LAW?

Animal law is the set of legal rules governing human practices that involve animals—what is done with these nonhuman beings. Humans have raised, trained, worked, fought, confined, lived with, slept with, experimented on, collected and displayed, bought and sold, and disposed of animals for thousands of years. And, of course, since *Homo sapiens* first walked the earth humans have killed countless animals for food, to fashion material goods, as sacrifices to hungry gods, and for recreation.

Animal Property and Animal Protection

The earliest animal laws were written by people who viewed animals entirely as property, as things to possess and use. These original rules regulated commerce and ownership—transferring, acquiring, and holding animals—and established liability for harm caused by owned beasts.

For example, the *Laws of Hammurabi*, from the eighteenth century B.C.E., specified how sheep, goats, cattle, and oxen were to be traded and branded. Hammurabi also ordered that a fine be paid by the owner of an ox that gores "a free-born man to death." Roman law of the fifth century B.C.E. allowed a herder to drive animals across another citizen's land if the road was impassable, and further stipulated that the owner of an animal that injures livestock belonging to another must surrender the offending beast to him. Animal laws of this nature are focused wholly on promoting human goals and interests by establishing rules to structure and guide these practices; they are not concerned with the welfare of the nonhumans involved.

Yet there are a few fleeting instances in which the laws of antiquity appear to have given some weight to the interests of the animals. In the Bible, which formed the legal foundation for Hebrew society and heavily influenced later European codes, King Solomon in his book of Proverbs announces that "[t]he righteous man cares for the needs of his animal." Also, the method of kosher slaughter, developed from the dietary rules set down in Leviticus and substantially reproduced by the halal slaughter of Islam, is widely regarded as a humane innovation of that biblical age. Kosher and halal demand a single cut across the jugular vein with a very sharp knife, a far easier death than a brutal beating, slow strangulation, or disembowelment.

Even so, concern for animal interests was far from the only motivation behind these specimens of ancient law. Because livestock supplied humans with food, comfort, and prosperity, among other things, it made good economic sense to take good care of one's animals. In that light, Solomon's aphorism could be simply a very early example of legal paternalism (restricting behavior that harms oneself) from an eminently patriarchal religious tradition. Similarly, killing animals by kosher and halal methods, in particular the requirement that the creature be alive and conscious, made for more hygienic meat, safer for human consumption at a time without refrigeration when fortuitously encountered carcasses presented a tempting but suspect source of nourishment.

These mixed motivations are manifested in animal law to this day, in which both human interests and animal interests are served to varying degrees, in the process sometimes pursuing complementary or conflicting legislative goals. Modern dog law and horse law provide many instances in which legal rules differentially weigh human and nonhuman concerns on a sort of sliding scale. Some have nothing to do with animal well-being, intending instead to promote human aims and ends exclusively. Others present a blend of motivations, benefiting both sorts of beings, while still others strongly emphasize animal protection. This yields a collection of laws that often have profoundly disparate orientations.

To illustrate these ideas, consider first that nearly every state code now includes an equine activity liability act (EALA), a statute that absolves operators of "horse-for-hire" businesses from legal responsibility when their customers suffer injuries while riding rented animals. From the same perspective, numerous city councils across America have enacted breed specific legislation (BSL) banning or severely restricting ownership of the dogs commonly called Pit Bulls. Both EALAs and BSL are intensely focused on human needs and desires concerning property and public safety, and neither gives animal welfare any weight. These are laws *involving* animals, but they do not have any *regard* for them; they do not give the interests of the nonhumans any consideration.

Yet, along with human purposes, other statutes do consider the animals. For example, leash laws preserve human property interests in dogs—containing them to ensure possession—while the control demanded also promotes community safety. At the same time, these laws also benefit the animals, as lost dogs often end up being euthanized in a pound or shelter, and loose ones often get hit by cars or injured by other animals.

On the other hand, some items of canine and equine law do fasten upon animal interests, and seem to care little for human well-being. For instance, the federal Animal Welfare Act (AWA) stipulates that dogs held at research facilities must be given regular opportunities for exercise and cannot be continuously locked away in a cage. Likewise, the federal Horse Protection Act bans "soring," a practice associated with competition in some horse shows, in which persistent pain is deliberately caused in a horse's feet, prompting the animal to accentuate its gait. Again, dogs and horses are covered by anticruelty statutes (every state has one), laws that in general prohibit torturing, mutilating, abandoning, failing to provide proper care, or otherwise mistreating animals. As a final example, the Marine Mammal Protection Act is a federal statute that outlaws harassing, hunting, capturing, or killing whales, dolphins, polar bears, sea otters, seals, and walruses. These sorts of legal rules—call them animal *protection* laws—have a different orientation than EALAs or BSL.

Animal Protection Law and Animal Rights

Looking across the sweep of human history, we see that animal protection laws are a very recent development. While, as previously noted, animal *property* laws are millennia old, legal rules specifically and essentially designed by legislatures to promote the interests of animals did not exist anywhere in the Western world until less than two centuries ago. Indeed, it is only within the last half of the twentieth century that the U.S. Congress has taken an active role in establishing standards for animal protection, having formerly relied on the states' anticruelty statutes to do the job on the rare occasions when lawmakers believed there was a job that needed doing. Today, many uses of wild and domestic animals are restricted at least to some extent by national laws that weigh nonhuman interests heavily, though our interests in our property and safety still figure prominently in contemporary animal law at all levels of legislation.

The rise of animal protection law in the United States over the last several decades is mainly a response by legislators to the heightened concerns of Americans about animal welfare, especially that of their pet dogs and cats. People also became worried about the treatment of other animals used in laboratories, and the fate of several highly social and intelligent wild species such as monkeys, apes, whales, and dolphins. The ascendancy of this type of legislation can be seen as a dimension of the environmental consciousness that developed in the 1960s, when many in the United States and in other nations became increasingly aware of the devastation wrought by human activity on the natural world. People looked to legal mechanisms to do something about it. During the 1970s and 1980s, ordinary citizens, along with activists working for animal protection organizations, marched and lobbied, demanding the attention of people with political influence, and new laws were written aimed at enhancing the quality of certain animals' lives.

Laws like these that strongly emphasize animal welfare, protecting the basic interests of nonhuman beings, suggest that lawmakers have created legal rights for these fortunate species. The Animal Welfare Act, say, gives certain animals a right to be provided with food and water every day, while anticruelty statutes give others a right to decent treatment, and, most strongly, some federal laws give whales and dolphins a right to life.

This idea is powerfully reinforced by such seminal works as *Animals and Their Legal Rights,* first published by the Animal Welfare Institute in 1968 and now in its fourth edition, with contents detailing legal safeguards for many domestic and wild species. Yet the conclusion that animal protection laws provide legal rights for nonhumans is not self-evident or uncontroversial. Although the issue of whether or not animals have *moral* rights has been hotly debated by philosophers, theologians, and other interested individuals for years, the matter of their holding *legal* rights is a relatively new topic for discussion.

Some legal scholars and commentators, scrutinizing the intentions of legislators and the opinions of judges, contend that at bottom *all* animal law is meant to serve human interests. They say that once one digs for the reasons *why* laws protecting animals are enacted, one finds that the ultimate motivation for these legal rules is to regulate the use of a rather curious object—a living, sentient being—to shield our property and our persons, not to benefit the animals themselves. Safeguards for animals are much more happy side effects than genuine legislative goals. This means that animals do not really have any legal rights at all.

This problem is addressed in the next chapter, where the possibility of legal rights for animals is explored. Even so, it is not necessary to settle the matter, and it is not the goal of this book to do so. Here, it is important to note only that "animal law" is not equivalent to "animal rights law." If indeed animals have no legal rights, this does not eliminate animal law as a legitimate and viable discipline that inventories both the regulation of property in animals, according to human interests, and the rules designed to protect the welfare of nonhumans themselves. In any case, how such laws can present a blending of these motivations has already been addressed.

Reflecting the recent concern for animal welfare, this book focuses on animal protection law, and presents a comprehensive survey of the legal rules with that orientation. Nonetheless, numerous occasions arise to discuss many of the laws involving animals that primarily or exclusively promote human interests in their own property, security, and general well-being. Consistent with the emphasis here, some items of animal property law are neglected in the coming pages, notably various issues relating to domestic animals in contract law and tort law. For example, the book does not discuss determinations of custody of pets following divorce, tenants' right to keep pets in rental property, the patenting of animals, or the nature of animal bailments (the responsibilities of persons possessing animals who are not their owners). Also set aside here are emotional distress claims and noneconomic damages for harm caused to animals, veterinary malpractice, and wills providing for companion animals.

SOURCES OF THE LAW

Most bodies of law are not static and fixed; they are fluid and dynamic. Animal law is no exception. Any discussion of animals and the law can at best offer only a snapshot of the current, and often temporary, state of affairs, along with views of what has gone before. This caveat should be kept firmly in mind while reading this book. To reinforce the idea the reader will often encounter such qualifying phrases as "currently," "presently," "at this time," and "at this writing" prefacing a description of some legal rule. Animal law in particular developed rapidly during the 1990s, and today it seems that something new arises every week. Back in 1980, there were no animal law texts, no law school courses studying animal law, and no lawyers specializing in the discipline. Two decades later, at least twenty books and one journal are devoted wholly to animal law, a dozen or more law schools offer animal law courses, including those at Harvard, Yale, and Georgetown, and hundreds of lawyers now focus on this legal arena.

Adding to its vitality, and unlike some other areas, Congress and the federal judiciary do not dominate animal law—to concentrate on that level is to miss much of the story. The activities of lawmakers and judges in the various states must be accounted for as well. Every effort has been made to present a survey of laws that is not only thorough, given this work's emphasis on animal protection, but also as up to date as possible. Nonetheless, it is likely that by the time these words are read, new laws will have been enacted, old ones modified, and key court cases decided that significantly alter the legal terrain. That is just the nature of the beast.

Fortunately, there are several ways to stay on top of the most recent developments. In print media, the *Congressional Quarterly Weekly* and the *Federal Register* are essential for tracking the progress of specific bills in Congress and for studying announcements of regulations issued by federal agencies, respectively. Major newspapers such as *The Washington Post, The New York Times,* and *The Los Angeles Times* often have timely reports of important events in the federal judiciary and in Congress. For electronic media, bills on Capitol Hill can be followed on the World Wide Web through the Thomas Legislative Information website at http://thomas.loc.gov, and the *Federal Register* is available through the Government Printing Office homepage, http://www.access.gpo.gov/su_docs.

Additionally, several animal protection organizations feature on their websites thorough updates for both federal and state legislation. The Animal Protection Institute (http://www.api4animals.org) and the Doris Day Animal League (http://www.ddal.org) are especially recommended. Government links on the homepages of all fifty states can provide access to bills moving through the legislatures of those jurisdictions, as well as to the rule-making process of state regulatory agencies.

This summary of media providing information on the continuing evolution of animal law indicates the three main sources for law generally: (1) acts of legislatures, both in Congress and in state capitals; (2) rules promulgated by federal and state regulatory agencies; and (3) the decisions of judges in federal and state courts. County commissioners and city councils also establish county and municipal ordinances, but, with a few exceptions (such as some items in dog law and horse law), these are not significant for animal law. The book discusses each of these sources, the basics of their procedures, and the recording of their pronouncements below.

Federal and state laws can exist independently of one another, so long as there is no inconsistency between them. If they are incompatible, the state law must give way, as authorized by Article VI, Section 2 of the U.S. Constitution. Known as the Supremacy Clause, this section declares that federal laws are the supreme law of the land, and state or local laws conflicting with them are unconstitutional. Also, only federal law can govern legal matters that cross state borders, in particular any sort of business activity that involves the exchange of goods or services for money, or simply that affects interstate commerce. The Commerce Clause in Article I, Section 8 of the Constitution gives Congress the power "to regulate commerce . . . among the several states."

Acts of Legislatures and Rules of Agencies

An act of Congress or a state legislature (often called an assembly) exemplifies the legislative branch of government as a source of law. Legal rules issuing from this source are called statutes. Such laws begin as "bills" introduced by one or more members of the legislature. The bill is then typically assigned to a committee or subcommittee that studies the subject matter addressed by the bill. After hearings and testimony concerning the proposal, and various drafts have been composed, the committee votes on the bill. If the committee vote is affirmative, it is then referred to all the members of the legislature for a full vote.

If the lawmakers pass the bill, it is then forwarded to the chief executive of the jurisdiction, either the president, in the case of federal legislation, or the governor of the state. When the chief executive signs off on a bill, it becomes a law or statute (bills can also become law if the legislature overrides a veto by the chief executive). The law is then "codified" or recorded in its final form in a "code book," an inventory of laws. At the federal level, the principal book of laws is the *United States Code* (USC), and each of the states has its own code book as well (the *Alabama Code,* the *Alaska Code,* etc.). The USC is arranged according to fifty different categories or "titles." State code books are also arranged by titles, though not necessarily the same ones or in the same order as the USC. Within each title, specific laws may be listed by chapter, subchapter, part, article, or section number, or by some combination of these divisions.

Legal citation at all levels of government is notoriously arcane and impenetrable for those outside of the profession, mainly because there are many different numbering systems with no standard format. There is, however, a general ordering principle that can make things clearer. The citation for a law in a code book typically contains two sets of numbers, usually separated by a dash, a dot, or an abbreviation for the code book. The first number indicates the title and the second the section, chapter, article, or other division. For example, the citation for the Animal Welfare Act of 1970 is 7 USC § 2131, indicating that this statute is found under Title 7 ("Agriculture") of the *United States Code*, beginning at section (§) 2131. Citations can be more specific. The Georgia law requiring that sodium pentobarbital alone be used to euthanize dogs and cats at animal shelters is cited as § 4–11–5.1, meaning it is in Title 4 ("Animals"), Chapter 11 ("Animal Protection"), Section 5.1.

The second source of law is federal and state administrative agencies. These government offices create laws when they issue regulations, as authorized to do so by a statute that the legislature has enacted. In animal law, the agencies of greatest significance are the Animal and Plant Health Inspection Service, a division of the U.S. Department of Agriculture; the U.S. Fish and Wildlife Service, located in the Department of the Interior; and their counterparts at the state level. Collectively, federal and state agencies regulate to varying degrees the care of some or all of the animals kept in laboratories, in zoos, in circuses, on breeding farms, at pet stores, at race tracks, in pounds, at shelters, and by animal dealers; the transportation and slaughtering of animals used for food; the safety of certain protected wildlife species; and the activities of hunters and trappers. Even so, the treatment of many animals is not regulated by any government office, notably those used for food and fur while they are still on the farm, animals performing in rodeos, and the creatures kept as pets in the homes of private citizens.

The point of administrative agencies is to form a group of professionals who are experts in a particular field. The application of their expertise is intended to effectively regulate a specific industry or area of commerce with rules that legislators, lacking the requisite aptitude, are not as well qualified to write. As required by the federal Administrative Procedure Act, and similar state laws, regulatory agencies must make proposed rules available to the public for comment, and the agency must duly consider these remarks before issuing a final rule. At the federal level, proposed rules and those that have been officially implemented are published each day in the *Federal Register*. Once finalized, federal regulations are compiled annually in the *Code of Federal Regulations* (CFR), a multivolume set organized and cited in the same manner as the USC. Each state also has numerous books of regulations of its own, again referenced by title and a division number (chapter, section, etc.).

The USC and the CFR can be found in university and municipal libraries all over the country, and in every law school library. Both resources are also available in their entirety on the World Wide Web at the Lexis-Nexis Academic Universe website under "Legal Research" (http://web.lexis-nexis.com/universe). State codes can also be searched here, but regulations from the fifty jurisdictions are much harder to come by. Even though most state agencies have homepages, easily accessed through the Findlaw state resources website (http://www.findlaw.com/11stategov), they may or may not include links to regulations. However, upon request, these agencies will send paper copies of regulations to interested individuals, usually free of charge. Law libraries typically have the regulations only for the state in which the school is located.

The relative impact of federal and state statutes and regulations, and the effect of legal rules generally on animal law, is far from uniform. Some dimensions of animal use are quite restricted and heavily regulated, while others are only lightly touched by the law. The Endangered Species Act, for example, occupies 36 pages of the USC and its implementing regulations cover 330 pages of the CFR (1999). On the other hand, the Humane Methods of Slaughter Act requires only 2 and 5 pages, respectively. Again, no federal law and only one state law places any restrictions at all on how mink are raised on fur farms. Furthermore, the federal government sometimes monopolizes a regulatory area in which the states have little involvement; other times these roles are reversed. To illustrate, consider that the states have little to do with standards for the care and treatment of laboratory animals, but are almost solely responsible for regulating recreational hunting and commercial trapping. At the same time, the federal government tightly controls the husbandry of animals at research facilities and has next to nothing to say to hunters and trappers of unprotected wildlife.

Decisions of Judges

The decisions judges make in state and federal courts are the third source of law, what is generally known as case law. Their judgments are based on a case-by-case interpretation of the state or federal constitution, and the relevant statutes and regulations. Judges look to these documents to guide and validate their opinions, and these decisions become law. Sometimes, however, judges must reach a conclusion in cases in which the constitution does not provide any explicit direction, and lawmakers have not supplied an applicable statute or regulation. In such "cases of first impression," judges must create the law by issuing a ruling that establishes a precedent. These precedent-setting decisions are examined closely by other judges in similar cases.

The determinations judges make in the absence of constitutional guidance, and when neither statutes supplied by lawmakers nor regulations promulgated by regulatory agencies apply, compose the common law. The rules of the common law are based on judges' understanding of prevailing social customs or practices, or what seems appropriate or reasonable in the particular circumstances of the case at hand. State and federal legislatures sometimes react to this "judge-made" law by writing the decision into subsequent legislation, or by passing laws that counteract a judge's decision with which they disagree.

Most opinions of judges in particular cases, whether forming the common law or interpreting codified statutory or regulatory law, are published in various court reporters. The federal judicial system is arranged hierarchically with the U.S. Supreme Court at the top. The decisions of the Supreme Court are published in the *United States Reports*, a publication of the federal government, and in the *Supreme Court Reporter*, issued by West Publishers of St. Paul, Minnesota. These opinions are cited by naming the parties to the dispute, followed by the volume and first page where the opinion appears in the publication, and the year the decision was rendered. For example, in *Lujan v. Defenders of Wildlife*, 504 U.S. 555 (1992), the first name refers to the "plaintiff" in the case, the party filing the complaint. The second name refers to the "defendant," the individual responding to the suit. The citation indicates that this case is in volume 504 of the *United States Reports* (abbreviated "U.S."), begins on page 555, and that it was decided in 1992.

Although the Constitution does not explicitly say so, since the historic *Marbury v. Madison* case in 1803 the Supreme Court has been regarded as having the power of "judicial review." This is the right to decide the constitutionality of every law, whether state or federal. Because the Supreme Court is the final arbiter of the law—there is no appeal from its judgments—it has the ultimate power to restrict legislative and regulatory activity. For these reasons, Supreme Court decisions are the most important items in case law.

Next in judicial importance below the Supreme Court is a system of federal appellate courts. These United States Courts of Appeals are divided into thirteen "circuits" according to twelve geographical regions and the federal circuit. Opinions of the various circuit courts are compiled in the *Federal Reporter*, also by West Publishing. For example, in *Stack v. Killian*, 96 F.3d 159 (6th Cir. 1996), Stack is the plaintiff, Killian the defendant, and the opinion is in volume 96 of the *Federal Reporter, Third Series* (abbreviated "F.3d"), beginning on page 159. The case was decided in 1996 by the United States Court of Appeals for the Sixth Circuit.

Below the circuit courts are ninety-six federal district courts. These are grouped geographically, and each state typically has one or two federal districts, depending on population. These opinions are cited in the same manner as those of the other federal courts: a volume and page number is sandwiched around an abbreviation for the relevant publication, with the year of decision and the court location tagged on at the end. District court opinions are collected in the *Federal Supplement,* also published by West, and cited as "F. Supp."

Finally, there are also many courts in each state's judiciary, including a supreme court, appellate courts, and superior and municipal courts. Many of these decisions are collected in West's National Reporter System that divides the country into seven geographical regions, with these abbreviations: Atlantic (A.), North Eastern (N.E.), North Western (N.W.), Pacific (P.), South Eastern (S.E.), Southern (So.), and South Western (S.W.). Citations here proceed in the familiar pattern, inserting the appropriate regional reporter abbreviation between the volume and page number. The court in which the case was decided appears in parentheses following the page number and before the year. For example, in *Hargrove v. State,* 321 S.E.2d 104 (Ga. 1984), the "Ga." indicates that the case was decided in the Georgia Supreme Court ("Ga." for Georgia). *Brackett v. State,* 236 S.E.2d 689 (Ga. Ct. App. 1977), on the other hand, was decided in the Georgia Court of Appeals, abbreviated "Ct. App."

Although any big city public library or major university library usually has one or both of the *United States Reports* and the *Supreme Court Reporter,* the federal and regional reporters tend to be harder to find outside of law schools. A library collection often contains only the reporters for the region in which the library is located. Fortunately, the Lexis-Nexis Academic Universe website (URL listed above) also contains full-text versions of both the federal and state cases (mainly high court and appellate levels) published in the court reporters.

The focus and importance of case law in the field of animal law varies a great deal depending on the area of animal use being considered. In wildlife law and in laws governing research facilities and exhibitors, the federal judiciary completely dominates state courts simply because the major legal rules that protect these animals are statutes enacted by Congress and regulations coming from federal agencies (especially the Animal Welfare Act, the Endangered Species Act, and the Marine Mammal Protection Act). On the other hand, the numerous opinions in animal cruelty cases, including animal-fighting litigation, almost exclusively originate with state judges who are interpreting the anticruelty laws of their jurisdictions.

Also, the sheer volume of litigation under various laws involving animals can be radically different, according to the species and what is being done with them. Court opinions under federal wildlife laws that protect certain species far outnumber those in any other area, totaling many hundreds, while the case law for rodeo animals, food animals, and fur farms is virtually nonexistent. The disparity is explained in large part by the fact that the use of wildlife is subject to a vast array of statutes and regulations while the use of animals in agriculture is almost completely unrestricted. These variations are reflected in the cases selected for inclusion in this book.

PLAN OF THIS BOOK

Animals thoroughly pervade human society, from its core to the margins and beyond. Animals are everywhere, they are all around us. This ubiquity spawns myriad opportunities for the law to regulate human practices involving nonhuman beings.

Animals are closest to us in our homes, where we keep them by the hundreds of millions—mainly domestic dogs and cats, but also rodents and birds, amphibians and reptiles. Here they live with us as pets or, more strongly, as "companions" cohabiting in a kind of extended family. Horses' lives too are closely connected with humans, these trusted beasts of burden boarded in stables or residing in our own backyards. These domestic animals have a high level of dependence on people, relying upon them for food, water, shelter, safety, exercise, and even some measure of psychological well-being. Such close associations bring humans and nonhumans into continuous contact, giving rise to legal rules governing how we treat our animal companions, especially when we house them in such numbers that they overflow out of our homes and exceed our capacity to responsibly care for them.

Animals are also pervasively present on our plates, as food. More precisely, body parts from millions of cattle, hogs, and sheep and from billions of poultry are in the meals that the vast majority of Americans eat every day. Before that, of course, these animals lived on farms or ranches, in feedlots, barns, warehouses, or other buildings, and were then transported to a processing facility, where they were slaughtered and packaged for consumption. Cow milk and chicken eggs are also featured in the diet of nearly everyone, and millions more individuals of these species are held in agricultural operations spread throughout the country. Mink and fox are cultivated on fur farms, their pelts to be stripped from their dead bodies and fashioned into garments for people to wear. Millions more wild animals suffer a similar fate in nature, trapped in unforgiving metal devices. Laws direct how the animals used in agriculture are raised, transported, captured, and killed.

Other wild species—elephants, dolphins, monkeys, bears, lions, and many more—are kept in cages or other forms of confinement; put on display in zoos to amuse and educate us; and presented as performers to entertain us in circuses and carnivals, on television, and in film. Cattle are put through their paces in rodeos, often chased by horses, which are also found, along with dogs, running races to feed our appetite for gambling. These animals are housed, moved from place to place, presented, exhibited, posed, trained, and ridden as spectator sports. Many different laws stipulate how these animal entertainers are to be kept and provided for, while on stage, in some type of conveyance, and between "acts."

Numerous wildlife species are pursued and shot, hunted as another kind of entertainment, recreational killing called a sport (this is rarely done for subsistence to stock essential food stores). The activities of the hunt are legally regulated in large part to ensure that a certain number of wild animals can be killed without decimating the species as a whole, trading the interests of individuals for the continuing existence of the group. Yet hunting regulations, and later blanket protections for particular species, came about as an exercise in crisis intervention when unrestricted human predation devastated the populations of various kinds of waterfowl and migratory birds, as well as eagles, wild equines, bears, fur seals, whales, dolphins, and then marine mammals generally. Some forms of wildlife were eliminated entirely, while others were brought to the brink of extinction before legal rules were enacted to stop their slide into oblivion.

Finally, millions of rats, mice, rabbits, hamsters, guinea pigs, dogs, cats, and monkeys are kept in research facilities as laboratory models for human physiology and psychology, as subjects in biomedical and psychological research, for toxicity and consumer products testing, and for biology education. These species are infected with numerous diseases, injected with many chemicals, subjected to manifold noxious substances, manipulated and injured, vivisected and dissected, sometimes with pain relief and sometimes without it. Inevitably, they are then euthanized. Laws answer the question of how all of these creatures should be sheltered and confined, handled and transported, and ultimately disposed of. There is also the question of the legal regulation of their treatment during the laboratory procedure that calls for the use of their bodies.

Ordering of the Chapters

Chapters 3 through 7—"Companion Animals," "Animal Agriculture," "Animal Entertainment," "Wild Animals," and "Laboratory Animals"—are ordered in progression from those animals closest to us to those most distant from our daily lives. These chapters begin at the heart of the human world—our own homes—where companion animals reside and food animals depart, and then move out through the urban venues where we confine animals to entertain us, and on to the wild animals inhabiting the fringes of our society, ripe for hunting or preserving as we so desire. Last, at the furthest remove from human experience, yet paradoxically abiding in our midst, are the laboratory animals that so very few of us ever see and about which we have little knowledge. Unlike the pets and farm animals we encounter every day, or the exhibited animals we can view at will after a short drive or by simply turning on the television, or the wildlife we can observe out in the country or even within city limits, laboratory animals exist behind the locked doors of research facilities, inaccessible to the public eye.

This sequencing principle for arranging these chapters does not, however, dictate any particular reading order. Each chapter is designed to be read independently of the rest, and none presuppose that any other part of the text has been read at all. The same applies to the main sections within the chapters, as listed in the table of contents. Although the section headings are organized within each chapter either chronologically or thematically (sometimes both), they can be read separately as self-contained units forming a discrete narrative, just like the chapters themselves. As a sourcebook, the text is designed to be readily digested piecemeal, though a cover-to-cover reading should go as smoothly as a pick-and-choose approach.

Chapter 2, "Animals and Rights," also need not be read immediately following this introductory chapter or before any of the others. Its section headings too can stand alone, though, above all the rest, perusal of this chapter in sequence is the most profitable approach for the reader. The subject matter here, as the name suggests, is the nature of legal rights and their relevance to animals. This is the most philosophical and polemical portion of the text. As it happens, despite the many laws designed to protect animals (the primary topic of this book) the status of nonhumans as genuine holders of legal rights is quite dubious. Often lawmakers have not been strongly motivated by concern for the animals themselves, and just as frequently it is unclear that they were. Moreover, courts at all levels have not recognized animals as rightsholders. Instead, some in the animal protection community have attempted to persuade judges that violations of certain laws safeguarding animal interests have injured people. Their goal is to vindicate human rights to benefit nonhumans.

General Structure of the Chapters

Some repetition across different chapters occurs, but none is verbatim. This is due to the sourcebook format, and the fact that a number of different topics in animal law overlap one another. For instance, the Animal Welfare Act (AWA) applies to both laboratory animals and exhibited animals, two different chapters here. Chapter 7 includes a section on AWA standards for the care and handling of dogs (and other species) used in research, one aspect of dog law, a subject treated in chapter 3. Also, cruelty issues arise in a variety of animal use contexts, though anticruelty laws are discussed in the chapter on companion animals.

Rather than distracting the reader with footnotes identifying these reiterations and overlaps, there are numerous parenthetical cross references scattered throughout the text. Similarly, the sources for each chapter are gathered at its end, and they are distributed in these categories: *Federal Laws; State Laws; Federal and State Cases; Books, Articles, and Guidelines;* and *World Wide Web.* A complete inventory of all sources is found in the appendices and the bibliography at the end of the book.

In addition to surveying laws and cases, the five chapters (3 to 7) forming the core of the text also contain extensive material describing the human practices that the various laws regulate, sketching the historical development of both the practices and the laws, and setting the stage for many of the court cases. Not only does this background material make for more interesting reading than a dry recitation of statutory language or a judge's opinion, it is essential for achieving a thorough grasp of animal law.

To illustrate this point, consider the Recreational Hunting Safety & Preservation Act. This federal law makes it illegal to "engage in any physical conduct that hinders a lawful hunt." A simple statement of this prohibition leaves unanswered questions about why Congress would write such a statute, exactly what sorts of activities are targeted, and how the problem the law seeks to remedy arose in the first place. Similarly, a rote presentation of the Humane Methods of Slaughter Act without some accounting of the history of slaughtering animals, the basics of the meat packing process, and the nature and significance of ritual slaughter leaves the law ungrounded and unmotivated. Why do we need to require "humane" techniques for killing food animals? What are these methods? How are they implemented? What is the religious exemption allowing? Where does it come from?

As is evident from the outline of this book, the text is concerned with animal law in the United States, neglecting legal protections and property laws established for nonhuman beings in other nations. A comprehensive treatise on global animal law has not yet been written. For readers interested in a multinational perspective, the website for the World Animal Net offers a page with links to animal protection laws in the Philippines, Taiwan, India, Korea, Switzerland, Australia, and New Zealand (http://www.worldanimal.net/legislinks.html). The best single source for animal law in England, which includes similar material on other nations of the European Union, is a book by Simon Brooman and Debbie Legge, *Law Relating to Animals* (1997).

Despite our focus on the United States, occasionally European counterparts to the American laws being discussed are mentioned for comparison purposes. Also, some laws worthy of attention that protect wildlife found within U.S. borders and territorial waters are really either international agreements or domestic laws with a significant international component. For example, the Migratory Bird Treaty Act, which restricts hunting of certain wide-ranging birds, is the Congressional ratification of a treaty with Canada, Japan, and Mexico. There is also the Agreement on the Conservation of Polar Bears, signed by the United States, Canada, Norway, Greenland, and Russia, that prohibits "taking" polar bears in the oceans and on the ice of the signatories. Again, the International Convention for the Regulation of Whaling, an agreement between thirty-five nations, the United States among them, has declared an indefinite moratorium on the killing of all whales, shielding cetaceans swimming almost anywhere in the world, including along American shores.

On the other hand, this book excludes wildlife laws that impact Americans but involve animals that do not naturally inhabit any part of the United States. Notable among these are the African Elephant Conservation Act, which prohibits importation of ivory from any country without an acceptable elephant conservation program, and the Rhinoceros and Tiger Conservation Act, which authorizes millions of dollars in public money to fund programs aimed at saving these species from extinction. Similarly, the Wild Bird Conservation Act bans the import of numerous exotic bird species to the United States. Finally, we do not consider legal restrictions on fishing here, either in the form of state regulations or as they are written into more than two dozen different federal laws.

2. Animals and Rights

WHAT ARE LEGAL RIGHTS?

Laws create legal rights. This is probably the single most important feature of any system of law—indeed one philosopher has called legal rights "indispensably valuable possessions." A few examples should give a sense of why this is so. The Nineteenth Amendment to the Constitution declares that "the right of citizens of the United States to vote shall not be denied or abridged . . . on account of sex," for the first time affirming that all women are entitled to vote. Or consider the Freedom of Information Act, which guarantees every citizen the right, upon request, to be provided with unclassified information about the activities of federal agencies. Then there is Title VII of the Civil Rights Act, forbidding decisions on hiring, firing, promotions, or job duties to be made on the basis of race, color, religion, sex, or nationality. This law gives current and prospective workers the right to be judged solely on their abilities and qualifications.

The opportunity to vote, the claim to information about the government, and the protection against discrimination in the workplace bestowed by these laws are not gifts or favors for which gratitude is the appropriate response. These immense benefits are *owed* to the rightsholders, and people can rightfully insist and demand that they be provided. If such legally valid entitlements are not forthcoming, it is just as proper for one so deprived to react with indignation, even outrage. The unwarranted denial of legal rights is thus a gross injustice and a severe personal harm. Rights are very special possessions indeed.

So what are legal rights? This is not to ask what our rights under the law are—to what do we have a right?—rather, this is an inquiry into the nature of rights themselves. What does it mean to say that someone has a legal right to something? Equally as crucial, how do individuals get them? What makes someone a holder of legal rights? And what does all this have to do with animals?

The Roots of Rights

These matters may be addressed initially by tracing the concept of a right back to the Romans, and the Latin word *jus*. Originally, this term generically referred to what is right or just, but over time it more specifically came to mean giving all people (all Roman citizens, really) what they were due, as required by Roman law. Thus, Romans had legal rights to own what they deserved, with the relevant laws validating this entitlement.

Much later, in the fourteenth century C.E., William of Ockham observed that *jus* speaks of a cognitive ability to recognize the moral law, which is given by nature, and to act according to what it dictates. For him, to have a right is to act rightfully, consistently with what the moral law requires; to have no right to do something is to defy this requirement. A right to defend oneself, for example, is the understanding that nature demands self-preservation in the face of deadly threats. Ockham saw an intimate connection between morality and the law: formal legal systems and the rights they bestowed were valid to the extent that they captured the moral law.

Two centuries later, Thomas Hobbes conceived of a right, not as the power of reason to grasp the moral law and act accordingly, but as the freedom to act without moral constraint. For him, to have a right is simply to be at liberty to act unencumbered by moral obligations. So a right to self-preservation obtains when there is no duty to refrain from forcefully defending oneself. Laws set forth legal obligations to act or abstain, and at the same time give citizens the freedom—it is their legal right—to do anything else without such constraints.

In contrast, some philosophers of law in the nineteenth century came to reduce all rights to duties. For example, John Austin and John Stuart Mill interpreted a right to self-defense as simply a duty held by all others to avoid interfering in the rightsholder's attempt to save himself or herself from harm. Legal rules impose this and other duties on people. In the next century another philosopher, Joel Feinberg, pointed out that identifying rights with duties held by others failed to account for what is most characteristic of rights, and what signals their greatest worth: the activity of claiming or demanding what one is due. The legal right to self-preservation now becomes a rightsholder's demand, an order authorized by law, to leave him or her alone in his or her pursuit of personal salvation.

Today, perhaps the most influential analysis of legal rights comes from a law professor, Wesley Hohfeld. Writing in the second decade of the twentieth century, Hohfeld noticed that the term "a right" was used by judges in several different ways, capturing many of the facets that philosophers had emphasized individually. He classified these variant meanings into four general categories.

Varieties of Rights

First, Hohfeld analyses a "claim-right," what he called "a right in the strictest sense," as one in which others have a duty not to interfere with the rightsholder doing or having something, most often some definite benefit. A right to life, for instance, carries with it an obligation on the part of others to avoid endangering that life, and the rightsholder can legitimately demand that they do so.

A second, more complex type of right, according to Hohfeld, is the "liberty-right." Here, unlike the claim-right, others have no duty to avoid interfering with the rightsholder, but they also have no (claim-)right that he or she not do or have something. For example, a woman's right to look at an attractive man in a public place is a liberty-right if he has no claim against her not to look at him; at the same time, he has no obligation to allow her to keep staring. He can simply walk away without violating her right to look.

A third concept is the "power-right," under which an individual has the authority to alter his or her own legal status, or that of another person. Judges have numerous power-rights, to imprison people, to free them from incarceration, to compel them to pay fines, to take away or return their children, or to marry or divorce them. Also, and crucially for animal law, each of us has the power to sue other people when they have violated our rights; this power changes us into individuals to whom others legally owe reparations.

Finally, Hohfeld's "immunity-right" insulates the rightsholder from the authority or control of another; no alteration can be validly effected in one so insulated. The Fourth Amendment to the Constitution, which affirms the security of the people in "their persons, houses, papers, and effects," grants to every citizen an immunity-right against "unreasonable searches and seizures." Unless a judge is convinced by law enforcement agents that unlawful activity has very likely occurred, the government cannot invade our homes and scrutinize or confiscate our property.

In light of Hohfeld's analysis, and before considering the issue of their legal rights (*see* this chapter: *Do Animals Have Legal Rights?*), it is worth noticing that animals logically *could* have at least some rights of each of these types. Starting with the first and last ones, there is no immediate conceptual or practical problem with animals having a claim to a host of beneficial conditions, such as life, freedom, bodily integrity, and noninterference, a basic right to be left alone. Laws could affirm these entitlements. Nonhumans cannot themselves *make* a claim or demand these benefits in court—neither can human infants or the mentally disabled, but that is no legal impediment to their rightsholding. Adult humans can make these claims for them in a court of law. Also, immunity-rights that protect individuals from invasions of their interests, such as the preservation of life and liberty guaranteed in the Due Process Clause of the Fourteenth Amendment are readily applicable to animals.

We can as well make sense of liberty-rights for animals. Wild animals could have rights to steal our food and tear up our campsites—so they should suffer no punishment—yet we have no duty to refrain from preventing their doing so. Or, a bear may have a liberty-right to block the trail ahead, but hikers are not obligated to avoid scaring it off the spot and let the beast just sit there (though this may be a prudent thing to do). As for the power-right, clearly no animal could effect a change in another's legal status the way a judge can. However, why couldn't a nonhuman be entitled to sue others—humans of course—when they violate the animal's claim-, liberty-, or immunity-rights? Again, animals are incapable of representing themselves in court, or pressing any claims against a defendant, but that's what lawyers do whether their client is human or nonhuman.

As it happens, this power-right to sue has become one of the most persistently and bitterly contested issues in animal law. In the lexicon of law, this debate is centrally concerned with the problem of "legal standing," both for the nonhumans themselves and for humans in the animal protection community (*see* this chapter: *Do Animals Have Legal Rights?* for more on this topic). However, prior to considering that problem, the discussion must turn to a different, more basic meaning of "legal standing," one that impacts the fundamental question at the core of the animal rights issue: Who has legal rights?

Rights and Legal Standing

The phrase "has legal standing" most commonly occurs in the opinions of judges to refer to a plaintiff who, as Hohfeld puts it, has the power-right to sue another party for violating one or more of her (usually claim) rights. To be entitled to bring a lawsuit, a plaintiff often needs to prove that there is a genuine "case or controversy" between himself or herself and the defendant. This requirement derives from Article III, Section 2 of the U.S. Constitution in which the federal judiciary is given the authority to adjudicate disputes among citizens and other litigants. A judge must dismiss a case if this is not proved, because the plaintiff has no legal standing to sue. Here, "legal standing" signifies a particular right held by a certain person in a specific set of circumstances.

On the other hand, "has legal standing" can also more comprehensively refer to any individual who has a bundle of legal rights, a rightsholder. United States citizens have numerous legal rights—to life, liberty, privacy, to vote, to a public education, to remain silent when arrested, to a trial by a jury of peers, and many others. An individual may fail to demonstrate a "case or controversy" to a court in a particular situation—so he or she has no legal standing there—yet that individual still retains his or her legal standing as a rightsholder. As law professor Christopher Stone once put the matter in his famous essay "Should Trees Have Standing?" to have legal standing in this sense is to "*count* jurally—to have a legally recognized worth and dignity in [one's] own right, and not merely as a means to benefit [others]."

Despite their different meanings, these two senses of "legal standing" have a close relationship. In the comprehensive sense, one who has no legal standing has no rights whatsoever, including the right to bring a lawsuit. Rocks and cars are rightless things, and perhaps trees are too, although Stone argued that trees and other natural objects could—and should—have legal rights. The core issue about animal rights is whether nonhumans are more like rocks, things without rights, or more like people, individuals with a worth and dignity who hold a variety of legal rights. Certainly, much like trees, their legal standing in this sense is highly controversial. So, too, for the other sense of the concept, in which saying that one has no legal standing is just to say that he or she has no power—the right to sue another in this case, though he or she does have some other (claim-, liberty-, or immunity-) rights that could be vindicated in court. When, if ever, are animals entitled to bring lawsuits against human defendants when they violate the rights of nonhumans?

Notice that animals can have legal standing to sue only if they have legal standing as rightsholders. The logically prior question then is whether animals have any legal rights at all. If they do not, then they cannot initiate a lawsuit against anyone because they have no rights to violate, and none to vindicate. In contrast, to reject the standing of a nonhuman in a particular "case or controversy" does not entail that the creature has no rights whatever. The fundamental problem then in animal law concerns the legal standing of animals as rightsholders, not their standing as holders of the power-right to sue. Nonetheless, an examination of the requirements for holding this right, as set out by the Supreme Court, will lead back to the conditions for identifying rightsholders, indicating how to answer the question, Who has legal rights?

Legal Standing and the Identity of Rightsholders

In 1857 the Supreme Court issued its pronouncement on a topic that had been vigorously debated in the young nation for decades. Chief Justice Roger Taney declared that a slave named Dred Scott—and by implication all of America's slaves—was not a U.S. citizen and therefore did not enjoy the legal rights afforded by the Constitution. The African Americans were not rightsholders (*[Dred] Scott v. Sanford*).

Within a few years, a civil war ignited over this proposition. During the middle of the bloody conflict, President Abraham Lincoln issued his Emancipation Proclamation, declaring in 1863 that the people held as slaves in the rebel states were legally free of their bondage and entitled to the protections of federal law. Two years later, after the abolitionist Union states had defeated the proslavery Confederate states, Congress ratified the Thirteenth Amendment, outlawing "involuntary servitude" in the United States. In 1868 the Fourteenth Amendment affirmed that all persons born in the United States were citizens of this country.

Since that time, there has been little discussion among American legal scholars, law professors, lawyers, and judges about the identity of legal rightsholders.

Who are they? Human beings of course. More significantly, it has just been assumed that *only* human beings (or collections of human beings, as

in corporations or nations) have legal rights. For many years, deliberations in courts, legislatures, law schools, and other venues have concentrated on questions concerning what specific rights are at issue, and on
whether or not this individual human (or group of humans) is entitled to
petition a court for damages. The focus on the narrower question of
standing to sue has come at the expense of investigation into the foundational problem of identifying who the legal rightsholders are. Yet this narrow focus can be instructive for reaching a solution.

The definitive characterization of legal standing to date was most recently detailed by the Supreme Court in *Lujan v. Defenders of Wildlife*, a
1992 decision. There, the justices asserted three basic elements in the definition, all of which must be satisfied before an individual can have the
power-right to sue—elements that the plaintiff bears the burden of establishing. For our purposes here, only the first criterion is important (for a
detailed discussion of this case, *see* this chapter: *Legal Standing under Federal Wildlife Laws*).

To have standing to initiate a lawsuit, an injury or harm must have
been suffered by the plaintiff. For the legal systems of the Western world,
an injury or harm is an invasion of the plaintiff's legally protected interests. In the United States, the Constitution, various statutes, and occasionally judges when rendering their decisions indicate what are the interests to be safeguarded. Consider again the Due Process Clause of the
Fourteenth Amendment. This assures us that no one's interests in life, liberty, or property can be justifiably thwarted by the government unless
certain legal procedures are followed, such as providing the opportunity
to confront one's accusers and ensuring a trial by jury, to be reasonably
expedited.

This example indicates perhaps the most basic and important of all
legally protected interests: those an individual has in his or her own life,
and in personal freedom and property. These are deep and abiding concerns that the framers of the Constitution substantially borrowed from
the Declaration of Independence, authored by Thomas Jefferson, who in
his turn was profoundly influenced here by the English political philosopher John Locke. To this list one can add such items as the interests people have in their health, reputation, personal privacy, emotional stability,
and bodily integrity, all of which are legally validated in some document
of law.

As further delineated in *Lujan*, this first feature of legal standing requires that the invasion of these legally protected interests, setting them
back or defeating them—the injury or harm—must have occurred "in
fact." The injury must be actual or at least imminent, one that is specific
and clear, rather than vague, dispersed, conjectural, or hypothetical. So in
a certain set of circumstances, one who has not been injured "in fact,"

which legally speaking is not to have been harmed at all, has no power-right to sue another party: that individual has no legal standing to sue anyone.

This element of legal standing tells how to identify individuals as rightsholders: they have *legally protected interests*. Human beings have interests of the sort mentioned above: life, liberty, property, health, reputation, privacy, and so on. These interests, and others, are protected by thousands of legal rules. Uncontroversially, humans are rightsholders because these documents of law underwrite the "worth and dignity," as Stone put it, of our interests. To put this in terms of Hohfeld's claim-rights, which are generally agreed to be the most important sort of rights, humans are the *direct* beneficiaries of legal duties. Laws impose obligations on others to respect our interests, just as we must respect theirs. The only issue remaining then is whether or not some particular person has the power-right to sue another in a specific set of circumstances: does he or she have legal standing here?

What about animals? Do any laws or judges' decisions legally protect their interests, creating legal rights for them? Do at least some nonhumans have the right to sue?

Some philosophers and legal scholars have contended that animals do not have interests, that, strictly speaking, they do not possess the requisite mental equipment to qualify as beings with interests. If these thinkers are correct, then laws could not really create rights for animals, since they have no interests to protect. However, other intelligent and reasonable people have argued for the opposite conclusion, finding the idea of animal interests plausible and even obvious. If one assumes that animals do have at least some basic interests, a number of critical concerns appear to be at stake for those creatures that humans routinely use every day. After all, animals are doubtless capable of sustaining a wide variety of injuries when they are killed, confined, controlled, or caused to suffer by humans.

Hundreds of millions of birds, cows, pigs, sheep, deer, mink, and other species are slaughtered in the United States every year for food and clothing (*see* chapter 4: *Animal Slaughter;* chapter 4: *Fur Farming;* chapter 4: *Commercial Trapping*), and for entertainment (*see* chapter 5: *Recreational Hunting*), which obliterates their interest in living. Millions of other animals—mice and rats, rabbits and hamsters, dogs and cats, among others—used in research, experimentation, and testing are often subjected to painful procedures and inflicted with diseases and toxic substances, thwarting an interest in health and bodily integrity (*see* chapter 7).

Many more animals are forcibly detained in cages and other confinement systems, a form of coercion incompatible with an interest in freedom, or they are compelled to perform for humans rather than simply being left alone (*see* chapter 5: *Circuses and Zoos;* chapter 5: *Rodeos;* chapter 5: *Greyhound Racing and Horse Racing;* chapter 5: *Cockfighting and Dog-fighting*). At the same time, various laws restrict human practices with animals in all these areas, while others prohibit harming eagles, whales, dolphins, seals, grizzly bears, and many other wildlife species (*see* chapter 6). Does all this mean that these animals have legal rights?

DO ANIMALS HAVE LEGAL RIGHTS?

Animals do not have a Declaration of Independence, an Emancipation Proclamation, or a Bill of Rights that would quickly and straightforwardly indicate both that they are rightsholders and what their rights are. Yet this book surveys dozens of animal protection laws, many of which are also found in a publication of the Animal Welfare Institute, *Animals and Their Legal Rights,* now in its fourth edition. Isn't it obvious that these laws provide animals with legal rights to the protections they afford?

Unfortunately, this is not obvious. Consider that every state in the United States requires dog owners to vaccinate their animals for rabies (*see* chapter 3: *Dog Law*). Rabies is fatal for any dog unlucky enough to contract it, so the law indisputably protects canines. Does this mean that it gives them the legal right to a vaccination? Probably not. The legislative goals of the immunization requirement are to promote public safety—rabid dogs are extremely dangerous—and paternalistically compel dog owners to take care of their property—a dog with a fatal disease is worthless. The legislators' concern is really for *human* well-being here, and canine health is at best a minor element. In light of that fact, it is difficult to see how these laws create any legal rights for dogs.

The lesson here is that one must try to determine the intentions and motivations that legislators had in writing animal protection laws. *Why* are lawmakers attempting to establish safeguards for animals? At least in large part, are they trying to benefit the animals themselves? Do they impose duties on humans directly to promote the well-being of these creatures? Are the interests of animals receiving legal protection for their own sakes, as ends rather than as tools for protecting human interests? Do these legal rules show that animals, in the words of law professor Christopher Stone, "have a legally recognized worth and dignity in [their] own right, and not merely as a means to benefit [others]"? (For further discussion of these ideas, *see* this chapter: *What Are Legal Rights?: Legal Standing and the Identity of Rightsholders.*)

Discerning the motivations of lawmakers is often a difficult task. Further, one cannot hope to canvas each of the dozens of animal protection laws discussed in this book in light of the questions above. We will not pretend to be settling the matter here. However, we can examine some especially important representative statutes, seeking the nature of the concern for animal interests that lies behind them, and in the process gain some insight on the legal status of nonhumans. From the legal point of view, are animals more like persons or are they just another form of property?

Animals as Property

Historically, it is clear that nonhumans had no legal rights. Animals have traditionally been regarded as property, or as potential property, which as such has no legally protected interests. This means that animals could never have the legal standing to sue in some particular situation to vindicate their rights to life, health, liberty, or other matters (for more on legal standing, *see* this chapter: *What Are Legal Rights?*). The failure to accord animals any legal rights whatsoever, and hence to divest them of all legal standing, weaves an unbroken thread through the fabric of the law, as determined by legislators and judges, stretching for millennia from Rome to England to America.

The Romans viewed animals as beings without free will or the powers of reason, and so classified them as *res*—things—rather than *personae*—persons. Under Roman law, as inventoried by such towering figures of classical jurisprudence as Justinian, legal title to an animal arose through a process called *occupatio*, where a person takes possession of a creature not already belonging to anyone, with the intention of owning it. As things, living wild animals originally became personal property when people "occupied" them: reduced them to human control through capture, followed by confinement, taming, or domestication. Justinian thought that domestic animals were the descendants of wild animals that had been seized and controlled long ago, with their offspring passed down through the generations from one person to the next according to legal rules governing the transferal of property. From an early period in the development of their empire, the Romans were intensely concerned with acquiring property, and evidently regarded all *res* as subject to such acquisition, including animals.

By 1000 C.E., these ideas had been imported to English common law essentially intact, and reinforced by certain passages in the Book of Genesis. Most impressive to early English jurists was God's gift to humanity of "dominion over the fish of the sea and over the birds of the air, and over the cattle, and over all the earth, and over every creeping thing which creeps upon the earth." Much later, at the end of the eighteenth century, William Blackstone, the author of the prodigiously influential *Commentaries on the Laws of England,* asserted that this passage from the Bible was the only genuine and incontrovertible justification for the human domination of animals. Blending this biblical validation with the Roman obsession with property, Blackstone proclaimed that "The Earth, therefore, and all things therein, are the general property of all mankind, exclusive of other beings, from the immediate gift of the creator."

One hundred years later, James Kent carried over into his own seminal study of the common law in the United States, *Commentaries on American Law*, both the Roman principle of *occupatio* and the scriptural justification located by Blackstone as the basis for the legal status of animals as property. For Kent, once seized or occupied, "tame animals" were property in perpetuity, while wild animals reverted to an unowned state if they were released or escaped from captivity. So we find that from Kent to Blackstone to Justinian, the legal status of animals as property, with no standing and no rights whatsoever, has been deeply embedded into the law of Western civilization for many centuries.

Yet the germ of legal rights for animals may be found in various anticruelty statutes, almost all of which have been written in the last century and a half. Although the Puritans of Massachusetts Bay Colony enacted the first anticruelty law in 1641, England had no such statute until 1822, and it would be another fifty years after that before most American states had outlawed cruelty to animals. By 1913 every state had done so.

Before such laws were passed, however, cruelty to animals was not an offense according to the common law, the collection of decisions made by judges in cases without a legal rule to follow. People who abused animals owned by others could be prosecuted under malicious mischief statutes for malevolently damaging someone else's property, thus causing the owner to lose some (or all) of the economic value to be derived from the beasts. Courts sought to compensate animal owners for these damages, and little or no thought was given to the interests of the creature that suffered the harm. This means that such statutes imposed only an *indirect* legal duty to treat animals in a certain way, while the true, direct beneficiaries were their owners, not the animals themselves. The direct obligation was to the human. Animal interests were not valued by the law for their own sake, but as a *means* to securing human interests in property (*see also* chapter 3: *Anticruelty Laws*).

Anticruelty statutes seem to depart from this scheme, suggesting that animals are more than just property, more than a means for human ends. Couldn't one say then that laws prohibiting cruelty to animals are designed to provide *the animals* with legal protections, making *them* the beneficiaries of direct legal obligations? And doesn't that entail that the animals so protected have legal rights, perhaps a right to decent, humane treatment, or, stated negatively, a right not to be treated cruelly?

State Anticruelty Laws and Animal Rights
Unfortunately, the notion that anticruelty statutes create legal rights for animals is deeply suspect. Furthermore, even if such entitlements are indeed generated by law, they appear to be narrowly confined. As suggested above, to understand the legal status of nonhumans here, one

must try to determine if anticruelty laws view them as direct beneficiaries, as valuable for their own sakes and not just as tools to serve human interests. To see this, we need to consider the purposes of anticruelty laws. Why did legislatures prohibit treating animals cruelly in the first place? Is the point to protect the interests of the animals themselves?

Although records of the deliberations that resulted in the enactment of anticruelty statutes either do not exist or are not available, over the last 100 years or so judges have occasionally offered their interpretations of the legislative intent behind these laws. Judicial opinions in this matter demonstrate a remarkable consensus approaching a unanimity: the ultimate purpose of anticruelty statutes is not really to protect animals and ensure that they are treated decently; it is to protect humans from harm and prevent the decay of their moral character.

Repeatedly, across decades of rulings, judges in widely disparate jurisdictions have observed that cruelty to animals sets one down a slippery slope toward perpetrating acts of cruelty against humans, while also "corrupting public morals" generally. This assessment from the Mississippi Supreme Court in *Stephens v. State* is representative: "Cruelty to [animals] manifests a vicious and degraded nature, and it tends inevitably to cruelty to men. . . . [H]uman beings should be kind and just to dumb brutes, if for no other reason than to learn how to be kind and just to each other."

The view that anticruelty statutes are much more about promoting benefits for humans than about safeguarding the interests of animals is further reinforced by the findings of the American Law Institute. This association of legal scholars canvassed state anticruelty legislation and drafted a paradigm statute for inclusion in their *Model Penal Code*. In the process, they commented that these laws appeared to be primarily aimed at "prevent[ing] outrage to the sensibilities of the community" rather than protecting animals. Again, numerous court cases have echoed this legal perspective. For example, in *Commonwealth v. Higgins*, the Massachusetts Supreme Court pointed out that such prohibited actions toward animals "have a tendency to dull humanitarian feelings and to corrupt the morals of those who observe or have knowledge of those acts."

These sorts of considerations, which pervade judicial interpretations of anticruelty statutes, indicate that the interests to be protected here are preeminently those of humans. The promotion of the well-being of animals is little more than a means or an instrument to enhancing civil relations between people, elevating their moral character, and shielding those who would be displeased or disgusted with demonstrations of cruelty to animals. Animals do not appear to be the beneficiaries of direct legal duties here, nor are they valued by the law for their own sakes, but as a means to benefit humans. This focus makes it difficult to see how laws prohibiting animal cruelty really do bestow legal standing as rights-holders upon the animals covered by the statutes. Difficult, yes, but perhaps not impossible to detect.

Making cruelty to animals unlawful because such behavior "tends inevitably to cruelty to men" clearly does not identify any legally protected interest of animals, and so does not by this avenue create any rights possessed by them. Yet if such mistreatment of animals really does cause "outrage to the sensibilities" and "corrupts morals" as well, so that outlawing it upholds moral standards and sensibilities, and if the outrage and corruption referred to here signifies more than just a propensity to commit acts of violence against other humans, then maybe animals do have some status above that of a mere means or tool to serve human interests.

In this instance, it would seem that acting cruelly or inhumanely toward an animal is morally wrong precisely because it wrongs the animal. If this were not so, why would perpetrating such an action have any effect whatever on the moral standards of a community, or the character of its members? This suggests that anticruelty laws, at least to some degree, have codified this moral regard for the animals themselves. If this is correct, then animals do have a legal right to humane treatment that is violated when they are abused.

Even so, it looks as though this right must be severely limited or exceedingly weak. State anticruelty statutes typically characterize "cruelty" as the "unnecessary" or "unjustifiable" infliction of pain and suffering, suggesting that a legal right to humane treatment is best understood as a right to be spared pain and suffering that is inessential and groundless. This, of course, implies that animals have no right to be spared necessary and justified harms. When is harming an animal necessary and justified, and when is it not? If, indeed, animal rights are generated here, to what exactly do these nonhumans have a right, and to what do they have no right? What precisely are humans legally obligated to avoid doing to them, and what are we legally permitted to do?

The laws do not offer any direct answers to these questions, but one can begin to understand the matter by first considering a few cruelty convictions, and then looking at the key statutory language. The following cases present instances of "unnecessary" or "unjustifiable" inflictions of pain and suffering.

In one, a man was convicted of animal cruelty for tying a puppy to the bumper of his truck and dragging the animal down the street (*Missouri v. Stout*). In another case involving a dog, a man chained a dalmatian to a tree, cut off its ears and tail, slashed its throat, and set loose a pit bull to attack it (*Commonwealth v. Tapper*). After burning his roommate's cat in a microwave oven and feeding it acetaminophen (which is poisonous to cats), a Houston man was successfully prosecuted for cruelty to animals

(*Celinski v. State*). In yet another instance of canine abuse, also in Texas, three men were found guilty of using cinderblocks to stone a stray dog to death. These cases suggest that if, indeed, an animal (or at least a dog or a cat) has a legal right not to be harmed, its protections extend only to the most extreme sorts of mistreatment.

State anticruelty laws also invariably exclude one or more of certain uses of animals from the scope of their protections. "Normal" or "accepted" agricultural practices, medical and scientific research and testing, and hunting and trapping are very commonly specifically placed out of reach of the statute, even though the law often covers "any animal." What do these exclusions say about the rightsholding of animals? That is hard to answer. They might be interpreted as meaning that any harms attendant upon *these* uses are necessary and justified, so that the animals' right that humans refrain from causing them gratuitous and wanton harms remains unscathed. On the other hand, they could mean that wildlife and the animals used in agriculture and in research have no rights at all.

Federal Laws and Animal Rights

This latter interpretation would be rejected by those who would point out that the animals used in agriculture and in research (setting aside the rights of wildlife for the moment) do have their own statutory guarantees of decent treatment. These are provided by the federal government independently of state anticruelty laws, so nonhumans are not bereft of legal rights after all.

The Humane Methods of Slaughter Act (HMSA) (*see* chapter 4), as the name proclaims, is supposed to ensure that animals used for food are killed humanely. The Animal Welfare Act (AWA) (*see* chapter 7) functions essentially as a national anticruelty law for animals used in research facilities and for exhibition. However, the notion that these two federal laws bestow legal rights on these animals is itself problematic. Consider the HMSA first.

Poultry are entirely excluded from the HMSA, so slaughtered birds at any rate do not have rights created by this law, even though they constitute over 90 percent of all animals killed for commercial food products (some state anticruelty laws specifically exclude poultry from their purview). The preamble to the HMSA and the legislative debates preceding its enactment speak of preventing "needless suffering," which is reminiscent of state statutes banning "unnecessary" harm. However, the scope of the slaughter law does not reach any treatment of livestock before the process of herding them to their imminent demise begins. Branding, castrating, dehorning, impregnating, roping, shearing, driving for other purposes, and additional "normal" agricultural practices that appear to cause varying degrees of pain and suffering are left entirely unregulated by this or any other federal statute (*see* chapter 4: *Legal Regulation of the Treatment of Farm Animals*).

Again, it is difficult to tell if this legal gap means that these practices are therefore needful and justified, so the right to be spared "needless suffering" is not touched here, or that livestock in this context have no rights at all guaranteed by state or federal law. In any case, if the HMSA does confer such a right on livestock, it is fairly plain that it is activated once the drovers start moving the animals into the abattoir; then "needless suffering" must be avoided.

Does the HMSA really create this right? This question might be answered by determining who the intended beneficiaries of the law are. Unfortunately, it is unclear what exactly the moral problem is that the law seeks to remedy by prohibiting the infliction of needless suffering during the slaughtering procedure.

Although there is no suggestion that inhumane slaughter tends to make slaughterhouse workers or anyone else more prone to commit acts of violence against humans—a consideration that would not give animals rights, as per state anticruelty laws—neither do we find the thesis that inhumane slaughter "outrages the sensibilities of the community" or "corrupts public morals." As we saw, this could plausibly serve as the foundation for the rights of animals. However, since very few members of the public ever witness the killing of food animals, what happens in the slaughterhouse would not have any sort of generally corrupting influence anyway. Perhaps, instead, the moral concern is not the widespread effect denoted by "public" corruption, but just to prevent *slaughterers* from doing something morally wrong to animals, whatever the broader consequences of their actions on the moral fiber of the community may be.

This is frankly speculative, but there is little else besides such conjecture to support the notion that the HMSA does generate animal rights. We cannot turn to judicial interpretations to help us here because a case involving an alleged violation of the HMSA has evidently never been litigated in a federal court, which means that no animal has ever been recognized as having legal standing of any sort under this law. One might say that the right issues from the principle that inhumane slaughter is just wrong—it wrongs the animal—irrespective of its effect on "community sensibilities" or "public morals." Perhaps, but no evidence exists that this principle was motivating the legislators who drafted the bill.

Moreover, there is a certain moral oddity about a legal system that provides no right to life, no right to freedom from confinement, and no right to humane treatment throughout the life of an animal until moments before it is slaughtered, yet does nonetheless supply a right to be killed compassionately. It is as if a person had no right to own property, but did have the right that his or her possessions not be taken by force or physical coercion, and only after he or she was first politely informed that they would be taken.

Many of the same reservations apply to the AWA. This federal law, too, speaks of ensuring that laboratory animals are "provided with humane care and treatment," and regulations issued under the authority of the statute detail standards for feeding, watering, housing, and transporting these creatures (*see* chapter 7: *Animal Welfare Act Regulations*). Yet it is not clear what the moral significance of this is.

Is the purpose, or a major purpose, of the AWA to benefit the animals themselves, thus indicating their legal standing as rightsholders? Do humans have direct legal duties to them to, among other things, feed them every day, ventilate the rooms in which they are housed, and confine them in appropriately sized cages? As with the slaughterhouse, the uses of animals in research facilities are hidden from public view, so the general deterioration of the moral character of the citizenry that could lead us to animal rights, as we found in the context of anticruelty legislation, is once more unavailable. There is here again the possibility that the AWA simply seeks to deter research personnel from committing immoral acts against animals because there is a basic moral dictum that abuse and mistreatment of lab animals is just wrong.

Were the sponsors of the AWA cognizant of this principle? No available document unequivocally indicates that they were. Yet if this really was motivating the enactment of AWA, despite the dearth of corroboration, there once again appears a strange ethical system that denies animals legal rights to life, liberty, health, bodily integrity, and freedom from coercion, but does give them the right to have their cages cleaned on a regular basis.

Other evidence points away from the notion that research animals have legal rights: no case litigated under the AWA has ever granted an animal legal standing to sue on its own behalf. Although this fact alone does not entail that lab animals are not rightsholders, one would think that if they were, and after better than thirty years in the *U.S. Code*, at least one lab animal would be granted standing to vindicate at least one AWA-conferred right. Yet this has not happened. Controversies over legal standing in litigation involving the AWA have always focused on whether or not some animal welfare organization or some individual human has the right to initiate a lawsuit in a specific case.

For example, in the first such proceeding under the AWA, and a case that proved seminal, the International Primate Protection League (IPPL) claimed that their membership would suffer financial and nonmonetary injuries if a research facility was allowed to reacquire monkeys that had been confiscated because the animals had been abused by personnel at the facility. In 1986 the Fourth Circuit Court of Appeals rejected the IPPL's arguments, and not only denied the group legal standing, but also ruled that the AWA did not provide for lawsuits by private individuals as an adjunct to the Department of Agriculture's authority to enforce the statute (*International Primate Protection League v. Institute for Behavioral Research;* for a detailed discussion of this case, *see* this chapter: *Legal Standing under the Animal Welfare Act*).

With this case reigning as a powerful precedent, several subsequent attempts by other animal welfare organizations in the late 1980s and early 1990s to secure legal standing as injured parties in cases of animal mistreatment proved entirely unsuccessful. This situation suddenly changed in September 1998 when the District of Columbia Circuit Court of Appeals ruled that a member of the Animal Legal Defense Fund had experienced an injury to a legally protected aesthetic interest as the result of viewing primates in conditions that violated provisions of the AWA (*Animal Legal Defense Fund v. Glickman;* for a detailed discussion of this and other standing cases, *see* this chapter: *Legal Standing under the Animal Welfare Act*).

This decision marks a watershed development in animal law and AWA litigation. However, it also emphasizes the point that animals themselves still do not have standing under this federal law.

Federal Wildlife Law and Animal Rights

Several *species* of wild animals, not individual creatures, have been named as plaintiffs in cases concerning violations of federal wildlife protection laws, which suggests that they have achieved legal standing and do qualify as rightsholders. Nonetheless, as with litigation under the AWA, the dominant controversy over legal standing in cases involving wildlife has been whether or not some animal advocacy organization is entitled to sue for damages arising from alleged violations of these laws.

To cite a single such example out of many, one of the first cases of this nature came under the Marine Mammal Protection Act (MMPA). This law bans killing marine mammals or importing them into the United States, but also allows the director of the National Marine Fisheries Service the discretion to waive the ban (*see* chapter 6). When Director Kreps decided to issue permits to the South African government for the taking of a certain number of Cape fur seals, the Animal Welfare Institute (AWI) sued, hoping to maintain the proscription. A ruling of the District of Columbia Circuit Court of Appeals in 1977 found in favor of the AWI on the grounds that allowing the hunt would invade their members' interest in observing, photographing, and delighting in the seals in their natural habitat, thus establishing their standing as an injured party (*Animal Welfare Institute v. Kreps;* for further discussion of this case, *see* this chapter: *Legal Standing under Federal Wildlife Laws: Can the Legal Standing of Humans*

Benefit Animals?). The interest the seals might have in not being killed was not considered, indicating that the animals themselves had no legal status of any sort. To date, no animal species has ever achieved standing under the Marine Mammal Protection Act.

A few wildlife species have appeared to gain legal standing as injured parties in a smattering of cases litigated under the Endangered Species Act (ESA) (*see* chapter 6), although no individual animal ever has. The ESA prohibits harming, killing, importing, or exporting members of species that have been designated by the secretary of the interior as likely to become extinct. In these proceedings, some animals so designated have themselves been named as the plaintiffs, and some courts have addressed the plausibility of the animals meeting the requirements for legal standing, which presupposes that they are already rightsholders.

In the first case of this sort, *Palila v. Hawaii Department of Land and Natural Resources* (*Palila I*), the habitat of a native Hawaiian bird, the palila, was threatened by a population of feral sheep and goats that the state was maintaining for sport hunters. In its 1979 decision, the federal district court ruled that the bird species was itself being harmed by the foraging sheep and goats, so by allowing this to occur the state was engaged in an act of taking prohibited by the ESA. The palila's status as the injured party was not contested or analyzed by this court, but in a revisitation of the issue nine years later the Ninth Circuit Court of Appeals asserted that "As an endangered species under the Endangered Species Act . . . the bird . . . also has a legal status and wings its way into federal court as a plaintiff in its own right . . . represented by attorneys for the Sierra Club, Audubon Society, and other environmental parties" (*Palila v. Hawaii Department of Land and Natural Resources* (*Palila II*).

Other litigation concerning the ESA has listed endangered animals as plaintiffs, including a species of owl (*Northern Spotted Owl v. Hodel*), a squirrel (*Mt. Graham Squirrel v. Yeutter*), the bald eagle (*American Bald Eagle v. Bhatti*), and a turtle species (*Loggerhead Turtle v. County Council of Volusia County*). Even so, such instances have proved far more the exception than the rule. In all these cases, as in *Palila I*, the standing of the animals is not analyzed by the court, and humans are always also named as plaintiffs. Moreover, when challenged, the standing of nonhumans under the ESA has been defeated every time. For example, in 1991 Secretary of the Interior Manuel Lujan successfully contested the legal standing of another endangered species of bird (the 'Alala). He convinced the District Court for Hawaii to reject the notion that the ESA gives animals any right to sue, and to hold that the ESA allows only "persons" to bring lawsuits, not animals (*Hawaiian Crow ('Alala) v. Lujan*). Two years later, the federal District Court for Massachusetts affirmed this view of standing under the ESA in *Citizens to End Suffering and Exploitation, Inc. v. New England Aquarium*.

This outcome should not be surprising, given the statutory language of the ESA. In its first section, the law states that certain species have aesthetic, ecological, educational, historical, recreational, and scientific value to the American people. Endangered and threatened species are worthy of conserving because we enjoy observing them, or regard them as a significant feature of our pastimes, or the existence of these species promotes our knowledge of the world. Nowhere in the ESA or its legislative history is there any statement or suggestion that these species have legally protected interests making them worthy of preservation for their own sakes or in their own right as the beneficiaries of direct legal duties.

Similar language is written into other, major federal wildlife protection laws. The statement of congressional findings in the preamble of the Marine Mammal Protection Act asserts that these creatures are "resources" of great aesthetic, recreational, and economic significance, and that they should be protected according to "sound policies of resource management." In the Bald Eagle Protection Act, the birds are touted as national symbols that represent "American ideals of freedom." Again, the Wild Free-Roaming Horses and Burros Act says that the animals "symbolize the historic and pioneer spirit of the West, . . . and enrich the lives of the American people."

These are not statements of respect and concern for the interests of animals; they are expressions of how certain species serve human interests in beauty, in entertainment, in money, in patriotism, and in nostalgia. This in itself does not necessarily mean that these wildlife species are entirely devoid of any legal standing, because there may be some other law not presently under consideration that does provide them with rights and under which they may have standing to sue. Unfortunately, no such alternative statutes come readily to mind.

It is perhaps appropriate then that the definitive pronouncement on the precise dimensions of the legal standing to bring a lawsuit, the Supreme Court decision in *Lujan v. Defenders of Wildlife*, concerned alleged violations of the ESA. The charges arose from construction projects that could have detrimentally impacted two officially designated endangered species residing in foreign countries, the Indian elephant and the Egyptian crocodile. The Defenders of Wildlife attempted to halt the projects on the grounds that neither the Department of the Interior nor the Department of Commerce had been properly consulted. The Supreme Court ruled that the wildlife organization had no standing to sue, because it had failed to show a specific, concrete injury to any of its membership. Injury to the elephants and crocodiles themselves was not considered as a salient factor (for a detailed discussion of this case, *see* this chapter: *Legal Standing under Federal Wildlife Laws*).

State Hunting and Trapping Regulations

Predictably, the situation looks even worse for wild animals subject to commercial trapping and recreational hunting. Even if such federal laws as the Endangered Species Act and the Marine Mammal Protection Act do not really provide these animals with legal rights, at least they are intended to protect the relevant species, albeit as grounded in human interests and not those of the animals. In starkest contrast, hunting and trapping laws are designed precisely to facilitate the destruction of wildlife designated as "game" species, typically during a specified time of year, the "open season."

As noted above, most state anticruelty laws exempt agricultural and laboratory uses of animals as well as "lawful" hunting and trapping from the category of prohibited actions. However, also noted was that it is unclear whether this exclusion implied that these practices involved "necessary" or "justifiable" inflictions of pain and suffering, and hence were not legally "cruel," or that the animals used in these ways were entirely without legal standing as rightsholders. In the consideration of food and laboratory animals, we examined other (federal) laws that purport to protect them, yet, arguably, these do not create any genuine animal rights either.

Although strictly speaking there are no federal or state "Humane Hunting and Trapping Laws," nor any other "animal welfare" statutes providing for the "humane care and treatment" of hunted and trapped animals, some state trapping regulations have been motivated by a compassionate concern. Do trapped animals in these jurisdictions have legal rights?

Several states have banned the use of the steel-jaw leghold trap, a device that typically causes extensive soft tissue damage, bone fractures, abscesses, and gangrene. Some states have also outlawed the body-gripping trap, which is supposed to ensure a quick kill by snapping the neck, but often fails to do so, and instead subjects the hapless animal to a lingering death as it is slowly squashed and suffocated. Snares, too, are prohibited by a number of states, since these tend to produce death by slow strangulation or a prolonged crushing of vital organs. Further, forty-five states require trappers to check their sets periodically in order to kill or release those animals who might otherwise continue to suffer while caught in them. Trap check times vary widely from state to state, from one to three or even four days, and also depend in many instances on where the trap has been placed (on land, in water, under ice) and the kind of trap that is set (*see* chapter 4: *Commercial Trapping*).

The handful of state legislatures that have approved trap prohibitions have declared them inhumane, but, as we know, this does not necessarily mean that the targeted animals have therefore been given legal rights. That depends on what the primary purposes of the laws are, either to provide protection for animal interests, and thus give rise to direct legal duties to them, or to benefit humans in some way, using animals as a means to that end. Unfortunately, there is virtually nothing to go on that would indicate which this is. There are no sources reporting the ultimate motivations of the relevant legislators. Furthermore, a thorough search of available databases has failed to yield a single reported opinion of a case involving a violation of either a trap ban or trap check limit. Apparently an illegally trapped animal (or species) has never achieved standing in a state court, and we cannot turn to a learned judge to discern legislative intent.

The situation here appears similar to that encountered above in the discussion of the Humane Methods of Slaughter Act and the Animal Welfare Act. The possibility of legal rights for animals found in the morally corrupting influence of the prohibited acts on the public conscience is unavailable here, because so very few people ever have occasion to observe a writhing animal, expiring in slow agony, pinned in a leghold or body-gripping trap, or in a snare.

Even if a right to be spared the needless suffering these traps produce is created by lawmakers who believe that treating animals this way does wrong to them, regardless of the impact of this behavior on the larger moral community, we would once more have a strange situation. An animal has *this* right, but no right to life, no liberty rights, and no right simply to be left alone. At any rate, it is clear that in those states with no trap bans—nearly 90 percent of them—targeted wildlife has no legal standing whatever.

Hunting regulations do not readily manifest any basis in humane considerations that might provide the foundation for the rights of hunted wildlife (*see* chapter 5: *Recreational Hunting*). Yet such a factor might be discerned in two regulated areas. The first is in the few states that have fairly recently adopted laws requiring hunters to make a "reasonable effort" to retrieve wounded animals from the field. This tempts one to the view that retrieval regulations compel hunters to end the suffering of their prey as soon as "reasonably" possible, motivated by a humanitarian concern for the interests of dying animals.

Unfortunately, the purpose of retrieval laws is not clearly distinguishable from that of the very similar "waste regulations," common in the hunting restrictions of many states. Waste prohibitions do not spring from a moral concern for animals' interests, but are instead primarily directed against market and trophy hunters who would leave a rotting carcass and take only the antlers or the hide or an internal organ, such as a gall bladder, considered valuable in some forms of Asian folk medicine (*see* chapter 6: *Legal Protections for Bears: Black Bears*). Also at work here in both waste and retrieval regulations is an aspect of "hunters' ethics" that simply abhors the squandering of wildlife resources, throwing away "good meat."

Some vision of hunters' ethics is also found at the bottom of a second region of state hunting regulations that could indicate a regard for the interests of animals: certain rules intended to enforce a standard of "fair chase," or giving the hunter's prey a "sporting chance." The point is to compel certain practices that reduce the probability of hunter success and enhance the opportunities of the hunted animal to evade destruction at the hands of the hunter. Toward that end, nearly every state prohibits the use of laser sighting devices, spotlights, crossbows, chemicals, explosives, and automatic weapons for taking wildlife. Baiting restrictions and curbs on the use of hunting dogs are also widespread, and likewise seem to be founded on some conception of "ethical hunting." Do these regulations lead us to the legal rights of wildlife?

Probably not. Once again, there is no available case law that might supply us with a judicial interpretation of this issue, and no "game" animal has ever been granted legal standing before the bar. At any rate, the notion that hunted wildlife actually has an interest in securing a higher probability of escape seems to be far too sophisticated an element of cognition to be credibly attributed to an animal. A simple interest in not being killed is much more plausible, but, of course, no hunting law protects that. Early wildlife agencies developed rules of "fair chase" in the late 1800s to prevent hunters from devastating wildlife with unfailingly lethal methods, which plainly does not engender direct duties to animals. Today, with "bag" limits deterring overkill, these regulations are more likely meant to impose standards of fairness with respect to other hunters, giving each a sort of equal opportunity to take animals, disadvantaging no one.

If retrieval regulations and those inspired by a principle of "fair chase" do not after all produce wildlife rights, then game animals have no legal status during the season in which the hunting of the particular species is permitted, the "open" season. For some animals—coyotes in almost every state, for example—there is no designated hunting season; it is always open season on them, so they have no legal rights at any time.

For other species that can only be legally hunted at certain times of the calendar year, it might appear that they have a legal right to life during the off-season, a right that vanishes when the off-season ends. However, even this rather curious idea—an intermittent right to life—evaporates when one realizes that allowing hunting only during certain times of the year is after all not motivated by any humane regard for the interests of the animals and is not intended to protect animal interests at certain times. Instead, restrictions on the days in which wild animals may be legally killed, as well as regulation of the number of animals that a hunter may kill, is driven by a desire to maintain wildlife populations in sufficient numbers to ensure that hunters will continue to have plenty of targets in the future, a management goal known as "sustained yield." Once more, we find laws using animals as a means for human ends.

LEGAL STANDING UNDER FEDERAL WILDLIFE LAWS

Despite the plethora of animal protection laws, it appears that most animals do not have any legal rights. At best, certain species—notably domestic dogs, cats, and horses—arguably have rights to be spared the most extreme forms of abuse and neglect (*see* this chapter: *Do Animals Have Legal Rights?*). Whether or not any laws really do provide rights for animals, the fact is that so far courts at all levels have been completely uninterested in the question of the rightsholding of nonhumans.

Instead, judges have focused on the rights of human plaintiffs who have claimed that *they* were injured by the manner in which various animals have been treated. The point of this strategy is not really to vindicate the humans, but to benefit animals that would otherwise be harmed.

In a series of landmark cases spanning the last thirty years of the twentieth century, a number of individuals and organizations have brought lawsuits seeking court orders and damages, ostensibly for themselves, but they were really suing on behalf of animals (*see also* this chapter: *Legal Standing under the Animal Welfare Act*). This historic sequence of decisions began in 1972 with a seminal case that had little to do with animals directly. Even so, it is one of the most important and influential in animal law, significantly impacting several subsequent cases focused on protecting animals.

Sierra Club v. Morton concerns the difficult and fundamental issue of "legal standing." In its most basic sense, to have legal standing is to have legal rights, to be a rightsholder. An individual with legal rights has certain interests that are protected by various laws: The U.S. Constitution, federal and state statutes and regulations, municipal ordinances, and judges' decisions all safeguard interests in life, health and well-being, safety and security, privacy, property, liberty, and others.

In a more narrow sense, to have legal standing is to be entitled to sue when one's rights have been violated: The plaintiff claims that his or her legally protected interests have been thwarted by the defendant in some specific set of circumstances. Now, of course, people—human beings—have such legally protected interests. Humans have legal rights that, when trampled upon, can be upheld in a court. Do *only* humans have these interests? (For more on these issues, *see* this chapter: *Do Animals Have Legal Rights?*)

Sierra Club v. Morton

Animals were not the subjects of this litigation; instead it was a swath of mountain wilderness on the west side of the Sierra Nevadas, in Tulare County, California. The Mineral King Valley was designated as part of the Sequoia National Forest in 1926, and during the late 1940s the U.S. Forest Service began to consider the valley as a potential site for recreational development. In 1965 the Forest Service invited bids from developers for the construction and operation of a combination ski resort and summer recreation area. Walt Disney Enterprises submitted the winning bid: a $35-million complex of motels, restaurants, parking lots, ski trails and lifts, and other structures designed to accommodate an estimated 14,000 visitors daily. A road 20 miles long, to be constructed by the state of California, was needed to provide access to the facility, and a high-voltage electricity line would be strung to supply power.

In 1969 the Sierra Club filed suit against Rogers Morton, secretary of the interior and chief administrator of the Forest Service. In the district court complaint, the Sierra Club claimed that the proposed development would violate several federal laws governing the preservation of national forests, and it sought permanent injunctions against the approval of the project. The district court granted a preliminary injunction, but the Ninth Circuit Court of Appeals vacated it on the grounds that the Sierra Club had failed to establish its standing as a party who would be injured by the development: it had not demonstrated that the Disney project would violate any legally protected interest of its membership. Since the suing party had no legal standing, there was no need for the court to consider the merits of the plaintiff's claim that laws would be broken if the project came to fruition. The Supreme Court agreed to review the case.

Justice Potter Stewart's majority opinion affirmed the judgment of the appellate court. The Sierra Club had no standing in this suit because it did not assert, much less prove, that any of its members would be affected in any substantial way by the project. "The Sierra Club failed to allege that it or its members would be affected in any of their activities or pastimes by the Disney development," Stewart noted. "Nowhere . . . did the Club state that its members use Mineral King for any purpose." Although the club did point out that the interests of future generations in the "aesthetic enjoyments" of the valley could not be realized if the Disney Corporation had its way, Stewart observed that a legally relevant injury did not consist in the invasion of any recognizable interest; it must be an *actual* injury. This is an "injury in fact," visited upon the person seeking judicial review of the matter. "The alleged injury," he wrote, "will be felt directly only by those who *use* Mineral King . . . and for whom the aesthetic and recreational values of the area will be lessened by the highway and ski resort." Because the Sierra Club was not suing on behalf of future generations, it needed to show that at least some of its membership who did frequent the valley would be harmed, and this was not shown.

Legal Standing for Nonhumans?

This case is also famous for producing one of the best-known dissents in the history of the high court, one that addressed the more fundamental issue of exactly *who* has legal rights, prior to considering the narrower question of whether any legally protected interests were thwarted in this case.

Justice William O. Douglas, a longtime devotee of wilderness preservation and conservation, argued that because natural objects—a wilderness area—can be injured in a legally cognizable way, they can be seen as having legal standing in themselves. Humans can speak for the rights of nature just as they do for individuals who are not legal persons, such as corporations and children. The Mineral King Valley itself, Douglas provocatively asserted, has legally protected interests that would be defeated by the resort development. The wilderness has a basic legal standing as a rightsholder, and, in this case, it has the right to sue the Department of the Interior as an injured party. Justice Stewart and the majority had not considered this alternative view of standing, simply assuming that the legal status of the humans was the only issue.

The notion that a wilderness area has legal rights has never been taken seriously in any subsequent court. It did, however, spark years of debate by philosophers, legal scholars, and law professors about the requirements for legal standing and whether or not some nonhumans qualify, especially animals. For his part, Douglas did not unequivocally assert that any animals in particular, or wildlife generally, do qualify, and it is indeed exceedingly rare to find a nonhuman listed as a plaintiff in any litigation.

Only a few circuit courts (never the Supreme Court) have produced these uncommon specimens of law for some wild animals protected by the Endangered Species Act (for example, *American Bald Eagle v. Bhatti, Loggerhead Turtle v. County Council of Volusia County, Mt. Graham Squirrel v. Yeutter, Palila v. Hawaii Department of Land and Natural Resources*). However, in these cases the injured party is a *species* of wildlife, not any individual animal, and humans are also listed as coplaintiffs. Moreover, these courts do not explicitly acknowledge or discuss the legal standing of the animal litigants. As in *Sierra Club,* humans are the ones with legally protected interests, and it is the humans who have the right to sue for redress.

Despite the fact that the Sierra Club had failed to demonstrate injury to any legally protected interest of their members, and notwithstanding the fact that the welfare of the wildlife in the valley was not really of prime concern, their suit did have two results favorable to those concerned with environmental protection generally. One of these was especially encouraging to animal advocates. First, the Mineral King project was never carried out, and that region of the Sierras remains undeveloped to this day. From a broader legal perspective though, *Sierra Club* produced a far more significant, landmark outcome. An environmental protection organization could achieve standing by proving that the regulation at issue in the case would adversely affect its members by thwarting their interest in the "aesthetic enjoyments" of the natural area.

"Aesthetic and environmental well-being," Stewart wrote for the majority, "are important ingredients of the quality of life in our society, . . . deserving of legal protection through the judicial process." Wilderness thus receives the protection it might not have otherwise gotten as a rightless thing. This seems to open a door for animal welfare organizations. If it could be shown that their membership was similarly harmed by the treatment of animals, the standing of humans as injured parties can secure benefits for the animals that might have eluded them.

Can the Legal Standing of Humans Benefit Animals?: *AWI v. Kreps*

The precedent set in *Sierra Club v. Morton* seemed to bode well for animal advocacy groups ready to take the next step and apply the evolving law of standing on behalf of animals. Their chance came just a few years later in 1976 when the Animal Welfare Institute (AWI), Defenders of Wildlife, the Fund for Animals, the Humane Society of the United States, the International Fund for Animal Welfare, the Committee for Humane Legislation, and the Friends of Animals sued Secretary of Commerce Juanita Kreps.

The director of the National Marine Fisheries Service (NMFS), an office in the Department of Commerce, had waived the Marine Mammal Protection Act moratorium on the taking or importation of marine mammals or marine mammal products for the Fouke Company, an importer of seal skins. Having secured the necessary waiver, Fouke then applied for a permit to import skins from the harvest of Cape fur seals taken off the coast of South Africa, subject to the NMFS condition that the kill not exceed 70,000 animals annually. The AWI and the other organizations sought an order preventing the importation, claiming that it violated several sections of the Marine Mammal Protection Act (*see* chapter 6). The district court threw out the case, ruling that the AWI and the others had no standing to sue. The plaintiffs promptly appealed the decision.

The District of Columbia Circuit Court of Appeals reversed the lower court ruling and in the process developed the law of standing for animal welfare organizations seeking to safeguard nonhuman species. After first finding that the federal animal protection law itself provided the AWI and its allies with standing, Judge Wright went on to show that even if it did not, the organizations were still entitled to sue. Upon analysis of several Supreme Court decisions, principally *Sierra Club*, Wright was able to distill three separate areas of inquiry, all of which must be satisfied to confer standing on a plaintiff: (1) the existence of an "injury in fact," (2) the defendant's action caused the plaintiff's injury, and (3) the thwarted interest—the injury—is protected by the law.

First, did the waiver injure the plaintiffs? Wright found that the AWI and the other groups would indeed be harmed by the deferment because it "impairs the ability of [their] members . . . to see, photograph, and enjoy Cape fur seals alive in their natural habitat under conditions in which the animals are not subject to excessive harvesting, inhumane treatment and slaughter." Second, the requisite causal connection also obtains, according to Wright, because, despite Kreps's claim that waiver or no, South Africa would continue to kill seals, Congress had decided that "denial of import privileges *is* an effective method of protecting marine mammals in other parts of the world." Finally, the Marine Mammal Protection Act is clearly intended to preserve aesthetic and recreational interests. Having established the legal standing of the organizations, Judge Wright went on to find that the waiver was illegal. The Supreme Court declined to review this decision, and Fouke was not permitted to import any sealskins.

Notice that here, as in the majority opinion in *Sierra Club*, the thought that the seals themselves might have standing to contest a decision promoting their own demise was not entertained.

More Benefits for Animals through Humans' Legal Standing: *HSUS v. Hodel*

The second major stage in the evolution of standing law that improved matters for animals, though once more *their* legal standing was not considered, came twelve years after *AWI v. Kreps* in the same D.C. Circuit Court (though with a new panel of judges). Once again, an animal protection organization sued the head administrator of a government agency.

This time, the Humane Society of the United States (HSUS) challenged a series of U.S. Fish and Wildlife Service (FWS) directives issued in mid-1984 that allowed hunting for the first time or expanded opportunities to hunt on twenty-two of the nation's wildlife refuges (*see also* chapter 6: *National Wildlife Refuge System Improvement Act of 1997: Hunting and Trapping in National Wildlife Refuges*). The HSUS complained that these agency actions were contrary to several different federal wildlife and environmental protection laws and sued Donald Hodel, the secretary of the interior, the home department of the FWS. The district court rejected the challenge, ruling that the HSUS lacked standing for two reasons. First, the "emotional injuries" that the hunting allegedly caused to its members were not constitutionally recognizable, and, second, the "recreational interests" the HSUS hoped to safeguard in this litigation were not "germane" to the overall mission of the organization.

Both these findings were reversed by Judge Patricia Wald of the appellate court. Although agreeing with the lower court that thwarting the "strong interest" of the HSUS membership in the preservation and humane treatment of wildlife was a "mere emotional injury" that enjoyed no legal protections, Wald noticed that this was not the only injury here. She pointed out that *Sierra Club v. Morton* had already established the legitimacy of aesthetic injuries. By compelling the HSUS members "to witness animal corpses . . . [and by] depleting the supply of animals and birds that refuge visitors seek to view," the hunting defeats "classic aesthetic interests, which have always enjoyed protection under standing analysis." However, in order for the refuge hunting to qualify as an "injury in fact" to the HSUS, Wald continued, it must also be shown that these defeated interests are "germane" to the purpose of the organization.

After a long discussion of the rigorousness of this condition and the meaning of the term "germane," the judge held that they are indeed. The lower court was mistaken to characterize the injuries to the HSUS members as "recreational." They are more accurately understood as impediments to aesthetic interests in observing wildlife, such interests being pertinent, closely connected, or "germane" to the humanitarian goals of the organization. The HSUS did have standing to sue, but Wald did not proceed to the merits of the group's claim that the hunting on the refuges violated federal laws.

Meanwhile, the justices of the Supreme Court confined their attention to the issue of the legal standing of plaintiffs concerned with animal well-being to a single remark, buried in a footnote of the 1986 majority opinion in *Japan Whaling Association v. American Cetacean Society*. Here, the whale preservation group had demanded that the secretary of commerce impose economic sanctions on Japan for refusing to abide by limits in whale take set by the International Whaling Commission (*see also* chapter 6: *Legal Protections for Whales*). In this aside, the Court acknowledged that the organization's membership would suffer an "injury in fact" by continued killing of whales since this would adversely affect their ability to watch and study the cetaceans.

Sierra Club and its immediate progeny, best represented by the D.C. Circuit in *AWI v. Kreps* and *HSUS v. Hodel*, as well as the footnote in *Japan Whaling Association*, offer the following lessons in standing law for animal protection organizations. First, the animals themselves have no legal standing, and they can only be helped when it is established that human litigants do have standing in the case. Second, the aesthetic interests in wildlife of the members of certain organizations are legally protected. Lastly, these interests can be injured "in fact" when animals are hunted and killed at the behest of the federal government, and provided these concerns are a significant part of the purpose of the organization. These results would subsequently come to be applied and significantly modified in two other key cases over the next decade, *Animal Legal Defense Fund v. Glickman* (*see* this chapter: *Legal Standing under the Animal Welfare Act*) and *Lujan v. Defenders of Wildlife*.

Lujan v. Defenders of Wildlife

This is the definitive statement to date by the Supreme Court on the requirements for legal standing. It explains exactly what is required for a human to achieve the status before the law that would protect the animals that the law does not value in their own right.

The law at issue here is the Endangered Species Act (ESA) (*see* chapter 6). Specifically, the ESA requires every federal agency to consult with either the Department of the Interior or the Department of Commerce to determine whether the projects or business enterprises they are promoting would imperil any endangered or threatened species. According to Section 7(a)(2) of the ESA, each agency must "insure that any action authorized, funded, or carried out by such agency . . . is not likely to jeopardize the continued existence of any endangered or threatened species or result in the destruction or adverse modification of habitat of such species."

In 1978 the Interior and Commerce Departments issued regulations stating that this requirement applied to projects undertaken in foreign lands as well as in the United States. Yet, just one year later, the regulations were rescinded and the consultation was demanded only for domestic enterprises. Shortly thereafter, U.S. funds were slated for two overseas operations, the Mahaweli irrigation project in Sri Lanka, and the rebuilding of the Aswan High Dam on the Nile River in Egypt. In the view of the Defenders of Wildlife, a wildlife protection organization, an endangered species of Asian elephant and a rare breed of Nile crocodile would be seriously menaced by these projects. However, because consultations with Interior or Commerce concerning their impact on these animals were no longer required, none had been done.

Alarmed, the Defenders immediately filed a complaint in the federal district court against then–Secretary of the Interior Donald Hodel, demanding that the new regulation be withdrawn and the original one, mandating wildlife assessments for both domestic and foreign projects, be restored. The organization anticipated that the funding would be withdrawn once the original regulation was reinstated and it was confirmed, as the Defenders believed it would be, that the two construction projects would be harmful for both of the ESA protected species.

Hodel moved to dismiss the suit on the grounds that the Defenders had no legal standing to make the complaint. Counsel for the group responded that since they represented members of an organization who had personally visited the sites in Sri Lanka and Egypt to study the endangered species, the matter of their standing had been established. The district court agreed with Hodel, rendering a decision favorable to the government in 1987.

On appeal, the Eighth Circuit Court of Appeals reversed the lower court, and sent the case back down to them to consider the merits of the Defenders' demand to revive the geographically sweeping regulation. The district court promptly ordered Hodel to restore the old regulation, and by mid-1990 the Eighth Circuit had affirmed this ruling (*Defenders of Wildlife v. Hodel*). In late 1991 the Supreme Court agreed to review the case, and by this time Manuel Lujan had replaced Hodel as the head of the Interior Department.

Requirements for Legal Standing

In a seven-to-two decision, the Supreme Court overturned the appellate ruling and dismissed the Defenders' suit for lack of standing. Justice Antonin Scalia's majority opinion for the first time delineated the authoritative view of the precise requirements for legal standing, or having a right to sue in a particular circumstance. As in every other case in which humans have sued to protect animals, the possibility that the nonhumans might themselves have such standing was not considered (*see also* this chapter: *Legal Standing under the Animal Welfare Act: International Primate Protection League v. Institute for Behavioral Research, Inc.*).

Scalia asserted three basic elements, all of which must be satisfied before an individual can be accurately identified as one with legal standing. First, and most importantly, to have the right to initiate a lawsuit, "the plaintiff must have suffered an 'injury in fact'—an invasion of a legally protected interest which is (a) concrete and particularized, . . . and (b) 'actual or imminent, not conjectural or hypothetical.'" The second requirement is that a causal relationship must obtain between the injury and the conduct alleged to be unlawful. The injury must be "fairly traceable" to the behavior of the defendant, and not the result of the actions of some third party not before the court. Simply put, the person being sued must be the one responsible for perpetrating the harm.

Third and finally, according to Scalia, there must be a high probability that the harm will be remedied by a decision favorable to the plaintiff. The prospect of obtaining compensation for the damage done has to be "likely" and not "speculative." The plaintiff bears the burden of establishing each of these three elements. Even though standing requires that each one of these elements be demonstrated, a case for standing immediately collapses if the plaintiff cannot show that an "injury in fact" has occurred.

Moreover, Scalia pointed out that standing becomes "substantially more difficult" to achieve when the object of the disputed government regulation is not the one challenging the law. This is because it is not so clear that this third party is really being harmed by the federal action. Such is the situation in this case, where Interior and Commerce promulgated regulations permitting *federal agencies* to proceed with foreign projects without assessing their effects on protected species. The government was not allowing the Defenders of Wildlife to do anything here, nor were they being restricted. This is in contrast to, say, a law that denies women the right to obtain an abortion, because here women—the objects of the law—can easily establish their legal standing as individuals whose interests are harmed by the restriction.

Why the Defenders of Wildlife Have No Legal Standing

Having set down these rather strict conditions, Scalia proceeded to consider whether the Defenders satisfied them. At the outset, he acknowledged that an aesthetic interest in observing and studying wild animals was undoubtedly legally protected. This had been established twenty years earlier in *Sierra Club v. Morton*. As noted above, the Sierra Club lost their suit, but the Court did recognize that "[a]esthetic and environmental well-being are important ingredients of the quality of life in our society, . . . deserving of legal protection through the judicial process." However, Scalia continued, to satisfy the first requirement for standing—the "injury in fact test"—the Defenders had to prove that such an interest of one or more of their members would be directly and detrimentally affected by the Mahaweli and Aswan Dam projects.

The Defenders tried to prove this through the affidavits of two members of the group, one who had traveled to Egypt in the past and intended to do so again in search of the crocodile, and another who had been to Sri Lanka and similarly planned to return in hopes of observing the elephant. Both individuals believed that the construction projects would harm them by denying them opportunities to see these animals, although neither had any specific plans for a journey to these lands. When asked when she would return to Sri Lanka, one answered, "I don't know. . . . Not next year, I will say. In the future." This was simply not enough to pass the "injury in fact" test for Scalia: "Such 'some day' intentions—without any description of concrete plans, or indeed any specification of when the some day will be—do not support a finding of the 'actual or imminent' injury our cases require."

Scalia also disposed of two other attempts by the Defenders to show that they had been harmed by the regulation. The first held that anyone who spends time in any part of the ecosystem where the elephant or the crocodile are found is thereby injured. Scalia said that this can only occur when someone uses the very same area inhabited by the animals, not some region in the vicinity. The second attempt claimed that anyone with a personal or professional interest in seeing or studying the animals can sue. This was completely unreasonable, Scalia scolded, because it implies that a person who likes to watch Asian elephants in the Bronx Zoo, and indeed the elephant keeper there, have legal standing in this case. "It goes beyond the limit," he wrote, "and into pure speculation and fantasy, to say that anyone who observes or works with an endangered species, anywhere in the world, is appreciably harmed by a single project affecting some portion of that species with which he has no more specific connection."

It might not seem unduly restrictive to reject both the notion that anyone anywhere with the requisite interest in animals could be harmed by a federal regulation impacting some area of the world, or the theory that a person a hundred miles up the Nile is injured by the demise of crocodiles downstream. Yet Scalia's focus on "actual or imminent" injury does represent a considerable tightening of standing law. This requires defendants hoping to protect animals by establishing their own standing as aggrieved parties to show exactly how and when the government regulation is going to thwart their aesthetic interests in the animals. On this view, the two leading cases discussed above, in which animal welfare organizations had convinced the District of Columbia Circuit Court that some of their membership would be harmed by actions of the federal government, were incorrectly decided.

Recall that in *Animal Welfare Institute v. Kreps*, the AWI was found to have standing because a waiver of the moratorium imposed by the Marine Mammal Protection Act on importing sealskins impaired the ability of their membership to observe living seals in the wild off the coast of South Africa. In the second case, *Humane Society of the United States v. Hodel*, the court ruled that members of the HSUS were harmed by federal regulations expanding hunting opportunities in some of America's wildlife refuges because they would be forced to observe dead animals killed by hunters.

In neither of these cases were the plaintiff organizations required to verify precisely when any of their members would be traveling to South Africa or to any of the wildlife refuges in question. Furthermore, no assessment was made of the probabilities of actually seeing animal corpses dispatched by hunters or not seeing seals that, but for the waiver, would otherwise have been available for viewing. Following *Lujan*, it would seem that such assessments and verifications must be provided before animal welfare groups can achieve standing on behalf of rightless wild creatures.

LEGAL STANDING UNDER THE ANIMAL WELFARE ACT

The Animal Welfare Act (AWA) and its implementing regulations, issued by the U.S. Department of Agriculture (USDA), set standards for the care and handling of certain species used by research facilities, zoos, circuses, and animal dealers (*see* chapter 7). Originally enacted by Congress in 1966 and subsequently amended several times, the AWA is intended to improve living conditions for animals in these operations and to ensure that they are treated humanely. The law is enforced by USDA inspectors, who are trained to detect violations and authorized to issue citations for noncompliance, the infractions punishable by a fine paid to the federal government.

What about the animals? When a provision of the AWA or one of its regulations is violated, the result is very often some harm to a protected animal. Do they have any right to sue when they are unlawfully injured by researchers, exhibitors, or dealers? Of course, no animal is capable of representing itself or testifying in court, but humans could provide representation for them, pressing claims in their interest.

To ask this question is to ask about the "legal standing" of the animals protected by the AWA, and whether or not they are entitled to vindication and compensation in court when legal wrongdoing harms their interests. The answer to the question is "no" (*see also* this chapter: *Do Animals Have Legal Rights?*). No animal has ever been recognized as a plaintiff in a case involving this federal law. Nonhumans have no standing before a court and have no right to sue when they are harmed. Indeed, it is extremely rare to find an animal plaintiff in any litigation under any federal statute. Yet this does not necessarily mean that the interests of animals are, paradoxically, left unprotected by the very laws that are supposed to benefit them. Humans, who indisputably have legal standing, can claim that certain AWA violations injure *them*, with the legal remedy advancing the interests of the animals. Will a court accept such a claim?

The Silver Spring Monkeys at the Institute for Behavioral Research

The long and winding road through the American judicial system that addresses this claim begins in 1981 at the Institute for Behavioral Research (IBR) in Silver Spring, Maryland. There, seventeen primates—sixteen crab-eating macaques and one rhesus macaque—would move into a national spotlight and become known as the "Silver Spring monkeys," unfortunate celebrities and perhaps the most famous lab animals in the history of science.

In the spring of that year Dr. Edward Taub, chief research scientist at IBR, received $180,000 from the National Institutes of Health (NIH) to continue his investigation of somatosensory deafferentation, a phenomenon he had been studying for more than two decades. Investigated by scientists since at least the 1890s, deafferentation is the deliberate severing of nerves leading out of the spinal cord to eliminate sensation in the extremities. By cutting nerves and then determining what limbs or parts of limbs were numbed, researchers could learn how the nerves control the body.

These sorts of inquiries have always been performed on animals, of course, typically dogs and cats, but Taub was using macaques, and had been since the late 1950s. After surgically numbing one arm in each monkey, Taub was trying to force the animals to use their crippled appendages. He strapped the good arm down and applied electric shocks until the damaged limb was moved. After a year of repeated trials, Taub planned to check the spinal cords of the monkeys for new nerve growth, the examination requiring that the animals be killed. The point of the experiment, Taub claimed, was to show that people who had lost function in their arms or legs due to stroke or injury could regain some use of their limbs.

Alex Pacheco appeared at the door of IBR on a morning in May 1981, touting his enthusiasm for research and asking for a job. Impressed but pleading a lack of funds, Taub offered him a volunteer position instead. Pacheco accepted without hesitation, and despite having made it clear that he had no experience in research using animals, he was almost immediately put in charge of several experimental procedures with the macaques and given keys to the facility. This was imprudent of Taub. Pacheco was a cofounder of the then fledgling People for the Ethical Treatment of Animals (PETA). His undercover mission was to plant himself in a federally funded research facility—IBR happened to be the closest one to his home—in search of abuses to lab animals.

He found what he was looking for. Rats and cockroaches skittered about freely in the animal-holding areas at the IBR, the surgery room was littered with garbage, and the macaques sat in tiny, filth-encrusted cages in a feces-spattered room. Most of the animals suffered from untreated or barely treated wounds—bloody, infected, and many of them self-inflicted. The numbing of the arms had provoked several monkeys to attack their dead limbs, chewing off the fingers and pulling apart the muscle tissue with their teeth. Animals commonly react to deafferentation of their appendages in this way, as scientists working in the area have long known.

By late summer Pacheco had begun documenting the sorry state of Taub's laboratory, returning after hours to photograph the squalor, the self-mutilation, and the dearth of medical care. He also brought several scientists experienced in working with primates into the facility under cover of darkness to corroborate his sense of outrage. In September, Pacheco decided he'd had enough. Armed with affidavits and photographs, he asked the Montgomery County police to investigate Taub for violations of the state anticruelty law. Having secured a warrant, a search was conducted at IBR shortly thereafter, and seventeen macaques—a dozen with deafferentated arms and five control animals—were confiscated. Several days later Taub was formally charged with seventeen counts of cruelty to animals (*see also* chapter 3: *Anticruelty Laws*).

Never before had a U.S. laboratory been raided by police, and it was the first time criminal charges of this nature were filed against a scientist conducting federally funded research.

State v. Taub **and** Taub v. State

Edward Taub stood trial in the District Court for Montgomery County, and in December was convicted on six counts of animal cruelty for failing to provide necessary veterinary care and acquitted on the other eleven counts (*State v. Taub*). He immediately appealed to the next level in the Maryland judicial system, where he was found guilty on just one count, with the conviction on the five others overturned. Not satisfied, Taub next petitioned the Maryland Court of Appeals requesting that the conviction on the single count be thrown out as well. The court obliged.

Unlike many states, Maryland's anticruelty statute did not contain a specific exemption for scientific research. This is in large part precisely why Taub was convicted by the lower courts in the first place: it was simply undeniable that he had not given the Silver Spring monkeys the "necessary veterinary care" required by the law. However, in 1983 the court of appeals determined that the Maryland legislature intended to prohibit only "unnecessary or unjustifiable physical pain and suffering." Despite their having written nothing about the matter into the statute, the court proclaimed that lawmakers in the Old Line State were certainly aware that animals are frequently used in research funded and regulated by the federal government, and sometimes "purely incidental and unavoidable pain" is inflicted upon them in the course of these investigations. In these circumstances, such as those that prevailed at IBR, the discomfort of the animals, no matter how extreme, was justified (*Taub v. State*).

Although Taub was completely exonerated, the appellate decision moved Maryland's General Assembly to make their legislative intentions in forming the state's anticruelty statute completely clear. In 1992 the law was amended to explicitly protect "all animals . . . [used in] federally funded scientific or medical activities."

Meanwhile, as Taub's case progressed through the Maryland courts, animal protection groups were not resting content. They sought federal jurisdiction in early 1982 by filing two separate lawsuits. In the first, the Humane Society of the United States (HSUS) and PETA argued that Taub had violated several provisions of the AWA regulating the care and handling of primates, and demanded that the USDA enforce the law, as directed by Congress, against IBR (*Humane Society v. Block*). In a second suit, the Fund for Animals contended that because Taub had acted in a manner contrary to the AWA, the federal district court in Washington, D.C., should prohibit the NIH from returning the macaques to IBR, which were at that time being held at an agency facility (*Fund for Animals v. Malone*).

The court dismissed both cases, reasoning against the HSUS and PETA that it was up to the USDA to decide when their enforcement authority should be brought to bear on a regulated entity—such an initiative was "wholly discretionary" for the agency. As for the request from the Fund for Animals, the court noted that the AWA neither states nor implies that the NIH has any legal duty to this or any other animal protection organization.

The Disposition of the Silver Spring Monkeys

When the police removed the seventeen monkeys from IBR in September 1981, they asked the National Zoo in Washington, D.C., to take them, but the zoo refused. Local animal shelters pleaded insufficient space and facilities, so the macaques were turned over to Lori Lehner, a member of PETA who had volunteered to house the animals.

Shortly thereafter, Taub, claiming that the monkeys were his property, asked Judge David Cahoon to order their return. Relying solely on recent USDA inspection reports of IBR that listed either no problems or a few insignificant ones, Judge Cahoon granted Taub's request and issued an injunction that the macaques be sent back to IBR the next day. Before they could be confiscated, the animals disappeared from Lehner's home. Negotiations between PETA and local law enforcement followed and an agreement was reached: the police would hold the monkeys and not turn them over to IBR. Cahoon wouldn't hear of it and once more directed the return of Taub's property. But when one of the seventeen died within days of arriving back at IBR, Cahoon ordered another relocation, this time to the NIH primate quarantine center at the Animal Laboratory in Poolesville, Maryland.

By now PETA had been joined in the struggle by the International Primate Protection League (IPPL), a nonprofit organization devoted to primate welfare, headquartered in Summerville, South Carolina. PETA and the IPPL wanted the macaques—now down to fifteen in number after another was euthanized at Poolesville—to be released to them so the organizations could move the animals to Primarily Primates, a wildlife sanctuary in San Antonio, Texas, where they could live out the rest of their lives in peace. Here, their daily care, as well as rehabilitation by a primatologist, would be paid for with private funds, rather than with the tax dollars needed to keep the monkeys at the NIH facility. The two groups even prevailed upon Republican Robert Smith of New Hampshire and Democrat Charles Rose from North Carolina—legislators in the House of Representatives—to draft a unique, bipartisan document, signed by 250 Congressmen, asking the NIH to send the macaques to the refuge.

The NIH was unmoved. The Silver Spring monkeys were the property of IBR, the agency retorted, and only IBR could give them away. Yet, at the urging of numerous allies in the research community, especially the American Medical Association and the National Association for Biomedical Research, IBR had refused to deal with any animal protection groups. Because neither the NIH nor IBR would relinquish the macaques for placement at Primarily Primates, PETA and the IPPL filed a civil lawsuit in Maryland at the start of 1984, requesting that the animal advocates be named as the legal guardians of the fifteen survivors. The case was removed to the federal district court at the end of the year, and in March 1985 it was dismissed on the grounds that neither the IPPL nor PETA had standing to sue. An appeal to the Fourth Circuit Court of Appeals followed, with the decision handed down in September 1986.

International Primate Protection League v. Institute for Behavioral Research, Inc.

Some "actual or threatened injury as a result of the . . . illegal conduct of the defendant" must be shown before a plaintiff can have standing to sue in a court of law (*see* this chapter: *Lujan v. Defenders of Wildlife*). Accordingly, the IPPL and PETA founded their case for standing on the claim that they would suffer financial injury as well as harm to their "aesthetic, conservational, and environmental interests" if IBR was allowed to reacquire the monkeys.

The IPPL and PETA argued that they would be damaged financially in two different ways. First, as taxpayers, they were entitled to an assurance that the law was followed by the NIH, a federal agency, and IBR, a federally funded facility. Second, they had contributed to the care of the animals before they were moved to the Animal Laboratory at Poolesville.

The plaintiffs also attempted to establish two sorts of nonfinancial injuries. First, what happened to the macaques thwarted their "personal interest in the . . . civilized and humane treatment of animals," and, second, returning the monkeys to IBR would disrupt their "personal relationship" with the animals.

Judge Wilkinson rejected each of these four claims of injury. Citing a Supreme Court pronouncement in another case, he quickly disposed of the first alleged injury: "Payment of taxes does not purchase authority to enforce regulatory restrictions." The second financial injury asserted by the plaintiffs did not fare any better. Wilkinson noted that any expenditures they had made for the care of the monkeys were done voluntarily and not in any way necessitated by Taub's conduct. The appeal to interests in humane treatment, conservation, the environment, and the aesthetic offense endured was similarly unpersuasive. Here, Wilkinson cited the Supreme Court decision in *Sierra Club v. Morton*, in 1986 the leading case on legal standing (*see* this chapter: *Legal Standing under Federal Wildlife Laws*). *Sierra Club* was to be supplanted in 1992 by *Lujan v. Defenders of Wildlife* (*see* this chapter: *Lujan v. Defenders of Wildlife*).

In *Sierra Club*, the wilderness conservation group attempted to halt a resort project in the Mineral King Valley of California's Sierra Nevada Mountains. The high court found that the group lacked standing despite its admitted interest and expertise in matters of environmental use and development. Quoting from Justice Stewart's majority opinion there, Wilkinson averred that the situation in *IPPL v. IBR* was identical, so "a mere interest in a problem, no matter how . . . qualified the organization is in evaluating the problem, is not sufficient by itself" to establish standing.

Finally, the judge found unpersuasive the notion that the plaintiffs would be injured if the macaques were returned to IBR because the bonds that had developed between them would be severed. The IPPL and PETA had attempted to support this claim with an analogy to *Sierra Club* of their own. The plaintiffs argued that the intrusion into their relationship with the monkeys was like the affront caused to nature lovers by developers disturbing national parks and forests, a form of injury accepted by the Supreme Court in that seminal case (though the Sierra Club failed to prove it was one suffered by its membership). Wilkinson denied the comparison because users of wilderness could enjoy the outdoors if the development was stopped, but even if the IBR lab scrupulously followed the AWA, the plaintiffs would have no contact with the animals kept there.

The Fate of the Silver Spring Monkeys

IPPL v. IBR was the first case in which human plaintiffs sought standing under the AWA, and the attempt was a failure. More than a decade would pass before this maneuver would meet with any success in *Animal Legal Defense Fund v. Glickman,* another case involving the welfare of primates (*see* this chapter: *Legal Standing under the Animal Welfare Act: ADLF v. Glickman*).

Meanwhile, the story of the Silver Spring monkeys was still not over. In July 1986, as the litigants were awaiting the decision of the Fourth Circuit Court of Appeals, five uninjured macaques were moved from Poolesville to the San Diego Zoo, and the remaining ten (two control animals and eight crippled ones) went to an NIH-funded facility in Covington, Louisiana, the Delta Regional Primate Center of Tulane University. Before the relocation, NIH Director James Wyngaarden sent a written assurance to Congress that the animals would live outside and "will not undergo invasive procedures for research purposes." Both promises were ultimately broken.

The monkeys were never housed outdoors. Instead they were confined to basic steel cages in a cinder-block room. Nor were they (not all of them anyway) spared further subjection to experimental procedures. They were just too tempting to NIH-supported scientists. Taub had planned to kill the monkeys and examine their spinal columns for new nerve growth after just one year, but by late 1988 legal and political circumstances—but for which they would have been long dead—had kept them alive for almost a decade after they had been originally crippled. No study of deafferentation had ever been conducted over such a time span, so the macaques presented a unique opportunity to investigate the long-term regenerative powers of the brain, one that neither Taub nor anyone else had envisioned.

In December 1988 the NIH announced that three of the monkeys would soon be euthanized, autopsied, and their spinal cords examined for any changes. When the plan became widely known, the NIH and the Bush administration were bombarded with criticism. Letters and telephone calls from thousands of angry citizens and dozens of congressmen came pouring in.

Even more incensed, the IPPL and PETA returned to the courts and filed suit in Louisiana, once more seeking custody of the animals so that they could be relocated to Primarily Primates. The Louisiana Civil District Court did not grant this request, but did issue a temporary restraining order in December 1989 prohibiting the euthanization of any of the monkeys. The NIH promptly moved the case to federal district court, as authorized for government agencies by a federal statute, but found no help there. The order of the state court was upheld and an injunction leveled against the agency to refrain from experimenting on or killing the macaques. The Fifth Circuit Court of Appeals agreed to hear the NIH's appeal in 1990.

There, the IPPL and PETA were defeated on the standing issue once again. The plaintiffs attempted to ground their standing, just as they had done in *IPPL v. IBR*, on the personal relationship they had developed with the Silver Spring monkeys and on their "long-standing, sincere commitment to preventing inhumane treatment of animals." This argument fared no better in the Fifth Circuit than it had in the Fourth. Once again, whether or not the Delta Primate Center acted lawfully in its treatment of the animals, the monkeys would be inaccessible in the confines of the lab, so the plaintiffs could not have any right to continue their personal relationships with them. And, again, citing *Sierra Club*, the fact that the IPPL and PETA had had a prolonged, bona fide commitment to animal welfare did not create standing. If it did, the consequence would be a precipitous slide down a slippery slope that would allow any organization—indeed, any individual—with the requisite interest the right to sue (*IPPL v. Administrators of the Tulane Educational Fund*).

This decision was rendered in March 1990 and in a little more than a year the Supreme Court reversed it, holding that the move from the state court to federal jurisdiction was invalid in this case. But it was too late for the Silver Spring monkeys. Three of them were euthanized in mid-1990 and two more were killed in April 1991 just before the reversal. All five were examined for nerve regeneration, and new nerve pathways were indeed detected, prompting a paper reporting these results that was published in the prestigious journal *Science*. Edward Taub was listed as one of the authors.

AWA Regulatory Definition of "Animal": *ALDF v. Espy I*

Our journey in the search for legal standing under the Animal Welfare Act continues at about the same time the Supreme Court invalidated the move of the Silver Spring monkey case from the Louisiana bench to the federal judiciary. We leave the IPPL and PETA behind for a new voyager through the courts, the Animal Legal Defense Fund (ALDF).

Along with several other animal protection organizations, the ALDF has frequently complained that the AWA and its regulations are too narrow, too vague, incomplete, and inadequately enforced, all such deficiencies ultimately harming the same animals the law is supposed to benefit. Because the animals have no legal standing of their own to petition a court for redress of grievances, members of the ALDF and others in the animal welfare community have tried to devise ways in which the shortcomings of the AWA "in fact" injure *them*. The legal remedy for the injury to humans will then make things better for the animals.

Several key decisions of the District of Columbia Circuit Court of Appeals in the still-evolving case law of standing have addressed this strategy, culminating in *ALDF v. Glickman*. Probably the two most critical cases in the succession leading to *Glickman* were decided by the D.C. Circuit Court just two months apart in mid-1994, both concerning ALDF challenges to AWA regulations issued by the USDA and both naming Mike Espy, secretary of agriculture, as the defendant.

In the first litigation the ALDF, joined by the Humane Society of the United States and two individuals, Patricia Knowles and William Strauss, objected to the exclusion of mice, rats, and birds from the definition of "animal" in USDA regulations specifying the range of species that the AWA's standards cover. The language of the AWA statute itself does not place these species out of bounds. (For the most recent developments on this exclusion, *see* chapter 7: *Animal Welfare Act Regulations: Laboratory Animals*). In 1991 the D.C. federal district court found that the ALDF and its allies had standing to sue, and the next year ruled that the exclusion of these species was indeed contrary to the AWA (*ALDF v. Yeutter* and *ALDF v. Madigan*, respectively).

The D.C. Circuit Court of Appeals overruled the lower tribunal, rejecting the claim to standing of each defendant, beginning with Knowles and Strauss. Dr. Knowles, a psychobiologist who had used rats and mice in her research, argued that because the care and treatment of these rodents was unregulated by the AWA, they would be subjected to inhumane treatment that would impair her ability to perform her professional duties in the future. To this appeal Judge Sentelle pointed out that, as established by the Supreme Court in *Lujan*, the injury required to achieve standing must be "imminent" or "certainly impending," and "[w]e cannot say that the injury she seeks to litigate is certainly impending." Knowles was not currently engaged in research using rodents and offered no immediate plans for doing so; in any case, she could avoid the alleged harm simply by choosing not to pursue such research. As for Strauss, Sentelle quickly dismissed his suit: It "amounts to nothing more than an attempt to compel executive enforcement of the law, detached from any factual claim of injury."

The ALDF and the HSUS premised their case for standing on their role as, among other things, disseminators of information to the public concerning laboratory conditions for animals. Because rats, mice, and birds were excluded from the requirements of the AWA, researchers were not required to provide the USDA with any data on the treatment of these species, which in turn made these facts unavailable to the two organizations. This constituted an "informational injury."

In response to this argument, Sentelle cited a number of previous D.C. Circuit Court decisions. These reveal that such standing can only be conferred by proving that either Congress intended the law in question to specifically protect this interest in distributing the information—creating a "right to information"—or that the organization is especially well suited to challenge agencies that neglect to provide it. The ALDF and the HSUS failed on both counts.

"[T]he general informational and educative interests in animal welfare," Sentelle wrote, "upon which the organizations base their suit are, by the terms of [AWA], the province of . . . oversight committees of private citizens, whose members 'represent society's concerns regarding animal welfare.'" This matter is pertinent foremost to the Institutional Animal Care and Use Committee, mandated by the AWA for each research facility (*see also* chapter 7: *Animal Care Committees*). It does not concern private, nonprofit groups with interests that happen to be consistent with the humanitarian purposes of the law.

AWA Regulations for Dogs and Primates: *ALDF v. Espy II*

ALDF v. Espy II was instigated by 1985 amendments to the AWA that directed the USDA to set "minimum requirements . . . for exercise of dogs, . . . and for a physical environment adequate to promote the psychological well-being of nonhuman primates" kept in research facilities, zoos, circuses, and by animal dealers. When three years had elapsed and the USDA had yet to issue any such regulations, the ALDF sued to grease the creaky, rusted wheels of the federal agency rule-making process. Three more years passed and finally, in 1991, the USDA published its final rules on these two items.

The ALDF leadership was not pleased. In their view, the USDA had basically told research facilities, exhibitors, and dealers to set their own standards. For canines, each is merely to "develop, document, and follow an appropriate plan to provide dogs with the opportunity to exercise . . . [that] must be approved by the attending veterinarian." Similarly, for primates they must "develop, document, and follow an appropriate plan adequate to promote the psychological well-being of nonhuman primates . . . [that] address[es] the[ir] social needs . . . [and provides a] physical environment . . . enriched by means of expressing noninjurious species-typical activities" (*see also* chapter 7: *Primates: Psychological Well-Being*).

A lawsuit was promptly filed, with the Society for Animal Protective Legislation, Primate Pole Housing, Inc., and its president Bernard Migler, Roger Fouts, and, once again, William Strauss joining the ALDF as plaintiffs. The district court agreed with the ALDF that the USDA had failed to provide the "minimum requirements" that Congress had ordered in 1985, and demanded that the agency do so. Upon appeal to the D.C. Circuit Court of Appeals, Judge Karen Henderson dismissed the suit because none of the plaintiffs had standing, and thus avoided considering the merits of their charge against the USDA.

Relying heavily on *ALDF v. Espy I*, Henderson pointed out that Strauss and the ALDF lacked standing here for the same reasons that they had no standing in the first case. Strauss was again not really claiming any factual injury, and the ALDF once more was neither the "peculiarly suitable challenger of administrative neglect" nor the appropriate body with the right to information that would confer standing upon them. These same organizational considerations ruled out standing for the Society for Animal Protective Legislation as well. Primate Pole Housing and Migler complained that they were injured because the USDA regulations did not require that primates be housed in pairs or groups, which provided no incentive for researchers or exhibitors to buy their products. To this, Henderson replied that she could not discern any intention by Congress to promote the sale of some particular form of primate housing system.

Finally, Henderson ruled that Fouts did not establish that he was injured with his claim that the regulations were too vague to ensure that he could design primate housing at his research facility that would be in compliance. This was because the AWA and its regulations apply to research *facilities*, not individual researchers. A person can qualify as a research "facility" under the AWA if he or she buys or transports animals, or receives federal funds to conduct research, but Fouts did not claim to be doing either. Even if he might have been harmed by failing to comply with the regulations, his injury, like that alleged in *ALDF v. Espy I*, was neither "imminent" nor "certainly impending," failing the test set down in *Lujan*. "Fouts' injury is remote and speculative," Henderson wrote, "couched in the language of uncertainty and futurity."

AWA Regulations in Exhibitions: *ALDF v. Glickman*

The lessons of *ALDF v. Espy I* and *II* were clear: Under the AWA organizational standing was out of reach and claims to standing by individuals would founder without a showing of actual, imminent "injury in fact." To concerned citizens, the situation seemed hopeless for animals used in research facilities, particularly primates. After all, lab animals are not accessible to the general public—nobody sees what is done to them—so it would be extremely difficult to show that the treatment of animals in labs causes any "imminent" or "certainly impending" injury to anyone in the animal welfare community.

Unable to establish standing in the context of AWA regulation of research facilities, the ALDF and others changed their tactics and turned to animal exhibitors, where the point of the whole enterprise is to display animals for paying customers. AWA restrictions apply to animal exhibitions and research facilities alike, so if the regulation of exhibitors could be altered, researchers would have to comply as well. The USDA standards concerning the psychological well-being of primates remained the target (the issue of exercise for dogs was not taken up).

Shortly after the decision in *ALDF v. Espy II*, Roseann Circelli, Mary Eagan, Audrey Rahn, and Marc Jurnove began regular visitations of animal exhibitors in Iowa, Ohio, New Jersey, and New York. Each person focused on one zoo and monitored the housing of the primates kept there. After nearly two years of observing conditions at these locations, the four and the ALDF filed suit in federal District Court against Daniel Glickman, now USDA secretary.

As in *ALDF v. Espy II*, the plaintiffs claimed that the AWA requires the Department of Agriculture to adopt specific, minimum standards to enhance the psychological well-being of primates, and simply allowing regulated entities to devise their own "plans" is not enough. But unlike in the prior case, Circelli, Eagan, Rahn, and Jurnove contended that they had each suffered "aesthetic injury" by viewing primates living in inhumane conditions at the zoos. In October 1996 Judge Charles Richey of the district court agreed with the plaintiffs on both counts (*ALDF v. Glickman*). However, before the year was out a split panel of three judges in the D.C. Circuit reversed the lower court and held that none of the four individuals, nor the ALDF, had standing to contest the regulations. Undaunted, the plaintiffs petitioned the appellate court for a rehearing in front of the full eleven-member panel. The request was granted in May 1998.

The court analyzes the claim to standing of just one of the plaintiffs—Marc Jurnove—needing no more than a single such determination to proceed to the merits of their argument against USDA rule making. Jurnove had visited the Long Island Game Farm Park and Zoo in New York on numerous occasions in 1995 and 1996, each time observing primates living in quite unpleasant, but apparently legal conditions. For example, one chimpanzee was confined in complete isolation from other conspecifics, the squirrel monkey cage was located adjacent to an area holding adult bears (a placement that often sent the monkeys into a frenzy), and the sole "enrichment" device for a snow macaque, also caged alone, was an unused swing. Jurnove repeatedly filed complaints with the USDA concerning these conditions, and government inspectors did investigate the Long Island Zoo four times, but in each instance found no violations whatever in the housing of the primates.

In their lawsuit Jurnove and the ALDF argued that, as directed by Congress, the USDA must promulgate concise, minimum requirements to protect the psychological well-being of primates, and since the agency had not done so, the current regulation was therefore unlawful. This was the same point made in *ALDF v. Espy II,* but now a second item signaled a crucial departure from all other AWA standing cases. Jurnove claimed that he had sustained an "aesthetic injury" by observing primates existing in social deprivation and psychological debilitation. This harm was caused by the failure of the USDA to produce the standards that Congress had demanded, and it would have been avoided had the agency done what lawmakers on Capital Hill told them to do.

Jurnove's Legal Standing
By a vote of seven to four, with Judges Sentelle and Henderson among the dissenters, the court found that Marc Jurnove has standing to sue. Judge Patricia Wald wrote the majority opinion, addressing Jurnove's legal status in terms of the three requirements articulated by the Supreme Court in *Lujan,* each of which must be satisfied: (1) an "injury in fact," that is (2) "fairly traceable" to the defendant, and that (3) a ruling in favor of the plaintiff will "likely" remedy the injury.

Citing *ALDF v. Espy I, Lujan, Sierra Club,* and another Supreme Court decision, *Japan Whaling Association v. American Cetacean Society (see* this chapter: *Legal Standing under Federal Wildlife Laws* and this chapter: *Legal Standing under the Animal Welfare Act),* Wald first noted that injury to an aesthetic interest in observing animals is well established as sufficient for qualifying a plaintiff for standing. More precedents found in the D.C. and other circuit courts—such as *Animal Welfare Institute v. Kreps, Fund for Animals v. Lujan,* and *Humane Society of the United States v. Hodel (see also* this chapter: *Legal Standing under Federal Wildlife Laws)*—further recognize an aspect of this interest consisting in the desire to see animals that are being treated kindly, and avoiding the sight of animals being subject to inhumane treatment. Because these were precisely the interests at stake for Jurnove, the only question that remained was whether his injury of this nature was suffered "in a personal and individual way . . . by seeing with his own eyes the particular animals whose condition caused him aesthetic injury." Clearly, this is exactly what happened to Jurnove at the Long Island Zoo.

Was Jurnove's injury caused by the USDA failure to supply minimum standards to govern humane treatment for primates? Wald held that it was. Familiar with the deeply social nature of these species, Jurnove was especially disturbed by witnessing a chimp and a macaque housed alone and out of sight of any other primates. This situation is permitted by the USDA regulations because they require only that exhibitors draw up a plan to "address the social needs of nonhuman primates," which can be done while keeping the animals caged alone. And although the government had stipulated that primates housed singly must be able to see and hear other conspecifics, this regulation could be safely ignored with a veterinarian's approval. This gave exhibitors plenty of room to find a vet willing to sign off on the exception, and allowed too much discretion to vets already employed by the exhibitor to adequately protect the well-being of the animals.

Jurnove was also distressed by the extreme agitation of the monkeys confined next to the bears, an arrangement permitted by the regulations that require only that incompatible species not be housed in the *same* enclosure, and say nothing about placing animals *next* to each other in separate cages. Finally, the installation of a solitary, largely rejected swing appeared to satisfy the requirement to "provid[e] means of expressing noninjurious species-typical activities." All these factors verify that the plaintiff's injury was "fairly traceable" to the USDA rules.

The last of the three necessary conditions for establishing standing is "redressibility," the likelihood that a decision in favor of Jurnove would provide a remedy for his injury. Because he had stated in his affidavit that he would continue to visit the Long Island Zoo, Wald ruled that this condition was satisfied as well: "[M]ore stringent regulations . . . would necessarily alleviate Mr. Jurnove's aesthetic injury during his planned, future trips to the [Zoo]." Having met all three conditions of legal standing, Wald ruled that Jurnove was entitled to sue the USDA and Secretary Glickman for violating the AWA, this issue being left to a future panel of the D.C. Circuit (*ALDF v. Glickman*).

ALDF v. Glickman II

This news was received with jubilation in the animal welfare community as a great legal victory for animals. Never before had a plaintiff achieved standing to sue under the AWA on behalf of animals, and it seemed to offer a very real possibility that legal protections for animals could be strengthened with a showing that current regulations injure the aesthetic interests of certain humans. Perhaps that will occur, but the rejoicing for this case might have been premature.

Establishing standing for Marc Jurnove was only half the battle here. The victory would not be complete until the court ruled on the merits and agreed with his claim, and that of the ALDF, that the regulations concerning the psychological well-being of primates were unlawful. In October 1999 once again a split panel of three D.C. Circuit judges (Wald was not among them, but Sentelle was) convened to consider this claim, and in February 2000 ruled in favor of Secretary Glickman and the USDA: the regulations were consistent with the intention of Congress and the mandate of the 1985 amendment to the AWA (*ALDF v. Glickman II*). The Long Island Zoo had done nothing illegal, at least on this score.

Yet the USDA may have also acted prematurely. Their adversaries expected an appeal to the Supreme Court following Judge Wald's majority opinion—instead, to the surprise of many, the agency drafted a new "Policy on Environmental Enhancement for Nonhuman Primates" and made it available for comment in July 1999. In light of the vindication of the old regulations bestowed by the D.C. Circuit Court, the attempt to modify the rules the preceding summer seemed unnecessary. At any rate, the new policy arguably does not represent a significant improvement, and it is difficult to see how its implementation would avoid injuries of the sort endured by Marc Jurnove. Although more detail is offered for providing social grouping arrangements, this additional information is still merely to assist in preparing a "plan [that] must address the social needs of primates," and no particular grouping is required; solitary housing is still permitted with a veterinarian's approval. Further, there is no stipulation concerning the placement of primate enclosures in the vicinity of incompatible species, such as the bears that so agitated the squirrel monkeys at the Long Island Zoo. On the other hand, a single swing as providing adequate "environmental enrichment" may not be acceptable any longer. The draft states that each primate should have "a *variety* of portable or movable items for manipulation" (emphasis added). At this writing, it remains to be seen what the final rule on this matter will be.

REFERENCES

Federal Laws
Animal Welfare Act of 1970, 7 U.S.C. §§ 2131–2157.
Bald Eagle Protection Act, 16 U.S.C. §§ 668–668d.
Civil Rights Act of 1964, 45 U.S.C. § 2000e.
Endangered Species Act of 1973, 16 U.S.C. §§ 1531–1544.
Freedom of Information Act, 5 U.S.C. § 552.
Humane Methods of Slaughter Act of 1978, 7 U.S.C. §§ 1901–1906.

Marine Mammal Protection Act of 1972, 16 U.S.C. §§ 1361–1421h.
United States Constitution, Fourth, Thirteenth, Fourteenth, Nineteenth Amendments.
Wild Free-Roaming Horses and Burros Act, 16 U.S.C. §§ 1331–1340.

Federal Regulations
Animal Welfare, 9 C.F.R. Chapter 1, Subchapter A.

State Laws
Anticruelty Laws
   See Appendix 3

Hunting and Trapping Regulations
   State Wildlife Agencies, http://www.wildlife.state.co.us/about/
   StateAgencyWebSites.htm.

Federal Cases
Supreme Court
   [Dred] Scott v. Sanford, 60 U.S. 393 (1857).
   Japan Whaling Association v. American Cetacean Society, 478 U.S. 221 (1986).
   Lujan v. Defenders of Wildlife, 504 U.S. 555 (1992).
   Sierra Club v. Morton, 405 U.S. 727 (1972).

Circuit Courts of Appeals
   American Bald Eagle v. Bhatti, 9 F.3d 163 (1st Cir. 1993).
   Animal Legal Defense Fund v. Espy (*ALDF v. Espy I*), 23 F.3d 496 (D.C. Cir. 1994).
   Animal Legal Defense Fund v. Espy (*ALDF v. Espy II*), 29 F.3d 720 (D.C. Cir. 1994).
   Animal Legal Defense Fund v. Glickman (*ALDF v. Glickman I*), 154 F.3d 426 (D.C. Cir. 1998).
   Animal Legal Defense Fund v. Glickman (*ALDF v. Glickman II*), 204 F.3d 229 (D.C. Cir. 2000) (unreported case at press time).
   Animal Welfare Institute v. Kreps, 561 F.2d 1002 (D.C. Cir. 1977), *cert. denied*, 434 U.S. 1013 (1978).
   Defenders of Wildlife v. Hodel, 911 F.2d 117 (8th Cir. 1990).
   Fund for Animals v. Lujan, 962 F.2d 1391 (9th Cir. 1992).
   Fund for Animals v. Malone, No. 81–2977 (D.C. Cir. 1982) (unreported case).
   Humane Society of the United States v. Hodel, 840 F.2d 45 (D.C. Cir. 1988).
   International Primate Protection League v. Administrators of the Tulane Educational Fund, 895 F.2d 1056 (5th Cir. 1990), *reversed*, 500 U.S. 72 (1991).

International Primate Protection League v. Institute for Behavioral
Research, Inc., 799 F.2d 934 (4th Cir. 1986), cert. denied, 481 U.S. 1004
(1987).
Loggerhead Turtle v. County Council of Volusia County, 148 F.3d 1231
(11th Cir. 1998).
Mt. Graham Squirrel v. Yeutter, 930 F.2d 703 (9th Cir. 1991).
Palila v. Hawaii Department of Land and Natural Resources (Palila II), 852
F.2d 1106 (9th Cir. 1988).

District Courts
Animal Legal Defense Fund v. Glickman, 943 F. Supp. 54 (D. D.C.
1996).
Animal Legal Defense Fund v. Madigan, 781 F. Supp. 797 (D. D.C. 1992).
Animal Legal Defense Fund v. Yeutter, 760 F. Supp. 923 (D. D.C. 1991).
Citizens to End Suffering and Exploitation, Inc. v. New England
Aquarium, 836 F. Supp. 45 (D. Mass. 1993).
Hawaiian Crow ('Alala) v. Lujan, 906 F. Supp. 549 (D. Haw. 1991).
Humane Society of the United States v. Block, No. 81–2691 (D. D.C. 1982)
(unreported case).
Northern Spotted Owl v. Hodel, 716 F. Supp. 479 (W.D. Wash. 1988).
Palila v. Hawaii Department of Land and Natural Resources (Palila I), 471
F. Supp. 985 (D. Haw. 1979), affirmed, 639 F.2d 495 (9th Cir. 1981).

State Cases
Maryland
State v. Taub, No. 11848–81 (Montgomery [Md.] County Dist. Ct. 1981)
(unreported case).
Taub v. State, 43 A.2d 819 (Md. 1983).

Massachusetts
Commonwealth v. Higgins, 178 N.E. 536 (Mass. 1931).

Mississippi
Stephens v. State, 3 So. 458 (Miss. 1888).

Missouri
Missouri v. Stout, 958 S.W.2d 32 (Mo. Ct. App. 1997).

Pennsylvania
Commonwealth v. Tapper, 675 A.2d 740 (Pa. Super. Ct. 1996).

Texas
Celinski v. State, 911 S.W.2d 177 (Tex. Crim. App. 1995).

Books

American Law Institute. 1985. *Model Penal Code*. Philadelphia: American Law Institute.

Animal Welfare Institute. 1990. *Animals and Their Legal Rights*. 4th ed. Washington, DC: Animal Welfare Institute.

Blackstone, William. 2001. *Commentaries on the Laws of England*. London: Cavendish (London: Callaghan, 1872).

Blum, Deborah. 1994. *The Monkey Wars*. New York: Oxford University Press.

Brooman, Simon, and Debbie Legge. 1997. *Law Relating to Animals*. London: Cavendish.

Favre, David S., and Murray Loring. 1983. *Animal Law*. Westport, CT: Quorum Books.

Feinberg, Joel. 1973. *Social Philosophy*. Englewood Cliffs, NJ: Prentice-Hall.

Francione, Gary L. 1995. *Animals, Property, and the Law*. Philadelphia: Temple University Press.

Frasch, Pamela D., et al. 2000. *Animal Law*. Durham, NC: Carolina Academic Press.

Gewirth, Alan. 1992. "Rights." In *Encyclopedia of Ethics*. Vol. 2. Edited by Lawrence Becker. New York: Garland.

Hohfeld, Wesley. 1919. *Fundamental Legal Conceptions as Applied in Judicial Reasoning*. New Haven, CT: Yale University Press.

Kent, James. 1894. *Commentaries on American Law*. St. Paul, MN: West Publishing.

Pacheco, Alex, and Anna Francione. 1985. "The Silver Spring Monkeys." In *In Defense of Animals*. Edited by Peter Singer. Oxford, UK: Blackwell.

Stone, Christopher. 1974. *Should Trees Have Standing?* Los Altos, CA: William Kaufman.

Wellman, Carl. 1992. "Concepts of Rights." In *Encyclopedia of Ethics*. Vol. 2. Edited by Lawrence Becker. New York: Garland.

Wise, Stephen. 2000. *Rattling the Cage: Towards Legal Rights for Animals*. Cambridge, MA: Perseus Books.

Articles

Favre, David, and Vivien Tsang. 1993. "The Development of Anti-Cruelty Laws During the 1800's." *Detroit College of Law Review* 1: 1–35.

Kelch, Thomas G. 1998. "Toward a Non-Property Status for Animals." *New York University Environmental Law Journal* 6: 531–585.

Mendelson, Joseph. 1997. "Should Animals Have Standing? A Review of Standing under the Animal Welfare Act." *Boston College Environmental Affairs Law Review* 24: 795–820.

Sunstein, Cass. 2000. "Standing for Animals (with Notes on Animal Rights)." *UCLA Law Review* 47: 1333–1368.

Wise, Steven. 1996. "The Legal Thinghood of Nonhuman Animals." *Boston College Environmental Affairs Law Review* 23: 471–546.

3. Companion Animals

ANTICRUELTY LAWS

In the United States legal rules to protect animals from cruel treatment at the hands of humans are dominated by laws of the individual states. Federal anticruelty legislation is confined to the Humane Methods of Slaughter Act, The Twenty-Eight Hour Law (*see* both in chapter 4), and the Animal Welfare Act (AWA) (*see* chapter 7), along with their implementing regulations. The Humane Methods of Slaughter Act requires certain techniques in killing cows, pigs, and sheep for human consumption (poultry are excluded), replacing traditional methods that are widely agreed to be cruel, notably repeated clubbing with sledge hammers or pole axes, and the cutting and bleeding of conscious animals. The Twenty-Eight Hour Law requires food, water, and rest at regular intervals for livestock that are transported by train, aircraft, or motor vehicle. The AWA is primarily intended to provide for the humane care and use of certain mammals (mice, rats, and birds are not covered) in research, testing, and education, and for exhibition purposes, primarily in zoos and circuses (rodeos are exempt; *see* chapter 5: *Circuses and Zoos;* chapter 5: *Rodeos*).

These three federal laws apply to the millions of animals that are slaughtered for food and used as subjects for experimentation and entertainment every year. Yet they still leave unprotected millions of others living in close association with humans—principally dogs, cats, and horses—that are not eaten by Americans and do not find themselves on public display or in a laboratory. State anticruelty laws are supposed to cover these creatures, at least to some extent.

There is no national database compiling cruelty complaints, prosecutions, and convictions, so no one knows exactly how many occur each year under the state laws. One credible estimate offered in the late 1990s is that the average big city has about 500 cruelty complaints annually. Less than 1 percent of these are tried before a jury, and guilty verdicts emerge in about 10 percent of the cases prosecuted. Assuming 100 major metropolitan areas in the United States, this figures to about 50,000 complaints, perhaps 500 prosecutions, and 50 convictions each year.

These numbers do not account for complaints and litigation arising out of rural America, where occasionally farm animals, especially horses, have been criminally neglected or physically abused. Given their location off the beaten paths of densely populated society, instances of cruelty in the countryside are likely underreported (*but see* this chapter: *Anticruelty Laws: Liability*). No estimates are available for the incidence of abuse or neglect here.

Early Anticruelty Laws and Their Origins

The first recorded law prohibiting cruelty to animals is in the Body of Liberties, a list of rules of conduct adopted by the Pilgrims of Massachusetts

Bay Colony in 1641. Concerned that after twenty years in the New World there was still no book compiling the laws of the colony, the town deputies turned to the Reverend Nathaniel Ward, who departed England in 1634 after receiving an Episcopal condemnation for heresy. In addition to being a Puritan minister, Ward was also a lawyer who claimed to have read nearly all the common law of his country, and thus seemed eminently qualified to produce a legal inventory.

The last section of the Body of Liberties is called "Off the Bruite Creature," and here under "Liberty 92" Ward wrote: "No man shall exercise any tirranny or crueltie towards any bruite creature which are usuallie kept for man's use." He also included a provision allowing drovers to rest and refresh their cattle "in any open place that is not Corne, meadow, or enclosed for some peculiar use." Ward's law was many years ahead of its time: no other colony ever enacted any sort of anticruelty statute, and nearly two centuries would pass before any of the newly minted states did.

Although Reverend Ward did not borrow exactly this legal idea from his homeland, it is in England that we find the roots of what would come to be pervasive American legislation intended to protect the welfare of certain animals. Curiously, despite Ward's professed familiarity with English common law, the origins of anticruelty laws are not to be found in this legal domain. The common law in England and America is "judge-made" law; it is the compilation of decisions rendered by judges in cases in which there is no legal rule to apply. What the magistrate says in these novel situations becomes law, establishing a precedent. Evidently, cruelty to animals did not exist as a criminal offense of the common law in England before 1800, at the earliest.

So where did Ward get the idea? Liberty 92 may have evolved out of various malicious mischief laws that had existed in England for centuries, and were occasionally used to prosecute people who had harmed animals. In these instances, individuals were sometimes convicted for mistreating animals, but the violation was really for malevolently destroying or damaging another person's property, not for being cruel to a "dumb brute." For example, a man who abused a borrowed horse could be sued for the economic loss the owner suffered from being unable to use the animal until it recovered.

Ward also may have been influenced by public nuisance laws, which could be violated when overt acts of violence against animals were perpetrated in the middle of town, offending the sensibilities or "injuring the moral character of those who witness it," as one eighteenth-century British judge put it. Of course, a man who abused his own horse, or at least did so in the privacy of his own stables, could not be indicted under such laws. Liberty 92 seems to take a dramatic step away from regarding animals as mere personal possessions or as props for human virtue and vice, and toward a view of them as holders of a legal right to decent, humane treatment.

In 1641 Ward was well ahead of the pace in England too, where the move from malicious mischief and public nuisance to anticruelty was not even attempted until 1800, and then again in 1802, when bills were introduced into Parliament to outlaw "bull-baiting." This was the practice of setting a pack of frenzied dogs on a bull, tormenting and torturing the animal for the pleasure and amusement of a group of people who watched the bloody melee. Both bills were narrowly defeated, mainly on the grounds that they unfairly deprived working-class people of a favorite form of entertainment. In 1809 a bill prohibiting "wanton cruelty, malicious wounding," beating, and other abuses of "domesticated" animals—horses and cattle foremost—passed the House of Lords, but lost in the House of Commons (for more on bull-baiting, *see* chapter 5: *Cockfighting and Dogfighting: Dogfighting and Baiting*).

Even as these bills went down, the industrial revolution had already caught fire in England, and animals, which had formerly supplied most of the energy required for agriculture, manufacturing, and transportation, began to be replaced by various steam-powered machines. As animal power became less crucial, attitudes concerning the treatment of certain species, especially horses and cattle, started changing. And so it was that in 1822 the "Ill Treatment of Horses and Cattle Bill" was approved by Parliament, and given royal assent by King George IV. Commonly known as "Martin's Act," the bill had been introduced by Irish Minister of Parliament Richard Martin, and it is widely regarded as the first significant animal protection law in the world. Though antedated by Liberty 92, the scope of Martin's Act was obviously far greater, applying to the whole of England. Specifically, the law prohibited "any Person [from] wantonly and cruelly beat[ing], abus[ing] or ill treat[ing] any Horse, Mare, Gelding, Mule, Ass, Ox, Cow, Heifer, Steer, Sheep or other Cattle." Punishment for violation was a fine not to exceed forty shillings.

Unfortunately, the practice of bull-baiting managed to evade the scope of the law as magistrates persistently refused to allow that the word *cattle* referred to bulls as well. It was not until 1835 when Joseph Pease's amendment was accepted that the baiting of any animal, as well as cockfighting, were declared illegal (*see* chapter 5: *Cockfighting and Dogfighting*). In 1849 legal protections for animals were further strengthened in England with the Cruelty to Animals Act. This law made it illegal to "ill-treat, over-drive, abuse or torture, or cause to procure to be cruelly beaten, ill-treated, over-driven, abused, or tortured, any Animal." Thus both the perpetrator and anyone who employed or directed others to engage in these activities were liable to prosecution, with a maximum penalty of a five-pound fine.

Early American Anticruelty Laws

Martin's Act is famous as the original anticruelty law, but not only did Liberty 92 long precede it, the Maine legislature had enacted a cruelty to animals statute the year before in 1821. This is the first U.S. law, one that provided a penalty of $2 to $5 and up to thirty days in jail to "any person [who] shall cruelly beat any horse or cattle." Although the law does not contemplate forms of cruelty other than beating, it also does not appear to be motivated by property interests in animals: *any* person who cruelly beats *any* horse or cattle is guilty. This achieves a more thorough separation from malicious mischief statutes, as Martin's Act had done, and seems to bring animals (cows and horses anyway) closer to having a legal status in their own right. On the other hand, the Maine law leaves the public nuisance foundation intact.

Many subsequent state laws retained an explicit focus on property. For example, Connecticut, Minnesota, and Vermont passed anticruelty laws in the 1850s, but all three prohibited only maltreating livestock that belonged to "another person." Presumably, one was still free to abuse one's own animals in these states. The second American anticruelty law combined the property concern with a suggestion of concern for the animal itself, notwithstanding the appeal to public nuisance. An 1828 enactment of the New York state legislature outlawed "maliciously" killing, maiming, or wounding horses, cattle, oxen, or sheep "belonging to another," and prohibiting anyone from "maliciously and cruelly" beating or torturing these animals "whether [they] belong to himself or another." This has the odd consequence that a person was allowed to kill his own horse with malice, but not beat it.

A number of other state legislatures modeled their anticruelty statutes on New York's 1828 version, but the revisions to the Empire State law written in 1866 and 1867 by Henry Bergh profoundly influenced virtually every subsequent state law and the amendments made to those already existing. As the founder of the American Society for the Prevention of Cruelty to Animals, Bergh dedicated his life to promoting compassionate treatment for domestic animals, and his concern is evident in nearly every line of the new law. Bergh removed the ownership limitation and expanded both the list of protected species by inserting the phrase "any living creature," and the inventory of prohibited actions by including such terms as overdriving, mutilating, and "depriving of necessary sustenance." This last proscription, indicating liability for neglecting an animal, marked a first in American legislation, as did another stipulation that outlawed abandoning "an old, maimed or diseased horse or mule . . . in any street, lane, or place of any city in this state."

All four of these elements, first appearing in the 1866–1867 New York law, are found in the majority of state anticruelty statutes today: the application to any animal and not just livestock (but there are exempted uses of animals; *see* this chapter: *Anticruelty Laws: Exceptions and Penalties*), a longer and more specific list of disapproved actions, liability for neglect, and a prohibition on abandonment. The explicit property basis ("belonging to another") vanished from Bergh's New York statute, and it cannot be found in any current state law.

Yet it would be hasty to conclude from this that animals then or now have legal rights, that they are recognized by anticruelty laws for their own sakes. There is still the grounding in public nuisance, which disapproves conspicuous displays of violence toward animals, not so much because they are seriously harmful to animals, but because they upset people and undermine their good character. Indeed, to this day the majority of anticruelty laws are arranged in state codes under titles such as "Offenses against Public Order," "Offenses against Public Order and Decency," "Crimes against Public Morals," "Offenses against Chastity, Decency, and Morality," and "Crimes against Chastity, Morality, Decency, and Good Order." Most of the rest are found in agricultural or food law titles (for a discussion of the legal rightsholding of animals, *see* chapter 2: *Do Animals Have Legal Rights?*).

When New York lawmakers accepted Bergh's revisions, twenty-one states had enacted anticruelty statutes, and at the turn of the century all forty-seven states, Hawaii (still an American possession), and the District of Columbia had done so. Today, each of the fifty states, as well as the District of Columbia, American Samoa, Guam, and Puerto Rico have their own anticruelty laws. The specifics are often different—some are quite brief while others are much longer and highly detailed—but all these laws address four distinct areas, along with the penalty for violations: (1) the kinds of animals that are protected, (2) the actions that are prohibited, (3) the mental state required to establish liability, and (4) the uses of animals that are exempted from the law. Discussion of anticruelty laws may be usefully pursued under these four headings.

Protected Animals and Prohibited Actions

Nearly every state law declares that "any animal" is covered, but several—Alabama, Florida, and Montana, for example—do not offer any further specification of exactly which species, if any, are excluded from the term "animal." Most states do define the word, some quite expansively.

For example, New Jersey stipulates that "'Animal' or 'creature' includes the whole brute creation." Arkansas says that "'animal' includes every living creature," while Colorado adds that "'Animal' means every living dumb creature." Other states narrow the definition a bit, such as Maine where "'Animal' means every living, sentient creature, not a human being." The qualification that *Homo sapiens* are not included is

common among state anticruelty laws, but still other states have more refined concepts, such as Hawaii, which specifically excludes "insects, vermin, and other pests" from the meaning of "animal," while Iowa excludes livestock, Louisiana exempts "fowl," Missouri sets aside
everything but mammals, Alaska leaves out fish, with Delaware adding
that "'Animal' shall not include fish, crustacea or mollusca."

All fifty states ban "cruel" actions, or acting "cruelly," or just plain
"cruelty," but none provide a clear account of exactly what these terms
mean. Many of the statutes do not offer any definition at all, and those
that do usually refer to killing, injuring, or causing pain that is "unnecessary" or "needless" or "unjustifiable." Exactly when killing, injuring, or
causing pain is necessary and when it is not, or when it is justifiable and
when it is not are left unspecified, but the exceptions listed in the statutes
(*see* this chapter: *Anticruelty Laws: Exceptions and Penalties*) suggest some
answers. Defendants charged with violations of anticruelty laws frequently attempt to exonerate themselves by appealing to the vagueness
of these terms, and then it is left to a court to pass judgment on their
meaning (for more on this defense, *see* this chapter: *Animal Hoarding: People v. Speegle*).

In addition to the proscription of cruel behavior, every state also explicitly prohibits certain acts perpetrated against the animals covered by
the law: maiming, torturing, mutilating, and tormenting are the specific
behaviors disallowed in nearly all of the statutes. Alabama and Arkansas
speak only of "cruel mistreatment" and "cruel neglect" as outlawed conduct without defining any of these concepts. Reflecting a bygone era
when animals were extensively used in agriculture and for transportation, most state codes also somewhat anachronistically (but *see* this chapter: *Horse Law: Carriage Rides*) forbid overdriving, overloading, or overworking animals. Those states that ban animal fighting staged for
entertainment usually place that prohibition in their anticruelty statutes
(*see* chapter 5: *Cockfighting and Dogfighting*).

Like the ban on killing, injuring, or causing pain, these other prohibited actions are very often explicitly or by implication qualified with such
adjectives as "unnecessary," "needless," "unjustifiable," "unreasonable,"
or done "without good cause." Once again though, the statutes supply
little guidance for determining when maiming, torturing, or tormenting
an animal is "needless" or "unreasonable." In legal practice, judges decide these matters when they rule on prosecutions of anticruelty laws,
and it is impossible to say beforehand what the ruling will be. For example, in 1974 the North Carolina Court of Appeals overturned the conviction of a man who had beaten a dog and repeatedly dunked its head into
a hole full of water. The court ruled the defendant had actually been involved in an "honest and good faith effort to train [the dog]" to stop dig-

ging holes, so his actions were *not* "without just cause, excuse or justification" (*State v. Fowler*). On the other hand, the Missouri Court of Appeals recently upheld the conviction of a man who had dragged a puppy tied by its leash to the bumper of his truck because he wanted to "teach the dog a lesson" about running away from his home (*Missouri v. Stout*).

Most states also proscribe either depriving an animal of "necessary sustenance" or "failing to provide proper food and water," with nineteen making both unlawful. The distinction between such a deprivation of an animal and the failure to provide for it is not easy to discern, and some of the states enjoining both do not distinguish the two. The others typically attach one or the other of the prohibitions to the actions of a person "having the charge or custody" of an animal or to one who "impounds or confines" an animal.

Over half of the states also require that shelter be provided, but currently only Delaware, Illinois, Maine, Maryland, Montana, Pennsylvania, Washington, and Virginia specifically mention that neglecting to provide veterinary or medical care to a needy animal is a violation (for more on animal neglect, *see* this chapter: *Animal Hoarding*). The withholding of other amenities is even less frequently prohibited: a smattering of states make reference variously to the provision of fresh air (Connecticut, Maryland, North Dakota, Ohio, Washington), exercise (California, Colorado, Kansas, Minnesota), and sanitary conditions (Maine, Wisconsin).

Better than two-thirds of the states also outlaw cruel methods of transporting animals. Most of these proscriptions are quickly stated in a single sentence without any examples or specifics. The Texas statute is typical: "A person commits an offense if he intentionally or knowingly transports . . . an animal in a cruel manner." Michigan and Minnesota offer the most detail, the latter by prohibiting conveyances without "suitable racks, cars, crates, or cages in which the animals can both stand and lie down during transportation." Michigan adds that the animals must have enough space in the vehicle to turn around.

A final category of prohibited actions is found in three-quarters of the states, which outlaw abandoning a protected animal. Surprisingly, the states usually do not define the term, but Delaware's explication of "abandonment" is representative of those that do: "completely forsaking or deserting an animal originally under one's custody without making reasonable arrangements for the custody of that animal to be assumed by another person." Some states narrow the scope of protection from abandonment. For example, although Iowa's anticruelty statute covers "domestic animals and fowl," only the abandonment of dogs or cats is illegal there. Similarly, while Nevada's law says that "animal" refers to "every . . . living creature" except humans, the Silver State prohibits abandoning "disabled" animals alone.

Liability

The third element in state anticruelty laws is the criteria for establishing the liability or blameworthiness of the accused. Half the states require one or more of the following mental states to attend the act of cruelty: it must be performed knowingly, intentionally, willfully, purposely, or recklessly. These are all highly technical terms in the legal lexicon with variant meanings, but in general they indicate in this context that the perpetrator acted deliberately, with the awareness that his actions were injurious to the animal, disregarding the risks of harm. A few states, California for example, add "maliciously" or "wantonly," suggesting that the accused acted with ill will or hatred toward the animal.

Cruelty convictions are often difficult to secure under this *mens rea* ("guilty mind") standard of culpability. It demands proof of the defendant's state of mind at the time of the alleged violation, something notoriously inaccessible in a courtroom well after the fact, and the awareness or malice can always be simply denied. Courts typically hold that these mental contents can be inferred from the circumstances and actions of the accused.

To illustrate this idea, consider the case of John Schott, a Nebraska rancher convicted in 1984 of two counts of cruelty to animals. After receiving several complaints from neighbors, the county sheriff and three veterinarians discovered forty cattle carcasses and seven dead hogs on Schott's property. The condition of the bodies and subsequent necropsies indicated that all had starved to death. Dozens of other animals at the ranch were clearly suffering from extreme malnutrition and dehydration. In his defense, Schott claimed that he had neither intentionally nor recklessly neglected his livestock, one or the other mental state being required to violate Nebraska's anticruelty law. Instead, he protested, severe winter weather had prevented him from providing the animals with sufficient food and water. The state supreme court rejected this appeal, holding that Schott's failure to adequately care for his livestock was not due to the weather because, despite its severity, there were numerous opportunities over a period of two months when he could have reached his animals without great difficulty. Rather, his neglect qualified as intentional and reckless because it "involve[d] a gross deviation from the standard of conduct that a law-abiding person would observe in [his] situation" (*State v. Schott*).

In a similar, more recent case, Glen Lykins appealed his 1999 conviction for three counts of animal neglect, arguing that he did not recklessly, knowingly, or intentionally ignore the basic needs of his horses. Lykins asserted that although he knew the animals were thin, he did "everything in his power to provide care for [them]" but had been unable to obtain hay. The Indiana Court of Appeals rejected this contention, pointing out that three different people had no problems acquiring hay for the horses, a sheriff's deputy had told Lykins where he could obtain hay and even offered to help haul it, and in fact Lykins had hay in his possession for over a month when a veterinarian determined the horses were still being neglected. "Clearly," Judge Messer concluded, "from the facts set forth in this case, the jury could infer that Glen knowingly, recklessly, or intentionally, neglected his horses" (*Lykins v. State*).

Several other states, such as New Hampshire, require only that the action was done negligently, that is, by acting the perpetrator ran an unreasonable risk of harm, whether or not there was any awareness of this effect or any malice in the action. Because this criterion does not require that a prosecutor prove that the defendant acted knowingly, intentionally, or maliciously, convictions based on negligence are easier to win. Those states that do not require any particular form of *mens rea* are usually taken to be maintaining a standard of strict liability for animal cruelty: the mere act of killing, injuring, beating, torturing, etc. the animal can be sufficient for conviction, no matter what was going on in the actor's head. That is not quite the whole story, however, since these actions must also be shown to be "unnecessary" or "unjustified." Strict liability offenses are thought to be the easiest to prove, but statistics comparing cruelty to animals convictions in *mens rea* states and strict liability states are not available.

Exceptions and Penalties

The fourth major element of state anticruelty laws concerns the uses of animals that do not count as violations. These exemptions are found in forty-seven states (Minnesota, Mississippi, and Oklahoma do not list any), a few expressing them with a simple "except as otherwise authorized by law" clause. Most jurisdictions stipulate that a charge of cruelty to animals can be successfully defended by proving that the action was done to protect humans or their property, to protect other animals owned by the defendant, or was necessary to terminate an animal's suffering.

The majority of states also designate certain activities as exempt from anticruelty prosecution. For example, a dozen exclude the treatment of animals involved in rodeos. Missouri and North Dakota exempt zoos and circuses, as does Michigan, which also specifically absolves horse racing (*see* chapter 5: *Circuses and Zoos;* chapter 5: *Rodeos;* chapter 5: *Greyhound Racing and Horse Racing*). Most often listed though are research or "experiments" using animals, in thirty states; veterinary practices, in half the states; "normal" or "generally accepted" methods employed in animal agriculture, such as slaughtering for food (in eighteen states), and driving, branding, dehorning, shearing, and castration (one or more of these in thirty states); and hunting and trapping in accordance with state wildlife law, in two-thirds of the states (for general hunting laws, *see* chapter 5: *Recreational Hunting;* for trapping, *see* chapter 4: *Commercial Trapping*).

Georgia's exception is typical, stipulating that the prohibition "does not apply to the killing of animals raised for the purpose of providing food nor does it apply to any person who hunts wild animals in compliance with the game and fish laws of this state. The killing or injuring of an animal for humane purposes or in the furtherance of medical or scientific research is justifiable."

Only two states presently impose a positive duty on individuals to report known or suspected cases of animal cruelty. Minnesota and West Virginia require veterinarians to do so when their examinations indicate animal abuse.

If none of these exemptions apply, and no other defense is successful, a person convicted of cruelty to animals will receive a legal punishment. Probably the most significant recent development in anticruelty law is the enhancement of penalties for violations. Animal advocates have often complained that legal punishments for abusing animals are much too lenient, providing little if any deterrent effect. Indeed, until the mid-1980s the harshest sentence that could be imposed in any state, no matter how atrocious the abuse or how many animals were harmed, was a fine of $1,000 and one year in prison, a transgression classified as a misdemeanor, the lowest level of criminal infraction. Such judgments were rarely passed by a court in any case. However, in the last decade and a half of the twentieth century, thirty states amended their anticruelty statutes to provide for felony convictions, seven of these in 2000 alone. At this writing, the Minnesota state legislature has moved into the second year of deliberations over a felony animal abuse bill.

The felony provisions usually distinguish different degrees of animal cruelty or abuse by specifying aggravating circumstances or in cases of repeated violations.

For instance, in 1995 Oregon's legislature added "aggravated animal abuse in the first degree" to the state code, a "Class C" felony (still a low level among felonious offenses) punishable by as much as five years in prison and a $100,000 fine. Oregon describes this form of animal abuse as the intentional killing or torturing of an animal "with a depravity of mind and reckless and wanton disregard of life." In Michigan, a second violation of the state anticruelty law automatically escalates the penalty to the felonious level, while a third conviction (or more) brings a maximum of four years imprisonment or a $5,000 fine or 500 hours of community service, or any combination of these penalties along with the costs of prosecution.

Wisconsin, the first state to provide for felony convictions in cases of animal cruelty, recently gained the distinction of meting out the most severe punishment ever inflicted upon an offender. In July 1998 Judge Richard Warner sentenced Barry Herbeck to twelve years in the state penitentiary after he was found guilty on five counts of felony mistreatment of an animal. Herbeck, already a felon for child abuse, had routinely tortured and killed cats and puppies by suffocation, drowning, and by hurling them against walls and down flights of stairs.

In states without felony penalties for cruelty to animals, creative prosecutors are finding other ways to secure sentences commensurate with the depravity of the crime. A case in point comes from Kansas, where in 1997 Marcus Rodriguez and three other individuals shot a terrier with a pellet rifle, placed the still living dog in a plastic bag, doused the bag with lighter fluid, set it on fire, and repeatedly hit it with a shovel. Police learned of this incident through an informant who supplied them with a videotape of the torture made by the perpetrators. Rodriguez pled guilty to one count of animal cruelty and received a sentence of one year in jail, the maximum allowable in Kansas. Unsatisfied with that punishment, the district attorney also successfully prosecuted Rodriguez for arson, proving that neither he nor any of the other three had a property interest in the terrier and they had not received the consent of the dog's owner to burn it. He was given a sentence of twenty-seven months in addition to the cruelty penalty, and the decision was upheld by the state supreme court (*State v. Rodriguez*).

Currently, ten states allow judges to order psychological or psychiatric counseling or treatment for individuals found guilty of abusing animals. Four others *require* such mental health care: California, for those on probation following a second conviction of animal cruelty; Illinois, for those convicted of torturing an animal, defined as inflicting "extreme physical pain, motivated by an intent to increase or prolong the pain"; West Virginia, as a condition of parole; and Colorado, after second and subsequent convictions. Nevada and New Mexico amended their respective anticruelty statutes in 1999 to require judges to order counseling for juveniles found guilty of a violation. The Michigan legislature is at this time considering a bill requiring psychotherapy for juveniles who commit an act of animal cruelty, even if the child is neither charged nor convicted of a violation.

Better than two-thirds of the states either bar offenders from any future ownership of animals or authorize the court to issue such a ban. All states except Alaska, Colorado, Georgia, Montana, and New Mexico have provisions that call for the seizure of animals that have been mistreated, and about half the states permit court orders compelling animal abusers to reimburse the state for the cost of caring for seized animals.

Other Recent Developments

Along with the trend to establish felony punishments, two other advances in anticruelty legislation occurred in the late 1990s, both involving interdictions of killing animals for entertainment.

Although performing an act of animal cruelty is illegal in every state, filming or photographing someone engaged in an act of animal cruelty, and then selling the images is not illegal anywhere. Why would anyone indulge in such media? For the money of course.

In the last few years, the existence of hundreds of "crush videos" has come to the notice of federal and state authorities. These are short video-tapes of women, often wearing stiletto heels but also shown barefoot, who proceed to stomp upon various rodents, mostly, crushing the animals to death with their feet. Mice, rats, guinea pigs, and hamsters seem to be the small animals of choice here, but frogs and snakes have also been used. Sometimes, the filming is done from below, through a glass plate, yield-ing a unique perspective on this grisly form of entertainment. Apparently, crush videos appeal to some men with a "foot fetish," where women's feet, and certain things they do with their feet, are experienced as sexually arousing. Such videos are currently available for purchase over the Inter-net, and indeed it was perusal of the World Wide Web that originally alerted concerned citizens to this particular perversion (*see also* this chap-ter: *Sexual Contact with Animals: Animal Cruelty, Obscenity, and the Law*).

In May 1999 Representative Elton Gallegly of California introduced a bill into Congress seeking to outlaw crush videos and other "depictions of animal cruelty." These are defined as "any photograph, motion-picture film, video recording, electronic image, or sound recording of conduct in which a living animal is intentionally maimed, mutilated, tortured, wounded, or killed, if such conduct is illegal under Federal law or the law of the State in which the creation, sale, or possession takes place." Gal-legly's bill garnered immediate, enthusiastic support by the overwhelm-ing majority of lawmakers, including a unanimous Senate; President Bill Clinton signed it into law in December 1999. The law bans the production or possession of a depiction of animal cruelty by anyone who has "the in-tention of placing the depiction in interstate or foreign commerce for commercial gain." Although the sale of a crush video is also illegal, pro-duction or possession of one for personal use is allowed. In such an in-stance, the woman doing the crushing could presumably be charged with violating an anticruelty statute.

The other recent development in anticruelty law concerns hunting, which, as we noticed above, is commonly exempted from the application of state laws. Many people have claimed that the suffering often endured by wild animals shot with bullets or arrows certainly qualifies as an "un-necessary" and "unjustifiable" infliction of pain—even more so for trap-ping, especially for those unfortunate creatures caught by steel-jaw leghold traps. Yet appeal to laws prohibiting cruelty to animals has not produced any lasting obstacle for individuals wishing to kill wildlife. This is evident in a recent case from New Mexico that could have had vast legal ramifications. Here, a man was found guilty by a trial court of violating the state anticruelty law when he killed two deer with a wire snare. However, on appeal the New Mexico Supreme Court overturned the conviction in March 1999, reasoning that the phrase "any animal" in the law referred only to domestic animals and captive wildlife, not deer running free in nature (*New Mexico v. Cleve*). Despite this absolution of hunting, one form of wild animal killing—many would not call it hunting—has been halted in a number of jurisdictions by anticruelty laws: pigeon shoots.

The pigeon shoot held every Labor Day in Schuylkill County, Pennsylvania, near the town of Hegins, has generated the most controversy over the years, and serves as a typical example of this particular form of entertainment. The event focuses on dozens of "shooters," each paying an entry fee to participate while other people pay for admission to watch. Thousands of pigeons are released one by one from trap boxes while the shooters take turns blazing away at them, receiving "points" if a stricken bird falls into a circled area. Several hundred pigeons are killed outright by the shotgun blasts, but hundreds of others fall to the ground wounded. These injured birds are eventually retrieved, often by boys who dispatch them by tearing their heads off, throwing or smashing them against various objects, or simply dumping them in barrels of dead and dying birds where they suffocate or bleed to death. This activity continues for most of the entire day.

The Pennsylvania Society for the Prevention of Cruelty to Animals (PSPCA) fought the Hegins pigeon shoot for more than a decade, in the courts and with protests on the killing grounds, always contending that the spectacle violates the state anticruelty law. Their battle had met with little success until July 1999 when the Pennsylvania Supreme Court ruled in their favor, although not with a finding that the event was an unlawful form of animal abuse. Instead, Chief Justice Flaherty, though clearly sympathetic to the PSPCA and the slaughtered pigeons, ruled on a purely jurisdictional question: Is an agent of the PSPCA empowered to enforce the state anticruelty law in Schuylkill County?

Pennsylvania law, like that of many states, allows courts to appoint agents of nonprofit organizations formed for the prevention of cruelty to animals to act as law enforcement officers, authorizing them to arrest anyone who violates an anticruelty law. The "Labor Day Committee," representing those supporting the pigeon shoot, claimed that the PSPCA agent, Clayton Hulsizer, was so authorized to act in Philadelphia County only, not in Schuylkill County. Judge Flaherty rejected this claim, and ruled that Hulsizer was entitled to exercise this policing function in Hegins (*Hulsizer v. Labor Day Committee*).

Before Hulsizer had a chance to arrest pigeon shooters for violating the Pennsylvania anticruelty law, his stated intention, the Labor Day Committee canceled the 1999 event, ending a string of sixty-five consecutive shoots. Initially unclear whether this was merely a temporary setback for the pigeon shooters, the Committee announced late in the year that the Labor Day carnage was permanently ended, and the group disbanded. Now they have no legal option in the matter. In July 2000 a bill prohibiting all pigeon shoots in Pennsylvania was signed into law. The state joins fifteen others that have already specifically banned such shoots as incompatible with their anticruelty laws. Legislation to that effect is currently pending in California and Texas.

ANIMAL HOARDING

No state or federal law places any limit on how many animals a person can keep on his or her own property. (The states do allow rental owners to restrict pet keeping by their tenants, and some municipalities have maximum numbers for pets in city residences.) Yet every state anticruelty statute contains a general prohibition against animal owners neglecting the basic needs of the creatures under their charge, or subjecting animals to "cruel mistreatment."

Many of these laws explicitly require that the animals be supplied with proper food, sufficient water, and adequate shelter (*see* this chapter: *Anticruelty Laws: Protected Animals and Prohibited Actions*). It is not easy for a private citizen to comply with this requirement when there are dozens of animals to feed, water, and house. In recent years, a certain kind of pet owner has come to light, one who fails to responsibly care for the animals and so causes them severe suffering, but one who at the same time claims to love them. Such an owner sometimes quite literally loves the animals to death. And that can indeed be against the law.

The Hoarder and the Hoarded

When an individual accumulates animals in such numbers that he or she is no longer able to provide them with adequate care, the mere collecting of animals is better understood as animal hoarding. The inclination is to think that such hoarding is simply good intentions gone awry, but it appears instead to be a form of psychopathology, probably a personality disorder (as yet, no psychological or psychiatric organization has officially so designated it). Unlike the hoarding of inanimate objects, animal hoarding has been little investigated. Until the mid-1990s there had been exactly one formal study of hoarding in the United States reported in the literature, a 1981 review of thirty-one cases occurring in New York City during the 1970s. Nonetheless, the phenomenon is not a new one, but it is only in recent years that this type of pathological collecting has received more attention, and certain patterns have emerged.

The average hoarder has thirty or forty animals, all dogs or all cats.

Usually a woman over forty, she lives alone in a single-family residence or apartment and is often unemployed and dependent on public assistance. This profile does suggest the stereotypical "cat lady," though the hoarded animals are frequently dogs and not cats, and some men have been documented as hoarders. Whether male or female, the hoarder seems to have an obsessive-compulsive or addictive personality that manifests itself in a preoccupation with the animals and acquiring more of them, with the process of accumulation ongoing for years. This personality profile also includes persistent denial that there is any addiction or obsession, isolation and alienation from society generally, and feelings of being unjustly persecuted.

The probability of recurrence here is also very high. When an intervention occurs and the animals are taken away from the hoarder, the individual will almost certainly begin collecting again. Perhaps remarkably, animal hoarders rarely have any previous history of institutionalization or diagnosed psychopathology. Since it has not been formally classified as a psychological problem and there has not been any systematic reporting of cases, the incidence of animal hoarding in the United States is presently unknown. Extrapolation from documented instances suggests that there are at least several hundred cases each year and perhaps as many as two thousand.

The collector gathers his or her animals through several avenues: visitations to local pounds and shelters, answering "free to good home" ads, taking in strays, and deliberate and unplanned breeding on the premises. By the time innocent collecting becomes pathological hoarding, the animals are almost always in a horrible condition: emaciated, starving, dehydrated, diseased, and infested with parasites and suppurating wounds. Not infrequently, the bodies of dead animals are found in the home, under beds, in closets or in the refrigerator, or simply lying out in the open. As the sheer number of animals has overwhelmed the hoarder's ability to take care of them properly, he or she also becomes incapable of maintaining a clean, orderly household. The dwelling is profusely strewn with debris of every sort, living spaces are squalid and food preparation areas filthy. A stench of urine and feces saturates the air.

Animal control agencies usually become involved in a hoarding case when the squalor and neglect are reported to them by a neighbor. Sometimes the police or a social worker will notice the situation and contact the local pound or shelter. Once confronted by authorities, a hoarder typically will not acknowledge the decay of the home or the suffering of the animals, and reject the idea of taking any of them to an animal control facility, fearing they will be euthanized there. If cited or arrested for cruelty to animals, hoarders have great difficulty understanding how the charge could be anything but groundless.

Hoarding and the Law

As mentioned above, animal hoarding is not in itself contrary to any state or federal law. However, it is unlawful in every state for a person to so neglect animals dependent upon him or her for their care that they live in pain and misery. Anticruelty statutes would seem to be the legal device of choice to stop such merciless disregard for the basic interests of the animals, but in fact this may not be the routine form of intervention here. Furthermore, concern for animal welfare may not be the primary motivation when interventions occur.

In a recent study of fifty-four animal hoarding cases in eight different states, one-third of the individuals were not prosecuted at all, and of those that were only three received any jail time, with six months the maximum. Much more common—75 percent of the cases—was some sort of court-ordered mental health or social service intervention on behalf of the hoarder: supervised or monitored living, psychiatric evaluations, or guardians. Just eight states presently allow judges to order psychological or psychiatric treatment for individuals found guilty of abusing animals, so most jurisdictions must use grounds other than animal welfare to secure this outcome, usually an appeal to public or personal (or both) health and safety. Moreover, even though thirty-five states either deny convicted offenders the right to own animals in the future, or allow the court to issue such a ban, only one-third of the reported cases resulted in courts commanding hoarders not to keep animals. It is hard to say what this study signifies for the legal disposition of hoarding generally—of course, the sample size is insufficient to support the claim that these statistics are broadly representative. There has as yet been no national compilation of data on pathological collectors prosecuted under anticruelty laws.

Even when hoarding is successfully prosecuted to the fullest extent of the anticruelty law, and even when such pathological collecting leads to reforms in these laws, society seems little closer to solving the problem. This is perhaps best illustrated by one of the most highly publicized hoarding cases, one that garnered substantial media attention in the region, and was picked up by the wire services and the major television networks.

It began in April 1993 in an unincorporated rural area near the town of Astoria, Oregon, northwest of Portland. On this spring day, a neighbor of Vikki Kittles noticed that the dilapidated school bus she had parked on her property was packed with dogs, one of which appeared to be having a seizure. Once alerted, county animal control officers and sheriff's deputies discovered that the bus contained 115 dogs, 4 cats, and 2 chickens. The dogs were severely malnourished and dehydrated, and many were obviously sick; 25 of them were either euthanized immediately or died while their owner was awaiting trial. (Several people close to the case noted how remarkable it was that so many of the animals had survived.)

Kittles was charged with first- and second-degree animal neglect, misdemeanors under Oregon's "Offenses against Animals" statutes. Throughout the lengthy litigation process and afterward, she was completely unrepentant. Serving as her own attorney, Kittles protested that her animal "collecting" was simply an alternative lifestyle unappreciated by the stodgy and repressed in law enforcement, one arising from a "religious" conviction that the dogs needed to be saved from murderous veterinarians. After a protracted, agonizing, and sometimes bizarre trial, she was convicted in 1995 on forty-two counts. The Oregon Court of Appeals rejected a review of her case without comment (*State v. Kittles*).

Judge Berkeley Smith imposed the maximum sentence then allowable: six months in jail (the term was extended by one month for numerous contempt of court citations Kittles received while representing herself). She also got four years probation, during which time she was not allowed to possess any animals, and Judge Smith ordered her to undergo counseling. After Kittles stubbornly refused to cooperate with state psychiatrists, this requirement was dropped in exchange for a little more jail time. Her period of incarceration lapsed in 1996, and, at this writing, her probation is ending too. Vikki Kittles is almost certain to hoard animals again. As mentioned above, high rates of recidivism are common with this disorder, and she already had a long history of accumulating animals in at least four other states on that day in 1993 when the neighbor peered into her bus. In any case, a few months in jail is a small price to pay for upholding a "religious" conviction that "saves dogs' lives."

For the purpose of thwarting and deterring pathological animal collecting, this is a bleak outcome, but the case motivated powerful legal forces to work for a considerable strengthening of the Oregon anticruelty law. Spearheaded by representatives of the Animal Legal Defense Fund, the Oregon Humane Society, and the Oregon legislature, people who had been particularly exercised by the Kittles affair, the so-called Kittles bill was drafted and enacted in 1995 by state lawmakers. The new law made "aggravated animal abuse in the first degree" a felony with the stiffest maximum penalty in the nation: five years in prison and $100,000 in fines. After five years on the books, no animal hoarder has been convicted or even charged with violating the new Oregon law, and ironically, given the source of its inspiration, a guilty verdict may be unavailable. A person is guilty of first-degree aggravated animal abuse in either of two circumstances: when he or she (1) "maliciously kills an animal," or (2) "intentionally or knowingly tortures an animal." This is known as a *mens rea* ("guilty mind") standard of culpability, where conviction requires proving that the accused had a certain mental state when the allegedly illegal action occurred (*see also* this chapter: *Anticruelty Laws: Liability*).

In the best of circumstances, this standard is not easy to achieve. The problem is even tougher here because a hoarder will vehemently deny that he or she had any intention of torturing the animals, and just as passionately reject the notion that he or she knew the animals were being tortured. Unlike any other person charged with animal cruelty, hoarders insist that, far from deliberately hurting them, they deeply love their animals. Proving otherwise in court would be very difficult.

The same problem arises for the other aggravating circumstance. The Oregon statute defines "maliciously" as "intentionally acting with a depravity of mind and reckless and wanton disregard of life." Again, a devoted animal lover, as the hoarder professes to be, would regard such an accusation as not merely false but utterly outrageous. Even if a jury could be convinced that a hoarder is depraved and reckless, *and* callously disdained the lives of the animals, a violation under this clause only occurs when an animal(s) *dies,* and not when it has merely endured pain and suffering. Yet hoarder neglect much more often causes misery in the animals rather than kills them. So this tough new anticruelty law appears to leave hoarding unscathed, or at least far from an easy reach.

Perhaps the most important hoarding case from the perspective of the law occurred in the jurisdiction next door to Oregon. There, in California, the defendant successfully appealed her conviction of cruelty to animals to the state appellate court. This is the highest advance of such litigation in a state judiciary with a legal influence extending across the nation (the California Supreme Court denied the defendant's petition for review). The case also strikes at two fundamental features of almost every state anticruelty law, as well as precisely what is at issue in the typical hoarding case: the prohibition on causing animals "unnecessary" pain, and failing to provide them with "sufficient quantities" of food and water, or "proper" shelter.

But what exactly is appropriate shelter for a dog, cat, horse, or other domestic animal? How much food and water is sufficient? And precisely when is causing pain and suffering to an animal unnecessary? The meanings of these key ideas are not obvious, and valid law cannot be completely obscure. In *People v. Speegle,* we find a defense of animal hoarding that could send shock waves throughout the preeminent form of animal protection law: the state anticruelty statute.

People v. Speegle

On July 27, 1993, in rural Butte County, California, north of Sacramento, animal control officers seized 200 poodles, 1 cat, and 3 horses from the property of Charlotte Speegle. Another 57 dogs were not retrieved until months later, some having been released by Speegle when the officers closed in and others evaded capture. Her freezer contained the frozen corpses of 2 adult dogs and 5 puppies—Speegle explained that she was saving the bodies for an undescribed "experiment." The floor of her trailer home was layered with feces, and neither food nor water was available for the animals. Speegle's own veterinarian remarked that in his 27 years of experience he had never seen an animal care facility in worse condition.

The confiscated animals were taken to the Northwest Society for the Prevention of Cruelty to Animals (NWSPCA), and there veterinarians found dogs with maggot- and flea-ridden fur, ear mites, intestinal parasites, rotted teeth, mouth disease, anemia, and suffering from severe malnutrition. Thirty-four of the poodles were soon euthanized or died from their debilitated condition; most of the remainder were eventually adopted. Meanwhile, the NWSPCA was financially and physically overwhelmed with caring for such a large influx of dogs, entirely to the exclusion of helping any other animals.

Speegle was charged with twenty-seven counts of animal cruelty under the California statute that allows felony status when anyone "causes any animal to be . . . deprived of necessary sustenance, drink, [or] shelter. . . . and subjects any animal to needless suffering, . . . or fails to provide the animal with proper food, drink, or shelter." She was also charged with 228 counts of misdemeanor animal neglect. The jury at the Superior Court of Butte County found her guilty of eight counts of felony animal cruelty for inflicting unnecessary suffering, and one count of animal neglect, a misdemeanor. In 1996 Judge William Patrick sentenced Speegle to two years in the state penitentiary, and ordered her to reimburse the NWSPCA for the cost of impounding the dogs, a sum of $265,000. She immediately challenged the decision to the California Court of Appeals.

Are Anticruelty Laws Too Vague?

The California anticruelty law, Speegle argued, is too general and unclear for the ordinary person of average intelligence to understand exactly what actions are legal and which are not. Statutes that outlaw failing to provide "necessary" or "proper" food and water, and prohibit causing "needless suffering" confront the average citizen with such vague directives that he or she can only guess at what the state demands. A law that engenders such uncertainty can only be unconstitutional. Interestingly and ironically, critics of anticruelty statutes, who are usually on the side of animals and would certainly find Speegle's actions abhorrent, have also complained of this ambiguity, especially in the prohibitions against causing "unnecessary" or "unjustifiable" pain, or doing so "without good cause" that are so common in the state laws. The only underlying principle they have discerned is that such terms seem to refer to practices through which animal suffering does not serve some well-accepted economic, entertainment, or other welfare interest of humans. The outcome of this case appears to reinforce both the ambiguity and the principle.

Speegle's defense, if successful, would have wide-ranging implications for litigation involving the hoarding of animals, and for cruelty cases generally, and not just in California. Every state anticruelty law includes language similar or identical to that found in the California statute at issue in this case. Events in the California judiciary, as well as in a legislature inspired by the decisions of Golden State judges, tend to have an impact on the legal proceedings in other less populated and less politically energetic and volatile states, though even states of like stature can be affected. No state court has a legal obligation to consider precedents in other jurisdictions, but given the prevalence of this language in anticruelty law, an appeal accepted in California on the grounds of its unconstitutional vagueness would certainly be noticed with great interest.

In a stunningly quick dismissal of an argument striking at the core of anticruelty law generally, Appellate Judge Davis rejected the notion that the California statute was unconstitutionally vague. Appealing to several precedents, he noted that a law does not have to specify every sort of action that it prohibits. First, that is impossible to do, especially so in anticruelty law since "[t]here are an infinite number of ways in which the callously indifferent can subject animals in their care to conditions which make the humane cringe." Furthermore, the terms "necessary," "proper," and "needless" each have a common meaning that is well understood by the ordinary person. They indicate in this context what is reasonable to provide for an animal in the way of food and water, and under what circumstances to avoid inflicting pain. Judge Davis called this an "objective standard of reasonableness."

Davis did not elaborate on this but apparently the idea is that there is a great deal of agreement about what the basic needs of animals (or perhaps just dogs) are, and what is appropriate for satisfying these needs. Although this is plausible, he did not indicate exactly what is reasonable here, or point out that what Speegle had done clearly was not reasonable. At any rate her felony conviction was not for failing to provide "necessary" or "proper" sustenance; it was for subjecting the animals to "needless suffering."

Here, however, an "objective standard of reasonableness" is not easy to see: there is *dis*agreement about when inflicting pain on an animal is needless and when it is not. For example, many people hold that the sufferings of animals used in research and in rodeos, for hunting and for commercial food products are precisely unnecessary, while many others deny this. Perhaps Judge Davis's point was that there is substantial agreement that the sort of thing Speegle had done causes suffering that is not necessary, but the uncertainty of that proposition is precisely Speegle's point. If this is Davis's reasoning, the critics mentioned above look to be correct because the most plausible basis for this agreement is that there were no financial benefits or enhancements for human well-being accomplished by the suffering of the poodles.

Was the Order of Restitution Excessive?
Speegle also challenged the order to pay the NWSPCA restitution for holding the animals. She claimed that her only responsibility was the expense for impounding the eight dogs she was convicted of abusing, not the cost for *all* of them. Furthermore, she said, the Humane Society should have euthanized the animals more quickly, rather than continuing to care for them while waiting for new owners, such delay driving up the cost of impoundment.

This defense also has the potential to send ripples through the calm legal waters of anticruelty law. Although not universal like the use of such terms as "necessary," "needless," and "proper," more than forty states do require those convicted of animal abuse to repay animal control facilities the cost of impounding the maltreated animals. When multiple animals are involved, as is always the case with hoarding but occurs in other sorts of cruelty cases too, Speegle's defense could drastically limit offenders' financial liability.

Davis looked to the letter of the law and the intention of the California legislature to reject this attempted evasion of liability. The California code states that "Upon conviction [for] . . . causing an act of cruelty, all animals lawfully seized and impounded with respect to the violation . . . shall thereupon be awarded to the impounding officer for proper disposition. A person convicted [for] . . . causing an act of cruelty, shall be liable to the impounding officer for all costs of impoundment from the time of seizure to the time of proper disposition." According to Davis, the phrase "costs of impoundment" does refer to "all animals lawfully seized with respect to the violation," such a reference being exactly what Speegle denied. "With respect to the violation" means only that there was a causal or general connection between the actual violation—which was abusing 8 dogs—and the impoundment of 200 dogs. There was then a violation concerning a subset of the total number of the dogs just because all of them were seized. This is different than the direct connection that would have been established if the law had been written so that "costs of impoundment" referred to "all animals lawfully seized *for* the violation," or *"as a result of* the violation."

Even if the phrase "with respect to" were not clear, Davis continued, the legislature has demonstrated an obvious intention to prevent cruelty to animals by authorizing agents of the state to take them away from people who are unfit to keep them. This means that the statute allows "the removal of *all* the animals in the keeping of a defendant found to be capable of cruelty, regardless of whether the other animals have been victims of a violation of the statute." This suggests that because the condition of some of the animals indicated that Speegle was or would be cruel to all them, the animal control officers were authorized to confiscate the whole lot.

In her defense, Speegle could certainly concede this point. After all, she was not challenging the impoundment power of the state, but the extent of her financial responsibility when this power was exercised. She could still legitimately wonder why she had to pay for the care of animals the jury had found her innocent of abusing.

As to the claim that the NWSPCA had a duty to euthanize the impounded animals instead of keeping them while the cost of their care mounted, Judge Davis simply pointed out that Speegle had offered no legal basis for this obligation, and dismissed the argument.

SEXUAL CONTACT WITH ANIMALS

In its original meaning the term *bestiality* signifies the demonstration of animal- or beast-like traits in a human being. The more modern sense of the term, which now seems to dominate, is sexual contact between a human and an animal. In this sense, it can denote a variety of actions but most commonly refers to the penetration of an animal's vagina or anus with the human penis or fingers, or with an object. In extreme cases, and especially in pornographic media, an animal may be injured or even killed for sexual gratification. Sexually explicit materials also feature the penetration of human females with an animal's penis, or oral-genital contact with an animal. Equivalent terms for all these actions are *zoophilia* and *zooerasty*, both from the Greek meaning "love of animals."

The Zoophile
Reliable data on the incidence of bestiality is sparse, and the psychological profile of the zoophile is not yet well developed, again for lack of solid information. Apparently, very few women ever have sexual contact with animals, even though, as just suggested, they are the participants routinely displayed in the sexually explicit material commercially available. It seems to be a predilection almost exclusively of men, perhaps residents of rural areas mostly, but exactly how many men have done this, or make a practice of it, is unknown—recent estimates have fluctuated wildly, from 1 percent to over 50 percent. More than half a century ago Alfred Kinsey and Wardell Pomeroy, basing their estimate on the testimony of a large sample, reported that 8 percent of American males have had at least one sexual encounter with an animal.

Many men may choose bestiality as an easy alternative to securing normal sexual contact with human females, such liaisons having proved difficult to establish or believed to be unattainable, while animals are accessible and readily subdued or coerced. Other zoophiles contend that they simply prefer sex with animals over sex with humans, regardless of the availability or cooperation of the sexual "partner." There also appears to be another category composed of sexual sadists who derive pleasure from hurting or killing animals. It is this latter group who are most plausibly charged with the sexual *abuse* of animals, escalating beyond mere sexual contact. On the other hand, many animal advocates argue that, because the nonhuman cannot consent to this activity, *any* sexual contact with an animal, regardless of physical harm, is abusive and more properly described as a form of sexual assault. At any rate, sexual sadism is not required to produce the rectal and vaginal tearing and rupturing observed in many animals subjected to this treatment.

Judging from cases in which a person has been charged with violating a state law prohibiting sexual contact with an animal, zoophiles prefer dogs and horses, due to their size and tractable nature, as well as the greater opportunities presented by two species living in such close association with humans. Even so, cats, cows, deer, pigs, rabbits, and sheep have also been used. Rodents, frogs, snakes, chickens and other birds seem to be the creatures of choice for the sexual sadist, especially those stimulated by detailed videos of these and other small animal species being crushed, a form of entertainment that has recently drawn the attention of Congress (*see* this chapter: *Sexual Contact with Animals: Animal Cruelty, Obscenity, and the Law*). The animals are obtained from all the usual sources from which humans can acquire them: pet shops, breeders, "free to good home" advertisements, animal shelters, and strays. In rural areas, zoophiles have been known to trespass on the property of livestock owners—"fence-jumpers"—in pursuit of the animals confined there.

Animals, Sex, and the Law

Sexual contact with animals has been traditionally viewed in the Western world with great abhorrence and opprobrium, an "unnatural crime" warranting the most severe punishment for both parties involved. Indeed, this activity was seen as so loathsome that when its proscription was written into the codes of many of the United States in the nineteenth century, the language of the statutes often referred only to the "abominable and detestable crime against nature" without saying anything about sex or animals. This rather vague phrasing is retained to this day in several state laws.

The loathing of bestiality traces back at least as far as biblical times and the Book of Leviticus, probably composed during the sixth century B.C.E., where it is written (New International Version): "If a man has sexual relations with an animal, he must be put to death, and you must kill the animal. If a woman approaches an animal to have sexual relations with it, kill both the woman and the animal." Because concern for animal welfare was not the motivation, it is unclear why these relations provoked such an extreme reaction, but it may be traced to outrage at the disruption of God's natural order that bestiality was believed to represent.

In the developing Christian world of Medieval Europe, the Jewish attitude was adopted and supplemented with the occult view that bestial intercourse results in demonic offspring intent on the proliferation of evil, a diabolical scheme cooked up by the devil himself. In this world, such horror could only be crushed with an ecclesiastical hammer, and church law became criminal law as kings accepted the doctrine.

So we find during a period lasting several hundred years, from the early Middle Ages until well into the nineteenth century, animals actually being prosecuted before European judges and juries for their involvement in sexual relations with some person, who was also called before the bar. Following the biblical injunction, and expressing the loathing and outrage mentioned above, courts almost invariably passed death sentences on both the human and the animal. The offenders were then summarily executed, first one then the other, often before large crowds. Indeed, two of the earliest cases adjudicated in the American colonies were a 1642 proceeding in which a teenaged servant boy was hanged along with the animals he had sodomized, and, twenty years later, the execution of three cows, three sheep, two pigs, a dog, and the man who had sex with them.

Today in the United States the legal view of bestiality has changed considerably. Only half of the states still have laws prohibiting sexual contact between humans and animals, counting two antibestiality bills presently under consideration by the Missouri and New Jersey legislatures; both are likely to pass. A number of state statutes criminalizing sodomy between consenting adults were repealed in the 1960s and 1970s, taking antibestiality provisions along with them. And, of course, violations in those states that continue to make sex with animals unlawful are not punishable by death for either the human or nonhuman participant. Instead, the animal is ignored entirely and the human is subject to a fine and/or prison time, penalties that vary considerably depending on the state.

For example, Delaware, Michigan, North Carolina, Oklahoma, South Carolina, and Virginia have designated sexual relations with an animal a felony (as does the Missouri bill), punishable by up to fifteen years in prison; yet of these, only South Carolina adds a fine, one of at least $500. Massachusetts and Rhode Island do not categorize the offense as a felony, but they have set their maximum penalty at twenty years. The Montana,

Mississippi, and Maryland codes each provide for up to ten years imprisonment; Montana also allows a fine of as much as $50,000, but Maryland's is only $1,000. In further contrast, Georgia says one to five years and no fine, and Minnesota has a maximum of one year in prison. Louisiana courts can impose as much as five years of hard labor and a $2,000 fine on a convicted offender. Whatever the maximum penalties may be, it appears that no offender in any state has ever received one. The case law in this area is extremely sparse.

The two dozen state codes that currently ban sexual contact with an animal approach this conduct in one of two different ways. Arkansas, Idaho, Kansas, Maryland, South Carolina, and Virginia have included bestiality in the general definition of criminal sodomy (not having repealed this law as other states have done). This is legally defined as any contact involving the mouth or anus of one individual and the genitalia of another. Aimed primarily at homosexual conduct, in these states the proscription is extended to encompass either a human or an animal.

Most of the other state codes have a statute explicitly addressing this behavior as a separate item. Some are very brief and general, such as a Pennsylvania provision that says simply that "any form of sexual intercourse with an animal" is outlawed. Others are much more specific and detailed, like Utah, where "[a] person commits the crime of bestiality if the actor engages in any sexual activity with an animal. . . . '[A]nimal' means any live nonhuman vertebrate creature . . . and 'sexual activity' means physical sexual contact: (i) between the actor and the animal involving the genitals of the actor or the animal and the mouth or anus of the actor or the animal; (ii) through the actor's use of an object in contact with the genitals or anus of the animal."

The Utah law is also noteworthy because this state joins Nebraska as the only jurisdictions that have specifically criminalized the use of an object to penetrate the anus or vagina of an animal. Georgia, Virginia, and Wisconsin seem not to have prohibited this practice at all, confining the offense to actions involving the mouth, anus, or genitals. In other states it is not clear if the use of an object would run afoul of the law. New York and North Dakota, for example, prohibit "sexual conduct" and "sexual contact" with an animal but do not indicate if penetration with an object qualifies. Similarly, along with the standard injunction against oral and anal sex, Maryland prohibits "any other unnatural or perverted sexual practice," while in Minnesota "[w]hoever carnally knows . . . an animal or bird is guilty of bestiality."

Still other states, harkening back to a time when sexual relations with an animal was "a sin too fearful to be named," do not articulate what exactly the prohibited action is. So we find that the Massachusetts, Michigan, Mississippi, Oklahoma, and Rhode Island codes detail only the punishment that awaits anyone convicted of an unspecified "abominable and detestable crime against nature."

Delaware, Kansas, and Montana have also made it unlawful for anyone to force another person to commit a sex act with an animal.

Animal Cruelty, Obscenity, and the Law

As mentioned above, in twenty-five states it is not illegal to have sexual contact with an animal. If, as some claim, any form of such contact qualifies as sexual abuse, a sexual assault, this suggests that state anticruelty laws should protect the violated animals. However, these laws appear to reach only the practice of the sexual sadist or other individual whose attack on an animal kills or injures it, causing the creature serious physical pain and qualifying as the "cruel mistreatment" proscribed almost everywhere (*see* this chapter: *Anticruelty Laws*). Yet it would be exceedingly difficult to prove in a court that an animal was cruelly mistreated when the sexual act did not cause obvious pain or injury. Moreover, most states exempt livestock and animals used in research facilities from the protections of their anticruelty laws in any case. Apart from these legal subtleties, there is no record of a case in which sexual contact with an animal—physically injurious or not—was successfully prosecuted as a violation of such a statute.

Nor is there any federal law prohibiting people from engaging in bestiality. Nonetheless, it has proved possible to prosecute the distribution of images on the Internet *depicting* sex acts involving humans and animals as a violation of federal obscenity laws. The World Wide Web currently contains dozens, possibly hundreds, of sexually explicit websites featuring graphic pictures of humans (again, overwhelmingly women) engaged in lewd activities with animals. Readily downloaded onto any home computer, most of these images involve oral-genital contact and copulation with a male animal. Though a few are offered free of charge to entice the consumer, the majority of these are available only to those who have paid a "membership" fee. Some links also offer emotional support to troubled zoophiles who feel embarrassed about their unusual tastes in sex (often referred to as being "zoo"), alienated from the larger society that approves only coupling between conspecifics. Whatever the precise menu, these sites seem to be quite popular: one boasts of receiving thousands of hits each day.

Federal law prohibits possessing with the intent to sell, transporting for sale, selling, mailing, importing, broadcasting, or distributing "obscene" material. Such material is not protected by the First Amendment guarantee of freedom of speech. The determination that some book, letter, pamphlet, picture, photograph, video, drawing, or other image is obscene must be made by a jury or a judge applying the three-part test devised by the Supreme Court in 1973. Legally obscene material is that which "the average person applying contemporary community standards" finds to (1) be "appeal[ing] to prurient interest"; (2) contain depictions or descriptions of sexual conduct that are offensive; and (3) "lack serious literary, artistic, political, or scientific value" (*Miller v. California*). To date, one court decision has found that images depicting bestiality are obscene, and that their distribution through personal computers is contrary to federal law.

In 1991, in the days before the Internet explosion, husband and wife Robert and Carleen Thomas operated Amateur Action Computer Bulletin Board System (AABBS) from their home in Milpitas, California. The AABBS "website" (as it would be called today) supplied sexually explicit images to individuals who, having paid a fee, dialed in through the phone lines and accessed the Thomases' inventory through a modem. By using a scanning device to convert numerous photographs from "adult" magazines into GIF (Graphic Interchange Format) computer files, the couple could send the pictures to any location in the country equipped with a computer and a modem. Among various images of oral sex, incest, and sadomasochism available from AABBS were depictions of people having sex with animals.

Tipped off by a complaint, in 1993 a U.S. postal inspector sent the Thomases money and managed to download many of these pictures. Within one year the Thomases had been charged in a federal district court in Tennessee (where the complaint had originated) with a dozen counts of violating federal obscenity laws, in particular one that prohibits anyone from "knowingly transport[ing by] means of . . . an interactive computer . . . any obscene . . . image." The jury in Tennessee found that the images, including those depicting bestiality, were indeed legally obscene, according to the standards of their community, and rendered a guilty verdict on ten of the twelve items. On appeal, the Thomases' convictions were upheld by the Sixth Circuit Court of Appeals (*United States v. Thomas*).

Although this case stands as a powerful precedent for deterring the commercialization of bestiality, so far, as evidenced by the high number of websites currently offering such images, no subsequent litigation has taken advantage of it. Interdiction of the offense seems to rank very low on the priority list of federal prosecutors. Even if this were not the case, convictions for obscenity are notoriously elusive and tainted with arbitrariness when secured, in large part because many American communities have radically different views on what sort of depictions are obscene. The denizens of San Francisco's "Tenderloin" neighborhood might find tame what the citizens of, say, Fairfield, Iowa, might reject as unadulterated smut. Notwithstanding a perennial concern about lax enforcement, a more solid foundation than obscenity law for discouraging the production and distribution of images of bestiality could be obtained by extending and supplementing recent federal legislation directed, not at animal sex, but at animal cruelty.

A gap has existed in anticruelty law, where, although every state prohibits cruelty to animals, neither the states nor the federal government have outlawed *making images* of people engaged in illegal cruelty, and selling them to consumers. This breach in the legal protections afforded to animals has allowed a market in "crush videos" to develop. These are videotapes of women in stiletto heels or barefoot crushing small animals with their feet. Most of the victims are mice, hamsters, and guinea pigs, but birds, frogs, and kittens have also been used. Some men with a "foot fetish" find such images sexually arousing, though no court has ever found them to be legally obscene.

To evade the vagaries of obscenity law, in July 1999 California Representative Elton Gallegly introduced legislation on Capitol Hill prohibiting the creation, sale, or possession of "depictions of animal cruelty," that is, videos of behavior contrary to state anticruelty laws or the federal Animal Welfare Act (*see* chapter 7). Opponents of the bill argued that crush videos are merely offensive speech protected by the First Amendment. The Supreme Court had already ruled, they noted, that the government interest in preventing cruelty to animals could be overridden by appeal to the right to free exercise of religion, also contained in the First Amendment (*see* chapter 4: *Legal Challenges to Ritual Slaughter: Church of Lukumi Babalu Aye v. Hialeah*). Unconvinced, lawmakers quickly approved Gallegly's bill, and President Bill Clinton signed it into law in December 1999 (*see also* this chapter: *Anticruelty Laws: Other Recent Developments*).

Similarly, measures independent of obscenity charges, and of cruelty, could be taken to criminalize the production of depictions featuring humans engaged in sexual activities with animals, applicable at least in those states already banning this activity. This could be accomplished by amending Gallegly's legislation to prohibit producing, selling, or possessing images depicting *any* activity involving animals that is contrary to state or federal law. A stipulation that such images lack "serious literary, artistic, political, or scientific value," as in the Supreme Court test for obscenity, would allow documentaries of cockfighting and dogfighting, for example, to be made, sold, and possessed (dogfighting is illegal in every state, and cockfighting is banned in all but four; *see* chapter 5). The amendment would also clearly reach the prevailing sexual conduct displayed on the Web, behaviors that arguably do not attain the level of cruelty to animals: women in oral-genital contact and having intercourse with animals.

So far, no such bill has been sponsored and none seems to be forthcoming. It would make commercial trafficking, by mail or cyberspace, in images of sexual contact with animals illegal everywhere except in and between states that have no antibestiality law. In these locations, appeal to obscenity and the relevant anticruelty laws would remain the only recourse.

ANIMAL CONTROL FACILITIES

The basic purpose of any animal control facility (ACF) is to provide a temporary repository for lost, unwanted, and nuisance animals. In the United States nearly every one of these unfortunate creatures is a domestic dog or a house cat. There is no national database, so precise figures are unknown, but estimates are that each year some 8 to 12 million individuals of these two species enter America's 6,000 ACFs, and about half of this number never leave—they are killed on the premises.

Legal restrictions on ACFs are dominated by a hodgepodge coming out of state and city codes. There is only one federal law regulating these facilities in any way. Further, a national organization imposing standards or policies throughout the industry does not exist. The National Animal Control Association (NACA) has a program for certifying ACFs, but it is strictly voluntary. The vast majority of these facilities are not NACA certified nor are they accredited by any other entity providing oversight or some form of governance. The NACA, the Humane Society of the United States (HSUS), and the American Humane Association each offer detailed guidelines for the operation of ACFs, but none are legally required to abide by them and many do not, at least not in their entirety.

Shelters and Pounds

All ACFs furnish society with transient housing for wayward animals, but in America two distinct sorts of agencies fulfill this function.

First, there is the ACF operated by a local or regional society for the prevention of cruelty to animals (SPCA) or humane society. (The HSUS is not an umbrella organization for these agencies and is not affiliated with any of them.) These are generic names for any nonprofit organization dedicated to animal welfare, authorized as such by a (local) government-issued charter, and managed by a board of directors. The size, and the range of activities and services offered varies widely among these societies. Some extend over a large city, others one or more counties, and still others cover an entire state, with branch offices and a full complement of directors, officers, staff, members, and volunteers working in various specialized capacities. Many are much smaller, covering only a single, lightly populated town or region, with little or no staff and the directors performing multiple, more general tasks. Some areas of the country are not serviced by any SPCA or humane society.

Regardless of size, at minimum these organizations are actively engaged in educating citizens on the principles of humane care and treatment, typically done through publications, mailings, public service announcements, and presentations. Also, many jurisdictions authorize SPCAs and humane societies to enforce anticruelty laws by conferring limited police powers on their agents. The larger operations also take positive measures to find the owners of lost or stray animals and place animals in the homes of responsible people. Finally, the majority of these organizations operate facilities for the temporary care and housing of lost or discarded pets: an ACF. Most people call this a "shelter," a term connoting caretaking and refuge, often intended to distinguish it from a "pound."

The pound is the second type of ACF, one operated by the animal control division of a city or county government, rather than by a private organization. Historically, the function of government animal control has been narrowly confined to enforcing laws providing for the collection and disposal of unclaimed and unwanted dogs and cats, especially those exhibiting symptoms of rabies or other disease.

Over the last couple of decades, however, the respective roles of SPCAs and animal control divisions have increasingly merged as local governments become more involved with humane education and the search for new and current pet owners. Anticruelty enforcement has traditionally been shared anyway, and both pounds and shelters destroy a lot of excess animals. Moreover, sometimes local governments contract with a humane society to perform animal control duties rather than set up or maintain their own facility. So now the major differentiating feature between these two types of agency is not so much any practical function but the economic structure. Humane societies and their shelters are primarily funded by charitable donations from private citizens, while animal control and their pounds are supported by taxation imposed on the general public. (A few ACFs in the United States are not connected with any animal welfare organization or with any government entity.)

Although government animal control officers are responsible for enforcing anticruelty laws, their primary legal obligation is to seize and impound (hence, the "pound") nuisance animals or those who are in some way menacing or endangering people. This is essentially an aspect of human health and safety, not animal welfare. Traditionally, these bothersome creatures have most often been dogs, earning the city or county officer the "dog-catcher" moniker, one the modern ACF employee disdains. This was the original form of animal control, developed in America's urban centers during the early 1800s, when municipal workers began patrolling the streets looking for diseased or vagrant animals, dogs with rabies in particular. The rural mentality that dogs could simply be left to roam at will did not transfer well to the new cities of America. Sterilization was unknown and wandering packs of canines in Boston, New York, Philadelphia, and other urban areas became not merely an extreme annoyance, but, as hosts of disease, posed a significant threat to public health.

In those days, pounds were essentially "catch and kill" operations. Dogs and cats were snared with nooses or nets, thrown into boxes for transportation to the impoundment yard, held there briefly (if at all) in complete squalor, and killed with hammers and clubs or hung with ropes. In New York City, for example, dozens of dogs were rounded up off the streets every day and loaded into crates. A crane lifted the containers out over the East River and lowered them into the water, submerging the animals until they drowned. The crates were then lifted back to the dock and the sodden mass of dead dogs dumped into carts and hauled to a dump or an incinerator. In New York and elsewhere, only a very few animals—and very lucky ones too—were ever recovered by their owners or adopted by others.

The Rise of the Animal Shelter
It was as a reaction to the brutal treatment and appalling conditions at the pound that the first SPCA providing a sanctuary for abused and homeless animals was created. Henry Bergh founded the American Society for the Prevention of Cruelty to Animals in 1866, but the ASPCA substantially emulated the Royal Society for the Prevention of Cruelty to Animals (established in 1824). The Americans followed the British model of dedication to humane education and the enforcement of anticruelty laws, rather than to an active sheltering endeavor. Similarly, state SPCAs established in Massachusetts, Pennsylvania, New Jersey, Illinois, and Minnesota during the late 1860s, and the first two municipal societies, in San Francisco and in Portland, Oregon, focused on fostering compassionate treatment of animals rather than operating facilities to house them.

In Philadelphia, Caroline White changed all that. The daughter of a prominent Quaker abolitionist, White had cofounded the Pennsylvania SPCA in 1868, but as a woman was not permitted to serve on the board of directors. Disgusted with the practices of the city animal control, and disgruntled with the management of the new organization—which encouraged women members to raise money yet would not allow them a voice in the allocation of the funds—White and several other members of the "Women's Branch" applied for and received a separate charter to form their own society. In 1870 the Women's Pennsylvania SPCA established the nation's first animal shelter as a humane alternative to the horrors of the pound. Here, dogs were provided with ample kennels, fresh air, running water, wholesome food, and medical care when necessary. Instead of beating, strangulation, or drowning, excess animals were painlessly killed with carbon dioxide gas or chloroform. (White went on to co-found the American Anti-Vivisection Society in 1883, the first organization in the United States dedicated to regulating the use of animals in research and experimentation.)

By the mid-1880s there were thirty-three private organizations devoted to the protection of animals in the United States, and when the century turned, there were over 200. Many of these, following the lead of Caroline White and the Women's Pennsylvania SPCA, set up sheltering facilities.

Even though the plight of dogs led to that first animal shelter, the early American humane movement focused more on the welfare of horses than that of canines. Horses were the most common animal in human society in those days, found on every street nearly all the time. As the preeminent conveyance for people and freight, coupled with an imposing size, the horse had a very high profile. Often, abusive treatment of overloaded and overworked animals was quite conspicuous. SPCAs labored diligently to promote humane handling of equines, while enforcing laws requiring it. The shelters accepted mistreated horses, or found farms where they could recuperate in peace. A number of hospitals and "rest homes" were established in the northeastern United States especially for the care of sick, old, and broken-down horses, notably Ryerss's Infirmary for Dumb Animals, Red Acre Farm, and the Animal Rescue League's hospital. Women were the driving forces behind these facilities: respectively, Anne Ryerss, Harriet Bird, and Anna Smith (for horse welfare law generally, *see* this chapter: *Horse Law*).

As motorized vehicles were developed and improved, the horses were gradually moved out into the country, disappearing entirely from the city by the 1920s (except for the commercial carriage rides, which persist to this day; *see* this chapter: *Horse Law: Carriage Rides*). SPCA members were overwhelmingly urban dwellers, so when the horses faded away in the concrete canyons, attention to equine welfare waned, to be replaced by a heightened awareness of the travails perennially inflicted upon the domestic dog. This realignment of humanitarian concern corresponded to a boom in canine ownership during the "roaring" (and barking?) 1920s, a surge that retreated in the Depression years and while the Second World War raged. But the war ended, the soldiers came home, and everyone, it seemed, wanted a dog.

Animal Seizure
The first significant legal regulation of ACFs began just after the Second World War, laws that had their greatest impact on the dogs held in these facilities. At this time, postwar prosperity was manifested in two dimensions that together conspired to produce a major change in the way ACFs operated.

First was a flood of money from the federal government to fund basic research, especially in the medical sciences. These investigations have nearly always proceeded by extrapolating from the results of tests done on animals, so the burgeoning number of research projects gave rise to a critical demand for animals to serve as subjects in the experiments. The second aspect of the affluence that followed the war was a large increase in the number of household pets, dogs in particular, kept by Americans, estimated as a 50 percent rise from the late 1930s to the late 1940s. Corresponding to the growth in the dog population were expanding numbers of canines arriving at local pounds and shelters, either picked up lost or as strays, or dropped off by owners who, for one reason or another, did not want them anymore.

The research community, led by the newly formed National Society for Medical Research (NSMR), saw the thousands of unclaimed animals languishing and dying in ACFs as a wasted resource. Yet operators of pounds and shelters were under no legal obligation to surrender the animals to anyone, much less to researchers desiring to use them as subjects in experiments. This was the state of affairs research interests worked to change.

In 1948 and 1949, after successful lobbying by the NSMR, Minnesota and Wisconsin passed the nation's first animal seizure laws requiring ACFs to hand over dogs and cats to research facilities upon demand. Within three years the NSMR and its allies had persuaded the city councils of Los Angeles, Washington, D.C., and Baltimore to pass ordinances, and the New York legislature to enact a statute mandating that ACFs relinquish their animals when the scientists or their minions came calling. By the early 1960s Connecticut, Iowa, Oklahoma, Ohio, Massachusetts, South Dakota, West Virginia, and a number of other municipalities had all followed suit, fueling a steady flow of animals to the laboratories from pounds and shelters all over the country.

The proliferation of animal seizure laws was a shocking development for the directors and staff of many animal shelters, and for much of the leadership of America's humane societies. They saw a terrible irony in the notion that a haven for animals should be compelled to surrender their charges to "vivisectors." Resistance to the new laws arose quickly out of the animal sheltering and welfare community, but it was mostly futile in those days. Nonetheless, although the early battles were all lost, in the long run the war was won, for the most part, in at least two main respects.

First, several new animal protection organizations were formed in the 1950s primarily as a response to the animal seizure laws. Some of these have become among the most effective proanimal lobbying forces in the nation. Foremost among them are the Animal Welfare Institute with its lobbying arm, the Society for Animal Protective Legislation, and the Humane Society of the United States, which, dissatisfied with its inaction on this and other issues, broke from the larger American Humane Association in 1954. The second ultimate victory was that nearly all these laws were eventually repealed, or at least significantly amended.

In 2000 fourteen states, mostly clustered in the Northeast, will not allow research facilities to acquire animals from ACFs, and it is illegal there for a shelter or pound to provide them: Connecticut, Delaware, Hawaii, Maine, Maryland, Massachusetts, New Hampshire, New Jersey, New York, Pennsylvania, Rhode Island, South Carolina, Vermont, and West Virginia. Only two states remain that require all ACFs to release animals for use in the labs: South Dakota and Utah.

In Oklahoma, Iowa, and Minnesota pounds must turn over animals on demand, but shelters are not so required (though they can if they wish to). Seven other states permit ACFs to surrender dogs and cats to research facilities if their management chooses to do so: Arizona, California, Michigan, North Carolina, Tennessee, Washington, and Wisconsin. Of these only California requires ACFs to inform the public that any animals they accept might end up in a laboratory. Pounds and shelters in the Golden State must conspicuously display a large sign that reads "Animals Turned into This Shelter May Be Used for Research Purposes." The remaining twenty-three states do not currently address the issue in their law codes.

Holding Periods

Winning the war against the state seizure laws fell short of a complete victory. Dogs and cats deposited at ACFs, even in those fourteen states, may still end up in a laboratory. Scientists for decades have had a powerful economic motive to mine pounds and shelters for animals: they cost little or nothing to obtain. Yet in these facilities there is no "quality control" of their overall fitness, a circumstance suggested by the standard industry designation for ACFs as "random sources."

It is mainly for this reason that within the last twenty years or so research operations have usually acquired their canine and feline subjects not from ACFs, but from animal dealers who supply "purpose bred" animals, the purpose being to serve as laboratory subjects. These dealers are business persons whose success depends in large part upon their reputation for providing their customers with a premium product: healthy animals in good condition without physical defects that might compromise the results of experimentation. No state or federal law prohibits pounds or shelters from selling dogs and cats to *dealers,* and when such a transaction occurs, the animals will almost invariably end up in laboratories. Nonetheless, it is in this area that the only federal law affecting the operation of ACFs is activated.

The Animal Welfare Act (AWA) and its regulations issued by the U.S. Department of Agriculture (USDA) mandate standards for the care, handling, and transportation of dogs and cats (and certain other species) by research facilities, zoos, circuses, animal dealers, animal breeders, and common carriers. First enacted in 1966 as the Laboratory Animal Welfare Act (a 1970 amendment changed the name), the original motivation for the AWA was to halt an epidemic of dog stealing by unscrupulous dealers, who then sold the canines for research and experimentation. Toward this end, the AWA demands that animal dealers be licensed by the USDA, and researchers are forbidden from buying animals from unlicensed dealers. Further, dealers must retain any dogs or cats they acquire for at least five days before selling them, a rule intended to deter the practice of moving animals swiftly from a "random source"—such as a pound or shelter—to a laboratory before the owners can track them down (for more on the AWA, *see* chapter 7).

A 1990 amendment to the AWA, named by its sponsors the Pet Protection Act, requires pounds and shelters to hold and care for all dogs and cats on site for at least five days before they can be legally sold to animal dealers. The intention of Congress is to give these species greater opportunities to be reclaimed by their owners or to be adopted by new ones, a provision that affords the animals ten total days before the one-way trip to the laboratory can commence. It also recognizes, perhaps years late, that ACFs are publicly available facilities easily located by prospective animal owners or by those searching for lost pets, while a dealer's private business is typically far less conspicuous or accessible. Anyone can find the local pound or shelter simply by looking in the telephone book. How would one determine where the nearest animal dealer conducts business?

Most state and local governments also dictate holding periods to their pounds, requiring them to keep animals on the premises for a certain amount of time before they can be adopted by a new owner or killed. Typically, these periods are four or five days for strays and a day or two less for pets brought in by their owners. Most shelter charters also specify a similar period in the same circumstances for their operations. Just as with the AWA stipulation, the general point is to decrease the likelihood that the animal will be destroyed instead of being reclaimed by its rightful owner.

In July 1999 California took steps to reduce this probability even further by establishing the longest required holding period for animals at any American ACF. Sponsored by state senator Tom Hayden, the new law directs that stray dogs and cats be held for at least six days, double the previous minimum of seventy-two hours. Animals brought in by pet owners wishing to relieve themselves of a burden must be held for at least two days. Like any mandated holding period, "Hayden's Law" is intended to increase adoptions and lower the number of animals killed, but it has thrown many Golden State ACFs into a panic. The space that might otherwise have gone to new arrivals is still being occupied by unclaimed animals, some of which are not nearly as "adoptable" as the unwanted individuals that now must be turned away.

Standards of Care

The majority of states do not regulate the housing and husbandry of animals kept at their ACFs in any detail. Presently only Colorado, Georgia, Iowa, Kansas, Louisiana, Michigan, Missouri, Nevada, and North Carolina have comprehensive standards of care for shelters and pounds, with compliance required for licensing. New Jersey and Pennsylvania also license ACFs but, like most states, stipulate only that the animals be given "appropriate" or "proper" care.

Colorado and Missouri are the leaders in this regulatory arena. The two states have the most complete and elaborate set of standards for keeping animals in pounds and shelters, beginning with general guidelines for the construction of the facilities. These structures must be soundly constructed and regularly maintained, readily cleaned and sanitized, and effectively prevent escape, access by other animals, or injury. Adequate ventilation and lighting, running potable water, and heating and cooling, are required for each facility. The seven other states substantially duplicate these general standards, but only Colorado adds that heat must be provided when the temperature in the facility drops below 50 degrees Fahrenheit for four consecutive hours, and cooled if it rises above 90 degrees Fahrenheit, while Missouri sets the limits at 45 degrees and 85 degrees Fahrenheit. North Carolina and Michigan also have a temperature minimum of 50 degrees Fahrenheit, but no other state demands cooling in an ACF. All these state regulations provide that outdoor housing protect the animals from the weather with shelters and shade, but only Missouri and Colorado expressly prohibit keeping animals outside that are not accustomed to the climate at the facility.

These two states also detail specifications for the "primary enclosure" of the animals: the construction and dimensions of their cages. As with the general housing standards, the cages should be safe, structurally sound, clean, dry, and provide ready access to water and food. Floors are to be constructed of materials that do not injure the animals' feet, which can include wire, so long as the gauge is thick enough to prevent sagging under the animals' weight, and the mesh is narrow enough so their feet will not pass through. Michigan and Louisiana are the only other states that mention flooring, but simply stipulate that the materials not injure the animals' feet.

Colorado and Missouri also specify the amount of cage space that each dog or cat must be given, a standard formula found in the federal Animal Welfare Act regulations, and one also utilized by Nevada, North Carolina, and Louisiana. Minimum cage area is the square of the number that is the length of the dog from the tip of the nose to the base of the tail plus 6, and then divided by 144. Georgia, Iowa, and Michigan have broad statements demanding "ample" or "sufficient" space to allow dogs and cats to turn around, stand, and lie down. The Kansas regulations for ACFs do not mention cage space.

Iowa joins Colorado and Missouri as the three states that require ACF personnel to exercise dogs. This must be done for at least twenty minutes each day in an exercise area with dimensions of no less than three times the length of the canine, one and one-half times the animal's height, and wide enough to "allow the dog to turn around easily." Iowa calls for twice-daily exercise, but Missouri offers simply the injunction "to provide dogs with an opportunity for exercise" and does not mandate the size of the runs used for this purpose or its frequency.

Although the North Carolina and Michigan regulations both mention that veterinary services should be available, Colorado and Missouri are also the only states that *require* ACFs to have an attending veterinarian. Furthermore, these are the sole jurisdictions, along with Iowa, that order daily cleaning of all animal cages. The other states offer general instructions to clean the enclosures "as often as necessary" or "often enough" to prevent illness or discomfort.

All nine states require pounds and shelters to offer the animals wholesome, palatable food and potable water at least once a day (if water is not continuously available). Eight of these—Kansas is the exception—require the separation of females in estrus from males and the isolation of "vicious" animals.

Sterilization

Most people who are well apprised of the situation agree that America has a serious pet overpopulation problem. The millions of dogs and cats killed in ACFs each year powerfully support this judgment.

Part of the difficulty is that very often people naively acquire pets, dogs especially, without having the appropriate inclination and sufficient time to adequately train the animals to coexist harmoniously with humans in their households. Intractable behavioral problems ensue, owners decide they cannot solve them, and so the luckless animals are turned over to the local ACF. The more significant factor in the predicament though is pet owners who do not responsibly control reproduction in their dogs and cats. These are two very prolific species: in just two years' time (assuming normal fertility and breeding at each estrus) one female dog, one female cat, and their offspring could produce a total of about 500 puppies and kittens. In two more years each of these 500 and their off-spring could produce 500 more, and in two more years . . .

No state law directs pet owners to spay or neuter, nor forbids them from dumping the excess animals of unplanned and unanticipated litters at the local ACF. Denver, Colorado, is currently the only jurisdiction in the United States that requires the sterilization of all dogs and cats housed within city limits. Recently, several cities have passed ordinances increasing the cost of licensing an intact animal by ten times or more over a license for a sterilized one, including Tucson, Arizona, from $8 to $75; Los Angeles, from $10 to $100; and Camden, New Jersey, where the license for a fertile dog or cat now costs $500.

At the present time twenty-four states stipulate that all dogs and cats adopted from ACFs must be sterilized. Among these, the New Mexico statute extends to "any animal" so adopted, Michigan includes ferrets along with dogs and cats, and in California the requirement applies only to counties with populations exceeding 100,000. Many who are troubled by pet overpopulation lament the fact that only about half of the states demand sterilization, complaining that all of them should, but there has been significant progress here: a decade ago just eight states had such laws.

Today, most of the states with the sterilization requirement direct the shelter or pound to spay or neuter before relinquishing the animal, or the adopter must sign an "agreement" (only Michigan calls it a "contract") promising to have the dog or cat sterilized, usually within thirty days; in practice, the latter alternative seems to be standard procedure. A dozen states add an incentive for keeping the promise by requiring the adopter to leave a deposit with the pound or shelter of some amount of money. For example, Massachusetts demands $10 to $30, California $40 to $75, in Michigan and New Mexico it's "at least $25," while in Ohio it's not less than $10. A few states simply note that the amount of the deposit is to be enough to pay for a sterilization procedure, but in any case the money will be returned when a document is presented, signed by a licensed veterinarian, verifying that the animal has indeed been spayed or neutered. The deposit is forfeited to the state if no documentation is produced.

A few states that do not require sterilization or any signed agreement have programs intended to encourage adopters to spay or neuter the animals they take home. For $45 Connecticut pounds (not shelters, which can set their own policies here) will turn over fertile dogs and cats along with a sterilization certificate. Of this total $20 is nonrefundable, but if the adopter comes back to the pound in thirty days or less with the certificate signed by a vet, the remainder will be returned; if the certificate is not signed within one month, the $25 is forfeited to the state "animal population control account." In New Jersey, individuals receiving various forms of public assistance—food stamps, Aid to Dependent Children,

Medicaid, and others—can have their adopted pets sterilized by a veterinarian participating in the state Animal Population Control Program for $25, less than a third of what such a procedure would normally cost. New York offers discount sterilization to any citizen who adopts a dog or cat from a pound or shelter in the Empire State.

New York and New Jersey also subsidize the cost of spaying and neutering with their own state "animal friendly" license plate programs. This is a new tactic in the battle against pet overpopulation, with Connecticut, Delaware, Louisiana, Maryland, Tennessee, Texas, and Virginia also developing similar programs in recent years. For a fee ($25 typically) drivers may buy a special license plate for their cars featuring dog and cat icons, and displaying such messages as "ADOPT 1" and "I CARE." All or most of the purchase price goes into state animal control programs so that low-cost or even free sterilization can be offered to people adopting dogs or cats from government-operated ACFs. A number of municipalities have also instituted low-cost or no-cost sterilization for dogs and cats, including Houston, San Jose, San Diego, Miami, and Spokane, Washington; in Raleigh-Durham, veterinary students at North Carolina State University sterilize pets for free.

Euthanasia

Until these and other mandated and encouraged sterilization programs become universal, or nearly so, there will be more dogs and cats in America than people are willing or able to care for adequately. What is to be done with the excess animals? At least for the foreseeable future, they will be killed—in the prevailing euphemisms, they will be "put to sleep" or "put down."

The more technical term for this killing of animals is *euthanasia*, derived from two Greek words, *eu*, meaning "good" or "happy," and *thanatos*, meaning "death." AWA regulations define euthanasia as "the humane destruction of an animal accomplished by a method that produces rapid unconsciousness and subsequent death without evidence of pain or distress." Similarly, the American Veterinary Medical Association (AVMA) Panel on Euthanasia explains that "euthanasia is the act of inducing a humane death in an animal. Euthanasia techniques should result in rapid unconsciousness followed by cardiac or respiratory arrest and ultimate loss of brain function . . . , [and] minimize any stress or anxiety experienced by the animal prior to unconsciousness."

For many people, thinking of euthanasia for humans, it is equivalent to "mercy killing," compassionately ending a life that is enduring unremitting suffering. However, according to the federal government and the AVMA, the key factor in euthanizing animals is not the *condition* of the individual killed, it the *method* of killing. Thus painlessly killing a perfectly healthy dog with a lethal injection qualifies as euthanasia, though few would call killing a perfectly healthy human euthanasia—indeed it would much more likely be called *murder.*

American ACFs euthanize a lot of dogs and cats. As mentioned above, it is uncertain exactly how many are killed, but even the lowest estimate of 4 million annually means that nearly 11,000 animals are destroyed at U.S. pounds and shelters *every day.* After the allotted holding period has expired, in the typical case unclaimed animals are removed from their cages and taken to a special room where they are restrained by one person while another intravenously injects an overdose of a barbiturate, usually sodium pentobarbital. The animal is rendered unconscious by the drug almost immediately, the central nervous system shuts down, respiration ceases, and the heart stops beating.

The AVMA has declared that injection with barbiturates like sodium pentobarbital is the "preferred method for euthanasia of dogs and cats" (the HSUS concurs). Those who regularly euthanize animals in this way agree that the death so caused appears to be one "without evidence of pain or distress." Sodium pentobarbital, and the less widely used but similar secobarbital, are "Schedule II" narcotics closely regulated by the federal Drug Enforcement Agency (DEA) and traditionally available only to licensed veterinarians. This classification has posed some problems, especially for private shelters because these often do not have a staff animal doctor, but do wish to euthanize animals as humanely as possible. Today, seventeen states allow ACFs to buy sodium pentobarbital directly from wholesalers rather than having to use a veterinarian as a middleman.

About half the state codes address the issue of euthanizing animals at the ACFs located within their borders. Of these, currently only Florida, Georgia, Maine, and Oregon demand that sodium pentobarbital or a barbiturate overdose alone be used as the exclusive method for killing animals in pounds and shelters. Most of the other states list the drug as one among several permissible alternatives. Arizona and South Carolina, for example, also allow nitrogen gas and "T–61 euthanasia solution," a nonbarbiturate, nonnarcotic mixture of three drugs combining general and local anesthetic properties with a curariform neuromuscular blocking agent.

Although not specifically condemned anywhere except Massachusetts, T–61 is impliedly illegal in the dozen or so states that either require only barbiturate injection or explicitly ban the use of drugs or drug mixtures with neuromuscular blocking properties. These drugs—such as succinylcholine, magnesium sulfate, nicotine, potassium chloride, or curare—paralyze the animal and cause respiratory arrest before inducing unconsciousness, producing pain and distress. However, the Maryland attorney general has declared that T–61 is not a curariform drug and the

AVMA does not condemn it, although the veterinarian organization does reject the use of all paralytic drugs for euthanasia. In any case, T–61 is no longer manufactured or commercially available in the United States.

Delaware and Oklahoma permit the use of chloroform for dogs and cats of any age while Tennessee approves this substance only for animals under four months old, and nitrogen or carbon monoxide inhalation for animals over this age. In Maryland and California the use of carbon monoxide chambers in ACFs is banned entirely, but Georgia and Rhode Island prohibit CO only when generated by internal combustion engines. Although this limitation is not explained by these two states, many believe that the CO in engine exhaust is impure and too hot to afford a humane death. The AVMA panel does not recommend euthanasia by this method, but does not unequivocally reject it either.

Tennessee allows euthanasia with the carbon monoxide emitted by burning gasoline, but addresses the problems of purity and temperature. The Volunteer State requires that the exhaust be percolated through a forty-gallon tank of water, the killing chamber be no warmer than 90 degrees Fahrenheit, and the engine be "carefully tuned and . . . operated only at an idling speed with the richest fuel-air mixture the carburetor will permit." Tennessee also has specifications for the carbon monoxide chamber, including internal lighting, a viewport, and separate compartments for each animal over twelve weeks old. Carbon monoxide must be introduced into the chamber in a manner that achieves a concentration of 5 percent within five minutes. South Carolina has similar requirements for the use of carbon monoxide.

Several states do not specify any particular method of killing dogs and cats in ACFs. Kansas, for example, instead prohibits all forms of destroying animals except those that employ "the most current approved euthanasia methods established by the American Veterinary Medical Association panel on euthanasia." Similarly, New Jersey allows only "a method of euthanasia generally accepted by the veterinary medical profession as being reliable, appropriate to the type of animal . . . , and capable of producing loss of consciousness and death as rapidly and painlessly as possible." Ohio simply bans all methods other than those "that immediately and painlessly render the domestic animal initially unconscious and subsequently dead."

One such widely banned method is the use of the decompression chamber, outlawed for the ACFs of twenty-nine states at last count. Formerly common, the states began moving to eliminate these devices in 1976. In the decompression process, air is rapidly sucked out of a sealed container, causing a sudden loss of pressure and asphyxiation for the animals loaded inside. ACF workers have long reported that dog behavior in decompression chambers indicates acute panic, severe distress, and serious pain. Puppies and kittens take an inordinate amount of time to die with this method. Ironically, at one time decompression (and carbon monoxide) chambers were lauded as humane alternatives to the standard techniques of the day: shooting, drowning, clubbing, and strychnine poisoning. Mechanical gassing and oxygen deprivation allowed minimally trained and relatively unskilled workers to swiftly kill large numbers of animals.

Even today, fully three-quarters of the states do not require any special training to kill animals in ACFs. On the other hand, a dozen states demand that all euthanasia be performed by either a licensed veterinarian or a person duly authorized by the state to humanely destroy animals in ACFs. Variously called "certified animal euthanasia technician" or "certified animal euthanasia specialist" or just "euthanasia technician," these individuals receive certificates from the state veterinary medical licensing board following a specified course of study. Included are such items as managing the stress of killing animals on a regular basis, animal restraint, the disposal of animal carcasses, DEA regulations, and the handling, inventory, usage, and storage of euthanasia drugs.

Most of these states do not specify any conditions for revoking the certification of a euthanasia technician. Among the few that do, Louisiana's are the most comprehensive, listing (among other things) having sold, given, or used sodium pentobarbital for recreational use, been found legally insane, "been shown to suffer from chronic inebriation or habitual use of drugs," or "performed acts of cruelty upon animals." Besides a blanket injunction against violating any rule prescribed by the veterinary board, West Virginia offers only two conditions of revocation: conviction for any felony, and conviction for cruelty to animals.

To Kill or Not to Kill

Animal control statutes and ordinances specify that unadopted animals are to be humanely destroyed after the designated holding period has lapsed, as do most SPCA and humane society charters. But while pounds are legally obligated to kill unwanted dogs and cats, private ACFs, unless they have contracted with a local government, are bound only by their own self-imposed policies concerning the ultimate disposition of the animals.

Since the mid-1980s a rapidly growing number of private shelters have made a radical—and quite controversial—change in their approach. Adopting a "no-kill" policy, these facilities refuse to destroy any of the animals they accept. Instead, the animals are kept on site throughout the duration of their natural lives or until they are adopted.

The prime motivation for this turnaround is that operators of "no-kill" shelters cannot endure the inconsistency they see in the work of the traditional "full-service" shelters. On the one hand, the traditional shelters counsel, even scold the public that dogs and cats are not disposable commodities to be frivolously discarded but sentient beings with an individual welfare and intrinsic value; on the other, each year these shelters routinely kill many thousands of healthy, normal animals whenever unenlightened and irresponsible pet owners bring them in. Because space is always at a premium, no-kill shelters do not accept every animal as the traditional shelter with an "open admission" policy typically does, but must turn some away, a "limited admission" policy. Further, even when space is available, the no-kills tend to refuse animals that are older, sickly, or with behavioral problems because these are not readily adoptable.

A mutual animosity, waxing and waning in its intensity, has developed between no-kill shelters and those that do euthanize. Operators and staff of shelters that will not destroy animals typically believe themselves to be morally superior and logically coherent, in contrast to the traditional shelters that labor under an inherent, and ethically problematic contradiction. They refuse to call the killing at the open-admission shelter "euthanasia," rejecting the AWA and AVMA definitions and reserving that label for the merciful ending of the life of an animal that is enduring untreatable suffering. Terminating the life of a robust and vigorous dog or cat because nobody wants it and there is no more "room at the inn" is just killing. Moreover, they say, the fundamental problem that has given rise to this controversy within the animal care community—overpopulation of dogs and cats—is neither solved nor even addressed by the mass destruction of pets. On the contrary, the availability of a service that willingly and easily disposes of surplus animals simply exacerbates the problem. It reinforces the repellent notion that dogs and cats are mere things that can be used for a time and then simply thrown away.

For their part, traditional shelters see the no-kills as "you-kills," facilities that refuse to become involved in the hard and tragically inevitable business of destroying unwanted animals, instead foisting the responsibility onto someone else, and then sanctimoniously claiming the moral high ground. Meanwhile, the limited-admission shelters trap animals with a terrible dilemma: once taken in, if never adopted they must spend their lives in cramped cages and stifling conditions, essentially living in an animal "warehouse." Yet animals refused by no-kill shelters will very likely endure a "fate worse than death" in the streets, such a destiny being the major justification for the euthanizing done at the traditional shelters. What is worse, they say, the no-kills will eventually send the unadoptable animals they are unwise enough to accept to the traditional shelter anyway. Despite these disturbing charges, the no-kill trend is accelerating. In 1993 there were about 200 limited-admission shelters, and within 5 years the total had more than tripled to over 700.

Although most of these shelters are apparently well run, ironically a few of them have run afoul of anticruelty laws by taking in more animals than the staff can care for in an appropriate manner, producing animal welfare problems similar to those found in cases of animal hoarding (*see* this chapter: *Animal Hoarding*). For example, a no-kill operation in Michigan called Aid to Animals was raided in July 1991 by three sheriff's deputies, an employee of the Michigan Anti-Cruelty Society, and three veterinarians, two of whom were working for the Michigan Department of Agriculture. Here they found conditions so egregious—starving and diseased animals, some with untreated, serious wounds—that 77 of the 300 dogs and cats kept on the premises were eventually euthanized.

In a plea bargain, Lydia Stack, the owner and operator of Aid to Animals, pleaded guilty to one count of animal cruelty. She later sued the deputies, the state humane society worker, and the civilian veterinarian present that day for violating her rights guaranteed under the Fourth and Fourteenth Amendments, bringing the matter into federal court. Stack contended that the warrant issued authorizing the raid was illegal because a television reporter and persons wielding videocameras accompanied the others; their presence meant the search was conducted in an unreasonable manner. Stack also argued that her right to due process was violated when she was denied the opportunity to contest the seizure of the animals before they were euthanized. The Sixth Circuit Court of Appeals rejected both these arguments (*Stack v. Killian*).

DOG LAW

The domestic dog (*Canis familiaris*) is the subject of more legal rules in the United States than any other single species, rivaled only by the horse (*see* this chapter: *Horse Law*). Most of these federal, state, and municipal laws have little or nothing to do with canine welfare, but are instead intended to regulate acquiring, holding, and transferring a very common but rather curious type of property: a living, sentient being.

In 2000 Americans owned 62 million dogs as pets or "companion animals," one for every four people, with 40 percent of all households containing at least one canine. The total number of feral dogs in the United States—those that have escaped or otherwise avoided domestication—is not known but almost certainly is in the hundreds of thousands. It is estimated that 4 to 6 million dogs, mostly pets, end up in a pound or animal shelter every year, and about half of these are euthanized there (*see also* this chapter: *Animal Control Facilities: Euthanasia*). Additionally, in 1999 just over 75,000 canines were used in American laboratories for research, testing, and education.

Dog Origins

The lineage of the domestic dog courses back some 50 million years to a large family of mammalian carnivores called the *Miacidae*. There were many kinds of Miacids, small animals about the size of a modern house cat that featured long, pointed teeth ("fangs"), sharp claws, and a simple digestive system, all nicely adapted to a diet of flesh. One member of this family, *Miacis*, is the primordial ancestor of every carnivorous mammal on earth today, including the dog.

About 45 million years ago, two main branches split off from *Miacis*, one eventually to form what we now know as the cat family (*Felidae*), the other becoming the *Mustelidae*—weasels, ferrets, mink, skunks, and other small animals with long, slender bodies, short legs, and small, rounded ears. At 30 million years before the present, *Miacis* faded as a distinct mammalian genera and evolved into three basic groups: *Procyonidis*, ultimately tracing forward to the raccoon, *Daphaenus*, the progenitor of the bear family, and *Cynodictus*, from which all modern canines are descended.

As the years passed and thousands of generations of animals lived and died in a changing world, *Cynodictus* dissolved into *Tomarctus*, a distinctly wolf-like creature with longer legs and feet, a shorter tail, and more compact body. Foxes (*Vulpes* species primarily) branched off from this line at about 10 million years ago, and within 2 million years from the present, *Tomarctus* too was gone. Many paleontologists believe that varying habitat and climate transformed this genus into the diverse *Canis* species we see today: the wolf (*C. lupus*), coyote (*C. latrans*), jackal (*C. aureus*), dingo (*C. dingo*), and the common dog (*C. familiaris*). Others argue that the *Tomarctus* line branched off in the direction of the hyena (*Hyaenidae* species), not *Canis*, and the ancestral canid is another wolfish creature called *Leptocyon*. These champions of *Leptocyon* also believe that the domestic dog descended directly from the wolf, or perhaps the jackal, because it is smaller and would presumably be less threatening to humans. The scientists on the other side hold that the dog developed as a separate species straight out of *Tomarctus*.

There is disagreement as well concerning precisely how *Canis familiaris* became domesticated. The standard theories include the adoption of orphaned puppies, or the gradual taming of camp followers, or cooperative hunting with wild dogs and the subsequent sharing of the kill. It is likely that all of these explanations, and others, account for the close association that developed between humans and dogs. Its highly social nature—the fervid willingness to submit to and obey a leader, an amiable disposition, and striking intelligence—made the animal an easy fit into human company. This may have occurred as long ago as 15,000 B.C.E., but as evidenced by fossils, dogs were certainly living with humans in North America by 8,000 B.C.E., in Asia and Europe by 7,000 B.C.E., and in the Middle East by 6,000 B.C.E..

After the third millennium B.C.E., many human groups had supplanted the nomadic hunting and gathering way of life with a more sedentary, agricultural existence. Selective breeding of dogs began around this time, mating particular individual animals to enhance certain physical characteristics in the offspring. This controlled reproduction earnestly pursued over several thousand years has led to the amazing medley of dog breeds we see today: over 160 are recognized by American dog associations, by far the highest number of races or varieties found in any mammalian species. The animals were designed, in effect, specifically customized to serve human interests and purposes.

Among these designer dogs are breeds made for chasing, tracking, and recovering wild animals (retrievers, pointers, greyhounds, bloodhounds, coon-, fox-, and wolfhounds), herding other domestic animals (Collies, sheepdogs, German shepherds), guarding homes and settlements (Mastiffs, Doberman Pinschers, Rottweilers), pulling loads (Great Pyrenees, Huskies, Malamutes), and providing a live, cuddly toy (Pomeranians, Pekingese, Chihuahuas).

The Development of Dog Law

American law is substantially modeled on the legal system of England, with the British common law especially influential. This is the body of legal rules that arose when British judges made decisions in cases in which there was no written rule to follow, simply because no lawmaking body had yet formulated one. In such "cases of first impression," the judges applied their understanding of prevailing social practices, or what seemed reasonable in the particular circumstances, and created the law by issuing a ruling that established a precedent.

Dog law originated in England in this way, with the results eventually adopted by the American colonies and carried over into the newly formed United States. These results were quite unusual, reflecting the unique and ambivalent relationship humans have always had with canines. Neither domestic nor wild according to the law, dogs had no legal rights but neither were they exactly property. Dogs hardly existed under the common law of England. The notion that they might be rightsholders with legal entitlements of their own was never seriously considered (*see also* chapter 2: *Do Animals Have Legal Rights?*).

Even so, for many years dogs were not given any clear status as property either. During certain periods of England's history robbery was punishable by death, so many courts mercifully limited the range of things that could count as property—capital punishment for stealing a dog seemed excessive to many British judges, so in such an instance they simply rejected the idea that anything had been unlawfully taken. Also, the judges of England consistently held for hundreds of years that a dog could not be personal property because it was not a domestic animal: dogs were not eaten for food, nor did they provide transportation or do any hauling work (herding sheep, or guarding houses, or catching rats apparently did not count). Neither did they qualify as wildlife, which would make them the property of the king. This same reasoning about the legal status of dogs prevailed in American courts through the 1800s, reaching its ultimate validation barely more than a century ago in a U.S. Supreme Court decision (*Sentell v. New Orleans & Carroliton Railroad Co.*).

Following a boom in pet ownership during the 1920s, American courts began to treat dogs just like any other domestic animal—as personal property. State legislatures and city councils all over the country enacted a plethora of laws to regulate buying and selling them, and for controlling the use and keeping of dogs. Today, dog law in the United States is dominated by these sorts of legal restrictions, primarily or wholly intended to promote human interests, particularly in their possessions, and secondarily or incidentally enhancing the well-being of the animals. Laws that are centrally motivated by concern for the welfare of dogs are much in the minority; we consider these below.

Dogs as Property

The license requirement is perhaps foremost among those dog laws that are designed to regulate property first, but also do have a positive effect on animal welfare. It is certainly the most common: between state, county, and municipal laws virtually every dog anywhere in the United States must be licensed and, as a condition of licensing, vaccinated for rabies (some cities require distemper shots, too).

Licensing has two main purposes: securing individuals' property interests in dogs, and promoting public safety. Dog licenses are obtained by giving money to the local government, usually about $10 for each animal, although some cities charge more than the standard fee to license dogs that are not sterilized (*see* this chapter: *Animal Control Facilities: Sterilization*). The revenue generated is used to supply some percentage of the funding for the local animal control program. The proportion varies from city to city, with some of these programs mostly paid for by license fees, while others derive little from this source.

The rabies vaccination requirement serves an obvious interest in both public health and canine health, because the disease is fatal for both man and beast. The license tag must be renewed each year (some jurisdictions now offer "lifetime licenses") and worn by the dog at all times. The tag is often imprinted with the owner's name and address, so it aids in the retrieval of a lost pet, which, like the rabies vaccination, benefits the owner, while also saving the dog from an unlucky fate in the pound or on the streets.

The "leash law" is nearly as ubiquitous as the mandate to license dogs, and while similarly intended to protect property and ensure public safety, it also has the happy side effect of benefiting the dog. Found in most state codes and in almost every municipal code, this law requires dogs to be on a leash and appropriately restrained whenever they are off their owner's property. Animal control officers are authorized to seize and impound any unleashed and uncontrolled animals wandering at large, and, following a stipulated holding period, unlicensed canines may be destroyed without any attempt being made to find the owner (*see* this chapter: *Animal Control Facilities: Holding Periods*). The Fourteenth Amendment guarantee that no person will be deprived of his or her property without due process of law prevents animal control from killing licensed animals before making a good faith effort to inform the owner of the impoundment. However, all the states allow livestock owners or their agents to summarily execute *any* dog found chasing, harassing ("worrying"), attacking, injuring, or killing their domestic animals. Also, anyone can legally kill any dog in self-defense or in defense of other people.

For other standard dog laws, there is no element of animal welfare apparent. Probably the best example is the "dog-bite law" appearing in just over half of the state codes. With just two exceptions (Hawaii and Louisiana) the states impose a standard of "strict liability" on owners when their dogs injure people by biting or in any other manner: it is not necessary to prove owners are negligent, irresponsible, or doing anything unlawful. For the rest of these states, the "one-bite" rule sets the standard. This is derived from a common law principle that owners are liable for injuries caused by their dogs only if they were aware or had good reason to believe that the animal was likely to hurt people. Already having bitten someone (the "one bite") is very solid evidence of this likelihood—it will move a judge to impose liability every time. Other sorts of "vicious propensities" will do just as well, including threatening, frightening, or jumping on people, and having a history of fighting other dogs.

Violations of dog-bite laws often activate "dangerous dog" laws, which are also common in American municipalities, and twenty-six states have them too. Obviously a pure public safety issue, such laws generally define a dangerous or "vicious" dog as one prone to unprovoked attacks on people (and not other dogs, usually), and require owners to confine, tether, or muzzle (or all three) the dog. Some of these statutes further demand that owners buy liability insurance, post bonds, obtain a special license, or erect "Beware of Dog" signs.

The dangerous dog laws of many cities also include restrictions or outright bans on the ownership of "Pit Bulls." This is the common name for three different canine breeds originally produced by combining the English bulldog with a now extinct variety of terrier. Rottweilers have also been targeted for restrictions in some areas. These forms of breed specific legislation (BSL), which began in the mid-1980s after a series of well-publicized attacks by Pit Bulls, are founded on the belief that the animals have an inherent propensity to be vicious, and present a constant threat to the public. Pit Bulls are the most common dog used in organized dogfighting, which is illegal in every state, no matter what dog is involved (*see* chapter 5: *Cockfighting and Dogfighting*). Despite the fearsome reputation of the Pit Bull, it is the Rottweiler breed that currently leads the nation in the number of dog biting incidents.

As property, dogs are just another consumer product to be bought and sold, so dog sellers are subject to general warranty laws, even though strictly speaking there is no manufacturer liable for defects. Nonetheless, many courts have held, and some state laws declare that an express warranty is created when the seller makes specific claims about a dog, say, that it is a particular breed. Further, an implied warranty arises without any overt statement, but a promise is suggested by merely selling the animal, such as that the dog is healthy or is suitable for the purpose, known to the seller, that the buyer aims to serve in acquiring a dog.

Currently, twelve states have so-called lemon laws, the main purpose of which is to protect dog buyers: Arkansas, California, Connecticut, Florida, Massachusetts, Minnesota, New Jersey, New Hampshire, New York, South Carolina, Vermont, and Virginia. Modeled after laws that allow a car buyer to receive a refund or replacement for a problem-plagued vehicle (a "lemon"), these dog laws entitle a buyer to similar compensation if he or she buys an animal with a serious disease or congenital defect. The state statutes generally require anyone trading in dogs—breeders, dealers, pet stores—to replace sick animals or refund the purchase price, as well as pay any veterinarian costs for diagnosing the problem or to relieve pain and suffering caused by the illness or defect.

Dog Breeding, "Puppy Mills," and Pet Stores

Like licensing and leash laws, dog "lemon laws" have been enacted primarily to safeguard human interests, in this case the consumer's interest in acquiring fully functioning property, but they may also advance the welfare of canines at the same time. The dog buyer protection laws arose in the early 1990s mainly as a reaction to the abuses of the "puppy mill."

This phrase has gained some currency recently to refer—pejoratively—to breeding facilities that mass produce pure-bred puppies in poor to horrifically bad conditions of housing and care. In a less derogatory sense, a "puppy mill" is any place that breeds a lot of dogs receiving pedigree papers from the American Kennel Club (AKC). There is, of course, a compelling economic incentive to breed as many animals as possible without significantly raising operating expenses. This reduces the "cost per unit" of production, which increases the profit margin. Problems of canine welfare arise when operating expenses are not adjusted to accommodate more animals, and adequate food, proper cleaning and maintenance, and veterinary services are neglected. In the dog breeding business, however, the "bottom line" often seems to be the most important number.

Breeders sell the young dogs at about eight weeks of age to brokers or dealers, who then resell most of them to pet stores. Perhaps 10 percent go to research facilities; breeders rarely deal directly with retail or research interests. Animals raised in a "puppy mill" with a substandard environment are often plagued with health problems, initially unknown to the new pet owner, but ones he or she must solve or pass on to someone else (buyers for research facilities are typically savvy enough to avoid getting animals from such breeders). Laws requiring that owners be compensated for sick or disabled animals are supposed to provide pet stores with a significant incentive to buy only from brokers or dealers who can supply healthy animals, and they in their turn should deal only with breeders who can do the same. This means, incidentally, better conditions and enhanced well-being for the dogs, as breeders pay less attention to the bottom line and more to the good of their animals.

Unfortunately, none of the states with the highest number of documented cases of mass producing puppies in poor facilities has a dog lemon law: Iowa, Kansas, Missouri, Nebraska, Oklahoma, and Pennsylvania. Missouri, Pennsylvania, and Kansas have legal standards of care for animals in breeding operations, as do Colorado, Georgia, and Iowa. These substantially duplicate, at least in part, the federal standards imposed on breeders by the Animal Welfare Act (*see* this chapter: *Dog Law: Federal Dog Protection Law*).

Producing large numbers of puppies of specific breeds for profit is not a new idea, and welfare problems attendant upon this enterprise is not a recent development. It all began shortly after the Second World War when the U.S. Department of Agriculture (USDA) initiated subsidies for farmers who, looking for a new cash crop after old standbys had failed, decided to raise puppies. The increased supply seemed to drive demand, or perhaps there was a happy correspondence between the two—in any case the family dog, pedigree registered with the AKC, became a fixture in American homes. New pet stores opened at a rapid rate throughout the 1950s and into the 1960s. Unfortunately, the new puppy farmers were not trained in canine husbandry—no law required them to be—and there were no state or federal regulations to follow. They housed their dogs in chicken coops and rabbit hutches, and treated them like another kind of livestock, often neglecting veterinary care because of the cost and, again, no such care was legally required.

Meanwhile, the AKC embarked on a nationwide campaign to convince prospective dog owners that the only dog worth having was a purebreed registered with their organization. Not coincidentally, the AKC also entered into agreements with breeders to receive money in exchange for validating registry papers on the animals the breeders sold. The arrangement continues to this day—the AKC receives over $26 million each year in registration fees—yet, critics have charged, the club has paid little or no attention to the conditions under which the animals have been raised. Seduced by the prestige that having a registered purebreed was perceived to bring, people came to believe, and still do, that the document was some kind of assurance that the dog they were getting was a physically superior animal. This is decidedly not the case, though, when the animal comes from a breeding facility where the care and handling is egregiously deficient.

The large-scale breeders are clustered mostly in rural areas of the Midwest, producing as much as 90 percent of all the puppies sold at retail pet stores. No one knows exactly how many animals that is—estimates run from 300,000 to 500,000 each year. Also, no one knows how many animals come from the nefarious "puppy mills," though some claim it is nearly all of them. At any rate, only California and Maine currently require pet shop owners to inform customers that registration papers from the AKC do not guarantee a healthy animal.

The care and handling of dogs (and other animals) in pet stores is unregulated in most states, and is expressly excluded from the provisions of the federal Animal Welfare Act. A few jurisdictions—Arizona and California among them—have brief statutory requirements demanding that owners of retail pet operations (sometimes called "dealerships") maintain their facilities in a sanitary condition, ensure that the animals receive adequate nutrition and hydration, provide them with sufficient space to make normal postural adjustments, and enlist the services of a veterinarian when necessary. In 2000 only eight states have detailed regulations for pet stores: Colorado, Georgia, Iowa, Kansas, Michigan, Missouri, Nevada, and North Carolina.

All these states have general guidelines for the construction of pet stores. These structures must be soundly built and regularly maintained, readily cleaned and sanitized, and effectively prevent escape, access by other animals, or injury. Adequate ventilation and lighting, running potable water, and heating and cooling, are required for each facility. As with the general housing standards, the cages where the animals are kept should be safe, structurally sound, clean, dry, and provide ready access to water and food. The regulations also specify the amount of cage space that each dog must be given, but only Colorado, Missouri, and North Carolina employ the standard formula found in the Animal Welfare Act regulations: the square of the number that is the length of the dog from the tip of the nose to the base of the tail plus 6, and then divided by 144. Georgia, Iowa, Michigan, and Nevada have broad statements demanding "ample" or "sufficient" space to allow dogs and cats to turn around, stand, and lie down. The Kansas regulations for pet stores do not mention cage space.

Colorado and Missouri are the only states that require pet stores to have an attending veterinarian, although the North Carolina and Michigan regulations both mention that veterinary services should be available. Along with Iowa and Nevada, Colorado and Missouri also order daily cleaning of all animal cages. The other states offer general instructions to clean the enclosures "as often as necessary" or "often enough" to prevent illness or discomfort.

All eight states require pet stores to provide the animals with wholesome, palatable food and potable water at least once a day (if water is not continuously available), and seven of these—Kansas is the exception—require the separation of females in estrus from males and the isolation of "vicious" animals.

Federal Dog Protection Law
The Animal Welfare Act of 1970 and its federal regulations (collectively, AWA regulations) were supposed to have solved the problems of the "puppy mill" decades ago. Under AWA regulations, a dog breeder must be licensed with the USDA, and is designated a "class A" dealer. This is defined in part as a person "whose business involving animals consists only of animals that are bred and raised on the premises in a closed and stable colony and those animals acquired for the sole purpose of maintaining or enhancing the breeding colony . . . [, and] any person who, in commerce, for compensation or profit . . . sells . . . any dog . . . for use as a pet." In 1971 breeders became subject to standards issued by the USDA for the humane handling and care of dogs. Similarly, "class B" dealers must also be licensed and comply with AWA regulations. These are essentially animal brokers or wholesalers who do not breed dogs or (usually) hold them in facilities but instead negotiate their sale to pet shops. Retail stores that sell dogs are not covered by any federal law, although, as explained above, there is some state regulation here.

Animal welfare advocates complain that for all practical purposes, dog breeders are hardly regulated by the federal government either. Enforcement is almost nonexistent, they say, and the few transgressions cited are lightly penalized. Evidence for this claim is found in the fact that there are about 3,000 class A license holders in the United States, but despite persistent charges by humane societies and other animal protection organizations that violations are rampant in the "puppy mills," the USDA stopped only twenty-nine of them from operating in 1996 and 1997. This agency has long been accused of indulging in multiple conflicts of interest, given their simultaneous mission to serve the economic interests of those engaged in animal agriculture—cattle growers, pig farmers, and dog breeders, among others—and their responsibility to uphold federal laws that promote the welfare of animals, including dogs.

Dog breeders, dealers, and brokers who hold animals, as well as research facilities, universities, and other organizations or institutions (which must be registered with the USDA) that keep dogs for testing, experimentation, or education must observe federal standards for the humane care, handling, and treatment of these animals (*see also* chapter 7: *Animal Welfare Act Regulations*). Additional regulations apply to carriers that transport dogs between these facilities and to pet stores. AWA regulations do not cover greyhounds (or any dogs) used in racing events; such standards as exist here are produced by state racing commissions (*see* chapter 5: *Greyhound Racing and Horse Racing*).

AWA regulations for dogs begin with general housing standards. The facilities in which dogs live are to be well constructed and regularly maintained, regularly cleaned and sanitized, and effectively prevent escape, access by other animals, or injury. Heating, cooling, ventilation, lighting, and running potable water are all required, as well as "disposal and drainage systems that are constructed and operated so that animal wastes are eliminated and the animals stay dry." Temperatures in indoor housing must not fall below 45 degrees Fahrenheit or rise above 85 degrees Fahrenheit for more than four consecutive hours, and dogs must be provided with a diurnal lighting cycle. Outdoor housing is permitted only for healthy, adult dogs that are adapted to the climate conditions found at the facility, and must include shelters to escape the weather. Dog shelters need to have a roof, four sides, and a floor, and enough space for each animal to stand, sit, and lie down normally, but "[m]etal barrels, cars, refrigerators or freezers and the like must not be used as shelter structures." Also required are wind breaks, adequate shade, and extra bedding material for when the temperature drops below freezing.

AWA regulations also detail the specifications for the dogs' "primary enclosure": the construction and dimensions of their cages or pens. As with the general housing standards, the cages should be safe, structurally sound, clean, and provide protection from the elements and other animals. Water and food should be easily accessible. Despite requiring for nearly three decades that floors be constructed of materials that do not injure the animals' feet, it was not until 1998 that the USDA specifically banned the use of uncoated wire 1/8 inch or less in diameter in the floors of dog cages. Permissible wire floors must have a solid resting surface "large enough to hold all the occupants of the primary enclosure at the same time comfortably." Floors made of mesh or slats need not include such a resting platform. Perhaps most importantly, these regulations stipulate "minimum space requirements." Besides directing that these enclosures have "sufficient space . . . to make normal postural adjustments with freedom of movement," the regulations specify precise dimensions in feet, inches, meters, and centimeters, depending on the weight of the animal. Required canine floor space is calculated by taking the measurement of each dog in inches from the tip of the nose to the base of the tail, adding 6, and then squaring the sum; dividing this product by 144 reveals the required floor space in square inches. In 1991 a minimum cage height requirement of six inches higher than the head of the tallest dog was adopted, and a ban on permanent tethering as a means of confinement was imposed. Groups of as many as twelve dogs may be housed together in the same primary enclosure, but they must be compatible; aggressive animals are to be isolated. Puppies less than four months old may not be housed with adult animals.

Following an amendment to the AWA in 1985, regulations were promulgated requiring that dogs be exercised on a regular basis, mainly by providing them with enough space to move about. Forced exercise devices like treadmills and carousels are not acceptable means of meeting this requirement. Further, any dog that is kept "without sensory contact with another dog, must be provided with positive physical contact with humans at least daily." The regulations do not explain what exactly "positive physical contact" is, nor do they state a required duration of this contact.

Dogs need to be fed at least once every day with "clean, wholesome, and palatable" food, appropriate to the species and in quantities sufficient for the age and size of the animal. Food receptacles must be cleaned and sanitized at least once every two weeks, while the primary enclosures must be cleaned daily of excrement and food particles and sanitized in the prescribed way twice a month. Water is to be made available either continuously, or for at least one hour twice a day.

AWA regulations also present standards for the enclosure and the conveyance used to transport dogs, as well as for care in transit. The cage or carton containing canines must be secure and strong, and one out of which the animal cannot put any part of its body. It must have either a solid, leak-proof bottom or a removable wire mesh floor. Adequate ventilation—calculated by a percentage of surface area—is required and the enclosure must be constructed so that the ventilation openings cannot be obstructed. Dogs over eight weeks old and weighing more than twenty pounds must be moved singly when transported by air, one for each cage; those less than this weight can go two at a time. When shipped by land, a maximum of four dogs older than eight weeks can be transported in the same enclosure. No size requirements are stipulated for the enclosures used to transport dogs.

The motor vehicle, rail car, aircraft, or marine vessel moving dogs must provide them with a sufficient supply of air for normal breathing, and the temperature of the cargo space has to be maintained between 45 degrees Fahrenheit and 85 degrees Fahrenheit. Dogs over sixteen weeks old must be offered food at least once every twenty-four hours, under sixteen weeks, every twelve hours; those of any age are to be given water every twelve hours. To ensure that the animals are alright, they must be observed by the operator of the conveyance, or some other person on board, at least once every four hours; aircraft with cargo holds that are inaccessible during flight are exempted from this requirement. Once the dogs arrive at their destination, holding facilities are required to be clean and sanitary, as well as sufficiently ventilated and heated or cooled to within the 45-degree-Fahrenheit to 85-degree-Fahrenheit range.

State Anticruelty Laws

Although not often mentioned specifically in the statutes, dogs are protected by the anticruelty laws found in all fifty states, and canines appear to be the animals abused in most successful prosecutions under state anticruelty laws. Nine of twelve cruelty convictions in 1996 and 1997 from randomly chosen lower-court decisions, and eight of the nine that were reviewed by state appellate courts involved one or more dogs.

State anticruelty laws vary widely in their length and detail (*see* this chapter: *Anticruelty Laws*). Some are short, broadly worded statutes that simply prohibit "cruel mistreatment," "cruelly beating," or "cruel neglect" without explaining exactly what behaviors qualify or what these key terms mean. Others provide much more information, defining "cruel" and other important concepts, and listing the specific conduct outlawed. Generally, illegal conduct includes torturing or overworking an animal, depriving it of "necessary sustenance" or "failing to provide proper food and water [or shelter in some instances]," abandoning an animal, causing one creature to fight another, and using a vehicle to carry an animal in a cruel or inhumane manner.

Most states expressly ban dogfighting in their anticruelty laws, although some have a statute that prohibits animal fighting generally. Currently, only California, Washington, and Oregon have laws specifically protecting dogs when they are being transported in a vehicle. All three jurisdictions require that canines be secured in the open back of a pickup truck or any "external" part of a vehicle rather than allowing them to move about freely.

Many cities and counties now have similar ordinances designed with canine welfare in mind, and some individuals have been successfully prosecuted under anticruelty laws for injuries suffered by dogs thrown from the back of pickups. It has been estimated that as many as 100,000 dogs are killed each year after jumping or falling out of the open bed of these trucks. Several states require drivers that injure or kill dogs with their cars to report the incident to the owner of the animal or the local police. Connecticut, New York, Oregon, and Rhode Island impose a further duty on drivers to render such aid as they can to the dog they have hit. About half the states also prohibit poisoning animals, and most of these list dogs as one of the species protected from noxious or toxic substances.

Police Dogs

Usually contained within the cruelty to animals statute, forty states also have laws that prohibit harming or interfering with dogs used by law enforcement personnel, the "police dog." These laws began in 1978 when Massachusetts became the first state to institute legal punishments for "[w]hoever willfully tortures, torments, beats, kicks, strikes, mutilates, injures, disables or otherwise mistreats a dog . . . owned by a police department." This language served as the basic model for many of the state laws that followed over the next twenty years.

The first recorded use of canines as aids for law enforcement is from 1907 on the Long Island district of New York. There, large dogs were simply turned loose in residential areas after midnight to rove through the neighborhoods, flattening anyone they encountered who happened to be out, and pinning the unlucky denizen of the night to the ground until their barking brought the canine handler to the scene. Today, the modern "K–9 Corps" found in virtually every city and state law enforcement agency is far more structured and multifaceted. Dogs are rigorously trained for use in patrolling, tracking, crowd control, search and rescue, investigating arson, apprehending criminals, finding hidden suspects and dead bodies, and detecting accelerants, explosives, firearms, and narcotics.

All of the state laws, except for those of Massachusetts and Rhode Island, explicitly prohibit killing a police dog. These two states have nearly identical statutes that detail a variety of proscribed actions that harm the dogs (as quoted above from the Massachusetts statute), some of which could plausibly lead to death. Of course, a dog could be killed instantaneously and painlessly, apparently evading this law, but no case has yet tested this aspect of the statute. Alabama, Connecticut, and Tennessee list causing the death of a police dog as the *only* illegal behavior in their statutes. Presumably, the general anticruelty laws of these states would protect a dog that was harmed, and not killed, in the course of its service in law enforcement, but, again, so far the matter has not been addressed by a court. All the states, with the exception of these last three, also specifically outlaw seriously injuring a police dog, and three-quarters of the forty additionally prohibit "interfering with" one.

Only Ohio makes it unlawful to *attempt* to harm a police dog, while New Hampshire and Utah are the sole states that prohibit attempting to interfere with the "duties" of a canine working in law enforcement. The forty jurisdictions offer a variety of mental states needed to establish legal liability, some depending on whether the police dog is killed, injured, or interfered with: intent, knowledge, willfulness, malice, recklessness, and negligence are all listed, either singly or in sundry combinations. This *mens rea* standard—a "guilty mind"—is nearly identical to that found in almost every anticruelty law (for more on this standard, *see* this chapter: *Anticruelty Laws: Liability*).

The punishments for infractions of these laws suggest that in many states police dogs have a legal stature elevated above that of the ordinary canine. In twenty-one states it is a felony to kill a police dog, typically punishable by up to five years in prison and a fine of $5,000. In Alabama and Virginia the maximum term is ten years, several states have a $10,000 fine limit, and in Arizona the limit is $150,000. On the other hand, the unlawful killing of a common dog in these states is a misdemeanor carrying at most a penalty of one year incarceration and a $1,000 fine. Oklahoma is the one state that provides a felony conviction for killing a nonpolice dog and just misdemeanor penalties for killing a police dog, so long as the death does not occur while the perpetrator is committing some other illegal act. Along with Michigan, Oklahoma makes harming a police dog a felony when done during the commission of a crime.

The legal disparity between members of the K–9 corps and pet dogs is also evident for the charge of causing serious injury to a police dog. A number of states that do not provide for felony convictions in their anticruelty statutes have three- to five-year terms for those guilty of seriously injuring police dogs (for more on felony penalties for anticruelty violations, *see* this chapter: *Anticruelty Laws: Exceptions and Penalties*). In general, guilty verdicts for this crime bring widely varying sentences depending on the state, from a maximum of eight years in Delaware, to a minimum of four months in North Carolina, with one year being the most common. Fifteen states allow courts to order persons convicted of killing or permanently disabling a police dog to pay restitution to the law enforcement agency, a sum that includes not only the value of the dog but the cost of training it.

In August 2000 President Bill Clinton signed the first federal law intended to enhance protections for police dogs, specifically those utilized by federal law enforcement agencies. Introduced in October 1999 by Representative Jerry Weller of Illinois, the bill passed through the House quickly and did not take much longer to win Senate approval. The Federal Law Enforcement Animal Protection Act provides a fine and one year in prison for any person who "willfully and maliciously harms any police animal, or attempts or conspires to do so." Killing, seriously injuring, or permanently disabling or disfiguring a police animal can be punished by up to ten years in prison. Although the act primarily covers dogs, the definition of "police animal" also includes horses "employed" by any federal agency.

HORSE LAW

The modern horse (*Equus caballus*) evolved from a dog-sized, four-toed leaf browser with an elongated skull, an animal taxonomically classified as *Hyracotherium* (more commonly known as *Eohippus*, from the Greek "oldest horse"). *Hyracotherium* roamed the woodlands of the North American continent during the Eocene epoch, beginning about 50 million years ago. Over time the creature became more horselike, growing larger in body and brain, becoming a grass grazer as savannas replaced forests, and evolving into two new genera, *Mesohippus* and then *Miohippus*. By 18 million years past, the species had moved north out of America and crossed the land bridge that then connected the Western Hemisphere with Asia, dispersing through that continent and on to Europe and Africa. The horse, as we know the animal today (*Equus*), disappeared from North America toward the end of the Pleistocene, perhaps eight or ten thousand years before the present, rendered extinct in the land by forces that remain largely unknown—overhunting by humans is a widely accepted theory.

By 3000 B.C.E. the horse had been successfully domesticated. Probably the first to do so were the people of the southwest Asian steppes, north of the Black and Caspian seas. Before long mounted warriors were easily subduing adversaries afoot. The horse proved especially effective both for expanding occupied territory by violent conquest, and for moving a population and their possessions into and around the newly acquired lands. Settlements and households then became larger as people, with horses to haul them, acquired more possessions.

The first major incursion facilitated by the horse, and one of the most significant events in global history, was the twentieth-century B.C.E. Aryan invasion of the Indus River valley, in modern-day Pakistan. From the steppes the Aryans crossed over the passes of the Hindu Kush in their chariots and swept down to the fertile flatland below, crushing the people they found there and changing the face of India, and the world, forever. In folklore and in historical fact, horse nations invariably prevailed, becoming masters of all they surveyed from the backs of their steeds.

Such has been the impact of the horse on human cultures, that a noted horse enthusiast once proclaimed, "Wherever man has left his footprint in the long ascent from barbarism to civilization we will find the hoofprint of the horse beside it." Perhaps this is overstated—among other plausible counterexamples, the Vandal hordes overran Rome on the backs of thousands of horses—but there is no denying the grand significance of the species. From Rome and Greece to Israel and Egypt, and from India to China the image of the horse was stamped on coins, sculpted in temples, elevated to pantheons and worshipped as divine. For centuries, only kings and aristocrats, priests and warriors, and the wealthy and powerful owned horses. In Europe the racing of horses was known as the "sport of kings" (*see* chapter 5: *Greyhound Racing and Horse Racing*). There peasants alone were without mounts, and horsemen ruled. The knight-farrier of King Frederick II wrote in the thirteenth century that "No animal is more noble than the horse, since it is by horses that princes, magnates and knights are separated from lesser people."

Legal Protections for Horses
Despite this veneration, as well as the ubiquitous presence of the horse in human society, it took nearly 5,000 years before the animals were expressly given any legal protections. This occurred in England in 1822, when Parliament passed the "Ill Treatment of Horses and Cattle Bill," which announced that anyone who "wantonly and cruelly beats, abuses or ill treats any Horse [among other livestock]" will be fined not more than 40 shillings.

In the United States, it has only been within the last three decades that any federal law has been passed specifically directed at protecting the well-being of equines (*see also* this chapter: *Horse Law: State Regulation of Horse Welfare*, for the application of the federal Twenty-Eight Hour Law to horses). The Horse Protection Act prohibits "soring" horses to accentuate their gait, and the Wild Free-Roaming Horses and Burros Act forbids capriciously harming these feral species on public lands (both discussed below, this chapter). Yet the Animal Welfare Act (AWA), in effect the federal anticruelty law, excludes horses "not used for research purposes" from its definition of "animal." The AWA protections do not extend to horse races, shows, fairs, or rodeos, events that are dominated by horses (*see* chapter 7: *Animal Welfare Act of 1970;* chapter 5: *Greyhound Racing and Horse Racing;* chapter 5: *Rodeos*).

State laws have not been much help either. By the end of the Civil War, most of the states had anticruelty statutes in their code books, yet horses seemed not to be enjoying their protections. The species was the prevalent animal in American society in those days, used for hauling every sort of freight and other materials, for public and private transportation, and for entertainment. Horses (and their excrement) were everywhere, conspicuously so given their size, and it was not uncommon to find the beasts overloaded and overworked in hard weather, underfed and underwatered at any time, beaten and abused in full view on city streets. Aged horses were often driven until they dropped dead, or, no longer capable of hauling anything, they were simply abandoned in the streets.

Indeed, the signal event in the history of the American humane movement occurred when Henry Bergh witnessed a cart driver brutally beating a horse. The atrocity moved Bergh to create the American Society for the Prevention of Cruelty to Animals (ASPCA) in 1866. The early ASPCA and the other local SPCAs formed by Bergh's inspiration focused much of their attention on promoting the humane treatment of horses, especially through the enforcement of anticruelty laws.

Today, enforcement in this legal arena remains a perennial problem, one exacerbated by the disappearance of horses from the city that attended the rise of the motor vehicle. The animals are now almost wholly confined to, and to some degree concealed in, rural America, behind fences, across swaths of pasture, or inside stables. Even if equine mistreatment could not be effectively hidden out in the country, as it could not be in a city running on horsepower, thirty of the state anticruelty laws exempt "normal" or "accepted" uses of animals in agriculture from their purview. In these jurisdictions, horses on the farm or the ranch are protected from almost nothing but the most hideous acts of abuse and neglect (*see also* this chapter: *Anticruelty Laws*).

In any case, for the state codes as well as the courts, horse law, like dog law (*see* this chapter: *Dog Law*), has few legal rules specifically designed to protect the well-being of the animal. Instead, equine law is dominated by statutory and common law rules for regulating commerce in horses, and especially for establishing the liability of owners, boarders, and users of horses.

Equine Law: Liability

Horses are large, powerful, and potentially dangerous animals that can easily injure or kill a human being. When this happens to a person as a result of the actions of someone else's horse, what is the extent of the owner's responsibility for the injury or death? A prominent and relatively new feature of equine law is a statute designed to limit the liability of horse owners who rent animals to people wanting to ride, or who for a fee provide instruction to others wanting to learn how. At last count, forty-three states have enacted some form of equine activity liability act (EALA). Most of these came in the 1990s as a response to an increasingly litigious society eager to sue somebody whenever something bad happens.

The main point of EALAs is to immunize the "equine professional" from liability when injury or death to a customer (or a veterinarian) results from the "inherent risks" of the "equine activity." These risks are generally defined to include such matters as the propensity of a horse to behave in ways that can harm people on or around the animal, the unpredictability of a horse's reactions to situations it encounters (for example, sounds, other animals, unfamiliar objects), and general riding conditions like the weather and the surfaces it treads upon. EALAs stipulate that so long as a sign has been posted at the stable announcing that participants in equine activities are voluntarily accepting these risks, the horse owner is not legally responsible for any harm caused by the animal. However, EALAs do impose liability on the equine professional when he or she provides a faulty horse or defective tack, fails to assess the ability of the rider to manage the horse safely, or intentionally causes injury.

Most other forms of liability for injuries and damages caused by horses are treated by the common law, under which judges' decisions in cases without an applicable statute function as legal rules. There are hundreds, possibly thousands of such cases in which individuals have been kicked or bitten or trampled by horses they tried to pet, or by ones they just happened to come upon. Traditionally, the common law has imposed liability on horse owners for all harms caused by their animals unless they can show that the injury resulted from the fault of the victim (his or her negligence or unreasonable actions), or from "fortuitous events." This doctrine made sense when the injured person was an innocent bystander or someone who passively encountered a horse. However, it very often also imposed liability on owners when people rented their horses, or paid for riding lessons from them, and then got hurt, even though these participants were neither innocent nor passive. EALAs evolved out of the common law tradition by combining the two defenses against liability into an assumption—announced by the posted signs—that the participant in the equine activity is aware of the risks endemic to riding horses: accidents can happen around these animals.

Much of the rest of equine law is concerned with contract law involving agreements between sellers and buyers, and between horse owners and operators of boarding stables. Major issues here include the form of ownership, the nature of the warranty (if any) with which the animal is sold, the role of a veterinarian in such sales, liens or security interests created in the horse by unpaid bills, and more liability issues, such as responsibility for the medical care of a sick or injured horse, or for property damage caused by the animal.

State Regulation of Horse Welfare: Transportation

The transportation of horses (and other livestock) across state lines must be done in compliance with the federal Twenty-Eight Hour Law (*see also* chapter 4: *Twenty-Eight Hour Law of 1994*). Horses must be "humanely" unloaded, fed, watered, and rested if their journey by rail or truck exceeds twenty-eight hours, but neither the statute nor its regulations define "humane." The regulations require holding horses in adequately sized pens that are clean, well drained, and provide protection from the weather, and further specify that each 40-foot carload of horses be supplied with 400 pounds of hay. However, the law does not set a maximum number of animals for any particular conveyance, and does not stipulate the design of cars or trailers used for transporting horses.

In 2000 about two-thirds of the states did not regulate the intrastate movement of horses (or other livestock) specifically by railroad or common carrier. At the same time, however, at least thirty-five states did include a ban on inhumane methods of transporting animals in their anti-cruelty laws. California, Connecticut, Maine, Massachusetts, Minnesota, New York, Vermont, and Virginia have the most detailed laws for travel by rail or road, each substantially modeled on the Twenty-Eight Hour Law, but each also extending the rule in important ways.

Connecticut appears to be the leader in this legal arena. In addition to prohibiting more than eighteen consecutive hours of travel without at least five hours for rest, food, water—the shortest interval of travel and the longest recuperation time in any jurisdiction—the Constitution State restricts the construction and dimensions of the vehicles used for transport. Horses must be conveyed in ventilated compartments with nonskid floors, partitions every ten feet, doors of sufficient height to allow the animals to pass through safely, and without any sharp or protruding surfaces. Small or young horses must be separated from large or mature ones, unless they are mare and colt, and these should not be loaded with other horses.

Vermont also prohibits travel in excess of eighteen hours without unloading the animals, but requires at least four hours for resting, eating, and drinking. For horses in particular, Vermont similarly requires that compartments be insulated, ventilated, equipped with partitions or stalls as well as loading ramps, and constructed with smooth materials and nonskid floors. New York's law regulating the transportation of horses is nearly identical to Vermont's; the Empire State has no further provisions protecting any other livestock when these species are transported.

The stipulations of California's horse transportation statute are similar to those of Vermont and New York, yet they apply only when equines are being taken to the slaughterhouse (California is the only state that has expressly forbidden the slaughter of horses for human consumption, but allows it for pet food). In Maine modes of conveyance "shall be sufficiently covered or boarded on the sides and ends to afford proper protection to the animals in case of storms or severe cold weather and shall be properly ventilated," and it is prohibited to load more horses than can "stand comfortably" in the transporting vehicle. Minnesota also demands that horses be given sufficient space to stand and lie down, and does not allow them to be transported with their legs tied together (with some exceptions).

Despite their attention to equine welfare, none of these laws prohibit moving horses during extremes of heat or cold, nor require heating or cooling in the rail cars, trucks, or trailers used to haul them. Minnesota does ban picketing a horse out in the open between November 1 and May 1 if its hair has been sheared or clipped within the previous sixty days. Notwithstanding a far milder climate, Rhode Island goes further and does not allow horses to be sheared at all between October 15 and March 1 unless approved in writing by a veterinarian. No other state has restrictions on shearing or clipping horses. Rhode Island and New Hampshire are also the only jurisdictions that require horse owners to provide their animals with a roofed shelter having at least three sides during winter.

State Regulation of Horse Welfare: Tail Docking and Tripping

A dozen states have banned the practice of docking the tail of a horse: California, Connecticut, Illinois, Maine, Massachusetts, Michigan, Minnesota, New Hampshire, New York, Ohio, South Carolina, and Washington. (Docking has been banned throughout Great Britain since 1949.) This involves cutting through the muscles, tendons, and bone in the solid part of the tail to shorten the appendage.

The operation has typically been done on certain breeds for shows and exhibitions. Harness horses and those used for draft purposes, such as the Percheron and Clydesdale, have traditionally had their tails docked to avoid interference and entanglement with the loads they were pulling. The alteration in the natural carriage of the tail has become a defining characteristic of these equine lineages. Despite the fact that the tail of any animal is highly sensitive, in years past the severing was done with little or no anesthetic. Even with complete numbing during the procedure, the loss of its tail makes a horse extremely vulnerable in the hindquarters and stomach area to flies and other biting insects.

The "steeplechase" originated in eighteenth-century England, inspired by the countryside riding that characterized fox hunting on horseback. It developed as a race, originally with a church and its steeple as the finish line, with courses that mimicked the varied terrain found on the hunt, frequently requiring the horses to jump over hedges, walls, ditches, streams, and other obstacles. In time the steeplechase became a regular event at horse shows in Europe and America, with expansive outdoor courses and more confined arena exhibitions, where riders put the horses through their paces one at a time. The equine participants in these competitions must be trained to jump these hazards, because a horse will naturally balk at the prospect, especially when it cannot see what is on the other side of the obstruction.

Training a horse to jump willingly and aggressively has commonly involved the use of wires, rails, ropes, or poles imbedded with nails, brads, or other sharp objects, a method generally known as "poling." In the training process, the animal is forced or enticed to jump over a hurdle topped with the spiked rail or wire, which, when contacted by its legs, causes significant pain. This induces the horse to jump higher the next time the opportunity arises. Currently, only California and Illinois specifically ban this practice entirely. Both of these states also prohibit tripping a horse, defined by California as "the use of any wire, pole, stick, rope, or other object or apparatus whatsoever to cause a horse to fall or lose its balance." Florida, Kansas, Maine, New Mexico, Oklahoma, and Texas have outlawed tripping a horse as well, but none of these expressly forbid poling.

The major effect of these laws is to make the performance of two events in the *charreada* illegal. More commonly known as the "Mexican rodeo," the *charreada* features a competition with the goal of roping the front legs of a horse for the purpose of causing the animal to fall (*see* chapter 5: *Rodeos: Legal Regulation of the Treatment of Rodeo Animals*). Florida has made horse tripping a felony, while the other states provide only misdemeanor penalties.

Carriage Rides

Businesses offering rides in horse-drawn carriages are found in many U.S. cities, among them New York, Boston, Chicago, Denver, Little Rock, Baltimore, New Orleans, Washington, D.C., Albuquerque, Cleveland, San Antonio, Honolulu, Atlanta, and in Charlotte, North Carolina, and Charleston, South Carolina. The practice began in 1877 in St. Augustine, Florida, for sight-seeing and romantic strolling, a creative alternative to the purely utilitarian function of horse-drawn conveyances common at that time.

Over the years conditions on the streets of America's cities have changed drastically, but there has been little corresponding improvement in the lot of the carriage horse. Lameness and hoof deterioration are a chronic problem as the animals spend eight to ten or even twelve hours a day pounding along on asphalt and concrete surfaces. Within the flow of traffic, the nose of a carriage horse dangles just three or four feet above the level of vehicle exhaust pipes spewing pollutants. Moreover, even though some cities do not allow operators to drive their horses when the thermometer hits 90 degrees Fahrenheit, the temperature on the baking streets is already far beyond that when this shade-temperature limit is reached.

Many carriage horses are discarded draft animals, large and heavy creatures physiologically ill suited for long and hard hours in an urban oven. Very few carriage horses are bred and trained for the purpose or pressed into service when young and vigorous. Most are cast off from the race tracks, too old to run anymore or produce colts with the bloodlines that could reasonably be expected to lead to competitive racers. In the 1990s, these and other humane concerns have moved councils to shut down carriage rides or refuse to grant licenses to new operations in more than a dozen cities, including Palm Beach and Key West, both in Florida; Santa Fe, New Mexico; and Reno, Nevada.

Legal regulation of carriage rides is a mosaic of ordinances, varying widely from one municipality to the next. Some cities, such as Denver and Charleston, have few laws regulating animal-drawn vehicles for hire, and none that have anything to do with the welfare of the horses. Others have more extensive rules, mostly for licensing, insurance, routes, and carriage equipment, but also a few that are intended to promote the health and well-being of the horse. Atlanta, for example, requires that carriage horses be free of open sores, wounds, lameness, "or any other ailment." Each animal must have "adequate flesh and muscle tone," be groomed daily, and provided with adequate water.

San Antonio, Texas, has perhaps the most thorough set of ordinances restricting the use of carriage horses while providing for their basic needs. In San Antonio, drivers must "ensure that appropriate and sufficient food and fresh, potable drinking water are available for each horse and that, while working, each horse is permitted to eat at reasonable intervals and have access to drinking water as necessary." The animals must be given a ten-minute rest between fares, and cannot be worked more than ten hours a day or when the temperature exceeds 95 degrees Fahrenheit. Owners of carriage horse operations are required to have their animals examined by a veterinarian every three months, treated for parasites every four months, and have their hooves trimmed and reshod every six to eight weeks. The horses and their tack are to be kept clean. Any lame horse, or one with open sores, wounds, evidence of emaciation, dehydration, or exhaustion, or a horse with loose shoes or no shoes at all, is considered unfit for work in San Antonio and cannot be used to pull a carriage. The city even mandates standards for stabling carriage horses: clean and dry, bedding at least 6 inches thick on concrete floors, continuous access to clean, fresh hay and water.

Currently, only Massachusetts has a set of statewide regulations, issued by the Department of Public Safety. These laws, as suggested by the agency where they originate and like most municipal codes, are predominantly concerned with regulating a business in order to protect the well-being of humans paying for this service and those traveling on the roads of the commonwealth. The regulations cover almost eight full pages of text, detailing dozens of licensing, certificate, insurance, and inspection requirements, while those benefiting the horse directly are reduced to just six short items. Even so, these rules do address several welfare problems that have plagued carriage horses.

Complaints that drivers overload the carriages to multiply fares have been common from horse advocates around the country. In Massachusetts horse-drawn carriages for hire are limited to no more than four adult passengers at one time. The state also requires that the harness of each carriage horse be cleaned every day, and sized and adjusted to fit the animal properly. Poorly fitting, dirty tack often causes sores and blistering from excess rubbing. Another frequent criticism of carriage rides is that drivers work their animals continuously without breaks because higher prices can be charged for longer rides and no money is made during downtime. Although rides cannot last longer than thirty minutes in Massachusetts, and the horse must be rested for at least five minutes between each fare, there is no maximum number of hours of work stipulated for the horses. Another regulation requires that a carriage horse's pace never exceed a "slow trot," and remain at a walk "[w]hen traffic permits."

Massachusetts has also adopted a maximum of 90 degrees Fahrenheit, the highest temperature in which the horses can be worked, but has added the humidity factor often overlooked in municipal codes. A combination of temperature and humidity totaling 140 or more suspends all carriage rides in the Bay State. A temperature of 25 degrees Fahrenheit, or a sum of the temperature and the wind chill equaling 25 degrees Fahrenheit will do the same. Finally, and rather redundantly, Massachusetts prohibits carriage horse operations during "adverse weather conditions, [such as] snow, ice, heavy rain, slippery conditions or extreme cold, heat, or humidity."

Soring

The gait of a horse—how it walks and runs—has long been regarded as one of the most attractive features of the animal, and a horse that prances along with a sprightly and lively step is highly desirable. The Tennessee walking horse was bred and trained in the southern United States to exaggerate its high-stepping gait into a kind of running walk, a flowing trot that is smooth and extended. This is known in the industry as the "big lick." The attribute came to be featured in horse competitions, and owners showing Tennessee walkers with the ability to perform the "big lick" received championship honors, the highest stud fees, and the best selling price.

For years the "big lick" was produced by training the animals with special weighted shoes, or with chains and rollers attached to the front legs.

But during the 1950s, many owners of Tennessee walkers authorized their trainers to increasingly employ a method that enhances the movement of a horse without a prolonged period of instruction. The technique is "soring," so called because soreness is deliberately induced in the front feet of the animal. When a horse has sore forelegs, it naturally lifts its front feet high and touches the ground as lightly as possible, trying to keep its weight off of its aching feet. This accentuates the normal stride of the animal and produces the distinctive characteristic of the Tennessee walking horse, one highly prized by show judges, breeders, and horse fanciers.

Sore feet in a horse can be deliberately caused by various mechanical and chemical means. Perhaps the most frequent method is the application of a substance to the pastern area (just above the hoof) that produces blistering, such as mustard oil, kerosene, or diesel fuel. Small chains or wires are then wrapped around the blisters, breaking them and creating a continuous source of irritation as they rub up and down with every step. Soring has also been done by making a thin, shallow incision around the circumference of the coronet band (where the skin meets the hoof) on both front feet. Salt, sand, or some other abrasive is applied to the cut to keep it from healing and maintain the soreness. Sometimes short nails or large tacks are driven into the bottom of the hoof under the pads, producing a constant dull pain even when the horse is merely standing.

As soring became more widespread in the 1950s and 1960s, and as owners willing to resort to it gained an obvious competitive advantage, horse advocates pleaded with state legislatures to ban the practice. They argued that soring was inhumane and, as such, contrary to already existing anticruelty laws. Moreover, it was simply unfair to owners who would not subject their animals to the painful procedure. Beginning with Kentucky in 1956, several states did enact laws to prohibit soring, among them Maryland, Virginia, and New York. Unfortunately, enforcement was lax, so owners were little deterred, and at any rate sored walkers continued to be shown in states that allowed them, such as Tennessee, Georgia, and the Carolinas. Horse owners and breeders, often wealthy and influential people with political connections, contended then and continue to do so today, that without soring there was nothing particularly noteworthy about the walking horse, and thus little reason to present the breed at horse shows.

Public condemnation of soring escalated in the late 1960s, spurred by a new animal welfare organization, the American Horse Protection Association. The persistence of soring in the walking horse industry incited concerned citizens to form the group in 1966, determined to stop the practice with a federal law. Due in large measure to their strenuous lobbying efforts on Capitol Hill, the Horse Protection Act (HPA) was signed by President Richard Nixon in 1970. The HPA is administered and enforced by the U.S. Department of Agriculture through its Animal and Plant Health Inspection Service (APHIS) office.

Horse Protection Act of 1970

The HPA begins with the Congressional acknowledgment of what horse advocates had been saying for years: Soring is cruel and inhumane, and produces an unfair advantage against horses who have not been made sore. On this moral foundation, the HPA prohibits showing, exhibiting, selling, auctioning, offering for sale, shipping, transporting, delivering, or receiving "any horse which is sore." Additionally, managers of horse shows, exhibitions, sales, and auctions must not allow sored horses to be displayed or sold in these venues.

Initially, the HPA exacted only a civil penalty of $1,000 for each violation, or $2,000 and no more than six months in prison, but punishments were significantly enhanced with amendments in 1976. Now, a maximum criminal penalty of up to three years incarceration and a $5,000 fine may be imposed, while, alternatively, the lighter civil punishment is still available. Offenders with one violation may also be barred for one year from showing or exhibiting any horse, or from managing or judging any horse show, exhibition, sale, or auction. Subsequent convictions can merit a disqualification of five years, or more. Management faces a $3,000 fine if a disqualified person is allowed to participate in any of these equine events.

Managers must maintain detailed records of the event, especially concerning the horses and their owners; these records must be made available for inspection by APHIS upon request. Horses that are sore, or are believed to be sore, may be detained by APHIS for up to twenty-four hours. Any equipment or devices used to sore horses may be seized.

Legal proceedings in federal courts and before administrative law judges have further delineated the scope of the HPA. Although a criminal conviction requires knowledge of the soring, a standard of strict liability was imposed for the civil penalty: owners and trainers of horses determined to be sore, as well as persons transporting or showing sore horses are all legally responsible even if they did not know the horse had been injured in this way, and had nothing to do with the actual soring. Furthermore, a person filing a complaint against one of these parties does not have to prove that the defendant was aware that soring had been done in order to establish a violation. Nor does the method of soring need to be determined, or that the owner, trainer, or exhibitor intended to sore the horse. Soreness can be confirmed by palpation alone—touching and handling the legs, especially the pasterns, feeling for swelling. The only evidence needed is that the horse attempted to withdraw both legs upon palpating them; no other behavioral responses are required.

APHIS was rather slow to issue regulations for the implementation of the HPA, taking nearly nine years to do so. Once promulgated, the regulations focused on two main factors: specific prohibitions and enforcement mechanisms. Any person who enters a horse in a show or exhibition, or sells or presents a horse for sale or auction is specifically prohibited from using certain devices and employing certain practices that commonly cause sore feet in horses. Among these are various sorts of apparatuses that are braceleted to the lower legs of a horse that slide up and down or rotate around the leg. Known as "action devices," these include beads, bangles, rollers, chains, boots, and collars weighing more than six ounces, rocker bars, hoof bands, and weights, as well as artificial extensions of toe length.

American Horse Protection Association v. Yeutter

The American Horse Protection Association (AHPA) was not pleased with APHIS. The new regulations did ban the use of substances that cause blistering when rubbed on a horse's legs—such as diesel fuel or mustard oil—while allowing only harmless lubricants like glycerine and mineral oil. However, action devices were not outlawed entirely. Instead, APHIS restricted the use of chains to those weighing no more than 10 ounces, and rollers up to 14 ounces.

This was not acceptable to the AHPA, so they sued the agency in 1984, demanding that all action devices of any weight be forbidden. The Circuit Court of Appeals for the District of Columbia reached a compromise position in 1987. Relying upon a study done at Auburn University showing that action devices weighing 10 ounces or more could cause soring while those of 6 or less did not, the court ordered the USDA to amend the regulations in light of these findings. The judges could not be persuaded to ban the devices entirely (*American Horse Protection Association v. Lyng*). In 1990 the USDA produced new rules with a revised allowance for action devices, this time setting the maximum at 6 ounces for all types of these apparatuses.

Still not satisfied, the AHPA filed suit again at the federal district court in Washington D.C., once more calling for USDA secretary Clayton Yeutter to issue regulations prohibiting the devices altogether. In June 1990 the district court complied with the wishes of the AHPA, finding that the regulations regarding action devices were "arbitrary and capricious." Secretary Yeutter was ordered to forbid them because "allowing their use can reasonably be expected to encourage or cause the soring of horses." This was a major victory, not only for the Horse Protection Association, but for a prominent faction within the walking horse industry that had rejected the drive to produce the showiest, most exaggerated gait—the "big lick"—one that led to soring. Instead, the "plantation" group favored the more sedate prancing characteristic of the breed when it was first developed in the eighteenth century. Outlawing action devices promised to revolutionize the industry. Yet district court decisions are always subject to appeal, and once more the USDA quickly turned to the D.C. Circuit Court for a review.

The appeals court did not find the arguments of the AHPA nearly as compelling as had the lower court. There, the association had opposed the 6-ounce limit, although not because devices of this weight caused soring—they accepted the results of the Auburn studies that weights at 6 ounces or less likely did not cause soring. Instead, the AHPA argued that allowing any action devices at all of *any* weight encourages owners and trainers to use chemical irritants banned by the Horse Protection Act. The devices and the irritating substances are so closely associated in the practices of the walking horse industry, the horse advocates contended, that the only way to ensure the end of soring was to absolutely prohibit both. Allowing boots, collars, and chains fosters the methods that the federal statute is supposed to prevent, and this is clearly inconsistent with what Congress intended in passing the law.

Judge Mikva of the D.C. Circuit rejected the principle that the Horse Protection Act directs the secretary of the USDA to bar any practice that might indirectly cause or perpetuate abuses. If it did, he wrote, then horse shows themselves should be eliminated, and the law clearly does not countenance this drastic step. All that is required of the USDA is to promulgate rules barring practices that "can reasonably be expected to directly cause soring." In light of the Auburn study, and in the absence of any compelling evidence that the employment of action devices of 6 ounces or less does have an immediate connection to soring, the USDA regulation is completely reasonable. Mikva agreed with the agency position that the answer is enforcement, rather than further prohibitions.

As to the charge that the USDA was acting in an arbitrary and capricious manner by permitting any action devices, Judge Mikva observed that the rule making by the agency just did not seem frivolous or ill considered. Although the district court that sided with the AHPA had concluded that "the Secretary failed to examine further the critical relationship between chemical soring and the use of action devices," the circuit court asserted that "the final rulemaking decision indicated an awareness of—and seemingly reasonable response to—comments . . . advocating an outright ban." In support of this claim, Mikva quoted a passage from the USDA's final rule announcement in which the agency reported that the horse advocates think the use of action devices encourages soring. Apparently, the judge believed that merely recognizing the existence of an opposing view indicates that it was carefully examined and given due consideration.

Enforcement of the Horse Protection Act

The enforcement of the HPA depends upon the timely inspection of the horses at shows, exhibitions, auctions, or sales. These inspections may be accomplished by APHIS veterinarians, who are entitled to unlimited access to all areas of the event, to examine the horses on demand, and to hold any animals for up to twenty-four hours for further scrutiny or testing. However, for policing the incidence of soring, government inspectors are much more the exception than the rule.

In a major concession to the industry, and as a realistic recognition that the USDA cannot provide inspectors for each of the hundreds of horse events presented each year in America (allocations of money for enforcing of the HPA have always been paltry), the regulations allow managers of horse events to appoint their own inspectors for the detection of soring. This option has been much exploited. Not quite complete self-regulation, this is a qualified or conditional form because this inspection program must conform to the requirements established by the federal government. Management-selected inspectors are called "designated qualified persons" (DQPs). The administrators of a horse show, exhibition, sale, or auction are not required to use a DQP, but it is an effective way of transferring legal liability if sored horses are presented in violation of the law: without a DQP, management is solely responsible.

The preferred qualification for a DQP is a doctorate in veterinary medicine, but farriers, trainers, or other experienced and knowledgeable individuals with substantial training in the care of horses can qualify as well. The veterinarian must be a large animal practitioner, or a member of the American Association of Equine Practitioners, or experienced in the diagnosis of lameness resulting from soring. In any case, DQPs must be licensed by a horse industry organization whose licensing program has been approved by APHIS. To receive this certification, APHIS demands that the program include at minimum ten hours of classroom instruction in the anatomy and physiology of the limbs of the horse, the HPA and its regulations, and the history of soring and its diagnosis. Four hours of practicum with live horses and a written examination are also required.

No person can obtain a DQP license who has been found in violation of the HPA or its regulations. The licensing organization must supply APHIS with a list containing pertinent information on all their DQPs, and the inspectors themselves are to inform the government of the owner, trainer, and exhibitor of each horse found to have been sored, and the event in which the animal was to be presented. DQPs are not permitted to show or sell their own horses in any venue where they are inspecting horses, or in one featuring animals belonging to the DQP's immediate family or employer.

DQP enforcement of the HPA does not appear to have been particularly successful. Anecdotal evidence from individuals within the walking horse industry indicates that soring is still pervasive. Perhaps as many as nine out of every ten horses in competition are subjected to the procedure. Hard data from the federal government itself as well as other sources lend some support to this bleak report. In a ten-year period from the late 1980s to the late 1990s, government inspectors diagnosed almost 700 incidents of soring—depressing figures that become more unsettling with the realization that as many as 90 percent of all horse inspections are done by DQPs, not agents of APHIS. Moreover, DQPs detected soring violations at a much higher rate when APHIS inspectors were present than when they were not. Perhaps worse, the practice seems to persist at even the highest levels of the industry. Since the early 1980s, better than half the winners of the Trainer of the Year award, and nearly all of the presidents of the Walking Horse Association have either been punished for soring or are being investigated for the offense.

In an effort to solve the enforcement problem, the USDA initiated a "Strategic Plan" in 1998, one intended to tighten its oversight of the horse industry and increase the accountability of DQPs. Certification of horse industry organizations such as the Walking Horse Association has become more rigorous under the plan, but USDA certificates keep government inspectors out of the shows, for the most part. This maintains the form of conditional self-regulation so desired by those engaged in showing and selling walking horses, where managers who work within the industry select the DQPs.

Among other requirements, horse industry organizations must produce and secure APHIS approval of a comprehensive set of rules that are consistent with the HPA and include standards of professional conduct. Two weeks prior to each event, the groups must submit to APHIS the names of individuals working as DQPs, records of violations written up by these people, and the penalties they assessed. APHIS must also be notified of any hearings concerning DQP performance so a government official can be present. Also required are lists, prepared and distributed monthly, of individuals who have been suspended for violations of the HPA and its regulations.

The Strategic Plan also calls for APHIS veterinarians to observe and evaluate DQPs at work during horse events while making announced and unannounced inspections of the animals at shows and auctions. The government vets also audit the records of horse industry organizations, especially those concerning the training and qualifications of DQPs, evaluations of these individuals by the organization, and their history of detecting violations and how these were penalized. The penalties for infractions have been enhanced under the plan, with first-time offenders barred from participation in shows or auctions for eight months, while a second violation gets two years, and a third receives a five-year suspension. Anyone with four violations of the HPA or its regulations is banned for life. If a transgression is confirmed after a show has concluded, any trophies, prizes, or points awarded must be forfeited.

It is too soon to tell how well the Strategic Plan will improve matters in the walking horse industry, but it seems to be a step in the right direction.

WILD FREE-ROAMING HORSES AND BURROS ACT OF 1971 (WHBA)

Hyracotherium, the primordial ancestor of the modern horse (*Equus caballus*), inhabited the forests of North America in prehistoric times. It evolved into several different equine species over the course of some 50 million years, culminating in *Equus*, and then vanished from the continent about eight thousand years ago. The reasons for the disappearance are still largely unknown, although the main factor was probably overhunting by the peoples who had crossed the Bering land bridge and drifted south through the Western Hemisphere.

Horses returned on January 2, 1494, when Columbus arrived at Hispaniola on his second voyage to the New World and deposited thirty-four of the animals on the island. Hernando Cortez brought horses to the mainland in 1519 when he landed at the Yucatan of Mexico on the way to the Spanish conquest of the Aztecs, and Coronado's 1540 expedition north from Mexico City into the American Southwest traveled on the backs of hundreds of horses.

North American Indians, who had known nothing of horses or burros, almost immediately began to acquire the animals by trade, gift, and theft, or by capturing those that had escaped or had simply been turned loose by the Spaniards. Many Indian peoples proved highly skilled at training and riding horses, and within 200 years the great horse cultures of the Lakota (Sioux), Cheyenne, and Comanche ruled a vast area on the North American plains. Meanwhile, the Indians of the eastern woodlands obtained horses from the French and English settlers who populated the seaboard, Appalachia, and the Great Lakes through most of the seventeenth and eighteenth centuries.

During 400 years of European colonization and subsequent American independence, horses and burros routinely abandoned domestication—by running away or human disowning—and developed flourishing populations of wild equines in the grasslands of the West. The decimation of large predator populations, especially those of the wolf and grizzly bear, left the animals virtually without enemies on the range. At the close of the 1800s, perhaps 2 million horses and burros were roaming an immense area, centered on Nevada, Utah, and northern Arizona, and including the arid regions of Colorado, California, Idaho, Oregon, Wyoming, New Mexico, and the Dakotas. The lineage of all of these animals is presumed ultimately to trace back to the herds of the Spanish conquistadors, although centuries of cross- and inbreeding had produced a creature with little resemblance to its Iberian ancestors. Perhaps foremost among the differences, the herds in the American West were wild animals, living on the land.

Decline of the Herds

When the Indian Wars ended in the 1880s, and with the demise of the buffalo, what remained of the formerly contested Western rangeland was gobbled up by ranching and farming interests. As the competition with domestic livestock for the open range intensified during the first half of the 1900s, and equine habitat succumbed to the plow, wild horse herds steadily though slowly declined. Ranchers throughout the West routinely shot or poisoned horses that they believed were destroying crops or depleting forage and water to be appropriated by their cows and sheep. The Nevada legislature officially authorized such actions with a statute permitting anyone to shoot wild horses on sight.

After the Second World War, equine attrition accelerated prodigiously as America's pet population burgeoned. Dog and cat food companies had discovered a ready source of cheap, unowned meat: the wild horses scattered throughout the mountain ranges and desert basins of the West. Hunters and herders under contract to the companies took to the field in droves, renting planes and trucks, gunning down or rounding up tens of thousands of the animals from the air and on land. Many horses were left mortally injured, dying a slow agonizing death, their bodies to be collected later. Those not killed outright or abandoned were packed into trailer trucks and shipped to slaughterhouses, usually without food or water. Although the Twenty-Eight Hour Law required transporters to provide livestock with sufficient food and water, at this time the provision applied only to animals shipped by railroad (*see* chapter 4: *Twenty-Eight Hour Law of 1994*).

Within a decade after the Second World War, wild horse numbers had been cut to less than 25,000. In the mid-1950s, after a chance encounter with a truckload of battered and bloodied horses that had been run down by a plane, a woman from Reno, Nevada, named Velma Johnston took on a one-person crusade to halt the human predation of wild horses. Nicknamed "Wild Horse Annie," Johnston garnered national attention for the plight of the horses, sparked by a deluge of letters from American school children and their mothers pleading with Congress to protect the animals. Eventually, Representative Walter Baring of Nevada was induced to sponsor a bill, and Mike Mansfield of Montana cosponsored it in the Senate. In September 1959, President Dwight Eisenhower signed the Wild Horse Annie Act into law.

Federal Protection for Wild Equines

Along with the Twenty-Eight Hour Law and the Humane Slaughter Act (*see* both in chapter 4), passed just the year before, at the time the Wild Horse Annie Act was one of only three federal laws designed to provide some protections for domestic (or normally so) animals. This law banned the use of aircraft or vehicles to hunt wild horses or burros on public land, and made it unlawful to "pollute any watering hole on any of the public land or ranges for the purpose of trapping, killing, wounding, or maiming any of such animals." Violations were punishable by a fine of up to $500 and six months in jail or both.

Then, as now, nearly all of these animals inhabited land administered by the Bureau of Land Management (BLM), so the protections afforded by the law were thought to be fairly comprehensive. Unfortunately, this proved not to be the case. Roundups on private land were not covered by the statute, nor were nonmotorized roundups on public land. Moreover, the Wild Horse Annie Act placed no obstacles to deter encroachment on wild horse habitat, and in any case the law suffered from lax enforcement. Ten years after the law was passed the wild equine population had been further reduced to less than ten thousand.

Velma Johnston continued to work on behalf of the animals. Assisted by horse protection groups, humane societies, and thousands more school children pleading with members of Congress, in early 1971 Johnston and her allies once again managed to prevail upon Representative Baring to sponsor a bill, this time aimed at strengthening the Wild Horse Annie Act. Senators Henry Jackson of Washington and Mike Hatfield of Oregon produced companion bills in the Senate. Following months of testimony and debate, President Richard Nixon signed the Wild Free-Roaming Horses and Burros Act (WHBA) in December 1971.

The WHBA proclaims that wild horses and burros are "living symbols of the historic and pioneer spirit of the West . . . that contribute to the diversity of life forms within the Nation and enrich the lives of the American people." As such, they "shall be protected from capture, branding, harassment, or death." The act went on to declare the crucial ecological status of the animals, that they "are to be considered in the area where presently found, as an integral part of the natural system of the public lands." The secretary of the Department of the Interior (overseeing the BLM) and the secretary of the Department of Agriculture (through the U.S. Forest Service) are authorized to enforce the WHBA on public lands and issue regulations administering it. The act survived a challenge to its constitutionality in 1976 (*Kleppe v. New Mexico; see* chapter 6: *Wildlife Law*, for a discussion of this case).

Recognizing the ongoing competition for forage with domestic livestock and other wildlife, as well as the need to prevent the deterioration of natural habitats, Congress charged the two secretaries with the responsibility of managing the wild equines. Given the distribution of the animals on public land, by far the bulk of the work falls to the interior secretary and the BLM. Wild equines found on land occupied by the Department of Defense or in national parks are not protected by the WHBA, even though these areas do legally belong to the American people.

Managing Wild Equine Herds
As authorized by the WHBA and federal regulations, the BLM has crafted an elaborate "Wild Horse and Burro Program." It divides wild equine habitat into 186 herd management areas (HMAs) covering some 44 million acres in ten states: Nevada, Utah, Arizona, Colorado, California, Idaho, Oregon, Wyoming, New Mexico, and Montana.

These 2000 totals are substantially reduced from thirty years ago when the BLM had identified 305 HMAs on 80 million acres in sixteen states. Also reduced are equine numbers—from about 50,000 then to 36,000 today, with better than three-quarters of this total living in Nevada. Most of the HMAs have formal management plans specifying such items as habitat requirements of the equines, their relationships with other public and private land uses, and the "management level"—the extent of human intervention in their lives—appropriate for the particular herd. The WHBA and regulations stipulate a minimalist approach to wild equine management, in keeping with their status as wild, not domesticated animals.

The stated goal of managing wild horses and burros as a genuine component of a region's wildlife population, usually sharing the range with livestock, is to "achieve and maintain a thriving natural ecological balance." This requires up-to-date inventories of their numbers and must include consultation with the U.S. Fish and Wildlife Service, state wildlife agencies, as well as due consideration of the recommendations of biologists and ecologists competent to offer a judgment on the matter. If after such consultation the secretary and BLM determine that there are too many wild equines on a given range, direct action must be taken to reduce their numbers to "appropriate management levels." The WHBA defines "excess animals" as those wild horses and burros that "must be removed . . . in order to preserve and maintain a thriving natural ecological balance and multiple-use relationship" in a given region.

The removal of equines from the wild must proceed in a certain order of priority, beginning with humanely destroying old, sick, or lame individuals. If still more animals must be removed to restore a natural equilibrium, the secretary is required to place these horses with private citizens, should there be any, who are willing and qualified to provide humane transportation, care, and treatment. After one year of demonstrating the ability to supply appropriate care, a person may then apply to the secretary for legal title to the animals. If granted, the person becomes the owner of the adopted horse or burro, and the animal is no longer protected by the WHBA. In the event that there is no adoption demand for excess animals, they may be "destroyed in the most humane and cost efficient manner possible." No methods for the humane destruction of equines are recommended by either the WHBA or its regulations, however "humane treatment" is defined as "handling compatible with animal husbandry practices accepted in the veterinary community, without causing unnecessary stress or suffering."

Owners of private land are entitled to have wild equines removed from their property by federal agents (typically BLM officers) upon written request. Ranchers sued the BLM in 1982, contending that the WHBA also imposes a duty on the government to prevent the animals from straying onto private land in the first place. However, the Ninth Circuit Court of Appeals, upholding the lower court decision, ruled that there is no such duty (*Fallini v. Hodel*). Under no circumstances may a trespassing animal be killed by the landowner. People may also maintain wild horses and burros on their property—this is known as "private maintenance"— so long as they protect the animals from "harassment" and supply the BLM (or the Forest Service) with information on the number of animals residing there. Wild horses and burros may not be deliberately taken from public lands or enticed onto private property.

The WHBA and its federal regulations specify that any of the following actions, when not authorized by the secretary, are illegal: killing a wild equine, "except as an act of mercy"; intentionally removing or attempting to remove a wild horse or burro from public lands; taming, breaking, or branding such animals; maliciously or negligently injuring or harassing them; processing their remains into commercial products (such as pet food); selling a wild horse or burro maintained on private land, or "commercially exploiting" one. Penalties for violations are up to one year in prison, or a fine of up to $2,000, or both.

Removing Animals from the Wild

Managing the herds by removing wild equines from public lands was immediately controversial, and continues today to be the most disputed aspect of the BLM Wild Horse and Burro Program. Indeed, the very first case litigated under the WHBA in 1975 saw a horse welfare organization challenging a BLM roundup of 400 wild horses in Nevada. The American

Horse Protection Association objected on the grounds that nothing proved that the animals caused the range deterioration that led to the roundup. The federal District Court for Nevada disagreed and authorized the removal of the horses (*American Horse Protection Association v. Frizzell*).

Part of the problem is that effective wildlife management requires accurate animal population figures, and it is not easy to obtain precise numbers of unclaimed and unbranded horses and burros living on a given HMA. Much of their habitat is gridded in a checkerboard pattern where public and private lands appear commingled in alternating parcels. Add to this highly mobile animals that are, of course, oblivious of property boundaries. The BLM has been accused by horse and burro advocates of willfully inflating wild equine numbers and overstating their impact on the environment. At the same time, the government agency has been accused by ranchers of underestimating wild equine totals and not fully appreciating how much damage they do to livestock interests.

In any case, the typical capture proceeds with a helicopter rounding up the number of animals judged to be in excess of the carrying capacity of the herd management area. Originally, the WHBA banned all use of motorized vehicles for managing the herds, but in 1976 Congress passed the Federal Land Policy and Management Act, allowing helicopters for gathering and vehicles for transporting wild horses and burros. A subsequent regulation further specified that *only* helicopters may be used for roundups. The animals are either driven directly to "preparation centers" or captured in portable traps and transported there. Old, sick, or lame animals may be destroyed on the spot but are in any event eventually sorted out from the healthy animals and killed. All animals are to be given a veterinary examination within four hours of their arrival at a preparation center, and those not designated for euthanasia receive vaccinations and medication for worms.

Since 1978 captured horses and burros have also received a "freeze-mark": a unique, painless way of affixing a permanent identification. The freeze-mark is applied by first super-cooling an iron in liquid nitrogen to a temperature of minus 320 degrees Fahrenheit, and then applying the instrument to a shaved area on the animal's neck. The hair grows back white on a dark-colored animal, and dark on a light-colored one. With a series of right angles and straight lines, rather than numbers or letters, the freeze-mark indicates that the equine is registered with the government, the approximate year of its birth, and its particular registration number, which also indicates the state in which it was captured.

The captured horses and burros remain at the preparation center for at least thirty days, allowing them the opportunity to become more accustomed to people and domestication. After that, they are shipped to the

Wild Horse and Burro Holding Facility at Elm Creek, Nebraska, or to an adoption site. The BLM instituted the Adopt-A-Horse program in 1973, originally only in Montana—the program went national in 1976. After twenty-five years, some 150,000 wild equines have been placed with private individuals, horses accounting for about 80 percent of this total. The most recent figures available show just over 10,000 total adoptions in 1998.

A person wishing to adopt a wild horse or burro must file an application form with the BLM. In order to qualify, the prospective adopter must be at least eighteen years old, without any prior conviction for inhumane treatment of animals, and have a facility with adequate space, confinement, shelter, and feed and water. If the application is approved, the adopter is invited to attend an adoption event to select a wild equine. Once the selection is made, a fee of $125 is paid and a "Private Maintenance and Care Agreement" is signed. As mentioned above, if after one year BLM is satisfied that the adopter has complied with the agreement, a certificate of title will be issued and the animal becomes private property.

Problems with Adopting Wild Horses

The Adopt-A-Horse program has also been troubled, almost from its inception. Interest in the animals has often failed to keep up with the numbers removed from the wild. Many horse enthusiasts are understandably reluctant to take on the task of training a wild animal. Moreover, the BLM exacerbated the problem in 1982 when it raised the adoption fee to $200, causing demand to plummet. The price was quickly returned to its original level just a year later.

The most serious charge leveled against the adoption program is that many of the animals end up at the slaughterhouse, though exactly how many do is much disputed. Animal protection groups have claimed that anywhere from 50 percent to as high as 90 percent of the rounded-up equines suffer this fate. The BLM puts the figure at only about 10 percent.

In 1985 the Animal Protection Institute (API) sued the Interior Department. The API alleged that the BLM was allowing the adoption program to be used as a supply source for pet food and for meat exports (horse meat is considered a delicacy in Japan, France, and several other countries), clearly illegal activity. The WHBA states that neither the animals nor their remains "may be sold or transferred for consideration for processing into commercial products."

A person can adopt no more than four wild equines each year, unless it can be demonstrated that the facilities provided for the animals are adequate for the number taken in. The API claimed that unscrupulous individuals were not only taking advantage of this stipulation to accumulate animals, they were also collecting powers of attorney from a number of people in order to exceed the limit of four. The horses and burros were held for a year in order to obtain title, and then shipped off to slaughter-houses at a considerable profit. Meat processors will pay at least $500 for a horse that cost the "adopter" the $125 BLM fee. What is worse, the API asserted that some animals were being slaughtered before title was trans-ferred. The federal district court ruled against the BLM, and on appeal the Ninth Circuit Court of Appeals affirmed that judgment in 1988. The BLM is prohibited from transferring title of wild horses and burros to individ-uals who had expressed the intent to use the animals for commercial pur-poses (*Animal Protection Institute v. Hodel*).

Nine years later the API was suing the BLM again, this time for ignor-ing the court's 1988 injunction halting the sale of adopted horses and bur-ros for slaughter. The disputants settled out of court in 1998, and much in the favor of the API and the equines. The BLM agreed to change the Pri-vate Maintenance and Care Agreement to announce that it will prosecute anyone who adopts a wild equine for slaughter or commercial exploita-tion. The BLM also said it would enter into agreements with American and Canadian slaughterhouses requiring them to notify the agency whenever an untitled horse or burro arrives on the premises. Finally, WHBA regulations were amended to prohibit the use of powers of attor-ney in the adoption process.

Who Will Manage Wild Horses and Burros?

Problems such as these with the adoption process, and the perennial com-petition between wild equines and livestock for water and forage, have won the BLM few friends on either the animal protection or the animal use side of the fence. It seems sometimes that no one is happy with the way the herds are managed.

Recently, an attitude expressed by the sentence "If you don't like it, see if you can do it better" has begun to build in Congress, where a move-ment to return management of the animals to the states is gathering mo-mentum. In September 1999, forty years almost to the day after Eisen-hower signed the Wild Horse Annie Act, Representative Jim Gibbons of Nevada introduced H.R. 2784, the "Wild Horse and Burro Preservation and Management Act." This bill would allow governors to assume on de-mand the authority to implement the WHBA formerly vested in the sec-retary of the interior.

Many observers noted the irony that a Nevada representative now ad-vocates a retreat from the same federal control that another Nevada rep-resentative had fought for in an earlier generation. Back then the states, particularly Nevada, had so clearly failed to conserve these "living sym-bols of the historic and pioneer spirit of the West." Would they do better in the new century? Those in the animal protection community think not. Their main fear is that the states will cave in to cattle growers, remove the horses and burros from the range so more cows can move in, and simply euthanize the equines without pursuing the adoption process.

Supporters of H.R. 2784 point out that the bill would have no effect on the current provisions of the WHBA and its regulations. Removal would only be permitted when horses or burros are overpopulating the range and upsetting its ecological balance, and cannot be done with impunity just to please ranchers. To this, their opponents respond that the states will likely have an economic interest in finding (or manufacturing) an equine-caused imbalance. The concern about preempting adoptions is supposed to be allayed by the bill directing the secretary to "conduct a national media campaign to increase public awareness of the . . . adoption program," and appropriating $4 million over three years to pay for the advertising. Coupling this measure with the WHBA regulation that allows euthanasia of healthy animals only when there is not a sufficient adoption demand, this concern may be unfounded.

REFERENCES

Federal Laws
Animal Welfare Act of 1970, 7 U.S.C. §§ 2131–2157.
Federal Law Enforcement Animal Protection Act, 18 U.S.C. § 1368.
Horse Protection Act, 15 U.S.C. §§ 1821–1831.
Obscenity, 18 U.S.C. §§ 1460–1469.
Punishment for Depiction of Animal Cruelty, 18 U.S.C. § 48.
Twenty-Eight Hour Law of 1994, 49 U.S.C. § 80502.
Wild Free-Roaming Horses and Burros Act of 1971, 16 U.S.C. §§ 1331–1340.
Wild Horse Annie Act, 18 U.S.C. § 47.

Federal Regulations
Animal Welfare
    Exercise for dogs, 9 C.F.R. § 3.8.
    Handling of animals, 9 C.F.R. § 2.131.
    Standards for humane handling, care, treatment, and transportation of
        dogs, 9 C.F.R. §§ 3.1–3.19.
Horse Protection, 9 C.F.R. §§ 11.1–11.41.
Wild Free-Roaming Horses and Burros: Protection, Management, and
    Control, 43 C.F.R. Part 4700.

State Laws
Anticruelty Laws
    Alabama, Ala. Code § 13A-11-14.
    Alaska, Alaska Stat. § 11.61.140.
    Arkansas, Ark. Code Ann. § 5-62-101.

California, Cal. Penal Code § 1-14-597.
Colorado, Colo. Rev. Stat. § 18-9-201.
Connecticut, Conn. Gen. Stat. § 53-247.
Delaware, Del. Code Ann. tit. 11 § 1325.
Florida, Fla. Stat. Ann. § 46-828.12.
Georgia, Ga. Code Ann. § 16-12-4.
Hawaii, Haw. Rev. Stat. § 37-711-1109.
Illinois, 510 Ill. Comp. Stat. 70/3.
Iowa, Iowa Code § 717B.2.
Kansas, Kan. Stat. Ann. § 21-4310.
Louisiana, La. Rev. Stat. Ann. § 14:102.
Maine, Me. Rev. Stat. Ann. tit. 7, § 739-4011.
Maryland, Md. Code Ann. § 27-59.
Michigan, Mich. Comp. Laws § 28.245.
Minnesota, Minn. Stat. § 343.21.
Mississippi, Miss. Code § 97-41-1.
Missouri, § 578.012.
Montana, Mont. Code Ann. § 45-8-211.
Nevada, Nev. Rev. Stat. 574.101.
New Hampshire, N.H. Rev. Stat. Ann. § 644:8.
New Mexico, N.M. Stat. Ann. § 3-18-1.
North Dakota, N.D. Cent. Code § 36-21-1.
Ohio, Ohio Rev. Code Ann. § 959.13.
Oklahoma, Okla. Stat. tit. 21-1685.
Oregon, Or. Rev. Stat. § 167.315.
Pennsylvania, Pa. Cons. Stat. § 18-511.
Texas, Tex. Penal Code Ann. § 9-42.09.
Virginia, Va. Code Ann. § 3.1-796.122.
Washington, Wash. Rev. Code § 16.52.205.
West Virginia, W. Va. Code § 61-8-19a.
Wisconsin, Wis. Stat. § 951.02.

Carriage Rides
   Atlanta, Georgia, Code of Ordinances, Animal-Drawn Vehicles,
      § 162-151.
   Massachusetts, Department of Public Safety, Regulations for the
      Operation of Horse Drawn Carriages, 520 C.M.R. 13.00.
   San Antonio, Texas, Code of Ordinances, Horse-Drawn Carriages,
      § 33-462.

Euthanasia in Animal Control Facilities
   Arizona, Ariz. Rev. Stat. § 11-1021.
   Delaware, Del. Code Ann. tit. 3-8001.

Florida, Fla. Stat. Ann. § 46-828.058.
Georgia, Ga. Code Ann. § 4-11-5.1.
Kansas, Kan. Stat. Ann. § 47-1718.
Louisiana, La. Rev. Stat. Ann. § 40-1041.
Maine, Me. Rev. Stat. Ann. tit. 17-1042.
Maryland, Md. Code Ann. § 27-59A.
Massachusetts, Mass. Gen. Laws ch. 20-151A.
New Jersey, N.J. Stat. Ann. § 4:22-19.
Ohio, Ohio Rev. Code, § 4729.532.
Oklahoma, Okla. Stat. tit. 4-502.
Oregon, Or. Rev. Stat. § 48-609.405.
Rhode Island, R.I. Gen. Laws § 4-19-11.1.
South Carolina, S.C. Code Ann. § 47-3-420.
Tennessee, Tenn. Code Ann. § 44-17-303.
West Virginia, W.Va. Code, § 30-10A-7.

Police Dog Laws
Alabama, Ala. Code § 13A-5-6; 13A-11-15.
Arizona, Ariz. Rev. Stat. § 13-707.
Connecticut, Conn. Gen. Stat. § 53-247.
Delaware, Del. Code Ann. tit. 11, § 4206.
Massachusetts, Mass. Gen. Laws. ch. 272, § 77A.
Michigan, Mich. Comp. Laws § 750.50c.
New Hampshire, N.H. Rev. Stat. Ann. § 625:9.
North Carolina, N.C. Gen. Stat. § 15A-1340.17.
Ohio, Ohio Rev. Code Ann. § 2921.321.
Oklahoma, Okla. Stat. tit. 21, § 649.2.
Rhode Island, R.I. Gen. Laws § 4-1-30.
Tennessee, Tenn. Code Ann. § 39-14-105.
Utah, Utah Code Ann. § 76-3-204.
Virginia, Va. Code Ann. § 18.2-144.1.

Sexual Contact with Animals
Arkansas, Ark. Code Ann. § 5-14-122.
Delaware, Del. Code Ann. tit. 11 § 777.
Georgia, Ga. Code Ann. § 16-6-6.
Idaho, Idaho Code § 18-6605.
Kansas, Kan. Stat. Ann. § 21-3505.
Louisiana, La. Rev. Stat. Ann. § 89.
Maryland, Md. Code Ann. § 554.
Massachusetts, Mass. Gen. Laws ch. 272-34.
Michigan, Mich. Comp. Laws § 750.158.
Mississippi, Miss. Code Ann. § 97-29-59.

Montana, Mont. Code Ann. § 45-5-505.
Nebraska, Neb. Rev. Stat. § 28-1010.
New York, N.Y. Law § 130.20.
North Carolina, N.C. Gen. Stat. § 14-177.
North Dakota, N.D. Cent. Code § 12.1-20-12.
Oklahoma, Okla. Stat. tit. 886.
Pennsylvania, Pa. Cons. Stat., § 18.3129.
Rhode Island, R.I. Gen. Laws § 11-10-1.
South Carolina, S.C. Code Ann. § 16-15-120.
Utah, Utah Code Ann. § 76-9-301.8.
Virginia, Va. Code Ann. § 18.2-361.
Wisconsin, Wis. Stat. § 944.17.

Shearing of Horses
Minnesota, Minn. Stat. § 323.46.
Rhode Island, R.I. Gen. Laws § 4-1-6.

Standards in Animal Control Facilities and Pet Stores
Arizona, Animal Care Requirements, pet dealer, § 44-1799.04.
California, Requirements for care of dogs, § 122155.
Colorado, Animal Shelters, § 18.00; Pet Animal Dealerships, § 11.00.
Georgia, Animal Protection, § 40-13-13.
Iowa, Care of Animals in Commercial Establishments, § 162.1-20.
Kansas, Animal Pounds and Shelters, § 9–22–1; Pet Shops, § 9-20-1.
Michigan, Pet Shops, Dog Pounds, and Animal Shelters, § 285.151.
Missouri, Animal Care Facilities, § 30-9.030.
Nevada, Care of Animals, § 574.210.
North Carolina, Animal Welfare Section, 52j.0200–0210.

Tail Docking, Horses
California, Cal. Penal Code § 597n.
Connecticut, Conn. Gen. Stat. § 53-251.
Illinois, 720 Ill. Comp. Stat. 315/1.
Maine, Me. Rev. Stat. Ann. § 17A-510.
Massachusetts, Mass. Gen. Laws ch. 272 § 79A.
Michigan, Mich. Comp. Laws § 28.255.
Minnesota, Minn. Stat. § 343.25.
New Hampshire, N.H. Rev. Stat. Ann. § 644:8-b.
New York, N.Y. Agriculture and Markets Law § 368.
Ohio, Ohio Rev. Code Ann. § 959.14.
South Carolina, S.C. Code Ann. § 47-1-60.
Washington, Wash. Rev. Code § 16.52.090.

Transportation of Horses
California, Cal. Penal § 597o.
Connecticut, Conn. Gen. Stat. § 22-415-2.
Minnesota, Minn. Stat. § 346.38.
New York, N.Y. Agriculture and Markets Law § 26-359-a.
Pennsylvania, 18 Pa. Cons. Stat. § 5511.
Vermont, Vt. Stat. Ann. tit. 13-387.

Tripping or Poling of Horses
California, Cal. Penal Code § 597g.
Florida, Fla. Stat. Ann. § 46-828.12.
Illinois, 510 Ill. Comp. Stat. 70/5.01.
Kansas, Kan. Stat. Ann., § 21.4310.
Maine, Me. Rev. Stat. Ann. tit. 7 § 3972.
New Mexico, N.M. Stat. Ann. § 30-18-11.
Oklahoma, Okla. Stat. tit. 21-1700.
Texas, Tex. Penal Code Ann. § 9-42.09.

Federal Cases
Supreme Court
   Kleppe v. New Mexico, 426 U.S. 529 (1976).
   Miller v. California, 413 U.S. 15 (1973).
   Sentell v. New Orleans & Carroliton Railroad Co., 166 U.S. 698 (1897).

Circuit Courts of Appeals
   American Horse Protection Association v. Lyng, 812 F.2d 1 (D.C. Cir. 1987).
   American Horse Protection Association v. Yeutter, 917 F.2d 594 (D.C.
      Cir. 1990).
   Animal Protection Institute v. Hodel, 860 F.2d 920 (9th Cir. 1988).
   Fallini v. Hodel, 783 F.2d 1343 (9th Cir. 1986).
   Stack v. Killian, 96 F.3d 159 (6th Cir. 1996).
   United States v. Thomas, 74 F. 3d 701 (6th Cir. 1996).

District Courts
   American Horse Protection Association v. Frizzell, 403 F. Supp. 1206 (D.
      Nev. 1975).

State Cases
California
   People v. Speegle, 62 Cal. Rptr. 2d 384 (Cal. Ct. App. 1997).

Indiana
   Lykins v. State, 726 N.E. 2d 1265 (Ind. Ct. App. 2000).

Kansas
Hearn v. City of Overland Park, 772 P.2d 758 (Kan.), *cert. denied* 493 U.S. 976 (1989).
State v. Rodriguez, 8 P.3d 712 (Kan. 2000).

Missouri
Missouri v. Stout, 958 S.W.2d 32 (Mo. Ct. App. 1997).

Nebraska
State v. Schott, 384 N.W.2d 620 (Neb. 1986).

New Mexico
New Mexico v. Cleve, 980 P. 2d 23 (N.M. 1999).

North Carolina
State v. Fowler, 205 S.E.2d 740 (N.C. Ct. App. 1974).

Ohio
State v. Anderson, 566 N.E.2d 1224 (Ohio) *cert. denied,* 501 U.S. (1991).

Oregon
State v. Kittles, No. 93–6346 (1995) (unreported case), *cert. denied,* 936 P.2d 363 (Or. 1997).

Pennsylvania
Hulsizer v. Labor Day Committee, 718 A.2d 865 (Pa. 1999).

Books

American Law Institute. 1985. *Model Penal Code.* Philadelphia: American Law Institute.
Beirne, Piers. 1998. "Bestiality." In *Encyclopedia of Animal Rights and Animal Welfare.* Edited by Marc Bekoff. Westport, CT: Greenwood.
Bestrup, Craig. 1997. *Disposable Animals: Ending the Tragedy of Throwaway Pets.* Leander, TX: Camino Bay Books.
Branigan, Cynthia A. 1997. *The Reign of the Greyhound.* New York: Howell Book House.
Brooman, Simon, and Debbie Legge. 1997. *Law Relating to Animals.* London: Cavendish.
Budiansky, Stephen. 1997. *The Nature of Horses.* London: Weidenfeld and Nicolson.
Bunting, Greta. 1997. *The Horse: The Most Abused Domestic Animal.* Toronto: University of Toronto Press.
Caras, Roger A. 1985. *Harper's Illustrated Handbook of Dogs.* New York: HarperPerrenial.

Curtis, Patricia. 1984. *The Animal Shelter.* New York: E. P. Dutton.

Fekety, Sally. 1998. "Shelters." In *Encyclopedia of Animal Rights and Animal Welfare.* Edited by Marc Bekoff. Westport, CT: Greenwood.

Francione, Gary L. 1995. *Animals, Property, and the Law.* Philadelphia: Temple University Press.

Frasch, Pamela D., et al. 2000. *Animal Law.* Durham, NC: Carolina Academic Press.

Leavitt, Emily Stewart, and Diane Halverson. 1990. "The Evolution of Anti-Cruelty Laws in the United States." In *Animals and Their Legal Rights.* 4th ed. Washington, DC: Animal Welfare Institute.

McCrea, Roswell C. [1910] 1969. *The Humane Movement.* New York: McGrath (New York: Columbia University Press, 1910).

Olsen, Stanley J. 1985. *Origins of the Domestic Dog.* Tucson: University of Arizona Press.

Randolph, Mary. 1995. *Dog Law.* 2d ed. Berkeley, CA: Nolo Press.

Stevens, Christine. 1990. "Dogs." In *Animals and Their Legal Rights.* 4th ed. Washington, DC: Animal Welfare Institute.

Toby, Milton C., and Karen L. Perch. 1999. *Understanding Equine Law.* Lexington, KY: The Blood-Horse, Inc.

Twyne, Pearl, and Valerie Stanley. 1990. "Horses." In *Animals and Their Legal Rights.* 4th ed. Washington, DC: Animal Welfare Institute.

Articles and Reports

American Veterinary Medical Association. 1993. "1993 Report of the AVMA Panel on Euthanasia." *Journal of the American Veterinary Medical Association* 202: 229–249.

Carmel, Krystyna M. 1994. "The Equine Liability Acts: A Discussion of Those in Existence and Suggestions for a Model Act." *Kentucky Law Journal* 83: 157–196.

Donald, Rhonda Lucas. 1991. "The No-Kill Controversy." *Shelter Sense* (September): 3–6.

Favre, David, and Vivien Tsang. 1993. "The Development of Anti-Cruelty Laws during the 1800's." *Detroit College of Law Review* 1: 1–35.

Frasch, Pamela D., et al. 1999. "State Animal Anti-Cruelty Statutes: An Overview." *Animal Law* 5: 69–80.

Handy, Geoffrey L. 1993. "Local Animal Control Management." *MIS Report* 25, no. 9 (September): 1–20.

———. 1994. "Handling Animal Collectors." *Shelter Sense* (May-June): 3–10.

Lake, Aaron. 2000. "1999 Legislative Review." *Animal Law* 6: 151–178.

Lockwood, Randall. 1993/1994. "The Psychology of Animal Collectors." *Trends* 9, no. 6: 18–21.

Maggitti, Phil. 1995. "Reining in the Carriage Trade." *The Animals' Agenda* 15, no. 4 (July-August): 16–19.

Marquis, Joshua. 1996. "The *Kittles* Case and Its Aftermath" *Animal Law* 2: 197–201.

Patronek, Gary J. 1999. "Hoarding of Animals: An Under-Recognized Public Health Problem in a Difficult-to-Study Population." *Public Health Reports* 114: 81–87.

Scheiner, Craig Ian. 1999. "Statutes with Four Legs to Stand On?: An Examination of 'Cruelty to Police Dog' Laws." *Animal Law* 5: 177–225.

Sturla, Kim. 1997. "Fixing the Feline." *The Animals' Agenda* 17, no. 5 (September-October): 33–36.

———. 1997. "The Role of Animal Shelters." *The Animals' Agenda* 17, no. 2 (March-April): 40–46.

World Wide Web

American Association for Horsemanship Safety, http://www.law.utexas.edu/dawson/index.htm.

Animal and Plant Health Inspection Service, USDA, http://www.aphis.usda.gov.

Animal Sheltering, http://www.hsus.org/programs/companion/animal_shelters.html.

Bureau of Land Management, National Wild Horse and Burro Program. http://wildhorseandburro.blm.gov/.

Dog Owner's Guide, Dogs and the Law, http://www.canismajor.com/dog/laws1.html.

Horse Protection Act, http://www.aphis.usda.gov/oa/pubs/fshpa.html.

Horse Protection Strategic Plan, http://www.aphis.usda.gov/oa/pubs/hpa.html.

Humane Society of the United States, http://www.hsus.org.

KBR's World of Wild Horses and Burros, http://www.kbrhorse.net/whb/blmhorse.html.

Puppy Mills, http://www.puppymills.com.

State Anticruelty Laws, http://www.law.utexas.edu/dawson/cruelty/cruelty.htm.

Tennessee Walking Horse Abuse, http://www.hsus.org/info/twhfacts.html.

4. Animal Agriculture

LEGAL REGULATION OF THE TREATMENT OF FARM ANIMALS

Animal agriculture utilizes several different domestic species to produce meat, milk, and eggs for human consumption, as well as hides and fur, mainly for clothing. In the United States during 1999 these commodities were generated from almost 9 billion animals.

Over 90 percent of this total were chickens: 8 billion "broilers" killed for food and 322 million "battery hens," egg-laying birds. Most of the remaining animals are other birds and mammals slaughtered for meat: 273 million turkeys, 23 million ducks, 101 million hogs, 37 million cows—including over 1 million calves eaten as veal—nearly 4 million sheep and lambs, 432,000 goats, and 77,000 horses (for dog and cat food, and for export to countries where horse flesh is consumed). Rounding out the sum are just over 9 million cows milked for dairy products, and 3 million mink killed for their fur (*see* this chapter: *Fur Farming*). Also to be accounted for in animal agriculture are about 4 million wild animals trapped in nature, their pelts stripped and sold into the garment industry (*see* this chapter: *Commercial Trapping*).

Such numbers are very difficult to grasp—to try to get a handle on them, consider that a stack of 2 billion $1 bills would be as tall as the Empire State Building. Despite the vast numbers, animal agriculture is the most lightly regulated domain of animal use in America today.

Cows and Hogs

The dairy industry exemplifies this dearth of legal attention to farm animal welfare. Currently, there are no state or federal laws specifically designed to safeguard dairy cows. About 90 percent of these animals are Holsteins, most held in strict confinement situations on farms in Wisconsin, Minnesota, New York, Pennsylvania, Michigan, and Ohio. Tied to a stall for twenty or more hours every day, standing on a concrete floor, dairy cows are given little or no opportunity to groom, exercise, or socialize with conspecifics. In the western states, especially California and Texas, the animals are often kept outdoors in groups where they can move about with some freedom, but there are no legal requirements to provide these animals with shade, heat, windbreaks, or shelter, nor to ensure that the corrals are adequately drained and cleaned. Dairy cows are milked by mechanical pumps two or three times every day for the ten-month period of lactation that follows the birth of a calf, an event biologically necessary to produce milk.

The calves born to dairy cows are usually removed from their mothers immediately, although some farmers allow a few days of suckling before separation. If the calf is female, it is likely to become another dairy cow;

if male, it is often taken to a veal stall. Here, the animal is tethered into a narrow space without straw or bedding of any kind, unable to turn around, lie down, or groom. During its entire three-month existence, it is fed an iron-poor diet of milk to make its flesh pale rather than beef-red, while the total confinement keeps the muscles soft and tender—the defining features of veal.

These methods of veal production are legal everywhere in the United States (the United Kingdom banned them in 1987). However, in May 2000 Representative Gary Ackerman of New York introduced a bill on Capitol Hill demanding humane living conditions for veal calves. H.R. 4415 requires farmers to allow calves the freedom to turn around, lie down, and groom normally. The bill further stipulates that "[t]he calf must be fed a daily diet containing sufficient iron." At this writing, the proposal is being studied by a House subcommittee on livestock.

The cattle that end up as steaks and hamburgers are born on ranches or beef farms. Every state produces beef cattle, but almost half of these animals are found up the middle of the country in Texas, Oklahoma, Kansas, Nebraska, Missouri, and Iowa. There are some thirty different breeds of beef cattle, with the Angus and Hereford varieties dominating. Usually within the first two months of their lives, cows of all breeds are branded with hot irons to identify them as the property of the ranch, and all males are castrated with a knife to make them less aggressive and to control bovine reproduction (this procedure produces a "steer"). Most cattle also have their horns removed to prevent lacerated hides and bruising. Dehorning of calves is done by chemical or hot iron burning of the budding appendage, or, in older animals, by instruments that gouge the horn out of the skull. No state or federal law prohibits any of these procedures—indeed cows *must* be branded in most western states—and no law requires pain relief during or after branding, castration, or dehorning. In practice, the use of anesthesia is rare at best.

Cattle usually spend eight or nine months with the herd, primarily fending for themselves on pasture or rangeland. When the rancher believes the time is right, the animals are rounded up and transported in large, tightly packed tractor-trailers to a feedlot for "finishing." Unless the journey lasts longer than one day, no state or federal law demands that the cattle be fed, watered, or rested before reaching their destination (*see* this chapter: *Twenty-Eight Hour Law of 1994*). The average feedlot holds about 10,000 cows in a series of corrals edged by a concrete feed trough. Here, they are fed a high-calorie diet consisting mainly of corn and soy meal, usually laced with a growth promotant to accelerate the process of bringing them to the market weight of about 1,000 pounds. Some beef producers buy "feeder calves" of four to six months old and ship them immediately to feedlots for fattening. There is no legal regulation of the conditions at feedlots, operations that are usually exposed to all the vagaries of the weather, and cloaked in dust and the stench of cattle waste.

When the market weight is attained, the cows are loaded onto the trucks once again and transported to the slaughterhouse. Upon arrival, the handling and killing of the animals becomes subject to state and federal laws requiring that the process be accomplished humanely, as legally defined (*see* this chapter: *Humane Methods of Slaughter Act of 1978*). Cattle are driven single file down a corridor into a restraint device, immobilized, stunned by a mechanical blow to the head, shackled and hoisted by one leg, and their throats cut. The animals then bleed to death.

The methods and structure of hog farming vary widely, depending on whether the operation is a small, family-owned farm of less than 100 animals, or a huge, corporate facility that processes hundreds of thousands of pigs each year. Like all animal agriculture, in the last twenty years or so the business has become concentrated into a number of large corporations. Due to this trend, most pigs spend their entire lives—about six months—in large, warehouse-like buildings that are designed to feed, water, and remove the manure of thousands of animals automatically. Iowa is by far the leader in these operations. To control their growth and development, and to facilitate this automation, some degree of confinement is required, ranging from complete detainment for each individual in a narrow stall, to small holding areas confining several hogs at a time.

Pregnant sows spend the sixteen-week gestation period in stalls or larger pens. During the last week of the pregnancy and the first two or three weeks after the birth of the piglets, sometimes longer, the sow is restricted to the tight quarters of a farrowing or "gestation stall," where she cannot walk or turn around. The Florida legislature is presently considering a bill to outlaw these stalls, but meanwhile they are legal everywhere. Newborn pigs are injected with antibiotics, their "needle" teeth are clipped, their tails removed, and their ears notched for identification. After weaning at about two weeks, males are castrated, and all pigs are taken to the automated growing building. They remain here for about twenty weeks, and are then shipped off to the slaughterhouse. Here, the pigs are typically rendered unconscious by an electric current, and then killed by bleeding. As with cattle, the treatment of hogs in the United States is essentially unregulated by law until they are transported, and once the process of slaughter begins.

Chickens

Chickens begin their brief lives in a hatcher. Once they break out of their eggs, their fate is a function of the facility in which they find themselves. If it is for egg production, males must first be separated from females. The males are usually killed: they may be decapitated, asphyxiated with carbon dioxide, piled into heavy-duty plastic bags and suffocated, or simply ground up alive as meal for other animals. There are no legal restrictions on the disposal of chicks.

The beaks of the females are immediately cut off with a hot blade so they will not peck and injure one another in the crowded conditions of a fully automated "layer house" holding as many as 80,000 birds. Debeaking is not regulated by law in any state. The laying hens are jammed into 12-inch by 18-inch wire enclosures known as "battery cages," three to five or even six birds in each cage, and stacked in tiers. In such a predicament, nearly every natural behavior of the birds is utterly thwarted: they cannot fly, walk, preen, stretch, roost, nest, dust-bathe, or peck or scratch for food.

Switzerland banned all battery cages in 1991, Sweden did the same in 1998, and the European Union announced in June 1999 that these cages will be illegal in all member nations by 2012. In contrast, neither the federal government nor any of the American states has prohibited the battery cage, or limited the number of birds per cage or stipulated its size. In the state of Washington, a bill requiring at least 86 square inches of floor space for each bird died in committee in July 2000. A battery cage with four birds gives each 54 inches of floor space, about the same area as the cover of a phone book.

To increase egg production, most egg farmers induce or "force" molting in their laying hens. This is done by withholding food from the birds for one or two weeks, and water for two or three days. The deprivation is quite stressful and causes the chickens to lose up to one quarter of their body weight and shed their feathers—the molt. Once food and water are restored, laying rebounds vigorously, with bigger eggs in greater quantities. The method is not restricted by any law. Concern about the intentional starvation that characterizes forced molting generated substantial criticism in the late 1990s, prompting one California state legislator to sponsor a bill banning the practice, and a poultry welfare organization to petition the U.S. Department of Agriculture (USDA) to do the same, so far to no avail. The California bill did not make it out of the Agriculture Committee, and the USDA claims to have no authority to prohibit forced molting.

For their part, "broiler" chickens, mostly males, are raised from one day old in large warehouses with populations of 10,000 to 20,000. About half of these birds are concentrated in Arkansas, Alabama, and Georgia. They, too, are debeaked and their toes are also removed, both measures to reduce injuries inflicted on other birds in their increasingly cramped quarters. At little more than six weeks, their rapid growth filling every inch of available floor space in the broiler house, they reach their market weight of about four pounds. The chickens are then packed alive into crates and shipped on trucks to the slaughterhouse. Here, they are hung by their feet from shackles on a conveyor line. Many poultry processors then dip the birds in an electrically charged water tank, intended to stun them to unconsciousness, but just one state requires stunning. From there, the conveyor takes the hanging poultry to a rotating circular blade that passes over their necks, and they bleed to death.

At this writing, California is the only state that has enacted a humane slaughter law for poultry, requiring processors to ensure that all chickens, turkeys, and ducks are unconscious before being cut, shackled, or hoisted (the ritual slaughter of poultry in the Golden State has been disputed as in violation of this law; *see* this chapter: *Legal Challenges to Ritual Slaughter: Farm Sanctuary, Inc. v. Department of Food and Agriculture*). Congress drafted the Humane Methods of Slaughter Act so that it does not apply to poultry, and state humane slaughter laws followed suit.

Similarly, the transportation of poultry is not covered by the federal Twenty-Eight Hour Law, and only four states regulate this practice: Connecticut, Pennsylvania, Rhode Island, and Wisconsin. The Connecticut and Rhode Island statutes are nearly identical, both requiring that poultry be shipped in "sanitary" crates or containers with "sufficient" ventilation and heating; "unnecessary suffering" must be avoided by providing "reasonable care." In Wisconsin, it is illegal "to so crowd and congest . . . chickens within any coop in any shipment so as to impair the well-being of such chickens during the course of transportation." Fines for violation in these states range from $10 to $100, with ten to thirty days in jail.

State Anticruelty Laws and Farm Animals

Every state prohibits cruelty to animals, and nearly all of these statutes are written to cover "any animal" (*see* chapter 3: *Anticruelty Laws*). Even so, thirty of the states have specifically excluded "customary," or "normal," or "accepted" uses of animals in agriculture from the protections of their anticruelty laws, with over half of these exemptions added since 1985. In these states, the farming practices briefly described above—branding, castration, forced molting, the use of the gestation stall and the battery cage, and the others—*could not* be found legally cruel by any court. A federal district court ruled in 1986 that hot iron branding on the face of cows is cruel and inhumane, but this is indisputably not the normal or customary location for a brand (*Humane Society v. Lyng*).

A provocative 1997 ruling by an English judge has eroded the legal principle that normal agricultural uses of animals are not cruel. Commonly known as the "McLibel Case," the decision culminated the longest litigation in the history of England's court system, a seven-year battle between the McDonald's Corporation and two working-class citizens of London. In 1991 McDonald's sued the defendants for libel after they distributed pamphlets containing numerous incendiary accusations against the company. Among other things, McDonald's was said to be responsible for destroying the rainforest, exploiting the poor and hungry, causing cancer and heart disease, and perpetrating the "torture and murder" of farm animals.

According to Mr. Justice Bell, the defendants failed to show that several of their claims were true, but he did hold that a number of standard farming practices were proved to be cruel. Among others, he cited the battery cage, the gassing of chicks with carbon dioxide, the crowding of "broilers" in their last days before slaughter, and the gestation stall for hogs (*McDonald's Corporation v. Steel*). No court in the Anglo-American world (or probably anywhere) had ever come to such a startling conclusion, and it remains to be seen what, if any, effect it will have on the legal regulation of animal agriculture on either side of the Atlantic.

In America individuals working in animal agriculture are very rarely charged with violating a state anticruelty statute, and convictions are even more uncommon. Guilty verdicts in these few cases are almost invariably for extreme neglect of farm animals, which courts find not to be customary or normal. For example, in 1984 a Nebraska rancher was convicted under the state anticruelty law for failing to provide food and water for dozens of his cattle and hogs; forty-seven of the animals starved to death (*State v. Schott*). More recently, a Pennsylvania man was found guilty in 1993 of cruelty to numerous horses he had stopped feeding. He unsuccessfully argued that withholding food was a standard practice for doomed horses, because he intended to send them off to a slaughterhouse (*Commonwealth v. Barnes*).

Convictions for positive acts of abuse of farm animals are the most infrequent judgments in an already minuscule collection. The first and so far only occasion on which a meat processor has been found guilty of cruelty to animals came in April 1993 when Lancaster Stockyards in Pennsylvania received a $222 fine for refusing to euthanize a downed cow. Most recently, in July 1999 three employees of Belcross Farms in North Carolina were charged with felony animal abuse for beating downed hogs with metal bars and pipe wrenches, and for skinning pigs that were still alive and conscious. This was the first time anyone working in animal agriculture had been indicted for a felony violation (no state provided felony status for an anticruelty violation before 1985; *see* chapter 3: *Anticruelty Laws: Exceptions and Penalties*). However, in a plea bargain agreement, the three defendants admitted guilt to misdemeanor charges, and were sentenced in May 2000. The harshest penalty was five months in jail and a $2,200 fine.

ANIMAL SLAUGHTER

Cows and pigs were aboard nearly every vessel carrying European colonists to the New World, the animals serving as provisions to be killed and eaten in due time. As early as 1627, there were several thousand head of cattle in Virginia, a stock begun twenty years before with the herds at Jamestown, the first British settlement in America. English cattle from Devon were first imported into the Massachusetts Bay Colony in 1624, and by the middle of the century most settlers in New England were well supplied with cows.

Hernando de Soto's expedition through present-day Florida, Georgia, and Alabama in 1539 and 1540 left behind scores of hogs, many of which turned feral, available to be appropriated and domesticated by anyone wishing to do so or simply shot wherever they were found. By the seventeenth century, the Carolinas and Georgia were nearly overrun with wild pigs flourishing on acorns and peaches, and the rich piedmont country also provided luxuriant fodder for the cattle driven down from Virginia. Sheep were much slower to catch on in the colonies—easily ravaged by wolves, the species often proved too fragile for the harsh extremes of weather found in the New World.

Livestock Slaughter in the Colonies and in Nineteenth-Century America

The killing of livestock was performed by the first settlers as they and their ancestors had done in Europe for centuries. This occurred in the fall and through the early winter, the "killing time" when the weather was cool enough to prevent the meat from spoiling in this era before refrigeration. Usually, the animals were beaten over the head with an ax or heavy hammer and then hoisted by one leg with a block and tackle attached to the stalwart beams of the barn or a stout tree limb out in the yard. Once dangled, their throats were cut, and, after the bleeding was through, the carcasses were "dressed"—beheaded, delimbed, eviscerated, skinned, and cut into manageable pieces. The meat was preserved for the coming year and the warm summer months by dry-curing with salt, smoking, or by pickling, this last the process of packing the meat in barrels filled with brine and saltpeter.

As the years went by and the immigrants proliferated, clusters of homesteads began to concentrate and evolve as towns in a steady process of urbanization, with livestock raising pushed to the fringes and out into the country. The new settlements were increasingly occupied by individuals with little or no connection to the farm, yet who still demanded meat. Initially, farmers would travel to the markets in Salem, Boston, New York, and Philadelphia to sell their already packed beef and pork, or they would bring live animals to be slaughtered and dressed on a spot near the market stalls, usually close to fresh water. Over time, ramshackle structures were thrown up at these customary killing spots, and the first slaughterhouses were born. Here farmers could perform the operation themselves or pay someone a small fee to do it for them. Early entrepreneurs of the fledgling meat industry claimed title to the property on which the killing was done and became the first proprietors in the business of livestock slaughter.

Eventually the sight of animals being destroyed in the middle of the city became abhorrent to the citizenry in numerous municipalities. Repelled by the stench and the gore, they passed laws banishing the nascent slaughterhouses to the outskirts of town. For example, slaughter was done just off Wall Street in New York for better than twenty years until it was ordered outside the city in 1676. This kind of restriction, akin to modern zoning laws, was the first form of slaughterhouse regulation, and obviously had nothing to do with animal welfare.

The disaffection with public slaughter provoking the legal exile of killing operations replayed a familiar pattern long established in cities and towns throughout Europe. There, the sentiment of the citizenry ultimately recoiled at the conspicuous display of animal butchery in their midst, a sight quite common in the Middle Ages, and the killing was moved to the periphery. Indeed, the definition of *abattoir* that appeared for one hundred years in every edition of the standard dictionary of the French language, after noting that it was a "[p]lace set aside for the slaughter of animals," observed that "[a]battoirs are located outside the surrounding walls of towns."

By the middle of the eighteenth century, slaughterhouses, raised in association with meat markets and packers, were common in and around the major urban centers of the eastern seaboard from Boston to Charleston, with one of the largest in Brighton, Massachusetts. After the Revolutionary War, the center of livestock raising, and therefore livestock slaughtering and packing, began to shift to the Ohio River country, a region substantially cleared of Indian resistance in the 1790s. Within a few decades Cincinnati was established as the frontier's foremost butcher and packer, especially of hogs, and by the 1850s it led the nation, slaughtering nearly half a million animals in a single, four-month season.

Chicago was not far behind. After the construction of the first slaughterhouse there in 1827, the community steadily grew, and two more decades saw new railroad spurs radiating out from the city to points east and south. As stockyards were built to confine the animals in excess of those needed to feed the local population, and competitors on the Illinois River languished without access to the rail lines, Chicago became the preeminent source of butchered and packaged meat, reaching the half million mark slaughtered in 1862. An early, and by now customary, sign of its emergence in the industry was an 1849 ordinance banning "the erection of slaughterhouses within the city of Chicago" and forbidding continued slaughter in already existing establishments.

Although the industry both in the east and the midwest began with slaughtering facilities separated from the meat packinghouses, the two operations usually combined very quickly to form a brutally efficient "disassembly" process. In the nineteenth century, as in the two centuries preceding, there was no legal regulation whatever of this disassembly or any of the preparations for it. Livestock were handled and slaughtered in any manner the packers chose.

In the typical hog operation, as exemplified in Cincinnati, the animals were driven with whips and clubs into a small pen connected to the slaughterhouse, crowded together until not one more animal would fit in the enclosure. Then a worker would walk over the backs of the pigs, striking them in the head, one after another, with a two-pointed hammer. It was not uncommon for stricken swine to have been merely knocked off their feet, rather than rendered unconscious or killed. Nonetheless, the animals were then impaled with hooks and dragged to a room where their throats were cut, and they were hung up to bleed out. After this, the carcasses passed to a huge vat of hot water, and then to a series of men, each performing a specified task: cutting out the inner ears, pulling off hair and bristles, hanging the bodies on hooks, stripping out the entrails, cutting off the head.

In Chicago, as in many other locations, the slaughtering of cattle proceeded by herding the animals single file to a man who stunned them with a sledgehammer or "pole ax," a two-headed tool with a spike or hammer opposite a blade. Notoriously, cattle often required multiple blows before they would go down, depending on the skill of the man at hitting a squirming, fractious animal. Once felled, however, as with hogs, the cow was then hoisted by one leg, cut, bled, and then shuttled from one worker to the next, by increments skinned, beheaded, eviscerated, and further processed into a food product. The largest slaughterhouses of the 1850s could kill and process 250 cows each day. In the late twentieth century, cattle could be transformed from living animals to ready-to-cook carcasses at the rate of 250 each *hour*.

Legal Regulation of Animal Slaughter

Were these methods of handling and slaughtering livestock in the 1800s cruel and inhumane? Illinois passed an anticruelty law in 1869 and Ohio did the same in 1880. Most of the northeastern states had done so before the Civil War, and all forty-six states of the Union had such a law before that century turned. However, most of these statutes specifically exempted "normal" or "accepted" agricultural practices involving livestock, or defined "animal" as not including those on the farm (*see also* this chapter: *Legal Regulation of the Treatment of Farm Animals: State Anticruelty Laws and Farm Animals*).

For the other states without explicit exclusions, it was simply assumed that killing animals for food did not qualify as an "unnecessary" or "unjustifiable" infliction of pain and suffering, the sort of offense prohibited by anticruelty statutes. Evidently, the slaughtering of livestock was never challenged in a court as a violation of one of these laws. In those days, federal regulation of the treatment of animals was confined entirely to the Twenty-Eight Hour Law, which required that livestock transported by rail be fed and watered if they were shipped for at least that length of time (*see* this chapter: *Twenty-Eight Hour Law*). Even though most European countries had passed some form of a humane slaughter law by the early 1950s—Switzerland leading the way in 1874—in the middle of the twentieth century the United States still had no legal restrictions of any kind on the killing of animals for human consumption.

This state of affairs slowly began to change in 1955. Senator Hubert Humphrey, appalled at slaughtering practices that were substantially unchanged since the rise of the industry over 200 years earlier, sponsored a revolutionary new bill. It required meatpackers to render animals unconscious before any cutting, hoisting, or shackling could be done; Representative Martha Griffiths proposed a companion bill in the House. This initial attempt was dismissed as unnecessary by the U.S. Department of Agriculture (USDA) and its secretary, Ezra Taft Benson, who claimed that business could promote humane slaughter better than lawmakers. These first bills never received a hearing.

The next year Humphrey chaired an agriculture subcommittee devoted to the issue, and hearings began in earnest. Over in the House, a similar subcommittee led by W. R. Poage decided to study the matter in the field by touring some Chicago slaughterhouses. The representatives witnessed for themselves the primitive and clumsy manner in which cows and pigs were bludgeoned and bled. For some hogs, no attempt was made at stunning—they were simply noosed by one leg with a chain and dragged to the man who slit their throats. Although much impressed and thoroughly appalled, Poage's subcommittee did not succeed in bringing the bill up for a vote in 1956, and neither did Humphrey's. Nonetheless, the forces for compulsory humane slaughter were gathering momentum.

In 1957 hearings were held before the full House Agricultural Committee, with the Animal Welfare Institute, the American Humane Association, the Humane Society of the United States, and many other animal advocacy organizations lining up against Benson's USDA, the American

Meat Institute, and the National Cattlemen's Association. The opposition was formidable, but the tide had turned and in February 1958 Poage's humane slaughter bill easily passed after a full House vote. Yet it still had to clear the Senate. There, the meat packers' lobbyists managed to influence the Senate Agriculture Committee to gut the proposed law of all the language mandating humane slaughter and replace it with a directive to continue researching the matter. After the maneuver was widely reported by the print media in June, the public was incited for the first time.

Sparked by newspaper editorials expressing shock and outrage, citizens bombarded their senators with demands to restore the deleted requirements. Hubert Humphrey and seventeen other senators championed a reanimation of the bill originally passed by the House, with Humphrey leading an all-day filibuster to defeat the new, severely diluted study bill that came out of the Senate committee. Finally, to the chagrin of the Agriculture Committee, Senate Majority Leader Lyndon Johnson called for a vote on the new Senate bill. It was narrowly defeated, forty-three to forty. With the last major obstacle cleared, the Senate overwhelmingly approved Humphrey's bill. The Humane Slaughter Act (HSA) was signed into law by President Dwight Eisenhower in August 1958, with a generous stipulation that it was not to go into effect until June 1960.

Humane Slaughter Act of 1960

The preamble of the Humane Slaughter Act (HSA) lists several justifications for legally regulating the killing of food animals, beginning with the acknowledgment that "humane methods in the slaughter of livestock prevent needless suffering." Section 2 announces that slaughter procedures must be humane, and goes on to identify the two methods found by Congress to so qualify. First, needless suffering is avoided when "all animals are rendered insensible to pain by a single blow or gunshot or an electrical, chemical or other means that is rapid and effective" before being gashed with knives, shackled, hoisted, or knocked down.

Although this core requirement of the HSA suggests that any animal used for food is to be killed humanely, in fact the law has never covered chickens or other poultry. Yet, at over 8 billion birds in 1999, these species account for about 95 percent of all animals slaughtered in the United States each year. The HSA applies just to the approximately 140 million hogs, cows, calves, sheep, and lambs annually killed for human consumption.

Also deemed humane in section 2(b) is ritual slaughter according to the tenets of any religious faith, specifically Judaism, that requires the "simultaneous and instantaneous severance of the carotid arteries with a sharp instrument." This provision of the act was insisted upon by Senator Jacob Javits of New York, who feared that the Humphrey-Poage bill would outlaw kosher slaughter. This is the standard method of killing the livestock permitted as food in the Jewish religion, which expressly requires that the animal remain conscious while its throat is cut. Halal slaughter, characteristic of Islam, directs a similar procedure and, because it is not explicitly mentioned, the HSA suggests that it, too, is humane. (For more on kosher and halal slaughter, *see* this chapter: *Ritual Slaughter of Animals.*)

Rather oddly, section 6 states that ritual slaughter is "exempted from the terms of this act," even though it had already been declared humane back in section 2. However, the point of section 6 is to permit the hoisting of conscious animals because 2(b) says nothing about *handling* during ritual slaughter counting as humane. A 1978 amendment to the HSA added a handling clause to 2(b) clearing up the ambiguity (*see* this chapter: *Ritual Slaughter of Animals*). Section 6 also provides an explicit assurance that the law does not inhibit the free practice of religion as protected by the First Amendment to the Constitution. (For more on the freedom of religion and animal killing as a religious practice, *see* this chapter: *Legal Challenges to Ritual Slaughter.*)

Finally, and rather ironically given his persistent opposition to the Humphrey-Poage bills, the HSA vested administrative authority in Secretary Benson of the USDA and ordered him to issue regulations specifying humane methods of slaughter by March 1, 1959. These regulations appeared in January 1959. Animal advocates have continuously questioned the wisdom of charging the USDA with implementing a humane slaughter law. After all, the agency steadfastly opposed the enactment of the HSA, and has traditionally supported the livestock and meatpacking interests that have always stubbornly resisted government regulation of their industry.

Congress also found that mandating humane slaughter not only smoothes and hastens business transactions involving livestock and the food products that come from them, it also "results in safer and better working conditions for persons engaged in the slaughtering industry." It is easy to see why this is so. Work in the slaughterhouse has always been among the most dangerous jobs in America, with one of the greatest risks of injury coming from the animals themselves. Once fitted with a manacle and lifted in the air, suspended by one leg, a conscious cow or horse will flail around wildly. Similarly, a pig, sliced open while still alert and aware, will violently thrash and strike out. Many workers have been battered by sharp hooves and teeth, or had their knives driven into their own faces, arms, chests, or other locations on their bodies, because they hoisted or cut conscious animals. The HSA is intended to promote occupational safety in the meatpacking industry by directing that only unconscious animals be processed. Although the incidence of on-the-job injuries in the industry has been reduced considerably since 1960, the rate for slaughterhouse workers is still one of the five highest of all occupations.

The HSA was quite radical at the time—recall that prior to its enactment there was no federal or state regulation of slaughter motivated by humanitarian concern—but it still contained two significant gaps. First, its scope was rather limited. The HSA applied only to packers supplying meat to the federal government, which left unregulated fully 20 percent of the companies slaughtering animals, and did not apply at all to the slaughter of animals in foreign countries importing meat to America. Second, the HSA provided no real mechanisms of enforcement, along with a very weak deterrent. It was viewed as "self-enforcing" because it required suppliers to sign a statement indicating that the meat came from animals killed in accordance with the HSA. Because making a false statement to the federal government is a felony, this was thought to provide a sufficient incentive to comply.

Even though by the mid-1970s better than three-quarters of American meatpackers reported that they had implemented humane slaughtering techniques, Senator Robert Dole of Kansas and Representative George Brown of California were not satisfied. Together, the two legislators authored amendments to the HSA in 1978 that expanded its range and created a device for enforcing the law.

HUMANE METHODS OF SLAUGHTER ACT OF 1978

The amendments to the Humane Slaughter Act (HSA) written by Senators Dole and Brown are mainly revisions of the Meat Inspection Act of 1906, which authorizes federal officials to scrutinize livestock for disease or other pathology before and after slaughter. These amendments, along with the surviving provisions of the HSA (two sections were repealed), are now collectively known as the Humane Methods of Slaughter Act (HMSA), signed into law by President Jimmy Carter in October 1978.

Strengthening the HSA

The HMSA expanded the coverage of the HSA, both domestically and abroad. Now, instead of relegating its protections to only those animals processed by companies with contracts to supply the federal government with meat, the new law declared that "No person, firm, or corporation shall, with respect to any cattle, sheep, swine, goats, horses, mules, or other equines . . . slaughter or handle in connection with slaughter any such animals in any manner not in accordance with [the Humane Slaughter Act]."

A serious weakness of the HSA had been that it did not supply any means of corroborating whether packers were employing methods of handling and slaughter identified as humane by the act and its federal regulations. Now, the HMSA charges USDA inspectors with the duty to examine slaughterhouse procedures and verify the humaneness of these methods. The inspectors work out of an office of the agency, the Food Safety and Inspection Service (FSIS). Further, FSIS inspectors are now empowered to "refuse to provide inspection or cause inspection to be temporarily suspended" if animals are not being slaughtered or handled humanely. This authority in effect gives inspectors the right to stop the production line—the flow of animals through the slaughtering process—preventing the product from reaching the market. This, of course, halts cash flow to the meatpacker and thus presents the company with a powerful economic incentive to comply with the HMSA.

These provisions of the HMSA are intended to ensure that nearly all slaughtering of livestock done in the United States is in compliance with the law. In 1999, 95 percent of the beef, veal, pork, and mutton packed and processed for human consumption came from 909 federally inspected slaughterhouses. This is less than half the total number of those facilities subject to federal review just a decade earlier. Like virtually every other dimension of agriculture in America, the transformation of living animals into food products has become increasingly concentrated in large corporations, as family-owned, small businesses either go under or are absorbed, unable to compete with the pricing system that trading in massive volumes allows.

Indeed, today one-half of all sales—over $40 billion—are enjoyed by the "Big Four" meat packers: Con Agra, Inc., of Omaha, Nebraska; IBP, Inc., of Dakota City, Nebraska; Cargill Meat Sector of Minneapolis, Minnesota; and Tyson Foods, Inc., of Springdale, Arkansas (dealing primarily in poultry). In 1980 fifty beef packing companies slaughtered two-thirds of the nation's cattle; in 2000, just Con Agra, Cargill, and IBP combined pack that much beef. A further concentration may be coming: in December 2000, IBP and Tyson began discussing a merger of the two food animal giants.

Most of the remaining 5 percent of nonfederally inspected operations come from about 2,400 very small packers overseen by state inspectors. State inspection is acceptable so long as the state has its own humane slaughter law—more than half of them do, and most of these are nearly identical to the federal law—and its standards of inspection for hygienic meat are consistent with those of the federal government.

The HMSA additionally required for the first time that imported meat be slaughtered according to the conditions of the act. Imports must also be inspected for disease, as specified by the Meat Inspection Act. In 1997 the United States imported over 2 billion pounds of meat from thirty-three countries, almost half of this total from Canada alone.

A foreign nation desiring to export meat to America is required to make a formal request to the FSIS, initiating an evaluation process of that nation's inspection system. The first step of the process is a review of documents included with the request detailing the foreign country's laws, regulations, resource allocation, and other information. A humane slaughter law consistent with the HMSA must be in place there. If the documentation reveals an acceptable inspection program of an efficient and legally humane meatpacking industry, FSIS officials travel to the country for an on-site review, evaluating their facilities, handling and slaughtering procedures, and in-plant inspection programs, verifying that the operation meets U.S. standards. Once approved by the FSIS, the foreign inspection program is "periodically reviewed" for continuing compliance; FSIS inspectors do not remain there.

American citizens bringing fifty pounds of meat or less from foreign countries for their own personal use are not required to prove that it came from an animal killed in a manner consistent with the HMSA. Exemptions from the directive to verify humane slaughter are also available for personal and "custom" slaughtering done domestically. Individuals who raise their own animals, such as on family farms, and do the slaughtering themselves to provide meat for personal or family consumption, or for their guests or employees, are not required to kill or handle these animals as prescribed by the HMSA and federal regulations. Similarly, such animals that are taken to a facility for a special, piecemeal slaughter are not protected by these laws, so long as the owner will not be selling the meat, but intends to feed it to his or her family, guests, or employees, or eat it himself or herself.

Livestock Slaughter and Humane Slaughter Regulations
Within little more than a year following the enactment of the HMSA in 1978, USDA secretary Bob Bergland issued regulations that for the first time governed the handling of livestock at FSIS-inspected facilities. Slaughter regulations have remained substantially unchanged since 1959 when they were first promulgated.

Animals typically arrive at meatpacking operations by truck, sometimes by rail, and are then off-loaded down ramps, through alleyways or driveways, and into holding pens or corrals before being driven into the slaughterhouse. HMSA regulations stipulate that corrals, ramps, chutes, gates, and driveways are to be maintained in good condition with splinters, broken boards, protruding nails, exposed bolts, or other sharp objects removed or repaired. Floor surfaces must be made slip resistant to provide secure footing, utilizing such materials as roughened or cleated cement for ramps and chutes, waffled floors, or sand.

The animals rarely spend more than twenty-four hours in a holding pen before they are killed, mainly because HMSA regulations demand that they must be fed if they are kept more than one day. Standard procedure at packinghouses is to deny livestock food for twenty-four hours prior to slaughter because the fasted (or "drift") animals bleed out more readily and are easier to "dress" (butcher). Whenever a holding period lasts all night, livestock need to be provided with sufficient space to lie down. Water must be available at all times in the corrals.

Livestock that arrive dying, diseased, or disabled must be separated from the healthy animals and moved to a covered area providing adequate protection from the weather. "Downer" animals—those unable to walk or stand due to injury or illness but remaining conscious—cannot be dragged to the shelter, instead they must be moved "on equipment suitable for such purposes." There, they await the FSIS inspector's decision on what is to be done with their bodies once they are killed.

In 1999 Representative Gary Ackerman of New York introduced legislation that would prevent "nonambulatory" livestock from coming to the slaughterhouse in the first place; a companion bill is being sponsored in the Senate by Daniel Akaka of Hawaii. Their proposal would amend the Packers and Stockyards Act to prohibit stockyard operators from transferring or marketing any animals that are unable to walk. Instead, the downed livestock must be humanely euthanized. At this writing, the "Downed Animal Protection Act" is still being debated on Capitol Hill. The federal bill is nearly identical to California's downed animal law; enacted in 1995, it is the only such state law in the country.

HMSA regulations also govern how the animals are to be driven into the holding pens, and then out of them and into the slaughterhouse—the rules for humane handling. This is to be done "with a minimum of excitement and discomfort to the animals," never forcing them to move faster than a normal walking speed. Metal pipes and sharp or pointed objects are not permitted for this purpose if the inspector believes their use would injure the animals or cause needless suffering. Electric prods, which send a jolt of current through the body when applied, are allowed so long as they are not turned up higher than fifty volts AC. All driving implements, such as switches and canvas slappers, should be used "as little as possible."

When the inevitable time comes, the animals are moved single file through a narrow driveway and into a chute leading to an apparatus that restrains each one individually. For cattle, the restrainer is known as a "knock box," and there the animal is rendered unconscious, usually with a blow to the head from a man called the "knocker" who wields a "captive bolt stunner." This device uses compressed-air or, less commonly, a 0.22 caliber charge to drive a steel bolt through a gun barrel and into the cow's skull, the bolt then immediately retracting.

The HMSA and its regulations demand that a stunner be applied only *once* for each animal—to dispense multiple hits for a single animal is illegal. There are two basic types of stunners, both approved by federal law: the nonpenetrating or concussion stunner has a flattened, circular bolt head (a "mushroom" stunner) that does not pierce the brain, while the penetrating type does. Regulations also note that "[t]he stunning operation is an exacting procedure that requires a well-trained and experienced operator. He must be able to place the stunning instrument to produce immediate unconsciousness." One of the most frequent criticisms of slaughterhouse procedures under the HMSA is that the stunners are incompetently employed, and either the animals are not knocked out before hoisting and cutting, or repeated hits are needed to produce unconsciousness.

Immediately after the stunning, the "shackler" attaches a manacle to one leg and the cow is hoisted by a chain attached to a conveyor belt, proceeding over to the "sticker," who makes a vertical (not horizontal) incision along the throat between the jaw and upper chest area. This cutting, called "sticking," severs the carotid arteries and the jugular vein, so the animal bleeds out as it slides along the "bleed rail." After the exsanguination (the actual cause of death) is complete, the carcass moves on to workers who skin out and remove the head, cut off the legs, remove the hide, eviscerate the internal organs, and cut the whole carcass in half.

According to HMSA regulations, cattle may also be stunned with electric devices (not permitted for horses); however, these are used infrequently on cows, and electrical stunning is much more often done with hogs, sheep, lambs, and calves. The typical electric stunner is a pincers-like mechanism with two electrodes that are placed on either side of the head. The regulations say only that "[s]uitable timing, voltage, and current control devices shall be used to ensure that each animal receives the necessary electrical charge to produce immediate unconsciousness" without specifying exactly what those parameters are. Standard practice in the industry is 70 to 90 volts and 0.3 amps for 2 to 10 seconds. In 1985 the FSIS approved electrical *slaughter* for hogs, sheep, lambs, and calves only, again without designating any values, although 400 volts with 1.7 amps at 5 seconds will cause cardiac arrest in these species. Chemical stunning with carbon dioxide is also permitted for these animals, and the HMSA regulations detail specifications for the gas, the "gas chamber," and its operator. Even so, this method—common in Europe—is rare in America.

Hogs are the most frequently slaughtered animal, with about 100 million annually accounting for nearly 70 percent of all livestock consumed in America (excepting poultry, which, again, are not covered by the HMSA). Before stunning, swine are driven into a "squeeze chute," a V-shaped contraption with moving sides that propel the animals to the stunner. Once unconscious, hogs are shackled, hoisted, and stuck. After bleeding, the bodies are conveyed to the "scalding tub" to loosen the hair on the carcass with hot water, and then on to a dehairing machine. Various butchers then remove the feet, skin, head, and internal organs, and the carcass is halved.

Finally, HMSA regulations approve the use of firearms for slaughtering livestock, including horses and mules, provided that "[t]he firearms shall be employed in the delivery of a bullet or projectile into the animal . . . so as to produce immediate unconsciousness in the animal by a single shot before it is shackled, hoisted, thrown, cast, or cut." No particular type of firearm or load is required or prohibited, recommended, or inadvisable. Even so, small-bore weapons must fire hollow-point bullets, frangible iron plastic composition bullets, or powdered iron projectiles, and black powder charges in muzzle-loading firearms must be fired "in close proximity with the skull of the animal." Other than these two stipulations, the regulations simply offer general directions to match the firepower used with the species, size, and gender of the animal so that immediate unconscious results from the shot. In any case, firearms slaughter is extremely rare in the meat industry because captive bolt and electrical stunners are so much cheaper to use.

RITUAL SLAUGHTER OF ANIMALS

Various religions around the world prescribe certain methods of killing animals before it is proper for humans to eat them. In America, such prescriptions from two of the great religious traditions have clashed with the aims of those concerned about animal welfare, a concern that has become written into statutory law. Both Judaism and Islam allow only certain animal species to enter the stomachs of their adherents, while prohibiting others. More importantly here, both faiths demand that the approved livestock first be slaughtered according to precise ritual specifications. For Jews, this is known as kosher slaughter, and for Muslims, acceptable slaughtering practices are halal. Although these practices are required by religious law, are they consistent with secular laws directing that food animals be killed humanely?

Kosher Slaughter

The term *kosher* derives from the Hebrew *kasher*, meaning "all right" or "permissible." Foods of any sort are called kosher if they are prepared and served according to the dietary rules of the Jewish religion. These rules were originally set down in the Torah (the first five books of the Christian Old Testament), specifically in the books of Leviticus and Deuteronomy. Kosher slaughter, or *Shehitah*, refers to a special method of killing animals for consumption by those who wish to abide by these dietary standards.

This method is not described in the Torah, but was later developed in the Talmud, a multivolume series of scriptural commentary. Cows, sheep, and chickens account for virtually all the animals currently subject to kosher slaughter. Jews are not permitted to eat pigs or any pork products.

To be designated kosher, the slaughter must satisfy two requirements. First, the animal must be killed by a man of recognized religious devotion (traditionally, women are not permitted to carry out this procedure). This individual is sometimes a rabbi, but more often he is an ordinary Jew of acknowledged piety who has received intensive training in the use and maintenance of a special knife resembling a straight razor, the *chalef*. Once the instruction is completed, the *shohet*, as he is now known, is qualified to slaughter permitted animals, not only to provide food for humans but as an act of veneration for God.

Kosher slaughter must be done by the *shohet* with a single, rapid cut, made without hesitation or delay, severing the jugular vein and the carotid artery. Burrowing, tearing, or ripping the animal are not permitted, and the incision must not be allowed to close back over the blade. When done properly, the stroke apparently causes little pain, and death follows in a minute or less as the animal bleeds out. The knife is sharpened and inspected regularly, eliminating any imperfections that would cause an increase of pain and inhibit making a clean incision; the blade must be free of any knicks, gouges, or dull spots.

The second condition for kosher slaughter is that the animal remain conscious during the cutting. Originally, the religious law stipulated that the animal be "moving" or, more accurately, that it be alive and healthy. This was intended to ensure that the meat was "clean," that people were not eating the flesh of animals dead for an indeterminate amount of time. The rule seems to have been based on hygienic concerns arising from a historic period long before refrigeration could preserve dead animal flesh and keep it safe for human consumption.

Critics of kosher slaughter have frequently charged that the requirement to cut only conscious animals is especially inhumane, a somewhat ironic objection because the original motivation for requiring conscious slaughter by an adept *shohet* was humaneness. This was thought to be more merciful than a bludgeoning that caused insensibility, or a clumsy or sloppy hatchet job. Nonetheless, kosher slaughter proved legally problematic in two different respects.

In the late 1950s a series of bills introduced on Capitol Hill insisted on a federal law requiring that animals be slaughtered compassionately. This was to be accomplished by first ensuring that livestock were unconscious before any cutting or bleeding was done, a measure precisely contrary to Jewish law that specifically prohibits the killing of an unconscious animal intended for use as human food. Senator Jacob Javits of New York and several Jewish organizations staunchly resisted this stipulation of the proposed legislation on the grounds that it would criminalize kosher slaughter, which, they argued, was a bona fide religious practice constitutionally protected by the First Amendment guarantee of the free exercise of religion.

In the spirit of compromise, the concerns of Javits and his allies were accommodated in the bill eventually passed by Congress and signed by President Dwight Eisenhower in 1958. The Humane Slaughter Act (and its 1978 incarnation, the Humane Methods of Slaughter Act) declares humane "slaughtering in accordance with the ritual requirements of the Jewish faith . . . whereby the animal suffers loss of consciousness . . . by simultaneous and instantaneous severance of the carotid arteries with a sharp instrument."

A second legal complication with kosher slaughter traces back to 1906. Early in that year, Upton Sinclair's novel *The Jungle* was published, causing an immediate furor. Set in turn-of-the-century Chicago and its immigrant community ("Packingtown") surrounding the Union Stock Yards and the giant meatpackers that ruled there, the book traces a fictional character through a harrowing and seemingly endless series of tragedies and misfortunes. Along the way, the shocked reader encounters graphic descriptions presented in sickening detail of the very real and abominably filthy conditions prevailing in the packinghouses, from meat scraps scooped out of floor drains and mixed in with canned beef to rats ground up with sausage.

Reforming legislation directed at cleaning up the egregiously unsanitary environment found in every packing plant had been pressed in the 1880s and 1890s with little success. Indeed, at the time of the publication of *The Jungle* a bill imposing standards for unadulterated food and drugs was stalled in the House, although it included no provision for meat inspection. President Theodore Roosevelt, who had been rather passive on the issue, read Sinclair's book and became just as appalled as everyone else. TR immediately devoted his considerable energies to pushing through Congress the Pure Food and Drug Act (PFDA) (substantially amended in 1938 and renamed the Food, Drug, and Cosmetic Act) and a newly minted Meat Inspection Act, both of which he signed in 1906. (Ironically, the point of Sinclair's book had little to do with cleaning up the industry, much less the welfare of slaughtered animals. A devout socialist and avidly prounion, he intended to move his readers with the plight of the oppressed worker. Sinclair once said that in writing *The Jungle,* he aimed for America's heart, but hit its stomach instead.)

The relevance of this episode in literary and legal history to kosher slaughter lies in sanitation regulations issued under the PFDA prohibiting slaughtered livestock from touching the packinghouse floor at any time. Traditionally, kosher slaughter had been performed on animals cast to the ground, but the federal law made such a posture during the killing illegal. There has never been any special dispensation for kosher slaughter here—this is a food safety for humans issue now—so to comply with the law, the animals were simply shackled and hoisted by a chain immediately before the *shohet* made his cut. Yet this seems to produce a serious animal welfare problem because, remember, these are fully conscious and aware animals, hanging by one leg with a profusely bleeding, slit throat. This was precisely the problem the Humane Slaughter Act is supposed to solve by directing that only *unconscious* animals be shackled and hoisted.

To solve the problem, lawmakers first chose to set it aside, and then later they defined it out of existence, a solution motivated at least in part by the fact that no humane restraint systems were available at that time (for such restraint, *see* this chapter: *Ritual Slaughter of Animals: Making Ritual Slaughter More Humane*). Again at the urging of Javits and his Jewish cohorts, section 6 of the HSA provides that "the handling or other preparation of livestock for ritual slaughter are exempted from the terms of this Act." The exemption was buttressed in 1978 with a clause stipulating that any handling of an animal during the kosher slaughter procedure also counts as humane.

According to the U.S. Department of Agriculture (USDA), the agency responsible for administering the HSA, in 1998 there were sixty-six plants in the United States using kosher methods to slaughter over 2 million animals annually. This accounts for just under 2 percent of all livestock killed for food in this country.

Halal Slaughter

The humane slaughter laws of 1958 and 1978 do not specifically mention any form of ritual slaughter other than that practiced by the Jewish religion. However, section 2(b) does designate humane the killing of animals with a "sharp instrument" that severs the carotid arteries when required by "any other religious faith." It is almost universally accepted that this provision includes the method of slaughter characteristic of Islam, halal slaughter. This inclusion has never been challenged in a federal court. USDA records indicate that there are fifty-seven halal slaughter establishments killing 2 million animals each year, or about 2 percent of the total.

Halal is an Arabic word meaning "permitted," "legitimate," or "lawful." It is contrasted with *haram* which means "prohibited," "illegitimate," or "unlawful." Halal and haram are two of the most important concepts in Islam, applying as terms of appraisal to a wide variety of behaviors and activities. Most salient here, of course, is the halal and haram of food. In general, Muslims are forbidden from eating anything that is recognized as having a debilitating or destructive effect on the mind, the spirit, or on the physical well-being or personal integrity of the individual: these substances are labeled haram. (Liquids are also identified as permitted or prohibited, with alcohol the leading haram drink.)

The foods that are halal and those that are haram are specified in four major sources: first is the Qur'an, the holy book of Islam; second in importance is the Hadith, a collection of the actions and pronouncements of the Prophet Muhammad; third, the Sunnah or the traditional teachings of Islamic clergy; and lastly, the Fiqh, the composite body of the several schools of Islamic law. Halal and haram foods for the Muslim are essentially the same as those for the Jew—indeed the Qur'an specifically states, "The food of those to whom the Book was given [the Jews] is lawful to you." For both, the main halal meats are lamb, mutton, poultry, and beef, while pork or pork products, the meat of carnivorous animals, as well as the blood from any animal are quite definitely haram.

As in Judaism, the devout Muslim must not merely be sure to eat only lawful meat, he or she must also be careful to consume only halal animals that were killed in a lawful way. Thus, the Qur'an further states that any animal is haram, even a cow or sheep, if it was beaten to death, strangled, or died from a fall or as the result of injuries inflicted by other animals. Halal slaughter, then, denotes the religiously proper method of killing permitted food animals. When halal meat is not available, Muslims are allowed to eat meat from animals slaughtered by Jews or Christians ("People of the Book"), but not by practitioners of any other religion.

Halal slaughter must be performed by a mature, clear-minded Muslim of unquestioned religious devotion who fully understands the nature of lawful slaughter and its requirements. Unlike Judaism, there is, however, no particularly detailed instruction or precise training regimen in the killing technique for the pious Muslim. Further, no special knife is required, so long as the instrument is very sharp and made of steel (a material requirement obviously arising out of the much more modern developments of Islamic law, as contained in the Fiqh).

The slaughter of an animal for food—called al-dhabh—must not be done in the presence of other creatures, and the animal to be killed must be conscious and healthy. Before the al-dhabh begins, the Muslim utters the sacred formula bismi-Llah, Allahu akbar—"In the name of God, God is most great"—which consecrates the killing. As in kosher slaughter, a single cut is swiftly made across the throat of the fully aware animal, severing the carotid artery, along with the jugular vein and the respiratory tract. The knife must be thoroughly rinsed after each kill. Halal slaughter is motivated by concerns similar to those for kosher foods: purity, cleanliness, and humaneness. The killing needs to be sanctified in the sight of Allah, while unwholesome and unsanitary food such as carrion must be avoided. The prescribed method of slaughter was thought to add compassion to a time when animals were simply objects to indiscriminately use and abuse at will.

The same inconsistencies, ironic though they may be, with humane slaughter laws observed above in the discussion of kosher methods also obtain here in halal slaughter, inconsistencies that are legally harmonized by exemption and definition. Although conscious animals may be cut and hoisted in halal slaughter, federal law has simply proclaimed that, as an exemplar of ritual slaughter, this is a humane method of killing food animals, and has also excused halal procedures from the restrictions applying to the rest of the meat industry. Nonetheless, Islamic authorities in Australia and New Zealand, apparently somewhat less dogmatic than their Jewish counterparts, have accepted certain forms of electrical stunning in those countries' plants catering to Muslim requirements. It is unclear whether the same dispensation has been allowed in America.

Making Ritual Slaughter More Humane
Halal and kosher slaughtering procedures that hoist and cut conscious animals are not illegal, but ritual slaughter can be made more humane with upright restraining systems that allow animals to be cut and bled to death before any hoisting is done, as well as meet standards of food safety.

In 1963 Cross Brothers Packing devised a special slaughter box that avoids hoisting and yet satisfies the religious prerequisites of both Judaism and Islam. The firm sold the patent for the device the next year to the American Society for the Prevention of Cruelty to Animals (ASPCA), and since that time it has been called the "ASPCA pen." One animal at a time enters the ASPCA pen, nudged forward by a rear pusher and supported below by a belly lift. Its head and neck extend through an aperture on one side of the box where a chin lift raises the head and secures it against a forehead bracket. The throat is then slit and the blood caught by a floor drain. After the animal collapses and the bleeding is complete, a discharge gate is raised and the animal can then be shackled, pulled from the box, and sent down the disassembly line.

A similar apparatus uses a double rail, conveyor restrainer invented by scientists at the University of Connecticut in the late 1970s. Here the animal is directed through a chute and to a cleated, inclined ramp from which the double rail conveyor extends horizontally. As the animal proceeds down the ramp it becomes suspended by the rail between its legs, to be moved to an opening at the end of the rail. There, a modification of the original conveyor design to accommodate ritual slaughter includes biparting doors that close around the neck, and a chain that raises a chin lift to expose the throat; the cutting and bleeding then proceed. Once completed, the doors open and the carcass can be moved through on the conveyor and hoisted. A third type of ritual slaughtering equipment, developed by Grandin Livestock Handling Systems, combines the chin lift and forehead bracket of the ASPCA pen with the double rail conveyor.

All three of these devices keep the animal off the floor, preventing its body or any exposed wounds from contacting unsanitary surfaces. Animal welfare concerns may also be met when certain conditions are fulfilled: the animals brought to the upright restrainers are placid and calm; the apparatus is fairly quiet, well illuminated, exerts the appropriate pressure, and prevents the animals from seeing people or other distractions; and a properly trained individual is adroitly wielding the knife. Physiological data and observation of behavior indicate that, when correctly performed, the cutting causes little or no pain, and unconsciousness follows within fifteen seconds or less for sheep, and somewhat longer for cattle.

None of these upright restraining devices are legally required at this time, and no statistics are available about how many are currently being employed. Anecdotal evidence suggests that most of the livestock ritually slaughtered in the more than 100 American packers of kosher and halal meat are not killed in these machines. Instead, the prevailing practice is the shackling and hoisting of conscious animals allowed by the HMSA religious exemption.

LEGAL CHALLENGES TO RITUAL SLAUGHTER

The First Amendment to the U.S. Constitution begins with this sentence: "Congress shall make no law respecting an establishment of religion, or prohibiting the free exercise thereof." The phrase preceding the "or" is known as the Establishment Clause, intended to guarantee American citizens that there will be no state-sponsored religion in their country. The phrase after the "or" is the Free Exercise Clause, an assurance that each person is entitled to pursue his or her vision of spirituality without interference from the government.

These clauses were at the center of the only two cases ever considered by the federal judiciary involving the slaughter of domestic animals traditionally used in agriculture. In each case, the plaintiffs charged government with infringing upon this First Amendment right, although one plaintiff sued to try and stop the slaughter, while the other went to court to continue killing animals. The first case focuses on the Humane Slaughter Act (HSA) and its exception for ritual killing, the challenger contending that this special provision amounts to a government endorsement of a religious practice, which is disallowed by the Establishment Clause. The other case reached all the way to the Supreme Court, where the plaintiff complained that a city ordinance prohibiting animal sacrifice violated the Free Exercise Clause.

Humane Slaughter and Kosher Slaughter

In the meat industry food animals have traditionally been killed by cutting and hoisting. The carotid arteries—the two major arteries in the neck carrying blood from the heart to the head—are severed and the animal is hung by a rear leg while it bleeds out. For many years, meat packers routinely stunned the animals with a blow to the head from a sledgehammer or a pole ax, slit their throats, and then suspended them for bleeding. Too often the stunning failed to produce insensibility or was skipped entirely, and the unfortunate creature was slashed, hung, and bled while still fully conscious and aware. Congress enacted the HSA in 1958 intending to ensure greater compassion in the killing of livestock for food. The United States Department of Agriculture (USDA) was charged with administering the Act (*see* this chapter: *Animal Slaughter: Humane Slaughter Act of 1960*).

The HSA prohibits any cutting or hoisting of animals before they have been rendered unconscious by mechanical, electrical, or chemical means. Even so, the law also contains a crucial exception to this ban. During Congressional hearings in the late 1950s concerning the bills that would become the HSA, Senator Jacob Javits of New York and several Jewish organizations protested the prohibition on cutting and hoisting conscious animals. This restriction, they pointed out, would make all kosher slaughter a federal offense. In Judaism, the traditional method of killing an animal permitted as food requires the slaughter of *conscious* animals by means of a single, rapid incision across the animal's throat.

Furthermore, food sanitation regulations issued by the USDA do not allow slaughtered animals to contact the floor after they have been cut. Thus, kosher slaughter not only demands that conscious animals be cut, but, given the federal regulation, they must also be hoisted while still awake and alert, both conditions clear violations of the proposed humane slaughter legislation. Such a law, Javits argued, would violate the constitutional right of Jewish people to the free exercise of religion, as guaranteed by the First Amendment.

Sufficiently persuaded, Congress passed a final draft of the HSA that included a special provision attempting to reconcile the concerns of the Jewish community with those of animal welfare advocates. Although section 2(a) of the law requires that livestock be "rendered insensible to pain . . . before being shackled, hoisted, . . . or cut," section 2(b) stipulates that ritual slaughter according to the tenets of the Jewish faith is humane; moreover, section 6 declares that "in order to protect freedom of religion, . . . the handling or other preparation of livestock for ritual slaughter [is] exempted from the terms of this Act" (*see* this chapter: *Ritual Slaughter of Animals*).

Jones v. Butz

Helen Jones, five other individuals, and three humane organizations filed suit in a federal district court for the state of New York early in 1974, naming USDA Secretary Earl Butz as the defendant. Jones and her allies, united in their commitment to the humane treatment of animals and the separation of church and state, contended that the HSA failed to satisfy either one of these principles. They challenged both the section 2(b) stipulation that kosher slaughter is humane, and the section 6 religious exemption on the grounds that these special provisions violate another aspect of the religious freedom protections afforded by the First Amendment. Jones claimed that, while the Free Exercise Clause may well provide Jews with the legal basis for a right to slaughter by kosher methods, the Establishment Clause denies them any such right.

Jones observed that while section 2(a) requires that livestock be rendered unconscious before they may be shackled and hoisted, sections 2(b) and 6 *allow* shackling and hoisting before unconsciousness is produced. These sections are therefore plainly incompatible not only with 2(a) but also with the declared policy of the United States, contained in the preamble to the HSA, that only humane methods shall be used in the slaughtering process. How can this inconsistency be accounted for? The only plausible explanation, Jones continued, was that Congress was legally enshrining a particular religious doctrine in sections 2(b) and 6, which is precisely what the Establishment Clause does not allow: the religious exemption is unconstitutional. Jones did not object to the cutting of conscious animals demanded by kosher slaughter—she conceded that to be humane. Rather, Jones insisted that the fettering and hanging of still sensible livestock was *not* humane. That sort of handling could only achieve the status of federal law if Congress had written a special religious purpose into the HSA. However, such a legislative import is prohibited by the First Amendment.

Judge Palmieri rejected this line of reasoning. He noted that lawmakers had considered "ample and persuasive" evidence that kosher slaughter, including the handling of animals during the slaughtering process, was indeed humane. Jones and her cohorts, Palmieri scolded, could not ask a court to determine which methods of handling animals are humane and which are not because "[w]e do not sit as a super-legislature to weigh the wisdom of legislation." In any case, Palmieri ruled it simply a legislatively appropriate "coincidence" that Congress finding a certain slaughter procedure humane, as described in 2(b), happens to be the same procedure as that required by a particular religious doctrine. The judge did not acknowledge that 2(b) makes no reference to preslaughter *treatment* of animals, the plaintiffs' concern here. A 1978 amendment to the HSA, cognizant of this case, appended a clause to section 2(b) that does mention handling of livestock in ritual slaughter, and similarly immunizes it from the prohibitions of the law.

What about the Establishment Clause and the exception created in section 6? Did Congress have a specific religious purpose in exempting kosher slaughter from the provisions of the HSA, thus running afoul of this aspect of the First Amendment? Although not referring specifically to section 6, Palmieri asserted that even if the legislators had allowed hoisting and cutting the throats of conscious animals out of deference to the religious tenets of Judaism, there was no violation of the First Amendment. This is because the Supreme Court has allowed Sabbatarians and conscientious objectors exemptions from the applicable laws on religious grounds. Some states have laws requiring certain businesses to be closed on Sundays, but Sabbatarians observe Saturday as the Sabbath (the original understanding of the Fourth Commandment in the Bible, Book of Exodus), and thus see no need to close their operations on Sunday. Similarly, individuals who can show a genuine commitment to a religious doctrine that prohibits participation in violence of any sort, such as that of the Quakers, are not required to serve in the armed forces. According to Palmieri, the ritual slaughter exemption is cut from the same cloth as these two sorts of religious exceptions.

More importantly, the judge continued, the Supreme Court has also devised a three-part test to determine whether a law offends against the Establishment Clause: (1) Does the statute have a secular purpose?; (2) Is its principal effect one that does not "advance or inhibit religion"?; (3) Does it avoid "excessive government entanglement with religion"? If the answer to all three of these questions is "yes," then the law is constitutionally innocuous. When this test is applied to the HSA provisions for ritual slaughter, Palmieri concluded, a trio of affirmative responses must be given.

This is a surprising conclusion. Although an exemption for ritual slaughter does not obviously result in "excessive government entanglement with religion," it is unclear how it serves any secular purpose or fails to promote religion. The permission to hoist and cut conscious animals is precisely designed to accommodate a particular religious practice, and is in another part of the HSA conceded to be inhumane. *Ensuring humane slaughter* is the secular purpose of the law, and sections 2(b) and 6 do not serve this goal. Moreover, this accommodation of course supports the practice it validates, which certainly seems to "advance" the religion. Despite these concerns, the case was affirmed by the Supreme Court without comment, and to date the federal judiciary has not been further troubled by the ritual slaughter exception.

Santería and Animal Sacrifice

The Supreme Court had much more to say about another case involving ritual slaughter, but one that did not address the HSA exemptions. Here, the First Amendment was again invoked, though this time the issue focused on the Free Exercise Clause, and the slaughter being challenged was to provide food for supernatural beings, not just human ones. Outside of many cases concerning federal protections for wildlife (*see* chapter 6), *Church of Lukumi Babalu Aye v. City of Hialeah* is the only occasion on which the high court has ever passed judgment on the use of animals for any purpose.

The Church of Lukumi is more commonly known as *Santería,* and is often generically labeled as "voodoo." The religion is fairly widespread throughout the Caribbean region and Brazil, but originally derived from a religious tradition indigenous to equatorial Africa. One of the more frequent and important activities for practitioners of Santería—and a common practice of the traditional religion in Africa—is the ritual killing of various animals, usually chickens and other birds. The animals are sacrificed to feed and propitiate a number of spiritual entities, called *orishas.*

During the seventeenth and eighteenth centuries, Portuguese and Spanish slave traders kidnapped large numbers of the Yoruba people along the west coast of equatorial Africa, in the present-day countries of Nigeria and Benin. The Yoruba were brought overseas to the islands of the Caribbean, principally Cuba, Haiti, Trinidad, and Puerto Rico; a substantial number were also sold to slaveholders in Brazil. Once in the new world, the Yoruba were forbidden from practicing their own traditional religion, and instead baptized into the Roman Catholic church. However, the Africans did not reject their native tradition but instead incorporated elements of Catholicism into it, and thus produced a religion blended from diverse elements.

Today, many of its practitioners regard the term *Santería* as derogatory, because it arose in this time of suppression and oppression. They believe the introduction of Catholic elements, especially the worship of a multitude of Catholic saints, was simply a subterfuge employed to make their captors believe they had converted, when in fact they were revering their own deities under the guise of the various saints. For those who subscribe to this view, the preferred term for their faith is *La Regla Lucumí,* the "Order (or Church) of Lucumi." In Brazil, the religion is called *Macumba.* Since *Santería* is the more widely recognized term, we retain that word here.

Santería is classified as a henotheism, in which a supreme being rules over a large number of lesser divinities, with these supernatural entities establishing close relationships with humans. Among the world's religions, the Yoruba are legendary for their expansive pantheon populated with hundreds of spirit beings. In the Santería system, God is known as *Olorun* or *Olodumare,* the "Owner of Heaven," and the subordinate divinities are called *orisha.* Since the time of the Yoruba indoctrination into

Catholicism, many orishas have been associated with specific saints, hence the name "Santería," "the Way of the Saints." For example, Babalz Ayi is St. Lazarus, Shangs is St. Barbara, and Oggzn is St. Peter. Additionally, each orisha is correlated with some natural force or human artifact (sickness, thunder, roads, money, for example), a number, a color, food, a dance posture, and an emblem. The orishas control all natural phenomena and every aspect of human life, so it is important to be on good terms with them and enlist their aid when needed.

A fundamental tenet of Santería is that each individual has a God-given destiny that is to be fulfilled through the facilitation of the orishas, so the faithful strive to cultivate a personal relationship with these beings. Communion with the orishas is accomplished by prayer, divination, and various ritual activities, the most prominent of which is the *ebo*. This term refers to a variety of sacrifices and offerings necessary to feed the orishas, who must have sustenance to survive and who would be displeased if deprived. The ebo may include prepared dishes, candy, fruit, or candles, but the most controversial form of this ritual is animal sacrifice.

The sacrificial animal is usually a bird—chickens are very common—but sheep and goats are also offered. Although animal sacrifice is most often performed as a propitiatory rite for extreme situations such as sickness or serious misfortune, animals are also killed when a new priest is consecrated in the service of her or his orisha, and during birth, death, and marriage ceremonies. The sacrifice is performed by the priest, who inserts a knife through the right side of the animal's neck between the esophagus and the vertebrae, intending to sever the jugular vein and the carotid artery. Some of the flowing blood is collected and drunk, and the flesh is cooked, part of which is offered to the orisha, with the remainder consumed by the initiate or penitent.

Church of Lukumi Babalu Aye v. City of Hialeah

In April 1987 the Babalu Aye branch of the Church of Lukumi leased some land in Hialeah, a south Florida city of some 200,000 residents, adjacent to Miami. Ernest Pichardo, the president and head priest of Babalu Aye, announced the intention of the church to construct a house of worship, along with a school, cultural center, and museum. He then began the process of obtaining the "required licensing, inspection, and zoning approvals. By August this process was complete, and construction was ready to begin.

Meanwhile, the Hialeah city council, aware of these developments, took several steps to deter the arrival of Santería into their midst. Cognizant as well of the prevalence of animal sacrifice in this church and desiring to prohibit the ritual, the council first sought the opinion of the state attorney general. The Florida attorney general opined that the ritual killing of animals for any purpose other than to provide food was not a "necessary" killing, and so was in violation of the state anticruelty law. A Hialeah ordinance banning the practice would therefore not conflict with the statute. (For more on state anticruelty laws, *see* chapter 3: *Anticruelty Laws*.)

In September the council unanimously adopted three ordinances, all specifically addressed to the practice of ritually killing animals. The first defined "sacrifice" as "to unnecessarily kill, torture, or mutilate an animal in public or private ritual or ceremony not for the primary purpose of food consumption." This ordinance also prohibited owning an animal with the intention of using it for food, but restricted the prohibition only to people who kill animals for ritual purposes, whether or not the animal is then eaten. Licensed businesses that raise animals expressly for food purposes were exempted from the ordinance. The second law declared that because animal sacrifice, as defined in the first ordinance, is incompatible with the health, safety, and welfare of the public, and is in any case immoral, it is illegal for anyone to sacrifice any animal within the city limits of Hialeah. Finally, the third ordinance defined "slaughter" as "killing animals for food" and prohibited the slaughter of animals outside those areas zoned for this purpose.

Pichardo immediately filed suit in the federal District Court for the Southern District of Florida, founding his complaint primarily on the allegation that the city ordinances were incompatible with the Free Exercise Clause of the First Amendment. In 1989 the district court ruled that although the ordinances were not "religiously neutral," neither were they unconstitutional because Hialeah's purpose was to outlaw animal sacrifice, not prohibit Santería from the city. In the judgment of the court, the city government had several compelling interests that outweighed Babalu Aye's interest in performing ritual sacrifices. First, animal sacrifice presents a significant health risk to the participants, who consume meat that has not be properly inspected, and to the public generally, who might contract diseases from improperly disposed, decaying bodies. Furthermore, it is traumatic to children who witness the killing, and it also qualifies as cruel and unnecessary.

On Pichardo's appeal of this ruling, the Eleventh Circuit Court of Appeals upheld it with a one-paragraph affirmation.

The Supreme Court on Animal Sacrifice

In a rare appellate progression, the Supreme Court unanimously rejected the lower court rulings. Justice Anthony Kennedy began his majority opinion by pointing out that a law restricting religious practice does not have to be justified by a compelling government interest if it is "neutral and generally applicable." Neutrality and general applicability are established when the law does not uniquely single out a religious practice it-self for proscription, but pertains to a variety of human activities.

This principle had been developed by the high court justices three years earlier in their landmark 1990 decision for *Employment Division v. Smith*. Here, two American Indians had been dismissed from their jobs for violating an Oregon drug law prohibiting possession of peyote, a hal-lucinogenic cactus. The Indians were members of the Native American church, where peyote is used ritually as a sacrament. Criminalizing pos-session of the cactus is unconstitutional, they argued, because it violates their freedom to practice their religion. The high court ruled that al-though the Oregon law did indeed ban the ritual use of peyote, the re-striction applied widely to the consumption of the drug in any context, not just in religious ones. Therefore, the state drug law was neutral and generally applicable.

However, when a law restricting religious practice is neither neutral nor generally applicable, to pass constitutional muster it must be sub-jected to the standard of "strict scrutiny." This is a penetrating judicial ex-amination activated when a fundamental right, such as the right to free exercise of religion, is threatened by a statute. In the face of such a threat, defenders of the law must show that it both furthers a compelling inter-est, and is "narrowly tailored" to promote that interest. What was the legal status of the Hialeah ordinances?

Kennedy found first that they did not pass the neutral and generally applicable test: "It is a necessary conclusion that almost the only conduct subject to [the] Ordinances . . . is the religious exercise of Santería church members." By using the words "sacrifice" and "ritual," the city laws clearly target a specific religious practice to the exclusion of other activi-ties. The various prohibitions, definitions, and exceptions to the ordi-nances further indicated that they were carefully crafted to apply to the ritual killing of animals by members of the Church of Lukumi, and not to any other animal killing. For example, the first ordinance, which banned ritual killing "not for the primary purpose of food consumption" was ob-viously intended to exempt kosher slaughter. Moreover, animal sacrifice was declared unnecessary, but hunting, fishing, the slaughter of animals for food, pest control, and euthanasia of unwanted pets were not touched by the ordinances.

Further, the Hialeah laws were at once overinclusive and underinclu-sive. They were overbroad because, if the city really was motivated by concern for public health, the council could impose a regulation mandat-ing the proper disposal of organic waste rather than prohibit animal sac-rifice. Similarly, Kennedy continued, animal welfare concerns could be ad-dressed with other regulations stipulating standards for the care, treatment, and slaughter of animals. In particular, the method of sacrifice employed by the Church of Lukumi, which was found not to be humane, "could be addressed by restrictions stopping far short of [prohibiting] Santería sacrificial practice."

The ordinances were also too narrow because they did not prohibit nonreligious conduct that presents just as great, or a greater risk to public health and animal welfare as animal sacrifice does. Again, hunting, fishing, exterminating rats and mice, and euthanasia in shelters and pounds were all permitted while the Santería ritual was not. Finally, a threat to public health was presented by any improperly discarded animal corpses, not just those coming from the Church of Lukumi, and hunters and fishermen could legally eat their take of wildlife without benefit of meat inspection.

Having established that the ordinances were not neutral or generally applicable, Justice Kennedy moved to the matter of strict scrutiny: "To satisfy the commands of the First Amendment, a law restrictive of religious practice must advance interests of the highest order and must be narrowly tailored in pursuit of those interests." Here, too, he found that the city council had failed. Although the government interests in public health and preventing cruelty to animals were indeed legitimate and powerful ones, for the reasons already presented, Hialeah did not closely draft the ordinances to advance those interests. Regulations dictating the disposal of organic waste, the treatment of animals irrespective of the purposes for their confinement, or the methods of slaughter could have promoted these compelling interests without proscribing the Santería ritual. The ordinances cited public health interests in preventing the disposal of animal carcasses in public places and the consumption of uninspected meat, but confined the furtherance of this interest to conduct motivated by the Santería religious conviction. Animal sacrifice is thus protected by the First Amendment.

Farm Sanctuary, Inc. v. Department of Food and Agriculture
A third challenge to ritual slaughter avoided any appeal to the First Amendment and instead charged that a special religious exemption afforded by a state law allowed inhumane methods of slaughter.

Like most states, California has its own humane slaughter law that essentially duplicates the provisions of the federal Humane Methods of Slaughter Act (*see* this chapter: *Humane Methods of Slaughter Act*). However, in 1991 the California legislature approved an amendment to the law that makes it unique in America: all chickens and other poultry, along with cows, pigs, and sheep, "must be rendered insensible to pain" before being butchered. No other humane slaughter law in the country covers birds in addition to these mammals.

In 1994 the California Department of Food and Agriculture issued reg-

ulations specifying procedures for killing poultry that are humane. Included there was a provision declaring humane methods of slaughter
prescribed by "the Jewish faith, Islamic and other faiths [that] cause the
poultry to lose consciousness through anemia of the brain resulting from
the simultaneous and instantaneous severance of both carotid arteries
with a sharp instrument." Crucially, the regulations further authorized
the chief of the Meat and Poultry Inspection Branch to allow "exemptions
for other methods of ritualistic slaughter of poultry."

In May 1996 Farm Sanctuary, an animal protection organization dedicated to ending the use of animals for food, filed a lawsuit against the Department of Food and Agriculture. Farm Sanctuary asked for a finding
that the exemption for "other methods of ritualistic slaughter" allowed
the chief to approve *inhumane* procedures for killing birds. After all, the
regulation in effect defines "humane slaughter" in the religious context as
one under which the arteries are severed when the throat is cut. In that
case, any other form of ritual slaughter would not qualify as humane.
Thus, the exemption is not consistent with a state law permitting only humane methods. The organization wanted a court order barring the issuance of any such "other" exemptions.

Judge Masterson rejected the claim that the regulation authorized the
chief to permit inhumane slaughtering techniques. Farm Sanctuary
failed to notice that the contested regulation endorsed other methods of
ritually killing poultry provided they "effectuat[e] the purpose of these
regulations." That purpose was to ensure that poultry are slaughtered
humanely. The plaintiff mistakenly interpreted the key sentences as saying that these other approved methods could be exempt from the restrictions of the state humane slaughter law. Instead, it meant that alternative
procedures could be exceptions to a list of specific methods of slaughter
that the department had already authorized. "[T]he use of the word 'exemptions,'" Masterson wrote, "simply reflects that the chief of the inspection branch can approve *additional* methods of ritualistic slaughter
that are *humane.*"

Farm Sanctuary could protest that the judge had missed the point. The
humane slaughter law and its regulations specify that poultry can be
killed humanely in several different ways, five found in secular operations and one in religious ones: gassing with carbon dioxide, electrical
stunning, electrocution, cervical dislocation, decapitation, and the severing of the carotid arteries characteristic of the Jewish and Islamic traditions. Any "other method" would therefore not be humane. Moreover,
neither the law nor its regulations offer a general definition of "humane,"
or give the chief inspector the discretion to determine when a slaughtering technique other than these six is humane.

TWENTY-EIGHT HOUR LAW OF 1994

When the Civil War ended in 1865, the cattle herds of the southern states were in a devastated condition: plundered, shot, lost. The northern herds had been seriously depleted to feed Union soldiers, and beef prices soared throughout the reconstructing and re-United States. Yet in Texas roamed literally millions of longhorn cattle. The question was: How to get them to a viable market?

Transportation of Livestock

Before the war, some Texas herds were driven up the middle of the country to Illinois and Ohio. Frequently though the trek proved too arduous even for the robust longhorns, plagued as it was by bandits, swollen rivers, severe thunderstorms, tornadoes, and other natural disasters, so such an endeavor was not regarded as profitable. Even worse, the longhorns often carried "Texas fever," a highly contagious disease that decimated other herds encountered on the journey. Citizens in Kansas and Missouri formed bands of armed vigilantes intent on intercepting Texas droves before they could infect their cattle, forcibly halting them at the border.

After four years of war, the more steady route to market had also become untenable. In the 1850s cattle had been driven to the Red River and then sent by steamer down to the Mississippi River and on to New Orleans. But now a destitute Big Easy offered few prospects for cattle sales to the impoverished south, and languished far from the more lucrative northern markets.

The answer was the railroad. Slowed during the fighting between the states, by late 1865 the Union Pacific was laying miles of track each day, determined to connect the country coast to coast with the iron road. Within two years, the northern branch was complete to Cheyenne, in Wyoming Territory, and the southern branch had extended 175 miles west from Kansas City to Salina. Just east of Salina lay the one-dirt-street town of Abilene, consisting of about a dozen earthen-roofed shacks. An Illinois cattle trader named Joseph McCoy visited Abilene in 1867, seeking a likely rail intersection with the newly established Chisholm trail. This dusty track looked like a promising route for moving cattle north out of central Texas and across "Indian Territory," present-day Oklahoma, to Kansas. McCoy judged that Abilene was the ideal location from which to ship Texas cattle east on the Union Pacific to the slaughterhouses in St. Louis, and especially those in Chicago.

In short order, McCoy prevailed upon the railroad to build a spur to Abilene and signed a contract with Union Pacific to pay him a commission on every carload of cattle shipped east. Next he convinced the governor of Kansas to rescind a quarantine on Texas cattle, and the Illinois legislature to amend a state law banning their importation, both restrictions having been provoked by fear of "Texas fever." After constructing holding pens and advertising the new railhead, the first load of cattle started east from Abilene in September 1867. This marked the inception of the mass transportation of animals in America. That first year about 35,000 longhorns were shipped, and by 1870 over 700,000 head were leaving Abilene, along with hogs and sheep.

At the time there were no laws or legal restrictions of any kind regulating how cattle or any livestock were to be transported. The first stock cars were 30-foot, converted coal cars without roofs or hayracks. If any fodder was provided, it was simply thrown over the animals, and sometimes tree branches were laid on the top to provide a bit of shade and shelter. Livestock were frequently loaded on these cars in mixed shipments of different species, with hogs on the floor and sheep on a temporary deck above them. When it was found that sheep frequently jumped out of the unroofed cars, the arrangement was reversed, but then the sheep were pummeled with pig excrement, hopelessly soiling the wool. This lead to the construction of permanent roofs on stock cars. Single-deck configurations for cattle were thought to waste space, so sheep and pigs were often crowded in under them, only to be knocked down and trampled by the larger animals—the fate of many weaker cows, too.

The railroad companies charged the same high rates per car no matter how many animals were loaded on, so a powerful economic motive led stockmen to pack as many on the train as possible. This was commonly done with a "prod pole." This instrument featured a six-foot rod with a spike on the end, and, perpendicular to the spike, a large screw that could be used to tangle into the tail hair, and by turning the pole, twist the appendage until the animal moved. Once loaded, the livestock were sent on a journey of three to six days, usually without food, water, bedding, adequate ventilation or heating, in every sort of weather. Upon arrival at the stockyards, three or four out of every ten animals were already dead, most of the others were seriously injured, sick, or diseased, and all had sustained substantial weight loss, as much as one-quarter of their body weight.

Regulating the Transportation of Livestock
Newspaper reports and editorials in the midwest and east, particularly in Boston and Chicago, publicized and criticized these methods of transporting livestock, raging against both the unsanitary conditions in which this food source was transported and the inhumane treatment inflicted upon the animals. George Angell, president of the newly formed Massachusetts Society for the Prevention of Cruelty to Animals, wrote a widely

distributed, scathing critique titled "Cattle Transportation in the United States."

In 1869 the Illinois legislature passed the first law regulating the conveyance of animals, requiring railroads to feed, water, and rest livestock after twenty-eight hours of travel. Congress reacted to the public outcry with a bill substantially modeled on the Illinois law, introduced in 1871. After much debate and opposition from the railroads and stockmen, the bill was finally passed in 1873 as the Twenty-Eight Hour Law, prohibiting livestock transporters from confining the animals for more than twenty-eight consecutive hours without food, water, or rest. What is perhaps most noteworthy about this statute is that it was the first federal law motivated, at least in part, by a desire to provide more humane conditions for animals, and to protect them from cruel treatment. Of course, the law was also intended to produce more hygienic meat for consumers.

Nonetheless, as originally written, the Twenty-Eight Hour Law was inadequate to accomplish either goal. Although conditions for the animals did improve, the gain was slight. There were no regulations for handling the animals during loading and unloading, and none for the pens and enclosures in which they were to be fed and watered. Drovers continued to use excessive force, including the "prod pole," while few of the holding pens provided any protection from the weather, and most were undersized quagmires of mud. Feed was typically dumped into the muck and water often came from contaminated potholes.

Amendments in 1906 solved some of these problems, but a significant gap remained, one that became most apparent after the Second World War. The law covered only animals moved by the railroads and did not apply to interstate transportation in trucks, a means of conveyance that had come to wholly dominate livestock transportation by the early 1950s.

After better than three decades in which the federal law was inapplicable to most of the transportation it was supposed to regulate, the Twenty-Eight Hour Law was finally repealed in 1994, revised and reenacted to account for all methods of livestock transportation. It stipulates that "a rail carrier, express carrier, or common carrier (except by air or water), a receiver, trustee, or lessee of one of those carriers, or an owner or master of a vessel transporting animals" across state lines "may not confine animals in a vehicle or vessel for more than twenty-eight consecutive hours without unloading the animals for feeding, watering, and rest." Further, transporters must load and unload the animals "humanely"—although humane methods are not specified—and allow them to recuperate for at least five consecutive hours before resuming the journey (increased from two hours in the original 1906 law).

Federal regulations further stipulate that the pens should have sufficient space for all the animals to lie down at the same time, provide suitable protection from the weather, and be clean and well drained. Ample quantities of potable water must be provided, as well as a sufficient supply of hay or corn, precise amounts depending on the size and type of animal being shipped. Livestock may be rested, fed, and watered in a railroad car as long as there is enough room for all the animals to lie down at the same time, and the feed is spread evenly throughout the car. The law does not apply to transportation within a state, or by aircraft or ship.

There are exceptions to the twenty-eight-hour rule. Carriers are permitted to confine sheep for as much as thirty-six consecutive hours if the twenty-eight-hour confinement period ends at night. This provision dates back to the original law, written on the advice of sheepherders who claimed that sheep were exceptionally skittish when moved at night and almost impossible to control. Also, the twenty-eight-hour period may be exceeded "when the animals cannot be unloaded because of accidental or unavoidable cause that could not have been anticipated or avoided when being careful." Finally, the owner of the animals may request in writing that the twenty-eight-hour period be extended to thirty-six hours.

This request is made to the federal office charged with enforcing the Twenty-Eight Hour Law, the Animal and Plant Health Inspection Service (APHIS), an agency of the United States Department of Agriculture. In the event that APHIS finds a violation of the Twenty-Eight Hour Law, the attorney general's office is charged with bringing a civil action against the accused, who may be fined $100 to $500 for each confirmed violation. There has been no reported litigation under the statute in nearly fifty years.

MAD COW DISEASE

"Mad cow disease" is the name given by the British press to what is known in the medical community as bovine spongiform encephalopathy, or BSE. The bovine-specific form of this malady is one of a family of diseases called spongiform encephalopathies, or spongy brain diseases. These incurable pathogens literally eat holes in the brains of those afflicted, making the cerebral matter look like a sponge, and wreaking psychological and physiological havoc on the mind and body.

The Rise of BSE

BSE appeared suddenly on a small farm in Kent, England, in April 1985, afflicting a handful of cattle with convulsions, lack of balance, and unusual aggressiveness. The beasts shook uncontrollably, had difficulty walking and eventually could not stand, and tried to attack their handlers. All had died or were destroyed within a few weeks. But that was far from the end of the matter. The disease began to spread through England's cattle like wildfire, abruptly surfacing throughout the nation's herds. Within two years dozens of cows were coming down with the ailment each week.

Even though BSE was unusual and not well understood, British public health officials were initially not particularly worried because it resembled scrapie, a much more familiar disease of sheep, so-called because the infected animals are seized by an intense itching that makes them scrape their skin raw. Another type of spongiform encephalopathy, scrapie had been well known in England for at least two centuries, and there had never been a documented case of any human contracting scrapie, or a scrapie-like disease, from eating contaminated lamb. BSE-infected cattle remained in England's food supply, with government assurances that the chance of transmission to humans was extremely remote.

As cases of BSE continued to proliferate across the country and public anxiety began to grow, in 1988 the English government brought together a group of eminent scientists to establish the Spongiform Encephalopathy Advisory Committee, charged with studying the matter and developing recommendations. The committee advised Parliament to burn or bury all clinically ill cattle, and to ban entirely, including for export, specific offals where BSE tends to accumulate—the brain, spinal cord, spleen, and intestines. These measures were legally instituted in 1989, and Parliament further directed mandatory reporting of all cases of BSE to the Ministry of Agriculture, Fisheries, and Food. By this time, the disease had been successfully transmitted to laboratory mice, thus proving that it could cross the "species barrier," a biological shield that, as determined by their physiological differences, often insulates organisms from the maladies of others. Scrapie had never been shown to be capable of scaling this obstacle.

Fearful that domestic herds would become infected, the United States banned the importation of British cattle in 1989, but still allowed packaged meat products from the United Kingdom. Two years later, after incidents of BSE had been reported from several other European countries, the U.S. Department of Agriculture (USDA) issued regulations prohibiting the importation of all cattle, meat, and meat products from the United Kingdom, Belgium, France, Ireland, Liechtenstein, Luxembourg, the Netherlands, Portugal, and Switzerland. Additionally, the USDA banned all such imports from the remaining nations of Europe, reasoning that because their "import requirements [are] less restrictive than those that would be acceptable for import into the United States and/or because of inadequate surveillance, [they] present an undue risk of introducing" BSE into America. Back in 1991, only Germany had halted all incoming shipments of British beef.

In 1990 up to 300 new cases of BSE were appearing in England each week. Two years later the weekly rate was 800. In 1994 the European Commission passed a resolution that no beef or beef products would be accepted from the United Kingdom without documentation that the meat originated in a herd free of BSE for at least six years. (The Commission runs the day-to-day affairs of the fifteen-nation European Union, proposes E.U. law, and enforces its implementation across Europe.) As more laboratory animals—including primates—were inoculated with BSE, grew ill, and died, and as British house cats also started developing the disease, it was becoming clearer that this was an extraordinary spongiform encephalopathy: it recognized little as a species barrier. Alarming suspicions began to develop that BSE could be transmitted to humans through eating contaminated beef, but equally powerful ethical considerations prevented the hypothesis from being tested.

Then in the spring of 1995 Stephen Churchill of Wiltshire, England, was stricken with convulsions, a loss of balance, and hallucinations. He died in May. The sudden onslaught of these symptoms drew doctors to the diagnosis that he had been killed by Creutzfeldt-Jakob Disease, or CJD, an uncommon brain disorder in the spongiform encephalopathy family named for the two German doctors who first described its occurrence. However, Stephen was only nineteen years old, while the typical CJD patient is at least fifty and usually in the sixties and seventies age range (CJD has sometimes been misdiagnosed as Alzheimer's disease). That same summer another British teenager exhibited similar symptoms and died shortly thereafter, and within another six months eight more young people—none older than their thirties—displayed classic manifestations of CJD and all were dead by late winter 1996.

The young age of the deceased was not the only anomaly exhibited by this form of CJD. Electroencephalogram recordings made of Stephen Churchill's brain, and of the other victims, showed slow, rounded waves of neurological activity. This is very different from the EEG displayed by the standard CJD-infected brain, which is characterized by sharp waves and rapid firing at once or twice every second. Further, the physical changes in the brain itself departed strikingly from the standard model. Along with the usual microscopic holes a spongiform encephalopathy punches in the cerebral matter, there was something completely new: large, rounded plaques of protein embedded in the brain.

Did Stephen Churchill and the other young people contract BSE by eating infected British beef? Can BSE cross the species barrier and kill humans? By mid-1995, compelling circumstantial evidence had begun to mount that pointed very clearly to the affirmative. After years of reassuring the public that BSE posed no threat to food safety, in March 1996 England's minister of health, Stephen Dorrell, made the shocking announcement that BSE almost certainly had been transmitted to humans as a new form of CJD. British beef could no longer be regarded as safe for human consumption.

The European Commission immediately banned all cattle and meat imports from the United Kingdom, finally following the regulatory path the United States had forged in 1989 and 1991. In July 1999 the commission agreed to rescind the ban after no new cases of BSE had appeared in England for over one year, and inspections of slaughterhouse practices proved satisfactory. However, France and Germany, unconvinced that British beef is now safe, have so far refused to allow any of the product into their countries, and the U.S. regulation remains in force. Meanwhile, the fifteen-year episode has cost the British government £1.5 billion (over $2 billion at current exchange rates), most of this in compensation to farmers for destroyed cattle, and the nation's beef industry is still far from recovering from the economic devastation wrought by BSE.

The Cause of New Variant CJD

In 1996 the anomalous form of CJD was christened nvCJD, or "new variant" CJD. More recently, as the novelty has worn off, some in the scientific community have dropped the "new" in favor of vCJD, while others claim there are too many new variants being discovered to warrant the abbreviation. The shortened version will be adopted here.

vCJD appears to be the product of a disease-causing agent unlike anything previously encountered in medicine. Although there are a number of theories competing for the explanation, scientific opinion has been coalescing around the view that a novel form of brain protein, rather than bacteria or a virus, is responsible. Named "prions" by Stanley Prusiner, a neurologist who won the Nobel Prize for his work in this area, these pathogens are virtually indestructible. Prions have no genetic material (DNA and RNA), so they are unaffected by radiation, and neither alcohol, detergents, boiling, burning, nor burying will destroy them. Lacking DNA, prions cannot reproduce themselves, however they appear capable of converting normal proteins into new prions, overwhelming the brain and turning it to sponge. It is not yet known how this conversion process takes place, and no one knows how to stop it.

By late 2000 eighty-four confirmed cases of vCJD had appeared in England and Europe; seventy-seven of these people are dead as of this writing. No confirmed cases of vCJD have occurred in the United States, but precautionary measures are in place. In addition to the import ban, in August 1999 the Food and Drug Administration (FDA) asked blood centers to refuse donations from anyone who lived in the United Kingdom for at least six months between 1980 and 1996, even though it is unclear whether vCJD (or CJD) is transmissible through blood products. At this writing, no verified instances of BSE have been documented among American cattle either. Even so, the low number of confirmed cases—hardly an epidemic—and the apparent absence of vCJD and BSE in

America are not good grounds for confidence that the scourge has been contained.

First, it is uncertain how widely cattle with BSE were dispersed through the food chain in England and Europe. Infected cows were being processed into food products for at least two full years before the Spongiform Encephalopathy Advisory Committee's recommendations were legislated, and it is unknown exactly how many cows contracted the disease. Nearly 175,000 BSE cases were diagnosed, but it would be naive to suppose this number represents all of them. Second, the incubation period of spongiform encephalopathies can be very long: ten, even twenty years or more is not uncommon. If vCJD developed in humans from meat contaminated and consumed in the middle and late 1980s, outbreaks in the middle and late 1990s are just what would be expected. What will the new millennium bring?

In December 1999 the National Academy of Sciences declared that BSE had indeed crossed the species barrier into humans: vCJD and BSE are the same disease. If that is so, then any risk of transmission can be reduced to zero by simply not eating beef or any beef products. But how did the cows get it in the first place? The route to answering this question takes us across the seas to some chilling social practices of an indigenous people, and ultimately to a practice of animal husbandry nearly as disturbing.

During the 1920s, the Western world became aware of a mysterious disease that had stricken the Fore people living in the highlands of Papua New Guinea, a huge island in the western Pacific. Strangely, the illness was afflicting women and children at a rate about thirty times that of adult males. Their major symptoms were steadily more debilitating incoordination until the victims could not stand, gradual loss of the ability to swallow, and persistent convulsions, followed by death in less than one year or, in some cases, within a few months. What the Fore called *kuru*—"tremble" or "shiver," usually denoting from cold or with fear—American doctors came to identify as a spongiform encephalopathy very much like CJD: the victims' brains were riddled with holes. Yet the cause of kuru eluded medical investigators for years until the disarmingly, and appallingly, simple explanation was discovered.

The Fore people were cannibals who ate the bodies of their deceased relatives as part of their funerary practices. Kuru probably entered the population after someone contracted CJD and was then eaten after expiring. The vast disparity in the rate of infection by gender and age came about because the women were responsible for disposing of dead bodies, so they reserved the brain, pancreas, liver, kidneys, and intestines, regarded as the choicest parts, for themselves and their children. Kuru, like spongiform encephalopathies generally, concentrates in the brain and internal organs. Women and children who ate infected brains and organs usually contracted kuru, and when they died, they too were eaten, passing on the disease to others who would die and then be eaten, and so on.

Hundreds of Fore were wiped out by kuru, some villages losing the majority of their women. This calamitous ritual was finally halted in the early 1960s when the Australian government, which owned Papua New Guinea at the time, banned the practice and enforced the prohibition. The incidence of kuru immediately dropped but, again as is typical of spongiform encephalopathies, the incubation period is prodigious and the final victims are still dying today.

Cattle Cannibalism and Food Disparagement

Cannibalism is very likely the cause of BSE as well—cattle cannibalism, that is. Throughout most of this century in England, and in America, cattle have been fed a cheap protein supplement substantially composed of the ground-up carcasses and by-products of cows and sheep. Included in this feed have been the corpses of "downer" livestock, sick animals that arrive at the slaughterhouse unable to stand and are condemned as unfit for human consumption.

The evidence is very strong that BSE is the product of cattle eating cattle, as well as scrapie-infected sheep. An escalation similar to that witnessed in the Fore ensued when cows with BSE were destroyed and fed back to healthy cattle, which then developed the disease, were killed, and turned into cattle feed, and so on. Once this connection was sufficiently established, or at least enough so as to err on the side of caution, in 1988 Parliament banned the use of animal products in livestock feed. Meanwhile, the American public was unaware that such cannibalistic feeding even existed in animal agriculture, and once the USDA had prohibited, by 1991, the importation of all English and European beef products, the prevailing legal view in the United States was that enough had been done.

Public ignorance and the prevailing view changed in the spring of 1996 when Howard Lyman appeared on the *Oprah Winfrey Show*. Taped in front of a studio audience in Chicago and shortly thereafter telecast across the country to millions of Oprah Winfrey devotees, Lyman revealed that American cattle are routinely fed road kill, euthanized pets, and sick cows that are rendered into feed. This is the same process of animal cannibalism that is widely acknowledged to be the cause of BSE in England, which then became vCJD when humans ate infected meat. Lyman denounced the practice and called for a government ban. Stunned, Oprah proclaimed, "It has just stopped me cold from eating another burger! . . . Cows should not be eating other cows!"

Almost immediately after the show aired, beef sales in the United States plunged to their lowest level in ten years. Within a couple more months a confederation of cattlemen calling themselves the "Texas Beef

Group" had filed suit against Winfrey, Lyman, and the Texas television station that carried the show, charging them with violating the state food disparagement law.

These statutes arose from another television program. In February 1989, *60 Minutes* reported on the dangers of Alar, a chemical that had been sprayed on apples for many years. Apples tend to fall off the tree before they are fully ripened, and Alar causes them to remain on the branches longer than they naturally would, extending the ripening process. Unfortunately, *60 Minutes* reporter Mike Wallace told viewers, scientific data has indicated that when Alar breaks down, the resulting compound is likely carcinogenic. Sales of apples and apple juice plummeted after the broadcast. Alar was officially banned by the Environmental Protection Agency in 1992, but not before Washington apple growers had filed suit against CBS. Ultimately, CBS prevailed in court because the apple producers could not show that the information presented on the program was false. Nonetheless, a number of states (strangely, Washington wasn't one of them) moved to head off potentially damaging activism on behalf of food safety.

Food disparagement laws prohibit any person from publishing or publicly announcing that a perishable commodity presents a hazard to human health when he or she knows it does not. Ohio's statute is representative: "Disparagement means the dissemination to the public in any manner of any false information that a perishable agricultural or aquacultural product is not safe for human consumption." Thirteen states have these laws, Texas among them, and it was for violation of this law that the Texas Beef Group sought to legally punish the defendants, claiming that Lyman's statements and Winfrey's endorsement of them, along with her substantial influence, had unjustly cost cattle growers in the state $11 million.

Even though the case was moved from a Texas state court to the federal district court in Amarillo, a center of cattle raising surrounded by feedlots and the location of one of the largest slaughterhouses in the country, Winfrey and Lyman won. After the presiding judge ruled that the Texas food disparagement law could not be applied because living cattle did not qualify as perishable commodities, in February 1998 the jury found the defendants innocent of a similar "business disparagement" charge (*Texas Beef Group v. Winfrey*).

In the meantime, the FDA finally acted upon the evidence out of Europe, and, perhaps, heeded the warnings of people like Howard Lyman. In July 1997 the agency issued regulations prohibiting the use of animal protein in feed for cattle, sheep, goats, buffalo, deer, elk, and antelope. The banned substance was defined as "any protein-containing portion of mammalian animals," but does not include blood, gelatin, cooked meat products approved for human consumption, milk products, or protein sources derived from pigs or horses. So far, BSE has not been shown to be transmissible to these two species.

FUR FARMING

Historically, the most recent development in animal agriculture is to raise certain species in captivity, kill them, remove their fur, and sell the pelts for a profit. The precise origins of fur farming (also called fur ranching) are hazy but it is apparently a modern enterprise that began in New York state just after the Civil War. Here, a few individuals in the far western county of Chautauqua and a few others in the Finger Lakes country of Oneida County caught mink alive and held them in confinement for breeding purposes.

Although Americans seem to have invented the business, it was really the Canadians who developed the industry in its infancy, dating from 1887 on Prince Edward Island, just north of Nova Scotia in the Gulf of St. Lawrence. Charles Dalton captured live "black" foxes (a naturally occurring phase of *Vulpes vulpes*, the red fox) in the forests of the island, caged them, and reared the animals for their pelts. Dalton eventually formed a kind of fur syndicate with four other Canadians, and together they made a fortune. Fox from Canada completely dominated the fur market initially, fetching ten or twenty times the dollar or two that the average mink pelt was worth at the turn of the century—some fox pelts sold for more than $1,000 each.

At the close of the twentieth century, America and Canada are minor players in the global fur market, producing only about 10 and 4 percent, respectively, of the total. Fox is now a small component of total production, with mink accounting for 24 million of the 28 million animals raised annually on the world's fur farms. The Scandinavian countries of Denmark, Finland, and Sweden account for nearly half of all pelts coming from the farm, with Russia and China at around 11 percent each, and Holland at 4 percent of world production. The remaining numbers are from such far-flung nations as Japan, France, and Argentina. Today, fox number only a little more than one-tenth of the whole at 3 million, while approximately one-half million chinchilla, sable, lynx, polecat, raccoon, dog, and nutria are also kept on ranches for their fur.

Mink Farming in America

The ascendancy of mink ranching in America can be traced to several key entrepreneurs who set up operations just before and immediately following the First World War. The first of these seminal figures was Frank Gothier, whose Iowa mink farm was established in 1911. In 1916 Jesse

Davis began raising mink he had trapped alive near his Vermont farm. That same year, also in Iowa, E. A. Schmalley bought breeding mink from a ranch in Nova Scotia.

Prior to the war, fox was the fur of choice in a variety of garments, and there was comparatively little interest in mink. During the Roaring Twenties, however, the capricious winds of fashion left fox fur becalmed, and invigorated the fledgling mink industry. Mink coats, stoles, and wraps became all the rage virtually overnight. Many trappers and entrepreneurs, inspired by leaders such as Gothier, Davis, and Schmalley, and cognizant of the economic potential, rushed to trap mink alive or import breeders from prime stocks in the Yukon, Quebec, and Nova Scotia. The price of a mink pelt doubled in just a few years' time. Although the depression era of the 1930s saw a small decline, by the end of the Second World War, more than 1 million mink pelts were coming out of America's fur farms every year. This total would continue to grow unabated for the next quarter of a century.

Today in the United States, as in the rest of the world, fur farming is nearly synonymous with mink, this species currently accounting for 93 percent of all ranch-raised pelts in America. The North American mink (*Mustela vison*) is a member of the Mustelid family of carnivorous mammals, characterized by long, slender bodies, short legs, and small, rounded ears. Its closest relatives are the weasel, ermine, and ferret (*Mustela nivalis, frenata,* and *nigripes,* respectively), but the family also includes the fisher (*Martes pennanti*), marten (*Martes americana*), and skunk (*Mephitis mephitis*). All these animals are usually solitary, primarily nocturnal, and demonstrate a level of ferocity out of all proportion to their diminutive size. For the wild mink, that is a body about one foot long, weighing less than three pounds. The average ranch mink is about half again bigger and heavier than its wild brethren, with some exceptional individuals at double the size.

Although most mink in their natural environment are a uniform dark brown, in the 1930s breeders discovered various genetic mutations that altered the natural color of the animal's fur. Today, mink are produced in about thirty different colors, including black, white, pearl, silver, violet, lavender, pink, sapphire, and gunmetal. The fur industry claims that there are significant behavioral differences as well, touting the ranch mink as a fairly tame creature, perhaps not quite docile but certainly not the hissing, gnashing bundle of fury one might encounter in nature. Indeed a number of states—Connecticut, Idaho, Illinois, Maine, Minnesota, Oregon, South Dakota, and Vermont among them—legally classify mink (and other fur-bearing animals) raised in captivity as "domestic" animals, not wildlife. This notion is quickly rejected as ridiculous by critics of fur farming. An animal species, they say, the product of countless millennia adapting to wild habitats, cannot become domesticated after little more than a century of confinement.

Fur farms in America are usually run by families two or three generations removed from the person who started the business, often a patriarch who began taking furbearing animals in the wild as a trapper. Many modern fur breeders have college degrees in agriculture, animal science, biology, or business. The farms they operate in America are structured much the same as those found anywhere else in the world, no matter the geographic location or size. Situated mainly in the colder latitudes of the earth, some fur farms house fewer than 100 animals while others (in Scandinavia) more than 100,000.

The standard layout features long, double rows of cages, or "pens" as they are called in the industry, ensconced beneath open-sided sheds about twelve feet wide, covered with roofing panels. To allow early morning and late afternoon exposure to the sun, the sheds are usually placed on a north-south axis. The cages, elevated off the ground on stands, are constructed of wire mesh, with bedding provided only in small, attached nest boxes. Mink pens are oblong shaped, measuring 2 or 3 feet long, and 1 1/2 feet wide and high. Fox cages are considerably larger to confine the bigger species. The animals are typically fed once a day with a wet mash of meat, poultry, and fish by-products not utilized for human consumption. Water is available in a cup fitted to the cage or through a small pipe valve. To prevent animals that have gotten out of their cages from leaving the property, and to stop predators or disease-laden wildlife from entering, the ranches are always surrounded by 5- or 6-foot-high fences, often chain-link woven with sheet-metal.

The major events on the fur farm through the year center on the reproductive cycles of the animals. Mink are usually bred in February—fox in March—with a litter of four or five "kits" born ("whelped") in April and May. The young ones are separated from their mothers after about six to eight weeks, and they begin shedding hair shortly thereafter. The molt continues through the summer and into early fall and, when completed, the animals' winter pelt starts to come in. By November or December, the fur is in prime condition, thick and luxuriant, and it is at this time that the breeder and his or her staff kill the nonbreeding animals and collect the pelts ("pelting"). This gives mink and fox an average life span of perhaps eight months. Especially healthy and fertile females are usually kept for up to five years, but they too will eventually be killed and skinned.

Traditionally, regardless of age, the animals were killed either by breaking their necks with a ratchet tool or through asphyxiation induced with carbon monoxide, usually exhaust fumes piped into an airtight box from an idling motor vehicle. In more recent times, there seems to be less neck breaking, and greater use of CO cylinders and lethal injections, although no hard data on methods are available. Once dead, the bodies are stripped of their pelts, which are then scraped ("fleshed") and dried to prevent decay, bundled, and turned over to a fur dealer, thus leaving the farm and entering the commercial market.

American Fur Industry
The fur dealer is paid a commission to handle the pelts and sell them for the breeder at auctions, most often in New York or Seattle (major international auction houses are in Toronto, Helsinki, Copenhagen, Frankfurt, St. Petersburg, and Hong Kong). The buyer is usually a dealer working for a fur wholesaler who will "dress" the pelts before reselling them to a manufacturer. The dressing is a complicated process of soaking, cleaning, softening, tanning, drying, and stretching, perhaps followed by dyeing. Manufacturers buy the dressed skins and then, working with a designer's pattern, stitch them into luxury garments, reserving the off-cuts to sew "plates" that will be fashioned into linings or cheaper sorts of apparel.

Constructing a full-length mink coat requires pelts from as many as seventy animals. A coat of similar size takes fifteen to twenty foxes to complete, although most fox is now used for trimming clothes. These finished articles are next purchased by a furrier or a retail department store, and then made available to the general public. The whole process may take a full year from the time the animals are skinned to the time the coat appears on a mannequin in a storefront window.

The American fur industry has suffered a precipitous decline over the last thirty years or so, a period that followed decades of continuous advances. The number of mink farms has shrunk dramatically from over 1,200 in 1968 to less than 450 in 1999, with decreasing numbers every year since 1980. Correspondingly, in the same three-decade period the number of mink pelts produced annually has tumbled from a peak of 6 million to less than 3 million. What is worse for the industry, the price of a raw pelt today is close to what it was in the late 1960s—about $24—even though production costs are now much higher and the dollar worth less (just before the stock market crash in 1929, mink sold at $20 a pelt). Total fur earnings have also dipped markedly, especially during the last half of the 1980s and into the 1990s. Revenue topped out at over $1.8 billion in 1985, just before antifur forces escalated their attack on the industry.

After five years of waging a persistent war in the press, through advertising, and in city streets—where those daring to wear fur risked being splashed and sprayed with red paint, while many fur retailers were vandalized—sales had been cut nearly in half, and the majority of fashion designers had stopped including animal pelage in the latest styles. Fur rebounded slightly in the mid-1990s, up to almost $1.3 billion in 1997, but then fell back closer to $1.2 billion in 1998, still an imposing figure that is

the envy of many American businesses. The numbers are a bit mislead-
ing however. The fur industry reports total income, not just garment
sales. Around 30 to 40 percent of earnings here are derived from various
"services" provided for owners of furs, such as storage, cleaning, repair,
and alterations.

Despite the slump from 1997 to 1998, designers seem to be intent on reviving the industry: more of them were using fur in 2000 than at any time
in nearly twenty years. This trend is likely to continue, provided, of
course, that consumers respond favorably, something those drawing fur
into their designs seem quite confident will occur. A few of the fashion
doyennes pursuing this course—Carolina Herrera, for example—had re-
nounced fur earlier in the decade, a change of mind and heart that has
also afflicted some of the world's celebrity "supermodels," such as
Naomi Campbell, who had once appeared nude in a provocative People
for the Ethical Treatment of Animals (PETA) ad claiming she would
rather be naked than wear fur.

The prevailing government restriction on the fur industry (other than
taxation) is imposed by the individual states in the form of statutes regulating commerce in animal pelts, laws that are directed at the fur dealer.
All states require dealers to purchase a license (sometimes called a permit) before they can legally trade in raw furs, with fees for residents of
the state ranging widely from a low of $1 (Alabama) to a high of $295
(Georgia); nonresident licenses typically cost three to ten times these
amounts. There are significant differences among the states concerning
what activities count as dealing in furs. Some define a dealer as anyone
who simply buys pelts, but others include buying *and* selling. Because the
fur farmer sells the animal skins, he or she is legally considered a dealer
in better than three-quarters of the states, and must also be licensed.

Utah and Wisconsin explicitly exempt the fur farmer from any licensing requirement, while Oregon and Idaho designate as dealers only those
who buy pelts. Washington requires a license just for those who "purchase, receive or resell" raw furs. Not coincidentally, these are five of the
top six fur-farming states in the country, accounting for about 75 percent
of domestic pelt production. The sixth, Minnesota, does direct anyone
who sells pelts to obtain a license. Several states—among them Alabama,
Maine, Nebraska, New Jersey, New York, and South Dakota—do not regard the fur farmer as a dealer, but still require a permit for raising and
breeding furbearing animals.

Legal Regulation of Fur Farms

In contrast to this ubiquitous regulation of commerce in fur, the *treatment*
of animals on fur farms is perhaps the most lightly regulated aspect of
any animal enterprise in America today—some have complained that

this dimension of the industry is essentially unregulated by law. Austria, on the other hand, banned fur farming entirely in 1998, and in 2000 the United Kingdom seems poised to do the same. The Ministry of Agriculture, Farming and Fisheries issued operating permits for an abbreviated three-year extension to Britain's sixteen mink farms, looking to make good on the Labor Party's pledge to end these operations.

For its part, the American government has not placed any restrictions whatever on how farmers raise and kill mink, fox, or other animals reared in captivity for their pelts: no standards are imposed for cage size, sanitation, heating, cooling, food, water, veterinary care, or methods of killing the animals. Moreover, U.S. wildlife protection laws do not extend to captive furbearers. They are not listed as endangered, they are obviously not marine mammals, migratory birds, or bald or golden eagles (*see* chapter 6 for the federal laws that cover these species), and no wild horses or wild burros are used for this purpose (*see* chapter 3: *Wild Free-Roaming Horses and Burros Act of 1971*). At any rate, and as suggested above, most of the states containing fur farms have officially designated their inhabitants "domestic" animals, not wildlife.

Even so, the federal laws that govern the handling and killing of domestic animals do not apply to these furbearers either. The Humane Methods of Slaughter Act (HMSA) and its regulations (*see* this chapter: *Humane Methods of Slaughter Act*), which require that only certain devices be used for stunning animals to insensibility and that the stunning occur before they are cut or hoisted, protects "cattle, calves, horses, mules, sheep, swine, and other livestock"—not poultry or, apparently, ranch-raised furbearers. No federal court has ever contemplated the issue of whether the HMSA applies to mink, fox, or other ranch-raised furbearers. Finally, the Animal Welfare Act (AWA) and its regulations (*see* chapter 7) stipulate that the term "animal" does *not* include those used for "food and fiber," thus placing all facets of animal agriculture, including fur farming, beyond the reach of the safeguards these federal laws afford.

The twenty-five states in which fur farms are currently located reinforce this federal exclusion by almost unanimously declaring that such operations are agricultural pursuits (Alabama law specifically directs that animal pelts are *not* farm products, and a few others do not have any stipulation). State humane slaughter statutes, which are often verbatim reproductions of the HMSA, follow the federal law in this respect also, by excluding captive furbearers from their protections, or so it seems anyway. No state court has ever pondered whether the restrictions on humane slaughter cover them.

The states' major form of legal constraint on the treatment of animals generally is the anticruelty statute (*see* chapter 3: *Anticruelty Laws*). Yet animals on fur farms find little if any relief from the law here either. Most state anticruelty laws, mirroring the AWA, exempt "normal" or "accepted" agricultural practices from any of the imposed restrictions, although none explicitly proclaim that fur farming is one of these exempted practices. A number of other states do not list an agricultural exception in their anticruelty statutes, and not every state that does have the exception has declared fur farming a dimension of agriculture. However, there is no record of any court ever convicting a fur farmer for violation of an anticruelty law in the operation of his or her facility or acquitting one so charged, nor any evidence that a state court has considered the question.

Even though there is a complete absence of case law that would settle the issue, several states appear to provide legal shelter for captive furbearers by defining exceptions to their anticruelty laws with language that fails to identify the fur farm, either explicitly or through a general agricultural exemption. The Georgia statute, for one, does not protect animals killed "for the purpose of providing food," "for humane purposes," for "the furtherance of medical or scientific research," or "wild animals" taken by lawful hunting. Because none of these exempt categories refers to the practice of raising animals to harvest their pelts, it would seem that there is legal space within Georgia's anticruelty law for captive furbearers. Alaska, Connecticut, Hawaii, and Iowa also list various exempt practices using animals that do not mention or imply fur farming.

A few states close any legal gap into which captive furbearers might enter to enjoy anticruelty protections with a catch-all exclusion that appeals to "customary" uses of animals. For a well-established industry at over 100 years old, this exception probably does capture fur farming, though, again, to date no court has ruled on the matter. Idaho, for instance, after listing eight different exceptions to the state anticruelty law, adds a ninth: "Any other exhibitions, competitions, activities, practices or procedures normally or commonly considered acceptable."

Many state anticruelty laws say very little about exactly what the exempted activities are, but nearly all of them prohibit mistreatment of animals that is done "without good cause," "maliciously," "needlessly," or "unjustifiably." The prevailing legal situation then seems to be one where it is just taken for granted that fur farming is necessary, justifiable, and is done for good cause and without malice. Currently, the one state that definitely does not make this assumption is Wisconsin, where we find the only semblance of an anticruelty law that applies specifically to ranch-raised furbearers. A Badger State statute provides that the Department of Agriculture "may examine all lands and buildings licensed as . . . fur farms . . . to determine whether wild animals held in captivity are treated in a humane manner and confined under sanitary conditions with proper care." Wisconsin is the largest producer of mink pelts in America.

Self-Regulation of Fur Farming

Fur farming is substantially, if not entirely, a *self-regulated* animal industry: the treatment of captive furbearers is primarily determined by the farmers themselves, rather than by any sort of government agency. Fur advocates often point out that federal or state regulation is not needed in this area because farmers have a powerful economic incentive to treat their furbearing animals well. After all, they say, one of the inevitable consequences of a poorly nourished, cruelly confined, and generally abused animal is a shabby, ragged pelt—for the fur farmer, this would mean a steadily diminishing or vanishing monetary value, striking directly at his or her livelihood. Critics retort that there is no similar economic incentive to kill mink and fox humanely.

The Fur Commission USA (FCUSA), an independent nonprofit association representing mink and fox farmers, stands today as the preeminent source of standards for fur farming as a self-regulating animal enterprise. In 1994 the FCUSA's Animal Welfare Committee revised a set of standards for operating mink and fox farms that were originally developed in the late 1980s by the Fur Farm Animal Welfare Coalition. A group of veterinarians, fur farmers, and animal scientists, the Coalition was exercised by the rising tide of antifur invective, most of which focused on animal mistreatment, and by slumping fur sales. The revisions of the FCUSA Committee were printed as *Standard Guidelines for the Operation of Mink and Fox Farms,* and a certification program was established for those facilities that were verified by an inspecting veterinarian as complying with the guidelines. Called the "Merit Award Humane Care Program," the FCUSA reports that in 2000 about 95 percent of mink pelts produced in America come from farms certified under the humane care program. Of course, these guidelines do not have the force of law, and there are no legal penalties for failing to follow them.

Most of the *Guidelines* address the major facets of the care and treatment of mink and fox in the operation of fur farms. Many of the standards are stated as procedures that "must" be followed, suggesting basic requirements, while others are put in the form of "should" statements, suggesting practices that are recommended but not required for certification. In the following survey of the Animal Welfare Committee's judgment, these two modal concepts will be interpreted accordingly.

The *Guidelines* begin with general principles of animal management. Farmers are required to be thoroughly versed in the natural history, behavior patterns, and nutritional needs of the animals. They must also be financially and materially equipped to provide appropriate housing, feed, water, and medical care for the mink and fox under their care. Further, farmers "must . . . ensur[e] that all employees and attendants on the farm are properly trained individuals who have a genuine concern for the welfare of the mink." This phrase does not occur in the discussion of fox farm management, nor does any other concerning the training of fox farm workers. Site selection for a fur farm must be a location with an adequate supply of clean water that also avoids areas with excessive amounts of noise and artificial lighting, both of which apparently disturb the animals. The Animal Welfare Committee requires that the farm be enclosed with an impenetrable fence, further specified for fox farms as one about six feet tall with a base buried to a depth of six or seven inches. Sheds must provide shelter from the weather and adequate ventilation. For mink, enclosed sheds are recommended only for areas frequented by severe weather, and must still provide sufficient natural lighting to promote the animals' normal life cycle.

The cages, or "pens," in which the animals reside need to be constructed in a manner that prevents the animals from escaping, and from injuring themselves or, especially for mink, injuring other animals in adjacent pens. Each cage must contain a fresh water source that is regularly maintained by the farmer, and readily accessed by the animal at any time. Proper feed must be provided and made easily available at least once a day, though the *Guidelines* add that once the mink are fully mature "it may be desirable to skip feed occasionally to aid conditioning," and "[u]nder certain conditions a daily feeding [of fox] may be skipped." The text does not explain what those conditions might be or why withholding food would enhance the quality of a mink's fur, but presumably these are items the fur farmer understands.

The Animal Welfare Committee requires that "furring pens"—cages of animals that will be killed for their pelts—for mink contain at least 2,000 cubic inches (a little larger than 1 cubic foot), while recommending 7 1/2 cubic feet for fox. Pens for breeding animals are to be at least twice these sizes, respectively for each species. All mink cages must have a nesting area, either made of wood or wire, large enough to allow the animal "to rest and sleep comfortably" and "designed to accommodate appropriate nesting materials." These materials are not specified. Only fox used for breeding must be provided with a nest box, which is also to have unidentified "suitable" nesting material. The pens must be elevated high enough off the ground so that feces fall clear of the cage. Manure under mink pens must be removed "regularly"—the *Guidelines* do not say how often that is, but do specify twice a month for fox. Pens should be cleaned "regularly" and "when necessary," without further designation of time intervals for either mink or fox.

Fur farmers are encouraged to work closely with a veterinarian and ensure that the animals receive appropriate vaccinations on a timely basis. Veterinary science should also be close at hand when the inevitable time comes to kill the animals and take their pelts. The *Guidelines* stipulate that killing furbearers according to methods approved by the American Veterinary Medical Association (AVMA) qualifies as "euthanasia, . . . a quiet, painless death . . . without causing fear and anxiety."

For mink, the Animal Welfare Committee endorses gassing with either carbon monoxide (CO) or carbon dioxide (CO_2). Manufacturer-sealed CO cylinders are "strongly recommended" for this purpose, rather than internal combustion engines; these produce CO as a by-product of burning gasoline. Car or truck exhaust is too hot and produces other chemicals in the combustion process that could cause the mink "irritation and discomfort." The *Guidelines* do not entirely reject internal combustion engines for killing mink—this method is allowed so long as the CO is "properly cooled and filtered." Either CO or CO_2 must be pumped into the "euthanasia chamber" in a concentration that will render the mink unconscious in 30 seconds or less; the *Guidelines* do not specify what that concentration is. Finally, it is recommended that only one mink at a time should be gassed, and each one must be examined individually to make sure it is dead.

The Animal Welfare Committee recommends that euthanasia for fox be performed by lethal injection, which is also approved by the AVMA. However, if the appropriate drugs (none are identified in the *Guidelines*) are not available, the fur farmer must use whatever method the veterinarian regards as humane.

COMMERCIAL TRAPPING

The legal regulation of trapping in America is mainly the responsibility of the individual states, although some federal laws do apply here. Under the Endangered Species Act, it is illegal to trap any animals designated by the U.S. Department of the Interior as either endangered or threatened. Also, bald and golden eagles, migratory birds, marine mammals, and wild horses and burros are generally shielded by the federal government through, respectively, the Bald Eagle Protection Act, the Migratory Bird Treaty Act, the Marine Mammal Protection Act, and the Wild Free-Roaming Horses and Burros Act (*see* chapter 6 for more on all of these laws, except the last, which is found in chapter 3; *see also* chapter 6: *National Wildlife Refuge System Improvement Act of 1997: Hunting and Trapping in National Wildlife Refuges*).

Congress has, however, written exceptions into all of these laws that allow the otherwise protected species to be live or lethally trapped under certain circumstances: to enhance the propagation and survival of endangered or threatened species, for scientific or exhibition purposes, for the protection of other wildlife, to promote commercial fisheries (marine mammals) or agricultural interests, and for religious (eagles) or subsistence purposes (marine mammals) by American Indians. Wild horses and burros may be trapped by government agents, in the sense of being rounded up and removed from the range when their numbers upset the "ecological balance" in certain areas.

Trapping for the purpose of selling the animal fur (or for recreation) is legal in every state except California. (Hawaii has no furbearing animals to trap.) In November 1998 California voters approved a ballot initiative, the most fundamental provision of which makes it unlawful for any person to trap any furbearing animal for commercial purposes or for sport, producing the first such statewide ban in the country. The Audubon Society and the California Waterfowl Association promptly filed suit in the U.S. District Court for Northern California, challenging a second stipulation of the new law that prohibits all government employees from trapping any mammal. The plaintiffs claim this violates the Endangered Species Act and the Migratory Bird Treaty Act by preventing federal agents from trapping predators that feed on endangered and threatened species and protected migratory birds. At this writing, the case remains in litigation.

Most of the state laws restricting trapping are regulations issued and enforced by wildlife agencies, traditionally called "Game and Fish Departments," but more recently known by such titles as "Department of Natural Resources" and "Department of Environmental Management." In several states, "game" or wildlife commissions rather than government agencies write these regulations, and some trapping laws come in the form of statutes authored by the legislature in the state capitol. Whatever their origin, these legal rules tend to be complicated and often vary widely from state to state. Trapping techniques and practices may have entirely different restrictions from one jurisdiction to the next, and those that are permitted or not even addressed by regulation in a particular state may be completely outlawed in another, perhaps even the one next door. Some states have many restrictions while others have very few.

Trapping in America

The history of trapping in the United States is closely associated with the westward incursions of Europeans and Anglo-Americans beyond the Mississippi River, across the Great Plains and over the Rocky Mountains to the Pacific. Throughout most of the eighteenth century and into the early nineteenth, trappers employed by the Hudson Bay Company, the North West Company, the American Fur Company, the Rocky Mountain Fur Company, and others probed the rivers and streams of the American west in search of beaver (*Castor canadensis*), mostly. Searching also for adventure, freedom, and money, the mountain men were at the vanguard of what many saw as the continental destiny of the white race. In their wake, the settlers and homesteaders were to follow, reinforced by the U.S. military, decimating the American Indian tribes that preceded them all.

Before very long, the beaver were decimated as well. By 1840, the rivers were trapped out, the bottom had fallen out of the European and American fur markets, and the mountain men and the fur traders were out of work. In the West during this time there were no legal restrictions on trapping, or hunting, or the taking of any animal at all by any means. Each man, each fur company, was free to kill as many animals as luck, skill, and ingenuity would allow. The notion of taking less now in order to ensure that there would be more in the future was not considered—the supply had seemed limitless. At the turn of the century, it was painfully clear that the supply of America's natural resources, including wild animals, was distinctly finite, and something needed to be done to address the growing problems of depletion and extinction.

The effort began in 1898 when Gifford Pinchot became head of the forestry division in the Department of Agriculture, soon to be reorganized under the administration of President Theodore Roosevelt as an independent agency, the U.S. Forest Service. Together, Roosevelt and Pinchot mandated America's first efforts at natural resource conservation, mainly by setting timber quotas, reforesting, and adding millions of acres of land to a highly regulated National Forest system. In 1908 Roosevelt convened a conference of state governors and urged them to tackle the problem of wildlife depredation. Two years later twenty-seven states had established game or conservation commissions that instituted hunting and trapping seasons, often setting limits on the number of animals that could be legally taken. By 1929 all forty-eight states had done so.

In 2000 there are about 150,000 trappers legally capturing and killing approximately 4 million wild animals every year. Most trapping is done for commercial purposes, namely, to sell the fur. Nearly half of the animals are taken in just four states: Wisconsin, Minnesota, Pennsylvania, and Ohio. These totals represent a dramatic decline from the late 1980s, when an estimated 20 million animals were taken by over 300,000 trappers. Informational campaigns and moral appeals launched by animal protection groups condemning trapping (and fur farming; *see* this chapter: *Fur Farming*) have apparently been successful, to some degree. Today, with demand dwindling and prices falling, very few people can count on trapping to make a living. Nearly all trappers engage in this activity only part time for supplemental income.

The animals most frequently targeted by trappers are coyotes (*Canis latrans*), rabbits (*Sylvilagus* and *Lepus* species), foxes (*Vulpes* species), raccoons (*Procyon lotor*), beavers, badgers (*Taxidea taxus*), muskrats (*Ondatra zibethicus*), nutria (*Myocastor coypus*, a large water rodent native to South America), bobcats (*Felis rufus*), fishers (*Martes pennanti*), and minks

(*Mustela vison*). The fur or "pelt" of these animals is usually sold to fur dealers who wholesale them to garment manufacturers, frequently located overseas. Additionally, squirrels (*Sciurus* and *Tamiasciurus* species), skunks (*Mephitis mephitis*), weasels (*Mustela* species), gophers (*Thomomys* and *Geomys* species), prairie dogs (*Cynomys* species), opossums (*Didelphis virgiana*), and other small mammals are often trapped to remove nuisances to human interests.

Traps

There are three basic types of traps subject to legal regulation. The most common, and most controversial, is the steel-jaw leghold (or foothold) trap. It is estimated that 80 percent of all animals trapped in the United States are taken by this device.

Basically unchanged since its invention in 1823, the leghold trap is intended to secure furbearing animals, later to be killed and retrieved by the trapper, without damaging the pelt. Its two spring-loaded jaws snap shut when the pan is depressed, releasing the trigger. Different varieties of these traps are distinguished according to the spring configuration—ranging from the single or double longspring, to the underspring, and the coiled spring—and size, measured by the distance between the jaws when the trap is set. Number 0 traps have a 3 1/2 inch jaw spread and a number 5 has a 12-inch spread, with various measurements in between. The largest bear traps may have a spread of 3 feet. Unlike the popular image of them, leghold traps are rarely manufactured with teeth, however, rows of teeth can be purchased and attached.

The National Trappers Association (NTA) claims that toothless legholds do not injure animals. On the other side, the American Veterinary Medical Association and the American Animal Hospital Association have both announced that, with or without teeth, this trap is inhumane, and both associations officially favor its legal prohibition. Despite the NTA assertion, documented injuries caused by these traps include extensive soft tissue damage, bone fractures, abscesses, and gangrene. It is well known that many animals will chew their own legs off to get free of them; a double jaw leghold is designed to prevent this.

The second type of trap is the body-gripping trap, variously known as killer traps, body-crushing traps, or by the trade name of its inventor, Conibear. These are constructed of two rectangular, square, or circular jaws made of metal with a spring attached to one or both sides. When an animal reaches or swims through the rectangle with the trigger, the trap is sprung, the jaws closing on the creature's body in a scissors-like action.

Body-gripping traps generally come in 3 standard sizes, 5, 7, and 12 inches, again measured by the jawspread when set. These traps are intended to kill the animal quickly, and avoid the lengthy suffering that may be endured by an animal caught in a leghold trap. This is supposed to be accomplished when the jaws rapidly shut on the spinal column at the base of the skull, breaking the neck and severing the spinal cord. However, it is widely acknowledged that body-gripping traps often fail to make the quick kill and instead clamp down on an animal's chest or pelvis, causing fractures and extensive blunt trauma injuries.

The snare is perhaps most problematic from the perspective of animal welfare, yet it also holds the promise of humane trapping. Essentially a wire looped at one end and attached to an anchor at the other, snares come in two basic types depending on the set. The leg snare is placed on the ground horizontally with a loop diameter of a few inches, and is activated when an animal steps in a pan; the neck or body snare is set vertically at some distance off the ground, looped at 6 inches or more. Most often, snares are made of uncoated cables, and neck or body snares slowly strangle animals to death or crush their vital organs, while leg snares tend to tear through the fur and skin all the way to the bone. Snares made of coated wire that are designed to constrict to a point short of causing death or serious injury hold the animal securely, avoiding needless pain and suffering. These have the added advantage that non-target animals caught in such a snare may be released without harm. Unfortunately, no state requires coated-wire snares, and they seem to be seldom used by trappers.

There is a fourth kind of trap, but there are few legal restrictions on its use. Variously known as cage traps or box traps, sometimes also called "live" traps, these are almost never used by commercial trappers; they are more expensive than other types of traps, difficult to disguise, and cumbersome to carry. Moreover, they present problems for the trapper intending to kill the confined animal. Unless the trap is set underwater, and the animal drowns, the cage itself tends to protect the creature from any lethal means employed by the trapper to dispatch it, and most are reluctant to extract the creature to end its life.

General Trapping Laws

All states require an adult to purchase either a trapping license or a general hunting (or small game) license, or sometimes both. License fees are reduced for minors, and some states exempt those who are underage from the license requirement, although that age varies from ten in Maine to eighteen in Colorado. Fees for residents generally run between $10 and $30, with nonresident fees usually costing five to ten times as much or more.

Trapping seasons are specified in state regulations, fluctuating somewhat according to the jurisdiction and the "target" species. Generally, though, the trapping season runs from late fall through early spring, or

November through March, the cold time when the pelts of furbearers are at their thickest and most luxuriant. Some species, such as the badger in Colorado, and the coyote in many states, may be legally trapped at any time of year. Limits are sometimes set on the number of animals a trapper may take, also depending on species and often on the particular "game unit"—an area of land—but frequently there are no limits for in-season trapping. With a few exceptions—such as Alaska, Florida, and Louisiana—the states require trappers to attach identification tags to their traps, typically listing the trapper's name, address, and license number.

Besides licensing, seasons, take limits, and identification, there are several other dimensions of trapping that are regulated by states. Foremost among them are these three: (1) the type and size of the traps allowed, which may depend on whether the trap is placed on land or in water, and trap placement, too, is sometimes restricted; (2) how often, if at all, the trap must be checked, which may also depend on where the trap is set; and (3) the status of wildlife liable to be trapped as "protected," or "unprotected," and rules concerning "nontarget" animals found in traps. In keeping with the multifaceted nature of trapping regulations, not all states specify rules for all these aspects, and two or more states may have very different regulations for the same item. Each of these is considered in turn, and some representative restrictions upon them are noted.

Trap Restrictions
In 1971 Rhode Island became the first state to ban steel-jaw leghold traps entirely. Florida followed with their own ban in 1973, and New Jersey enacted theirs in 1986. These three were enactments of the respective state legislatures, but in the late 1990s citizen initiatives in California, Colorado, Massachusetts, and Arizona led to prohibitions in these states on the use of these traps (on public land only in Arizona, about 80 percent of the state). Voters in the state of Washington did the same in 2000, bringing the total to eight. Connecticut and Delaware prohibit leghold sets on land, but they are allowed in water.

At the federal level, bills to outlaw these traps entirely have been introduced on Capitol Hill many times, beginning in 1957 and continuing to the time of this writing in 2000. No such proposal has ever survived long enough to be called up for a vote on the floor of Congress; the current version is mired in various committees. In contrast, at last count eighty-nine other countries around the world have banned leghold traps, including all fifteen nations of the European Union.

Most of the remaining forty-two states that permit steel-jaw leghold traps place various restrictions on their use. About one-third of the states prohibit using them with teeth, and about two-thirds of the states have size limits for these traps. The limits vary considerably, from 5 5/8 inches in Ohio to 9 inches in Alaska and Oregon. Size limits often depend on whether the trap is set on land or in water. New Mexico, for example, allows 6 1/2 inches on land and a 12-inch spread for water sets, the largest specified measure for any state. Several jurisdictions impose one size limit no matter where the trap is set, while others restrict the size only for land sets, and have no limits for those placed in water.

New Mexico, along with Indiana and North Carolina, require that the jaws of the traps be offset, so they do not meet when sprung but leave a small space between the jaws. Either offset or padded jaws are required in Arizona (on private land), Tennessee (except in burrow entrances and water), Utah, and Washington. Idaho, Kansas, Michigan, Mississippi, Montana, New Hampshire, South Dakota, Texas, and Wyoming currently have no such restrictions whatever.

California, Colorado, Florida, and Oklahoma have declared the body-gripping trap inhumane, and have outlawed its use entirely. Arizona will not allow it on public lands, and Delaware, Maryland, New Jersey, South Dakota, and West Virginia have banned it from land use, but it is permitted in these jurisdictions in water. Massachusetts voters had rejected the Conibear-type trap in 1996; however, the legislature of the Commonwealth passed a bill in early 2000 bringing it back. As with leghold traps, most states have size restrictions on body-gripping traps, from no more than 4 1/2 inches in Ohio to 11 inches in Alaska. Some variations on this regulated area include Iowa, where body-griping traps larger than 8 inches must be completely submerged; North Dakota, with the same rule, but only between certain dates; and New Hampshire, which allows traps larger than 7 inches for bear only. Half the states have no size restriction for water sets, and one-third have no restrictions of any sort on body-gripping traps.

Like nearly all trapping regulations, restrictions on snares differ markedly from state to state. Minnesota's are the most complex, stipulating that, among other things, fox can be taken with a snare only in the northeast forest zone of the state, water snares are only permitted in the central zone, snare loop diameter must be 10 inches or less, snare cable diameter at 1/8 inch minimally, and bobcats and bears cannot be trapped with snares. A few states specify loop diameter, and these may be a maximum—such as in Minnesota, also Ohio's 15-inch limit—or a minimum, as in Arkansas, Missouri, and South Dakota, where a lock must be attached to snares preventing them from closing to less than 2 1/2 inches in diameter. Rarely, states also stipulate a minimum diameter of snare cable, as Minnesota does, for example 1/16 of an inch in North Dakota and 5/64 in Missouri.

Nine states prohibit the use of any snare, anywhere: California, Connecticut, Massachusetts, New Hampshire, New York, North Carolina,

Oklahoma, Pennsylvania, and Rhode Island. Arizona and Indiana do not allow snares on public land, while Maryland bans them in seven specific counties. Alabama and Wisconsin prohibit their use on land, but have no restrictions on snares set underwater. Arkansas has banned leg snares but not body snares. Georgia, Maine, South Carolina, and Michigan allow snares underwater and only for beaver. Twenty-eight states have no restrictions on the use of snares.

Some states have specific distance restrictions on the proximity to areas frequented by humans that a trap may be set; as usual, there is great variation here too. For example, Arizona prohibits setting a trap within 25 yards of an established road, or within 50 feet of mapped trails, and will not allow any sets within 1/2 mile of picnic or camping areas, or roadside rest stops. New Mexico makes it 25 yards from either roads or trails, and 1/4 mile from picnic or camping areas, or roadside rest stops. New York's regulation prohibits only traps set on public roads. South Carolina's regulation prohibits only traps set on trails or paths. Kansas bans traps closer than 50 feet from roads and 5 feet from fences bordering roads. Maryland says nothing about roads, fences, trails, picnic or camping areas, or roadside rests, but prohibits setting traps within 150 yards of a human habitation. Maine makes it a minimum of 200 yards from an inhabited dwelling, unless the resident gives permission to set the trap closer, or it is completely submerged, or it is set for beaver; Maine also prohibits a person from trapping outside of his or her own property within 1/2 mile of a town. Colorado outlaws sets within 500 yards of dwellings or structures. In Iowa, the distance restriction for dwellings applies only to body-gripping traps and snares, and there is no mention of such a restriction around towns. Surprisingly, most states do not have any such distance restrictions on trap sets, unlike the hunting regulations of the states, every one of which prohibits the discharge of firearms in close proximity to buildings or roads, typically within 100 to 150 feet (for hunting laws generally, *see* chapter 5: *Recreational Hunting*).

Trap Check
Wildlife caught in traps—whether leghold, "killer," or snare—can suffer through prolonged, excruciating deaths from blood loss, shock, and exposure. In an attempt to make their trapping laws more humane, most states mandate that trappers examine their sets periodically in order to kill or release those animals who might otherwise slowly expire in misery. Here we find another motley collection of regulations with trap-checking requirements varying enormously from state to state.

About one-third of the states require trappers to visit all their traps, no matter where they are set, every twenty-four hours. In contrast, Alabama, Alaska, Kansas, Montana, and Michigan do not require trappers to check any of their sets at any time; North Dakota merely "recommends" that they do.

The two most common variables for check requirements, however, are trap placement and trap type. Minnesota, for example, mandates a daily check for land traps, every three days in water, and no requirement at all for traps set under ice. Maine says the same, but it is every five days for water sets. Wisconsin has this regulation too, but at four days in water. New Hampshire rules call for daily checks of any trap, but seventy-two hours if it is under ice. Arkansas and Iowa also require that all land traps be inspected every day, yet have no requirements at all for water sets. Washington requires trappers to check legholds and snares every forty-eight hours, unless they are set in urban areas, in which case they must be checked daily, while body-gripping traps must be examined every seventy-two hours. In Utah legholds and snares set on land must be checked every two days, but only every four days for body-gripping and underwater traps.

Some states ignore these factors. Nevada says ninety-six hours for all traps no matter the type or placement; Idaho says seventy-two hours; in Mississippi, Tennessee, and Texas, thirty-six hours; Ohio, Oklahoma, and Rhode Island, twenty-four. There is even a variation on this minimal theme: New Mexico requires a check every twenty-four hours by a trapper or his or her "representative, " but the trapper himself or herself must examine the sets every other day.

Protected, Unprotected, and Nontarget Species

Each state's trapping regulations contains a list of "furbearers." Sometimes this list is included as part of an inventory of "protected" species of wildlife, and other times it is distinguished from the "protected" animals. A number of states make no mention of either "protected" or "unprotected" species. This somewhat confusing terminology arises because wildlife agencies tend to use the word "protected" indiscriminately to refer to wildlife with two very different sorts of legal status.

In one sense, "protected" signifies species for which there is a "closed" and an "open" season—a time in the calendar year when it is illegal to trap or hunt those animals, and a time when all taking is regulated by a permit/license system. In the other sense, "protected" refers to species that may not be legally taken at (almost) any time—there is no open season—typically animals designated as endangered or threatened under federal or state laws, and marine mammals. Strictly speaking, then, there is a "closed-season protected status" and a "no-kill protected status." On the other hand, the term "unprotected" has a fairly uniform meaning as those species that trappers are permitted to take throughout the year, and this often includes some of the listed furbearers. So furbearing animals liable to be trapped may be either "protected" or "unprotected."

The animal most commonly unprotected from trappers is the coyote, listed as such in about half of the states, followed by the skunk and the raccoon. Ground hogs, opossum, beaver, weasel, and jackrabbits have a year-round open season in a number of states. Arizona, Wisconsin, and Minnesota simply note that all animals for which no closed season has been declared are unprotected. The protected species—meaning protected from being killed by trappers—run toward large and medium-sized carnivorous mammals, some of which are legally designated as endangered in all or part of their range: for example, the black bear (*Ursus americanus*), grizzly bear (*Ursus arctos*), mountain lion (*Felis concolor*), lynx (*Lynx canadensis*), gray wolf (*Canis lupus*), black-footed ferret (*Mustela nigripes*), wolverine (*Gulo gulo*), and river otter (*Lutre canadensis*).

Some states have outlawed trapping certain species that may be lawfully taken in other states. For example, several states prohibit trapping black bears—among them Alabama, Connecticut, Louisiana, Maryland, Missouri, New Jersey, and Oklahoma—while most western and Great Lakes states offer no such protections to the bruins (*see also* chapter 6: *Legal Protections for Bears*). A few jurisdictions prohibit trapping animals that are actually extinct in that state, such as Texas, where it is illegal to traps wolves or jaguars even though neither species has been spotted in the Lone Star State for decades.

The concept of a "nontarget species" is rarely defined in state trapping regulations. Idaho is one of the very few states in which this term basically refers to protected wildlife: "any species for which the season is closed." A more inclusive characterization would mention domestic animals as well: any species not classified as wildlife for which there is neither an open nor a closed season. Unlike hunting, in which the person with the weapon can refrain from shooting a nontarget animal, traps take any creature that happens to come too close. No one knows how many dogs, cats, livestock, endangered species, and animals caught out of season end up in traps. Estimates range from a ratio of two nontargets for each target animal, to five for every one. Taking the lower figure means that 9 million protected and domestic species are trapped every year.

Nonetheless, half of the states have no laws addressing the issue of the accidental trapping of nontarget species, and a third of those that do direct their provisions only to the taking of wildlife out of season. Utah, Washington, and Wyoming require trappers to release such animals "unharmed," but offer no suggestions about how to do that. Washington adds that if the creature cannot be released unharmed, it should be left in the trap and officials of the state Department of Fish and Wildlife notified. But in Idaho, which requires wildlife to be "released immediately," dead animals are to be removed from the trap, "taken into possession," and the

Department of Fish and Game notified within three days. Similarly, Colorado tells trappers to "release immediately . . . [any] wildlife accidentally captured alive. It cannot be killed." If the animal is dead, the carcass is to be delivered to a Division Wildlife Officer within five days. Trapping a "protected furbearer" in South Dakota means only that the Department of Fish and Game must be informed within twenty-four hours.

For those states that do consider domestic animals in their regulations, some of these are quite narrowly written while others are more expansive. Missouri simply prohibits setting traps in "paths made or used by persons or domestic animals." Likewise, Louisiana tells trappers to "avoid setting traps in areas where domestic animals may be caught." Georgia requires trappers to carry choke sticks—a pole with a loop on one end—to release domestic animals. In Montana snares must not be set where they might catch livestock; no other trap or nontarget species are mentioned for Big Sky country. Arizona's law is probably the broadest, requiring trappers to both "release without additional injury all animals [they] cannot lawfully take" and carry a device to assist in the removal of nontarget animals from the trap.

None of these states provide any express penalty for trapping nontarget species. Indeed, Idaho offers trappers $5 for turning in lynx and river otter carcasses, both endangered species. Alabama, Montana, and New Hampshire impose liability for damages to domestic animals.

REFERENCES

Federal Laws
Animal Welfare Act of 1970, 7 U.S.C. §§ 2131–2157.
Exemptions from inspection requirements, personal and custom
  slaughtering, 21 U.S.C. § 623.
Humane Methods of Slaughter Act of 1978, 7 U.S.C. §§ 1901–1906.
Humane Slaughter Act of 1960, 7 U.S.C. §§ 1901–1906.
Meat Inspection Act, 21 U.S.C. §§ 601–623.
Twenty-Eight Hour Law of 1994, 49 U.S.C. § 80502.
United States Constitution, First Amendment.

Federal Regulations
Animal proteins prohibited in ruminant feed, 21 C.F.R. § 589.2000.
Bovine Spongiform Encephalopathy: Prohibited Importations, 9 C.F.R.
  § 94.18.
Humane Slaughter of Livestock, 9 C.F.R. §§ 313.1–50.
Twenty-Eight Hour Law regulations, 9 C.F.R. §§ 89.1–5.

State Laws
Anticruelty Laws. *See* Appendix 3, State Anticruelty Laws.
Ohio, Disparagement of perishable agricultural or aquacultural food
    products, Ohio Rev. Code Ann. § 2307.81.
Transportation of Poultry. Connecticut, Conn. Gen. Stat., § 53-249;
    Rhode Island, R.I. Gen. Laws, § 4-1-7; Wisconsin, Wis. Stat., § 134.52.
Trapping Regulations. *See below,* World Wide Web, State Wildlife Agencies.
Wisconsin, Humane, adequate and sanitary care of wild animals, Wis.
    Stat. § 29.879.

Federal Cases
Supreme Court
    Church of Lukumi Babalu Aye v. City of Hialeah, 508 U.S. 520 (1993).
    Employment Division v. Smith, 494 U.S. 872 (1990).

District Courts
    Humane Society v. Lyng, 633 F. Supp. 480 (W.D.N.Y. 1986).
    Jones v. Butz, 374 F. Supp. 1284 (S.D.N.Y.), *affirmed,* 419 U.S. 806 (1974).
    Texas Beef Group v. Winfrey, 11 F. Supp. 2d 858 (N.D. Tex. 1998).

Foreign Cases
McDonald's Corporation v. Steel, English High Court of Justice, Queen's
    Bench Division (Q.B. Div'l Ct. 1997).

State Cases
California
    Farm Sanctuary v. Department of Food and Agriculture, 74 Cal. App. 4th
        495 (1998).

Nebraska
    State v. Schott, 384 N.W.2d 620 (Neb. 1986).

Pennsylvania
    Commonwealth v. Barnes, 629 A.2d 123 (Pa. 1993).

Books
American Meat Institute. 2000. *Meat and Poultry Facts.* Washington, DC:
    AMI.
Brooman, Simon, and Debbie Legge. 1997. *Law Relating to Animals.* London: Cavendish.
Clemen, Rudolf Alexander. 1966. *The American Livestock and Meat Industry.* New York: Johnson Reprint Corporation (New York: Ronald Press,
    1923).

Dale, Edward E. 1960. *The Range Cattle Industry*. Norman: University of Oklahoma Press.

Eisnitz, Gail. 1997. *Slaughterhouse*. Amherst, NY: Prometheus Books.

Frasch, Pamela D., et al. 2000. *Animal Law*. Durham, NC: Carolina Academic Press.

Garner, Robert. 1998. *Political Animals: Animal Protection Politics in Britain and the United States*. New York: St. Martin's.

Gillespie, James R. 1995. *Modern Livestock & Poultry Production*. 5th ed. Albany, NY: Delmar.

Grandin, Temple. 2000. "Handling and Welfare of Livestock in Slaughter Plants." In *Livestock Handling and Transport*. 2d ed. Edited by Temple Grandin. New York: CABI.

Hodgson, Robert G. 1945. *The Mink Book*. 2d ed. Toronto: Fur Trade Journal of Canada.

Katme, A. M. 1987. "An Up-To-Date Assessment of the Muslim Method of Slaughter." In *Humane Slaughter of Animals for Food*. London: Universities Federation for Animal Welfare.

Leavitt, Emily Stewart, and Diane Halverson. 1990. "Humane Slaughter Laws." In *Animals and Their Legal Rights*. 4th ed. Washington, DC: Animal Welfare Institute.

Liss, Cathy. 1998. "Trapping." In *Encyclopedia of Animal Rights and Animal Welfare*. Edited by Marc Bekoff. Westport, CT: Greenwood.

Lyman, Howard. 1998. *Mad Cowboy: Plain Truth from the Rancher Who Won't Eat Meat*. New York: Simon & Schuster.

Mason, Jim, and Peter Singer. 1990. *Animal Factories*. New York: Harmony Books.

Mench, Joy A. 1998. "Chickens." In *Encyclopedia of Animal Rights and Animal Welfare*. Edited by Marc Bekoff. Westport, CT: Greenwood Press.

Musgrave, Ruth, and Mary Anne Stein. 1993. *State Wildlife Laws Handbook*. Rockville, MD: Government Institutes.

Rhodes, Richard. 1997. *Deadly Feasts: Tracking the Secrets of a Terrifying New Plague*. New York: Simon & Schuster.

Rollin, Bernard. 1995. *Farm Animal Welfare*. Ames: University of Iowa Press.

Romans, John R., et al. 1994. *The Meat We Eat*. 13th ed. Danville, IL: Interstate.

Sinclair, Upton. 1906. *The Jungle*. Urbana: University of Illinois Press, 1988 (New York: Doubleday, 1906).

Smith, Bruce W. 1981. *Nature's Jewels: A History of Mink Farming in the United States*. Brookfield, WI: National Board of Fur Farm Organizations.

Toby, Milton C., and Karen L. Perch. 1999. *Understanding Equine Law*. Lexington, KY: The Blood-Horse, Inc.

Vialles, Noel. 1994. *Animal to Edible*. Translated by J.A. Underwood. London: Cambridge University Press.

White, Richard. 1994. "Animals and Enterprise." In *The Oxford History of the American West*. New York: Oxford University Press.

Wolfson, David J. 1999. *Beyond the Law: Agribusiness and the Systematic Abuse of Animals Raised for Food or Food Production*. Watkins Glen, NY: Farm Sanctuary, Inc.

Articles, Guidelines, and Reports

American Veterinary Medical Association. 1993. "1993 Report of the AVMA Panel on Euthanasia." *Journal of the American Veterinary Medical Association* 202: 229–249.

Animal Welfare Committee, Fur Commission USA. 1997. *Standard Guidelines for the Operation of Mink and Fox Farms* (September).

Aulrich, Richard J. 1998. "Michigan's Fur Bearing Industry." *Michigan State University Extension Special Report*, SR 499201 (July 28).

"BSE Watch." *The Animals' Agenda*, bimonthly continuing feature.

Collins, Earl K. 1937. "The History of Fur Farming." *The Black Fox Magazine* (January): 31–33, 66–67.

Goodwin, J. P. 1997. "Opening the Cages: Freedom from Fur Farms." *The Animals' Agenda* 17, no. 1: 22–23.

Grandin, Temple, and Joe Regenstein. 1994. "Religious Slaughter and Animal Welfare." *Meat Focus International* (March): 115–123.

Holzer, Henry Mark. 1995. "Contradictions Will Out: Animal Rights vs. Animal Sacrifice in the Supreme Court." *Animal Law* 1: 83–108.

Kaufman, Marc. 2000. "Cracks in the Egg Industry." *Washington Post*, 4 April, at A1.

NOVA, "The Brain Eater." Production of WGBH Boston, PBS affiliate. Broadcast transcript, February 1998.

Wolfson, David J. 1999. "McLibel." *Animal Law* 5: 21–60.

World Wide Web

Animal and Plant Health Inspection Service, USDA, http://www.aphis.usda.gov.

Animal Liberation Front, http://www.enviroweb.org/adl/alf.html.

Coalition to Abolish the Fur Trade, http://www.banfur.com.

Food and Drug Administration, http://www.fda.gov.

Food Safety and Inspection Service, http://www.fsis.usda.gov.

Fur Commission USA, http://www.furcommission.com.

Fur Information Council of America, http://www.fur.org.

The Fur Trade, http://www.worldanimal.net/fur-trade.html.

Humane Farming Association, http://www.hfa.org.

Kosher Slaughter, http://www.whit.org/shofar/html/kosher.html.

Mad Cow Disease Homepage, http://mad-cow.org/.

National Agricultural Statistics Service, http://www.usda.gov/nass.

National Trappers Association, http://www.nationaltrappers.com.

Santería, http://religioustolerance.org/santeri.htm.

State Wildlife Agencies, http://wildlife.state.co.us/about/StateAgency WebSites.htm.

United Poultry Concerns, http://www.upc-online.org/.

5. Animal Entertainment

CIRCUSES AND ZOOS

The Animal Welfare Act of 1970 (AWA) (*see also* chapter 7) and its implementing regulations impose standards for the care and handling of animals used by exhibitors. The AWA defines an animal exhibitor as "any person (public or private) exhibiting any animals . . . to the public for compensation, . . . and such term includes carnivals, circuses and zoos exhibiting such animals whether operated for profit or not." Specifically excluded from this definition of an exhibitor are owners and operators of pet stores (*see* chapter 3: *Dog Law: Dog Breeding, "Puppy Mills," and Pet Stores*), and any person participating in rodeos (*see* this chapter: *Rodeos*), horse, dog, or cat shows, and in livestock shows or fairs. The federal government does not impose any legal restrictions on these uses of animals.

As originally written by Congress, the AWA says nothing about animal acts generally, such as the use of trained animals in traveling shows, in television, the movies, and in other entertainment venues. However, federal regulations issued in 1972 under the authority of the statute inserted the phrase "animal acts" between "circuses" and "zoos" in the definition of "exhibitor." Similarly, the AWA does not mention horse or dog races, but these animal exhibitions later appeared in the regulatory definition as *excluded* from the provisions of the law (*see* this chapter: *Greyhound Racing and Horse Racing*). The addition of animal acts as regulated entities was challenged in 1976 when Hal Haviland, the owner of a professional "dog and pony show," argued that Congress did not intend the AWA to embrace the type of animal performance he operated.

Judge Robinson of the District of Columbia Circuit Court of Appeals disagreed, ruling that animal acts are similar enough to circuses, carnivals, and zoos to have been targeted by Congress for legal restrictions. Curiously, the judge did not address the similarities between Haviland's operation and the excluded exhibitions, rodeos and dog shows in particular. Why is the animal act at issue more like the regulated performances and less like the exempt ones? Haviland also complained that the AWA exemptions for other forms of animal exhibition, such as rodeos, unfairly discriminates against the restricted exhibitors. In response, the judge opined that AWA protections have broadened over time "as the national interest seemed to warrant," suggesting that there was no significant public concern about the treatment of animals in the exempted exhibitions (*Haviland v. Butz*).

Forms of Animal Exhibition

The AWA does not make any legal distinctions between circuses and zoos, but in practice the two can be differentiated according to how the animals are exhibited. In circuses and in some carnivals, they are usually trained to perform, or at least the animals are coaxed or coerced into displaying certain behaviors. Carnivals and circuses have common origins (*see* this chapter: *Circuses and Zoos: A Brief History of Circuses*), although circuses typically have more animal acts, and more elaborate ones, too, while carnivals have games of chance.

In contrast to circuses, carnivals, and other animal acts, animals in zoos are not trained nor are they customarily compelled to act in any particular way; they are simply on display. Animal exhibitions of this sort include: all sizes of zoos, from those containing hundreds of animals to "roadside" zoos with a dozen or fewer; nature preserves and wildlife parks, where for a fee wild animals (often exotic species) are available for viewing within large tracts of enclosed land; and aquariums, which feature maritime species.

The distinction between a circus and a zoo does sometimes get blurry. Nearly every aquarium has marine mammals—dolphins mostly—that are trained to perform in front of an audience, but they and other sea animals are also on display without performing. "Petting zoos" have domesticated animals that may be handled and ridden, and in some parks and preserves the animals may be coerced to appear for the paying customers. Some circuses and carnivals have a few animals that are simply presented without being made to "do" anything.

Most of the features taken to distinguish these two forms of animal exhibition produce an overlap in some operations. For example, zoos are often defined as places where animals are displayed to educate the public about various species, but it would be difficult to establish that no one learns anything about animals at a circus. Relatedly, some say that animals are used in circuses purely for entertainment, yet it is likely that this is precisely the motivation for most zoo visits. It might be thought that the conservation of species distinguishes zoos from circuses, but if that just means that certain species are being maintained, insulated from the vagaries of the wild, then circuses do that too. If conservation includes captive breeding programs, the fact is that a number of zoos do not have such programs while some circuses do.

Whatever the disposition of the animals utilized there, the AWA and its regulations provide nearly all of the legal restrictions impinging upon the approximately 2,100 circuses and carnivals of all sizes, zoos large and small, aquariums, nature preserves, and wildlife parks operating in the United States today. Enacted by Congress in 1970 and subsequently amended several times, the AWA marked the first time that the care and treatment of animals in American exhibitions had been regulated in any way. Indeed, it was not until the twentieth century that these creatures were protected by laws anywhere in the world—starting with Britain's Performing Animals Act of 1925—despite a sometimes sordid and suspect history tracing back many centuries.

A Brief History of Circuses

Circus is a Latin word for "circle" or "ring," yet the original circus, the *Circus Maximus* of Rome, was U-shaped rather than circular. The circus began there in the fourth century B.C.E., with horses as the featured animals. Spectators delighted in demonstrations of equestrian skill, and were especially thrilled by chariot races. Occasionally during the show overzealous or careless drivers would send the speeding chariots smashing into one another or cause them to topple while rounding a corner. The organizers of these events discovered that their audiences very much enjoyed witnessing these disasters. Within a few generations, the presentations in the Roman circus had evolved from mere competition to see who was the quickest to complete the course, to choreographed displays of spectacular chariot crashes. Designed to amuse the crowd, these often resulted in serious injuries or death for the luckless humans and horses.

From here it was a short step to a circus dominated by violent confrontations between humans and animals, and between different animal species, as epitomized by the notorious events staged in the Coliseum. Among them: the *venatio* featured the "hunting" of animals turned into the ring; gladiators made names for themselves fighting and slaying bulls, bears, lions, and other animals; criminals, and later Christians, were thrown into the arenas to battle the beasts, with the hapless humans sometimes provided with weapons and sometimes not; and strange combinations of animal species were provoked into fighting each other to the death. Over a span of more than 700 years of the Roman circus, hundreds of thousands of elephants, lions, leopards, cheetahs, wolves, hippos, bears, crocodiles, antelope, tigers, rhinos, seals, bison, horses, even ostriches, and other species were slaughtered. All this to entertain a volatile citizenry best mollified with, as the poet and satirist Juvenal put it, "bread and circuses" (for more on animal fighting staged to entertain humans, *see* this chapter: *Cockfighting and Dogfighting*).

After the fall of Rome in the fifth century C.E., organized exhibitions of animal fighting and killing declined drastically. It was left to itinerant animal trainers and handlers to wander the rutty roads of Europe and Asia, drifting from one village to the next, searching for people who would pay to watch an animal perform. Beginning in the seventh century, the fairgrounds of Europe proved the most fertile source of revenue for the traveling animal acts. Originally a gathering place for merchants selling their wares, the fairgrounds also featured animal acts and other performers as accompaniments to these business transactions. Over time, entertainment came to dominate these gatherings as the tradesmen abandoned them for standardized retail markets in the rapidly developing urban areas. By the 1300s, the foundations of the modern circus had been laid at the Euro-

pean fairs, where animals—horses mostly—did the bidding of their trainers, alongside jugglers, tumblers, tightrope walkers, and magicians.

It was not until the eighteenth century, however, that all these features
were put together under one show and dubbed a "circus." Like the original Circus Maximus, the modern circus began with horses and feats of
equestrian skill. An Englishman named Philip Astley is widely regarded
as "the father of the modern circus"—the first person to display his own
prodigious talents at trick riding, and those of other riders in his employ,
in an open ring for paying customers. By 1770 these demonstrations were
supplemented with the acrobatics, rope dancing, and juggling that have
since become standard circus fare. About ten years later, one of Astley's
former horsemen, Charles Hughes, opened up his own show and called
it "The Royal Circus." The idea proved immensely popular, especially as
a traveling show that brought amusement and excitement to the dreary
and boring village existence of the European countryside. At this time
there were no legal restrictions whatever on the use of animals in any
human endeavor, either in England or anywhere in Europe.

"The father of the American circus" was a student of Charles Hughes,
a Scotsman called John Bill Ricketts, who staged shows in Philadelphia
and New York City in 1793. Americans are credited with first displaying
wildlife as circus animals in the first few decades of the 1800s. Before this
era, the early circuses presented horses almost exclusively—sometimes
also dogs trained to do various stunts—and traveling exhibitions of exotic species were separate entertainment endeavors. These mobile zoos
were commonly called "menageries" or "museums," where the animals
did not perform but were merely shown. Gradually, to the great delight
of audiences everywhere, wild animals were added to the circuses, and
not simply as a static display. The first to pursue this course was Isaac
Van Amburgh, who in 1833 strolled into a cage of lions and bullied them
into obedience and submission. As big cats were increasingly displayed
in the circus repertoire, Van Amburgh's style and costume were widely
imitated, especially what became the standard "lion tamer" outfit: jungle
fatigues, pith helmet, whip, and a pistol firing blanks.

In 1835 a confederation of menageries known as the "Zoological Institute" formed, a syndicate that quickly monopolized the business of renting out exotic animals to circuses. By the 1850s dozens of circuses were
traveling across America. Infused by menageries, nearly all of them featured wild animals, sometimes as exhibits but usually as performers, especially lions, tigers, leopards, and chimpanzees, but including bears, giraffes, and camels. The most popular circus animal was quickly
established as the elephant, a stature that remains to this day (*see* this
chapter: *Circuses and Zoos: Elephants*).

Phineas Taylor Barnum bought a menagerie in 1860 and began touring throughout the eastern states, featuring the first hippopotamus to appear in America. Within little more than ten years he had wedded his collection of animals to a retinue of clowns, acrobats, and jugglers and called it "Barnum's Great Traveling Museum, Menagerie, Caravan, Hippodrome and Circus." In the 1880s, five brothers from Baraboo, Wisconsin, began presenting circuses and variety shows, the precursors of what would turn into the great circus dynasty of the twentieth century. Eventually, these Ringling Brothers would join forces with Barnum and by the 1920s own or claim title to a dozen different circuses, their eponymous show featuring a huge menagerie that at its height included 40 elephants and 400 horses. Today, the Ringling Brothers and Barnum & Bailey Circus is the premier traveling show in the United States, displaying a modern menagerie of some 250 animals.

A Brief History of Zoos

The keeping of wild or semidomesticated animals for exhibition purposes, motivated primarily by curiosity, traces back at least 4,500 years to the rulers of Old Kingdom Egypt, although these collections also had some religious significance. Pictures and hieroglyphics unearthed at Sakkarah show that these ancients had taken numerous species from the wild and raised them in captivity, including hyenas, monkeys, several kinds of antelope, ibex, and gazelles. By 1200 B.C.E., a series of later Egyptian kings had added lions, lynxes, leopards, cheetahs, various smaller wild cats, hares, giraffes, ostriches, and many species of birds to their collections.

In China the Emperor Wen Wang created a large garden about 1000 B.C.E., and called it *Ling-Yu*, the "Garden of Intelligence," or, in other translations, the "Divine Park." Details are lacking but apparently the Ling-Yu contained antelope, goats, several species of deer, many fish, dazzling white birds, and other animals thought to promote communication between humans and spirits. At about this same time in the Near East, King Solomon's Jerusalem menagerie included deer, horses, apes, and peacocks, and the kings of Babylonia kept monkeys, rhinoceroses, camels, and antelope.

The Greeks started collecting animals in the seventh century B.C.E., and within three hundred years, most Greek city-states contained a zoo, typically dominated by birds housed in sophisticated aviaries. The world's first great zoo was founded by a Greek, a general of Alexander the Great whom the boy king named Ptolemy I. Though located in Egypt, it was nonetheless in the deeply Helenized city of Alexandria that the zoo was established around the turn of the third century B.C.E.. Within a generation, the inventory of animals found there would be the envy of most modern zoos: elephants, lions, leopards, cheetahs, camels, giraffes, rhinoceroses, bears, oryxes, goats, sheep, oxen, and a very large snake that was probably a python.

Roman zoos began to develop as early as the third century B.C.E., but within a few generations appear to have become little more than holding areas for restocking the bloody shows in the Coliseum and other such circuses. With the demise of the Empire in the fifth century C.E., the zoos faded as well, and it was several centuries before a revival of animal collecting was seen in Europe. In the interim, the Emperor Charlemagne stands alone as the major patron and sponsor of the medieval zoo. His three menageries of the eighth century, located in present-day France and Germany, housed elephants (the first seen in Europe), monkeys, lions, bears, camels, falcons, and many exotic birds.

Zoos began to spring up again throughout the thirteenth and fourteenth centuries in Florence, Naples, Milan, Nicosia, Lisbon, and other European cities. Meanwhile, in Asia and the New World, the keeping of animal collections never faded. Marco Polo visited the personal menagerie of Kublai Khan, one populated with elephants, rhinoceroses, hippopotamuses, tigers, leopards, bears, deer, boars, camels, monkeys, and other species. In Mexico, at the vast gardens of Moctezuma, Hernan Cortes found aviaries stocked with raptors, waterfowl, and pheasants, and paddocks for jaguars ("leopards"), foxes, snakes, monkeys, sloths, caimans, turtles, llamas, deer, armadillos, and antelope.

As the Renaissance progressed back in Europe, it became quite fashionable among aristocrats, royalty, monarchs, and even popes to establish zoos in their preferred locations. So we find that within a period of little more than 250 years, menageries were opened in the Vatican, Chantilly, Paris, Versailles, Madrid, London, Dublin, Berlin, Dresden, Antwerp, Prague, Vienna, and many other cities, several of which are still operating today. For its part, America did not begin creating formal zoos until after the Civil War, but by the turn of the century there were eighteen in the United States, mostly in the major cities of the Northeast, but including Denver, Chicago, Cleveland, Dallas, and Cincinnati.

Whether in the New World or the Old, almost all of the animals inhabiting these facilities had been captured by collectors and their crews, who were dispatched to Africa, India, and the wilds of the Americas specifically to stock the big city zoos. At the time there were no laws to regulate the taking, exportation, importation, transportation, or housing of wild animals. Any creature could simply be appropriated with impunity and brutality, and shipped in any manner deemed acceptable.

Baboons, for example, after being lured into large traps and pinned by the neck with forked poles, were bound and gagged for transit: hands and feet lashed, jaws muzzled with cord, and then the entire body tightly wrapped in cloth. Baby hippopotamuses were usually captured by killing the mother and then disabling the youngster with a harpoon wound. Infant animals were preferred for the zoos, and it was standard procedure to secure them by simply destroying one or both of the parents. For every animal that survived the capture and transportation to an American zoo, dozens died in the field and on the ships and railroads. And upon arrival at the zoo, the animals faced bleak accommodations: cold cement, ceramic tiles, iron bars, stale air. Such housing had of course prevailed for hundreds of years.

Then in the 1960s, ideas in zoo architecture first developed at the turn of the century started to gain currency, and the designs were turned into reality. Back in 1907, an animal dealer from Germany opened the first zoo without bars. Carl Hagenbeck had been supplying zoos and circuses with thousands of animals over the course of twenty years, but he decided he wanted to build his own zoo, incorporating a unique vision of how to keep animals in captivity. His enclosures used moats, hedges, fake rocks, and serpentine paths to produce the illusion that there were no barriers between the human spectators and the animals. Especially startling, predator and prey species seemed to be residing in the same enclosure.

This novel approach to zoo design was largely ignored for better than half a century until the "back to nature" movement hit its stride, and the conservation of species and their habitat began to replace the capture and collect philosophy that had prevailed in the zoo community. Today, no zoo is without at least a few "naturalistic" enclosures influenced by Hagenbeck's vision, and in many, bars and cages cannot be found. Such measures seem to enhance the quality of the animal's lives—especially by promoting breeding in captivity—and zoogoers like them, but they are not required by any federal or state law.

The Animal Welfare Act and the Regulation of Animal Exhibitors

When Arizona was admitted to the Union in 1913, all forty-eight states, as well as the territories of Alaska and Hawaii, now had statutes prohibiting cruelty to animals. Few of these laws has ever provided a specific exemption for circuses and zoos, so technically they all applied to the use of animals in these forms of entertainment. Even so, instances in which circus personnel have been convicted of cruelty to any animals under their charge in violation of a state law are quite rare, and none exist for zookeepers. Two recent examples are a trainer working for King Royal Circus in 1995 who entered a no contest plea to second-degree animal abuse charges in Oregon for beating a juvenile elephant, and, in 1998, another trainer convicted in California of cruelty to eight ponies in his care at the Sterling & Reid Circus.

Idaho allows an exemption from the provisions of its anticruelty statute for animal exhibitions "normally or commonly considered acceptable," while New Mexico does the same for uses of animals "not otherwise prohibited by law," both concessions having been interpreted to include circuses and zoos. Missouri, North Dakota, and Michigan specifically exempt zoos. At this writing, no state has banned animal exhibitions outright, though a bill to prohibit the display of elephants, lions, tigers, and bears (except in accredited zoos) is making its way through the Rhode Island legislature. In comparison, the only animals that may legally appear in a circus anywhere in Finland or Sweden are domestic dogs and cats, and tame horses. During the 1990s a number of municipalities passed ordinances prohibiting circuses featuring "exotic" animals within city limits. These include Corona, California; Hollywood and Lauderdale Lakes, both in Florida; Stamford, Connecticut; Collinsville, Illinois; Quincy and Revere, both in Massachusetts; Takoma Park, Maryland; and Redmond, Washington. In 2000 a similar law almost made it through the Seattle city council, which would have been by far the largest city with such a ban, but the measure failed by one vote.

It was not until 1970 when Congress passed the Animal Welfare Act (AWA) that circuses and zoos were expressly targeted for federal regulation, done under the auspices of the U.S. Department of Agriculture, the agency responsible for administering and enforcing the law. The AWA requires that all circuses and zoos obtain a class C exhibitors license from the Animal and Plant Health Inspection Service (APHIS), an office of the U.S. Department of Agriculture. Animals cannot be legally exhibited until the license has been issued, and this requires proof that all the applicable federal regulations are being observed. Compliance is verified by an APHIS official who performs an on-site inspection of the facilities. Further, neither circuses nor zoos can buy, sell, or transport any animals without a license. Renewal of the license must be done each year by filing an application and an annual report with APHIS. The cost of this certificate is very low, a fee determined by the number of animals being exhibited, ranging from $30 for one to five animals, up to $300 for 501 or more.

Before proceeding to an overview of selected species-specific items, a couple of general provisions of the AWA regulations pertinent to circuses and zoos should be noted here, beginning with record keeping. The primary motivation behind the enactment of the AWA was to protect the interests of pet owners, some of whose dogs and cats were turning up in laboratories, so federal regulations require that exhibitors keep detailed records concerning any domestic dogs or cats they acquire. Among other things to be noted are the name and address of the person from whom each dog or cat was obtained, APHIS license or registration number or the driver's license number of this person, any veterinary care the animal received, and a physical description, including breed, sex, date of birth or approximate age, and distinctive markings. Also, any dog or cat acquired by an exhibitor must be held on the premises for at least five days before it can be sold or transferred.

These rules are intended mainly to oversee animal dealers, particularly those that trade in dogs and cats, because some of the unscrupulous ones had been stealing people's pets and selling them to research facilities. Although some circuses use trained dogs, zoos do not display these animals or domestic cats. Exhibitors must record the same information for all other animals they hold, except a simple listing of the individual species is sufficient rather than a detailed description of each animal.

The handling of circus and zoo animals must be done in a way that prevents "trauma, overheating, excessive cooling, behavioral stress, physical harm, or unnecessary discomfort." Animals are to be spared physical abuse, and training methods cannot include the deprivation of food and water *unless* this is done for abbreviated periods and the animals receive adequate nutrition every day. When animals are performing or on public display, the regulations require that barriers be in place or "sufficient" distances provided to separate them from the audience. After each performance, an animal must be given a rest period at least as long as the duration of the act, and "dangerous animals" must be controlled by handlers at all times during any public exhibition. The customers and patrons of circuses and zoos are permitted to feed the species on display only if the exhibitor provides food "appropriate to the type of animal and its nutritional needs."

After these general items, the bulk of the AWA regulations prescribe minimum requirements for housing, feeding, watering, and veterinary care for protected species. One section or subpart is devoted to marine mammals, and another to primates; these species are some of the most important zoo and aquarium animals.

The subject of a third, catch-all portion of the regulations is "Warmblooded Animals Other Than Dogs, Cats, Rabbits, Hamsters, [and] Guinea Pigs." The creatures named here are of greatest interest to research facilities, not animal exhibitors, and standards specific to them are detailed elsewhere (*see* chapter 7: *Animal Welfare Act Regulations*). The "other warmblooded animals" do, however, preoccupy those who exhibit animals in circuses and zoos, covering numerous popular and economically valuable species. The only species of birds, reptiles, and amphibians that are protected by federal laws are those officially listed under the Endangered Species Act (*see* chapter 6).

AWA Regulations for the Exhibition of Marine Mammals
In a bygone era harbor seals could be found in many circuses, catching and throwing balls, and posing on drums. A few shows had trained polar bears, and one circus even had an enormous elephant seal weighing a ton and a half called "Goliath." Today, marine mammals have disappeared from the traveling circus animal acts, and are exclusive to zoos and aquariums.

The latest APHIS figures available show that in 1997 there were 110 of these establishments containing 1,429 marine mammals, with two dolphin species (*Tursiops truncatus* and *Delphinus delphus*), harbor seals (*Phoca larga*), California sea lions (*Zalophus californianus*), and polar bears (*Ursus maritimus*) accounting for almost all of them. Currently, South Carolina is the only state that has placed any restrictions on the exhibition of marine mammals, banning all public displays of captive dolphins and whales. A bill introduced in the Washington state legislature prohibiting the display of whales, porpoises, and dolphins did not fare well in 2000, but it is likely to be revived in 2001.

In 1999 AWA regulations for the exhibition of marine mammals underwent a number of revisions. No substantive changes had been made in almost fifteen years, during which time animal advocates, led by the Humane Society of the United States (HSUS) and the Animal Welfare Institute (AWI), peppered APHIS with criticism. The outcome of these concerns, as well as data gathered by the agency, was a set of standards with nearly every section revised to some degree, written with the participation of the HSUS and the AWI.

General facilities requirements call first for fencing or other barriers to completely enclose lagoons or other natural seawater areas. All operations exhibiting marine mammals must have fences, walls, glass partitions, distances of space, or other obstacles to protect the animals from "abuse and harassment from the viewing public." Exhibitors lacking such physical barriers must employ conspicuous, uniformed individuals whose job is to keep the public from troubling the animals. Various objects used to amuse or stimulate the animals—"environmental enhancements" or, simply, pool toys—cannot be ingestible, easily breakable, or harmful. Natural water areas do not need to be drained, but adequate drainage of all primary enclosure pools is required for cleaning, to be done "as often as necessary to maintain proper water quality." The bacteria content and salinity of the water in which marine mammals live is to be tested at least weekly, and maintained at levels appropriate for their health and well-being. Sufficient amounts of water and electricity must be provided for the housing of marine mammals, and all exhibitors are required to submit contingency plans to APHIS, subject to agency approval, detailing measures that would be taken in the event of a power failure or loss of water source. These plans need to describe evacuation and relocation procedures, and back-up systems.

Indoor facilities must have air and water adequately heated or cooled "to protect marine mammals from extremes of temperature . . . and to prevent discomfort." Ventilation should be provided and, since marine mammals breathe oxygen, every enclosure is required to have a vertical air space above the water averaging at least six feet in height. Diurnal lighting is not required here, but "overexposure . . . to excessive illumination" should be avoided, and ideally interior housing should be illuminated in a manner that approximates the natural habitat of the animal. Outdoor housing is allowed only for those marine mammals who would not be harmed by the air and water temperatures found at the exhibition site. So that the animals may enter and leave the water, pools for polar bears and seals cannot be allowed to freeze over; whale and dolphin pools must be kept clear of all ice.

Space requirements for marine mammals are the most exacting of any species protected by the AWA and its regulations, though curiously, none of these specifications were revised in 1999. Enclosures for cetaceans (whales and dolphins) may consist entirely of a pool of water. For cetaceans, the dimensions of the pool depend on the species confined and a series of formulae that are ultimately a function of the average length of an adult representative of the species.

To take a simplified example, a beluga whale (*Delphinapterus leucas*) has an average adult length of 14 feet. This figure, according to a table in the regulations, yields a "minimum horizontal dimension" (MHD) of 28 feet and a minimum required pool depth of 7 feet. These numbers in turn are used to calculate the minimum required volume of water in a pool containing up to two beluga whales. This volume is the MHD divided by 2, squared, and then multiplied by 3.14, the product then multiplied by the depth. Thus, a beluga whale, or two, must have a pool containing at least 4,308 cubic feet of water. Other tables give additional water volumes for each animal in pools holding more than two animals. Surface areas for cetacean pools are calculated with the same formula, except a value of 1.5 is used instead of the depth.

Primary enclosures for pinnipeds (seals mostly, but including walruses and sea lions) must consist of a pool and a "dry resting area" (DRA) where the animals can haul themselves out. The size of the DRA is calculated according to several variables, beginning with the average length of adults of each species, a figure that is in turn a function of gender because there are wide disparities in size among many pinniped species according to sex. For almost all pinnipeds, this number is then squared for each animal in the enclosure and the results are added. So, to take another simple example, consider an enclosure with ten harp seals (*Phoca groenlandica*). According to another table in the regulations, both male and female of this species have an average length of 6.1 feet; squaring this number, and then multiplying it 10 times yields a DRA of 372 square feet. The surface area of the pool must be at least as large as the DRA, and its depth at least 3 feet or one-half the average adult length of the longest pinniped species in the enclosure. The MHD for pinnipeds must be at least one and one-half times the average adult length of the largest species confined there.

Polar bears must be provided with a pool, a DRA, and a den (for more on the law and polar bears, *see* chapter 6: *Legal Protections for Bears*). Here, there are no formulas to calculate, just clear-cut minimum sizes mandated: an 8-foot MHD, 5-foot depth, and 96 square feet of surface area for a pool holding one or two bears, 40 more square feet for each additional bruin; 400 square feet for the DRA of up to two bears, 40 more for each animal in excess of two; 6 feet in width and depth, and 5 feet in height for the den. The interior of the den must not be visible to the viewing public, and a fertile female housed with a male must be provided with her own den. Strangely, these housing and space requirements seem not to apply for polar bears used in circuses. The regulations stipulate that "[f]emale polar bears in traveling acts and shows must be provided a den when pregnancy has been determined." One might suppose that the impracticality of providing polar bears on the road with pools, dry resting areas, and dens would legally preclude the use of this species in that capacity altogether, but this is apparently not so. In any case, there are no polar bears currently being used by circuses.

All these minimum enclosure sizes can be ignored and smaller areas utilized so long as these are "temporarily used for nonmedical training, breeding, holding, and transfer purposes." A veterinarian's authorization is required if housing in smaller enclosures for training, breeding, or holding exceeds two weeks. Confinement for transfer extending beyond one week must be justified by a veterinarian every week. The approval of a vet is also required before a marine mammal can be housed alone. Husbandry, training, and other pertinent staff of the zoo must draw up a written plan justifying the duration of the isolated confinement, and detailing enrichment measures to be taken for the animal. Most marine mammal species are highly social in the wild, and for these animals the regulations further direct that they be housed at least in pairs, provided the individuals are compatible. Incompatible animals of any species should never be confined together.

When a zoo or aquarium acquires a new marine mammal, it must be kept separately from the resident species of the facility until the attending veterinarian determines the animal is in good health and poses no medical threat to the others. Any contagious disease discovered in the new animal must be cured before it can be housed with the residents, "unless, in the judgment of the attending veterinarian, the potential benefits of a resident animal(s) as a companion(s) to the newly acquired animal outweigh the risks to the resident animal(s)."

The regulations require that medical records be kept for each animal, detailing its species, USDA identification number, age, sex, markings or scars, the animal's weight, length, all diagnostic test results, and the course of treatment taken for any medical problems that have occurred.

The vet must visually examine each marine mammal at least twice a year, and all cetaceans must be given a physical examination at least once each year. When any marine mammal dies at a zoo, the vet is required to prepare a complete necropsy report, to be kept for at least three years and available for perusal on request by APHIS.

All marine mammals must be offered "wholesome, palatable" food, appropriately formulated for the species, at least once a day. Employees of zoos and aquariums who feed these species are required to be sufficiently knowledgeable to ensure that the animals are receiving adequate nutrition. If a marine mammal does not eat for over twenty-four hours, this must be immediately reported to the attending veterinarian. Exhibitors must keep records of the estimated individual daily consumption of each animal for one year. Feeding by members of the general public can be done only with food provided by the zoo, and this must be supervised by learned, uniformed employees.

All employees of zoos and aquariums caring for marine mammals are required to successfully complete a program of instruction focused on husbandry and handling techniques appropriate to the species housed at their particular facility, and on proper procedures for reporting medical concerns. Experienced trainers who meet professionally recognized standards must directly supervise all training of the animals.

AWA Regulations for the Exhibition of Primates

Monkeys and apes have perennially been among the most sought after animals in animal exhibitions, and at one time nearly every zoo and circus had at least a few of them. In 1999 there were 5,075 primates held by 290 class C exhibitors in the United States, with over 90 percent of the animals kept in zoos and in "zoological" and "wildlife" parks. Rent-an-animal services and private individuals accounted for most of the rest.

Curiously, APHIS lists only one circus as a class C license holder with primates. Anecdotal evidence suggests that there are perhaps a dozen primates currently being used by American circuses, but apparently no one really knows. The numbers seem to have waned over the last couple of decades and it is likely that those few circuses still exhibiting primates are leasing the animals from individuals who keep and train them (for the legal regulation of primates used in research and testing, *see* chapter 7: *Primates*).

General housing and nutrition standards for primates require that they be provided with dwellings that are well constructed and regularly maintained, regularly cleaned and sanitized, while effectively preventing escape, access by other animals, or injury. Housing facilities must be equipped with electricity supplying ventilation, lighting, running potable water, and "disposal and drainage systems that are constructed and operated so that animal wastes are eliminated and the animals stay dry." Primates must be fed at least once every day with "clean, wholesome, and palatable" food, appropriate to the species and in quantities sufficient for the age and size of the animal. Drinking water is to be made available either continuously or "provided as often as necessary for the health and comfort of the animal." Cleaning and sanitization of food receptacles is required at least once every two weeks, while the "primary enclosures"—cages, pens, or confinement areas—must be cleaned of excrement and food particles every day, and sanitized in the prescribed way twice a month.

More precise housing specifications for primates are also described. For example, those housed indoors cannot be exposed to temperatures below 45 or above 85 degrees Fahrenheit for more than four consecutive hours; outdoor shelters, such as those found today in most zoos keeping primates, must be heated or cooled if the temperature falls outside of this range. A diurnal lighting cycle, uniformly diffused throughout the facility, is required. Outdoor housing is permitted only for primates that are adapted to the climate conditions found at the facility, and this must include shelters to escape the weather. Zoos are required to place a barrier between primate enclosures and any public viewing areas. Primates used in circuses, whether merely uncaged or allowed physical contact with the audience, must be controlled and supervised at all times by an experienced handler or trainer. Moreover, exterior housing for primates must be enclosed by a fence, 6 feet tall, or more, unless approved by APHIS.

AWA regulations detail further specifications for the primary enclosure. As with the general housing standards, the enclosures should be safe, structurally sound, clean, and provide protection from the elements. Water and food should be readily accessible. Floors are to be constructed of solid materials that do not injure the animals' feet. These regulations also stipulate precise "minimum space requirements" for primates that are a function of each animal's weight, affording "sufficient space . . . to make normal postural and social adjustments with adequate freedom of movement." For example, a primate weighing between 33 and 55 pounds must be housed in a cage at least 3 feet tall with 8 square feet of floor space, while one over 55 pounds gets 25 square feet of floor area and 84 inches in height. The regulations also direct that great apes weighing more than 110 pounds be given "an additional volume of space in excess of that required for [primates over 55 pounds] . . . to allow for normal postural adjustments." The "additional volume" is not specified.

A 1985 amendment to the AWA directed APHIS to develop standards for "environmental enhancements to promote [the] psychological well-being" of primates. Much to the displeasure of primate advocates, the regulations did not appear until 1991, and when they finally did, many were still unsatisfied by the generality and ambiguity they saw there. These regulations include allowances for the social grouping needs of primates, so long as the species can coexist harmoniously; primates kept individually in cages are supposed to be able to see and hear other primates of compatible species. Also called for here are devices for enriching their enclosures by means of such items as perches, swings, mirrors, and other objects to manipulate. Such enrichment also includes allowing primates the opportunity to forage for food, and giving unspecified "special attention" to infants, primates housed alone, and great apes. Primates are never to be maintained in restraint devices unless this is necessary for "health reasons."

After several more years of debate and criticism concerning the environmental enhancements requirement, in July 1999 APHIS issued a "draft policy statement" adding much more detail to the standards published in 1991, and calling for comments. At this writing, the final rule on the matter has not yet been published, so nothing contained in this document is legally binding (for more on this issue, *see* chapter 7: *Primates: Psychological Well-Being*; chapter 7: *Primates: A New Policy for the Psychological Well-Being of Primates?*).

As traveling shows, circuses with primates regularly transport the animals from place to place, and sometimes zoos exchange or transfer animals as part of cooperative agreements, moving species under their own auspices rather than consigning them with a carrier. AWA regulations also present standards for the enclosure and the conveyance used to transport primates, as well as for care in transit. The cage or carton containing primates must be secure and strong, and one that the animal cannot open or out of which put any part of its body. It must have either a solid, leak-proof bottom or a removable wire mesh floor. Adequate ventilation is required and the enclosure must be constructed so that the ventilation openings cannot be obstructed. Unless a mother and infant or a male and female that are pair bonded are being transported, primates must be moved singly, one for each cage. Size requirements are not nearly so precise here, the regulations stipulating only that each animal should have enough space to turn around and sit upright, and there must be clearance between the head and the top of the enclosure.

The motor vehicle, rail car, aircraft, or marine vessel that transports primates must provide the animals with a sufficient supply of air for normal breathing, and the temperature of the cargo space has to be maintained between 45 and 85 degrees Fahrenheit. Primates can be shipped with other animals, but if these other species are predators or enemies, they must be kept out of their sight lines; the regulations say nothing about hearing or smelling these antagonists. Primates over one year old must be offered food at least once every twenty-four hours, under one year every twelve hours; those of any age are to be given water every twelve hours. To ensure that the animals are alright, they must be observed by the operator of the conveyance, or some other person on board, at least once every four hours; aircraft with cargo holds that are inaccessible during flight are exempted from this requirement. Once the primates arrive at their destination, holding facilities must be kept clean and sanitary, as well as sufficiently ventilated and heated or cooled to within the 45-to-85-degree-Fahrenheit range.

AWA Regulations for the Exhibition of "Other Warmblooded Animals"

Most of the animals exhibited in circuses and zoos are covered in a very broad category of AWA regulations meant to capture any "warmblooded" species other than marine mammals, primates, and the dogs, cats, rabbits, hamsters, and guinea pigs widely used in research facilities. Lumping so many and such different species together under one set of standards—creatures with the diverse habits and habitats of, say, tigers, gazelles, bears, kangaroos, rhinoceroses, prairie dogs, and giraffes—has been seen by some as a serious defect, since the "specifications," paradoxically, have to be very general.

Elephants, which also fall in this wide-ranging area, have been of special concern for a number of people both inside and outside of the animal exhibition business, particularly circuses. AWA regulations do not mention this species. However, there have been some interesting legislative developments of late on both the state and federal level that impact the exhibition of elephants, as discussed in the following section.

Regulations for indoor and outdoor housing facilities are generic versions of the standards set forth for the other species: structures strong enough for the animals confined there, "reliable and adequate" water and power, "adequate" ventilation, and "ample" lighting are required without further details. The temperature of the housing facilities must be "compatible with the health and comfort of the animal," and no further indication is given of what those temperatures might be. Space requirements, while quite precise for other protected species, are here to be simply enough "to allow each animal to make normal postural and social adjustments." These other species are to be fed once a day with "wholesome, palatable" food, and water is to be available at all times or "be provided as often as necessary for the health and comfort of the animal." Transportation standards are as well essentially generic statements of those found for primates: sufficient air and ventilation provided, food offered every twenty-four hours and water every twelve, observation of the animal in transit every four hours, temperatures maintained in holding areas between 45 and 85 degrees Fahrenheit.

One new development in the regulations for these other "warm-blooded" species has occurred, adding some uncharacteristic specificity in this category. APHIS has recently adopted fencing requirements here, where formerly there had been none. Effective May 2000, all outdoor housing of "dangerous" animals—listed examples are lions, tigers, leopards, cougars, bobcats, bears, wolves, rhinoceroses, and elephants—must be enclosed by a fence at least 8 feet tall; shorter barriers require authorization by APHIS. All other warmblooded animals confined outdoors need to have a 6-foot fence as a "secondary confinement system for the animals in the facility." All fences must be 3 feet or farther from the animals' primary enclosure unless, again, an exception is granted by the federal government. No fences are necessary for these animals if the outside walls of the enclosure are sufficiently strong and high enough, or if a natural barrier is adequately restrictive. The new regulations add that the fence requirement does not apply when housing domestic livestock.

Elephants

P. T. Barnum once said, "Elephants . . . are the pegs to hang a circus on." The two are so closely associated in the American mind that most people immediately identify the elephant as the quintessential circus animal. Indeed, the first elephant born in captivity in the United States was delivered at a circus in March 1880 at the winter quarters of James Bailey's show. Barnum, already internationally known for his circuses and cognizant of how profitable elephants were in the entertainment business, offered Bailey $100,000 for the baby and its mother. The proposition was rejected but the birth was apparently a prime motivation for Barnum and Bailey to join forces a year later and create the world-famous circus—"the Greatest Show on Earth"—that still carries their names today.

Many American zoos keep elephants, of course. In 1999 there were 270, the total close to evenly split between the African and Asian species, distributed among approximately eighty zoos. Even so, at least sixty zoos in the United States do not have any elephants. In contrast, even the humblest "mud show" (small outfits that set up on dirt lots) has at least one pachyderm, and a mammoth circus such as the Ringling Brothers might have twenty, while no zoo in the United States currently houses more than six elephants. This is why, despite the fact that there are many more zoos, the numbers are nearly the same: at last count, about 240 elephants, almost all of them females of the Asian species, could be found in two dozen different American circuses. And it is safe to say that for most Americans, exposure to a live elephant is at a circus. It is also in the circus context where the captivity of this species is most controversial.

Elephants were first exhibited in the United States as the main attraction of the precursor to the modern circus, the traveling menagerie. In

April 1796 Jacob Crowninshield, captain of the *America*, sailed into Boston harbor with a 3-ton Indian elephant, a female bought in Bengal for $450. He immediately sold the animal for $1,000 and within ten days "The Elephant," as she was unimaginatively billed, was on display in New York City. For nearly a quarter of a century, the beast was exhibited up and down the east coast, drawing large audiences that happily paid for the opportunity to view an enormous exotic animal. The first pachyderm to appear in a circus was a female African elephant called Old Bet, exhibited by the Cayetano and Company circus in 1812. Her owner leased her to numerous menageries and circuses, transactions that proved to be very lucrative. Old Bet's "career" ended prematurely when she was shot to death by a Maine farmer.

By the 1820s most menageries had an elephant, and the crowds loved them. In 1850 Barnum and two partners sent a ship to Ceylon for the express purpose of retrieving at least a dozen elephants to perform in circuses. They got thirteen and managed to return to New York with ten still alive. Within twenty years, elephants had become fixtures in nearly every circus in America, and in thirty years a circus elephant became the first nonhuman celebrity. At that time, Barnum learned of an African elephant named Jumbo, kept at the Royal Zoological Gardens in London, that had abruptly become cranky and hard to manage. Over the protests of England's citizens, press corps, and queen, the zoo sold the animal to Barnum for $10,000. Almost immediately, Jumbo became the most famous animal in America, indeed, one with star power unmatched before or after, although perhaps rivaled in the 1960s by a dog called Lassie or Flipper the dolphin. In the first six weeks he was on display, Jumbo made $336,000 for Barnum, an immense sum for that time comparable to millions today. When Jumbo was hit by a train and killed just four years later in St. Thomas, Ontario, both his hide and his skeleton were mounted and displayed. On the centenary of the accident, the city of St. Thomas erected a monument to the animal. The adjective "jumbo," popular in the lexicon of marketing to denote large-sized products, is taken from the name of this elephant, who was the biggest captive animal of his day.

Jumbo's irritable and intractable disposition at the Zoological Gardens had gotten him branded a "rogue," and even though he became much more docile once Barnum acquired him, there is a storied history of numerous circus elephants "going bad": attacking their trainers, handlers, or members of the audience, often with fatal results. Most legendary of all is probably Queen, also known as Mary, who is documented to have killed at least thirteen people in the first decade of the 1900s, including a small boy who ran in front of her during the circus parade in Buffalo, New York. These rogue elephants were usually destroyed soon after they began demonstrating such belligerent and deadly behavior, some of them dispatched in the style of public executions. Especially notable here is Tops who, after she had killed two trainers and a circus fan, was electrocuted before a crowd of hundreds of people at Coney Island in 1903. The event was filmed with one of the earliest motion picture cameras.

Much more recently, the last decade of the 1900s has seen an increasing number of incidents in which circus elephants have suddenly become quite aggressive, injuring and killing trainers, grooms, spectators, and, perhaps most disturbing, members of the general public who are riding on the animals. More than a dozen such incidents occurred in the United States during the 1990s, and there were many more in other parts of the world. For example, on New Years Day 1996, a high school principal in Comfort, Texas, was thrown from the back of an elephant belonging to the King Royal Circus, sustaining two broken ribs and arm and wrist injuries. Elephant rides have long been a staple of circus attractions, and one of the most popular, yet their increasing hazardousness in recent years has provoked lawmakers in some jurisdictions to ban them entirely.

As of 2000 elephant rides (as well as camel rides, which are featured in a few circuses) were prohibited in Delaware, Georgia, Maine, Mississippi, Missouri, New Jersey, and in two Virginia counties, Spotsylvania, which is mainly rural, and Fairfax, the location of Alexandria and Arlington, just across the Potomac River from Washington, D.C. All these statutes specifically outlaw "public contact between people and animals." Similar laws were considered by the legislatures of Florida and Maryland in 2000, but did not make it out of committees.

At the federal level, Representative Sam Farr of California introduced legislation in September 1999 that would make elephant rides anywhere in the United States illegal. The bill, titled the "Captive Elephant Accident Prevention Act," would impose a fine and up to one year in prison on anyone who, for a fee, "knowingly makes available any elephant for . . . the purposes of allowing individuals to ride that elephant." Congress adjourned in December 2000 before any action could be taken on this bill.

GREYHOUND RACING AND HORSE RACING

In 1970 Congress enacted the Animal Welfare Act (AWA) (*see* chapter 7) "to insure that animals intended for use in research facilities or for exhibition purposes or for pets are provided humane care and treatment." The U.S. Department of Agriculture (USDA) was charged with the responsibility to devise, implement, and enforce standards for the care and treatment of animals used for these purposes. Lawmakers did not mention horse or dog racing in the AWA, but USDA regulations issued two years later did.

The AWA first defines an animal exhibitor broadly to mean anyone who places animals on display for money, and identifies circuses and zoos in particular as regulated entities (*see* this chapter: *Circuses and Zoos*). The law then quickly stipulates that several forms of animal exhibition are excluded from the requirements of the AWA, notably rodeos (*see* this chapter: *Rodeos*) and pet stores (*see* chapter 3: *Dog Law: Dog Breeding, "Puppy Mills," and Pet Stores*). In 1972 USDA regulations inserted the phrase "horse and dog races" between "pet stores" and "rodeos" in the list of *excluded* operations. At that same time, the USDA also inserted the phrase "animal acts" between "circuses" and "zoos" as *included* exhibitions, subject to the requirements of the AWA. A subsequent challenge in federal court to this inclusion failed (*see* this chapter: *Circuses and Zoos*). The exemption for horse racing and dog racing has never been legally contested.

Legal Regulation of Animal Racing

No other federal law intended to promote animal welfare restricts horse racing or dog racing either. Individuals who breed horses and dogs for the tracks, or house the animals in stables or kennels are also not regulated by any federal animal protection law. Although the AWA does govern the "class A animal dealer," defined as any person who breeds and sells animals, and many breeders sell Thoroughbreds and greyhounds, not just any animal is protected by the law.

The term "animal" in the AWA refers *only* to dogs and horses that are "being used, or [are] intended for use for research, testing, experimentation, or exhibition purposes." Racing dogs and horses are obviously not bred for the laboratories (though greyhounds have often ended up there; *see* this chapter: *Greyhound Racing and Horse Racing: The Fate of the Racing Greyhound*), and remember, these races do not count under the AWA as regulated forms of animal exhibition. The same considerations absolve the stable or kennel operator: AWA housing standards apply only to research facilities and the stipulated forms of animal exhibition. In any case, the numerous breeders of Thoroughbreds and greyhounds who do not sell the animals are not subject to the federal law.

Legal regulations for the care and treatment of racing horses and dogs are left entirely to the individual states, mainly in the form of rules handed down by state racing commissions. These are government agencies whose membership is typically appointed by the governor. The major task of the racing commissioners is not to provide for animal welfare, but to structure and standardize the procedures for conducting horse races and dog races. Their focus is on the tracks and the stables and kennels there, rather than the farms and ranches where the animals are born and trained. A few states do have regulations for the care and treatment of animals at breeding facilities, but a large majority do not, and those that do have excluded animals used for racing from their purview.

Racing commissioners write rules to govern the activities of the many participants in the races: bettors, pari-mutuel managers, animal owners, jockeys, trainers, starters, lead-outs, lure and camera operators, stewards, veterinarians, kennel and stable masters, and paddock judges, among others. Animal racing is a form of government-regulated gaming—betting on games of chance—and racing commissions determine the rules for playing these games. Just like all state-controlled gambling (lotteries, bingo, slot machines, casinos), horse racing and dog racing are businesses that are supposed to generate revenue for state coffers. So, a primary concern of the commissions is the management of the money that flows into and out of the tracks and remote betting sites.

Racing commission rules are voluminous: every state has hundreds of them. Yet only a tiny percentage of these have anything to do with protecting the animals. The minuscule proportion also varies with the type of racing. During the 1990s, following revelations of hideous abuse and neglect, the treatment of greyhounds came under close scrutiny and heavy criticism from the media, animal protection organizations, and the general public. As dog racing revenues declined precipitously, commissioners in several states reacted with new rules intended to enhance greyhound welfare.

In contrast, horse racing has never suffered from pervasive bad press or widespread societal condemnation, and the critical gaze of the animal welfare community has hardly lighted upon it. On the contrary, this form of entertainment has always been accorded a high level of prestige, and in the late 1990s it is making more money for the states now than ever before, in excess of $3 billion a year, with over $13 billion in total betting (much of this is off-track wagering, though, as attendance on-site has fallen significantly). Consequently, as seen below, there are very few rules designed to protect racing horses.

We begin then with the more controversial and more regulated form of animal racing, the running of greyhounds.

The Greyhound and Greyhound Racing

The greyhound is one of the oldest dog breeds, dating at least as far back as 5000 B.C.E. to the ancient Near East. Originally developed as a hunting dog, this canine is a "sighthound" rather than a "scenthound," one bred to rely on its visual acuity to notice rabbits, rodents, antelope, deer, and other medium-sized ungulates, and then run them down with its incredible speed. With long legs, deep chest, and slender physique, the average greyhound can run nearly twice as fast as the swiftest human.

The Egyptians, Greeks, and Romans all prized the greyhound highly as a hunting dog and household companion, and only the wealthy and powerful owned them. In ancient Egypt, where one of the most important deities was the half-man half-dog Anubis and earthly canines were revered, the god Set was depicted as a greyhound with a forked tail. Some centuries later, in the Greek city-states and in the Roman Empire, greyhounds had a social status far above any slave or foreigner. Yet it was the ancient Celts and Etruscans to the north and northwest of Rome that first developed formal competitions between dogs around the first century C.E., pitting the animals against one another in contests of speed and ability. This earliest form of what came to be known as "coursing," and the basis for modern dog racing, saw two or more greyhounds set loose in a field containing rabbits. The winner was whichever animal caught a rabbit first, or at least the one that appeared to be the quickest and most agile.

The nobility of medieval Europe enthusiastically pursued coursing, as well as hunting, with their cherished greyhounds. Indeed, the English so adored the breed that for a period of almost 400 years only members of the aristocracy were legally permitted to own the dogs and use them for coursing or hunting. Coursing was practiced much as the Etruscans and Celts had done centuries before, with few formal rules and no legal ones regulating the event. Finally in 1561, appalled at a coursing event in which a pack of greyhounds slaughtered sixteen deer, Elizabeth I declared that the dogs had an unfair advantage that must be eliminated. Shortly thereafter, the "Law of the Leash" appeared, declaring, among other things, that coursing greyhounds could not be released until the prey was at least 50 yards in the lead. This is the first known regulation of any sporting event using greyhounds, and it remains in force in England to this day.

Greyhound racing as it is conducted today was created by Americans, although the first recorded race between the dogs occurred in Hendon, England, in September 1876. Here, a straight, grooved rail 400 yards long and mounted with an "artificial hare" was laid in a field. As the lure was mechanically propelled along the rail, the dogs chased after it, with the first to reach the end of the rail the winner. However, this new form of racing was not well received in England, mainly because coursing aficionados disdained the notion of a winning dog being simply the one that runs to a target first—this requires no agility or intelligence, they complained.

In America it was this same idea of an artificial lure that lead to the rise of greyhound racing. Some thirty years after the inaugural event in Hendon, O. P. Smith invented a lure consisting of a stuffed rabbit skin attached to a motor that ran around a rail on the outside of a circular track. He called it the "Inanimate Hare Conveyor." The device was first used in 1907 at a small track in Salt Lake City, Utah. Within five years, Smith had received the first of the many patents he would be awarded for the mechanical lure, and in 1919 the first bona fide dog track opened near Oakland at Emeryville, California, featuring Smith's conveyor. The artificial lures in operation today are substantially the same as the basic design crafted by O. P. Smith nearly a century ago.

Greyhound racing caught on quickly, founded upon the system of pari-mutuel wagering originally developed for horse racing (*see* this chapter: *Greyhound Racing and Horse Racing: A Brief History of Horse Racing*). During the 1920s, dog tracks, usually in some association with the horses, were springing up in many of the states that had legalized this form of gambling, especially in Florida. One of these tracks in St. Petersburg—Derby Lane—remains in operation today, seventy-five years after its opening night. Following an ebb during the Great Depression and the Second World War, greyhound racing rebounded in the late 1940s and into the 1950s, and by 1960 dogs were running at twenty-eight tracks in seven states. In another thirty years, the industry had reached its apogee, with sixty-two tracks operating three to five days a week in nineteen states, and an annual betting "handle" (total amount of money wagered) of over $3 billion. A lot of dogs were needed to keep all these races running, and nearly half a million greyhounds were born in the 1980s.

But then in the last years of that decade and the first few of the next, the mainstream media and several animal protection organizations, which until that time had largely neglected dog racing, began to enlighten the public to horrendous abuses of animals within the industry. Among the most egregious incidents were the 100 starving greyhounds discovered in 1990 at a kennel near the Tucson track, 60 of which could not be saved, and in 1992, also in Arizona, a killing field south of Phoenix littered with 143 dead greyhounds, each with a bullet hole in the right temple. Also during this period, Americans became aware that many racing dogs end up in laboratories as tools for research and testing. This realization began in 1989 when a report widely broadcast in the regional media described how two animal dealers had collected over 600 greyhounds and sold them to a dozen different research facilities, mainly in California.

In light of these and other disturbing episodes, several state legislatures moved against dog racing, and much of the public moved away from the tracks. Maine outlawed dog racing in 1993, Virginia and Vermont did the same two years later, followed by Idaho and Washington in 1996, and Nevada in 1997. A ballot initiative that would have made Massachusetts the seventh state in less than a decade to reject dog racing was narrowly defeated in November 2000. North Carolina banned greyhound racing back in the 1950s, although the motivation was opposition to gambling rather than concern for animal welfare.

By 1998 attendance at greyhound races had dropped by one-quarter, the betting handle on the dogs had decreased to about $2 billion (a sizable sum but less than one percent of the total gambling market in the United States), and thirteen tracks had closed. Today, the industry is left with fifteen states running dogs on forty-nine tracks, better than a third of these in Florida. The other states are Alabama, Arizona, Arkansas, Colorado, Connecticut, Iowa, Kansas, Massachusetts, New Hampshire, Oregon, Rhode Island, Texas, West Virginia, and Wisconsin.

Legal Regulation of Racing Greyhound Welfare: On the Farm

Racing dogs begin their lives on one of America's 2,000 greyhound farms. In 1999 just over 33,000 puppies were born on these farms, annual numbers that have been reduced by more than one-third during the 1990s. Critics of the industry have long complained that too many pups are whelped each year, producing an excess number of dogs that must be disposed of, many either ending up in laboratories or simply killed (*see* this chapter: *Greyhound Racing and Horse Racing: The Fate of the Racing Greyhound*). Most of the greyhound breeding operations are located in the states with tracks, especially along the sunbelt in Arizona, Texas, Kansas, Arkansas, Alabama, and Florida, but farms are also found in a few states without dog racing, such as Oklahoma and Nebraska.

As mentioned above, greyhound racing is not a regulated animal exhibition under the federal Animal Welfare Act, and since only animals bred for exhibition purposes (and laboratory use) are protected by the law, greyhound breeders are not subject to AWA standards of care. Furthermore, few states have such standards of their own, and the two with the most comprehensive set of legal rules to promote the welfare of animals at breeding facilities—Colorado and Kansas—have specifically exempted greyhounds from the provisions of their regulations. However, under intense public pressure following the revelations of greyhound abuse, and faced with plummeting revenues at the tracks, in 1993 the National Greyhound Association (NGA) developed guidelines for the care and treatment of greyhounds at the breeding facilities.

Although these guidelines do not have the force of law, and there are no legal penalties for violation, all the dog racing states require that greyhounds be registered with the NGA before they can begin their racing careers at an official track. The NGA can rescind the dog registrations of a breeder who is not in compliance and deny him or her the opportunity to race his or her greyhounds or lease them to someone else for racing. This form of self-regulation is thought to present a powerful economic incentive to follow the association's standards. Compliance is verified by one full-time and seventy-five part-time NGA inspectors who make announced and unannounced visits to the farms. There is no set time interval between inspections, but the current schedule has each breeding facility visited every other year.

The NGA guidelines require breeders to provide "adequate heat, insulation, bedding and cooling" for the greyhounds in their housing facilities. However, unlike some of the state standards for track kennels (*see* this chapter: *Greyhound Racing and Horse Racing: Legal Regulation of Racing Greyhound Welfare: At the Track*), no temperature range is specified beyond which the dogs must be provided with heating or air conditioning. Puppies under eight weeks old, and pregnant females within two weeks of delivery have to be kept indoors in "climate controlled" housing, but there is no indication of what that "climate" is supposed to be. Similarly, the NGA does not stipulate a precise minimum cage or "crate" size for the dogs, just that the enclosures must "afford ample space for the Greyhounds to comfortably turn about, stand erect, sit or lie." Also, breeders are required to remove the animals from their crates at least three times every day, but the guidelines do not say that the dogs must then be given an opportunity to run, play, or even stretch.

Typically, though, greyhounds are released from their cages into larger enclosures—"turn-out pens," runs, or exercise areas—and allowed to move about. These more spacious confines must be fenced, cleared of debris and brush, and have shelters with shade and some protection from inclement weather; water must be available here at all times. There is no food requirement in the NGA guidelines. Although breeders are required to clean the pens, runs, and exercise areas at least once in each twenty-four-hour period, in contrast the general housing facilities need be cleaned only "on a regular basis," without specifying how often that is.

After about six months in these facilities, the training of the young dogs begins, sometimes at a special facility separate from the dog farm. Greyhounds basically need to "learn" one thing: run as fast as they can around a track in pursuit of a lure. For decades this training was done with the use of living creatures, usually rabbits, but sometimes with cats, guinea pigs, or chickens. The dogs naturally chased the fleeing animals with great enthusiasm, and once caught, they were encouraged to shred the mangled body as a reward. It is not known exactly how many rabbits and other small animals died during these exercises, but it is certain that thousands were killed every year.

Beginning in the 1980s, the state racing commissions in Alabama, Arizona, Connecticut, Idaho (prior to banning racing in the state), Iowa, Kansas, Massachusetts, New Hampshire, Oregon, Texas, and Wisconsin have prohibited the use of live lures. The Florida anticruelty statute outlaws baiting animals to provoke fights between them, and includes the use of live lures as a form of baiting. Oklahoma, Maine, Minnesota, and Vermont have a similar proscription in their respective anticruelty laws (none of these states have any dog tracks, but Oklahoma has numerous greyhound farms). On the other hand, neither the racing commissions nor the legislatures in Arkansas, Colorado, Rhode Island, and West Virginia have banned live lures. The remaining thirty states do not address the issue.

A greyhound is registered by the NGA at about eighteen months to two years old and after the dog has finished in the top four in two "schooling races." These are essentially practice runs to determine which greyhounds might be lucrative racers. Once registered, each dog receives a "grade" that indicates the level of its success in racing. Rookie greyhounds are graded M for "maiden class," but after the dogs leave the farm, move to the tracks, and start running races regularly, they can advance up through the grades D, C, B, and A. This is accomplished as the canines put together strings of consecutive first-, second-, or third-place finishes.

Legal Regulation of Racing Greyhound Welfare: At the Track

Greyhounds spend virtually all of their racing lives—about two years—housed in privately owned kennels at or near the tracks where they are run. An individual dog rarely runs more than two races a week, and since the 1/4 or 5/16 mile oval is traversed in about thirty seconds, the running itself is a tiny fraction of a dog's life—there is a lot of downtime at the kennels.

The number of kennels servicing each track, and the number of dogs held at each kennel varies depending on the size of the dog racing operation, which is a function of the length of the racing season, the number of races run, the amount of the betting handle, and other factors. Average figures for a standard track are about 500 greyhounds split between 10 or 12 kennels, although a large track like Derby Lane would double these numbers. Most kennel operators lease these dogs from their owners in exchange for a substantial share of the animals' winnings, usually about two-thirds. A low percentage of greyhounds are the property of the kennel operators, but the majority of racing dogs are owned by people who have purchased them as an investment; some may never see their property at work.

As with breeders, only a small handful of states regulate the care and treatment of animals held at commercial kennels, whether they house pet poodles or racing greyhounds. Colorado and Kansas, the leaders in this regulatory area, with 7 dog tracks between them kenneling perhaps 3,000 animals, have again both made specific exceptions here for greyhounds. Similarly, in Iowa, despite having fairly detailed regulations for commercial kennels generally, these standards do not apply to the housing of greyhounds at the state's two tracks. At the greyhound kennel compounds, animal welfare is left entirely to the rules issued by the state racing commissions.

There is a great deal of variation among the dog racing states in the scope of the rules for the care of greyhounds. At one end of the spectrum is Arkansas, with one track, where there are no rules whatever of this sort. Close to this same pole is Florida. Even though the Sunshine State leads the nation with seventeen tracks where several thousand dogs are kept, concern for greyhound welfare is essentially confined to a single sentence in the statute on pari-mutuel wagering: "It is the intent of the Legislature that animals that participate in races . . . be treated humanely, both on and off racetracks, throughout the lives of the animals." Texas says little more than kennels "must be well-ventilated[,] . . . constructed to be comfortable in all seasons[,] . . . kept clean and in good repair, [and provided with] . . . adequate lighting." West Virginia merely notes that greyhounds must not be mistreated, abandoned, injured, or deprived of sustenance, shelter, or medical care.

Moving toward the other end of the spectrum is Alabama, which has charged kennel personnel with ensuring that greyhounds are treated humanely, and borrows the description of inhumane treatment from the state anticruelty law. Alabama adds that each kennel can contain no more crates than "will allow adequate runway space, airflow, and the general well-being of the greyhounds being housed." Similarly, the Wisconsin Gaming Commission has also incorporated language from the cruelty to animals statute into the rules for "Humane Treatment of Racing Animals" (see also chapter 3: Anticruelty Laws). None of the states specifically exempt racing greyhounds from the protections of their anticruelty laws, but prosecutions are quite unusual in the industry and successful ones even rarer. The only such case in the last several years is from August 2000, when Texas physician Harry Roland pled guilty to animal cruelty charges. He had failed to provide veterinary care for one of his greyhounds that had broken a leg in a race two months previously. Roland's farm contained eight or ten greyhound carcasses, apparently killed by bludgeoning with a metal pipe.

In Arizona, after the well-publicized incidents mentioned above and others, the state racing commission moved to develop stringent rules for the care of greyhounds both at the breeding farm and at the track kennels. The standards published in 1995 represent the most comprehensive directions for breeders and kennel operators in the industry today. Unfortunately, they apply to only about 5 percent of all the dogs used for racing in America.

Arizona greyhounds must be housed in well-ventilated, amply lighted facilities that are cleaned and disinfected at least once each week. The indoor temperature must not exceed 85 degrees Fahrenheit at any time, and heat, bedding, or insulation must be provided when the temperature drops below 50 degrees Fahrenheit. Water must be constantly available, and food and water dishes must be kept free of mold and slime. Curiously, Arizona has no requirement to provide food at regular intervals. A minimum size of 31 inches wide, 42 inches long, and 32 inches high is stipulated for the cages or "crates" in which the animals are confined. Breeders and kennel operators must clean and sanitize these cages every day, and ensure that they are constructed of materials that allow the dogs to stay clean and dry.

Until March 2000, when the Oregon Racing Commission adopted rules closely modeled on Arizona's, the Grand Canyon state was the only one requiring that greyhounds be taken out of the crates at least four times in each twenty-four hour period. This is typically done to release the dogs into turn-out pens, runs, or exercise areas where they can stretch, run, and eliminate bodily waste. Arizona further requires that these areas be fenced, cleaned daily, cleared of brush and weeds, and provide enough shade so that all the dogs can avoid direct sunlight.

Arizona and Oregon are also the only jurisdictions to establish standards for the intrastate transportation of greyhounds. Crates used for transporting the canines must be well maintained, cleaned and sanitized each day or more frequently if necessary, and cannot be smaller than 2 feet wide, 3 feet long, and 34 inches high. Two dogs, at most, are allowed in each crate, so long as there is enough space for both animals to "comfortably" sit and lie down, turn around, and stand. The dogs must be checked no less often than once every four hours of the journey, and offered water at each interval. In hot weather, exceeding 90 degrees Fahrenheit, Arizona requires that vehicles transporting greyhounds be equipped with cooling systems, and when the temperature falls below 50 degrees Fahrenheit, heat, bedding, or insulation must be provided. Oregon does not mention cooling systems or heat, but instead sets absolute limits at 45 degrees and 95 degrees Fahrenheit.

The Fate of the Racing Greyhound

A greyhound that achieves the A grade due to its prowess at the track will inevitably tumble back down the grading scale as it begins to lose races, and then fail to place at all in competition with younger, faster dogs. Other dogs never advance far up the scale. Once a greyhound drops out of the D class, it is said to have "graded off"—the animal is failing to make any more money for its owner. This usually happens after about two years of racing, and then a decision must be made about what to do with the animal. After all, the greyhounds were created to run at dog tracks, and when they cannot do that profitably, their existence appears pointless.

For many years, most of these "retired" racers—three- or four-year-old dogs—were either killed outright, or sold or donated to research facilities, including medical and veterinary schools. No one knows how many greyhounds have been disposed of in these ways since the 1920s when the industry began in America. After the enactment of the Laboratory Animal Welfare Act (the precursor to the AWA) in 1966, research facilities have been required to record, among other things, the number of dogs of each breed they have obtained. However, labs are not required to include this information in their annual report to the USDA, so it is not available to the public through that federal agency.

On the other hand, some states have freedom of information laws that can be used to access the records of public institutions. For example, the *Greyhound Network News* wielded such a statute in 1998 to learn that the School of Veterinary Medicine at Colorado State University had acquired over 2,600 greyhounds for the school laboratories during a three-year period in the mid-1990s. Back in the 1980s, the New England Anti-Vivisection Society estimated that about 2,000 greyhounds were appropriated by Massachusetts labs every year. Estimates today vary depending on whether the NGA or greyhound advocates are consulted, but in 1999 somewhere between 8,000 and 14,000 graded-off dogs exiting the racing system were not adopted, and perhaps one-half of these went to research facilities. These figures of 4,000 to 7,000 greyhounds killed outright each year do not represent the total because they do not include puppies that never make it off the farms. When these animals are taken into account, here too we find disputed sums, ranging from 9,500 to over 20,000 greyhounds euthanized every year.

Whatever the precise number of canines eliminated, there is no disputing that greyhound adoptions have increased drastically since the 1980s. Yet again there is little agreement about exactly how much. The NGA reports that the adoption rate more than tripled in the 1990s to an annual total of about 18,000, while greyhound advocates say the number is closer to 12,000 a year. After various greyhound abuses came to light in the late 1980s, the NGA formed the American Greyhound Council (AGC) "to provide for the welfare of the racing greyhound and the betterment of the greyhound industry." Among other responsibilities, the AGC finances the Greyhound Adoption Fund, a program that has granted thousands of dollars to adoption groups around the country, though none to those that expressly reject dog racing as a legitimate use of the animals.

Currently, only Arizona's racing commission has written an official program into its rules "to promote the adoption of racing greyhounds as domestic pets." The program provides for up to 25 percent of the license fees generated from track operators to be distributed to nonprofit canine adoption groups. Approved groups cannot sell the dogs, give them to a research facility, pound, or animal shelter, or "allow the greyhounds to be used for racing, wagering, or hunting." However, the adoption organization must be associated with a race track. This seems to be a deliberate attempt to shut out independent greyhound advocacy groups, which do tend to be highly critical of the entire dog racing enterprise.

Vaccinations, if necessary, and sterilization are required for each canine accepted into Arizona's program. Furthermore, measures must be taken to acclimate the dogs to life as companion animals, including exposure to cats, a new diet, and common household objects such as furniture and stairs. The program requires a representative of the adoption group to inspect the home of a prospective adoptee, verifying that the housing situation there for the greyhound is in compliance with the commission regulations.

A Brief History of Horse Racing

The first written account of a race between horses comes from the *Iliad*, Book 23. Possibly composed as long ago as the thirteenth century B.C.E., the story suggests that the chariot race described was one in a longstanding tradition of such contests. First prize, to be awarded by Achilles, was a woman highly skilled at needlework, and a tripod of "two-and-twenty measures" with handles. The original record of a mounted horse race for which there is solid historical evidence is also from Greece, at the Thirty-third Olympiad, held in 644 B.C.E.

The Romans became especially fanatical about horse racing. After a modest beginning in the fourth century B.C.E. with a few chariot races at the Circus Maximus, a kind of major league of racing had developed by the start of the common era, one featuring numerous teams, ample funding, and famous drivers whose celebrity can only be compared to the most acclaimed contemporary American athletes. No doubt horses had been run against one another for many centuries before the Romans or the Olympic games, particularly by the highly skilled equestrians of the Asian steppes, where the species had been domesticated at least 3,000 years earlier.

The foundations of modern horse racing are found in Britain, however, where the oldest surviving description of such a contest comes from 1174 C.E.. The riders were professional jockeys, and the venue was a London horse fair held every Friday for years, so it is certain that formal racing had begun much sooner than this date. Before the twelfth century was done, money prizes were being offered to winners. By 1500 a horse race was run every year at Chester on a site that to this day still presents annual racing. The signal event for British coursing was the ardent patronage of the monarchy, beginning with James I in the early 1600s and especially Charles II at the end of that century, making it "the sport of kings."

The 1700s saw the crystallization of horse racing into the basic structure that prevails today and its rise to the level of a national pastime. Perhaps most important was the development of the "Thoroughbred" racing horse, a mixture of Arabian, Turk, Mediterranean, and native English horses (the lineage of every Thoroughbred in the world today traces back to three stallions of the 1750s). The *General Stud Book* was first published in 1791, meticulously recording the Thoroughbred bloodlines. The creation of the "Jockey Club" also came in this period, an organization that still exercises control over racing and breeding. Numerous "turf" courses were laid out, many of which continue to be used today. Unlike the standard American flat, dirt oval, English courses have always been on grass with widely varying shapes and gradients.

In America the Puritans who dominated the early colonists rejected horse racing as sinful and actively suppressed it throughout the 1650s. Then in 1665 Colonel Richard Nicolls, who had commanded the forces that wrested New Amsterdam from the Dutch and renamed it New York, set up a course on Long Island and organized races there for the spring and fall. With this precedent and a greater influx of more secularly minded colonists south of New England, the popularity of American horse racing grew parallel with its rise in England, though initially on a much smaller scale. By the time of the Revolutionary War, "the sport of kings" was the favorite pastime of landowners in Maryland, Virginia, and the Carolinas. The War of 1812 and the Civil War dampened coursing spirits, but racing expanded following both interruptions.

In the 1870s the Americans developed a "stud book" to track the ancestry of the Yankee Thoroughbreds, established their own Jockey Club, and introduced the system of pari-mutuel wagering. Originally devised by a Frenchman, the basic pari-mutuel method is to pay off gamblers who backed first- ("win"), second- ("place"), and third-place ("show") horses from the total sum of money bet on all runners in the race, less a commission. In French, *pari* is "bet" and *mutuel* is "mutual." At this time, governments in states along the eastern seaboard from Florida to New York began forming racing commissions to formalize the conduct of races, and especially to ensure that the state treasury received its share of the losers' money.

Legal Regulation of Racing Horse Welfare

State-sanctioned Thoroughbred races are held somewhere in America nearly every day of the year among the approximately 100 tracks currently operating in 32 states. In 1999 over 68,000 horses ran nearly 55,000 races. Based on national studies from the early 1990s, perhaps 800 or 900 of these animals were fatally injured while running in a race, and about 5 percent hurt so seriously that they were unable to finish. Many more injuries are only discovered later, after the race is completed.

These injuries are almost always to the legs of the horse—muscle tears, ligament damage, fractures of varying severity—although the fatalities are sometimes due to broken vertebrae suffered in a horrible fall. The ankles of a horse are scarcely larger than those of an adult human, yet the animal weighs 5 or 6 times as much and can run 40 miles per hour. The stresses on those appendages are immense, and coupled with running on hard, weather-proof tracks, some lameness, fractures, and deaths are inevitable.

All the racing commissions allow owners or trainers to treat their animals with pain relievers on race day, typically specifying phenylbutazone, or "bute," as it is known in the industry. Lasix (furosemide), a diuretic prescribed to reduce swelling and bleeding, is also uniformly permitted. However, the dosage of both of these substances is strictly limited by racing rules. Excessive use of bute in particular has allowed horses to run with injuries that would otherwise have prevented them from competing, thus aggravating the condition. Racing rules demand blood or urine tests from all the horses "carding" (finishing first, second, or third) in each race. The samples are checked for one or more of the dozens of banned drugs (various amphetamines, tranquilizers, bronchodilators, decongestants, and painkillers) and for illegal concentrations of approved drugs. A horse running with good odds that finishes well back in the pack may also be tested.

No racing commission limits the number of races a horse can run over any interval of time, whether the same day, week, or year. Even so, the number of starts per runner has declined markedly from the 1960s when the average Thoroughbred might compete in a dozen races a year. In 1999 the figure stood at a little more than seven. All the state commissions require that a designated veterinarian assess the physical condition of each racehorse prior to running, what is often called a "racing soundness examination." This is supposed to ensure that every animal is sufficiently healthy and fit to, as the California rule puts it, "exert its best effort to win." In California, vets must closely inspect the eyes and legs of each horse, record its temperature, and observe the animal at rest and while in motion.

Several states also have specific rules for dealing with animals hurt during the running of a race. In Kansas, for example, disabled horses must remain on the track until retrieved by a horse ambulance, which vehicle must be kept on the premises. Euthanasia of a racehorse must be done "out of the vision of the public," either from behind a "large portable screen" that the ambulances are required to carry, or by removing the animal from the track. Minnesota's rule is nearly the same.

The most common racing commission rule addressing horse welfare concerns the jockey's use of a whip while riding in the race, although some states do not mention this issue. None of the states *require* whips in horse racing, but most do stipulate that an announcement be made to the audience identifying which jockeys are not riding with whips. Restrictions on whips vary in their detail. Kentucky has a comprehensive rule that forbids whipping "(a) on the head, flanks, or any part of [the horse's] body other than the shoulders or hind quarters; (b) during the post parade except when necessary to control the horse; (c) excessively or brutally causing welts or breaks in the skin; (d) when the horse is clearly out of the race or has attained its maximum placing; or (e) persistently even though the horse is showing no response under the whip." The whip rules in California, Massachusetts, and Texas are identical to this one. In contrast, Colorado says only that "a whip shall not be applied by anyone in an abusive manner at any time," Iowa prohibits "excessive or indiscriminate whipping," and Wyoming will not allow more whipping "than is reasonably necessary."

Very few of the states have rules addressing the humane treatment of racing horses generally. Virginia does minimally attend to this issue, noting that "[t]he conduct of racing, with pari-mutuel wagering, shall be . . . humane to the horses." In Idaho, the commissioners direct that tracks be maintained with "special consideration for the comfort and safety . . . of the horses. . . ." The Minnesota commission mentions facilities maintenance "with consideration for the . . . safety and health of horses."

Oregon's provision here is by far the most thorough, declaring that no racing animal shall be subjected to "cruel or inhumane treatment," defined as inadequate food, water, and shelter, any form of neglect, or "conditions which cause the animal to give the appearance of physical pain or suffering." Alone among all the racing commissions, Oregon's rules also reference the state anticruelty statute for descriptions of prohibited conduct toward racing horses. In contrast, Michigan and Nebraska specifically exclude horse racing from the provisions of their anticruelty laws. About half the state laws exempt "normal," "accepted," or "customary" uses of animals, and the practices surrounding horse racing would seem to qualify (*see* chapter 3: *Anticruelty Laws*).

Prosecutions of trainers, jockeys, or other racetrack personnel under state anticruelty laws for abusing racehorses appear to be exceedingly rare, and guilty verdicts are even more unusual. The only case on record in recent years involved a trainer who subjected a horse to "milkshaking," force-feeding a mixture of water and baking soda with a tube inserted down the animal's throat. The concoction is believed to delay fatigue, but here the feeding tube curled back and emptied the substance into the animal's lungs. The horse was euthanized and the trainer received six months in jail for his cruelty-to-animals conviction.

Stabling and Transportation of Racehorses

Thoroughbreds spend most of their five- or six-year racing "careers" in stables and in horse trailers. The animals are housed in barns at the tracks and in training centers, and they are often transported between these facilities, and between them and the farms of horse breeders and owners.

Nonetheless, standards of care in stabling and in transportation are spotty. Racing commissions rarely establish rules for keeping Thoroughbreds at stables, and they are not authorized to regulate the movement of animals within the state. Most states have no such regulations anyway.

California leads the nation in number of race tracks (sixteen, at last count), yet the Golden State's horse transportation statute applies only when equines are being taken to the slaughterhouse. New York has some of the most demanding laws in this area, but has only four tracks. The Empire State prohibits transporting horses for more than eighteen consecutive hours without giving the animals at least four hours for rest, food, and water. Vehicles used to transport horses in New York must have ventilated and insulated compartments, nonskid floors, partitions, loading ramps, doors of sufficient height to allow the animals to pass through safely, and no sharp or protruding surfaces. Vermont and Connecticut have similarly rigorous laws but neither state has any horse racing.

Interstate transportation of racehorses (and livestock generally) is subject to the federal Twenty-Eight Hour Law (*see also* chapter 4). If racehorses are moved by rail or truck for at least twenty-eight hours of travel time (state laws can be more stringent but not less so), the animals must be "humanely" unloaded, fed, watered, and rested. Federal regulations require corrals of "adequate" size for holding the horses, pens that are clean, well drained, and that provide protection from the weather. Each 40-foot carload of horses must have 400 pounds of hay, but the law does not set a maximum number of animals for any particular conveyance. Thoroughbreds typically run in the region where they were born and trained, so journeys of sufficient duration to activate this federal law are quite uncommon for them.

No federal laws regulate the stabling of horses or any other animal. Only a handful of racing commissions have anything to say about housing racehorses, and here the instructions are quite minimal. For example, tracks in Colorado and Iowa must provide individual box stalls with separate feeding and watering areas for each animal. Additionally, the stables must be adequately drained, and "manure and other refuse . . . promptly and properly removed." Kentucky horse trainers are responsible for maintaining the stables "in a clean, neat, and sanitary condition at all times." Similarly, New York stables must be "maintained in a clean and sanitary condition," and every stall has to be "thoroughly disinfected" after each horse has used it. Florida has charged its veterinarians with the responsibility to inspect the stables "for general health and safety requirements," yet no such requirements are found in the Sunshine State's racing rules.

The Fate of the Racing Horse

Some Thoroughbreds begin racing as two-year-olds, but most start at three or four. Few horses can run competitively past the age of ten. Many others are withdrawn from the tracks well before this time due to injuries or simply because they do not win or at least card. Horse racing is a business, and the animals that do not make money for their owners are not kept in the industry. Unlike the greyhounds used in dog racing (*see* this chapter: *Greyhound Racing and Horse Racing: The Fate of the Racing Greyhound*), it is not known how many Thoroughbreds are removed from horse racing every year. In the United States the Jockey Club maintains records on the number of colts foaled annually—just over 33,000 in 2000—but no organization tracks how many leave the system, or their individual fates upon exit. What becomes of them?

Horses that have had long and lucrative racing careers are usually returned to farms for breeding (not geldings of course), on the theory that their success has a strong genetic component that can be passed on. Other, lesser animals, especially injured ones, are often sold to meat packers—their final destination is a slaughterhouse. About 75,000 horses are killed for meat in the United States every year, mostly for export to foreign countries (such as Japan and France) where horsemeat is a highly regarded meal, but also for rendering into commercial pet food. The U.S. Department of Agriculture, which regulates the meat processing industry, does not require records on the source of the animals sold for slaughter, so no one really knows how many racehorses suffer this fate. One recent estimate figures that about 10 percent of horses sold for slaughter are retired Thoroughbreds.

More fortunate horses are adopted and used in other equine activities, such as riding for personal pleasure or as rented mounts, as polo horses or for shows, for hunting, as law enforcement animals, and as carriage horses (*see* chapter 3: *Horse Law: Carriage Rides*). In the past, placement in these "second careers" was accomplished in a mostly haphazard and generally fortuitous fashion for the horses, but in recent years the endeavor has become much more organized.

Although the original equine adoption organization devoted to racehorses, the Thoroughbred Retirement Foundation, was established in 1982, the 1990s saw a surge in coordinated efforts to place former racers in decent environments. The United Pegasus Foundation, based in California, Michigan's Second Career Racehorses, the Horse Protection Association of Florida, and Rerun, located in Kentucky, are a few of the many groups now focused on saving retired racehorses. In July 2000 the National Thoroughbred Racing Association announced the formation of the Racehorse Adoption Referral Program, a nationwide "clearinghouse" intended to facilitate horse adoptions by connecting owners, potential adopters, and "equine retirement agencies."

To date, at least two tracks have also established programs to promote the adoption of racehorses, Sam Houston Race Park in Houston and Suffolk Downs in Boston. No state racing commission has yet mandated a horse retirement program, as Arizona has for greyhounds (see above), so all of these efforts are strictly voluntary. Also, there is currently no established national organization overseeing and accrediting the various regionally oriented groups, so there is no data on how many Thoroughbreds are adopted each year in America. The Thoroughbred Adoption and Retirement Association (TARA) may change this situation. Newly formed in late 2000, TARA aspires to coordinate and promote racehorse adoptions on the national level.

RODEOS

American rodeo is a substantially self-regulating animal enterprise, one in which most of the rules guiding human conduct toward the animals are written and enforced by groups of people who are members of rodeo associations. Prior to the last half of the twentieth century, when most of these organizations were created, there were no formal standards of this nature whatever and even today at least half of all rodeos are not governed by any sanctioning body. Legal rules written by elected representatives of American citizens have touched rodeo only very lightly, and in the early days of this sport (as many call it) neither federal nor state laws affected rodeo at all.

The Origins of Modern Rodeo

The word "rodeo" is derived from the Spanish verb *rodear* meaning "to surround" or "to encircle." In the seventeenth- and eighteenth-century vernacular of northern Mexico, *rodear las vacas* referred to the activity of rounding up cattle.

Livestock raising had been imported into this region and developed by Spaniards—landed aristocrats and Catholic missionaries who discovered that ranching in New Spain was very different from what they had left behind in Andalucia or Murcia. In the Old World ranges were small and the gathering of livestock could be done on foot by peasants. Anyway, only the wealthy owned horses and nobility did not deign to herd cows. In the New World cattle were dispersed over vast tracts of land, requiring men mounted on horses to accomplish the seasonal gathering of the animals for branding, breeding, and ultimately for processing into hides, tallow, and meat. So the *hacendados* and *padres* equipped their servants and the newly baptized Indians with horses, provided minimal instruction, and told them to bring in *las vacas*. The mounted herdsmen were known as *vaqueros*—those who attend to cattle—and we may suppose that in the early days of the *rodear las vacas* there was a considerable amount of on-the-job training.

As the years passed and the great *estancias* spread north into what is now the American Southwest, generations of *vaqueros* perfected their craft, especially the more exciting and technically demanding skills of roping cattle and calves, taming wild horses, and training young horses for the saddle. Some individuals became quite proficient at these tasks and were well known for their skills. Friendly (and sometimes not so friendly) competition arose among *vaqueros* on the same *estancia*, and then spilled over to include rival operations, the men vying for superiority in the techniques of the trade. These contests often attracted the attention of other *vaqueros* as well as the local population, who enjoyed the entertainment—always in short supply out in the country—and admired the abilities displayed. The seeds of modern rodeo are found in such informal gatherings on the Mexican frontier, where spectators delighted in the exhibition of these talents demonstrated on cows and horses, all evolved out of the fundamental ranching activity, the *rodear las vacas.*

During the first half of the 1800s, English-speaking Americans steadily drifted into the Southwest, many of them hiring on with the Mexican outfits. They adopted much of the culture and language of the cattle-raising way of life, each becoming a "cowboy" or, corrupting the Spanish *vaquero*, a "buckaroo." After the annexation of Texas in 1845, the enormous cession of land that followed the war with Mexico in 1848, and the Gadsden Purchase of 1853, much of this territory became United States territory. Once the internecine hostilities of the Civil War ceased, American and European landowners began earnestly pursuing ranching throughout the West.

The cowboy and his craft became much in demand, and, not coincidentally, the first recorded American rodeo was held. This is generally recognized as a "bronc riding" contest that took place in 1869 on the high plains of eastern Colorado in the vicinity of a town called Deer Trail. ("Bronc" is from the Spanish *bronco,* meaning "rough" in general or, when attributed to horses, "unbroken.") Cowboys from two different ranches competed for the distinction of the longest ride on the back of a bucking horse, replaying for fun the common ranch chore of "breaking" feral horses. As the *vaqueros* had already been doing in Mexico for perhaps two centuries, such cowboy competition certainly occurred in other locations in the states and U.S. territories of the West, and probably at earlier dates as well, although there are no written records of these.

American rodeos became much more common during the 1880s, although they were usually called "cowboy tournaments" or "round-ups," or, in California and Arizona, "fiestas." The term *rodeo* did not gain currency until after the turn of the century. Various western towns—Prescott, Arizona; Alpine and Pecos, both in Texas; Montrose and Denver, two Colorado communities—claim credit for presenting the first formal rodeos in certain years of the 1880s, with paying spectators and prize money or trophies for winners in several events. This decade also saw the rise of the "Wild West Show," a major impetus to establishing rodeo as a lucrative form of entertainment.

The pioneer here was William F. Cody, more popularly known as "Buffalo Bill," who first produced a demonstration of riding and "bronc busting" for the 1882 Fourth of July celebration near his home in North Platte, Nebraska. The program was a great success. In little more than a year, Cody, always a shrewd entrepreneur, had a touring company staging the Indian-Anglo conflicts and cowboy skills of the Old West before full houses in amphitheaters all along the east coast. "Buffalo Bill's Wild West and Congress of Rough Riders" was quickly and widely imitated, with such retinues as the "101 Ranch Wild West Show" and "Pawnee Bill's Wild West Show" presenting a standard mix of Western melodrama and riding and roping exhibitions.

Wild west shows proved expensive to stage, so many producers turned to doing rodeos instead, where not only did the spectators pay to see the show, the cowboys also ponied up entry fees to display their talents. Eventually though, independent producers with traveling rodeos shuttling from town to town were no match for the local rodeo committees. Usually composed of prominent, influential, and well-heeled citizens and ranchers, these committees financed and organized the production for their own region. This remains today the principal mechanism for making a rodeo into a reality. One of the longest-running rodeos, and probably the most famous, the Cheyenne Frontier Days Rodeo in Wyoming, was put together by just such a local committee in 1897. Within five years, Cheyenne's Frontier Days was drawing crowds in excess of 20,000, an enormous figure at the time, eclipsing the attendance at any other entertainment event.

After three decades of growing popularity, as best represented by such showcases as the Frontier Days and the Pendleton Roundup in Oregon, a number of the more successful rodeo committees banded together in 1929 to form the Rodeo Association of America. This alliance for the first time standardized and codified rodeo rules—which tended to vary depending on the location and were often inconsistent—and established a ranking system, awarding points based on prize money won. At the end of the year, an individual from each rodeo event who had accumulated the most points in competition was designated the "world champion" cowboy in that category.

Stung by unscrupulous promoters who would, among other nefarious deeds, skim entry fees to enhance their profits, the cowboy contestants got themselves organized in 1936, calling their group the "Cowboys' Turtle Association." Renamed the Rodeo Cowboys Association (RCA) in

1945, the RCA endorsed forms of competition, wrote rules for fairly promoting and conducting rodeo contests, and appointed their own "world
champions." The Rodeo Association of America went under in 1947 and
the rodeo committees were absorbed into the RCA, which became the
PRCA in 1975—the Professional Rodeo Cowboys Association. For over
fifty years, the PRCA has been the largest and most influential sanctioning organization in American rodeo.

Modern American Rodeo

A rodeo is held somewhere in America every weekend of the year. Indeed, pick any Thursday or Friday afternoon through Sunday night
stretch on the calendar and there is likely to be such an event in a couple
of dozen different locations, primarily scattered around the western
states. The PRCA sanctions over 700 rodeos annually, but this is far from
representing all the events that occur. The total number is unknown but
is probably three to five times higher. Of the remainder, perhaps a third
are governed by other, smaller sanctioning bodies (such as the International Rodeo Association) with standards that are substantially modeled
on those of the PRCA. It is very likely that at least 1,000 rodeos each year
are not authorized or overseen by any rule-making association.

Most of these events are "little rodeos," with tiny prize purses (perhaps a few hundred dollars) and "weekend warriors" for contestants.
Having only a local reputation at most, with correspondingly limited
promotion, these events are held outdoors in rural communities well off
the mainstream of the rodeo circuit. At the other end of the spectrum are
the fifty or so "big name" rodeos, all PRCA events, with total prize money
near or exceeding $100,000, and featuring performers who make their liv-
ing rodeoing. Known by even the casual rodeo fan, these major rodeos
are heavily promoted in a variety of media throughout a region, or even
across the country as in the National Finals Rodeo held every December
in Las Vegas. Staged in larger urban areas, often with expansive, covered
amphitheaters, these include the prestigious rodeos found in Denver, San
Francisco, Phoenix, San Antonio, Houston, Fort Worth, Miami, and New
York City. Also in this upper echelon are the famous "sentimental rodeos"
of smaller cities such as Cheyenne, Prescott, Greeley (Colorado), Salinas
(California), and Dodge City (Kansas).

Although the PRCA claims 5,000 contestant members, only about 5
percent of these earn more than $10,000 a year competing in rodeos.
These 200 or 300 cowboys, the top money makers in all of rodeo, take
home more than half of the millions of dollars of total prize money available ($30 million in 1998). For this elite group, who consider themselves
professional athletes, rodeo is a professional sport, not a mere pastime of
cowhands who are back riding the range on Monday morning. This first

tier of modern rodeo is the main focus of the TV contracts (ESPN and TNN), the corporate sponsors (Wrangler jeans, Winston cigarettes, Coors beer, Dodge trucks, and Copenhagen-Skoal smokeless tobacco, among others), the official licensed products (such as hats, T-shirts, coffee mugs, and shot glasses), the Pro Rodeo Hall of Fame (in Colorado Springs), and the rodeo groupies ("buckle bunnies").

American, PRCA-sanctioned rodeos are defined in large measure by six standard events, which also form the core of virtually every rodeo, whether endorsed by the national organization or not. In the early days of rodeo, the riding of bucking horses and roping of cattle were always featured in the performance, these two most nearly approximating the ranch work from which rodeo originally derived. Several other kinds of events were also common back then, exhibitions that have since faded from the rodeo scene, though not disappeared entirely. Among these are horse racing, relay racing, trick riding and roping contests, and "wild cow" milking, in which the cowboy attempted to squirt a few drops of milk from a trussed range cow into a bottle. Today, the regular exhibitions are divided into two categories of three events each. In the timed events the contestants try to perform a specific task as quickly as possible, while in the "rough stock" events the winners are determined by judges' assessments of their riding styles during a set time interval.

Rodeo Events and Their Restrictions

Bull riding is the centerpiece of the rough stock competition, and probably the most popular rodeo event, saved for last on the typical program. This exhibition seems to evoke something of the same fascination one finds in those who enjoy anticipating car wrecks at a motor speedway. Not surprisingly, it is the most dangerous event for contestants, the one in which the most rodeo fatalities have occurred.

The standard bucking bull is a Brahma mix, weighing 1,500 pounds or more, a fertile male bovine specifically bred to lunge and leap, plunge and spin whenever a human has the temerity to sit on its back. The man who does this at the rodeo has only a plaited rope to grip, one fastened around the animal's chest. As the bull bucks his way across the arena, the contestant tries to stay on for eight seconds.

Additional style points are awarded if he rakes the bull with his spurs during the ride. According to PRCA rules, the rowels (disks with pointed projections) of the rider's spurs must be blunted and locked, and electric prods cannot be used to provoke the bull out of the "chute" (the holding pen where it awaits release into the arena). In September 2000 California became the first state to prohibit the use of prods on any animal in the chute; currently, no other state or federal law restricts electric prods or spurs in rodeos (some city ordinances do, *see* this chapter: *Rodeos: Legal*

Regulation of the Treatment of Rodeo Animals). Here, we must also remind ourselves that about half of all rodeos staged in the United States are not subject to any rodeo association rules.

Spurring is *required* by PRCA rules in the other two rough stock events, which also feature bucking animals: saddle "bronc" riding and bareback riding. The rider in either event will be disqualified if he does *not* use his spurs on the horses in the proper manner. The instruments must have dulled rowels, as in the bull riding, but here they must also spin loose. In the saddle ride, the contestant holds onto a rope attached to the horse's bridle, and for bareback, a kind of rawhide suitcase handle fixed to a strap serves as the handhold. In both events, riders must keep their other hand free of the horse and the rigging, and they are given eight seconds to demonstrate their ability to ride a fractious, lurching equine.

Whether saddled or not, the bucking horses—bulls too—wear flank or "bucking" straps that are tightened moments before the chute opens. These strips of leather, encircling the animal's stomach and back just behind the rib cage, irritate and annoy the animals, enhancing their tendency to buck. The PRCA dictates that flank straps must be lined with sheepskin or neoprene, have quick-release buckles, and are never to be used with sharp or cutting objects. Although it has often been charged that these belts are placed to exert pressure on the genital area of the horse or bull, rodeo people always reject this allegation as ridiculous. Electric prods can only be used for "chute stalls," according to PRCA rules. These are horses that suddenly freeze up and will not leap out into the arena.

Calf roping is the oldest and most common timed event. It is found in every rodeo, usually as the initial event, and dates from such perennial ranch chores as securing young cows for branding, and retrieving, or rescuing them from thick brush or mud wallows. Here, a Hereford calf, typically, four to six months old and weighing 200 or 300 pounds is released from the chute. The PRCA allows the use of electric prods here, but asserts that this measure is seldom necessary. As the animal runs across the arena, a contestant on horseback takes off after it, swinging a loop of rope over his head. The rider is permitted by the rules to rope any part of the calf's body, but usually the head is caught. Once that is accomplished, the horse abruptly stops, taking slack out of the rope but trying not to jerk the calf off its feet, though this usually happens. A "busted" calf must be raised upright again (if it doesn't get up on its own) and then manually thrown down, which takes more time. Ideally then, the calf is just standing there as the rider dismounts, runs over, throws it to the ground, takes another length of rope (the "pigging string") and ties it around three of the animal's legs. The point of this exercise is to be the fastest to do it; eight to nine seconds is considered an excellent time.

The object of team roping is the same, but its structure is a little differ-ent. In this event, instead of a calf, a corriente "steer" is used—this is an adult, male bovine of a special breed that has been castrated and weighs about 600 pounds. This time, two riders pursue the running animal, one to rope its horns (the "header") while the other aims for the hind legs (the "heeler"). A five-second penalty is assessed if only one leg is caught, but in any case the event is over when the steer is stretched out between the two riders and their horses.

Corriente steers are also used in the third timed event, but here they are "wrestled" rather than roped. Once more, the animal breaks into a run across the arena—prodded if necessary—followed by a contestant on a galloping horse, and kept running in a straight line by a second rider on one side (the "hazer"). At what is judged to be the appropriate moment, the rider leaps from the horse, grabs the steer's horns, digs in his feet, and, by twisting the animal's neck over, topples it into the dust. Com-pleting the exercise in less than five seconds is a fast time.

Steer wrestling did not originate in routine ranch work, because this would be a very strange thing for a cowboy to do. It was invented by one of the earliest black rodeo contestants, Bill Pickett, who first demon-strated the procedure while working for the 101 Ranch Wild West Show in 1907. Legend has it that Pickett drew his inspiration for pulling steers down from the ranch bulldogs, who would swarm a cow, sometimes using their teeth to latch onto the hapless animal's snout and drag it to the ground—hence the nickname for the steer wrestling: "bulldogging."

Interestingly, the bulldog was bred in England during the Middle Ages especially for fighting with cattle, providing humans with a form of en-tertainment known as "bull-baiting" (*see also* this chapter: *Cockfighting and Dogfighting: Dogfighting and Baiting*). The dog's lower jaw projects well in front of the upper one, affording a powerful vice-like grip, while its deeply set nose allows for sufficient air inhalation as the mouth clamps down on the bull. It is said that Pickett himself would sometimes grip the steer with his teeth, but this maneuver is contrary to PRCA rules today.

Legal Regulation of the Treatment of Rodeo Animals

None of these events is subject to any pervasive legal regulation. The manner in which rodeo animals are treated is largely unrestricted by ei-ther state or federal law. The Animal Welfare Act (AWA) (*see* chapter 7) primarily regulates the use of animals in research, testing, and experi-mentation, and explicitly announces that it does not apply to rodeos. Al-though the AWA and its regulations do also dictate the care and treatment of animals used by an "'exhibitor'. . . , such term includes carnivals, cir-cuses, and zoos . . . , but such term excludes . . . rodeos." Moreover, be-cause livestock are generally excluded from the definition of "animal" under the AWA, the federal law provides no protection for horses or other farm animals "not intended for research purposes."

Currently, Rhode Island is the only state with a set of legal rules imposing a substantial amount of external regulation on how rodeos are conducted; violation carries a fine of $50 to $500. The Ocean State's most comprehensive measure is a requirement that a licensed veterinarian be present at every rodeo, and he or she must have at least two years of experience in the treatment of large animals. PRCA rules stipulate that a vet be present at each rodeo, but do not demand any particular expertise or length of work experience of this individual. Rhode Island also directs that the vet attending a rodeo be given unrestricted access to every event using animals, and has the authority to declare any animal unfit for use in any event; the decision of the doctor on this matter is final. The rodeo promoter is responsible for any expenses related to having this on-site medical expertise. The new California law mentioned above that prohibits prodding animals in the chute also requires that a veterinarian be in attendance or on call at every rodeo held in the state.

There is a widespread misconception that many states prohibit the competition known as steer roping, but, in fact, at this writing only Rhode Island has banned this event. Although it was once a regular event in most rodeos, steer roping is now mostly confined to rural settings in several western states—Colorado, Kansas, Oklahoma, Wyoming, New Mexico, and Oregon, mainly.

Steer roping is much like calf roping except for one crucial difference: while the calf is supposed to be thrown to the ground by the contestant, a running steer is to be dropped by tripping with the rope. After the rider has thrown his loop and secured it on the animal's horns, he veers to the left, lowering the rope along the steer's right side. As horse and rider move away at a sharp angle, the rope catches the sprinting animal just below the hip, and the hind legs are abruptly pulled out from under it. The steer's higher center of gravity, one-quarter-ton weight, and sprinter's speed increase the probabilities of injury resulting from the tripping—dislocations and broken bones and horns are not uncommon. The event seems to have been moved out into the country to venues where audiences are more accepting of what urban dwellers tend to regard as brutal and cruel, so today it is quite rare to find steer roping displayed at a city rodeo. Except in Rhode Island, this absence is a voluntary reaction by the rodeo community to the discontent of a certain segment of the public, not one legally compelled by state legislators.

Rhode Island is also the one state that does not allow the traditional form of calf roping in which the animal is subjected to a sudden stop or fall after being secured with a lariat loop. "Breakaway" roping is allowed—instead of cinching tight, the loop slips through when pulled—

but because the calf cannot then be thrown and trussed, the PRCA does not consider this a legitimate calf-roping event. Because a PRCA-sanctioned rodeo must include all six of the standard events, this provision of the Rhode Island statute, along with the stringent veterinarian requirements, has virtually eliminated rodeo in the Ocean State. Finally, Rhode Island alone stipulates that any individual who has been convicted of cruelty to animals while participating in a rodeo is not permitted to be a rodeo contestant.

Although this last condition makes sense, there is no record of any person in any state, including Rhode Island, ever having been convicted of cruelty to animals in the course of a rodeo performance. Indeed, a dozen states explicitly exempt rodeo from the provisions of their anticruelty laws, so such a conviction is impossible in these locations: Arizona, Colorado, Kansas, Missouri, Montana, Nebraska, New Mexico, New York, Oregon, Utah, Washington, and Wyoming.

Eleven of these twelve states immunize rodeo events specifically from the provisions of the law, just as the AWA does. The twelfth, Utah, perhaps also inspired by the AWA, simply excludes rodeo animals from the definition of "animal" in the anticruelty statute designating those creatures it protects. Idaho is a thirteenth state that in effect places rodeo beyond the reach of its anticruelty law by declaring that "exhibitions . . . normally or commonly considered acceptable . . . shall not be construed to be cruel nor defined as cruelty to animals." Undoubtedly, rodeo qualifies as such an exhibition, although this exclusion has never been tested in a state court (*see also* chapter 3: *Anticruelty Laws*).

Ohio is the only state besides Rhode Island that restricts some basic practices of American rodeo, having outlawed the use of unpadded flank and bucking straps, and electric prods on horses and cattle. A major rodeo producer questioned the constitutional validity of the ban in 1984. The Ohio Court of Appeals held that because the statute advances the state's legitimate interest in preventing the mistreatment of these animals, it stands as valid law (*State v. Longhorn World Championship Rodeo, Inc.*).

The most sweeping restrictions of rodeo come from St. Petersburg, Florida, which has banned the events entirely from within the city limits—in 2000 this is the sole, complete proscription of rodeo in America. For comparison, no rodeo performance has been legally staged anywhere in the United Kingdom since 1934 when Parliament passed the Protection of Animals Act. After a disturbing video was aired on NBC showing a bull breaking its leg at a 1991 rodeo in Pittsburgh, the city outlawed the use of electric prods, flank straps, and spurs with sharpened or fixed rowels. Similarly, Baltimore also bans electric prods, flank straps on horses, and the use of spurs. Southhampton, New York, and Pompano Beach, Florida, have disallowed prods, straps, sharpened spurs, or bullwhips.

These prohibitions have effectively ended rodeo in these cities. In 1998 Woodstock, Illinois, passed an ordinance that prohibits a person from fighting or wrestling with any animal, thus making steer wrestling illegal in that community.

In contrast to the American rodeo so far described, none of whose standard events are banned in any state, Mexican rodeo—called the *charreada*—has found some of its traditional events condemned by the law of several states. The *charreada*, popular especially in the border states of California, Arizona, New Mexico, and Texas, is defined by ten different exhibitions using horses and cattle. Two of these events have drawn the ire of citizens and state legislatures because the object of both is to trip a horse. In the *manganas*, the contestant tries to bring a running horse crashing to the floor of the arena by roping its two front feet, either while chasing the animal on foot (*manganas a pie*) or while riding another horse (*manganas a caballo*). As in steer roping, a large, fast animal with a high center of gravity is being compelled to suddenly lose its balance, pitching headlong into the dirt. Again, fractures, broken bones, dislocations, and lacerations are a regular occurrence.

At this writing, Florida and Illinois (both of which have also seen *charreada* performances), California, Kansas, New Mexico, Maine, Oklahoma, and Texas all prohibit tripping a horse. In these statutes, "trip" is generally defined as using a rope, pole, wire, stick, or other object to cause a horse to fall or lose its balance. Florida has made violation of this law a felony, while the other states provide only misdemeanor penalties (*see also* chapter 3: *Horse Law: State Regulation of Horse Welfare: Tail Docking and Tripping*). As suggested above, no state except Rhode Island has outlawed tripping cattle.

Legal Regulation of the Transportation of Rodeo Animals
Unlike rodeo events, the movement of animals to and from rodeos is often subject to legal regulation, and it is the stock contractor who may be liable. Although the contestants in the roping events almost always ride their own horses, most of the other animals used in rodeos are supplied by stock contractors. These are independent operations of varying size, typically run by a single individual or a family, in business to provide rodeo committees with sufficient bulls, steers, calves, and horses to stage an exhibition of the desired size.

The largest and most successful stock contractors also produce their own shows. The average PRCA rodeo might use 200 or so bucking horses, 100 bulls, and 200 to 250 steers and calves. Add a few dozen pick-up horses as well as the mounts owned by each of the perhaps 50 contestants in the roping events and this totals to over 600 animals. A major, large-scale rodeo such as in Ft. Worth or Denver would call for at least twice this number. Smaller rodeos have far fewer animals, of course, but in these events the same calves and steers are used over and over again. No PRCA or any rodeo association rule, let alone legal rule, limits the number of times a particular cow can be roped or wrestled at any given event. The PRCA does prohibit using the same cattle during successive calendar years, and will not allow roped cows to be used for wrestling also.

In the early days of rodeo when stock contracting was developing as a business, bucking horses were obtained from ranchers and farmers desiring to rid themselves of cantankerous animals whose inclination to buck made them useless for work or riding. Wild horses roaming on the open range were free for the taking then, and these, too, were rounded up by the contractors' crews and pressed into service. But after the Second World War machinery replaced many working horses, tens of thousands of wild horses were slaughtered to supply a burgeoning pet food industry, and rodeo became increasingly popular (*see also* chapter 3: *Wild Free-Roaming Horses and Burros Act of 1971: Decline of the Herds*). These factors significantly diminished the pool of rogue horses that could be provided for rodeos. Reacting to an increasingly dire situation, the most enlightened stock contractors began breeding their own animals, applying basic principles of genetics to select for horses prone to buck. Today, most stock contractors breed their own bucking horses and bucking bulls, while the cows to be roped or wrestled are usually purchased from ranchers.

Stock contractors are constantly moving their animals from their base of operations to various rodeos, from show to show, and back home again. It is here that the care and handling of rodeo animals is first impacted by legal rules. Any journey exceeding twenty-eight hours in which cattle or horses are transported across state lines must be done in compliance with the federal Twenty-Eight Hour Law (*see also* chapter 4). This requires that livestock be "humanely" unloaded, fed, watered, and rested if their travels last longer than that amount of time. The law does not define "humane." The PRCA has a similar rule, which also does not define "humane," that allows only twenty-four hours of confinement. Federal regulations implementing the Twenty-Eight Hour Law require that the pens where livestock are held for a feeding and watering interval be of adequate size, clean, well drained, and that they afford shelter from the weather. Further, the amount of feed to be provided for them in each conveyance, depending on the species being transported, is specified.

The Twenty-Eight Hour Law does not contain any instructions for the maximum number of animals permitted in any particular conveyance, nor are there any stipulations regarding the construction of cars or trailers designed for transporting animals. Furthermore, often the transportation of rodeo animals does not cross state lines, and so does not activate the federal statute. Yet about two-thirds of the states do not have laws regulating the intrastate movement of livestock by railroad or common carrier. At the present time, only Maine, Minnesota, and Vermont have comprehensive laws of this nature, each substantially modeled on the Twenty-Eight Hour Law, but each also extending this legal arena in important ways.

All three state statutes apply to all livestock, and prioritize animals over any other type of freight. In Maine, modes of conveyance "shall be sufficiently covered or boarded on the sides and ends to afford proper protection to the animals in case of storms or severe cold weather and shall be properly ventilated," and it is prohibited to load more animals than can "stand comfortably" in the transporting vehicle. Minnesota also requires that animals be given sufficient space to stand and lie down, and will not allow large animals to be transported with their legs tied together. Vermont prohibits a trucker from traveling more than eighteen consecutive hours without unloading the animals from the trailer, and allowing them at least four hours for rest, eating, and drinking. Livestock transported by either rail or truck must be separated according to species. Vermont also specifies conditions of transportation for horses in particular, requiring, among other items, that compartments be insulated, ventilated, equipped with partitions or stalls as well as loading ramps, and constructed with smooth materials and nonskid floors.

New York's law regulating the transportation of horses is nearly identical to Vermont's, but the Empire State has no further provisions protecting cattle or any other livestock when these species are transported. Similarly, Connecticut has a thorough law prohibiting "inhumane transportation," but it only protects horses, and no other animals are included. The stipulations of California's horse transportation statute are close to those of Vermont and New York, yet they apply only when equines are being taken to the slaughterhouse (*see also* chapter 3: *Horse Law: State Regulation of Horse Welfare: Transportation*).

Although Massachusetts and Rhode Island each have their own "Twenty-Eight Hour Law," and Michigan and South Carolina both have a "Thirty-Six Hour Law," all of these apply only to the transportation of animals by rail, and not by truck. The federal Twenty-Eight Hour Law, first enacted in 1873, was directed at the railroads and did not cover the movement of animals by truck until it was amended in 1994. Nonetheless, as of 2000, the USDA has not issued any regulations specific to truck transportation of livestock. Also, none of these four states have any provisions for the conditions of transportation, as we find in the Maine, Minnesota, and Vermont codes. Alabama proscribes the "transport [of] animals in any manner not consistent with humane methods of treatment," but only when the destination is a livestock market, which leads ultimately to the slaughterhouse, not a rodeo.

Finally, the anticruelty statutes of about two-thirds of the states outlaw "transport[ing] an animal in a cruel manner" or "carr[ying] in or upon any vehicle any animal in a cruel or inhuman manner." However, very few of these laws specify exactly what qualifies as a cruel mode of conveyance.

At any rate, apparently no stock contractor or his or her agent has ever been convicted of violating any federal or state Twenty-Eight (or Thirty-Six) Hour Law or a state anticruelty law in the process of moving animals to or from a rodeo.

COCKFIGHTING AND DOGFIGHTING

Humans have pitted animals against one another in violent and often fatal confrontations as a form of entertainment for many centuries. There is solid evidence that staged fighting between animals began in Asia some 3,000 years ago when semiwild jungle fowl were thrown together in battle, usually to the death; wagers were made on which bird would triumph. Cockfighting has carried on in Malaysia, Sumatra, Bali, Borneo, the Philippines, and other places in the southern islands and peninsulas of the continent from that day to this.

In the Western world, the Greeks started animal fighting sometime in the fourth century B.C.E., placing dogs in arenas with lions and elephants, and delighting in the spectacle as the animals ferociously fought one another. In ancient Rome, from at least the first century B.C.E., fights between exotic animals captured in Africa and the Near East were a regular bill of fare in the Coliseum: rhinoceroses against bears, bulls against elephants, bears against bulls, and other combinations of species. The Romans also invented staged fighting between humans and animals in the Coliseum and other *circus* venues in the Empire, where gladiators, criminals, and later Christians battled a host of species, usually large, carnivorous mammals (*see also* this chapter: *Circuses and Zoos: A Brief History of Circuses*).

Origins of Cockfighting

The Greeks and Romans also enjoyed bringing together male chickens with a serious antipathy toward one another to watch them flail away until one died or quit fighting. The rooster, or cock, is a highly territorial bird, and extremely possessive of his hens. He will instantly attack perceived interlopers with astoundingly relentless fury, slashing with his clawed feet and especially with the hooked spur that grows from the back of each leg. The Greeks are thought by many to have been the first to attach a sheath to this spur, enhancing its durability and sharpness. Such sheaths, as well as knives or gaffs that replace the removed spur, are common in cockfighting today.

The Greeks may have borrowed this pastime from the Persians or possibly the ancient Syrians, who seem to have deified the fighting bird. Legend has it that the Athenian general Themistocles elevated cockfighting to something close to a national sport. A chance encounter of two birds at war with one another as his army marched on the Persians apparently inspired the Greeks to a decisive victory. To commemorate the event, Themistocles later had an amphitheater devoted to cockfighting constructed in Pergamus.

Like most things Greek, the Romans zealously adopted cockfighting. Indeed their ardor for it was evidently so great that Pliny, the famous historian of the first century C.E., could gush that "there is not a mighty Lord or State of Rome, that dare open or shut the door of his house, before he knows the good pleasure of these fowls." A later Roman historian claimed that the empire began to decline when cockfighting fell into disrepute among its governors. It is said that the Roman emperor Severus prepared his sons and officers for the conquest of Britain by commanding them to witness cockfights every day, an exercise that was supposed to steel them against the perils of the impending assault.

Cockfighting may have been introduced to the British Isles by the Romans, or it might have already developed there by the time the invaders arrived. In either case, it was not until the twelfth or thirteenth centuries that combat between cocks gained some measure of popularity in England, and then it was primarily a form of entertainment for schoolboys. Typically, the boys were treated to cockfighting as an annual event associated with religious celebrations, such as Lent. This practice continued in the schools for hundreds of years, although a few institutions would not allow it, mainly as a frivolous waste of time rather than from any concerns about its humaneness. Objections to cockfighting are rare in written records from the time, and no laws existed then protecting chickens or any other animal.

Adult (male) interest in cockfighting—or "cocking" as it came to be called—seems to have grown over the years as boys excited by the events in school maintained their enthusiasm as men. By the sixteenth century, cocking had become quite popular in England, having received validation from Henry VIII, who commanded that a cockpit be built at the palace of Whitehall. Within another hundred years, as subsequent monarchs endorsed it, cockfighting blossomed into a major spectator "sport" in the country, rivaling and later eclipsing horse racing, with which it was often paired (*see* this chapter: *Greyhound Racing and Horse Racing: A Brief History of Horse Racing*). In Scotland, Ireland, and Wales, as in England, thousands of people from all social classes watched, bet on, and participated in cocking. Nearly every city and hamlet had pits where the fighting occurred, and the newspapers lavished attention on the activities there.

The English, and especially the Irish, imported cockfighting into America, probably in the late seventeenth century and certainly by the early eighteenth. It quickly became a favorite diversion of the colonists, including no less a personage than George Washington. By the 1830s, another president, Andrew Jackson, was presenting cockfights in the White House, and the exploits of pugilistic poultry had become the original national pastime. Birds of British heritage—called "gamecocks"—were fighting in countless urban and rural pits up and own the Atlantic coast, from New York through the Carolinas. Predominantly Spanish strains fought in all the Gulf Coast states, brought north from Cuba, Haiti, Puerto Rico, and other Caribbean islands where the Spaniards had introduced the pastime. They had done the same in Mexico and Central America, and from here cockfighting had infiltrated north into the territories of the American Southwest.

As in England, there is little documentation of any opposition to the feathered fracas in colonial America or during the first several decades of the new nation. Even so renowned a humanitarian as Abraham Lincoln (yet another chief executive) refereed cockfights as a young man. He once remarked: "As long as the Almighty permits intelligent man . . . to fight in public and kill each other while the world looks on approvingly, it is not for me to deprive the chicken of the same privilege."

The American setting for a cockfight, and the rules of the contest were established in the early 1800s and have changed little since then. The pit is circular or octagonal, 18 or 20 feet across, with a circle marked in the center. About a foot away from the circle on opposite sides is a line; it is here that the birds are placed by the "setter," facing one another, and turned loose on a signal from the referee. Once the birds clash, the fight typically goes on until one of them flees or dies. This often happens within a few minutes or even a few seconds, when a rooster, fitted with a knife or gaff, strikes a fatal blow. Somewhat like human boxing, a loser is also one that gets knocked senseless for three ten-counts, and once for twenty. Cockfighters and their advocates vehemently deny that the birds are incited to attack—the rules forbid doing so and in any case, they say, you cannot force a cock to fight. Furthermore, they have difficulty finding anything cruel about their avocation. Against such charges they protest that gamecocks fight not out of fear or panic but because the birds *enjoy* it.

Early Regulation of Cockfighting

Perhaps it is appropriate then that the first recorded legal restriction on cocking anywhere in the world was probably not strongly motivated by abhorrence of animal cruelty. In 1835 England's Parliament passed "An Act to consolidate and amend the several Laws relating to the cruel and improper Treatment of Animals," providing a fine of up to five pounds (or two months at "hard Labour" if the convicted did not pay) for anyone staging a cockfight "within Five Miles of temple bar" (a court of law). The main target of this act, however, was animal baiting (*see* this chapter: *Cockfighting and Dogfighting: Dogfighting and Baiting*), which by this time had generated considerable moral outrage among the wealthier classes. Many condemned this activity as barbarous and cruel, but baiting was almost exclusively a pastime of working people and the poor, and the gentry regarded it as low class and undignified.

In contrast, people of every economic station patronized and participated in cockfights, as mentioned above, and in the early nineteenth century very little ethical concern had been expressed against it. The ban on running a cocking show—there was no penalty for owning the birds or for observing a fight—seems to have been founded mainly on a desire to stifle other illegal activities often surrounding the event. Defeated "cockers" frequently refused to pay on the bets they had made, and various forms of cheating were common; disorderly conduct and even rioting typically followed. Disagreements on matters of judgment in a cocking regularly lead to fisticuffs. Alcohol tended to fuel these altercations, so by 1835 most municipalities had already prohibited cockfighting in "public houses" (bars).

For some years after this the law was not enforced and cocking carried on in England much as before. But in 1849 the Cruelty to Animals Act strengthened the ban on the fighting, and during the 1860s and 1870s popular sentiment against the use of animals in laboratories spilled over to encompass the treatment of "all creatures great and small," including chickens. Enforcement improved, and offenders were successfully prosecuted. By the time the Protection of Animals Act was passed in 1911, which unequivocally prohibited all animal fighting, cocking had gone completely underground in Britain. It remains there today, suppressed but not extinct.

In America only three states had outlawed cockfighting by the time of the Civil War: Massachusetts, Delaware, and Vermont. Massachusetts and Vermont rejected animal fighting when their respective legislatures first passed a cruelty to animals law, with the Bay State leading the way in 1835. The state had a high proportion of Puritans, of course, and these Calvinists were some of the few who had voiced any objection to cockfighting back in England, beginning as early as the mid-seventeenth century, although it is not clear how much of their concern stemmed from humaneness rather than a disgust with gambling. The Massachusetts anticruelty law was the second of its kind in America (Vermont's did not come until 1854) and just the third one in the world. Most of the subsequent bans on cocking and animal fighting generally came within the anticruelty statutes of the various states, although they were rather slow to come. At the turn of the century, nearly half the states permitted cockfighting, and in 1920 a dozen still did.

Contemporary Cockfighting Laws

Today, forty-six states prohibit cockfighting, the latest additions coming in the November 1998 referenda voting when citizens of Arizona and Missouri approved new laws prohibiting it. Actually, Missouri had first outlawed animal fighting in 1873, but in 1985 the state supreme court declared the statute unconstitutionally vague because it seemed to proscribe merely being present at a place where a cockfight had been held, even if no such fight occurred at the time of the visitation (*State v. Young*). A group called Missourians Against Cockfighting succeeded in placing on the 1998 ballot an initiative to enact a new cockfighting law, one carefully drafted to pass constitutional muster; the initiative passed easily. Following a legal challenge from a cockfighting group, the state supreme court affirmed that the initiative had been properly prepared (*United Gamefowl Breeders Association v. Nixon*).

Kansas, Louisiana, New Mexico, and Oklahoma are the only remaining jurisdictions in 2000 that permit battles between male chickens for human entertainment. Oklahoma looks likely to leave this group, as a citizen initiative similar to those that changed the laws in Arizona and Missouri has been gathering momentum and may appear on the ballot in 2001.

By September 1999 the Oklahoma Coalition Against Cockfighting had gathered nearly 100,000 signatures on their petition to ban cockfighting, more than enough needed to present the issue to the general voters. As in Missouri, however, gamefowl advocates brought the petition to court, charging that it did not properly identify the proponents of the initiative. Also as in Missouri, the supreme court of Oklahoma ruled in June 2000 that the petition did comply with the law (*In re Initiative Petition No. 365*), but an election board official then declared that it was too late to put the question to voters in November. Meanwhile, the Oklahoma Gamefowl Breeders Association has gone back to the supreme court, this time arguing that thousands of signatures on the petition are invalid. At present, the court has not yet ruled on this matter.

No such initiatives are currently in the works for Louisiana or New Mexico, and cockfighting seems firmly ensconced in both states. Bills banning the blood sport in Louisiana did not make it out of the committee stage in 1997 and the next year received a decisive thrashing in the state senate. Over forty years ago New Mexico quashed the strategy of prosecuting cockfighting as a violation of the animal cruelty law. In 1958 the state supreme court ruled that a gamecock does not legally qualify as a protected animal in the Land of Enchantment (*State v. Buford*). Arizona, which as mentioned above allowed cockfighting until 1998, had also been operating under a similar decree from its supreme court, one issued within weeks of the New Mexico decision, excluding chickens from the state ban on animal abuse (*State v. Stockton*).

Many believe that Kansas has prohibited cockfighting, but this is not so. The Sunflower State has no such law, nor any general ban on animal fighting that includes birds. Furthermore, in 1973 a Kansas Supreme Court judge ruled as Arizona and New Mexico had, holding that the state anticruelty law is intended to cover "beasts of the field," "beasts of burden," and "hair-bearing animals," not gamecocks (*State v. Claiborne*). A Georgia appellate court reached the opposite conclusion for that jurisdiction in 1977. There is no specific cockfighting law in Georgia, but the judges ruled that this particular use of roosters is a form of cruelty to animals (*Brackett v. State*).

As defendants involved in cockfighting have attempted to exonerate themselves from cruelty charges by claiming that the law does not extend to gamecocks, several other state high courts have addressed this question. For example, forty-seven people charged with cruelty to animals in Hawaii argued that the state law only disallows "keeping or managing" a place for cockfighting, not setting two roosters to attack one another. The Hawaii Supreme Court rejected this reasoning in 1979, finding that fighting birds are included in that state's definition of "animal," which refers to "every living creature," and that cockfighting is itself one of the actions prohibited by the state anticruelty law (*State v. Kaneakua*). Most recently, a California court of appeals held in 2000 that roosters and other birds are protected by the state's animal cruelty statutes because they fall within the category of "every dumb creature" (*People v. Baniqued*). Although California does outlaw cockfighting, it provides only misdemeanor penalties for violation and prosecutors had secured a felony conviction of Modesto Baniqued under the anticruelty law. (*See also* chapter 3: *Anticruelty Laws*.)

The basic prohibition in the state laws forbids instigating, promoting, sponsoring, or encouraging cockfighting, keeping cockpits, or causing the birds to fight. After that, the statutes are arranged according to three main variables: the seriousness of the offense, the legality of attending a cockfight, and whether possession of gamecocks is outlawed. Before 1975 no state had felony penalties for any aspect of cockfighting, and as recently as twenty years ago, only a few did. In 2000 seventeen states provide felony convictions for causing or using fowl to fight, or operating a cockfighting business. Most of these provide a maximum penalty of five years in prison and a $5,000 fine. Half the states criminalize possession and thirty-one do not allow witnessing a cockfight. Eleven states with misdemeanor penalties also ban spectating and possessing gamecocks.

Currently, only Michigan has designated cockfighting, spectating, and possession of fighting birds as all felony offenses, punishable by up to four years in prison, a $50,000 fine, and 1,000 hours of community service. This qualifies as the toughest animal fighting law in the nation.

After Michigan, the strictest laws are found in Alaska, Arizona, Delaware, Minnesota, and Pennsylvania, all of which made cocking and possession felonious while also banning attendance at fights. Indiana, Maryland, Maine, North Dakota, New Jersey, New York, Rhode Island, Wisconsin, and Wyoming are next with felony penalties for causing birds to fight while also prohibiting watching and possessing them. The southern United States, long a cockfighting stronghold, has the most lenient laws. All of the states except Texas, the Carolinas, and Florida have designated the staging of cockfights a misdemeanor offense while not providing any penalties at all for either possession or spectating. Both Carolinas do prohibit watching the fights, but allow the possession of gamecocks. Florida is the only southern state providing a felony conviction, yet it is also lawful in the Sunshine State to own a fighting bird.

As just suggested, the combinations among these three variables found in some state laws indicate a certain legislative ambivalence toward cockfighting. Hawaii, Iowa, Idaho, and Nevada are four more jurisdictions that permit their citizens to keep gamecocks, but do not allow causing birds to fight or watching them do it. Yet why else would people have the roosters? Montana has made cockfighting a felony, and does prohibit possession, while permitting people to observe their battles. Texas does the same, though operating the fights is only a misdemeanor in the Lone Star State. These laws seem not to recognize that cockfighting is substantially fueled by members of the audience betting on the birds. Perhaps the strangest law comes from Colorado, where cockfighting is a felony, indicating that the state regards the offense as a serious one, yet at the same time observing a cockfight and possessing fighting birds are both perfectly legal there.

Cockfighting laws have occasionally been challenged as unconstitutional, usually on the grounds that they are too vague to be fairly enforced. For example, thirty-nine individuals jointly indicted for spectating at a Tennessee cockfight argued in 1984 that the statute was so unclear that completely innocent people, such as investigative reporters and farmers happening upon two animals fighting in a barnyard, could be in violation. The state supreme court disagreed, pointing out that the law prohibits "knowingly" attending a cockfight "as a spectator" (*State v. Tabor*; for the same issue in dogfighting laws, *see* this chapter: *Cockfighting and Dogfighting: Dogfighting in the Courts*). In a similar case, an Oregon court of appeals ruled in 1993 that the state law making it a crime to watch the "preparations" for a cockfight is not unconstitutionally vague; a person of "common intelligence" could determine that the activities presented were leading to a fight between roosters (*State v. Albee*).

In Ohio another collection of defendants appealed their convictions by asking the court to find that the state cockfighting law was void for vagueness. Their request was granted, but only in part. The court of appeals invalidated the specific ban on being "present thereat" a place kept for the purpose of cockfighting because it was not clear whether it applied only when a cockfight was in progress. However, the remainder of the statute was not infected by this problem and the convictions were upheld (*State v. Bryson*). Interestingly, the Missouri Supreme Court decision mentioned above that invalidated the state law based the ruling on the fatal ambiguity of the same phrase, "present thereat." Unlike their brethren in Ohio, the Missouri judges decided that this bit of imprecision contaminated an entire statute of nearly 100 words.

Dogfighting and Baiting

In Europe instigating animal fights for human amusement evolved mainly from the common practice of employing packs of dogs for hunting large mammals, especially bears, wolves, boars, stags (male deer), and the aurochs (an extinct wild cow). When the dogs cornered the hunters' prey, a bloody melee would ensue as the animal defended itself against the swarming canines. The hunters would eventually arrive on the scene and often derived pleasure from observing the combat. Over time, aristocrats with many dogs to spare began to stage such confrontations deliberately as a kind of entertainment, called "baiting."

This staging can be traced in written records as far back as 1050 C.E. when Britain's Edward the Confessor presented a fight between a bear and six mastiffs to an audience. Bull-baiting, destined to become the most popular type of animal fighting, dates from the early 1200s, soon after the aurochs disappeared. By the Middle Ages, especially in England, baiting had become a favorite pastime of royalty and commoners alike. Usually a bull, less often a bear or badger, was tethered or chained to a stake and set upon by one or several dogs loosed by their owner. People gleefully observed the exhibition, often wagering on its outcome. Would the attacked animal prevail or would the dogs? How many dogs would it take to bring down the animal? How many would be injured before the bull was subdued? The well-known English bulldog was especially bred for participation in these fights, having a lower jaw projecting far in front of the upper jaw, which supported a powerful vice-like grip, along with a deeply set nose, allowing the dog to get sufficient air as it clamped down on the bull.

In the seventeenth century organized fighting between dogs developed in a similar manner, beginning as a purely utilitarian exercise and then becoming adapted to provide a human pastime. Initially, dogs were set against one another as a method of testing them for their ferocity, indicating which dogs would be most effective for guarding property or protecting human life (in contrast, cockfighting was always simply a diversion in Europe, as in Asia). Before very long, people began to provoke dogs into fighting one another solely for the entertainment value they derived from the contest, apart from any functional purpose it might serve. Betting on the outcome became standard.

Around 1800, seeking a faster and more agile fighting animal, English breeders began to cross the bulldog with a form of terrier, and thus produced the bull and terrier. This is the dog that came to be known in the United States as the bull terrier, or simply and infamously, the "pitbull."

Excepting a 1634 law of the Massachusetts Bay Colony prohibiting "tiranny or crueltie to any bruite creature which are usuallie kept for man's use," the first attempt at animal welfare legislation anywhere in the world was specifically aimed at the practice of animal baiting. In 1800 Sir William Pulteney introduced a bill into Parliament to outlaw bull-baiting specifically, on the grounds that it was inhumane and debasing of the citizenry. The bill was ably opposed by Secretary of War William Windham who countered that such a law would be unfair to the working class, with whom by this time baiting had become widely associated. Windham magnanimously argued that the ban would deprive the underprivileged of one of their few sources of recreation. The bill was narrowly defeated.

It was not until 1835 when Joseph Pease's amendment to the 1822 Martin's Act was accepted by Parliament that baiting was outlawed throughout England. The new law provided that anyone who "shall keep or use any House, Room, Pit, Ground or other Place for the Purpose of running, baiting or fighting any Bull, Bear, Badger, Dog or other Animal . . . , shall be liable to Penalty not exceeding Five Pounds." Baiting in England faded away fairly quickly after 1835, but apparently dogfighting surged as followers of the baiting "sports" turned to the pits for their amusement. Dogfighting required only a small and easily secluded area, so enforcement of the law was a continual problem.

Organized dogfighting and bull and bear baiting for gambling and entertainment were widespread in America by the early 1800s. Cockfighting, too, was extremely popular throughout the country, particularly in the south. Although by the time the Civil War had ended, twenty of the thirty-five states had enacted anticruelty laws, only three of these specifically addressed animal fighting: Massachusetts, Delaware, and Vermont, with the Bay State leading the way in 1835. Instead, the other state laws proscribed violence against farm animals primarily, especially horses. In 1867 New York revised its anticruelty law to include a ban on animal fighting and baiting, a statute that would become the model for many other states. Section 2 declared it a misdemeanor to be involved in any way with a commercial enterprise promoting fights between "any bull, bear, dog, cock, or other animal" (*see also* chapter 3: *Anticruelty Laws*).

Like cockfighting, the rules of dogfighting have changed little since the nineteenth century. In the standard case, individuals "contract" with one another to fight their dogs, the agreement stipulating the rules governing the battle, especially the weight of the animals, the principles of the wagering, and what constitutes victory and defeat. Dogs must be close to the same weight—a scale has always been standard equipment at every contract fight—and odds and betting limits are established for each. The criteria for declaring winners and losers vary somewhat, but in general dogs lose that at any time jump out of the pit, as do those that refuse to fight, or that are picked up by their handlers. Of course, dead dogs also lose, though, unlike cockfighting, fatalities are reportedly rare.

The fighting is conducted in an enclosure (the "pit") about 15 feet wide, with sides 2 1/2 or 3 feet high; carpeting often covers the floor area. Two dogs are brought to the pit by their respective handlers, usually the owners, who hold the canines in opposite corners behind a line. Sometimes a referee is present, and he gives the signal for the fight to begin. This commences as a simultaneous "scratch," in which the dogs are released at the same time to rush at each other across the pit and join conflict. When one dog pins the other with an immobilizing bite hold, the two are pried apart with a "breaking stick," a wedge-shaped rod used to separate the jaws, and they are taken back behind their respective lines. Now, alternate "scratches" begin, with the leading dog given the opportunity to attack first. This continues until one dog has been vanquished, as defined by the agreed upon rules. Also unlike cockfights, dogfights may go on for an hour or more, the handlers down in the pit all the while, close by the grappling dogs, shouting exhortations in their ears.

Contemporary Dogfighting Laws

The "gamedog" of choice is the "pitbull," the commonly used generic name for three different canine breeds: the American Staffordshire terrier, the bull terrier, and the Staffordshire bull terrier. As mentioned above, the pitbull is the product of crossing the English bulldog with a now extinct breed of terrier.

After a rash of maulings in the mid-1980s, some resulting in the death of toddlers, many American cities have severely restricted ownership of pitbulls, or banned them entirely. Known as "breed-specific legislation," these laws have been regularly, and sometimes successfully challenged in the courts. At least two states—Minnesota and Oklahoma—do not allow their municipalities to regulate ownership of dogs according to breed. On the other hand, the U.S. Supreme Court has declined to review two state supreme court decisions—in Kansas and Ohio—upholding ordinances that forbid people from keeping pitbulls (*Hearn v. City of Overland Park* and *State v. Anderson*).

In the world of dogfighting, one who owns, breeds, or fights game-dogs is called a "dogman" (and it is overwhelmingly men who do this). Because dogfighting is illegal everywhere, it is not known exactly how many dogmen there are in America, nor the total number of gamedogs. Estimates range from 10,000 to 50,000 individuals who either fight dogs for a living (the "professionals") or as a hobby; the dog population would equal at least five times that total.

All fifty states have criminalized managing, sponsoring, promoting, or operating a dogfighting enterprise, or causing dogs to fight. Many of these laws specifically exempt the use of dogs for managing livestock and for hunting (*see also* this chapter: *Recreational Hunting: Taking Restrictions: Baiting and Dogs*). As with cockfighting, nearly all dogfighting laws are found within the anticruelty statutes of the states, and some of them are written broadly to include fighting between any animals. There are significant variations among them, falling along the three dimensions noted above in cockfighting laws. Some of the admixtures of restrictions on spectating at a dogfight, possession of a dog intended for fighting, and their status as felonies or misdemeanors are likewise a bit strange.

As recently as 1975, no state provided a felony conviction for any aspect of dogfighting. In 2000 participation in a dogfighting business is felonious in forty-five states, punishable by a fine of up to $10,000 and as much as five years in prison. In July 1999 a Sacramento, California, superior court judge handed down the most severe punishment ever imposed for dog-fighting, and one of the harshest for any animal abuse, sentencing Cesar Cerda to seven years in a state prison after his no contest plea. Investigators had seized fifty-five dogs (mostly pitbulls) at Cerda's residence, all of which the court declared unadoptable and ordered euthanized.

Only Idaho, Iowa, Maryland, Vermont, and West Virginia retain misdemeanor penalties for dogfighting in 2000. Iowa and West Virginia take the offense the least seriously of any jurisdiction: along with having the lightest maximum penalties for staging a dogfight (one year and $1,000), neither state has restrictions on attending one or owning a gamedog. Hawaii, Montana, and Virginia are the only other states that allow individuals to be spectators at canine conflicts without imposing any legal penalties. In a startling contrast, a dozen states regard merely watching a dogfight a felony, including Wisconsin, just across the Mississippi River from Iowa, where such spectating is perfectly legal.

The most stringent dogfighting laws in America are found in the ten states that have placed across-the-board felony status on all three of these aspects of the blood sport: Alabama, Alaska, Arizona, Colorado, Mississippi, New Hampshire, Ohio, Pennsylvania, and Rhode Island. The tenth is New Mexico, where dogs and roosters are apparently viewed very differently—recall this is one of only four states that has legal cockfighting. Kansas and Oklahoma, too, allow the rooster battles, but make dogfighting and possession of gamedogs felonious and ban spectating. Similarly, Mississippi has one of the toughest dogfighting laws but one of the weakest cockfighting laws, ranking it just a misdemeanor and placing no restrictions on owning gamecocks or watching them clash. Alaska, Colorado, Connecticut, Maine, Massachusetts, Michigan, Minnesota, Montana, New Jersey, New York, North Dakota, Pennsylvania, Rhode Island, Wisconsin, and Wyoming have made fighting between all animals felonious offenses.

This sort of legislative schizophrenia about species can be seen within the dogfighting domain as well. For example, Georgia and Virginia both rate it a felony, but neither has legal rules prohibiting observation of the fights or possessing dogs intended for fighting. Montana has designated both holding the dogs and the fighting itself felonies, but does not criminalize spectating at all, while Nevada makes spectating illegal, but not possession. In Georgia, conducting a dogfight and watching it are both felonies, but owning a gamedog is legal. Forty states prohibit the possession of dogs for the purpose of fighting, and most of these have made the offense a felony. In this variable, too, one finds some lawmakers with divided minds: Florida, Kentucky, Louisiana, and Nevada all classify dogfighting as a felony and observing a fight a misdemeanor, yet a person who keeps the dogs in any of these states is doing nothing illegal.

Dogfighting in the Courts
Like cockfighting, dogfighting laws have sometimes been questioned on constitutional grounds. One of the first such challenges came before the Georgia Supreme Court in 1984, when three men convicted under the state law argued that its provision making it a crime to "allow" a dogfight to occur is too vague for "men of common intelligence [to determine] the conduct which is forbidden." The court disagreed, holding that the term "allow" in the statute encompasses knowing that a dogfight is taking place, and consenting to it, a definite meaning plain to those of "common intelligence." The defendants also objected to their convictions by appeal to equal protection, pointing out that while dogfighting is a felony in Georgia, cockfighting (as included in the state anticruelty law) is only a misdemeanor. This appeal, too, was rejected with the assertion that the state legislature acted within its discretion in establishing penalties of differing severity for these violations (*Hargrove v. State*).

In 1990 an Ohio man also tried an equal protection argument to invalidate the Buckeye State's dogfighting law. Kenneth Gaines cited the general animal fighting statute, under which violation carried misdemeanor penalties, and compared the felony punishment he received for dogfighting. Like the Georgia court, the Ohio Supreme Court found that the legislature had a legitimate option to choose the appropriate sanctions for unlawful behavior. Gaines also claimed that the term "dogfighting" was not defined in the statue, so it was unclear what conduct was being prohibited. To this, Judge Jones opined that the law "sufficiently reflects the proscribed conduct in terms which do not require men of common intelligence to necessarily guess at its meaning" (*State v. Gaines*). The same attempt to void the state law due to the vagueness of "dogfighting" failed for an Alabama man in 1985 (*Jones v. State*).

State laws that prohibit watching dogfighting have also occasionally been charged with unconstitutionality. For example, defendants in Michigan argued that the ban on spectating would make witnessing any violent altercation between any two dogs a criminal act, producing a vague and overbroad statute that outlawed otherwise legal activity. A state appellate court upheld the ban in 1978, finding the statutory language narrow enough to focus on attendance at an illegal dogfight, and clear enough to give citizens fair notice of the prohibited actions (*People v. Cumper*).

The most recent such case comes from 1994, when an investigative reporter for a Colorado television station appealed her conviction for dogfighting. As part of her report on the activity in the Denver area, Wendy Bergen had attended two dogfights arranged at her request. Bergen contended that under the state law, spectating at a dogfight is only illegal when done for entertainment or for monetary gain, and neither motive applied to her. Without these motivations, she continued, the statute was too broad because someone who inadvertently found herself at a dogfight would be doing something unlawful. A Colorado court of appeals did not agree with this reasoning, pointing out that, for a violation, the statute requires a person to be "knowingly present" at a dogfight. It does not matter if he or she is there for fun, for money, or for information; and someone who simply stumbled onto a dogfight would not be "knowingly present" there (*People v. Bergen*).

Animal Welfare Act

Besides being contrary to these state laws, animal fighting is also a federal offense. Hearings began in 1974 on Capitol Hill, with testimony documenting interstate dogfighting rackets stimulated by intense gambling. Films taken by undercover investigators revealed the blood and brutality of these spectacles. Representative Tom Foley introduced a bill primarily aimed at prohibiting dogfighting, although all mammals were included. The Ninety-third Congress adjourned before any action could be taken.

The bill was reintroduced the next year. This time around, a companion bill was championed in the Senate by Lowell Weicker, focused entirely on the transportation of animals involved in fighting. Over in the House, Congressman John Krebs added a rider to the Foley bill that extended protections against fighting to birds as well. This addition led to a not uncommon bit of political maneuvering in the House. A contingent led by Steven Symms, steadfastly opposed to the prohibition on dogfighting, even so supported the Foley bill along with the cockfighting rider, thinking that the bird ban would render the bill impotent. The strategy did not work: the antidogfighting provisions were accepted in both the House and the Senate, although the cockfighting addendum was modified, as seen below. In April 1976 the Animal Fighting Venture Prohibition Act was enacted as an amendment to the Animal Welfare Act (AWA) (*see also* this chapter: *Circuses and Zoos;* chapter 7).

Section 26 of the AWA bans sponsoring or exhibiting an animal in an "animal fighting venture," defined as "any event which involves a fight between at least two animals and is conducted for purposes of sport, wagering, or entertainment." The amendment stipulates that the use of dogs (or any other animal) for hunting purposes does not count as an animal fighting venture. Further, the term "animal" refers to "any live bird, or any live dog or other mammal, except man."

Specifically outlawed are intentionally selling, buying, transporting, or delivering an animal for the purpose of enlisting it in a fighting venture, or receiving one for transportation from one state to another. Also prohibited is using the U.S. mail, the telephone, or any media outlet for promoting or in some way advancing animal fighting. Violations of any of these provisions can be punished with a fine of up to $5,000 and one year in prison, or both. The secretary of agriculture, who is charged with administering and enforcing all the provisions of the AWA, has the authority to investigate allegations of animal fighting through the FBI, the Treasury Department, and any other law enforcement agencies he or she may call upon. To date, there has never been a case litigated in a federal court under this section.

What about cockfighting? At the time of the amendment, several states still had not prohibited it, and as already seen, in 2000 there remain four states permitting such events. In the congressional debates, the Senate insisted that those states allowing rooster battles should continue to do so if they wished. Therefore, section 26 of the AWA includes a special exemption for them: "fighting ventures involving live birds [shall be unlawful] only if the fight is to take place in a State where it would be in violation of the laws thereof."

Unfortunately, this concession to states' rights opened a significant loophole. It allows the movement of birds from a state where cocking is outlawed into the four states—Kansas, Louisiana, Oklahoma, and New Mexico—where it is legal, thus perpetuating the very practice that Congress clearly intended to reject. So in the states adjacent to these four that allow possession of fighting birds—Arizona, Arkansas, Mississippi, Missouri, Tennessee, and Colorado—the AWA amendment means only that cockfighters have to travel to a neighboring jurisdiction to stay within the law. Coupled with the state permission, the Animal Fighting Venture Prohibition Act offers little or no deterrent in this region, which is the heart of cockfighting country.

Trying to close the loophole, in March 1999 Senator Wayne Allard of Colorado introduced a bill that would change section 26 to ban *all* interstate transportation of birds for use in cockfights, no matter the legality of the practice in the states. After better than eighteen months wending its way through various committees, Congress adjourned in December 2000 before a vote could be taken on the amendment. This means that it will have to be reintroduced in 2001.

RECREATIONAL HUNTING

In America the legal regulation of pursuing and killing wild animals is dominated by a vast array of state laws, emanating from all fifty jurisdictions. At the same time, a number of federal laws prohibit hunting selected species, ban a particular method of hunting, and regulate the pursuit of wildlife in certain public lands.

It is illegal to hunt any animal listed as either endangered or threatened under the Endangered Species Act. Bald and golden eagles, some migratory bird species, marine mammals, and wild horses and burros are also shielded by the federal government through the Bald Eagle Protection Act, the Migratory Bird Treaty Act, the Marine Mammal Protection Act, and the Wild Free-Roaming Horses and Burros Act (*see* chapter 6 for more on all of these laws, except the last, which is found in chapter 3). The states where any of these species occur list them as protected under their own wildlife laws.

Additionally, the Airborne Hunting Act is a federal law that makes it illegal for a person in any state to shoot any animal from an aircraft. Persons employed or licensed by state or federal governments to protect humans, land, water, other wildlife, domestic animals, or crops are exempt from the prohibition. Finally, hunting of any species is not allowed in National Parks or in some National Wildlife Refuges, although federal regulations permit hunting in many other refuges (*see also* chapter 6: *National Wildlife Refuge System Improvement Act of 1997: Hunting and Trapping in National Wildlife Refuges*).

In 2000 about 14 million Americans (6 percent of the total population) bought hunting licenses, numbers that have been slowly dropping through the last decade. Nearly all of these pursue wildlife as a form of recreation, a pastime ("sport" hunting), rather than for subsistence or survival. As a group, hunters are aging, with the average now at an all-time high of forty-four years old; 94 percent are men. At last count, 134 million wild animals are killed by hunters in the United States annually. About half of these are doves, ducks, grouse, quail, and partridge, and about one-third squirrels, rabbits, and raccoons. Over 6 million deer and more than 24,000 bear are also slain each year (*see also* chapter 6: *Legal Protections for Bears*).

Hunting Laws in England and the Colonies

Pervasive hunting laws are a relatively recent phenomenon in America. When British colonizers began settling along the eastern seaboard in the seventeenth century there was little reason to follow the English model and write hunting laws. In England two main concerns justified regulating the taking of wildlife, and neither applied to the New World.

One was essentially a desire to maintain the privileges and powers of the ruling classes. This was accomplished by "qualification statutes" that prohibited the poor and landless specifically from taking wild animals. The earliest such English law on record comes from 1389, and allowed hunting only for persons owning land producing an income of at least forty shillings a year; in 1604 the minimum was raised to 100 pounds. Moreover, these laws also prohibited poor people from using various weapons, notably firearms. This proviso was intended to keep firearms out of the hands of the lower classes, a group infamous among the aristocracy for spawning dissidents who railed against the prevailing social order, one controlled by the wealthy and powerful. Qualification statutes were to persist until 1831 when they were officially banned.

The second major reason for hunting regulations in England was to ensure that wildlife populations would not be seriously depleted or even wiped out by excessive preying upon them. This goal became known as "sustained yield," an idea found at the core of modern wildlife management or conservation. The elimination of the British wolf, ordered by King Edgar in the tenth century, proved that intensive hunting could destroy an entire species, although the demise of this particular animal was not a cause for concern among people of that age. Sustaining a continuing harvest of wild animals was promoted not only by instituting legal restrictions on who could hunt—as with the qualification statutes—but more importantly by stipulating time periods when certain species could not be legally taken by anyone: "closed seasons." English laws also placed a maximum number on the quantity of some animals that could be legally killed, commonly called the "bag limit."

In America the wildlife circumstances were so radically different from England that legal restrictions on hunting were initially unnecessary. The animals were spread throughout a huge, largely unmapped wilderness, peopled with often hostile Native Americans, so a hunt was typically both difficult and dangerous. As Samuel Johnson famously remarked, "Hunting was the labour of the savages of North America, but the amusement of the gentlemen of England." Those English gentlemen who settled on the fringes of the forbidding American forests in the 1600s had little incentive to legislate hunting as their exclusive right, and even if they had done so an enormous natural resource (as hunters have always viewed wild animals) would have been wasted. Moreover, wildlife was superabundant in America, with an apparently inexhaustible supply that would have made concern about sustained yield seem almost neurotic.

In the New World, then, the reasonable policy toward wildlife for the European immigrants was no different from the daily practice of the Indians: a principle of "free taking," where everyone, no matter their wealth or station, was entitled to kill as many wild animals as they wanted, whenever they wanted to, supposing a willingness to take on the rigors of the hunt. The doctrine of free taking, with a few isolated exceptions in the mid-Atlantic region, prevailed throughout the colonies and indeed the rest of the continent over the subsequent years of westward expansion. It applied even to private holdings, so that American landowners had no special claim to wild animals inhabiting their property. For a quarter century after the 1620 landing of the Pilgrims at what they called Plymouth, there were no laws whatever to restrict the taking of wildlife in America.

An inkling of change to this situation appeared in the middle of the seventeenth century, gathering momentum during its waning and into the early years of the eighteenth. Decades of steady hunting in the colonies had begun to deplete certain preferred species, especially those close to the rapidly growing settlements. The first recorded hunting law in America comes from the year 1646 and the Colony of Virginia, which established a closed season on deer hunting. This was the only regulation on hunting for nearly fifty years until the Massachusetts Bay Colony did the same in 1694. The first closed season on birds comes from a few New York counties in 1708, and just two years later Massachusetts prohibited the taking of wild birds close to towns. In 1741 New York outlawed deer hunting "near Christian settlement." By the time of the Revolutionary War, every colony except Georgia had designated certain seasons of the year in which deer could not be legally hunted.

The Development of Modern Hunting Laws

During the 1800s worry about sustained yield—ensuring that plenty of animals remain to be hunted—motivated a host of new hunting laws throughout the American states and territories. The closed season was the restriction of choice, while bag limits were rare until the late nineteenth century.

With the westerly expansion of the European-Americans, the human population exploded across the plains and mountains, and wildlife populations suffered a corresponding decline. To satisfy the demands of palate and fashion, market hunting became a popular occupation, particularly decimating buffalo, elk, antelope, bighorn sheep, pigeons, and various plumed water birds, especially swans and egrets. So one finds an 1852 California law declaring a closed season on antelope and elk, Nevada proclaiming a closed season on mountain goats and bighorn sheep beginning in 1861, and three years later Idaho legislating the first buffalo protection by making it illegal to kill the beasts from February 1 to July 1. Arkansas banned all hunting of waterfowl in 1875, and in 1879 Michigan declared a ten-year moratorium on elk hunting.

As the nineteenth century faded, it had become apparent to lawmakers across the country that if the most desirable wildlife species were not to be hunted out of existence, the days of totally unregulated free taking must end. The near extinction of the buffalo in the space of a decade was a hard lesson that impressed many. In 1878, at opposite ends of the country, California and New Hampshire created the first government agencies devoted entirely to conserving wildlife by controlling hunting, built on the foundation of sustained yield.

By 1895 a number of states had realized that promoting sustained yield required more than simply telling hunters that they could not kill certain animals at certain times—it required money to pay for administrators and their staff, law enforcement officers ("game wardens" or conservation officers), and for the development of animal populations and their habitat. Thus, in this year the modern system of licensing for state residents and for nonresidents was set up, compelling people to pay the state for the privilege of hunting its wildlife. From that time to this, hunters have shouldered the majority of the financial burden for maintaining wild animals in their natural environment.

Sources of Legal Restrictions on Hunting

Today, hunting is tightly controlled by the states through a complicated multitude of legal restrictions. These take the form of either statutes or regulations. Hunting statutes are written and approved by state legislators, while hunting regulations are promulgated by state wildlife agencies or commissions. Similarly, federal statutes controlling hunting (such as those mentioned above) are produced by Congress, while the regulations come from government agencies, especially the U.S. Fish and Wildlife Service.

This different authorship indicates a major distinction between the two: regulations are created or amended much more easily and quickly. A statute, whether at the state or federal level, is typically the result of extensive and lengthy study, debate, and revision by a legion of politicians in the state (or the nation's) capital. In contrast, regulations are simply declared by a department director or wildlife commissioner (or a federal agency), though with due consideration, it is assumed, and typically the opportunity for public comment is provided. Regulations nonetheless do have the force of law, just as statutes do, because agents of the state (and the nation) are charged with enforcing them and legal penalties are provided for their violation.

The restrictions on hunting that are a matter of statute and those that are a matter of regulation vary considerably from state to state. In one state, Maine for example, the legislature may determine requirements for hunting licenses and how much they cost, while in another, such as Arizona, this may be left to the Wildlife Department. Pamphlets or booklets distributed by the states that describe their hunting restrictions do not distinguish their legal ancestry, but this is of little significance to the hunter. Overall though, the bulk of state hunting restrictions are regulations coming from a wildlife agency, not statutes written by the legislature. For convenience, the terms "regulation" and "law" will be used interchangeably in the coming discussion.

Traditionally, these state wildlife agencies were called "Game and Fish Departments," but within the last decade or so there has been a definite trend to rename them with a more comprehensive label. The favorite seems to be "Department of Natural Resources," with variations such as Department of Environmental Conservation (New York), Department of Environmental Management (Massachusetts), Department of Wildlife and Parks (Kansas), and Department of Conservation (Illinois). Several states retain the old terminology. In 2000, for example, Alaska has a Department of Fish and Game, while Arizona and Wyoming both have a Game and Fish Department.

Sometimes, a state's wildlife management office does not consist in a department of state employees but a "commission" of five to eight private citizens appointed by the governor, such as Florida's Game and Fish Commission, Pennsylvania's Game Commission, Nebraska's Game and Parks Commission, and Tennessee's Wildlife Resource Commission. More often, a state has both a wildlife department (or division) and a commission: California, Colorado, Idaho, Montana, New Mexico, Oklahoma, and Oregon are examples. In these instances, it is the commission that is charged with the responsibility of issuing hunting regulations, while the wildlife department, whose director is usually selected by the commission, is essentially an administrative, enforcement, and information-gathering body.

Whatever the agency structure, field work is done by state conservation officers, also occasionally called game wardens, each of whom has the authority to enforce the wildlife laws of that jurisdiction.

Contemporary Hunting Laws

A comprehensive survey of the fifty states' hunting laws is far beyond the scope of this book. Indeed, no such thorough treatment exists today. This is not surprising because there are thousands of hunting laws in America, along with their many qualifications and exceptions. To illustrate, consider that Arizona has a tract of hunting regulations that currently runs to eighty-three pages (including advertising), and California's is sixty-nine pages long. Nonetheless, some common features and patterns can be noted here that will give a general understanding of the contours of this legal landscape.

Nearly all the states require individuals between the ages of sixteen (for some, fourteen or even twelve) and sixty-five to buy a license before they can legally hunt a wild animal. Those younger than sixteen or older than sixty-five need not obtain a license, but most states stipulate that children who hunt must be accompanied by an adult who does have a license. One notable exception here is that Maine does not allow children less than ten years old to hunt in any circumstances. The states also exempt military personnel and those hunting on their own property from the license requirement. Hunting licenses can be purchased annually at a cost of about $15 to $25 for residents of the state, or a "lifetime" license is available, typically for several hundred dollars (some states offer five-year licensing periods).

Nonresidents must pay five to ten times as much, or more in some states, for their hunting licenses. In the mid-1970s, an out-of-state hunter challenged the fairness of this very large difference in Montana, claiming that it was unconstitutional. Charging nonresidents so much more for licenses, he argued, violated both the Equal Protection Clause of the Fourteenth Amendment, which guarantees all citizens the equal protection of the laws, and the Constitution's Privileges and Immunities Clause. Article IV, Section 2 of that document provides that "The Citizens of each State shall be entitled to all Privileges and Immunities of Citizens of the several States." The Supreme Court disagreed. A majority of six justices found that the privileges, immunities, and equal protections provided by the Constitution apply only to a "fundamental right," and recreational hunting is not a fundamental right (*Baldwin v. Fish and Game Commission*).

Merely buying a license does not guarantee that a person may legally hunt—for that one must also secure a "permit," a permission granted by the state to attempt to kill a particular species of wild animal. Permits are allocated according to the results of random drawings similar to lottery systems. An individual's chances of being drawn vary considerably, depending on how many prospective hunters are also seeking to pursue that species, and the number of animals of the species the state wildlife agency has determined may be killed while still sustaining the yield. This conservation of wildlife is additionally promoted by setting a bag limit for each wildlife species. Bag limits also diverge widely according to the kind of animal hunted, from a single individual—common for large mammals such as bear or elk—to a dozen or more—as with many sorts of birds. These maximums for a given species often change from state to state, as an animal that is plentiful in one state may be much rarer in another.

State hunting regulations contain a list of "protected" species of wildlife. This catalogue usually, and somewhat confusingly, lists animals that may not be legally taken at certain times—they are "protected" during a closed season—as well as endangered and threatened species, which may not be recreationally hunted at any time. Some states clarify the quite different legal status of these two wildlife categories by distinguishing protected species from "game" species. The "nongame" species of a state often refers to those animals that may not be killed, but are not ordinarily hunted anyway. On the other hand, some states use the term "nongame" as synonymous with "unprotected" species, for which there are no hunting restrictions whatever. It is always open season on these animals, and they may be legally killed in any manner. Coyotes and crows, for example, appear on almost every state's list of unprotected or "nongame" species. The hunting regulations in each jurisdiction must be carefully studied to understand what is meant there by wildlife that is protected, unprotected, game, or nongame.

In recent years, many states have begun requiring hunters to take "hunter education" courses before they venture into the field, and to wear bright orange garments when they get there. The clothing requirement occurs in better than two-thirds of the states' hunting laws, and is found in several versions. Most go so far as to specify how much of the fluorescent material must be worn, from 100 square inches above the waist in Virginia to 500 square inches in Georgia. Other states simply tell hunters to wear the color without saying how much. New Mexico merely recommends donning orange hunting garb. Waterfowl and archery hunters are generally exempted from the clothing rule.

Presently, only a handful of states do not compel attendance at a hunter education course. These classes emphasize shooting safety for the most part, but some also mention basic principles of conservation and "hunting ethics." A few states, such as Ohio and North Carolina, include an exposition of fundamental hunting laws in the curriculum. In deference to older hunters, typically only those born after a certain date need take the course.

Taking Restrictions: Seasons and Weapons

The major feature of state hunting regulations is a wide range of restrictions on "taking" wild animals. In wildlife law, "taking" denotes such activities as disturbing, pursuing, capturing, killing, or attempting to kill an animal—most of the behaviors commonly associated with the practice of hunting. The broadest and most unequivocal taking restriction found in all the states is that hunting any game species during its closed season is forbidden (Connecticut, Maine, and Virginia also forbid hunting at any time on Sunday). Likewise, every state prohibits hunters from carrying loaded weapons in a vehicle, and outlaws discharging weapons within a certain distance from human habitations (100 to 150 feet) or across roadways. Also, every state forbids hunting from a vehicle, though this rule has an important exception for the physically disabled. The states permit these individuals to shoot from a vehicle so long as it is not moving.

It is illegal to hunt most designated game species at night, standardly defined as the time between one half-hour after sunset and one half-hour before sunrise, but many states do allow night hunting of various nocturnal mammals, principally the raccoon, and including the opossum, fox, and bobcat. On these hunts, lights may be used even though artificial illumination is prohibited while tracking or shooting other animals. The states have banned the practice of "spotlighting" or "jacklighting," particularly on deer hunts. Deer can be frozen in their tracks when caught by the beams of a bright light, making a normally flighty prey an easy target. Many states also prohibit the use of laser sighting devices or any other sort of light attached to a weapon for the purpose of enhancing marksmanship, although Michigan has approved the use of laser sights for legally blind persons. Alaska and Montana are two of several states that will not allow night vision equipment on hunts conducted after dark.

Taking restrictions such as these, and others to be cited below, suggest another basis for the legal regulation of hunting that goes beyond sustained yield. This basis is generally seen as an "ethical" one, and is often captured with the term "fair chase." The idea is to compel standards of behavior that diminish the probabilities of hunter success and provide the hunted animal with enhanced opportunities to evade its own destruction at the hands of the hunter, also known as giving the animal a "sporting chance." In the late nineteenth century, such standards were intended as another mechanism for promoting sustained yield by preventing hunters, especially those hunting for the market, from decimating wildlife with unfailingly lethal methods. With the advent of bag limits and legislation specifically directed at impeding and then eliminating market hunters, the motivation behind these laws became less biological, enforcing a vision of "hunters' ethics." (For more on fair chase, *see* chapter 6: *Legal Protections for Bears: Hunting Black Bears*.)

Many taking restrictions concern the weapons that hunters use, and also have more to do with standards of "sportsmanship" than with conservation. With very few exceptions, the states have outlawed silencers, fully automatic weapons, semiautomatic firearms holding more than five rounds, and the use of explosives or chemicals for taking wildlife. Some weapons restrictions are a bit odd. New York has banned the use of spears for hunting, while Alabama allows them, so long as the blade is at least 2 inches wide. No other states mention spears.

Other constraints on weapons concern their size, firepower, and their targets. A maximum shotgun size of 10 gauge is common, and most states have a minimum caliber for muzzleloaders, ranging from 0.40 in California to 0.45 in Montana. In Connecticut a hunter cannot legally use a handgun to hunt deer, while Florida and Washington have banned handguns for game birds. Alabama says a hunter after deer with a handgun must make sure the weapon is at least 0.40 caliber. In North Carolina, New Hampshire, and New Mexico, among others, turkey cannot be taken with a rifle, and Virginia says no rifles for migratory birds and waterfowl. California and Wisconsin require a hunter's rifle barrel to be at least 16 inches long. The states have also written the federal nontoxic shot requirement into their regulations for hunting waterfowl and migratory birds with shotguns. This rule is imposed under the authority of the Migratory Bird Treaty Act (for more on the nontoxic shot issue, *see* chapter 6: *Migratory Bird Treaty Act of 1918: Subsistence Hunting and Nontoxic Shot*).

Archery specifications are also found in all the states' hunting regulations. Oklahoma's are fairly typical: bows must have at least 40 pounds "draw weight" and arrow points must be at least 7/8 inches long and 1 1/2 inches wide; laser or light sights are prohibited, as are any devices that mechanically draw the bow, as is characteristic of the crossbow. A ban on crossbows is nearly universal, but so is a significant exception to this law. In recent years state wildlife agencies have been courting physically disabled hunters (for instance, as mentioned above, by allowing them to shoot from vehicles), for whom the use of standard archery equipment and heavy firearms is impractical or impossible. With verification of paralysis or amputation, most states will issue a special crossbow permit to a disabled person or "challenged hunter" as some call such individuals. In contrast, Alaska will allow anyone to use a crossbow, though not during an archery season, and Texas's only crossbow restriction is that the weapon cannot be employed to hunt migratory birds.

Taking Restrictions: Baiting and Dogs

Nearly every state addresses the issue of baiting in their hunting regulations: using food, scents, calls, or decoys in an attempt to lure animals into the close proximity of the hunter's firearms. About one-third of the states have banned baiting entirely, except for various mechanical bird calls, and most of the others do not allow electronic bird calls or live decoys. A federal regulation, also honored in state hunting laws, prohibits hunting migratory birds by sowing fields with seed, grain, salt, or other bird food (*see* chapter 6: *Migratory Bird Treaty Act of 1918: Baiting*).

The use of bait to take bears has generated a fair amount of controversy over the last decade as a number of state initiatives have sought to outlaw the practice, most recently Oregon in 1995. Bears are easily lured by mounds of rotting meat, fruit, and vegetables, replete with the odor of decay that attracts bruins like a magnet. The hunter awaits concealed nearby, usually in a tree stand. Currently, ten states permit bear-baiting: Alaska, Arizona, Idaho, Maine, Michigan, Minnesota, New Hampshire, Utah, Wisconsin, and Wyoming. The nineteen other states in which bears may be legally hunted have banned it. (For more on baiting bears, *see* chapter 6: *Legal Protections for Bears: Hunting Black Bears.*)

The use of dogs for tracking and cornering wildlife is also heavily regulated by the states, with a variety of different restrictions. For example, in Arizona and New Mexico hunting dogs are illegal for pursuing any animals except bear and mountain lions, while Iowa's sole restriction is that dogs cannot be used in state-owned game management areas between March 15 and July 15 and they must have a rabies vaccination. In Alaska dogs are permitted only for hunting large mammals ("big game"), but Oregon does not allow hunting dogs to pursue any mammals at all. Texas, Indiana, Michigan, and Wisconsin allow dogs for hunting any game species except deer, while in Oklahoma they are permitted for any species except deer, elk, antelope, and turkey. Alabama allows canines just for the pursuit of bobcat, and in California only elk hunters may use dogs.

California has banned outfitting dogs with "treeing switches," a device that sends an electronic signal to the hunter when a dog looks up into the branches at the animal brought to bay. The states also have regulations for training hunting dogs, usually requiring that this be done in certain areas at certain times, with unloaded or blank loaded weapons, if any, and ensuring that the animals do not harm game species out of season.

Finally, about half of the states have laws that prohibit allowing the carcass or edible parts of a wild animal to go to waste. The main purpose of these laws is to prevent individuals from wastefully exploiting certain animals in order to sell their body parts for profit—one of the measures intended to deter market hunting—but they are also directed at promoting a standard of hunter ethics that abhors useless despoliation. Most of these waste statutes prohibit removing the head or antlers from deer or elk and leaving the remainder of the body. Several states have begun to include "retrieval" requirements in their waste statutes. Michigan, Texas, Georgia, and Iowa, for example, demand that a hunter make a "reasonable effort" to retrieve an animal wounded in the field. This requirement seems to be motivated by a humane concern for injured wildlife, rather than by a prudent interest in efficiency or to deter avarice.

Violation of any of the states' many hunting laws is almost always a misdemeanor, calling for the payment of a relatively small fine, a leniency that has opened up wildlife agencies and state legislatures to considerable criticism. Some states provide felony convictions for multiple offenses and for taking endangered species.

"Canned Hunts"

Scattered across half of the states in the United States are areas of private land inhabited by gazelles, cape buffaloes, angora goats, corsican sheep, red deer, lions, tigers, giraffes, and other large mammals not native to America. Ranging in size from a few acres to thousands of acres, there are perhaps 1,000 or more of these ranches where nonindigenous, exotic animals live confined by fences, cages, or chains or other tethers.

The animals are here, far from their homelands, to serve as prey for people who come from all over the country and pay hundreds, even thousands of dollars for the opportunity to kill an exotic animal and procure a "trophy": the head, horns, or hide of the dead animal. In most of these operations, there is no "fair chase" or "sporting chance" provided to the nonnative mammals, the basic standard of "ethical" hunting. Instead, they have virtually no chance at all of eluding the hunter. The animals are captives, typically born and raised on the ranch, so they tend to be much more tame than wild, with little fear of humans. And after all they are confined by the fenced borders of the property. Some of these hunting ranches have a "no kill, no pay" policy, and a guaranteed dead animal is what their customers come for. This is "hunting in a can," a sordid equivalent to "shooting fish in a barrel."

Killing a captive, exotic animal under such conditions has been widely condemned by animal advocates and conservationists alike, and the term "canned hunt" is meant to express that opprobrium. Organizations with as widely divergent and often incompatible goals as the Izaak Walton League, a strongly prohunting group, and the Humane Society of the United States, just as adamantly opposed to hunting, have both demanded that canned hunts be outlawed. They are especially disturbed by the unsportsmanlike conduct of the practitioner in such an endeavor and the threat of disease that nonindigenous animals present to native wildlife.

In an unprecedented alliance, the two organizations have joined many other voices in expressing unqualified support for a bill sponsored by Representatives George Brown and Porter Goss, introduced to Congress in January 1999. The Captive Exotic Animal Protection Act would make it a federal offense to knowingly transfer, transport, or possess in interstate or foreign commerce a confined exotic mammal, those not "historically indigenous to the United States, . . . for the purpose of allowing the killing or injuring of that animal for entertainment or the collection of a trophy." The provisions of the bill apply only to exotic animals that have been held in captivity for either the majority of their lives or for one year, whichever is the shorter period. Also, ranches larger than 1,000 acres would not be subject to the ban because, the bill's sponsors believe, the larger area provides the animals with a higher probability of escaping the hunter, opening up the "can" as it were. Violations would be punishable by a fine of as much as $100,000 or one year imprisonment, or both. At this writing, the bill is under consideration by various congressional committees.

A number of states have already outlawed canned hunting, including California, Connecticut, Maine, Nevada, New Jersey, New York, North Carolina, Oregon, Wisconsin, Wyoming, and most recently (November 2000) Montana. Nonetheless, without federal regulation to control interstate commerce, the proprietor of one of these ranches located in a state that permits canned hunting can legally obtain an exotic animal from a state where the practice is prohibited. Moreover, supporters of the Brown-Goss bill argue that a federal law is needed because exotic animals tend to slip through the legislative cracks of the states: fish and game agencies are traditionally responsible for native species of wildlife while state agriculture departments manage livestock.

RECREATIONAL HUNTING SAFETY & PRESERVATION ACT OF 1994

Unlike legislative reforms to enhance the welfare of animals used in entertainment (see this chapter: Circuses and Zoos), agriculture (see chapter 4), and in the laboratory (see chapter 7), there is little that can be done to improve the lot of the wildlife that are prey for hunters. State hunting laws have some "fair chase" restrictions that increase the likelihood that animals will evade the hunter—bans on laser sights, explosives, automatic weapons, and spot lights (see this chapter: Recreational Hunting: Taking Restrictions: Seasons and Weapons). Even so, no legal assurance can ever be provided that wild animals running at large will be treated humanely or killed without pain and distress.

There seems to be no middle ground for the law to occupy between the total abolition of hunting and allowing an activity that often inflicts fear and suffering on animals. Yet the total legal abolition of any human endeavor is almost always exceedingly difficult to accomplish, especially one that has been deeply embedded in numerous cultures for millennia.

Active opponents of hunting are then, of necessity, involved in a movement to completely abolish a profoundly entrenched use of animals. Not surprisingly, from the legal perspective this movement has always been an utter failure.

In a kind of desperation over this state of affairs, over forty years ago some adversaries of hunting began turning to extra-legal methods to stop the carnage—there seemed nothing else that could be done. During the summer of 1958 in England, members of the League Against Cruel Sports (LACS) first laid down a "secret chemical" to confuse the hounds used to hunt stags (male deer) and foxes across the British countryside. The false scent trails sent the trackers on a wild goose chase, so to speak. This tactic met with some success, and after a few years, younger and more militant members of the LACS called for increasingly aggressive actions. Discouraged by the older and more conservative faction dominating the group, the militants splintered off and formed their own organization, boldly named for the mission they would pursue: the Hunt Saboteurs Association (HSA)

Hunt Sabotage
Throughout the 1960s HSA representatives—dubbed "sabs" by the media—were fixtures at stag and fox hunts around England. Their principal methods distracted and bewildered the dogs: throwing meat in their path, indiscriminately blowing hunting horns, and broadcasting high-frequency sounds. Additionally, the sabs would lay down in front of hunters' vehicles, block roads to hunting areas, and detonate smoke bombs.

Even these forms of sabotage proved too tame for some of the HSA membership, and in the early 1970s a new and yet more radical group formed devoted to thwarting hunters. Calling themselves the "Band of Mercy," after a nineteenth-century antivivisection group, these saboteurs indulged in slashing the tires and smashing the windshields of hunters' vehicles, and began to perpetrate further property damage on other *loci* of animal exploitation, notably laboratories. By the end of the 1970s, the Band of Mercy had been transplanted to the United States and evolved into the Animal Liberation Front, whose covert operations moved away from subverting hunts to concentrating on research facilities and fur farms, vandalizing the premises and releasing the animals found there. (For more on the Animal Liberation Front, *see* chapter 7: *Animal Enterprise Protection Act of 1992.*)

Meanwhile, corresponding to the rise of the animal protection movement and a growing concern for the well-being of animals generally, opposition to sport hunting had been steadily building in the United States during the late 1960s and into the 1970s. Some animal activists grew tired of lobbying legislators or writing essays or engaging city and suburban dwellers in debate. They had learned what their English brethren had realized two decades earlier: none of these more passive intellectual exercises did anything to stop hunting, and there seemed to be a far more assertive and effective method of protecting game animals. Inspired by the HSA (though no formal organization with this focus has ever been established in the United States), foes of recreational animal killing took to the woods, fields, and mountains in an attempt to directly hinder hunters, and save animals' lives. This type of public protest came to be popularly known as "hunter harassment."

Techniques for sabotaging hunts had to be adapted to conditions in America, where it is rare to find hunters on horseback with dogs in small areas. Instead, American sabs mainly focused on scaring targeted animals away from the guns, strolling through hunting units while talking loudly, singing, playing portable radios, or plying noise makers of various sorts. Another common field tactic, which also scattered wildlife out of harm's way, was to form a kind of meandering picket line, the saboteurs carrying signs, wearing orange clothing emblazoned with antihunting slogans, and talking to the hunters as they attempt to stalk animals, explaining arguments against hunting and asking them to defend their actions.

Sometimes, these methods were preceded with a gathering at some central location where hunters tend to begin their pursuit of wildlife, such as in campgrounds or at the entrance of a natural area, where signs and banners were displayed, and attempts were made to engage the hunters or their supporters in debate. Similarly, as a straightforward form of registering disapproval rather than a direct act of sabotage, some protesters confronted the hunt with silence, saying nothing to either the shooters or the animals, carrying no signs, wearing no slogans. Instead, the objector, often alone, simply walked or stood quietly in the area, perhaps placing himself between an animal and the hunter.

Making Hunt Sabotage Illegal

When hunt sabotage and protests began spreading in the United States during the mid-1970s, none of the sabs' or protesters' activities were unlawful. Making noise in a hunting area or talking to armed men who are looking for wildlife to kill or standing between a hunter and his prey did not violate any state or federal statute. As long as they did not trespass, these opponents of hunting were acting in a perfectly law-abiding manner. Hunters in several states began to complain bitterly to legislators and to commissioners on wildlife boards that their hunting, also a legal activity, was being severely impeded and even thwarted entirely.

The situation came to a head in southern Arizona during the late 1970s. There, the protest of the annual bighorn sheep hunt, held every fall, had been recurring and escalating for several years. Protesters would fan out through the bighorns' mountainous range, tracking and tailing the hunters, shouting, singing, and banging pots. The sheep hunters were outraged, especially those who were paying thousands of dollars for equipment, supplies, transportation, and nonresident licenses to pursue the animals. The Arizona legislature heard their outcry and responded in 1981 with the first hunter harassment statute, prohibiting any activity that disrupts a lawful hunt. Georgia and Vermont enacted similar laws that same year.

Other states were energized by these measures, and as the legislative momentum grew, the Wildlife Legislative Fund of America drafted a model hunter harassment law and accelerated their lobbying efforts at both the state and national levels. By July 1995, when Hawaii passed its own law, every state in the Union had made all forms of in-the-field hunting protest illegal.

Some of these state statutes have been challenged as unconstitutional, with varying results. Federal and state courts have found the hunter harassment laws of New Hampshire, Idaho, Montana, and Connecticut to be invalid, mostly on the grounds of vagueness and excessive reach of the prohibited actions. For example, the Connecticut law was ruled "unenforceably vague in its overly broad scope." It made unlawful not only interference with the hunt itself, but also "acts in preparation" for hunting. This could include hindering hunters buying food for the hunting trip, making plans in the lunchroom at work, or even trying to get a good night's sleep before the trip (*Dorman v. Satti*).

In a more narrowly focused approach, the Minnesota Court of Appeals decided against invalidating the entire statute. Instead, the judges struck down only that portion of the law that prohibited attempting to dissuade hunters or enjoying the outdoors in some way that interfered with them (*State v. Miner*). In response to these setbacks, legislatures invariably redrafted the appropriate language. The Wisconsin Court of Appeals is currently the only tribunal that has ruled the state's law constitutionally sound, without need of further amendment.

While these more parochial matters were being litigated, the issue moved to the national stage. On Capitol Hill, the Wildlife Legislative Fund had begun as early as 1989 to solicit support for a federal hunter harassment law from the Congressional Sportsmen's Caucus, a group of prohunting legislators. A number of them would become sponsors of bills that would eventually coalesce into the Recreational Hunting Safety and Preservation Act, swiftly passed by Congress and signed into law by President Bill Clinton in September 1994.

More commonly known as the "Hunters' Rights Amendment," the federal statute is in its main features very much like the various state laws. Its core prohibition is the "[o]bstruction of a lawful hunt: it is a violation . . . intentionally to engage in any physical conduct that hinders a lawful hunt." This transgression merits a civil penalty, punishable by a fine of up to $10,000 if force or violence against the hunter or his or her property were used or threatened, and not more than $5,000 for any other infraction. The act also provides for injunctive relief—a court order that the hunting protest, in whatever form, must cease or not commence at all. These injunctions may be sought by the head of wildlife management in the state, the attorney general of the United States, or any person who is or would be the target of a hunt protest.

Is the Hunters' Rights Amendment Constitutional?

After six years in the U.S. Code, surprisingly, there has been no litigation under the Recreational Hunting Safety and Preservation Act, so the federal judiciary has not yet had the opportunity to determine if the law is consistent with the Constitution. Critics complain that the statute offends against the First Amendment guarantee of free speech because it punishes individuals for expressing a particular opinion, one that condemns hunting. Indeed, once the fundamentals of free speech law are understood, it is not difficult to raise suspicions about the "Hunters' Rights Amendment."

In two seminal cases involving protesters, each of whom burned an American flag (*Texas v. Johnson* and *United States v. Eichmann*), the Supreme Court developed a multifaceted test for deciding when government regulation impermissibly suppresses speech, contrary to the First Amendment. There are several basic aspects of this test. It begins with judges determining two things: the outlawed action is intended to "convey a particularized message," and the audience of the message is very likely to understand it. If these two conditions are met, the conduct qualifies as "expressive," it is communicating something meaningful.

Next, having established that expressive conduct is being restricted, a court must conclude that the regulation is aimed at suppressing the *content* of the message: government is trying to stop the speaker from saying something. If the challenged statute does indeed prohibit behavior that makes a certain statement because of what it expresses, the law must be subjected to a standard of "strict scrutiny." This is an especially penetrating judicial examination, searching for a "compelling government interest" promoted by the law, one that would justify interfering with expression based on the content of the statement, overriding the First Amendment protection.

On the other hand, a finding that the statute is "content-neutral" does not necessarily avoid strict scrutiny. If the government interest in proscribing the behavior is only activated when a message with a particular meaning is conveyed, even though the law does not specify that a certain point of view is illegal, judges must still closely examine the statute.

The Recreational Hunting Safety and Preservation Act looks to be readily susceptible to the high court test. Certainly the primary forms of hunt sabotage qualify as expressive conduct. Walking around a natural area brandishing antihunting signs while challenging hunters to defend their practice demonstrates an obvious intention to "convey a particularized message" that even the dullest shooter could comprehend. The same goes for deliberately scaring animals away from the guns. So does the act seek to interdict this expressive conduct based on its content? Evidently not, because the statute says only that intentional action hindering a hunt is prohibited. This could be done by someone who happens to enjoy singing in the wilderness, or, like St. Francis, preaching to animals. Indeed a sycophantic hunting advocate could thwart hunters by glomming onto them in the field, loudly encouraging and exhorting successful killing.

This sort of behavior is clearly not the target of the act, so to avoid being overbroad it would seem that the "Hunters' Rights Amendment" *must* be content based at bottom: it is the meaning of what is being expressed by this conduct that government is seeking to censor. If this is true, to pass the test of constitutionality, the act must be subjected to the standard of strict scrutiny where judges search for the overriding government concern that the law promotes. What is that predominant federal interest?

The *state* interest most often identified as behind hunter harassment laws is the critical role of hunting in wildlife management, reducing animal populations that would otherwise overburden habitat, while generating revenue through license fees to fund conservation efforts. Unfortunately, there is no general agreement among wildlife biologists that recreational hunting efficaciously manages wild animals. One major problem is that doves, ducks, and squirrels typically will not overpopulate to the detriment of their habitat, yet these species represent more than half of all wildlife killed by hunters. Setting that issue aside, however, the question remains about the strength of the government interest in conservation: is it weighty enough to override the First Amendment? At any rate, the triumph of such an interest over speech of this nature supposes that hunt saboteurs have been effectively foiling American hunters, yet there is little evidence indicating that this has been the case.

Another possible interest advanced by some states is the significance of hunting to American culture. For instance, in 1996 in Alabama and 1998 in Minnesota, a majority of citizens, convinced that effective legislative forces were at work pushing lawmakers to ban hunting entirely and alarmed at the efforts of hunt saboteurs, voted to respond to the perceived threat with constitutional amendments expressing the critical role of hunting in their way of life. As the Minnesota amendment puts it, "Hunting . . . and the taking of game . . . are a valued part of our heritage that shall be forever preserved for the people and shall be managed by law and regulation for the public good." Voters in North Dakota and Virginia approved measures with similar language in November 2000.

Accepting this proposition as it stands, we still have the question of whether this interest should be prioritized over the right to freely express oneself as hunt saboteurs do. More centrally, there is not likely to be a popular or judicial consensus that hunting really is such an overriding value in the many dimensions of our national heritage. After all, 94 percent of Americans do not hunt and the Supreme Court has already ruled in *Baldwin v. Fish and Game Commission* that hunting is not a fundamental legal right.

Inevitably, these and other facets of the Recreational Hunting Safety and Preservation Act will exercise federal courts in the not-too-distant future. Indeed a trip to the Supreme Court is likely.

REFERENCES

Federal Laws
Animal Welfare Act of 1970, 7 U.S.C. §§ 2131–2157.
Obscenity, 18 U.S.C. §§ 1460–1469.
Punishment for Depiction of Animal Cruelty, 18 U.S.C. § 48.
Recreational Hunting Safety and Preservation Act of 1994, 16 U.S.C. §§ 5201–5207.
Twenty-Eight Hour Law of 1994, 49 U.S.C. § 80502.

Federal Regulations
Animal Welfare Act Regulations, 9 C.F.R. Chapter 1, Subchapter A.
    Standards for humane handling, care, treatment, and transportation, §§ 3.1–42 (Part 3).
        Marine mammals, §§ 3.100–118.
        Nonhuman primates, §§ 3.75–92.
        Warmblooded animals other than dogs, cats, etc., §§ 3.125–142.
Twenty-Eight Hour Law Regulations, 9 C.F.R. §§ 89.1–5.

Federal Register
Animal Welfare; Marine Mammals, 64 Fed. Reg. 35: 8735–8755 (Feb. 23, 1999).
Marine mammals and certain other regulated animals; Perimeter Fence Requirements, Final Rule, 64 Fed. Reg. 200: 56,142-56,148 (Oct. 18, 1999).

State Laws
Alabama, Handling of livestock, Ala. Code § 2-15-110.
California, Penal Code, Poling or tripping a horse, Cal. Penal Code § 1–14–597g.

Florida, Cruelty to Animals, tripping a horse, Fla. Stat. Ann.
§ 46-828.12(4).
Illinois, Horse Poling or tripping, 510 Ill. Comp. Stat. Ann. 70/5.01.
Kansas, Kan. Stat. Ann., Horse tripping, § 21.4310.
Maine, Unlawful use of animals, Me. Rev. Stat. Ann. tit. 7-3972.1(F).
Ohio, Ohio Rev. Code, Ban on certain devices to stimulate animals,
§ 959.20.
Oklahoma, Horse tripping, Okla. Stat. tit. 21-1700.

Anticruelty Laws
  Arizona, § 13-2910.
  Colorado, § 18-9-201.
  Florida, § 46-828.12.
  Idaho, § 25-35-14.
  Kansas, § 21-4310.
  Maine, § 7-739-4011.
  Michigan, § 28.245.
  Minnesota, § 343.21.
  Missouri, § 578.012.
  Montana, § 45-8-211.
  Nebraska, § 28-1001.
  New Mexico, § 3-18-1.
  New York, § 69-26-353.
  North Dakota, § 36-21-1.
  Oklahoma, § 21-1685.
  Oregon, § 167.315.
  Utah, § 76-9-301.
  Vermont, § 13-352.
  Washington, § 16.52.205.
  Wyoming, § 6-3-203.

Cockfighting
  Alaska, Alaska Stat. § 11.65.145 (animal fighting).
  Arizona, Ariz. Rev. Stat. § 13-2910.03–.04.
  Colorado, Colo. Rev. Stat. § 18-9-204 (animal fighting).
  Delaware, Del. Code Ann. tit. 11-1326 (animal fighting).
  Florida, Fla. Stat. Ann. § 828.12 (animal fighting).
  Hawaii, Haw. Rev. Stat. § 711-1109(1)(c) (animal fighting).
  Idaho, Idaho Code § 25-3506.
  Indiana, Ind. Code §§ 35-46-3-8 to 35-46-3-10 (animal fighting).
  Iowa, Iowa Code § 725.11.
  Maine, Me. Rev. Stat. Ann. tit. 17-1033 (animal fighting).
  Maryland, Md. Code Ann. § 27-59.

Michigan, Mich. Comp. Laws § 28.244 (animal fighting).
Minnesota, Minn. Stat. § 343.31.
Nevada, Nev. Rev. Stat. 574.070 (animal fighting).
New Jersey, N.J. Stat. Ann. § 4.22-24 (animal fighting).
New York, N.Y. Agriculture and Markets Law § 26-351.
North Carolina, N.C. Gen. Stat. § 14-362.
North Dakota, N.D. Cent. Code § 36-21.1-07.
Pennsylvania, Pa. Cons. Stat. § 18-5511-H.1 (animal fighting).
Rhode Island, R.I. Gen. Laws §4-1-9.
South Carolina, S.C. Code Ann. § 16-17-650.
Texas, Tex. Penal Code Ann. § 42.09 (animal fighting).
Vermont, Vt. Stat. Ann. tit. 13-352 (animal fighting).
Wisconsin, Wis. Stat. § 951.08.
Wyoming, Wyo. Stat. Ann. § 6-3-203(c)(ii)(iv).

Dogfighting
    Alabama, Ala. Code § 3-1-29.
    Alaska, Alaska Stat. § 11.65.145 (animal fighting).
    Arizona, Ariz. Rev. Stat. § 13-2910.01, 02.
    Colorado, Colo. Rev. Stat. § 18-9-204 (animal fighting).
    Connecticut, Conn. Gen. Stat. § 53-247.
    Florida, Fla. Stat. Ann. § 828.12 (animal fighting).
    Georgia, Ga. Code Ann. § 16-12-37.
    Hawaii, Haw. Rev. Stat. § 711-1109.3.
    Idaho, Idaho Code, § 25-3507.
    Iowa, Iowa Code § 725.11.
    Kentucky, Ky. Rev. Stat. Ann. § 525.125, 130 (animal fighting).
    Louisiana, La. Rev. Stat. Ann. § 14:102.5.
    Maine, Me. Rev. Stat. Ann. tit. 17-1033 (animal fighting).
    Massachusetts, Mass. Gen. Laws ch. 272-88.
    Michigan, Mich. Comp. Laws § 28.244 (animal fighting).
    Minnesota, Minn. Stat. § 343.31.
    Mississippi, Miss. Code Ann. § 97-41-19.
    Montana, Mont. Code Ann. § 45-8-210 (animal fighting).
    Nevada, Nev. Rev. Stat. 574.070.
    New Hampshire § 644: 8-9.
    New Jersey, N.J. Stat. Ann. § 4.22-24 (animal fighting).
    New Mexico, N.M. Stat. Ann. § 30-18-9.
    New York, N.Y. Agriculture and Markets Law § 26-351.
    North Dakota, N.D. Cent. Code § 36-21.1-07.
    Oklahoma, Okla. Stat. tit. 21-1696.
    Pennsylvania, Pa. Cons. Stat. § 18-5511-H.1 (animal fighting).
    Rhode Island, R.I. Gen. Laws §4-1-9.

Vermont, Vt. Stat. Ann. tit. 13-352 (animal fighting).
Virginia, Va. Code Ann. § 3.1-796.125.
West Virginia, W. Va. Code § 61-8-19a (animal fighting).
Wisconsin, Wis. Stat. § 951.08.
Wyoming, Wyo. Stat. Ann. §§ 6-3-203(c)(ii)(iv).

Hunting Regulations
See below, World Wide Web, State Wildlife Agencies websites

Racing Commission Rules
Alabama, Greyhound Care, § 2-2, 4.
Arizona, Greyhound Care, §§ R19-2-324-331.
California, Use of Whips, § 1688; Racing Soundness Examination,
     § 1846.
Colorado, Veterinary Practice, § 5.208; Use of Whips, § 7.740.
Florida, Veterinarians inspect stables, § 61D-6.009(h).
Idaho, Safety, § 060.06.
Iowa, Facilities Responsibilities, Stalls, § 491-10.2(1); Jockey, Conduct,
     § 491-10.5(2)j(4).
Kansas, Post to Finish, Disabled Horse, § 112-7-22(n).
Kentucky, Trainers, Duties and Responsibilities, § 810-1:008(3)(8); Use
     of Whips, § 810-1:1016(15)(2).
Massachusetts, Use of Whips, § 4.11(VI)(6).
Minnesota, Facilities, Maintenance, § 7875.0100(2); Horse becomes
     disabled, § 7883.0160(14).
New York, Receiving Barn, § 4003.17; Whips, § 4117.8(c).
Oregon, Prohibited Conduct, § 462-130-0010; Care of Greyhounds,
     §§ 462-180-0010-0060.
Texas, Whips, § 313.405(d); Kennel Buildings, 309.313(b).
Virginia, Conduct of horse racing, 10-100-10; Use of whip, § 10-140-290.
West Virginia, Cruelty to racing animals, § 45.1.6.
Wisconsin, Humane Treatment of Racing Animals, § 15.02(1)(c).
Wyoming, Use of whip, § 15f.

Transportation of Animals
Maine, Me. Rev. Stat. Ann. tit. 7-3981.
Michigan, Animal confined on railroad cars, Mich. Comp. Laws
     § 28.246.
Minnesota, Cruelty in transportation, Minn. Stat. § 343.24.
New Mexico, Unlawful tripping of an equine, N.M. Stat. Ann.
     § 30-18-11.
New York, Agriculture & Markets, Transportation of horses, N.Y.
     Agric. & Mkts Law § 26-359a.

Rhode Island, Rodeo animals and livestock, R.I. Gen. Laws § 4-20-1.
Texas, Cruelty to Animals, tripping a horse, Tex. Penal Code Ann.
§ 9-42.09(8).
Vermont, Transportation of horses, Vt. Stat. Ann. tit. 13-387.

Federal Cases
Supreme Court
Baldwin v. Fish and Game Commission, 431 U.S. 288 (1978).
Miller v. California, 413 U.S. 15 (1973).

Circuit Courts of Appeals
Haviland v. Butz, 543 F.2d 169 (D.C. Cir. 1976).
United States v. Thomas, 74 F.3d 701 (6th Cir. 1996).

District Courts
Dorman v. Satti, 678 F. Supp. 375 (D. Conn.), *affirmed*, 862 F.2d 432 (2d
Cir. 1988).

State Cases
Alabama
Jones v. State, 473 So. 2d 1197 (Ala. Crim. App. 1985).

Arizona
State v. Stockton, 333 P.2d 735 (Ariz. 1958).

California
People v. Baniqued, 101 Cal. Rptr. 2d 835 (Cal. Ct. Ap. 2000).

Colorado
People v. Bergen, 883 P.2d 532 (Colo. Ct. App. 1994).

Georgia
Brackett v. State, 236 S.E.2d 689 (Ga. Ct. App. 1977).
Hargrove v. State, 321 S.E.2d 104 (Ga. 1984).

Hawaii
State v. Kaneakua, 597 P.2d 590 (Haw. 1979).

Kansas
Hearn v. City of Overland Park, 772 P.2d 758 (Kan.), *cert. denied*, 493
U.S. 976 (1989).
State v. Claiborne, 505 P.2d 732 (Kan. 1973).

Michigan
People v. Cumper, 268 N.W.2d 696 (Mich. Ct. App. 1978).

Minnesota
State v. Miner, 556 N.W.2d 578 (Minn. Ct. App. 1996).

Missouri
State v. Young, 695 S.W.2d 882 (Mo. 1985).
United Gamefowl Breeders Association v. Nixon, 19 S.W.3d 137 (Mo. 2000).

New Mexico
State v. Buford, 331 P.2d 1110 (N.M. 1958).

Ohio
State v. Anderson, 566 N.E.2d 1224 (Ohio), *cert. denied,* 501 U.S. (1991).
State v. Bryson, 605 N.E.2d 1284 (Ohio Ct. App. 1992).
State v. Gaines, 580 N.E.2d 1158 (Ohio 1990).
State v. Longhorn World Championship Rodeo, Inc., 483 N.E.2d 196 (Ohio Ct. App. 1985).

Oklahoma
In re Initiative Petition No. 365, 9 P.3d 78 (Okla. 2000).

Oregon
State v. Albee, 847 P.2d 858 (Or. Ct. App. 1993).

Tennessee
State v. Tabor, 678 S.W.2d 45 (Tenn. 1984).

Books
Animal Welfare Institute. 1990. *Animals and Their Legal Rights.* 4th ed. Animal Welfare Institute.
Branigan, Cynthia A. 1997. *The Reign of the Greyhound.* New York: Howell Book House.
Brooman, Simon, and Debbie Legge. 1997. *Law Relating to Animals.* London: Cavendish.
Croke, Vicki. 1997. *The Modern Ark: The Story of Zoos.* New York: Scribner.
Encyclopaedia Britannica. 14th and 15th eds. S.v. "Horse Racing."
Fisher, James. 1967. *Zoos of the World.* New York: Natural History Press.
Fleig, Dieter. 1996. *The History of the Fighting Dogs.* Translated by William Charlton. Neptune City, NJ: T. F. H. Publications.
Frasch, Pamela D., et al. 2000. *Animal Law.* Durham, NC: Carolina Academic Press.

Friend, Ted. 1998. "Circuses and Circus Elephants." In *Encyclopedia of Animal Rights and Animal Welfare.* Edited by Marc Bekoff. Westport, CT: Greenwood.

Johnson, William M. 1990. *The Rose-Tinted Menagerie.* London: Heretic Books.

Kreger, Michael D. 1998. "Zoos, History of Zoos." In *Encyclopedia of Animal Rights and Animal Welfare.* Edited by Marc Bekoff. Westport, CT: Greenwood.

Lawrence, Elizabeth Atwood. 1982. *Rodeo: An Anthropologist Looks at the Wild and the Tame.* Knoxville: University of Tennessee Press.

Lund, Thomas. 1980. *American Wildlife Law.* Berkeley and Los Angeles: University of California Press.

Mullan, Bob, and Gary Marvin. 1999. *Zoo Culture.* 2d ed. Urbana: University of Illinois Press.

Musgrave, Ruth, and Mary Anne Stein. 1993. *State Wildlife Laws Handbook.* Rockville, MD: Government Institutes.

Ogden, Tom. 1993. *Two Hundred Years of the American Circus.* New York: Facts On File.

Phelps, Norman. 2000. *Body Count: The Death Toll in America's War on Wildlife.* New York: The Fund for Animals.

Scott, George Ryley. 1983. *The History of Cockfighting.* London: Triplegate.

Wooden, Wayne S., and Gavin Ehringer. 1996. *Rodeo in America.* Lawrence: University Press of Kansas.

Articles and Guidelines

Bilger, Burkhard. 1999. "Enter the Chicken: On the Bayou, Cockfighting Remains Undefeated." *Harper's Magazine* 298, no. 1786 (March): 48–57.

Crecente, Brian D. 2000. "Fashionable Brutality: Dogfighting on the Rise." *APBnews.com* (17 July).

Eidinger, Joan. 2000. "Nowhere to Run: Dog Racing in Decline." *The Animals Agenda* 20, no. 5 (September/October): 30–35.

Hessler, Katherine. 1997. "Where Do We Draw the Line between Harassment and Free Speech?: An Analysis of Hunter Harassment Law." *Animal Law* 3: 129–162.

Hubert, Cynthia. 1999. "Seven-Year Term for Dog Fighting." *Sacramento Bee,* 26 July.

Larson, Peggy W. 1998. "Rodeo is Cruel Entertainment." *Pace University Environmental Law Review* 16: 115–123.

National Greyhound Association Board of Directors. 1993, 2000. "NGA Inspection Guidelines." National Greyhound Association.

Professional Rodeo Cowboys Association. 1998. "Official Rodeo Rules" (November).

Provance, Jim. 2001. "Drugs: Racing's Dark Horse." *Toledo (Ohio) Blade,* 28 January.

Samuels, David. 1999. "Going to the Dogs." *Harper's Magazine* 298, no. 1785 (February): 52–63.

Weisberg, Lisa. 1998. "Legislative Proposals Protecting Animals in Entertainment." *Pace University Environmental Law Review* 16: 125–132.

World Wide Web

American Greyhound Council, http://www.agcouncil.com.

Animal and Plant Health Inspection Service, USDA, http://www.aphis.usda.gov.

Animal Protection Institute's Circus Campaign, http://www. api4animals.org/IssuesAnd AdvocacyCampaigns/Entertainment/ CircusCampaign.

Bans on Animal Acts in the United States, http://circuses.com.

Cockfighting in Oklahoma, http://commerce.tulsaworld.com/search/searchform.html.

Complete Guide to Horse Racing, http://www.equineinfo.com/horseracing.htm.

Greyhound Network News, http://www.greyhounds.org/gnn.

Greyhound Protection League, http://www.greyhounds.org.

Humane Society of the United States, http://www.hsus.org.

Animal Fighting, http://www.hsus.org/current/

Circuses and the Law, http://www.hsus.org/current/circus_law.html

Facts about Greyhound Racing, http://www.hsus.org/whatnew/sadog_facts.html.

Hunt Saboteurs, http://www.enviroweb.org/HSA.

International Species Information System, http://www.worldzoo.org.

The Jockey Club, http://home.jockeyclub.com.

National Greyhound Association, http://nga.jc.net.

People for the Ethical Treatment of Animals, Media Center—Factsheets, Animals in Entertainment, http://www.peta.org/mc/facts.

Professional Rodeo Cowboys Association, http://www.prorodeo.com.

State Wildlife Agencies, http://wildlife.state.co.us/about/StateAgency.

6. Wild Animals

WILDLIFE LAW

Legal protections for wild animals in America are dominated by federal laws approved by Congress and signed by the president. Today, the federal government's authority over the states to regulate the use of wildlife within their borders is unquestioned. This was not always the case. For generations after the colonies won their independence from Great Britain, the individual states made their own decisions about the disposition of wild animals found within their jurisdictions, free from interference originating on Capitol Hill. So what gives Washington, D.C., the right to dictate to the states how they are to manage wildlife?

Federal Regulation of Wildlife

The earliest answer to this question given by the federal judiciary is that the government has no such right, a reply that for years would render the matter of federal power over wildlife confusing and unsettled.

In 1889 Connecticut convicted Edgar Geer of violating a state law prohibiting the possession of game birds with the intention of transporting them out of the state. In his defense, Geer appealed to Article I, Section 8 of the Constitution. Known as the Commerce Clause, this provision empowers the federal government to regulate trade between the states. Geer contended that because the Commerce Clause reserves the right to restrict interstate trading to the federal government, the Connecticut law was invalid. The Supreme Court rejected this argument in 1896, with Justice Edward White proclaiming that each state had the right to control and regulate "the common property in game," and the obligation "to preserve for its people a valuable food supply" even if this required imposing some restrictions on the movement of animals out of the state (*Geer v. Connecticut*).

This ruling presents a puzzling jumble of several distinct issues: the comprehensiveness of federal governance over commerce, the scope of state authority to control wildlife, the nature of property rights in wild animals, and the relationships between these matters. Nonetheless, *Geer* became famous as the seminal case announcing the "state ownership doctrine": wild animals are the property of the states in which they reside, and as the owners of these animals, the states have the exclusive right to regulate what is done with them. Such a doctrine seems to severely impede or even preempt federal wildlife law altogether. However, just four years after *Geer*, with some irony, this same Commerce Clause provided the basis for one of the earliest pieces of federal wildlife legislation. And, in fact, at the time *Geer* was decided, the president and Congress had already ordered restrictions on the use of some wildlife.

In 1900 Congress passed the Lacey Act (*see* this chapter: *Lacey Act*), prohibiting interstate trafficking in (mostly) birds killed or captured in violation of state laws. As a clear assertion of federal power over what may be done with certain creatures living in the wild on public lands, the authority for the Lacey Act is straightforwardly derived from the Commerce Clause. Yet almost all federal wildlife laws then and now are not of this secondary and dependent nature, in which a legal rule from the state is required as a substrate, and they are not wholly concerned with the movement of species across state lines. Instead, U.S. law has always been more directly concerned with protections for wild animals themselves, essentially the same sort as the state statutes that the Lacey Act sought to reinforce.

This began in 1892 when President Benjamin Harrison declared Alaska's Afognak Island a reserve where wildlife is protected, followed in 1894 by the Yellowstone Protection Act prohibiting hunting in the National Park. During the first quarter of the twentieth century, other presidents and Congresses created numerous wildlife refuges where hunting is restricted or banned entirely (*see* this chapter: *National Wildlife Refuge System Improvement Act of 1997*). In 1940 Congress prohibited (with certain exceptions) pursuing, shooting, possessing, trapping, or molesting bald eagles, and in the 1970s wild horses and burros, all marine mammals, and numerous endangered wildlife species received similar protections (*see* chapter 3: *Wild Free-Roaming Horses and Burros Act of 1971*; this chapter: *Marine Mammal Protection Act of 1972*; this chapter: *Endangered Species Act of 1973*). For decades, the federal government has continuously asserted its sovereignty over the use of wildlife, and remains the preeminent source of legal protections for wild animals.

Even so, *these* sorts of restrictions cannot be underwritten by the Commerce Clause (or not entirely). Again we have the question: from whence do they derive their authority? For years, despite the holding in *Geer*, no one seriously addressed this inquiry. It seemed to be taken for granted that the federal government was entitled to unilaterally establish legal safeguards for wild animals, yet at the same time the state ownership doctrine appeared to say otherwise (*but see* this chapter: *Migratory Bird Treaty Act of 1918: Implementing the Treaty*). This problem remained essentially unresolved for decades until finally, inevitably, a conflict arose between state and federal law.

The Property Clause and the Regulation of Wildlife

Tracing the long road to a resolution takes us back to 1900 again. That year, the Arizona territorial government banned all deer hunting on the Kaibab Plateau, a spruce- and fir-cloaked tableland north of the Grand Canyon. Decades of unrestrained, excessive hunting there through the 1800s had reduced the mule deer (*Odocoileus hemionus*) population to no more than 4,000 animals. After twenty-five years of the ban, and the extermination of the region's major predator, the gray wolf (*Canis lupus*), the number of deer had exploded to over 100,000, nearly 100 for every square mile on the Kaibab. The forest was stripped of available forage, leaving a ravaged and stricken ecosystem—the deer were starving.

Attempting to restabilize this ecological community, the secretary of agriculture ordered government hunters to kill thousands of the animals, but when they began to do so, Arizona law enforcement agents arrested them. Now a state (accepted into the union in 1912), Arizona still retained the territorial prohibition for the Kaibab Plateau, so hunters working for the United States there were in violation of state law. The federal government protested the arrests, and soon the dispute went to the courts, ascending through the district and appellate levels, eventually arriving at the Supreme Court in 1928.

At each venue, Arizona officials had rested their case primarily on *Geer v. Connecticut:* the states were entitled to regulate and control the wildlife found within their borders or, put simply, the states owned the animals and could do with them what their elected officials wished. This state ownership doctrine, Arizona argued, entailed that the federal government had no right to impose rules for managing wildlife on public lands, so the culling of deer on the Kaibab was illegal. However, the Supreme Court of 1928 was not like that of thirty-two years earlier. In *Hunt v. United States,* Justice Sutherland's majority opinion proclaimed that "the power of the United States to thus protect its lands and property does not admit of doubt . . . the game laws or any other statute of the state . . . notwithstanding." Arizona lost.

The notion contained in *Geer* that the states had some sort of pervasive and preeminent claim on wildlife was severely undermined. The force behind this judicial excavation was another special principle contained in the Constitution. The Property Clause in Article IV, Section 3 states that "Congress shall have Power to dispose of and make all needful Rules and Regulations respecting the Territory or other Property belonging to the United States." In *Hunt,* the Property Clause was held to underwrite the removal of animals that were damaging U.S. property, thus overturning a significant portion, but not the entirety of *Geer.* The federal government evidently did have the right to manage wildlife adversely affecting public land, no matter the state's wishes. This did not however negate the core proposition asserted in *Geer:* the states own the animals. Yet a serious erosion of that idea had begun.

Who Has Authority over Wild Animals?

The sequence of events that resulted in a decisive blow to the state ownership doctrine began years later on a chilly February morning in 1974. That day, Kelley Stephanson rode over to Taylor Well to inspect his cattle. There at the northern New Mexico watering hole, he found that his cows

had some company: a small herd of wild burros drinking the precious liquid and feeding on the scattered forage in the immediate area. Stephanson leased about 8,000 acres surrounding the well from the federal government to graze his livestock. This was public land supervised by the
federal Bureau of Land Management (BLM), and, indeed, officials from
the BLM had first informed him of the presence of the burros in the vicinity of Taylor Well. Stephanson came to believe that the wild burros were
molesting his cows and depriving them of feed, so he asked the BLM to
remove the equines. When the agency refused, the rancher turned to the
New Mexico Livestock Board.

The Livestock Board responded quickly. As empowered by the New
Mexico estray law, agents of the state rounded up nineteen burros and
sold them all at a public auction within a week. The federal government
responded almost as fast. The BLM demanded that the Livestock Board
retrieve the sold animals and return them immediately to public lands.
As the authority on which to base this command, the BLM cited the Wild
Free-Roaming Horses and Burros Act (WHBA) (*see* chapter 3). Enacted in
1971, the WHBA protects "all unbranded and unclaimed horses and burros on public lands of the United States" from "capture, branding, harassment, or death." The BLM is responsible for managing these herds on
public lands as integral components of the natural environments where
they live. Only the secretary of the interior (the BLM is housed within the
Interior Department) or his or her delegates may direct that any of these
animals be removed from BLM-managed regions, and this must be done
according to federal regulations.

A showdown between the federal government and the state of New
Mexico had been brewing for some time. The Livestock Board had signed
an agreement with the secretaries of the interior and agriculture in August 1973 promising to cooperate with federal efforts to manage the wild
equines. But just three months later, the board reneged and stated its intention to enforce the state estray law, even if this required entering public land and seizing wild horses and burros. The roundup and sale of the
burros from Taylor Well was calculated to force the issue of state sovereignty over animals inhabiting natural areas. Then in March 1974 New
Mexico filed a complaint in a federal district court against Secretary of the
Interior Thomas Kleppe, requesting an injunction to halt enforcement of
the WHBA and a declaration that it was constitutionally invalid. The
court acted as requested.

Kleppe v. New Mexico

New Mexico successfully argued to the lower court that U.S. authority to
control wild animals was limited to regulating their movement in interstate commerce, pursuant to the Lacey Act, or preventing them from

damaging public lands, as affirmed in *Hunt*. Because neither objective applied to the WHBA—this law is designed to protect the *animals* and not the land—Congress had exceeded its power to regulate wildlife.

A unanimous Supreme Court rejected this argument in 1976 and offered what stands as the definitive word to date on the extent of the federal mandate provided by the Property Clause. Writing for the unified bench, Justice Thurgood Marshall first disposed of New Mexico's appeal to *Hunt*. He pointed out that it was a mistake to read this decision as holding that damage to federal property *must* be shown before the property power could be legitimately invoked. Instead, *Hunt* merely indicated that this was a *sufficient* cause for federal regulation of wildlife, not that it was necessary or required. So what is required? Marshall admitted that the extent of federal power over public lands under the Property Clause had not been conclusively delineated (and still has not been at this writing), yet he noted that it is apparently unlimited. At any rate, that authority is not confined to protecting the land from damage caused by wild animals, such as the deer tearing up the Kaibab, and is indeed expansive enough to include protecting wildlife inhabiting the public domain.

To New Mexico's charge that, if the WHBA is a legitimate exercise of federal power according to the Property Clause, then state sovereignty has been seriously and illegally compromised, Marshall was equally dismissive. He noted that a state retains jurisdiction over public land within its borders unless it agrees otherwise, but at the same time the federal government reserves the authority to pass laws in accord with the Property Clause regarding those lands. So what happens when state and federal law conflict, as the New Mexico estray law was incompatible with the WHBA? "[T]he state is free to enforce its criminal and civil laws on [public] lands," Marshall wrote, "[b]ut where those state laws conflict with the Wild Free-Roaming Horses and Burros Act, or with other legislation passed pursuant to the Property Clause, the law is clear: The state laws must recede."

This conclusion indicates that the Supreme Court judgment here, and federal control of wildlife generally, are based on more than just the Property Clause. The depths of the issue plumb farther than the matter of federal power over wild animals to the equally vexing problem, as seen so clearly here in *Kleppe*, that arises when state and federal laws are incompatible. This particular dilemma is, after all, what sparked litigation challenging federal authority for the regulation of wildlife in the first place, as was seen above in *Hunt*. On such occasions, it is not merely the Property Clause that rules the day, but that principle conjoined with the Supremacy Clause of the Constitution. Article VI, Section 2 declares that federal laws are the supreme law of the land, and state laws conflicting with them are superseded. This is what allowed Justice Marshall to assert that "federal legislation necessarily overrides conflicting state laws," finding in favor of the WHBA and the interior secretary's administration of the law, and against New Mexico.

There remains another matter, one mixed in with the authority over wildlife question since the time of *Geer:* who owns wild animals, the state or the federal government? This question was not answered in *Kleppe*. Although Marshall observed that it was not at all clear that wild horses and burros are not the property of the United States, he also failed to say exactly whose property they are.

LACEY ACT

On two occasions in 1896 an ornithologist named Frank Graham walked about the streets of Manhattan closely observing ladies' hats. He counted them. Of the 700 hats perched on the heads of the women he encountered on his strolls, 542 of them contained bird feathers, representing some 40 different species. This was a serious problem. (Almost all of the remaining 158 featherless hats belonged to the elderly or women in mourning.)

In 1886 the American Ornithologists Union estimated that 5 million birds were being killed every year so that their plumage could serve as a favorite Victorian ornament, satisfying the palate of fashion at the cost of an alarming depletion of many species. That same year, New York passed one of the first laws protecting "nongame" species. The New York Bird Law, intended to stop the slaughter for feathers, prohibited killing, wounding, or capturing "any bird of song or any linnet, blue bird, yellow hammer, yellow bird, thrush, woodpecker, cat bird, peewee, swallow, martin, blue jay, oriole, killdeer, snow bird, grass bird, grosbeak, bobolink, phoebe bird, humming bird, wren, robin, meadow lark or starling or any wild bird." The statute also banned selling, buying, or possessing any of these creatures. Plainly, birds of every sort were being plundered for their plumes, and if they were to be protected, laws of long reach had to be written.

Yet state laws like this one, and others of similar construction that were inspired by New York's example, could not reach far enough: they could not grasp a wrongdoer who had departed for another jurisdiction. So a market hunter could illegally shoot flamingos in Florida, or exceed the bag limit for pheasants in Illinois, and legally sell parts of both species in New York City. At the turn of the last century, the birds seemed doomed unless some regulation of interstate trafficking in feathers and other avian by-products could be established. But no state had the legal authority to do that.

The Lacey Act of 1900

Iowa Congressman John F. Lacey found the answer to the problem in the Commerce Clause of the U.S. Constitution. Article I, Section 8 of the Constitution gives the federal government the authority to govern interstate commerce: "The Congress shall have the power . . . [t]o regulate Commerce with foreign Nations, and among the several States, and with Indian Tribes." The movement of dead birds and their body parts across state lines for sale and trade, he reasoned, is clearly interstate commerce well within the purview of lawmakers on Capitol Hill.

Congress agreed with Lacey, and so the Commerce Clause provided the first explicit authorization for the federal government to regulate wildlife. Unlike the Property Clause of the Constitution (Article IV, Section 3; *see* this chapter: *Wildlife Law*), federal regulation of wildlife as authorized by the Commerce Clause has never been seriously challenged. Lacey's bill was signed into law by President William McKinley in 1900, and named for its sponsor.

Evoking the constitutionally validated federal control, section 5 of the new statute outlawed a standard maneuver designed to thwart state game laws: marketing in one state feathers from birds protected in another, where the act of commerce itself is not contrary to any state law. For example, in Alabama herons were protected, so a person who killed one and then sold its plumes was breaking the law. However, it was not illegal in Alabama to sell heron feathers from a bird killed in Georgia, so the nefarious shooter had simply to head west from Okefenokee, say, crossing into the other jurisdiction to avoid the law. The Lacey Act foiled this scheme: animal bodies or body parts brought into a state acquired the same legal status as those originating in that state. Further, this provision also barred transport for sale of a species, not protected in one state and thus legally taken there, into a state in which it was protected, and where it could not be legally killed. After Lacey, any carrier who delivered such contraband across the borders of a state, or the person who turned it over to a carrier, was now committing a federal offense.

The international component of the Commerce Clause also supplied the authority behind another provision of the Lacey Act. This one prohibited the importation of various species that the secretary of agriculture, charged with administering the law, "may . . . declare injurious to the interest of agriculture or horticulture" (*see also* this chapter: *Lacey Act: Injurious Wildlife;* this chapter: *Nonindigenous Aquatic Nuisance Prevention and Control Act of 1990*). Mongooses (*Mungos mungo*), fruit bats, starlings (*Sturnus* spp.), and English sparrows were among the first such species disallowed for importation. The secretary was further empowered to pursue methods of preserving and restoring populations of "game birds and other wild birds," so long as these measures did not conflict with current state and territorial law. Finally, the packaging of dead animals or body parts for interstate shipment had to include clear markings of the contents.

The Lacey Act did not present a robust deterrent. Congress provided light penalties for violation ($500 maximum fine for carriers and no jail time), and demanded a high standard of culpability. Conviction required *scienter,* that is, proof that the defendant knew his or her actions were unlawful and that he or she intended to violate the law. Although the Lacey Act is credited by some with ending illicit trade in plumage and thus reinvigorating many bird species, a likelier explanation for the recovery is that the fickle whims of fashion turned away from feathered hats and boas. The federal law in any case had no impact on commerce between states without laws protecting the targeted birds. Moreover, it was too late to save the Carolina parakeet (*Conuropsis carolinensis*) or the passenger pigeon (*Ectopistes migratorius*), the last individuals of both species expiring in 1914. Nonetheless, this statute is the progeny of national lawmakers embarking on a very early foray into wildlife management. Along with an 1894 act of Congress that banned hunting in Yellowstone National Park (John Lacey also sponsored this bill), the Lacey Act of 1900 represents the federal government exerting its authority over American wildlife for the first time.

Through the first few decades of the twentieth century, federal influence in the governance of wildlife in the United States increased markedly. Dozens of reserves and sanctuaries that would eventually be organized as the National Wildlife Refuge System were created by acts of Congress and executive orders from the White House, areas where hunting was strictly regulated or completely banned (*see* this chapter: *National Wildlife Refuge System Improvement Act of 1997*). In 1911 an international agreement with Russia, Japan, and Great Britain restricted the numbers of, and the manner in which, fur seals in Alaskan waters could be taken (*see* this chapter: *Fur Seal Act of 1966*). The Migratory Bird Treaty Act of 1918 (*see* this chapter: *Migratory Bird Treaty Act*) protected dozens of species crossing numerous state and national borders. In light of these and other developments, a 1935 amendment extended the scope of the prohibitions contained in the Lacey Act, outlawing interstate commerce in wild animals killed or captured in violation of federal laws or those of any other nation.

Reflecting a greater concern with wildlife trade between the United States and other nations, an addition in 1949 prohibited transporting animals into the country in an "inhumane and unhealthful" manner. The secretary of the treasury, who has the responsibility for regulating imports, was directed to promulgate requirements for compassionate and hygienic modes of exporting wild animals to America. The amendment did not define "inhumane and unhealthful," but declared that solid evidence of a violation is any shipment containing "a substantial ratio of dead, crippled, diseased, or starving" animals.

The Lacey Act Amendments of 1981

The statute underwent a major overhaul in 1981, with virtually every section altered to some degree except the one banning imports of injurious wildlife. Congress removed section 5 entirely, which asserted that animals transported into a state are to be regarded as though they originated there.

Perhaps the most significant change is that now trafficking in *any* sort of protected animal is forbidden, either wild or bred in captivity, and including fish, reptiles, amphibians, mollusks, crustaceans, and invertebrates (plants either on state endangered species lists or protected by the Convention on International Trade in Endangered Species are also covered). A further strengthening of the prohibition makes the mere possession of animal contraband illegal, if so enjoined by state law, where formerly this provision had been confined to taking, transporting, or selling specimens.

Penalties for violating the Lacey Act are dramatically enhanced to a maximum fine of $20,000 and five years in prison, provided the market value of the animal traded is at least $350. Offenses that qualify for this magnitude of punishment are felonies, and the guilty party is liable to the seizure of all equipment used in the unlawful activity. Rewards may be offered by the secretary of the treasury for information that leads to an arrest or conviction. The amendments also weakened the *scienter* requirement for conviction; the Lacey Act can be violated even if the offender did not know that interstate commerce in species protected by state law is forbidden, and even if he or she had no intention of doing anything illegal. Nonetheless, to be blameworthy under the Lacey Act, an individual must be aware that in killing or capturing an animal he or she has broken a *state* law.

These 1981 modifications, and others, produced a retooled Lacey Act that has become one of the most powerful weapons in the arsenal of federal wildlife law enforcement. Charges brought under the act were uncommon before the amendments, but frequent afterwards. Subsequent litigation has ranged over several puzzling issues; for example, whether certain customs laws of foreign nations are motivated by wildlife conservation (which activates Lacey) or economics (which does not). Another problem is how to determine the market value of wildlife. A third addresses the constitutionality not only of the laws of foreign countries under their own constitutions, but also the laws of the states under ours: if such laws are unconstitutional, then there is no underlying violation upon which to base an offense against the Lacey Act.

One of these complications produced conflicting judgments from two federal appellate courts. In 1984 the Fifth Circuit Court of Appeals ruled that someone who provides service as a guide for an illegal hunt is in effect offering to sell wildlife in violation of the Lacey Act (*United States v.*

Todd). Two years later the Ninth Circuit Court of Appeals disagreed and declared that the sale of guide services is not equivalent to selling wild animals, so a guide on an illegal hunt could not be charged with a violation (*United States v. Stenberg*). Congress decided to settle the matter. A 1988 amendment to the Lacey Act makes it quite clear that "a person who for money or other consideration offers or provides guiding, outfitting, or other services . . . for the illegal taking . . . of fish or wildlife is deemed to have conducted a sale in violation of the Act."

Injurious Wildlife

The original Lacey Act outlawed the importation of "birds or animals" harmful to agricultural interests. An amendment in 1960 clarifies the sort of wildlife contemplated as injurious by specifying "wild mammals, wild birds, fish (including mollusks and crustacea), amphibians, reptiles, or the offspring or eggs of any of [these]" as subject to the ban. Further, the interests to be safeguarded from harmful wildlife are expanded beyond agricultural ones to encompass human well-being, forestry, and those of other wildlife.

The 1900 act also authorized the secretary of the treasury to promulgate regulations implementing the prohibition on injurious wildlife. None were produced until 1973, and by that time this responsibility had been shifted to the secretary of the interior. These regulations list some eleven mammalian genera, four bird species, a family of fish (*Clariidae*), a genus of crab (*Eriocheir*), and the brown tree snake (*Boiga irregularis;* currently found only on Guam) as banned from the United States. However, the director of the Fish and Wildlife Service can issue a permit allowing the importation of these animals "for zoological, educational, medical, or scientific purposes." Any exotic wildlife other than those listed in federal regulations may be imported for these purposes, and for exhibition and propagation, provided that they are declared to Customs at the port of entry and are held in captivity.

Interestingly, it is also contrary to federal regulations under the Lacey Act to import any uneviscerated fish of the salmon family unless they are certified as uncontaminated by any one of a variety of viruses, notably *Oncorhynchus masou*. The regulations contain two full pages of detailed instructions for performing the proper virus assay tests. This provision is, of course, not directed at the salmon but arises from fear of a life form harbored by the fish that could produce an epidemic.

MIGRATORY BIRD TREATY ACT OF 1918

By the early years of the twentieth century, it had become obvious to many scientists, conservationists, concerned citizens, and lawmakers that unrestricted hunting, both for sport and for markets in meat and feathers, had seriously depleted populations of migrating bird species. The question was what to do about it. The answer, regulating the hunting of migratory birds to conserve their numbers, was very easy to say but much harder to put into practice.

Initial Attempts to Conserve Migratory Birds

Nomadic flocks of birds travel hundreds of miles, even thousands of miles for some species, crossing the boundaries between states and international borders, too. Who is legally empowered to restrict taking them?

In the first decades of the 1900s, the federal government had yet to assert its authority over the states to comprehensively manage wildlife through regulation, and an international treaty for the same purpose was still in the experimental stage. Indeed, the historic case of *Geer v. Connecticut,* decided just before the century turned, saw the Supreme Court asserting that the individual states had the right "to control and regulate the common property in game" (*see also* this chapter: *Wildlife Law*). This ruling received strong reinforcement from the high court in 1912 in *United States v. The Abby Dodge.* The Fur Seal Treaty of 1911 (*see* this chapter: *Fur Seal Act of 1966: Fur Seal Treaty*), the first multinational agreement aimed at wildlife conservation, was quite limited in scope and dubiously effective, prohibiting only the hunting of fur seals on the open ocean.

In 1913 Congress boldly forged ahead into uncharted legal waters and passed the Migratory Bird Act, announcing that all migratory birds were under the care and protection of the U.S. government, and could be hunted only according to federal regulations. Ill-fated and short-lived, within two years two different district courts had declared this law unconstitutional because the Supreme Court had already ruled in *Geer* that wildlife not on federal land was the property of the states (*United States v. Shauver* and *United States v. McCullagh*). While the high court mulled over whether to review these lower court decisions, the United States signed the Convention for the Protection of Migratory Birds, an agreement with Canada to regulate hunting the birds, though the other signatory was Great Britain, the sovereign over our neighbors to the north.

The Canadian Convention divides migratory birds into three groups: game birds, nongame birds, and insect-eating birds. It stipulates that hunting is not allowed for insectivorous or nongame birds, except by permit for scientific reasons or to propagate the species. Inuit ("Eskimo") and American Indians may hunt some species of nongame birds for personal use as food and clothing. The same restrictions and exceptions apply to taking nests or eggs. Any migratory birds may be killed if they "become seriously injurious to agricultural or other interests in any particular community." According to the treaty, Canada and the United States can establish open hunting seasons on the game birds of 107 days (or less) at any time between September 1 and March 10; for the rest of March through August, all taking of these birds is banned. The dates of an open season do not have to be consecutive, so there can be multiple hunting seasons over this span on the calendar, as long as the total does not exceed 107 days.

In later years other nations became parties to the convention: Mexico in 1936, Japan in 1972, and the Soviet Union in 1976. The terms of the treaty remained substantially unchanged when these countries signed on, with a few minor variations. For example, the Mexican treaty sets the season at four months maximum, while Japan simply requires that hunting be prohibited during the primary nesting season of the species. Similarly, Russia (which accepted the treaty obligations of the U.S.S.R. after it became defunct) allows hunting seasons of unspecified duration so long as they are consistent with preserving the flocks. The Japanese and Soviet conventions also added broadly worded exhortations to the signatories to protect and preserve habitat.

Implementing the Treaty

In 1918 Congress passed the Migratory Bird Treaty Act (MBTA), executing and ratifying the Canadian Convention as federal law. Just as the 1913 Migratory Bird Act had been immediately challenged, it did not take long before a state argued that the MBTA represented an unconstitutional exercise of federal power over property that did not belong to the government in Washington, D.C.

Relying heavily on the *Geer* decision, Missouri sought a restraining order against a federal game warden who had attempted to enforce the MBTA there. Counsel for the United States appealed to the Supremacy Clause of the Constitution (Article VI, Section 2), which announces that duly enacted federal statutes "shall be the Supreme Law of the Land." Repudiating *Geer,* Supreme Court Justice Oliver Wendell Holmes asserted for the majority that "[w]ild birds are not in the possession of anyone, and possession is the beginning of ownership." He added that given the depleted condition of bird populations, the states clearly could not be relied upon to protect these species. *Missouri v. Holland* validated the MBTA while beginning to sound the death knell for the state ownership of wildlife doctrine.

The MBTA strengthens and adds more detail to the Canadian Convention, and authorizes federal agencies to devise regulations to achieve its goals. Section 2 declares that it is illegal to pursue, hunt, take, capture, kill, or to attempt to take, capture, or kill any migratory bird. Further, possessing, offering to sell, purchasing, bartering, transporting, exporting, or importing any bird, part of a bird, nest, or egg is prohibited. The Canadian Convention had merely prohibited the "shipment or export" of unlawfully taken migratory birds or bird parts. Section 3 empowers the secretary to issue regulations specifying the extent to which migratory birds may be hunted, taken, captured, killed, possessed, sold, purchased, transported, or exported. The "secretary" here was originally in the Department of Agriculture, but in 1939 Congress transferred rule-making authority under the MBTA to the Department of the Interior. Since that time MBTA regulations, in particular hunting restrictions, have been promulgated by the U.S. Fish and Wildlife Service (FWS), a division of the Interior Department. Also, the states are free to write their own laws or regulations to protect migratory birds, even more stringent ones, so long as they are consistent with the convention and the federal statute.

The MBTA provides for both felony and misdemeanor penalties. For many years, the legal condition of *scienter,* or "knowledge," that is, awareness of what one is doing, was not required to secure a felony conviction. However, in 1985 the Sixth Circuit Court of Appeals ruled that a felony conviction for violation of the MBTA without proof of *scienter* violated the right to due process of law as guaranteed by the Fourteenth Amendment (*United States v. Wulff*). Congress wrote an amendment the next year to account for this ruling. Now, to prove a felony violation prosecutors must show that the defendant knew he or she was taking, selling, bartering, or offering to sell a bird or bird part; at the same time, it is not necessary to prove that the accused knew he or she was violating the MBTA or that the bird was protected.

At about the same time as this amendment, the Sentencing Reform Act of 1984 significantly increased the punishment for federal crimes. Previously, MBTA maximums were a fine not to exceed $2,000 or incarceration for up to two years, or both, but with the sentencing reform the limits are now $250,000 and three years. A misdemeanor is any nonfelonious infraction of the MBTA and does not require *scienter* (*but see* this chapter: *Migratory Bird Treaty Act of 1918: Baiting*)—it is punishable by, at most, $5,000 (increased from $500) and six months in jail.

Hunting Migratory Birds

The MBTA was enacted to *control* the hunting of migratory birds, not to stop it. The statute, like all hunting regulation, is directed at the conservation of species, not the preservation or protection of individual birds (for more on general hunting laws, *see* chapter 5: *Recreational Hunting*). Although the MBTA does ban killing certain insectivorous and nongame species (with the exceptions noted above), most of these birds are too small and too dull to be desirable as food or for feathers, so they were rarely the target of hunters anyway. Today, of the approximately 800 species covered by the law, 170 are classified as game birds—liable to be pursued by shooters during the designated time period. Even so, over the last decade the

FWS has established hunting seasons for just forty-two species, and nearly all the migratory birds taken by hunters come from about half of this number: a dozen duck species (*Anas, Histrionicus, Aythya,* and *Aix* spp.), six of geese (*Branta* and *Chen* spp.), four of doves (*Zenaida* spp.), and two kinds of swan (*Cygnus* spp.). In 1999 hunters killed over 54 million of these birds. The wildlife species most frequently taken are of the genus *Zenaida:* one out of every four wild animals hunters slay is a dove.

The complicated process of writing the intricate hunting regulations that set the length of open seasons and "bag" limits (the maximum number of birds each hunter may legally kill) must be reprised each year, as the ecological status of the bird populations changes. It begins in May when the FWS conducts breeding surveys to determine how well the species have reproduced, followed by a census of bird numbers in July. At the end of this month, the FWS holds its annual Waterfowl Population Status meeting to clarify the present situation for ducks, geese, and swans. Data and recommendations for hunting rules are then passed on to four Flyway Councils, each composed of scientists and conservation officers from the wildlife agencies of the states over which migratory birds cross on their seasonal travels. North America's four major "flyways"—the Pacific, Central, Mississippi, and Atlantic—are routes consistently taken by most birds, generally north in the spring for breeding and then back south in the fall for wintering. In early August the councils and other representatives of state wildlife agencies gather with FWS officials to collaborate in formulating regulations for the flyways, the three "management units" (western, eastern, and central), and for Alaska. These are then proposed in the *Federal Register,* and just as with any rule making by a federal agency, interested parties have the opportunity to comment on them.

Final dates for the "early" hunting seasons and their bag limits are published in the *Federal Register* by September 1; "late" seasons and limits appear by October 1. The MBTA gives the FWS three and a half months to work with, so hunting seasons can be split, and some species are pursued over two or three different time periods. The FWS typically stipulates the dates of the early hunts, while the states are given blocks of days or "frameworks" that they can divide into two or three late seasons.

For example, in the eastern management unit, 1999 regulations for Louisiana allowed dove hunters to take this bird from September 4 to September 12, October 16 to November 15, and from December 13 to January 9; in Tennessee, it was September 2 to September 26, October 9 to October 24, and December 18 to January 4. In the flyways, ducks and geese had early hunting seasons of about ten days to two weeks during specified September dates. On the other hand, for the 1999–2000 late duck seasons, the states in the Atlantic, Mississippi, and Central flyways were given "outside dates" of October 2 and January 23, between which they could schedule up to sixty days of hunting, except in the Central, which got seventy-four days. In the Pacific Flyway, for ducks the states were allotted the entire 107-day period originally specified by the MBTA. Late goose hunting in 1999 was much more fine tuned, with seasons determined by the species hunted, the state in which the hunting was to be done, and often by "zones" within particular states.

Goose bag limits are also a function of these variables, ranging in 1999 from twenty "light geese" (Ross's and snow geese, *Chen rossii* and *C. caerulescens*, respectively) a day on late season hunts throughout the Mississippi and Central flyways, to three a day for the same species in the Pacific. For early hunts, the maximum take of Canada geese (*Branta canadensis*) was two in numerous states, but five in many others. Bag limits for most game birds do vary a great deal, depending on the species and the region. Other examples from 1999 include dove limits, set at ten per day in the western management unit and twelve to fifteen in the eastern and central; twenty-five rails (*Rallus* spp.) could be killed daily in any of the thirty-seven states with an open season on the bird, while the woodcock (*Scoloplax minor*) take was set at three; in New Mexico, hunters were allowed just one moorhen (*Gallinula chloropus*) a day, but next door in Texas the maximum for the same bird was fifteen.

Subsistence Hunting and Nontoxic Shot

Back in 1918 the MBTA did not include any special exemptions for Alaskan natives. Many of these people lived in remote areas and depended on game birds for food during the closed season, especially several species of geese. No such exceptions were subsequently written into MBTA regulations. Nonetheless, the FWS had an unwritten policy for years not to enforce the ban on hunting during the closed season in certain rural regions of Alaska, especially on the southwest coast in the vast delta formed by the Yukon and Kuskokwim Rivers.

In 1976 when the U.S.S.R. signed on to the Convention for the Protection of Migratory Birds, the Soviets insisted on a provision allowing subsistence hunting to accommodate indigenous peoples living in Siberia. Congress amended the MBTA two years later to authorize regulations permitting subsistence hunting, but no such regulations were ever produced. Instead, the FWS made it their official policy not to prosecute violations by subsistence hunters in Alaska. Then in 1984 some of these hunters living in the Yukon-Kuskokwin Delta region made an agreement with the FWS to reduce their subsistence take of four goose species, emperor (*Chen canagica*), white-fronted (*Anser albifrons*), brant (*Branta bernicla*), and Canada. The geese inhabit the delta of these two great rivers only between April and August, just the time the MBTA declares all migratory bird hunting ended.

Shortly after the FWS and the hunters struck this bargain, several conservation groups sued the Service, claiming that both the agreement and the failure to interdict subsistence hunters violated the MBTA. A federal district court decision upheld the deal. On appeal, however, the Ninth Circuit Court of Appeals ruled that regulations issued pursuant to the international treaty must be consistent with the terms accepted by all four signatories, and the Canadian Convention contained no allowance for subsistence hunting during the closed season. Although the court did not address this item, the principle also invalidates another federal regulation, one allowing Inuit and Alaskan Indians to take auks at any time (a family of water birds, *Alcidae*, protected as "nongame" species under the MBTA). The terms of the treaty with Mexico also had no special provision for hunting by indigenous peoples, probably because most Mexicans are *mestizos*, of mixed Spanish and Indian ancestry, and the nation has a large native population. The Ninth Circuit sided with the FWS on the enforcement issue, however, because the MBTA did not supply any guidelines for upholding the law. The Supreme Court declined to review this case (*Alaska Fish and Wildlife Federation and Outdoor Council v. Dunkle*).

In the years following this decision, the FWS was instrumental in drafting amendments to the Canadian and Mexican conventions that approved subsistence hunting and the taking of nongame species by Alaskan natives. The changes were accepted by the two nations and ratified by the Senate in 1997. In August 1999 the FWS produced a "Closed Season Enforcement Policy in Alaska" with special provisions for the Yukon-Kuskokwim Delta. For the rest of the state, the FWS asserted a diligence in enforcing the closed season and all other regulations for hunting migratory birds. In the Y-K Delta region, with certain exceptions, any migratory bird may be killed by subsistence hunters at any time, including the spring and summer months. Spectacled eiders (*Somateria fischeri*), Steller's eiders (*Polysticta stelleri*), and emperor geese must not be taken at any time, and brant, Canada, and white-fronted geese must not be taken during nesting, brood-rearing, or when flightless (after molting); taking the eggs of any of these species is also prohibited. With an assurance that "we will give enforcement priority to the[se] . . . violations," the FWS policy also bans the assistance of aircraft in hunting migratory birds, and, for the first time, affirms the active prosecution of hunters using lead shot.

The lead shot issue has been even more contentious than subsistence hunting out of season. Bird hunting is almost always done with a shotgun. When discharged, this weapon sprays a swath of 225 to 350 pellets (the "shot"), making it easier to take down a small, moving target. A bird hit with a shotgun blast is actually struck by only a portion of the pellets packed into the shell, and some or most of the little balls miss the mark and fall to the ground fairly quickly. Of course, all the shot descends to earth when the quarry is missed completely, and hunters rarely drop a bird with just one pull of the trigger.

As long ago as the 1870s (and probably earlier) people noticed that waterfowl often ingest spent pellets that drop into the lakes and ponds of their feeding areas. These birds need a certain amount of grit in their digestive tracts to aid in the breakdown of food, so they consume pebbles and sand, usually scooped up from the bottom of the wetlands they inhabit. The problem with this, one well documented by the 1920s, was that all shotgun pellets were made of lead, a metallic element that is toxic to birds (and mammals). Estimates diverged widely, but by the 1970s each year hunters were very likely depositing several thousand tons of lead pellets into America's wetlands, and several million waterfowl were dying from lead poisoning.

Convinced and alarmed by the data, the FWS issued regulations in 1976 banning lead shot in certain areas of all four flyways where the incidence of lead poisoning had been particularly high. Various hunting organizations, notably the National Rifle Association (NRA), and some state wildlife agencies staunchly opposed this measure. The states contended that they were not properly consulted on the matter and they were already overburdened with federal regulation of their wildlife. The hunters complained that nontoxic shot—such as steel pellets—damages the guns, creates a safety hazard to hunters, and costs more than lead. The NRA promptly sued the FWS, alleging that the ban on lead shot was arbitrary, capricious, and an abuse of agency discretion. The federal district court disagreed, and the appellate court affirmed that ruling (*NRA v. Kleppe*). Even so, in 1978 Congress attached a rider to the Department of the Interior appropriations bill that expressly denied funds to the FWS for enforcing the regulations, thus allowing the states to ignore them without fear of reprisal.

Undaunted, the Service continued to work for a complete ban on lead shot, and in 1986 announced a plan to gradually spread nontoxic shot zones across the nation over the next five years. States that resisted the program would find themselves bereft of all waterfowl hunting in these zones when the FWS unleashed the MBTA, the Bald Eagle Protection Act, and the Endangered Species Act to close down the shooting seasons there. So, as planned, in 1991 the FWS issued a rule requiring all migratory bird hunters everywhere to fire only nontoxic shot in their guns. Since that time, legal shot must be made of steel, tin, bismuth-tin, or tungsten alloys. Federal regulations detail a complex process of toxicity testing by which the FWS may approve shot of other metal compositions.

The FWS has placed two other prohibitions on the use of shotguns for hunting migratory birds: they cannot be larger than 10 gauge, or capable of firing more than three shells. Additional weapons restrictions include bans on rifles, pistols, swivel guns, machine guns, explosives, poisons, drugs, and any "stupefying substance." Migratory birds cannot be legally taken from any type of concealment below water level or from any motor vehicle, including aircraft, and hunters are not permitted to use electronic or recorded bird calls or live birds to lure waterfowl or other migratory birds closer to the guns.

Baiting

The lead shot versus steel shot issue did generate considerable debate in the 1970s and 1980s, but the deepest and most abiding source of controversy surrounding the hunting regulations for migratory birds has been focused on baiting (for more on baiting, *see* this chapter: *Legal Protections for Bears: Hunting Black Bears*).

An area of land or water liberally sprinkled with seed, grain, salt, or other feed is an irresistible attraction to birds, which naturally want to settle in and eat. Deliberately spreading food to attract the birds can also be a tactic very difficult for hunters to resist. Unlike most other forms of hunting, where the main task is to find the wildlife to shoot, bird hunting is largely about finding opportunities to fire on targets within shooting range. Migratory birds are not often hard to locate, but as winged creatures that routinely travel vast distances in a multidimensional world, they can take to the skies, or stay up there, and very easily avoid being shot. Baiting brings them down to earth, right where the hunter wants them.

Or some hunters want them there anyway. There seems to be little consensus on the propriety of baiting among those who take wildlife for recreation. There are those who reject baiting any species, including migratory birds, as "unsportsmanlike" while others opine that it depends on the animal pursued or on how sure the attraction is. Certainly fish are OK, some say, but not bears; and plastic decoys are fine, but not a bag of corn spread on a field. Unlike standards of "ethical" hunting, standards of legal hunting are codified, and FWS regulations on this matter have been quite clear since the 1920s: "No persons shall take migratory game birds . . . [b]y the aid of baiting, or on or over any baited area."

Even this seemingly straightforward directive contains complications. First, does a person violate the law if he kills migratory birds in an area that he does not know is baited? Neither the MBTA nor its regulations answered this question, so the federal judiciary had to decide. The prevailing opinion of these courts, dating back to at least the late 1930s, has been that *scienter* is not required to violate the baiting regulation (a misdemeanor). This establishes a strict liability status for these offenses: shooting birds over bait is illegal whether the hunter knows the area is baited or not. A *scienter* requirement is usually quite difficult for prosecutors to satisfy, since it demands proof of the contents of an individual's mind, and a defendant can always simply deny having the relevant knowledge. Most courts have rejected the notion that in writing the MBTA Congress expected federal prosecutors to accomplish this formidable task. Instead, those who wish to hunt migratory birds within the confines of the law must take it upon themselves to determine the conditions of the fields or wetlands where they pursue these creatures. A notable dissident from this counsel is the Fifth Circuit Court of Appeals, which ruled in *United States v. Delahoussaye* that the regulation is violated only when the hunter "should have known," or "could reasonably have . . . ascertained" that the area was baited.

A second legal puzzle in the baiting issue concerns two agricultural exceptions to the prohibition. For many years, federal regulations have allowed migratory bird hunting in croplands, and where grains or salt have been scattered so long as the presence of this bird-attracting feed is "solely the result of normal agricultural planting or harvesting; [or] . . . as the result of bona fide agricultural operations or procedures." So, say a farmer scatters grain in a nonstandard or abnormal way, aiming to produce a crop and without any thought of luring birds, but little or nothing grows. Meanwhile, a hunter shoots birds in the field. Is he in violation or do the exceptions protect him? The farmer did not intend to bait any birds, and believed the seeding would result in the growth of plants. Do these facts about the farmer's state of mind matter? There has been far less litigation and little judicial consensus on this question. In two of the most recent cases, one appellate court answered "yes" and another said "no."

The affirmative answer comes from the Fourth Circuit. Two hunters had been cited in 1993 for illegally killing birds in a field sown with wheat. They defended their actions by appeal to the agricultural exceptions, claiming that the farmer had scattered the seed so the resulting plants would curtail erosion in the field, not bait birds. The court rejected this defense, holding that the farmer's intentions were irrelevant: Because the wheat was unlikely to grow and would not prevent erosion even if it did, the scattering of grain here could not be a "normal" or "bona fide agricultural operation" (*United States v. Boynton*).

The Fifth Circuit Court, on the other hand, has held that the farmer's intentions are precisely the issue. Here, a Louisiana farmer seeded his field with winter wheat in late August 1997 and shortly thereafter hunted doves in the acreage. FWS agents charged him with hunting with the aid of bait. Citing *Boynton*, the district court asserted that it was immaterial what the farmer's intentions in sowing the seed were. What mattered was that the planting had occurred over three weeks earlier than the date for starting winter wheat recommended by the Louisiana State University Extension Service, so it was neither a "normal" nor a "bona fide" agrarian practice. On appeal, the Fifth Circuit reversed this decision, holding that a "bona fide agricultural operation" is one conducted "in good faith" or "without fraud," terms that incorporate for this exception a "subjective prong . . . [that] looks at the intent of the person scattering the grain." Accepting testimony that the defendant planted the wheat at the same time and in the same way that he and his father had done for many years, the court found that this qualified for the second agricultural exception, and vindicated the farmer (*United States v. Adams*).

Recall that in *Delahoussaye* the Fifth Circuit had also required a form of *scienter* for conviction under the baiting prohibition, indicating a bench enamored of a "subjective" element in the interpretation of this regulation. It is an interpretation quite congenial to numerous bird hunters, apprehended and convicted in other courts for hunting over bait, who pleaded ignorance about the condition of the areas in which they were shooting. Over the years, as successful prosecutions of the allegedly ignorant mounted, bills were often proposed in Congress to amend the MBTA to include a *scienter* requirement to the baiting offense. All failed until Alaska Representative Don Young's "Migratory Bird Treaty Reform Act" won approval in 1998, resulting in a redefinition of illegal baiting: Hunting of migratory birds is prohibited "[by] the aid of baiting, or on or over any baited area, where a person knows or reasonably should know that the area is or has been baited."

Moreover, in June 1999 the FWS restructured the agricultural exceptions and redefined some of the key terms, building in both a subjective element of intent, and an objective aspect determined by authoritative standards. Now, the second exception for a "bona fide agricultural operation" is jettisoned in favor of the "normal agricultural operation." This is defined as "a normal agricultural planting, harvesting, post-harvest manipulation, or agricultural practice, that is done in accordance with official recommendations of State Extension Specialists," such as those at LSU in *Adams*. In turn, a "normal agricultural planting, harvesting, or postharvest manipulation" is defined as "a planting or harvesting undertaken for the purpose of producing and gathering a crop, . . . that is done in accordance with official recommendations of State Extension Specialists."

The first exception is now separated into four aspects, beginning with a permission to hunt in "lands or areas where seeds or grains have been scattered solely as the result of normal agricultural planting, harvesting, or post-harvest manipulation." Because this is an agrarian practice "undertaken for the purpose of" yielding a crop, the farmer's intent is crucial for establishing this exception; but conformity of the practice to the views of the Extension Service is also needed. Additional exemptions are provided here for hunting from blinds camouflaged with natural vegetation or with vegetation from crops, so long as these do not serve as bait, or where grain is "inadvertently" scattered by the movements of the hunter. The new rule for the second exception is a bit perplexing. It allows hunting in areas spread with grain or seed only when this was caused by a "normal agricultural operation." Under the new definition, this operation is just a "normal agricultural planting, harvesting, or post-harvest manipulation," so it is not apparent how the second exception is distinct from the first one. The FWS explains that the first exception applies to the hunting of *any* migratory game bird, including waterfowl, while the second applies to the hunting of birds, *except* waterfowl. Yet a single exception for a "normal agricultural operation," defined as "a planting, harvesting, or post-harvest manipulation undertaken for the purpose of producing and gathering a crop, that is done in accordance with official recommendations of State Extension Specialists," along with the blind and accidental scattering provisions, would seem to cover everything.

At this writing, it remains to be seen how the federal judiciary will react to the new regulations.

BALD EAGLE PROTECTION ACT OF 1940 (BEPA)

In 1782 the Continental Congress adopted the bald eagle (*Haliaeetus leucocephalus*) as the national symbol, despite the objections of Benjamin Franklin whose preference was for the wild turkey (*Meleagris gallopavo*). Bald eagles are so called, not because their heads lack feathers but because colonists from England described them using the Middle English word "balled," meaning "shining white." In those colonial days, there were perhaps half a million nesting bald eagles spread throughout North America (except the desert southwest), 400,000 in Alaska alone. Over the next century and a half, the symbol of America was rampantly shot, trapped, and poisoned across its entire range. Fairly and unfairly blamed for predations on fisheries and young domestic animals, especially sheep, as well as providing a favored target for sport hunters and feather collectors, by the late 1930s the bald eagle had become exceedingly rare in the lower forty-eight states.

Legal Protections for Bald Eagles

Recognizing this, and asserting the value of the eagle as a symbol of freedom and strength, in 1940 Congress passed one of the earliest wildlife protection laws, the Bald Eagle Protection Act (BEPA). By enacting this legislation, Congress made it a federal offense for any person to "take" any bald eagle; that is, to pursue, shoot, shoot at, wound, kill, possess, capture, trap, molest, or disturb the bird. Also protected are the eggs and nest, as well as any part of the bird. The Department of the Interior and its secretary have the responsibility for administering and enforcing

BEPA, duties that are substantially fulfilled by an agency of the Interior Department, the U.S. Fish and Wildlife Service (FWS).

In 1940 violation of BEPA was a misdemeanor punishable by a maximum fine of $500 or six months in prison or both. Following an amendment in 1972, criminal penalties were added, raising the maximums to $5,000 or one year in prison, or both, for each violation. Also added in 1972 were the provisions that anyone who supplies information on an infraction that leads to conviction is entitled to collect half of the fine, and an individual found guilty of any violation who holds a livestock grazing agreement with the federal government may have the permit canceled.

Congress granted the secretary of the interior the authority to make two sorts of exceptions to the prohibition on taking bald eagles. First, the secretary may allow taking "for scientific or exhibition purposes of public museums, scientific societies, and zoological parks," and, second, "for the protection of wildlife or of agricultural or other interests in any particular locality." These exceptions are granted and a permit issued once a lengthy application has been approved by the director of the FWS. Taking applications for science or exhibition purposes must explain why the current number of bald eagles at the institution is insufficient. Applications to take eagles preying on livestock must specify the damage alleged to have been done by the birds. In either case, a permit will be issued only if the available data indicates that the taking will not adversely effect the preservation of the bald eagle.

BEPA Amendments
For almost twenty years following its enactment, BEPA did not succeed in halting the decline of the bald eagle. After an initial stabilization of eagle populations, the species suddenly confronted a new menace: DDT. This and other organochlorine insecticides were used in prodigious quantities following the Second World War for mosquito control, soaking coastal areas and wetlands. Bald eagles consumed contaminated fish and small mammals, which caused the shells of the birds' eggs to grow paper thin; the eaglets did not survive. By the late 1950s, there were only a few hundred nesting pairs in all the lower forty-eight states. There were troubles in Alaska too. As originally written, BEPA exempted the state from its provisions, despite the fact that, although it had the largest bald eagle population, Alaska also had the highest incidence of human depredations on the bird. An estimated 100,000 more bald eagles were killed in the Last Frontier before a 1959 amendment included the fiftieth state within its restrictions.

An amendment in 1962 extended the act's protections to cover golden eagles (*Aquila chrysaetos*), not so much because these raptors were in danger of extinction but more to protect immature bald eagles, which closely resemble goldens. Young bald eagles were being killed unwittingly by ranchers, mostly, who thought they were dispatching unprotected golden eagles. Since 1962, BEPA has often been called the Bald and Golden Eagle Protection Act. That year's amendments also included two new exceptions to the taking prohibition. The first authorized the secretary to allow the taking of golden eagles, upon request by a governor, to safeguard livestock populations in a given state. The second provided that the secretary could permit taking of both eagle species "for the religious purposes of Indian tribes." This second exception was later the subject of much debate in the courts, as we'll see below.

In the early 1970s a number of ranchers in Wyoming declared war on bald and golden eagles. Initially, this was waged furtively, but the media caught wind of the carnage and broadcast the sordid details throughout the country. Dozens of eagles were poisoned by thallium sulfate, consumed after the ranchers liberally laced sheep and lamb carcasses with the deadly substance and placed the bait on the open range. Even more brazen, the ranchers employed hunters to shoot from helicopters, and some 800 eagles were blasted from their nests and perches, and right out of the sky.

Although the helicopter hunting was clearly an unauthorized taking contrary to BEPA, as well as a breach of the then brand new Airborne Hunting Act, the Interior Department did not pursue the ranchers on the poisoning issue. This was because BEPA, the secretary contended, did not allow prosecution unless it could be shown that the person who placed the poison intended to kill the eagles, and this could not be demonstrated here. Congress reacted with a 1972 amendment that substantially lessened the degree of intent necessary to prove a violation; now whoever "knowingly, or with wanton disregard for the consequences of his act" takes any eagle is breaking the law. Moreover, just to be sure, Congress added the word "poison" in the definition of "take." The amendments of this year also enhanced the penalties for violation, as mentioned above, and allowed golden eagles, who are confirmed livestock predators, to be taken and used for falconry (traditionally employing the gyrfalcon and the peregrine, "falconry" more generically refers to training any bird of prey to hunt).

Still another exception to the taking prohibition was added in a 1978 amendment. At a time when America was struggling to meet its growing energy needs, and the OPEC oil embargo of just a few years earlier was a fresh and troubling memory, Congress discerned a potential conflict between the provisions of BEPA and the increasing reliance on domestic coal. Accordingly, language was added to the act empowering the secretary to permit the destruction of golden eagle nests (but not those of bald eagles) that would otherwise stand in the way of "resource development or recovery operations." Critics of this stipulation have seen it as a serious weakening of protection for golden eagles and have often pointed out that the amendment does not define what the phrase "resource development or recovery operations" means.

Bald eagle numbers began to rebound significantly in the mid-1970s following the Environmental Protection Agency's 1972 order banning the use of DDT in the United States. Further revitalization came in 1978 when, acting under authority of the Endangered Species Act (*see* this chapter: *Endangered Species Act*), the secretary of the interior added the bald eagle to the list of endangered species in forty-three states and designated the bird as threatened in Michigan, Minnesota, Oregon, Washington, and Wisconsin (bald eagles have never been imperiled in Alaska and they do not occur in the Hawaiian islands). More diligent enforcement and successful FWS restoration projects in the 1980s helped the species to flourish yet more. In 1995 the bald eagle was downgraded from endangered to threatened in those states where it had previously been so listed. Then the FWS announced in July 1999 that the bald eagle population stood at nearly 6,000 nesting pairs, and proposed that the raptor be removed entirely from the list of threatened and endangered species. At this writing, the lengthy process of delisting the threatened species continues.

BEPA and American Indians

Various treaties made with the U.S. government during the nineteenth century have, among other things, granted Indians rights to take wildlife on and off reservation lands. These treaty rights have sometimes clashed with both state and federal wildlife laws, raising the basic issue of whether the legislation abrogates or annuls the rights conferred by the treaty. Eventually, indeed inevitably, BEPA was tested on this issue in the courts, with incipient rulings producing contrary results. In 1974 the Eighth Circuit Court of Appeals held in *United States v. White* that BEPA did not annul treaty rights, but six years later the Ninth Circuit Court of Appeals demurred and ruled in *United States v. Fryberg* that it did. The Supreme Court agreed to settle this matter in 1986.

The case began several years earlier when the FWS launched an undercover investigation into illegal trafficking of eagle feathers by Indians in South Dakota. At that time, a single eagle feather might fetch up to $100 on the black market, and a full-length war bonnet as much as $5,000. The FWS discovered that from 1980 to 1983, over 300 eagles had been killed in and around the Lake Andes Wildlife Refuge in South Dakota, the feathers (and talons) sold to tourists and collectors. In 1983 fifty people were charged with various violations of BEPA and the Endangered Species Act. One of the accused, a Yanktonai Dakota (Sioux) named Dwight Dion, admitted that he had shot four bald eagles and one golden eagle. However, he defended his actions by appealing to the 1858 "Treaty with the Yancton," which created the Indian reservation where the shooting occurred, and entitled all Yanktonai to unrestricted hunting there. A federal district court accepted this defense and dismissed the charges. Predictably, given their verdict ten years earlier in *White*, the Eighth Circuit Court of Appeals affirmed.

Justice Thurgood Marshall wrote the opinion for a unanimous court in *United States v. Dion*, reversing the lower tribunals. He sought first to determine if Congress in writing BEPA intended the law to abrogate conflicting treaty rights. Although there was no explicit statement of such an intention in either the language of the act or in the legislative history, abrogation was "strongly suggested" by the 1962 amendment establishing a permit system allowing Indians to take eagles for religious purposes. After all, Marshall reasoned, why have a permit system if BEPA does not in other instances ban Indians from taking eagles? The conclusion was inescapable that the 1962 amendment expressed an "explicit legislative policy that Indian hunting of the bald and golden eagle, except pursuant to permit, is inconsistent with the need to preserve those species." Therefore, since Congress has the power to modify or eliminate treaty obligations, whether with foreign nations or Indian nations, the drafters of BEPA intended to do just that when treaties conflict with it.

The exemption for ceremonial use by Native Americans has itself generated a fair amount of controversy. Indians have contended that the permit system allowing them to take eagles for religious purposes is an unconstitutional infringement on their right to practice their religion free from government constraints, as guaranteed by the First Amendment: "Congress shall make no law respecting an establishment of religion, or prohibiting the free exercise thereof." They believe the acquisition of feathers for this end should be entirely unregulated by the government. A federal district court agreed with them in 1986, declaring that the application procedure for the permit was "unnecessarily intrusive and hostile to religious privacy" (*United States v. Abeyta*). However, that year another district court rejected this argument, and the Ninth Circuit Court of Appeals affirmed that ruling without comment (*United States v. Thirty-Eight Golden Eagles*).

Most recently, in 1997, the Ninth Circuit did feel compelled to issue an opinion endorsing the conviction of two Crow Indians, brothers named Frank and William Hugs, for violating BEPA (*United States v. Hugs*). The Hugses admitted trapping, shooting at, shooting, and killing a number of bald and golden eagles on the Crow Reservation in Montana. Nonetheless, they claimed that their right to free exercise of religion is denied both by BEPA's taking prohibition, and by a burdensome permit system in which as much as two years might elapse between the time an application is submitted and its subsequent approval. Although the evidence indicated that the Hugses were far more interested in selling eagle parts for profit than using them in religious ceremonies, Judge James Browning accepted their defense appealing to the right to free exercise of religion. To evaluate this appeal, Browning looked to the Religious Freedom Restoration Act (RFRA), designed in 1993 to adjudicate conflicts between government legislation and religious practices. The RFRA forbade laws that substantially burden the free exercise of religion unless imposing the burden advances a "compelling government interest and is the least restrictive means of furthering that interest."

Browning conceded that BEPA and the permit system presented a substantial impediment on the practice of some Native American religions, but the law did indeed further a very important government concern in the health and flourishing of these raptor species. He went on to list the basic information required on the application—including the nature of the ceremony, the applicant's authorization to participate in it, and verification of his tribal affiliation—but asserted that this was the least restrictive method of promoting that compelling interest. In any case, since the Hugses did not attempt to secure a permit, they were barred from challenging its constitutionality.

At this writing, the Supreme Court has not yet considered BEPA in light of the right to free exercise of religion; the judgment of the Ninth Circuit stands as the benchmark on this matter. (For more on the right to free exercise of religion and the use of animals, *see* chapter 4: *Legal Challenges to Ritual Slaughter*).

FUR SEAL ACT OF 1966

North of Alaska's Aleutian Archipelago in the eastern Bering Sea lie four small, rocky islands named for a Russian navigator, Gerassim Pribilof. When the Russians discovered the Pribilof Islands for the Western world in 1786, they were primarily in pursuit of the sea otter (*Enhydra lutris*) and the money to be made in trading the luxuriant fur of the species, but here they found something that proved quite lucrative as well.

On one of the four islands, which came to be called St. Paul, they found hundreds of thousands of northern fur seals (*Callorhinus ursinus*), perhaps as many as 4 million in all. As the Russians quickly learned, each summer the seals came in enormous numbers to these tiny speckles of land to mate and bear their pups. Although these rookeries are found on a few other islands scattered about the Bering Sea, for reasons that are still not well understood the seals congregate in the Pribilofs at a rate triple that of all other sites combined.

The pelt of the sea otter is incredibly lush, containing about 500,000 hairs in each square inch, and hence was worth forty or fifty times as much as that of the seal, whose hair density was perhaps half of the otter's. Yet the seals were so unfailingly gathered at the Pribilofs in such vast numbers, and were so easy to kill, the Russians could not resist exploiting the resource. Agile and swift in the water, the pinnipeds are clumsy and slow on land. The slaughter of a seal (then as now) was accomplished simply by walking up to one, clubbing it on the head—crushing the thin skull—and following that with a stab in the heart so the animal would bleed out. The Russians took to this grim task with alacrity, employing Aleut Indians to kill and skin about 70,000 seals every year, this despite the relatively low demand for seal fur in the late eighteenth century. Within two decades after sealing began on St. Paul Island, nearly 1 million sealskins were stored away in warehouses, rotting to pieces.

The Russian government finally put a stop to the unrestricted killing in the 1820s. The Russian-American Company, which had received a charter from the czar in 1799, was ordered to take no more than 50,000 fur seals annually, and to take none at all every five years so that the herd could recover. This early effort at government-imposed wildlife conservation worked, for the most part, and by the time Secretary of State William Henry Seward had negotiated the 1867 purchase of Alaska from Russia, the Pribilof seal population was probably close to the preexploitation number of between 2 and 4 million animals.

American Sealing in the Pribilof Islands

The Pribilof Islands were part of Seward's deal (or his "folly," as the shortsighted derisively called it), instantly transforming the rocks into American territory, and the seals into American property. Within a few years, Congress had authorized the Treasury Department to bestow the exclusive right to harvest fur seals upon the Alaska Commercial Company (ACC).

ACC's twenty-year lease stipulated a maximum take of 100,000 annually, none at sea, none with guns, and only male yearlings or older. When the lease expired in 1890, slightly more than 2 million seals had been killed at a profit margin for ACC stockholders of nearly 80 percent. For its part, the United States derived more money in taxes and tariffs from the Pribilof seal trade alone—over $10 million—than the country had paid for all of Alaska itself—$7.5 million. None of this wealth could have been acquired if the demand for sealskin garments had not exploded in the 1870s, increasing tenfold within a decade. The first modern fur coat was probably made from sealskin.

This lust for fashion, fueled by a government-supported monopoly in the days before antitrust law, along with seriously mistaken population estimates, proved terribly costly to the seals. In 1890 there were no more than 800,000 animals in rookeries that had once contained four or five times that number. ACC's lease was not renewed. The North American Commercial Company (NACC) got the prize instead, under similar terms, though the annual quota was reduced to 60,000. However, by this time the fur seal population was so depleted that only once in the twenty-year life of NACC's lease were even half that many taken; the average was only 17,000. Even so, demand for sealskin coats and capes remained high and NACC cleared several million dollars in profit.

Meanwhile, another source of decimation to the fur seal population came in the form of "pelagic sealing," the practice of hunting seals on the open sea. During forty years of a U.S.-sanctioned fur seal monopoly in the Pribilofs, enjoyed first by the ACC and then the NACC, hundreds of vessels operated by Russian, Japanese, Canadian, and independent American sealers plied the eastern Pacific Ocean, hunting the pinnipeds with spears, harpoons, shotguns, and rifles. This method is extremely wasteful, and, coupling the high demand with the total absence of any legal regulation, was guaranteed to cause a crisis for the fur seal as a species.

The major problem with pelagic sealing is that once a seal is fatally shot or struck, it invariably and irretrievably sinks. Conservatively, two animals are lost for every one that is taken. Records indicate that over those forty years, at least 1.3 million skins were sold by pelagic sealers, which, given a two-to-one kill-to-take ratio, means a total of almost 4 million were destroyed. Add to this number the seals taken in the Pribilofs by the Russians, the ACC, and the NACC and we have the astonishing figure of over 10 million fur seals killed between 1786 and 1911. With the exception of the white-tail deer, no other wild mammal species of the United States has been slaughtered in such numbers.

The Fur Seal Treaty of 1911

By the mid-1880s, it was clear that the northern fur seal was in trouble. The federal government decided the problem was unrestricted pelagic sealing. American Revenue ships began seizing vessels found seal hunting in the Bering Sea, nearly setting off an international incident with Great Britain when several Canadian schooners were apprehended. The Americans held the view, untenable from the perspective of international law, that fur seals in the open ocean were rather like cattle strayed from the home pasture (namely, the Pribilofs), and not like whales, which belonged to whoever caught them. Despite this flimsy argument, the United States and Great Britain agreed in 1892 to prohibit their citizens (including especially Canadians) from sealing pelagically in the north Pacific and Bering Sea from May through July of each year, and at any time within sixty miles of the Pribilof Islands.

This measure did little to solve the problem of fur seal decline. Canada did nothing to enforce the seasonal ban, and many American sealers simply ignored it, taking their chances at being caught—a good bet since the United States could not adequately police the entire Bering Sea. What is more, the Japanese had entered the fur seal business from their side of the north Pacific, an area that was in any case not subject to the Anglo-American agreement. The Russians had never stopped sealing. As the first decade of the twentieth century ended, there were perhaps 300,000 northern fur seals remaining on the globe.

Finally, after several years of urging by Secretary of State Elihu Root and the Taft administration, the principal sealing nations—America, Great Britain, Russia, and Japan—managed to agree upon the articles of a "Treaty for the Preservation and Protection of Fur Seals." Designed to regulate the harvest and save the species, pelagic sealing was the main target of the Fur Seal Treaty of 1911, the congressional ratification of the international agreement. The signatories consented to a complete ban on pelagic sealing for at least fifteen years, leading to a prohibition in perpetuity if there were no subsequent objections; there have been none, and the ban remains in effect to this day. Further, the treaty empowered each nation to seize any vessel engaged in pelagic sealing, unless the offending ship was in its own territorial waters. Apprehended pelagic sealers were to be delivered expeditiously to the nation under whose flag they sailed, and only that nation could prosecute and penalize the wrongdoers. The treaty further stipulated that Aleuts, Indians, Ainos "and other aborigines" were exempt from the ban, so long as they pursued seals in muscle- or wind-powered boats and did not use firearms.

The agreement mandated compensation in exchange for mutual restraint on pelagic sealing. Canada (as represented by its sovereign, Great Britain) received a percentage of the land sealing take from the United States, Russia, and Japan. Russia and the United States shared a portion of their harvest with the other two nations but not with each other, while Japan was required to hand over a percentage to all three of the other signatories. Another major provision prohibited importing sealskins that had not been officially stamped and certified as being the product of a government-authorized harvest. However, the treaty did not provide any formula by which seal harvest quotas would be established; instead, each nation was given complete discretion to set their own maximums.

Such freedom might have spelled a return to the days of overexploitation, but the lesson seemed to have been learned. Within twenty-five years after the treaty was signed, seal numbers had returned to around 2 million. Never thoroughly satisfied with the agreement and in any case preparing for war, Japan withdrew from the treaty in 1940, which led to its expiration one year later. Canada and the United States reached a temporary agreement in 1942, allotting 20 percent of the Americans' take to the Canadians each year. This covenant governed the Pribilof harvest until 1957.

The Fur Seal Act of 1966

Canada (now her own sovereign), Japan (recovered from the ravages of war), the Soviet Union (having replaced the Russian Empire), and the United States entered into a new agreement in 1957. The Interim Convention on the Conservation of North Pacific Fur Seals adopted all the basic tenets of the 1911 treaty, but added something new: an explicit mission statement for managing the pinnipeds. This mandated "maximum sustainable productivity of the fur seal resources . . . so that the fur seal population can be brought to and maintained at the levels which will provide the greatest harvest year after year." Also original to the 1957 convention was the creation of the North Pacific Fur Seal Commission, which was directed to make recommendations on harvest quotas while developing and implementing an elaborate research program; one representative from each nation sits on the commission.

The 1957 convention was labeled "interim" because initially it was intended to govern fur sealing for just six years, but the agreement was extended in 1963 for another six years and another extension was ratified in 1969, this time for seven years. In 1966 Congress passed the Fur Seal Act, officially codifying at the domestic level U.S. obligations contained in the compact with Canada, Russia, and Japan. These were substantially the same as those articulated in the 1911 treaty, as listed above, but included an explicit prohibition on taking seals, possessing, transporting, importing, or offering seals or parts of seals for sale unless authorized to do so by the secretary of commerce. In 1976 the interim convention was extended yet again, and the United States persuaded its treaty partners to accept amendments calling for research into how seal populations were affected by commercial fisheries and environmental changes resulting from human activity.

The 1976 continuation lasted until 1981 when the fifth and final extension was agreed upon, but only for a four-year period. Meanwhile, the Pribilof harvest steadily declined through the 1970s, cutting the annual take in half by 1983. The total fur seal population in the north Pacific was estimated at only about 800,000. The precise causes were not clear, but may have been due to a pinniped epidemic, seals drowning in lost or discarded fishing gear, or the increased take of pollock by commercial fisheries, a prime prey of fur seals in the north Pacific. Probably all these factors, and others, worked in concert against the seals.

Recognizing the decay of fur seal numbers and anticipating more, Congress amended the Fur Seal Act in 1983, establishing a $20 million

Pribilof Islands Trust Fund for the benefit of the Aleuts living on the islands, some families having done so for several generations dating to the time of the Russians. The point of the fund was to prepare the Indians for the demise of the industry by promoting a "stable, self-sufficient, enduring, and diversified economy not dependent upon sealing." Further amendments in 1988 and 1990 added another $12.2 million.

The End of Commercial Sealing in the Pribilof Islands

By 1984 public outrage at sealing generally had been building for nearly twenty years since film of the Canadian harp seal (*Phoca groenlandica*) slaughter near Newfoundland first received a wide viewing in Europe and America. Book-length accounts of the carnage soon followed, notably Brian Davies's *Savage Luxury: The Slaughter of the Baby Seals*. Additional graphic film footage showed harp seal pups, prized for the white fur of their infancy, being pounded with gaffs and clubs, only to be skinned apparently alive and conscious.

To the American public, it made little difference whether the particulars involved harp seals harvested by Canadians in the north Atlantic or fur seals dying by American hands in the north Pacific—the killing had to stop. Tactics had to vary, of course, because U.S. jurisdiction did not extend to Canadian waters. When Orwell's special year arrived, American and European objections and boycotts had prompted import bans on harp sealskin in those nations, and Canada had outlawed both the gaff and the taking of "whitecoat" pups. Nonetheless, harp sealing near Newfoundland continued through the 1980s and into the late 1990s, when the annual kill rate stood at just under 200,000 animals. Yet for reasons that are not clear, the seal slaughter plummeted in 2000 to only 91,000 taken, resulting in a slashing of pelt prices to half the value of 1999.

Back in 1984 and the north Pacific, commercial taking of fur seals in the Pribilofs ended. That year, for the first time, the Senate did not ratify another perpetuation of the interim convention. Rallied by various animal welfare groups, such as Greenpeace and Sea Sheperd, which had tried and failed to have the fur seal listed as threatened under the Endangered Species Act (*see* this chapter: *Endangered Species Act*), public sentiment against killing any seals at all had reached a strident pitch and the Senators heard the cry. With the international agreement evaporated, and the Fur Seal Commission defunct in effect, regulation of the Islands' herd fell entirely to the Fur Seal Act and the Marine Mammal Protection Act (MMPA) (*see* this chapter: *Marine Mammal Protection Act*). Enacted in 1972, the MMPA placed a moratorium on all taking of marine mammals—including pinnipeds, of course—unless the secretary of commerce issued a waiver for various purposes, none of which applied to the fur seal. Moreover, the Fur Seal Act prohibits such taking unless authorized by the secretary through regulation, and no such authorization appeared.

Both federal laws do, however, permit the Aleuts (as well as "Eskimos and Indians") to take fur seals for subsistence purposes only, defined as taking "for food, clothing, shelter, heating, transportation, and other uses necessary to maintain the life of the taker or for those who depend upon the taker to provide them with such subsistence." The Aleuts have killed about 1,600 fur seals each year since 1985 for these purposes, and at the turn of the twentieth century the species now numbers about 1 million individuals.

LEGAL PROTECTIONS FOR WHALES

For countless millennia whales swam the world's oceans unmolested. Although their existence was well known at least as early as biblical times (the Book of Genesis specifically notes their creation by God), and in the fourth century B.C.E. Aristotle wrote in the *History of Animals* that they were air-breathing fish, it was not until the third or fourth centuries C.E. that the Japanese began actively pursuing whales on the open sea. In the eleventh century, Basques venturing out of the Bay of Biscay and Norwegians from the Scandinavian Peninsula began hunting large cetaceans in the north Atlantic Ocean. By 1650 the Dutch, English, and Americans had joined them, plying the warm waters of the Gulf Stream under sail power, hurling iron harpoons when they chanced to get close enough to the beasts that the strength of an arm might prove sufficient to doom some of the biggest living things on the earth. These early whalers mainly targeted the slower and more tractable right whale (*Balaena glacialis*), so named because it was the "right whale" to hunt. Nonetheless, success in this sort of hunt was not common.

In the nineteenth century everything changed. Ships equipped with steam-powered engines and guns firing grenade-tipped harpoons efficiently destroyed tens of thousands of whales, feeding an enormous demand for whale oil and baleen. It is said that these ships, sailing under the flags of many countries (including the United States), killed more whales between 1870 and 1910 than *Homo sapiens* had managed to slay in all of human history prior to that four-decade period. After that, whales became increasingly difficult to find.

First Attempts at Whale Protection

By 1925 concern that whales were disappearing led the League of Nations to recommend international control of the whaling industry with regulations designed to halt excessive exploitation of cetaceans. Toward this end, the Bureau of International Whaling Statistics was formed in 1930 with a mission to provide the world community with accurate numbers on whale populations and how many were being taken. The next year, the Convention for the Regulation of Whaling was signed by twenty-two nations, the first multinational agreement to curb whale killing. Unfortunately, the 1931 convention did not provide effective protections, largely because the two dominant whaling nations—Japan and the Soviet Union —refused to sign it. Also, the stipulations of the convention were rather weak, confined to such items as sparing calves and nursing mothers, and avoiding the waste of whale carcasses. In 1932 at least 43,000 whales were killed.

Little was accomplished to rectify the situation until after the Second World War, although the war itself considerably slowed commercial whaling. Finally, in December 1946 a new and improved agreement was ratified that substantially governs whaling to this day: the International Convention for the Regulation of Whaling. Fewer nations signed this compact than had done so in 1931, but Japan and the Soviet Union were two that did, holding out promise that the tide could be turned in favor of the whales. The convention created the International Whaling Commission (IWC), an administrative and regulative body charged with overseeing whale conservation around the world, wherever the leviathan is found. The IWC consists of one representative from each signatory nation, and has the authority to designate protected whale species, declare open and closed seasons and ocean regions, specify whaling methods, and determine size and take limits.

As the nation had done in 1931, the United States signed the 1946 agreement. It remained then for Congress to write a statute that would provide the legal framework for implementing American obligations under the convention. The Whaling Convention Act of 1949 (WCA) is founded on the judgment that whales have enormous scientific and aesthetic value, and are essential components of the marine ecosystem. The act authorizes the president to appoint a commissioner to the IWC, and the secretary of state to register objections to IWC regulations. American citizens and persons sailing in U.S. waters are prohibited from killing or wounding whales, transporting, purchasing, selling, or offering to sell whales or whale products in violation of IWC regulations or regulations issued by the secretary of commerce.

The United States has not issued a license for taking whales since shortly before its self-imposed moratorium on whaling in 1972, but the WCA does authorize the secretary to issue such licenses. Applicants must prove that the whale-catching vessel is appropriately equipped and staffed to pursue whales in a manner consistent with the convention, and with regulations issued by the IWC and the federal government. Further, compensation for the crew of the whaling vessel cannot be a function of the number of animals caught. Licenses may also be granted, under sim-

ilar constraints, to ocean-going vessels capable of processing whale carcasses at sea ("factory ships") and to factories that process whale remains
into various products ("land stations"). Finally, the WCA empowers
Coast Guard or U.S. Custom officers, or U.S. marshals to conduct warrantless searches on any vessel in U.S. waters that an officer has reasonable cause to believe is engaged in illegal whaling. Individuals committing acts in violation of the WCA, the convention, or relevant regulations
who are observed by law enforcement officers may be immediately arrested. Convictions are punishable by up to one year in prison and a
$10,000 fine, or both.

Whales Continue to Decline
From within a decade of its inception in 1946 to this day the IWC has
been subjected to much criticism from conservationists and whale advocates generally. Particularly impressive and depressing to these critics has
been the fact that a number of cetacean species continued to decline for
years after the IWC was in place. For example, after two decades of "regulating" the whaling industry, the IWC was compelled to issue a ban in
1966 on all taking of blue (*Balaenoptera musculus*) and humpback
(*Megaptera novaeangliae*) whales, for fear the two species would fade into
extinction. Such failures led some to derisively label the commission "the
whalers' club."

Part of the problem has always been that the IWC was given an arguably incompatible set of convention objectives, calling for both increased whale populations and the expansion of the whaling industry.
Moreover, the regulatory structure with which the IWC must work is
hardly conducive to conservation: any IWC proposal can be defeated if
more than one-quarter of the representatives reject it, and a nation can
safely ignore any approved directive simply by registering an objection to
it within ninety days. This escape clause has been exploited many times.

Especially outrageous for many was the IWC's refusal to endorse a
moratorium on whaling, beginning in 1972. During the late 1960s, with a
heightening environmental awareness and the much-publicized plight of
such species as the blue and the humpback, whales captivated Americans
in a manner unprecedented for any wild animal before or since. "Save the
Whales" T-shirts and bumper stickers appeared everywhere. "Whale
watching" became a favorite pastime off both coasts (and indeed today is
a multimillion dollar business, a dimension of "ecotourism"). Hordes of
naturalists and photographers, led by Jacques Cousteau, took to the seas
with cameras and sound equipment to record the creatures' amicable disposition and eerie, yet alluring, "songs."

With public opinion overwhelmingly sympathetic and its commercial
whaling industry extinct, America became the foremost defender of big

cetaceans on the planet. The United States enacted the Marine Mammal Protection Act of 1972 (see this chapter: *Marine Mammal Protection Act*), outlawing virtually all taking of any type of whale by American citizens or in territorial waters. And so it was that U.S. insistence that year led the United Nations Conference on the Human Environment, held in Stockholm, to forcefully recommend that the IWC impose a ten-year moratorium on all commercial whaling. The IWC stubbornly resisted the "Stockholm Declaration," as it was called, for ten years.

Meanwhile, determined to exert an influence that would lead to a total ban on whaling, the United States turned to the only practical mechanism available on the international level, short of war: trade sanctions. The "Pelly Amendment" to the Fishermen's Protective Act of 1967 empowered the president to severely limit imports of fish products from nations "certified" by the secretary of commerce to have "diminished the effectiveness" of conservation measures aimed at "any living resource of the sea," including, of course, whales. Although nations were certified on two occasions during the 1970s, no trade sanctions were ever imposed, so in 1979 Congress decided to add some muscle to the law with the "Packwood-Magnuson Amendment" to the Fishery Conservation and Management Act. This revision made sanctions mandatory: when a nation was certified as setting back whale conservation, the president was required to cut their fishery allocation in half throughout the 200-mile wide U.S. conservation zone along both coasts.

The Moratorium and Its Aftermath
The IWC met in Brighton, England, in 1982 and finally obtained the three-fourths majority needed to approve the indefinite cessation of commercial whaling anywhere in the world, effective in 1986. There was much jubilation from all those concerned with cetacean welfare, but their joy quickly dampened when the Soviet Union, Norway, and Japan all filed objections to the moratorium, stating that they had no intention of halting whaling at any time.

Even so, in 1985 the Soviet Union announced that it would end commercial operations within two years; however, the Soviets then promptly exceeded their allocation of minke whales (*Balaenoptera acutorostrata*). In accordance with the Pelly and Packwood-Magnuson Amendments, the secretary of commerce immediately certified the Soviet Union, costing them millions of dollars in lost revenue from fish that would have been taken in the U.S. conservation zone. The certification was revoked in 1987 when the Soviets did as they said they would and stopped whaling. Norway too was certified under similar circumstances, and when they also agreed to cease whaling in 1987, the sanction was withdrawn.

For its part, Japan rejected an IWC directive reducing the sperm whale

(*Physter macrocephalus*) quota to zero in 1984. When the United States threatened trade sanctions, the Japanese succeeded in negotiating an agreement with the Americans in which they pledged to reduce their sperm whale kill and, beginning April 1, 1988, abide by the moratorium. In exchange, the United States would not certify Japan and no penalties would be levied. The deal was contested by whale advocates, who claimed the law clearly demanded that Japan be certified; the Supreme Court disagreed and allowed the negotiated arrangement (*Japan Whaling Association v. American Cetacean Society*). Nonetheless, the future looked bright for the whales: the three remaining whaling nations had all agreed to the moratorium.

Yet a loophole existed in the convention, and Japan exploited it to the fullest. Article VIII stipulates that any signatory nation may issue permits that authorize killing whales for scientific research, known as "research whaling." Moreover, the remains of whales taken for research purposes may by processed and sold in whatever manner the nation prescribes. Instead of observing the moratorium as promised, in 1988 Japan proceeded to award its fleets permits for research whaling, and have done so every year since that time. Up to the close of the 1999 season, Japan has killed 4,554 whales, mostly antarctic minkes in the IWC-designated Southern Ocean Whale Sanctuary. Incredibly, although Japan has been certified by the United States on several occasions since 1988, no significant trade sanctions have ever been imposed.

Likewise for Norway. Following Japan's lead, Norway began issuing scientific permits for whaling in 1988. Then in 1993, despite having committed to the moratorium, Norway changed its mind and, eschewing the "research whaling" maneuver, began a blatantly commercial harvest of minke whales in the northeast Atlantic Ocean. Each year since then, Norway has set rapidly escalating quotas for its minke take, numbers that stand in 1999 at 750 whales annually. Like Japan, Norway has been certified more than once, but without having suffered any trade sanctions, perhaps because it could easily retaliate by withdrawing exploration licenses to U.S. oil companies. In March 1999 Iceland's Parliament passed a resolution to resume commercial whaling within its territorial waters. Iceland is not a member of the IWC.

In 1992 the IWC began to pave the way for a resumption of commercial whaling for its membership by developing "revised management procedures." By 1994 a plan was in place whereby large-scale whaling could begin when a given whale stock increased to at least 54 percent of its population total in the "pre-exploitation" days before overhunting decimated the cetaceans. The United States has opposed the plan and, indeed, the Marine Mammal Commission has issued a report, approved by Congress, emphasizing that the value of whales goes beyond their use as natural resources, that moral considerations speak against a return to commercial whaling at any time. In any case, the "revised management procedures" have to this date never been implemented, but they may not be long in coming. At the July 1999 meeting of the IWC, it was noted that before the scheme could be executed "work on a number of issues, including specification of an inspection and observer system must be completed." One year later, however, Japan and Norway exerted sufficient pressure at the July 2000 meeting to persuade the IWC to accelerate the drafting of a new whale management plan. The two nations and a number of other countries interested in pursuing commercial whaling will meet in Japan in early 2001 to complete the work on this project.

Aboriginal Subsistence Whaling

The moratorium adopted by the IWC admits of only two exceptions. One of these—scientific research—has been used by Japan and Norway to continue hunting, violating the spirit if not the letter of the whaling suspension, as we have seen. The other exception has been nearly as controversial. It allows taking whales "when the meat and products of such whales are to be used exclusively for local consumption by the aborigines" and when a continuing subsistence need has been proved. "Aboriginal subsistence whaling" is defined as "whaling . . . carried out by or on behalf of aboriginal, indigenous or native peoples who share strong community, familial, social, and cultural ties relating to a continuing dependence on whaling and on the use of whales."

The controversy started mildly enough in Alaska, where Inuit whaling communities on the north slope had been engaged in unregulated and unrestricted hunting of bowhead whales (*Balaena mysticetus*) for many centuries. The IWC determined in 1977 that bowhead numbers in the Arctic Ocean could be as low as 600 individuals, and quickly asserted a complete prohibition on all bowhead hunting. With support from the federal government, the newly formed Alaska Eskimo Whaling Commission managed to prevail upon the IWC to lift the ban in 1978 and allow the Inuit to take twelve whales each year, as permissible aboriginal subsistence whaling. Since then, bowhead numbers have increased, and the annual quota is now fifty-four.

Contention over the aboriginal subsistence exception began to build in 1994. Inspired by both the success of the Inuit in managing whales while maintaining a key cultural element, and by the signal event of the removal of the gray whale (*Eschrichtius robustus*) from the Endangered Species list, the Makah Indians of Washington's Olympic Peninsula decided to take up whaling again. For nearly seventy years, the Makah had abandoned whaling following the severe depletion of gray whales by commercial whalers and increased pressure by the Bureau of Indian Affairs to pursue farming. Now, the tribe needed the approval of the IWC and the bestowal of the aboriginal subsistence exception before they could legally return to this hunting tradition.

Several tribal members accompanied the U.S. delegation to the 1996 IWC meetings in Aberdeen, Scotland, seeking the subsistence exception. To almost everyone's surprise, the U.S. delegates withdrew their proposal to permit whaling by the Makah, citing concerns about the training of the Indian whalers and their methods of hunting. However, the Americans pledged their support of the Makah and their willingness to press the matter the following year at the meetings in Monaco.

After the IWC adjourned in October 1997, it was widely reported that the commission had granted the Makah a subsistence exception to hunt four gray whales each year. In fact, no such proposal was ever presented, let alone approved. A clear majority in the IWC did not believe the Makah had "strong community, familial, social, and cultural ties relating to a continuing dependence on whaling and on the use of whales." Instead, the Clinton administration cut a deal with the Russian Federation, exchanging four gray whales from the allotment slated to go to the Chukotka of eastern Siberia for an equal number of bowhead whales allotted to the Inuit of Alaska. Thus the IWC quota of 124 gray whales for aboriginal populations in the Pacific remained unchanged, and the Makah could go whaling again. By spring 1998 the National Marine Fisheries Service (NMFS) had issued the Makah a license for aboriginal subsistence whaling, and the National Oceanic and Atmospheric Administration (NOAA) had published regulations for subsistence whaling that included the Makah.

Nonsubsistence Aboriginal Whaling

Anticipating this outcome, Representative Jack Metcalf of Washington, some concerned citizens, and several animal protection organizations had already filed suit against NMFS, NOAA, and the Commerce Department, asking for an injunction to halt the Indian's whale hunt. Metcalf argued that the federal defendants had failed to adequately assess the environmental impact of the planned hunt on the gray whale population, and was therefore in violation of the Whaling Convention Act and the National Environmental Policy Act (NEPA). A number of Makah elders, one of whom was a plaintiff in the lawsuit, also opposed the hunt on different grounds. They pointed out that traditionally whale hunting was preceded by months of various ritual activities, including regular fasting and sexual abstinence, rites that would not be observed by the modern whalers. For these elders, the profound religious and cultural significance of the whale hunt was irretrievably lost.

The Commerce Department, NOAA, and the NMFS emphasized that

an environmental assessment of Makah whaling had been prepared, as required by NEPA, a determination made that the hunt would not significantly affect the environment, and a "Finding of No Significant Impact" (FONSI) issued. In September 1998 the federal District Court for Western Washington accepted this and allowed the hunt to proceed. Intending to set out after the whales in October, the Indians soon realized that none of their number had hunted cetaceans before, indeed, no living Makah ever had, so more preparation was necessary. In May 1999 Makah hunters struck and killed a 30-ton gray whale with harpoons and 0.50 caliber machine-gun bullets. As it turned out, this may be the only whale the Indians will be allowed to take.

Meanwhile, Metcalf appealed the lower court decision to the Ninth Circuit Court of Appeals, and in June 2000 the plaintiffs finally received the injunction they had sought for nearly three years. Judge Stephen Trott ruled that although NOAA did produce an environmental assessment, NEPA was violated nonetheless. The assessment was prepared a year and a half *after* the agency had formally agreed to support the Makah's endeavor to resume whaling.

Specifically, NOAA contracted with the Indians in March 1996 to present their case for whaling to the IWC, to assist them in collecting information and specimens from killed whales, to monitor the hunt, and to promulgate the appropriate regulations authorizing it. The agreement was renewed in October 1997 and four days later the FONSI was issued. But NEPA regulations and the relevant case law clearly demand that environmental assessments be done "at the earliest possible time" and "before any irreversible and irretrievable commitment of resources" have been made. According to Judge Trott, this is exactly what the federal defendants did not do. "It is highly likely" he wrote, "that because of the federal defendants' prior written commitment to the Makah . . . , the environmental assessment was slanted in favor of finding that the Makah whaling proposal would not significantly affect the environment."

Trott quashed the FONSI and suspended the agreement with the Makah, which removes regulations authorizing the whaling. He ordered the preparation of a new environmental assessment (*Metcalf v. Daley*). This process continues at this writing.

MARINE MAMMAL PROTECTION ACT OF 1972 (MMPA)

By the middle 1960s, the world's marine mammals had reached a state of extreme crisis. Throughout the nineteenth and twentieth centuries, millions of blue, gray, humpback, right, and sperm whales, fur and harp seals, walruses, sea otters, and polar bears had been hunted and killed in their habitat of ice and ocean, the rocky coasts and frigid waters of a dozen nations, including the United States. The sea-dwelling mammals were exploited for oil, baleen, fur, fat, and meat, and for sport. After the Second World War, spinner and spotted dolphins too were slaughtered by the hundreds of thousands as a mere side effect of tuna fishing in the tropical Pacific Ocean.

International efforts to save these severely depleted species began in 1911, when America joined three other nations in consenting to the articles of a treaty that restricted the taking of fur seals, already reduced by 90 percent to perhaps a quarter million (*see* this chapter: *Fur Seal Act of 1966*). After thirty-five more years had passed, another international agreement finally attempted to regulate whale hunting with a special whaling commission, but instead of leading to replenished cetacean numbers, all those species mentioned ultimately became imperiled (*see* this chapter: *Legal Protections for Whales*). Then the dolphin slaughter began in earnest. It eventually peaked at over 200,000 annually in the 1960s, a period that also found sea otters and polar bears in danger of disappearing.

At this time, only the Migratory Bird Treaty Act of 1918 (see above, this chapter) provided a comprehensive federal law designed to protect a large class of wildlife, and marine mammals were obviously not included. Even though some National Wildlife Refuges (*see* this chapter: *National Wildlife Refuge System Improvement Act of 1997*) did completely ban hunting of certain animals such as elk or buffalo, the preserved species were overwhelmingly birds (mostly waterfowl). In any case the prohibitions were highly localized and covered only a small fraction of the territory where American wildlife lived and might die from human hands. Domestic legislation had ratified the whaling treaty in 1949, but that amounted to agreeing with whatever the whaling commission did, and the little that was accomplished by the group did not include effective conservation measures.

The international, piecemeal approach to conservation had largely failed to competently manage highly mobile populations of wild animals inhabiting a vast area of oceans and their coastal fringes. Moreover, a capacious federal law providing effective safeguards for any wildlife other than game birds was essentially absent.

Federal Protection for Marine Mammals

This situation began to change when President Lyndon Johnson signed the Endangered Species Preservation Act of 1966, followed three years later by President Richard Nixon's signature on the Endangered Species Conservation Act of 1969 (*see* this chapter: *Endangered Species Act of 1973*). For the first time, the American Congress was making a concerted effort to protect entire species of mammals found anywhere in the United States, and indeed the world—not just birds, and not just in the nation's wildlife refuges.

Nonetheless, the endangered species laws still left unprotected wildlife not officially identified as at risk. Perhaps more importantly, during the 1960s and early 1970s many people became convinced that marine mammals—especially whales and dolphins—were intelligent, sensitive creatures living in complex social systems, and hence worthy of protection in their own right, whatever their economic value as a natural resource might be. Others demanding legal action argued in a more traditional vein, contending that conservation of marine mammals was needed to sustain an important commercial and food resource, while still others appealed to the crucial role of these mammals in maintaining healthy ecosystems.

With these diverse pressures brought to bear on Capitol Hill over four long years of hearings, debate, and compromise, a receptive Congress finally passed the Marine Mammal Protection Act in 1972 (MMPA). Only the Endangered Species Act eclipses the MMPA and its implementing regulations for length and complexity in the realm of animal law, reflecting the wide array of ideological commitments it is supposed to appease. By 1996 the MMPA had been amended fifteen times.

The MMPA is administered by two federal agencies, the Department of Commerce and the Department of the Interior, with ultimate authority vested in their respective secretaries. The National Marine Fisheries Service (NMFS) is the administrative branch of the Commerce Department charged with implementing the MMPA, and is responsible for whales, dolphins, porpoises, and seals. Over at the Interior Department, the Fish and Wildlife Service (FWS) oversees walruses, sea otters, polar bears, and manatees. To achieve the objectives of the MMPA, the two agencies are required to consult with the Marine Mammal Commission, an advisory body intended to be impartial, without any political allegiances. The three members of the commission are appointed by the president, who chooses them from a list of experts provided by the chairperson of the Council on Environmental Quality, the secretary of the Smithsonian Institution, the director of the National Science Foundation, and the chairperson of the National Academy of Sciences.

At the core of the MMPA is a "complete cessation" of all taking and importing of marine mammals and products made from these animals, a suspension commonly known as a moratorium. The MMPA defines "to take" as meaning "to harass, hunt, capture, or kill" or to attempt to do so. In 1972 the prohibition on harassing marine mammals was an entirely new sort of government regulation on human activity involving animals, yet Congress did not define the term. It was not until a 1994 amendment that "harassment" was specified as "any act of pursuit, torment, or annoyance which (i) has the potential to injure a marine mammal [this is 'level A harassment'] . . . ; or (ii) has the potential to disturb a marine mammal . . . by causing disruption of behavioral patterns ['level B ha-rassment']." Federal regulations now include within the meaning of "take," and thus identifying prohibited behavior, detaining or restraining marine mammals for any length of time, feeding or attempting to feed them, and collecting dead animals or their body parts.

In addition to the basic taking prohibition, according to the MMPA it is unlawful to possess, transport, sell, offer to sell, buy, import, or export any marine mammal or product made from any marine mammal. Fur-ther, it is illegal to import any marine mammal that is nursing, pregnant, or less than eight months old, unless the secretary has issued a permit for scientific research or to enhance the survival or recovery of the species. The MMPA also prohibits any "inhumane" taking of marine mammals, but rather than define this concept, leaves the determination of what is humane and inhumane to the judgment of the secretary. Subsequent reg-ulations characterize "humane" as the infliction of the "least possible de-gree of pain and suffering practicable to the animal involved." Violations of these provisions are punishable by up to one year in prison and a fine of $20,000.

Waivers to the Moratorium

Although the point of the MMPA is to bring a halt to human activities that adversely affect marine mammals, the act also provides a byzantine system of waivers from the taking prohibition, as well as many excep-tions to it. Apparently, Congress intended the waiver procedure to be the primary device by which marine mammals might be taken for commer-cial or recreational hunting purposes, but it has turned out that waivers are very seldom sought. None have been granted in over twenty years, though they remain available. Perhaps this is what lawmakers had in mind when they devised the arduous process.

It begins with a request for a waiver made to the secretary of com-merce or the interior. The secretary must first determine whether the pro-posed taking is consistent with the antecedently determined "optimum sustainable population" (OSP) for that species, either as a whole or for a local population group. The OSP is "the number of animals that will re-sult in the maximum productivity of the population or species." This refers to how many animals are needed to replace individuals lost due to natural morality. If the secretary decides that granting the waiver and is-suing a permit authorizing the taking will not reduce the animal popula-tion below the OSP, regulations are then declared for waiving the mora-torium and authorizing the taking.

Unlike other federal agencies, whose regulations are simply made available for public comment, regulations attendant upon a waiver to the MMPA are subject to a much more rigorous process of review, including the right to cross-examine the secretary or his or her representatives in an administrative hearing. The subject of the interrogation can also extend beyond the proposed regulations and include the legitimacy of the waiver itself. If the regulations pass muster, the secretary is then free to issue a permit that authorizes the taking. Before doing so, however, notice of the waiver application must be published in the *Federal Register*, and thirty days must be allowed for public comment. The decision to grant or deny a waiver may be challenged by any person, and the debate may wind up in the chambers of an administrative law judge, who will then make a final decision. When a waiver is granted, the permit issued must indicate in precise detail the number of animals to be taken, where this will occur, and over what time period.

Although waivers have been extremely rare, exceptions to the moratorium for commercial fisheries are quite common. The MMPA, its subsequent amendments, and implementing regulations allow taking of marine mammals "incidental" to fishing operations. Incidental taking results from normal fishing operations or when marine mammals are prevented from interfering with fishing activities. Over the nearly three-decade life of the MMPA, these exceptions have been rewritten, refined, and elaborated many times. Today, they are bewilderingly complicated, varying considerably depending on such factors as the species of marine mammal incidentally taken, the "stock" or population group of a species impacted by the fishing, the frequency of the incidental taking, where it occurs, and whether the fishing vessel is foreign or American. Extensive amendments written in 1994, and over fifty pages of the *Code of Federal Regulations* are devoted to these exceptions.

Exceptions to the Moratorium for Commercial Fishing
It began simply enough in 1972. The MMPA provided that during the first two years following its enactment, all taking of marine mammals incidental to commercial fishing was exempted from the prohibition while methods of reducing incidental mortality were studied. This research had made little progress by 1974, and at that time all forms of incidental taking became illegal, except for those specifically authorized by regulation.

In those days, the incidental taking garnering the most regulatory attention, and the loudest public outcry, was the killing of thousands of dolphins in the process of fishing for tuna in the eastern tropical Pacific Ocean (*see* this chapter: *Legal Protections for Dolphins*). In response to public pressure following the expiration of the two-year exemption, the NMFS began to issue regulations requiring certain methods and equipment that appeared to reduce incidental mortality among dolphins. However, these regulations were tailored to circumstances in the tuna fisheries, where many thousands of marine mammals were being killed to the serious detriment of entire populations of animals. Most other sorts of commercial operations were not taking nearly that many marine mammals and there appeared to be little impact on their populations.

In due time, the killing of dolphins by the tuna boats lead to an amendment to the MMPA, the Dolphin Protection Consumer Information Act of 1990, which defined "dolphin safe" seafood products. Meanwhile, the federal regulations designed for tuna fisheries were widely ignored by other sorts of fishing operations. None attempted to avail themselves of the convolutions and uncertainties of the waiver procedure, as described above. Illegal incidental taking persisted, and because such violations were difficult to interdict, their biological impact on marine mammal populations could not be determined.

Hoping to solve this problem, Congress amended the MMPA in 1981 to allow American fishing operations to take "small numbers" of marine mammals so long as this had no more than a "negligible impact" on the animal population. Unfortunately, within a few years this too proved unsatisfactory. Fishing vessels could rarely confine their incidental take to marine mammal stocks whose numbers were not already depleted or about which population data was known. For several more years, fisheries were in effect allowed to ignore restrictions on incidental taking, so long as they participated in a research program intended to gather information on the effect of commercial fishing on marine mammals. In 1994 Congress finally wrote a new set of rules to regulate the incidental take of marine mammals by commercial fisheries.

These 1994 amendments introduced several new concepts of wildlife management. They begin with an order to the secretary to produce a "stock assessment" for each population group of marine mammals residing in American waters. This assessment contains the secretary's judgment on the size and distribution of the species as well as ecological factors affecting it, and is then used to determine the "potential biological removal level" of the animal. As the phrase suggests, this is the number of animals that could be taken from a population group while still maintaining the OSP. This allows the identification of "strategic stocks": population groups where the number of deaths caused by humans exceeds the potential biological removal level.

Next, the secretary must classify all commercial fisheries into one of three categories, according to the frequency with which they incidentally take marine mammals. For those strategic stocks subject to a high or occasional frequency of incidental take, the secretary must design a "take reduction plan," the immediate goal of which is to decrease incidental mortality and serious injury below the potential biological removal level. The long-term goal is reducing these impacts to "insignificant levels approaching a zero mortality and serious injury rate." Fisheries that regularly take strategic stocks must comply with the plan. Those not impacting strategic stocks must register their vessels with the Department of Commerce, submit periodic reports, and comply with observer requirements.

Other Exceptions to the Moratorium
The taking prohibition may also be avoided by securing a permit for species or stock "enhancement," for scientific research, for public display, for photography, or by being an Alaskan native. As the law was originally written, capturing and relocating marine mammals (or even trying to) for the purpose of repopulating stocks or reviving a species was technically in violation of the MMPA. Unlike the Endangered Species Act, it contained no provision for measures "enhancing the survival or recovery of a species or stock." This omission was rectified with a 1988 amendment that included the further stipulation that any marine mammals held captive for this purpose must be returned to the wild as soon as possible.

Originally, the MMPA allowed the secretary to issue permits for taking, including lethal taking, any marine mammal for scientific purposes, even those that were pregnant, nursing, or less than eight months old. This permission was tightened a bit with the 1994 amendments that prohibited lethal taking of any individuals from *depleted* stocks. However, this too can be evaded when "the Secretary determines that the results of such research will directly benefit the species or stock, or that such research fulfills a critically important research need." On the other hand, permit requirements were loosened somewhat in 1994 when Congress authorized the secretary to promulgate regulations allowing taking marine mammals for scientific purposes without a permit so long as it involves only disturbance ("level B harassment") and not injury or death to the targeted animals.

Marine mammals may also be lawfully taken when the secretary issues a permit for public display. To secure such a permit, the prospective permittee must show that the animals will be presented in an education or conservation program judged acceptable according to the "professionally recognized standards of the public display community." Additionally, anyone desiring to hold marine mammals for these exhibition purposes must be registered or licensed according to the Animal Welfare Act (*see* chapter 5: *Circuses and Zoos*). Finally, their facilities must be open to the general public on a regularly scheduled basis.

Although the MMPA contained no prohibition of photographing marine mammals and required no permit to do so, photographers' efforts to capture the animals on film can qualify as an illegal taking when their normal behaviors are disrupted by a person with a camera, amounting to "level B harassment." The 1994 amendments thus authorized the secretary to issue permits "for photography for educational or commercial purposes involving marine mammals in the wild."

Alaskan Indians, Aleuts, and Inuit (Eskimos) have relied upon marine mammals—especially whales and seals—for food, clothing, and for much of their material culture for many centuries. Determined to accommodate this traditional way of life, which would have been radically altered otherwise, Congress has exempted Alaskan Natives from the taking prohibition of the MMPA. These people are free to hunt, kill, capture, or harass any marine mammal without a permit or any other authorization, provided that the point of these activities is either for subsistence or to create and sell "authentic native articles of handicrafts and clothing." The taking must also be accomplished in a manner that avoids any unnecessary waste of the animal carcass.

LEGAL PROTECTIONS FOR DOLPHINS

In the warm tropical waters of the Pacific Ocean, off the west coasts of Central America, Columbia, Ecuador, and Peru, enormous schools of yellowfin tuna are found, shoals of fish numbering into the hundreds of thousands. Unlike anywhere else in the world, and for reasons that are not well understood, the tuna congregate here in the eastern tropical Pacific (ETP) directly under groups of spinner and spotted dolphins (*Stenella longirostris* and *S. attenuata*). Since the dolphins are air-breathing aquatic mammals, they tend to stay fairly close to the surface, where they are often plainly in view. Fishermen had known of this phenomenon for centuries, but it was not until the years following the Second World War that the presence of dolphins in the ETP as a certain indicator of tuna below was widely exploited. A multinational tuna industry developed during the late 1940s, no longer hindered by the difficulty of finding tuna in the vastness of the open ocean. Here was a conspicuous, living beacon pointing straight at prolific harvests of fish.

Purse Seining in the 1950s and 1960s

Tuna fishing on a grand scale initially employed long lines knotted with thousands of hooks played out over miles of water, the fish to be snagged individually. However, by the late 1950s this method had been replaced by purse seining, a technique that uses huge nets deployed by speed boats around entire schools of surface-swimming dolphins and the tuna beneath them. The bottoms of the nets are then winched snugly with steel cables, pulling them tight like a drawstring on a purse, and preventing the tuna from escaping to deeper water.

Although highly efficient for catching tuna, purse seining also traps the dolphins. As air-breathing marine mammals, the dolphins often drowned after becoming entangled in the nets underwater, or they would bleach dry in the sun on the deck of the tuna vessel when pulled on board with the fish. For years, this fatal side effect of tuna fishing was unknown to the general public. By the time the Marine Mammal Protection Act (MMPA) (*see* this chapter: *Marine Mammal Protection Act*) was passed in 1972, an estimated 5 million spinner and spotted dolphins had died as a direct result of purse seining.

Congress specifically exempted "incidental taking" of dolphins in the course of tuna fishing from the provisions of the MMPA, while ordering two years of research investigating how to reduce dolphin mortality caused by purse seining to near zero. When the two years had elapsed and this research had yielded few results, the secretary of commerce issued regulations requiring the U.S. tuna industry to use equipment and methods that appeared to reduce dolphin mortality to some degree, but without specifying any limit to the number of dolphins that could be killed. Animal welfare groups sued the Department of Commerce, demanding that a maximum number be established. They prevailed in 1976 when the District of Columbia Circuit Court of Appeals ordered the commerce secretary, through the National Marine Fisheries Service (NMFS), to set a limit to the number of dolphins that could be legally taken by tuna boats (*Committee for Humane Legislation, Inc. v. Richardson*). Initially fixed at 78,000, by 1985 the quota had been reduced to 20,500, a fraction of the approximately 350,000 dolphins killed each year by the tuna industry in the early 1970s.

This remarkable progress in dolphin conservation predictably put the U.S. tuna fleet at a serious economic disadvantage. As the number of American vessels declined, foreign tuna boats increased dramatically, especially those flying under the flag of Mexico. Unencumbered by the strictures of U.S. legislation, these fleets utilized purse seining with impunity, and the dolphin kill began to rise again. Congress reacted to this situation in 1984 with a "comparability requirement," an amendment to the MMPA that imposed an embargo on tuna imports from countries whose dolphin kill rates exceeded 1.25 times that of the U.S. rate. The embargo was also extended to other countries that imported tuna from foreign nations that did not comply with the MMPA standards.

"Dolphin Safe" Tuna

Throughout the 1980s American consumers became increasingly aware of dolphin deaths associated with tuna fishing; expressions of outrage, boycotts of canned tuna, and public protests proliferated. In April 1990 in an unprecedented corporate decision, the StarKist, Chicken of the Sea, and Bumblebee brand companies announced that they would cease buying any tuna caught in association with dolphins. The three companies, together controlling over 80 percent of the U.S. tuna market, declared that all of their tuna products would henceforth be labeled "dolphin safe," signifying this self-imposed restriction. The nature of the tuna industry was radically altered: U.S. and foreign fishing fleets that legally killed dolphins, as allowed by the MMPA, could find few buyers with access to the lucrative American market.

A rare turnabout came swiftly after the corporations' announcement: Congress was spurred to follow the lead of business. Technically an amendment to the MMPA, the most important provision of the Dolphin Protection Consumer Information Act (DPCIA) was a definition of the term "dolphin safe": all tuna in the product must be from a fishing expedition in which dolphins were never encircled with nets, not even one time, and regardless of whether or not any dolphins were killed. In other words, if a purse seine or any other fishing net was deployed just once by a tuna boat, and even though no dolphins were killed, none of the tuna caught at any time during that voyage could be labeled "dolphin safe."

Foreign nations with tuna fleets were not happy with these new policies and regulations, especially the embargo for failing to meet the comparability requirement. Mexico in particular reacted strongly by claiming that the MMPA restrictions violated the General Agreement on Tariffs and Trade (GATT), and filing a complaint with the dispute panel. The GATT is an international agreement that regulates trade among the various nations that sign, intended to promote commerce between them by removing certain economic obstacles. In September 1991 the GATT dispute panel ruled in favor of Mexico. However, such a ruling does not mean that the prohibited trade practice must stop; instead, it authorized Mexico to retaliate against the United States with economic sanctions of its own. Since the United States was in the process of reforming and improving its trade relations with Mexico, diplomatic efforts were accelerated to resolve the dispute.

These efforts produced the La Jolla Agreement of 1992. Named for the southern California community where the negotiations occurred, this was the first multinational agreement to protect the dolphin species. The ten signatories to the compact, which included Mexico and the United States, resolved to set steadily diminishing dolphin kill quotas so that by 1999 annual dolphin mortality would be less than 0.1 percent of the estimated population, or about 5,000 individuals (as it happened, this death rate was reached within one year). The agreement also established an international review panel to monitor compliance with the quotas, a scientific advisory board to assist research aimed at reducing dolphin mortality, and required that every tuna boat have an internationally accredited observer on board to verify that the standards have not been exceeded.

A New Definition for "Dolphin Safe"?
Even as the discussions in La Jolla proceeded, Congress was writing its own dolphin protection plan. In a series of amendments to the MMPA,

the International Dolphin Conservation Act of 1992 (IDCA) encouraged an agreement between nations to declare a "global moratorium" on purse seining tuna around dolphins for at least five years, an agreement that was to be reached by March 1, 1994. The IDCA also declared that meanwhile there would be a ban in the United States on the sale or importation of all tuna not qualifying as "dolphin safe" under the definition established in 1990 by the DPCIA. Nations that expressed a commitment to honor the moratorium were exempt from the embargo.

No nation ever agreed to the moratorium, and by 1995 the DPCIA and the IDCA had produced a U.S. market with virtually no tuna caught in association with dolphins or by foreign vessels. Several parties to the La Jolla Agreement continued to be disgruntled with the American embargoes and the strict definition of "dolphin safe." They urged Congress to lift the bans and loosen the definition, warning that continued restrictions might well undermine the progress toward dolphin protection initiated in La Jolla.

As further incentive to American lawmakers, twelve nations, including Mexico, Costa Rica, Honduras, Panama, Columbia, and the United States, signed the Declaration of Panama in October 1995. The declaration reaffirmed the objectives of the La Jolla Agreement, including the 5,000-dolphin kill limit, and stipulated a number of provisions for tightly regulating tuna fishing in the eastern tropical Pacific while protecting the dolphin species. Supported by several environmental organizations, such as Greenpeace and the World Wildlife Fund, the declaration was recognized as legally binding so long as the United States lifted the embargoes and appropriately revised the meaning of "dolphin safe."

This contingency was met in August 1997 when President Bill Clinton signed the International Dolphin Conservation Program Act (IDCPA) into law. The two main provisions of the IDCPA are, first, a lifting of the tuna embargoes from countries that are in compliance with the La Jolla Agreement and the Declaration of Panama, and, second and most controversially, a new definition of "dolphin safe."

Now "dolphin safe" is to refer to tuna caught during a fishing voyage in which neither a qualified observer nor the captain of the vessel observed a dolphin killed or "seriously" injured in the process of using purse seines or other sorts of nets. This is a radical revision of the concept. Under the DPCIA, consumers could rest assured that "dolphin safe" meant that the primary cause of dolphin mortality in the tuna industry—purse seining—was *never* employed. Under the IDCPA, consumers now must trust that the relevant personnel did not actually *see* a dolphin death or injury during purse seining. The IDCPA also requires that, between July 2001 and December 2002, Congress scrutinize scientific research concerning the detrimental effects of purse seining on dolphins in the eastern tropical Pacific.

Crucially, the IDCPA stipulated that the import sanctions could not be rescinded, nor the meaning of "dolphin safe" changed until the NMFS had made an initial finding that there were no serious, long-term harms to dolphin populations as a result of purse seining. Of particular concern to Congress were the physiological effects of stress caused by repeated chasing and encircling, even though no dolphins were witnessed killed or severely injured in the process. Due by March 1999, the IDCPA required that the investigation consist of population surveys and stress studies to determine whether encirclement by nets is having a "significant adverse impact" on dolphin reproduction.

"A Significant Adverse Impact"?
In April 1999 Secretary of Commerce William Daley announced the results of the NMFS research. He reported that the total population of spotted and spinner dolphins (about 2.3 million) in the ETP had not increased in the previous several years. On the contrary, the numbers had remained stable or even slightly decreased, this despite the fact that mortality associated with purse seining had been dramatically reduced, down to about 2,000 animals in 1998.

Why had there not been a dolphin population boom? One plausible answer would be stress due to continued net fishing, where mother and young become separated, social groups are splintered, net confinement provokes mutual aggression, and physical exhaustion sets in. However, Daley said that NMFS findings on this factor were inconclusive. Though one might think this uncertainty would lead government officials to err on the side of caution, the secretary reasoned otherwise: "NMFS has determined that there is insufficient evidence to conclude that intentional deployment on or encirclement of dolphins with purse seine nets is having a significant adverse impact on any depleted dolphin stock in the ETP. Because of this initial finding, the 'dolphin safe' labeling standard . . . will change . . . to implement the IDCPA." The new definition of "dolphin safe" was officially enshrined in federal regulations, effective February 2000, and the embargoes were lifted before 1999 ended.

Meanwhile, incensed by Secretary Daley's decision, ten animal welfare organizations and two private citizens—including Defenders of Wildlife, the Animal Welfare Institute, the Humane Society of the United States, the International Wildlife Coalition, and environmental activists David Brower and Sam LaBudde—filed suit in the federal District Court for Northern California in August 1999. The plaintiffs contended that Daley inadequately appraised the biological information gathered by the NMFS, and thus abused his discretion with the arbitrary and capricious finding that purse seining had "no significant adverse impact" on the dolphins. If this were true, they claimed, then dolphin numbers should have appreciably increased, yet this had not occurred.

Judge Thelton Henderson ruled in favor of the dolphins in April 2000. Congressional approval of the IDCPA, he noted, was conditional upon the results of specific stress studies, and this research had to show the animals were not being harmed by purse seining before the meaning of "dolphin safe" could be legally altered. In particular, the NMFS was ordered to review the literature on dolphin stress, place trained necropsy technicians on fishing vessels to collect tissue samples from dead dolphins, analyze demographic and biological data on dolphin populations, and perform experiments in which dolphins were repeatedly chased and captured by circling them with nets.

Somewhat incredulously, Henderson pointed out that, of these researches, the NMFS pursued only the literature review. The necropsy study was never done, allegedly because foreign fishing vessels were uncooperative (no U.S. boats were using purse seines). Yet on several occasions Mexico had affirmed its willingness to cooperate with the Americans in advancing this study. The analysis of the demographic and biological information was "underway," but would not be complete until 2002, despite Congress's directive that this was to be a one-year study to commence in 1997. Finally, the NMFS did not even begin the formal planning of the chase and recapture research until *after* the secretary's initial finding, and stated that the experiment would not be conducted until spring 2001.

What is worse, the relevant literature on dolphin stress perused by the NMFS clearly indicated that the operations of tuna fisheries are probably "psychological and social stressors" for dolphins, potentially leading to suppressed immune systems, disruptions in the reproductive cycle of females, and unobserved deaths. "The stress literature," Judge Henderson wrote, "demonstrated that it was likely that dolphins experience a multitude of harmful stress effects from the chase and capture process, and that it was scientifically plausible that such effects could be causing population level effects." Indeed, the NMFS's own report on these studies concluded "the information suggests . . . that the fishery has been the source of significant adverse impact on these two populations [of spinner and spotted dolphins]." The report did not present any evidence contrary to this conclusion. Henderson ruled that Secretary Daley's initial finding, which triggered the new definition of "dolphin safe," was unwarranted and unlawful. Both were therefore discarded (*Brower v. Daley*).

Irrespective of this outcome, the StarKist, Bumblebee, and Chicken of the Sea brand companies had already pledged to abide by the definition of "dolphin safe" signifying that the tuna were caught without purse seines or net encirclement. Several grocery stores and restaurants joined them in this commitment, including Safeway, IGA Stores, Red Lobster, and The Olive Garden. Whatever elected representatives and Cabinet secretaries in Washington, D.C., decide, powerful business interests in America are apparently convinced that consumers want all dolphins to remain unharmed.

ENDANGERED SPECIES ACT OF 1973 (ESA)

The most comprehensive, controversial, and perhaps the most complicated wildlife protection law in the world, the Endangered Species Act (ESA) mandates a wide range of measures to preserve species that are perilously close to becoming extinct. When the ESA was enacted in December 1973, a list of 109 such imperiled species was compiled; 27 years later there are 1,788 species from around the world on the list, 495 of which are animals found in the United States, our focus here. Over this time, just thirty-one species have been removed from the tally, and only eleven of those because they are no longer in danger of vanishing. Thirteen were either incorrectly listed or renamed to secure taxa. Seven others were not saved; they became extinct.

Extinction is a very common natural process. As many as 98 percent of all the animal and plant species that have ever existed on the planet have disappeared. In one massive die-off some 65 million years ago at least eight out of every ten animal species expired when a large meteor collided with Earth, ending the reign of the dinosaurs. Usually, however, extinctions have occurred gradually at a rate of about thirty animal species per millennium, a pace that has been substantially accelerated by human activities over the last few centuries, though one far from meteoric.

Since the Pilgrims arrived in North America in 1620, approximately 125 species of birds and mammals have been eliminated, mainly by excessive hunting. The most recent victims are the passenger pigeon (*Ectopistes migratorius*) and the Carolina parakeet (*Conuropsis carolinensis*). Once flocking by the millions, the pigeons were blasted from the skies for food and fun, while the parakeets were shot primarily so that their brilliant feathers could adorn ladies' hats, although they also proved an eliminable nuisance in farmers' fields and orchards. The last specimens of both birds died in zoos in 1914, a pigeon named Martha and a parakeet called Incas.

Yet it was not until the early 1960s that Congress seriously attempted to do anything about the loss of species. Hearings at that time acknowledged that various kinds of wildlife in the United States had become extinct during the twentieth century, among them the passenger pigeon and the Carolina parakeet, and that a number of other species were at risk of falling to the same fate. In light of these findings, Congress announced that these depleted taxa were of "aesthetic, ecological, educational, historical, recreational, and scientific value to the Nation and its people." The federal government would therefore pursue means of preserving them and the ecosystems on which they depend.

Initial Attempts to Preserve Depleted Wildlife

The first federal measure that protected vanishing wildlife was not primarily intended for that purpose, rather it was designed to safeguard the country's first national park, Yellowstone, established in Wyoming Territory in 1872. Although boundaries had been drawn, no laws were created to regulate conduct in the park, so in 1893 Representative John Lacey of Iowa sponsored a bill prohibiting mining, logging, and hunting in Yellowstone. One of the last remaining bands of American bison or "buffalo" (*Bison bison*) inhabited the park at that time. Numbering a couple of hundred individuals, the Yellowstone herd represented most of what was left of a species that in a few decades had catastrophically declined from a total of perhaps 50 million, gunned down by market hunters for their hides, their tongues, and for sport. When President Grover Cleveland signed Lacey's Yellowstone Protection Act in May 1894, the new law in effect provided the world's first legal shield for an endangered species.

A long period of legislative quiescence followed in which next to nothing was done to save disappearing wildlife. Finally, in 1966, after finding that urbanization, burgeoning human populations, and increasing reliance on technology had exterminated some wild animal species and severely depleted others, Congress passed the Endangered Species Preservation Act. This law directed the secretary of the interior to identify each "fish and wildlife" species native to America whose "existence is endangered" so that "its survival requires assistance." It also consolidated various wildlife refuges, ranges, and management areas administered by the Interior Department into the National Wildlife Refuge System (this stipulation was later designated the National Wildlife Refuge System Administration Act of 1966; *see also* this chapter: *National Wildlife Refuge System Improvement Act*).

Beyond these items, the new law was timid and tentative. Its sole substantive provision authorized the interior secretary to protect habitat by buying land with money drawn from the Land and Water Conservation Fund, capped at $5 million annually and limited to $750,000 for any single acquisition. This is a severe constriction of a project intended to preserve species. Habitat loss can be devastating, but it is merely one of several critical factors that threaten wildlife. Others include overhunting, predation, disease, introduction of nonnative species, and severe weather. Moreover, there are many other ways to protect habitat besides simply buying land.

Incredibly, the 1966 act also failed to prohibit killing, injuring, or removing any of the taxa identified as "threatened with extinction" except those found on federal lands; this authority in other jurisdictions was left entirely to the individual states, then the traditional source for regulations on taking wildlife. Finally, no restrictions were placed on the commercial movement of endangered species across state borders, or the importation of such species from foreign lands. Few were satisfied with the 1966 law, and it did not take Congress long to produce a supplement to it.

The Endangered Species Conservation Act of 1969 corrected some of the flaws, notably by prohibiting interstate commerce in endangered species, and by raising the ceiling on single acquisitions of land to $2.5 million. It also clarified the meaning of "fish and wildlife," originally interpreted by the Interior Department as referring only to vertebrates, to include "any wild mammal, fish, wild bird, amphibian, reptile, mollusk, or crustacean." The most important feature of the 1969 act, however, was to significantly expand the duty to protect species, extending the shield beyond the borders of the United States, and authorizing the secretary of the interior to draw up a list of wildlife threatened with extinction anywhere on the planet. Importation of these species into this country was outlawed. Nonetheless, the act also specified several exceptions to the ban on importation, empowering the secretary to allow the introduction of foreign endangered species for zoological, educational, and scientific purposes, and to produce breeding populations in captivity.

Although an improvement, the 1969 Act had its own shortcomings. Unfortunately, it also permitted the states to devise their own regulations concerning the taking of endangered species in their jurisdictions. Another unsolved problem was that most federal agencies were not required to ensure that their projects and activities did not detrimentally affect endangered species and their habitats. Finally, by the early 1970s it was obvious that many plants were also at risk of extinction, yet neither the 1966 nor 1969 acts provided any protection for endangered plant species even though their continued existence would clearly promote the same values as did the preservation of wild animals.

Federal Protection for Threatened and Endangered Species

In December 1973 President Richard Nixon signed the Endangered Species Act (ESA), remedying the defects of the earlier statutes and providing far more extensive protections. Now, *any* animal or plant species can be safeguarded, *all* federal agencies are directed to avoid activities that harm protected species, and the taking of endangered species *anywhere* is expressly forbidden by federal law.

Primary responsibility for the administration and enforcement of the ESA and regulatory action in accordance with it is vested in the Fish and

Wildlife Service (FWS). A branch of the Department of the Interior, the FWS is the major actor in the legal moves authorized by the ESA. The National Marine Fisheries Service in the Department of Commerce is responsible for certain maritime species. Ultimately, administrative and regulatory responsibility traces back to the secretary of the interior, who must approve the initial listing of a taxon as protected by the ESA, FWS regulations, and any human activity impinging upon a listed species.

The ESA mandates cooperation between the states and the federal government. The secretary must enter into cooperative agreements with the states to manage and acquire land for the conservation of threatened and endangered species. Federal assistance may also be offered to states that establish conservation programs. Although the states are consulted before species found in their jurisdictions are listed, they have no veto power, and the final decision belongs to the secretary.

Attempts must also be made to influence foreign governments. Communicating through the secretary of state, the secretary of the interior must exhort foreign countries to take steps to conserve various wild animals and plants, including those listed as threatened or endangered. With the approval of the president, the secretary may also provide financial and technological resources to other nations to encourage the protection of wildlife and plants. The ESA also implements the terms of the Convention on International Trade in Endangered Species of Wild Fauna and Flora (CITES), an international agreement that currently has 132 nations as signatories. CITES seeks to regulate trade in imperiled species by requiring the "Management Authority" of both the exporting and the importing nation to register their approval before any individuals of such a species can be exchanged between them. The ESA designates the secretary of the interior as the "Management Authority" for the United States.

The basic purpose of the ESA is to save wildlife from extinction, so at its core is a list of species that are designated as being at risk. The listing process that forms the foundation of the ESA divides imperiled species into two general categories. An "endangered" species is one "which is in danger of extinction throughout all or a significant portion of its range" unless recovery and rehabilitation efforts are implemented. "Threatened" species are those that are "likely to become endangered species in the foreseeable future." The term "species" here includes not only subspecies of animals and plants, but also "any distinct population segment of any species of vertebrate fish and wildlife." The inclusion of populations under the definition of species recognizes that one group of animals may be endangered in a particular area while another of the same species may be thriving somewhere else. For example, the brown bear population is healthy in Alaska, but threatened in the lower forty-eight states.

The process of adding a species to the ESA list usually begins with a petition submitted to the secretary of the interior asking him or her to declare the species as an endangered or threatened one. Petitions concerning marine wildlife and plants are presented to the secretary of commerce, who may then direct the secretary of the interior to list a species. Either secretary may also propose the listing of a species. In practice though, the processing, evaluation, and federal initiation of petitions are done by the FWS. A petition for ESA protection of a species may be tendered by anyone, but typically representatives of wildlife organizations, and scientists working in both the public and private sectors take the initiative. Whoever presents the petition, to be successful it must be based upon the best scientific and economic data available and clearly indicate that due to predation or disease; habitat loss or modification; overutilization for commercial, recreational, scientific, or educational purposes; or any other natural or human-caused factors, the species warrants protection.

Once received, the secretary has up to ninety days to determine whether the status of the species is worthy of deeper investigation. If it is, the decision to propose that the taxon be designated as threatened or endangered, or one not to issue such a proposal, must be made within one year. A decision not to propose any listing of the species may be reviewed by an administrative law judge. If the secretary decides otherwise, a notice of a proposal to list a species must be published in the *Federal Register*, the governors of the affected states notified, and a summary of the proposal printed by a local newspaper. Any interested parties then have three months to submit their recommendations and comments on the proposal. A public hearing may also be held upon request. Within one year, the secretary must issue a final rule, also appearing in the *Federal Register*, declaring that the species is endangered, threatened, or that it will not be listed at all.

The Prohibition on Harming Endangered and Threatened Species

Once a species is classified as endangered or threatened, section 9 of the ESA declares it unlawful for any person to take, or to try to take any protected species within the United States, in U.S. territorial waters, or on the open ocean. To "take" is defined as "to harass, harm, pursue, hunt, shoot, wound, kill, trap, capture, or collect, or to attempt to engage in any such conduct." The ESA also prohibits importing, exporting, possessing, selling, delivering, carrying, or transporting threatened or endangered wildlife, or violating any regulation promulgated by the secretary concerning protected species.

With the exception of "harass" and "harm," the prohibited actions in the definition of "take" are the standard sorts of human interventions with wildlife that traditionally have been regulated by conservation laws. Forbidding "harming" and "harassing," however, introduces new terms into the legal equation, yet Congress did not further refine the meaning of "take" by explaining the significance of these novel ideas. This is puzzling because including "harm" in a definition that also lists "shoot," "wound," and "kill" is plainly redundant, unless lawmakers had some other injurious activity in mind. Similarly, "to harass" can denote many different kinds of conduct, and it is unusual to find the verb used to refer to something done to an animal.

The FWS eventually defined "harass" as any "intentional or negligent act or omission which creates the likelihood of injury to wildlife by annoying it to such an extent as to significantly disrupt normal behavior patterns." Surprisingly, this definition has remained essentially unchanged, and federal courts have had few occasions to dissect its denotations.

This is not so with the word "harm." The endeavor to understand this concept took years of analysis in the Department of the Interior and in the federal courts, culminating in a Supreme Court decision. The controversy began in 1975 when the FWS issued a regulation defining "harm" to an endangered or threatened species as any action or failure to act "which annoy[s] it to such an extent as to significantly disrupt essential behavior patterns." As examples of these behaviors, the FWS listed "breeding, feeding or sheltering." Also, "environmental modification or degradation" that "disrupt[s] essential behavior patterns" counts as harm to a protected species in violation of the ESA. This regulation went unchallenged and uninterpreted until 1979. Then the Sierra Club, the National Audubon Society, and the Hawaii Audubon Society initiated legal action on behalf of a rare bird species, the palila (*Loxioides bailleui*).

A variety of Hawaiian honeycreeper, the palila is found only in the forests of mamane and naio trees around Mauna Kea, on the "Big Island" of Hawaii. The bird first appeared on the endangered species list in 1967. The state Department of Land and Natural Resources had been keeping herds of feral sheep (*Ovis aries*) and goats (*Capra hircus*) on the slopes of Mauna Kea since 1950, selling permits to parties interested in hunting the animals. The plaintiffs contended that these half-wild, nonnative sheep and goats were damaging the native forests by eating mamane shoots and saplings, and because these trees are nearly the exclusive source of food for the palila, this in turn placed the continued existence of the bird at considerable risk. Maintaining the herds thus caused "environmental degradation," constituting a harm to the palila that fell under the definition of prohibited taking. The federal district court agreed with the plaintiffs, and ordered the state "to eradicate the feral sheep and goats from the palila's critical habitat." In 1981 the Ninth Circuit affirmed that judgment on appeal (*Palila v. Hawaii Department of Land and Natural Resources* or *Palila I*).

Apparently displeased with this outcome, the FWS quickly revised the definition of "harm," allowing "habitat modification or degradation" to qualify as taking in violation of the ESA only "where it actually kills or injures wildlife by significantly impairing essential behavior patterns." This conceptual tightening was clearly intended to rule out the notion that action causing deterioration of the environment could be equivalent to an unlawful taking. Indeed, the FWS had initially tried to extract any mention of "environmental modification or degradation" from the definition, but relented to vigorous objections.

Despite the new emphasis on an actual kill or injure standard, the same plaintiffs prevailed again several years later when they demanded that, in addition to the feral animals, domesticated mouflon sheep also be removed from Mauna Kea, and the state resisted. In 1988 the same district and circuit courts concurred that the survival of the palila could not be ensured as long as the mouflon sheep were present in the same area. Once again both benches ruled that Hawaii had violated the ESA and the regulation prohibiting harm caused by environmental degradation. Even so, neither court asserted that the damage to the palila habitat directly resulted in death or injury to any of the birds. In light of the 1981 regulation, this would seem to be the finding necessary to rule against the state, yet these judges saw it otherwise (*Palila v. Hawaii Department of Land and Natural Resources* or *Palila II*). In any case, the issue was far from settled.

Babbitt v. Sweet Home Chapter of Communities for a Great Oregon
In 1992 a coalition calling themselves the Sweet Home Chapter of Communities for a Great Oregon filed suit in the District Court for the District of Columbia against Secretary of the Interior Bruce Babbitt. Composed of logging companies, small landowners, logging industry organizations, and families whose livelihood depended on timber cutting, the Sweet Home Chapter complained that the federal government had deprived them of opportunities to make money. The ESA regulation banning harm through environmental degradation, they said, had prevented them from cutting trees in some of Oregon's old-growth forests.

The northern spotted owl (*Strix occidentalis* var. *caurina*) occurs only in the ancient spruce and fir forests of the American West, where it is completely dependent for food on the small mammals and birds found in this biotic community. Declared a threatened species in 1990, northern spotted owl numbers had been steadily declining for years as more and more of their forest habitat fell to various firms in the timber industry. Once classified under the ESA and their critical habitat designated, the bird effectively halted logging activity in these areas (*see also* this chapter: *Endangered Species Act of 1973: Critical Habitats and the Northern Spotted Owl*). This situation with the owl in the spruce-fir forests of Oregon was very closely analogous to the palila in the mamane-naio forests of Hawaii, and *Palila II* demonstrated clearly that the federal judiciary was interpreting the harm regulation as prohibiting impacts on an ecosystem detrimental to ESA-protected species.

The Sweet Home Chapter wanted the regulatory definition of "harm," especially the reference to habitat modification, declared invalid. The coalition argued that in writing the ESA Congress never intended the concept to include the idea of "environmental degradation" that the FWS foisted upon it. In support of this claim, the plaintiffs pointed out that a Senate draft of an ESA bill defining "take" did contain this idea, but it was deleted in the final version. Moreover, the Senate had added the term "harm" to the definition of "take" without discussion. In any case, the Sweet Home Chapter concluded, Congress really intended that habitat degradation would be prevented by the federal purchase of private land, not by such an expansive regulation.

The district court was not convinced. The understanding of the FWS that habitat modification counted as "harm" was a reasonable elaboration of ESA prohibitions, the court ruled. After all, Congress had the opportunity to change the definition of "take" in the 1982 amendments, following the decision in *Palila I*, but did not do so. This suggested that lawmakers were untroubled by the judicial interpretation that the Sweet Home Chapter believed to be improper. The lawsuit was dismissed.

To the surprise of many, upon appeal the D.C. Circuit Court reversed the lower court ruling. Judge Williams's majority opinion held that the word "harm" should be read as denoting only "the perpetrator's direct application of force against the animal. . . . The forbidden acts fit, in ordinary language, the basic model 'A hit B.'" Environmental degradation does not fit this model, so the regulatory definition is invalid.

Williams based this construction on a number of factors. Among them, he agreed with the plaintiffs that the legislative history of the ESA and its provision for land acquisition told against the definition. Williams also found compelling the narrow interpretation of the term "harass" recently given by the Ninth Circuit Court in a case examining a Marine Mammal Protection Act (MMPA) prohibition (*see* this chapter: *Marine Mammal Protection Act*). There, a fisherman had been convicted of harassing porpoises in violation of the MMPA after he fired two shots at the animals to scare them away from his fishing line. The Ninth Circuit overturned the conviction by appeal to a legal principle called *noscitur a sociis:* literally, "one is known from one's associates." Its significance here is that a word takes its meaning from the words around it. The court reasoned that since the other prohibited actions in MMPA—killing, hunting, and capturing—"involve direct and significant intrusions upon normal, life-sustaining activities," illegal harassment must do so as well (*United States v. Hayashi*).

Ironically, the Ninth Circuit had upheld the expansive regulatory definition of "harm" in *Palila I* and *II*, a definition in part now nullified by a principle the same bench had used in another case to *narrow* a different key prohibition in different federal wildlife law. At any rate, the Ninth and the D.C. Circuit Courts were clearly in conflict over the validity of the regulation, so the Supreme Court stepped in to settle the matter.

What Does "Harm" Mean?
The high court ruled that the FWS interpretation of the meaning of "take" was reasonable, and causing harm in violation of the ESA does not require the "direct application of force against the animal." Writing for a six-to-three majority, Justice John Paul Stevens advanced three reasons for the decision to overturn the D.C. Circuit.

First, a simple consultation of a dictionary. Webster's says that "harm" means "to cause hurt or damage: to injure." This definition obviously includes habitat modification resulting in actual injury or death, and makes no mention of the "direct" or "immediate" causation favored by the Sweet Home Chapter. A second reason, Stevens continued, is the broad and comprehensive purpose of the ESA to protect endangered and threatened species from activities harmful to them. Prominent among these protections is the conservation of the ecosystems that sustain them. Finally, Justice Stevens observed that the 1982 amendments to the ESA authorized the interior secretary to issue permits for taking listed species as long as "such taking is incidental to, and not the purpose of, the carrying out of otherwise lawful activity." Incidental taking makes no sense if protected animals could *only* be taken through direct and deliberate action intending to harm them in some way, or to engage in some other prohibited conduct. Thus, the allowance for incidental takes "strongly suggests that Congress understood [ESA] to prohibit indirect as well as deliberate takings."

Stevens scolded the D.C. Circuit for making several errors in their decision in favor of the Sweet Home Chapter. For example, the appeal to the canon of *noscitur a sociis* was misguided, supposing as it did that the function of "harm" in the regulatory definition was basically the same as that of the other concepts appearing there. But the context in which "harm" is used indicates that "Congress meant that term to serve a particular function in ESA, consistent with, but distinct from, the functions of the other verbs used to define 'take.'" Even if the principle was correctly applied, Stevens noted, it provides no support for the Sweet Home Chapter. Several of the other words in the definition refer to types of conduct that do not necessarily involve direct applications of force, such as "harass," "wound," and "pursue."

Also, Stevens pointed out that, far from undermining it, the legislative history of the ESA *supports* the FWS definition of harm. Both the Senate and House reports on bills that would eventually become the ESA noted how "take" was defined "in the broadest possible terms," so broad, indeed, that *unintentional* harassment was included. This clearly indicates that Congress was interested in regulating much more than the deliberate actions of hunters and trappers. As for the fact that a phrase about the modification of habitat was deleted from the Senate bill, Stevens did not find this particularly relevant. There was no indication in the legislative history why the habitat provision was removed, and in any case it was far more expansive than the regulation the Sweet Home Chapter was currently challenging. The deleted prohibition was against *any* adverse habitat modification, unqualified by the actual kill or injury standard later inserted.

Exceptions to the Taking Prohibition
In 1973 the ESA provided four different exceptions to the prohibition on taking endangered and threatened species. Today these four remain, and subsequent amendments have added several more.

Among the original exceptions is the stipulation that the restrictions do not apply to anyone holding an endangered or threatened species in captivity or in a "controlled environment" on the date President Nixon signed the ESA into law (December 28, 1973). Also exempt are individuals keeping animals at any time before they are placed on the list, so long as these creatures are not being held for commercial purposes. Further, the secretary (in practice, the director of the FWS) may issue a permit for taking endangered or threatened species "for scientific purposes or to enhance the propagation or survival of the affected species." The lengthy applications for these permits must appear in the *Federal Register* and the public given the opportunity to comment on them.

Indians, Aleuts, or Inuit ("Eskimo") born in Alaska and residing in the state, as well as nonnative residents of aboriginal villages in Alaska are exempted from the provisions of the act under certain conditions: the taking of listed species must be done "primarily for subsistence purposes," without wasting animal products, and by those who are "primarily dependent" on the wildlife "for the creation and sale of authentic native articles of handicrafts and clothing." Such items are defined by ESA regulations as articles commonly made before the law's enactment, constructed mainly of natural materials, and not mass produced. The FWS can rescind any or all of these exceptions for Alaskans, if their taking of listed species brings the animals too close to extinction.

American Indians residing elsewhere in the United States are *not* exempt from the ESA, yet various treaties written in the 1800s have guaranteed them the right to hunt, typically without regard to species. Do these treaty rights override the federal law? The question has not yet been answered by any tribunal. When a Lakota (Sioux) Indian was prosecuted in 1985 for capturing bald eagles, then an endangered species, the Supreme Court ruled that the Bald Eagle Protection Act does abrogate treaty rights, but did not decide the issue of the ESA's priority (*United States v. Dion; see* this chapter: *Bald Eagle Protection Act of 1940: BEPA and American Indians*). Native Hawaiians, however, have been told by the Ninth Circuit Court of Appeals that the ESA does not permit them to exercise their aboriginal rights to hunt threatened and endangered species (*United States v. Nuesca*).

Other exclusions were written into the ESA with amendments in 1976, 1978, and 1982. Among these is one for any person holding raptors in captivity, either as pets or for commercial purposes, on or before the date the ESA was enacted. Artifacts made from parts of listed species that are at least 100 years old may be legally possessed, bought, sold, imported, or exported, as may most scrimshaw products (carvings or etchings made from whale bones or teeth), regardless of age, held when the ESA became law.

A 1978 amendment allows taking listed species if necessary to protect human well-being, such as defending oneself or another person against an aggressive grizzly bear (a threatened species). However, in a subsequent case testing this "self-defense" exception, the Ninth Circuit Court rejected the notion that the amendment applies to the protection of property as well. A sheep rancher was charged with violating the ESA and assessed a fine after he killed a grizzly that had preyed upon his livestock. He claimed that, far from being liable for the grizzly's death, if the government did not compensate him for his losses, he would be deprived of property without due process. The court was not convinced (*Christy v. Hodel*).

One of the more innovative exceptions, established with a 1982 amendment, is the "experimental population." These are populations of endangered species that the FWS introduces into areas outside their current range to enhance the survival and propagation of the species generally; usually these species are reintroduced to formerly occupied habitat. Although these are members of officially endangered species, the experimental population status affords the animals fewer protections, primarily by designating them as threatened, which allows the FWS to design less restrictive regulations for them.

The FWS also distinguishes these experimental populations as either "essential" or "nonessential." Essential populations are those "whose loss would be likely to appreciably reduce the likelihood of the survival of the species in the wild," and it is these that are considered threatened in their new habitat. However, most experimental populations are "nonessential," they are treated as species that are *proposed* to be listed. This means that no "critical habitat" is designated for these animals, and federal agencies or federally funded activities need not avoid destroying or modifying the areas where they have been placed (*see also* this chapter: *Endangered Species Act of 1973: Critical Habitats and the Northern Spotted Owl*).

The rationale for downgrading protections for experimental populations is to promote the acceptance and cooperation of private landowners and lessees of public land, who would presumably see reintroductions with all the standard ESA restrictions as unduly burdensome or costly. For example, the FWS has established experimental populations of the gray wolf in parts of Wyoming, Montana, Arizona, and New Mexico, a species traditionally viewed by local ranchers as predaceous vermin to be eradicated (for more on experimental populations, *see* this chapter: *Legal Protections for Bears: Grizzly Bear Recovery*).

Finally, a 1982 amendment authorized the FWS to issue permits for the taking of listed species that is "incidental to, and not the purpose of, the carrying out of otherwise lawful activity." This exception reflects congressional recognition that many customary human activities in nature could result in the unintended and unplanned taking of endangered or threatened species. Examples of such activities include trail and road maintenance, the erection of structures, tree cutting, dam operations, commercial and sport fishing, and hunting of unprotected species. Remember, under the ESA's definition of "take," and as affirmed by the Supreme Court in *Sweet Home* (*see* this chapter: *Babbitt v. Sweet Home Chapter of Communities for a Great Oregon*), a violation may occur even though no direct physical injury is caused to an animal and even if the prohibited acts are done accidentally.

The application for an incidental taking permit must detail a "habitat conservation plan," explaining how the applicant will lessen the number of incidental takings that may occur, and how the funding for this plan will be supplied. Before the FWS can approve the permit the agency must verify that the incidental taking will not "appreciably reduce the likelihood of the survival and recovery of the species in the wild."

Critical Habitats and the Northern Spotted Owl
When a species is listed, the ESA requires the secretary to identify its "critical habitat" for federal protection. This key idea would become one of the most difficult and contentious ones in the statute, yet Congress did not define it in 1973, and no method for its determination was offered. Instead, lawmakers simply wrote a broad injunction in section 7, addressed to all federal agencies, that they "insure that actions authorized, funded, or carried out by them do not jeopardize the continued existence of endangered or threatened species or result in the destruction or modification of habitat of such species which is determined by the Secretary . . . to be critical."

A 1978 amendment stipulated that "critical habitat" referred to geographical areas either currently occupied by the animals or ones not yet occupied that are "essential to the conservation of the species." A subsequent regulation further detailed the criteria for designating critical habitat. These include adequate space for normal behavior and population growth, availability of basic physiological requirements (food, water, air, light, nutrients), cover or shelter, and areas for breeding, reproduction, and rearing of offspring.

Ironically, this 1978 amendment also seriously hindered the listing process. It additionally demanded an accounting of the economic impact of designating an area as critical habitat, and allowed the secretary to refrain from making this designation when economically beneficial to do so. Given the already existing statutory requirement, this had the practical effect of stifling the appearance of species on the list: if no critical habitat, then no listing. Moreover, the economic analysis of critical habitat for numerous listing proposals proved so complicated that after two years they were still not complete, and the ESA requires that proposals be withdrawn if the secretary has not made a final determination within that time. In 1982 these obstacles were overcome with an amendment allowing listing without simultaneous designation "if critical habitat is not then determinable."

Yet the failure to specify critical habitat, even though a species is listed, can have its own disadvantages for imperiled wildlife. The famous case of the northern spotted owl illustrates this problem well. Weighing a pound or two and standing about a foot and a half tall, this subspecies is found only in the old-growth spruce and fir forests fringing the western slope of the Cascade Mountains, from southwestern British Columbia down through Washington, Oregon, and into northwestern California. The owl lives in the large conifers, lining its nesting holes with alpine debris, feeding on squirrels, mice, and small birds. The big trees are also much prized by the logging industry.

As timber cutting in the northwestern United States steadily continued through the 1950s, 1960s, and into the 1970s, scientists began to take notice of a marked decline in spotted owl numbers. The bird, they discovered, is an "indicator species," a barometer of forest health: if it is thriving, so are the woods, and if the trees disappear, so does the northern spotted owl. Nonetheless, during the 1970s the United States Forest Service (USFS) flatly rejected several proposals to save the *Strix* variety by setting aside tracts of land in several national forests. These are public lands where some three-quarters of the nation's old-growth forests are found.

Finally in 1988 the USFS announced that nearly 1 million acres of northern spotted owl territory would be placed off-limits to loggers, but about 25 percent of the other 6 million or so acres of prime owl habitat would be logged after fifteen years, and 60 percent after fifty years. Both tree cutters and "tree huggers" were infuriated by this arrangement. Almost immediately, representatives of the timber industry, led by the Washington Contract Loggers Association, sued the USFS for *banning* logging in *any* part of the old growth forest. At the same time, the Seattle Audubon Society and other environmental organizations sued for *allowing* logging in *any* spotted owl habitat. After first issuing a preliminary injunction ordering the USFS not to sell any timber to logging firms, the federal district court then removed the order when Congress attached a rider to a 1989 appropriations bill protecting the USFS from legal challenges to its utilization of spotted owl habitat. On appeal, the Ninth Circuit Court of Appeals ruled that the rider was unconstitutional. However, by this time—late 1990—nearly all the timber had already been sold, and in any case the Supreme Court subsequently determined that Congress had done nothing illegal (*Robertson v. Seattle Audubon Society*).

Meanwhile, undaunted, environmental groups had been trying another tactic: bringing the ESA to bear on the controversy by forcing the FWS to list the spotted owl as an endangered species, and thus secure the protections of the federal law. In January 1987 an environmental organization called Greenworld submitted a petition to list the bird as endangered throughout its range. The idea was reinforced that summer when twenty-nine other such groups filed a second petition for listing the species as endangered in parts of Washington and Oregon, and threatened elsewhere. The FWS rejected both petitions in December with the pronouncement that listing the owl was "not warranted at this time."

Greenworld and most of the other organizations—including the Seattle chapter and several other regional chapters of the Audubon Society, the Wilderness Society, and the Sierra Club—promptly sued Interior Secretary Donald Hodel and the FWS. The plaintiffs argued that the rejection of the petitions was "arbitrary and capricious." Judge Thomas Zilly agreed with them. The FWS had failed to provide any explanation or justification for denying the listing, and had seemingly ignored the opinion of its own population biologist that "continued old-growth harvesting is likely to lead to the extinction of the [spotted owl] subspecies in the foreseeable future." Judge Zilly did not order the FWS to list the species; instead he gave the Service ninety days to explain why it wasn't (*Northern Spotted Owl v. Hodel*).

Rather than attempt to do that, the FWS relented and listed the northern spotted owl as threatened in June 1990. Yet, still evincing a certain obstinacy, the FWS did not designate any critical habitat for the bird on the grounds that it was not "determinable," an omission apparently allowed by the 1982 amendment. This prompted many of the same plaintiffs from *Hodel* to file suit again in the same federal district court. Secretary Manuel Lujan, now head of the Interior Department, and the FWS were named as defendants.

The plaintiffs complained that the ESA demands the identification of critical habitat for the owl concurrently with the listing unless compelling reasons for not doing so are provided, and no such reasons had been offered. Once more, Judge Zilly found for the environmental organizations. "The federal defendants," he wrote, "fail to direct this Court to any portion of the administrative record which adequately explains or justifies the decision not to designate critical habitat for the northern spotted owl." This time, however, the judge directed the FWS to produce a critical habitat plan within sixty days. This was done, and in early 1992 the appropriate areas were officially identified (*Northern Spotted Owl v. Lujan*).

The FWS's motivations for refusing in 1990 to designate habitat crucial for the spotted owl are not transparent, but this failure did allow logging on federal lands inhabited by the bird to continue for nearly two years after the listing. After all, section 7 of the ESA appears to impose one duty upon every federal agency to avoid "the destruction or adverse modification of critical habitat," and a second duty to avoid actions "likely to jeopardize the continued existence" of any listed species. If no critical habitat is specified, the first obligation cannot be violated, and without that specification it is not clear how merely cutting down trees imperils an entire species of owl. On the other hand, it is also unclear that section 7 states completely distinct legal duties because detrimental impacts on critical habitat would seem necessarily to create a hazard to an endangered or threatened species.

The FWS and Congress labored over this distinction with guidelines, regulations, and amendments through the 1970s and 1980s. Finally, when the FWS designated critical habitat for the spotted owl in 1992, as so ordered in *Lujan,* the agency produced what remains the current government understanding of these section 7 duties. If some activity destroys or unfavorably alters the habitat of a species that is near to becoming extinct, both the critical habitat duty *and* the jeopardy duty have probably been violated. If a species has nearly recovered from its endangered or threatened status, such activity likely violates only the critical habitat duty.

What ESA-imposed obligation, if any, is violated when a nearly complete, multimillion dollar public works project will imperil a small population of three-inch, snail-eating fish? Answering that question would take five contentious years, and involve the Congress of the United States, the Department of the Interior, the Tennessee Valley Authority (TVA), environmentalists, and, finally, the Supreme Court.

The Jeopardy Duty and the Snail Darter

The fish that ignited the controversy is one of about 130 species in the perch family commonly known as "darters," so-called from their habit of streaking through the water in short bursts after prey. This famous species is *Percina tanasi,* named the "snail darter" by its discoverer, University of Tennessee ichthyologist David Etnier. In August 1973, four months before the ESA was enacted, Dr. Etnier was exploring the waters of the Little Tennessee River several miles upstream from where it empties into the Tennessee River, about an hour's drive southwest of Knoxville. There he came upon a previously undescribed fish living in shallow, clear water, eating snails out of the gravel riverbed. After due study and confirmation of its uniqueness, in January 1975 Etnier and several others petitioned the secretary of the interior, as provided by the new federal law, requesting that the snail darter be listed as an endangered species. The secretary determined that the fish was very likely worthy of ESA protection, and published the proposal for listing in the *Federal Register*. Numerous reactions to the proposal came from various quarters, including the TVA, and in October 1975 the snail darter was officially listed as endangered.

Meanwhile, TVA construction of the Tellico Dam and Reservoir Project entered its final stages. The dam portion of the plan was located near the confluence of the Little Tennessee and Tennessee rivers, and although building had begun shortly after Congress appropriated funds for the project in 1967 and by 1975 it was virtually completed, the Tellico Dam had never been put into operation. Environmental organizations and local citizens had opposed the project from the start, not out of concern for the snail darter, which was still unknown then, but to save the farmland and natural areas that would be drowned by the 17,000-acre, 30-mile-long reservoir that would be created when Tellico's gates were closed.

Led by the Environmental Defense Fund, the opposition banded together and convinced the federal courts that the TVA's environmental impact statement for the project did not comply with the National Environmental Policy Act. An injunction was issued in 1972 ordering a halt to the construction (*Environmental Defense Fund v. TVA*). Nearly two years elapsed before the courts found that the TVA was in compliance, and the building began again, just about the same time that President Nixon signed the ESA. By then, the snail darter had been discovered less than ten miles upstream from Tellico Dam.

When the snail darter was listed, its critical habitat was determined to be along the Little Tennessee River precisely where the Tellico Reservoir would fill once the dam became operational—the fish was found nowhere else. Secretary Kleppe's pronouncement on the emergent conflict was unequivocal and preemptory: "The impoundment of water behind Tellico Dam would result in the total destruction of the snail darter's habitat. . . . All federal agencies must take such action as is necessary to insure that actions, authorized, funded, or carried out by them do not result in the destruction or modification of this critical habitat area." Even so, the TVA had steadfastly maintained that the ESA did not prohibit completion of an approved project, paid for and nearly finished before the law was signed, arguing that the term "action" in section 7 did not encompass the final phases of ongoing projects. For their part, Congress had continued to appropriate money to finish the job, with the approval of President Gerald Ford. It seemed that Tellico would not be stopped, and the fish were doomed.

In February 1976 the Association of Southern Biologists, the Audubon Council of Tennessee, and three concerned citizens and residents of the Little Tennessee Valley, one of whom was named Hiram Hill, filed a lawsuit in the federal District Court for Eastern Tennessee. They alleged that, if the dam was put into service, the TVA would violate the ESA-imposed duty not to jeopardize the existence of an endangered species. The plaintiffs requested a permanent injunction against its completion.

TVA v. Hill: The Dam v. the Darter

The district court agreed that the Tellico Dam would very likely extinguish the snail darter. Nonetheless, the suit of Hill and the other plaintiffs was dismissed and their request denied. Their complaint would lead to an absurd result, the court reasoned, one that Congress could not possibly have intended—that is, that an injunction must be issued to halt an impoundment of water if an endangered species is discovered the day before the gates are scheduled to close. Impressed that $53 million would be lost if the dam were scrapped, the court concluded that "[a]t some point in time a federal project becomes so near completion and so incapable of modification that a court of equity should not apply a statute enacted long after inception of the project to produce an unreasonable result." That time had arrived (*Hill v. TVA*). Bolstered by this decision, in June 1976 Congress appropriated more money for Tellico.

Yet the Sixth Circuit Court of Appeals had an entirely different opinion. In January 1977 that court handed down the permanent injunction sought by the plaintiffs, with instructions that the order remain in effect until either Congress legislatively exempted Tellico from the restrictions of the ESA, or the snail darter was removed from the endangered list. Rejecting the TVA's understanding of the limited range of application for the word "actions" in section 7, the appellate court also could not accept the proposition that the ESA requires judges to weigh the value of an endangered species against the cost of a public works project in progress. Further, the fact that Congress had continued to allocate funds for the dam was irrelevant.

Lawmakers responded to this decision that summer by earmarking more money for Tellico. Persuaded by the TVA, this apportionment included $2 million to facilitate the relocation of the snail darter to another waterway. The Supreme Court agreed to review the case shortly thereafter.

The chief justice himself, Warren Burger, wrote the six-to-three majority opinion, holding that the TVA would indeed violate the ESA by completing and operating the dam, and that a permanent injunction was the appropriate judicial response to the prospect of this violation. Quoting the section 7 duty that federal agencies avoid jeopardizing endangered species or destroying their habitat, Burger wrote that "one would be hard pressed to find a statutory provision whose terms were any plainer. . . . This language admits of no exceptions." The meaning of this plain language is solidly supported by a study of the legislative history of the ESA. There one finds, again and again, reports from both houses of Congress that the descent of species into extinction must be reversed, that, no matter the effort and resources required, the "genetic heritage" of life on earth must be preserved. As one House report put it, "The value of this genetic heritage is, quite literally, incalculable." The commentaries Burger cited indicated that species have this enormous worth because they are valuable to human beings, a view that nature is a vast, largely untapped medicine chest, an apothecary with many presently unknown remedies, a bounty that we risk at our own peril.

Moreover, Burger pointed out that drafts of ESA bills contained phrases qualifying the duty of federal agencies to preserve endangered species only "insofar as is practicable and consistent with [their] primary purposes." Yet, sensitive to concerns that such qualifications would be read as permissions to prioritize agency purposes whenever they conflicted with the well-being of endangered species, Congress deleted these reservations in the final versions of the bills that would become the ESA. The general obligation of federal agencies is clearly stated in section 2, demanding that each of them "seek to conserve endangered species," where "conserve" means "the use of all methods and procedures which are necessary to bring any endangered species . . . to the point at which [ESA protections] are no longer necessary." The operation of the Tellico Dam is incompatible with this obligation, the duty imposed by section 7, and the intention of Congress in writing the ESA.

Finally, the chief justice addressed the TVA's contention that the repeated allocations of money made by Congress for the dam, even after being fully apprised of the situation involving the snail darter, amounted to an "implied repeal" of the ESA. He conceded that reports from the House and Senate Appropriations Committees did suggest that the legislators either believed the ESA did not apply to Tellico or that it should be completed despite the law. Whatever the committees' attitude, Burger pointed to several high court precedents establishing that repeals by implication are deeply suspect and that a legislative intention to repeal must be "clear and manifest." These features are entirely absent from the records of the congressional committees.

Exempting Federal Agencies

Reacting with unexpected circumspection in the wake of *TVA v. Hill*, Congress did not simply authorize a blanket exception for Tellico as many anticipated would happen. Instead, lawmakers quickly wrote up a formal process for federal agencies seeking an exemption from the section 7 duties, approving it as one of the 1978 ESA amendments just before adjourning at the end of the year. Although the ESA had always provided exclusions from section 9 prohibitions (both discussed below), these are primarily addressed to individual or corporate actors, and no exceptions had ever been stipulated for federal agencies.

Part of the new exemption process involved detailing the nature of the consultation with the secretary that federal agencies had been required to undertake since 1973, although the procedure for those deliberations had never been explained. Now, before starting a federal project, agencies must ask the secretary—the FWS really—whether threatened or endangered species live in the area to be developed. If any listed species do occur there, the agency and the FWS must collaborate to produce a "biological assessment," ascertaining how the species would be affected by the project, if at all. Once it is determined that the agency action would affect a threatened or endangered species, the agency must discuss the matter further with the FWS, which will draft a "biological opinion" describing the likely impact of the project on the species and its critical habitat. If, in the judgment of the FWS, the agency will violate either or both of the section 7 duties in pursuing the project, the biological opinion must recommend "reasonable and prudent alternatives to the agency action."

It is only at this point, after the biological opinion has been produced, that federal agencies unwilling to settle for these alternatives may attempt to secure an exemption from section 7 by submitting an application to the FWS. If the Service determines that the application has appropriately addressed the consultation process, the biological issues involved, and the matter of the agency's "irreversible commitment of resources," hearings are conducted with the applicant. The FWS then prepares a report on these hearings and submits it to the "Endangered Species Committee" (ESC), which has the final authority to approve exemptions for federal agencies.

Also created by the 1978 amendments, the ESC is chaired by the secretary of the interior, and includes the secretaries of agriculture and army, the chair of the Council of Economic Advisors, the administrators of the Environmental Protection Agency and the National Oceanic and Atmospheric Administration, and a representative, appointed by the president, from each state affected by the particular action. Exemptions are granted if at least five of the committee members agree that each of several conditions have been met. Among them are these: (1) there are no reasonable and prudent alternatives; (2) the benefits of the project outweigh those of alternatives that are consistent with the ESA; (3) the project is in the public interest of the region or the nation; and (4) there is no irreversible commitment of resources.

The TVA submitted the first application under the new exemption process for Tellico, and, again to the surprise of many, the ESC unanimously rejected it. Undeterred, Congress speedily drafted and approved a bill directing the completion of the Tellico Dam and waiving all federal laws that might halt it. President Jimmy Carter did not veto the bill.

Meanwhile, several hundred snail darters had been removed from the Little Tennessee River and transplanted into three other rivers nearby. In November 1979 the dam's gates closed and the Tellico Reservoir filled where the lower reaches of the Little Tennessee had once approached the Tennessee River. One year later, Dr. Etnier discovered snail darters in South Chickamauga Creek, and over the next few years other watercourses in the area revealed additional populations of the fish. In 1984 the FWS reclassified the snail darter as threatened, which it remains today, and removed the Little Tennessee River from ESA protection as a critical habitat.

Recovery Plans

Removal from the list, or at least a downgrading from endangered to threatened status, would seem to be the ultimate goal of the ESA, one preferably accomplished through the recovery of the imperiled species. Nonetheless, in its original 1973 version, the act said nothing about what must be done, if anything, to provide for the recovery of listed species. The revitalization of an entire species almost always requires many different biological and social measures undertaken over an extended time, so early on the FWS started on its own initiative to produce documents detailing the "recovery plans" for certain species as they were listed.

It was not until the 1978 amendments that Congress decided to require the secretary to devise some strategy of recovery, directing him or her to "develop and implement plans for the conservation and survival" of endangered and threatened animals and plants. No further guidance in this process was then offered. Later amendments through the late 1970s did add more detail. Threatened or endangered species most likely to benefit from recovery plans are to be given priority, especially those whose survival conflicts with development projects or some other economic activity. Also, recovery plans must include site-specific management actions, "objective, measurable criteria" of recovery that, when met, would result in removal of the species from the protected list. Estimates of the cost to implement the plan and how long it will take are further required. These plans vary widely in their length and complexity, some are just a couple of dozen pages long, while others are well over 100 pages.

The recovery plan for the black-footed ferret (*Mustela nigripes*), for example, addresses each of the main aspects mandated by Congress. First, its recovery has been given priority due to a friction, not directly between the ferret and economic interests, but between black-tailed prairie dogs (*Cynomys ludovicianus*) and farming and livestock raising. It has been widely believed in agriculture for decades that prairie dogs do excessive damage to food crops, and successfully compete with cattle and sheep for grass; their extensive network of burrows also presents a hazard to livestock who might blunder into the holes and injure themselves. Consequently, prairie dogs have been intensively hunted and trapped, such predation severely depleting the black-footed ferret population. There is probably nothing this ferret likes better for any meal than a plump, juicy prairie dog, and the two species live in very close association. The endangered status of the ferret is a direct result of the concerted attack by agriculture interests on prairie dogs.

Among other things, the recovery plan calls for releases of captive-bred ferrets into suitable reintroduction sites, locating and maintaining potential habitat, and establishing at least thirty breeding adults in each wild population with a total census of 1,500 mature ferrets by 2010. Meeting this goal would constitute the recovery of this species. The program costs over $2 million. (*See* this chapter: *Legal Protections for Bears: Grizzly Bear Recovery.*)

Although since 1978 Congress has clearly demanded that recovery plans be written, about two-thirds of all listed animal species have as yet no such plan. Moreover, no further standards have ever been imposed for the composition or implementation of recovery plans. There is a dearth of case law in this area, but the prevailing opinion from the federal bench seems to be this: recovery plans must be formulated; however, the secretary has wide discretion to alter the timetable and the actions detailed in the plan. In what appears to be the leading case at this time, a federal district judge ruled that "[t]he recovery plan presents a guideline for future goals but does not mandate any actions, at any particular time, to obtain those goals" (*Oregon Natural Resource Council v. Turner*). Even so, it is clear that once a plan is published, the FWS must do something and cannot sit on the design indefinitely.

Penalties

The ESA provides some of the stiffest punishments available for violations in animal law. Criminal penalties of up to $50,000 in fines or one year in prison, or both, may be assessed against a person who is proven in district court to have knowingly violated any provision of the ESA concerning endangered species. Civil penalties of $25,000 are also provided for this type of infraction.

After the Sentencing Reform Act of 1984, which increases criminal penalties for federal crimes, the maximum fine for a violation of the ESA is $100,000. Each violation concerning threatened species may bring a $25,000 fine and six months incarceration for criminal penalties, or a civil punishment of half this dollar amount. Importers and exporters are liable to the same civil penalties for trading in endangered and threatened species, whether they knew they were violating the ESA or not, but an unwitting offense by any other person cannot be punished with a fine greater than $500. Additionally, any aircraft, vehicles, boats, weapons, and other equipment used while committing an illegal act may be seized and forfeited to the federal government. Finally, the secretary must suspend for up to one year or cancel the federal hunting or fishing permits of a person convicted of a criminal violation of the ESA.

The secretary must also pay reward money to individuals providing information that leads to the arrest and conviction of perpetrators. Rewards are to be funded by money collected from fines and forfeitures, and these revenues are also to be used to pay for the care of wildlife held during legal proceedings.

Any person may file a civil suit against any other person, organization, or government entity alleging violations of the ESA, and private citizens may also charge the secretary with failing to list an appropriate species as threatened or endangered, or with failing to remove a recovered species from the list.

The scope of the citizen suit provision was recently tested in the Supreme Court. Two ranchers and the administrators of two irrigation districts in northern California were dismayed by a 1992 FWS recommendation. The Service wanted to maintain a minimum water level at a lake and a reservoir in the Klamath Irrigation Project to protect two endangered species of fish, the Lost River (*Deltistes luxatus*) sucker and the shortnose sucker (*Chasmistes brevirostris*). A series of lakes, rivers, dams, canals, and reservoirs, the Klamath Project was frequently tapped by agricultural interests for growing crops and watering livestock, a supply that would be curtailed by the FWS restriction.

The plaintiffs principally argued that setting a minimum water level in effect established critical habitat for the fish, yet no economic analysis had been done, as required by the ESA. The district court and the appellate court dismissed the suit, holding that only plaintiffs alleging an interest in preserving endangered species were entitled to sue on this basis. The Supreme Court reversed that ruling, reading the ESA provision quite literally: "any person" means *any person* may file a lawsuit under the ESA, not just environmentalists or those concerned about endangered animals (*Bennett v. Spear*).

LEGAL PROTECTIONS FOR BEARS

The origins of the modern bear genus *Ursus*, Latin for "bear"—date back at least 50 million years to a large family of carnivorous mammals known as the *Miacidae*. The miacids were small animals whose pointed teeth, sharp claws, and simple digestive systems effectively adapted them to a diet of flesh. One member of this family, *Miacis*, is the ancestor of every meat-eating mammal presently inhabiting the planet, including bears.

Two main branches split from *Miacis* perhaps 45 million years ago, one that would become the cat family (*Felidae*), the other the *Mustelidae*—weasels, ferrets, mink, skunks, and other slinky animals with long, slender bodies, short legs, and small, rounded ears. At 25 to 30 million years before the present, *Miacis* disappeared, dissolved by the inexorable processes of evolution into three main groups: *Procyonidis*, eventually morphing into the raccoon; *Cynodictis*, the parent of today's wolves, coyotes, foxes, jackals, and domestic dogs; and *Daphaenus*, the progenitor of the bear.

The first creature that we would recognize as a bear, the first *Ursus*, appeared in central Europe sometime between 5 and 8 million years ago. As the species name suggests, *U. minimus* was still on the smaller side like *Daphaenus*, about as big as a medium-sized dog, but in other respects the animal was much different from the canines. When walking, this bear planted its whole foot—a dog strides on its toes. Its bigger skull contained larger teeth, with molars suitable for grinding vegetable matter, and a longer intestine, signaling the movement to an omnivorous diet.

At about 2 million years ago *U. minimus* became *U. etruscus*, the "Etruscan bear." It is with this species that we begin to see a blossoming into the large and powerful animal we know as the modern bear. Evidently, this was a physiological response primarily to the vast climatological and geographical upheavals wrought by the Ice Ages. The weather grew colder and the glaciers stripped away the forests of northern Europe. A general rule of mammalogy states that a body retains heat more efficiently when the ratio of surface area to mass increases. This means that in the radically altered, glacial environment a larger frame is easier to keep warm.

As the tens of thousands of icy years passed, the Etruscan bear faded away, evolving into *U. arctos*, the brown bear, and *U. thibetanus*, the black bear. Both species spread across Asia, with the larger, more aggressive brown bear dominating on the steppes in the center of the continent and throughout the vast Siberian taiga. The black bear populated the subglacial forests in the south, but the highly adaptable brown was common here as well. Eventually, the two species migrated over the land bridge that connected northeast Asia with North America and infiltrated the

New World, first *U. thibetanus* at perhaps a million years before the present, and *U. arctos* much later, at about 50,000 B.C.E..

When the last glaciers receded around 10,000 B.C.E., the American bears embarked on an evolutionary course that separated them from their Euro-Asian brethren as decisively as the continents were now sundered, so much so that taxonomists say the New World black bear is a different species, *U. americanus*. On the other hand, the scientists see the brown bears as closer relations, dividing the American members of the family into subspecies, and featuring the darkly christened *Ursus arctos horribilis*, more commonly called the "grizzly" bear. Nonetheless, all agree that the grizzly and its North American siblings are bigger, smarter, and more aggressive than the comparatively more docile and diminutive Old World brown bear.

The evolution of the polar bear, *Ursus maritimus*, is not as well understood. The generally accepted account is that the advancing glacial ice sheet isolated a population of brown bears, probably in Siberia, some 200,000 to maybe a quarter million years ago. Living constantly close to the water, responding to the ever-present snow and ice, this group of *U. arctos* quickly developed into a rather different animal, a sea bear. The head shrank somewhat and the neck elongated, apparently to streamline the body for recurrent swimming; the molars and canines grew longer and sharper as vegetation exited the diet; fur bleached of all color proved the most effective camouflage in a world of endless white; a prodigious layer of blubber sheathed the body against the arctic cold; and that frigid climate produced a further heightening of the surface-to-volume ratio, yielding a beast of enormous proportions.

Polar Bears
Weighing three-quarters of a ton and standing 10 feet tall, the adult male polar bear is the largest mammal outside of Africa that does not live in the ocean. Even so, this bear spends few of its waking hours on land, and during those infrequent visits to *terra firma* the sea is never far away. When not seeking cover in deep snow drifts from inclement weather, or denning with cubs, polar bears are almost always found on the frozen surface of the Arctic Ocean, hunting ringed seals (*Phoca hispida*) along the ice leads and on the floes. The total number of *Ursus maritimus* in the world today is not precisely known; at most, no more than 30,000 inhabit the circumpolar region above Alaska, Canada, Greenland, Norway, and the Russian Federation. The American population, located in the Chukchi and Beaufort seas off the north coast of Alaska, is estimated at some 3,000 to 5,000 individuals.

Although data is absent (for obvious reasons), perhaps 200 or 300 polar bears were killed every year for centuries by the native populations of

North America, Europe, and Asia. Then in the late 1800s commercial seal and whale hunters sailing under the flags of the United States, Russia, Norway, and Japan began to slaughter polar bears in earnest, mainly to reduce competition for an economically valuable prey species, but also for "sport" and meat. After the turn of the century, recreational hunting of the white bear in far northern Europe became a popular pastime for wealthy sportsmen. In the 1940s guides with airplanes began delivering shooters to its Alaskan haunts, further depleting the species. By the middle of the century, several hundred polar bears were being killed every year in Alaska alone, and the annual take worldwide was well over 1,000. Since females give birth to only one or two cubs every four years at best, and infant mortality can reach 50 percent, the pace of the killing far exceeded the reproduction rate. At this time, there was no legal regulation whatever of polar bear hunting, nor of any activity adversely affecting the animals.

Finally, in 1955 the Soviet Union implemented the first restrictions on taking polar bears, banning all hunting entirely. In 1961 Alaska established a closed season on polar bear hunting, prohibited the use of aircraft for pursuing the animal, and outlawed the killing of cubs and females with cubs. Four years later, at the initiative of the United States, scientists from Canada, Norway, Denmark (on behalf of Greenland), and the U.S.S.R. met with the Americans in Fairbanks, Alaska, to discuss the fate of the now beleaguered bear species. Further meetings in 1968, 1970, and 1972, conducted in consultation with the International Union for the Conservation of Nature and Natural Resources (IUCN), produced a series of recommendations and resolutions for the protection of polar bears, but no legal action. Not long after the fourth meeting, Congress urged President Richard Nixon to negotiate a treaty to preserve the animals with the other nations claiming possession of areas inhabited by polar bears.

Polar Bears and the Marine Mammal Protection Act
Meanwhile, Nixon signed the Marine Mammal Protection Act (MMPA) (*see* this chapter: *Marine Mammal Protection Act*) that year, 1972, with joint administration of the law assigned to the U.S. Fish and Wildlife Service (FWS) in the Department of the Interior and the National Marine Fisheries Service in the Department of Commerce. Management authority over polar bears is vested in the FWS, which also issues regulations concerning the animals.

Instituting safeguards for all marine mammals found within the jurisdiction of the United States, including polar bears, the MMPA protects the Chukchi-Beaufort population from "taking"; that is, from hunting, capture, killing, or harassing by any person subject to American law. "Harassment" is defined as pursuing, tormenting, or annoying the animals in a manner that may injure them or disrupt their behavior patterns. Strictly speaking, the MMPA does not provide an outright or absolute ban on taking polar bears or other marine mammals. Instead it imposes a "moratorium," a (presumably) temporary halt to all the listed activities, one that can in principal be rescinded when these species have sufficiently recovered from the dire situation in which excessive hunting has placed them. Further, the MMPA provides several exemptions to the moratorium, allowing polar bears to be legally taken notwithstanding the restrictions of the federal law.

First, the MMPA authorizes Alaskan Indians, Aleuts, and Inuit ("Eskimos") to hunt, harass, capture, or kill any polar bear at any time "if such taking is for subsistence or handicraft purposes and is not accomplished in a wasteful manner." Over the past 20 years, Alaskan natives have killed an average of about 100 bears annually, including 10 to 15 cubs. Despite this broad permission, a council of Canadian Inuit has made a pact with the Alaska Fish and Game Department, agreeing to follow stricter rules governing polar bear management in the Beaufort Sea region. These Inuit have pledged not to molest bears constructing or inhabiting dens, and to spare cubs and females with cubs or yearlings. However, most taking of polar bears by native peoples occurs in the Chukchi region, and there the size of the population is unknown.

An amendment in 1981 created a second exception to the MMPA moratorium, one that allows "incidental taking," that is, unintentional or accidental harassing and killing of polar bears. Permissible incidental takes must be in "small numbers" that have a "negligible impact" on the species, and must "not have an unmitigable adverse impact" on the use of the animals by natives. A "negligible impact" is defined as one "that cannot be reasonably expected to, and is not reasonably likely to, adversely affect the species." An "unmitigable adverse impact" causes polar bears to leave or avoid hunting areas, displaces native hunters, or puts physical obstacles between the hunters and the polar bears.

In March 2000 the FWS found that the oil and gas exploration, development, and production operations of BP Exploration, Inc., ARCO Alaska, Inc., and Exxon Corp. would have a negligible impact and no unmitigable adverse impact on polar bears (and pacific walrus) in the Beaufort Sea and along the north coast of Alaska. Consequently, the FWS issued a three-year authorization to the companies for the incidental take of "small numbers" of these animals. This is a continuation of an exemption period originally granted in 1993 to BP and a dozen other oil and gas corporations (including Exxon, Amoco, Mobil, and Texaco). Although the incidental taking approved here includes lethal taking, the FWS reports that through 1999 no polar bears (or walruses) had been killed by the work of the oil firms. Incidental taking associated with commercial fisheries is also allowed by the MMPA, but currently the Chukchi-Beaufort habitat is not affected by these operations.

The law also provides a permit system that authorizes taking bears for scientific research, to enhance the survival or recovery of the species, and for public display. Although numerous permits have been awarded for research and species enhancement, none have been issued to capture polar bears in the wild for public display. Even so, the Anchorage zoo received one in 1998 to acquire an orphaned cub (the mother had been shot, reportedly in self-defense) and a number of zoos have been granted this permission to import captive-bred bears. As of 2000 there are 111 specimens of *Ursus maritimus* confined in 40 American zoos. Standards for their care, treatment, and transportation are given by regulations issued under the authority of the Animal Welfare Act (AWA) (*see* chapter 5: *Circuses and Zoos: AWA Regulations for the Exhibition of Marine Mammals*).

In the past, some circuses have exhibited trained and untrained polar bears, which often received top billing as the featured animal act. Indeed, one of the first exotic animals ever displayed in America was a polar bear. Advertised as the "ferocious Greenland Bear," it toured the colonies in the 1730s as the star attraction of a traveling menagerie, one of the precursors of the modern circus. Today, no circus has a polar bear, and it has reportedly been at least twenty years since any did. Permits are also required to photograph polar bears, which can illegally take the bruins by "harassing" them. Despite the thousands of images of the bears commercially available, no such permissions have ever officially been given.

The MMPA moratorium may also be waived entirely. The complicated process of obtaining a waiver involves a detailed application, the thorough biological assessment of the impact of the taking on the species, the promulgation of appropriate regulations, notice and comment on both the waiver application and the proposed regulations, and possibly a cross-examination of the secretaries of commerce or interior by parties opposing the waiver. The whole issue may end up in the court of an administrative law judge. In any case, to date a waiver authorizing a polar bear take has yet to be issued.

The MMPA also established a ban on the importation of polar bears and products made from the animals, but this, too, may be overridden by all the exemptions noted above, except the one for incidental take. Polar bears that are pregnant, nursing, or less than eight months old cannot be imported under any circumstances, nor may any bear be taken in an "inhumane way." MMPA regulations define "humane" as the infliction of the "least possible degree of pain and suffering practicable."

In 1994 the National Rifle Association and the Safari Club lead a successful lobbying effort amending the MMPA to permit sport hunters to import polar bear parts from Canada, specifically from the Northwest

Territories where the bears are found. The amendment generated much controversy, inspiring rancorous debate in Congress. Hunting advocates contended that the permit fee—$1,000—and other expenses would promote bear conservation and enhance the well-being of native Canadians. Their opponents charged that the revision was just a ploy to accommodate American trophy hunters desiring to bring polar bear heads, skins, and claws back home.

Hunters apply for importation permits once they have killed a bear, and issuance is subject to certain conditions. Foremost among them is that the Northwest Territories must have a "scientifically sound" bear management program that will sustain hunted populations, one that is consistent with the purposes of the International Agreement on the Conservation of Polar Bears (*see* this chapter: *An International Agreement to Protect Polar Bears*), and can provide verification that the bear was legally taken. In the initial determination of early 1997, the Interior Department found that these criteria were met for five polar bear populations in the far reaches of the Northwest Territories; two more were added in early 1999. That year, ten permits to import sport-hunted bears were issued, down from the 1997 high of twenty-four.

Finally, although the MMPA attaches particular importance to the acquisition, improvement, and protection of marine mammal habitat and the larger ecosystem where these creature are found, very few regulations preserving the homelands of marine mammals have been issued. Such regulations designed specifically for polar bears have not been produced.

An International Agreement to Protect Polar Bears
Perhaps motivated by the enactment of the MMPA in 1972, shortly thereafter the five circumpolar nations finally formalized a plan that would protect *Ursus maritimus* around the world, signing the Agreement on the Conservation of Polar Bears in late 1973. The Senate ratified the treaty in 1975 and the appropriate governing bodies of all five signatories had done the same by 1978.

The articles of the agreement are similar to many of the provisions of the MMPA, but there are significant differences, too. Article I prohibits "taking" polar bears, here defined as hunting, killing, and capturing them. Unlike the U.S. federal law, there is no injunction against "harassing" bears in the agreement, and the prohibition is not a "moratorium" but an indefinite ban, though one that is nonetheless qualified with several exceptions, as in the MMPA. For example, article III stipulates that each nation may allow taking for "*bona fide* scientific . . . or conservation purposes" and "to prevent serious disturbance of the management of other living resources." This latter exception was added to authorize removing nuisance bears that disrupt commercial operations such as seal harvesting, while the reference to "living resources" prevents it from absolving oil and gas exploration or development.

Two other article III exceptions proved to be quite contentious. One entitles the signatories to permit "local people using traditional methods in the exercise of their traditional rights" to hunt, kill, or capture polar bears. Canada pushed through this first exception, desiring both natives and nonnatives who use the bear for their material culture, for subsistence, or who might come to depend on the animal as a resource to escape the ban. Further, soon after ratification Canada announced that it understood the "traditional rights" of "local people" to include their entitlement to sell polar bear permits to nonnatives for sport hunting, as long as native guides and dogs were used in the pursuit.

The second exception ambiguously allows taking "wherever [the bears] have or might have been subject to taking by traditional means by that [country's] nationals." The Canadian government insisted on interpreting this exception to allow polar bear hunting by *any* person, provided this is done in a region where nationals have taken bears "by traditional means." An alternative reading of the exemption permits taking only by citizens of that nation.

The outcome of this analysis is a Canadian interpretation of the agreement that permits sport hunting of polar bears by foreign nationals, Americans especially, in areas accessible by dog teams and snowmobiles—the "traditional means." In effect, this makes the open oceans and the ice floes scattered among them an inviolate polar bear sanctuary protected by the article I prohibition simply because dogs and snow machines cannot reach the bears in these regions. On the other hand, the near-shore sea and land areas that can be reached by these modes of travel become hunting grounds opened by the article III exceptions.

None of the other signatories has ever contested Canada's reading here. Recreational hunting of polar bears by foreign nationals has continued uninterrupted in the Northwest Territories since the agreement was signed. As mentioned above, the MMPA originally made the importation of bear trophies into the United States illegal. That ban ended with the 1994 amendment and the subsequent finding by the Department of the Interior that the hunting program in Canada was compatible with the purposes of the agreement.

Other articles are addressed to methods of take, polar bear research, and habitat protection. Airplanes and "large motorized vehicles" may not be used to take the bears under any of the exceptions, and all parties to the treaty are required to conduct research programs focused on the conservation and management of polar bears. The signatories agreed to pursue "appropriate action" to safeguard the ecosystems where the bears reside, to give "special attention" to critical aspects of their habitat, such as

denning sites, and to manage polar bears by means of "sound conservation practices." None of the quoted phrases are defined or explained in
the agreement.

Also missing from the articles, surprisingly, is a ban on hunting cubs
or females with cubs, and neither is there any such proscription to protect
denning bears. Instead, these concerns were appended to the document
as a resolution after the authors, apparently, forgot to include them in the
articles. The practical effect of this oversight is that the cub and denning
provisions are not legally binding on the parties to the agreement.

Black Bears

Historically, black bears inhabited at least some areas in every one of the
United States, except Hawaii. Today, they are still found in much of
America. Perhaps as many as half a million black bears live in varying
concentrations in no less than thirty-eight states. Most of them are in
Alaska, the Rocky Mountain states, and in the coastal ranges and Cas-
cade-Sierra Nevada mountain chain that run through Washington, Oregon, and California. Significant populations of the bears are also located
in the upper Great Lakes region, the Appalachian Mountains from Pennsylvania to Georgia, the Ozark Mountains in Arkansas, in the Adiron-
dacks and Catskills of New York, and throughout most of New England.
Small pockets of *Ursus americanus* may be found in Florida, Alabama,
Mississippi, Louisiana, and Texas. Essentially an arboreal creature, black
bears are absent from the western deserts and the grasslands of the Great
Plains and Midwest.

Despite the common name, many black bears are not black, instead
they are brown, cinnamon, honey, or even blond. The size of adult bears,
male and female, also fluctuates considerably depending on their habitat
and diet, ranging from about 150 to 400 pounds, with the average somewhere in between. Although always close to trees—the black is the only
bear that can climb—the woods that are home to the species range from
the temperate rain forests on the West Coast to the alpine forests in the
Rockies to the scrub woodlands of the Southwest to the cypress swamps
of the Southeast.

True omnivores, black bears eat many different kinds of plants and
enjoy the flesh of other animals as well. Among their favorite vegetables
are skunk cabbage, dandelions, grasses and roots of all varieties, acorns,
beechnuts, hickory nuts, pine nuts, raspberries, chokecherries, crowber-
ries, blueberries, and, appropriately enough, bearberries. Black bears will
not only climb trees to eat the new leaves and the catkins of poplar, aspen,
and willow, but they will even eat the bark, too. They do not often kill
other animals, and many a black bear has gone a long time between
meals of meat, but they do relish almost any carrion, from deer to mice to

domestic dogs. Ants, termites, beetles, ladybugs, and other insects are also fair game.

Legal Protections for Black Bears

Unlike polar bears or grizzly bears (*see* this chapter: *Legal Protections for Bears: Grizzly Bear Recovery*), no federal law or international treaty safeguards individual members of *Ursus americanus* wherever they are found. Federal protections for black bears presently extend only to the Louisiana subspecies, *U. a. luteolus,* and to other bears inhabiting the adjacent states of Texas and Mississippi.

In 1992, under the authority of the Endangered Species Act, the FWS declared the Louisiana black bear a threatened species—one likely to be at great risk of extinction in the foreseeable future—and thus one shielded by the federal statute. Primarily, this means that the 200 or 300 black bears in Louisiana may not be pursued, hunted, shot, wounded, killed, trapped, captured, or harassed at any time (with certain exceptions, such as in self-defense or for "incidental taking" associated with mining, logging, or road building; *see* this chapter: *Endangered Species Act of 1973*). Because no one but a bear biologist can distinguish *U. a. luteolus* from any other subspecies, and given their proximity to the imperiled population in the state next door, all black bears in southeastern Texas and in southern Mississippi, no matter their variety, have received this protection from the FWS as well.

Besides these three jurisdictions, six other states where black bears occur have either officially designated the animal as protected or do not provide shooters an open season on the species in their hunting regulations. In 1999 one of these six—Nevada—faced down a proposal by pro-hunting groups, excited by a well-documented resurgence of *U. americanus* in the western mountains of the state, to create a bear season there. After much debate, the Nevada Board of Wildlife Commissioners abandoned the idea. Similarly, Maryland rejected a proposed bear hunt for fall 2000, and will instead pay compensation for bear-related losses to rural people, whose complaints had prompted consideration of the hunt. After a dramatic tenfold surge in black bear numbers in New Jersey, and hundreds of reported bear disturbances, for the first time since 1971 the state Fish, Game, and Wildlife Council had decided to establish a black bear season for 2000. However, as opening day approached, the Council accepted Governor Christine Todd-Whitman's plan to have police kill bears posing an immediate danger, and to tag and relocate "nuisance" bears. The New Jersey hunt was canceled.

In 1999 just over 24,400 bears were killed by American hunters in 28 states. This is a significant decline from the late 1980s when about 40,000 were being slaughtered annually.

It is illegal to kill black bears at any time other than during the hunting season designated by state regulations, or at any time at all in jurisdictions where the animals are fully protected, such as in Louisiana. Yet, according to many observers, the poaching of black bears has reached epidemic proportions. Since this is a clandestine criminal activity, reliable numbers here are not available, but it has been estimated that at least one bear is poached for every one that is legally taken. Why so many? For the explanation, we must look across the Pacific Ocean to Asia.

Parts of bears have been used in the traditional medicines of China, Korea, and Japan for many centuries. Bear flesh, fat, blood, bones, paws, and spinal cords were once routinely prescribed for a variety of ailments, but the most sought-after remedies today are derived from the gall bladder and liver bile. Many Asians living in North America and in the Far East believe that these bear viscera contain special properties for effectively treating heart disease, liver disease, colon cancer, ulcers, stomach and digestive disorders, diabetes, hemorrhoids, and other maladies. As populations of the Asian black bear (*U. thibetanus*) have been devastated by habitat loss and human predation, the market value of bear gall and bile has skyrocketed to outrageous heights. For example, in Korea bile sells for $100 to $150 a gram, or more, which is about the same price American drug dealers charge for that quantity of cocaine. A gall bladder weighing just four ounces, taken from a bear killed in the Rocky Mountains, might fetch $1,000 at a traditional market in San Francisco's Chinatown, and $10,000 in Tokyo.

Evidently, poachers are targeting American black bears (Alaskan brown bears, too) in increasing numbers, harvesting their viscera, and selling them at great profit to purveyors of traditional Asian medicines. Currently, thirty-two states ban all trade in bear parts, but sixteen allow it and two others have no laws addressing the issue. Even though such commerce in these sixteen states must be in parts from legally killed bears, either taken inside or outside the state depending on the jurisdiction, it is nearly impossible to determine the species and origin of gall bladders and bile. In fact, because of this difficulty, there is strong evidence of a thriving trade in counterfeit viscera. The answer to this poaching problem would seem to be federal legislation to override the patchwork of state laws. In May 1999, for the third time in three congressional sessions, Senator Mitch McConnell of Kentucky introduced the Bear Protection Act, a bill that would prohibit importing, exporting, or domestic trading in bear viscera.

McConnell first filed a similar bill in 1995, but no committee considered it. He tried a second time in 1997, the bill making it out of the Environment and Public Works Committee in 1998, but Congress adjourned before the Senate took any action. After two more years, having been joined by Illinois Congressman John Porter's companion bill and many cosponsors, the Bear Protection Act is currently back in several congressional committees, but now seems likely to pass. It bans all foreign and domestic selling, buying, possessing, transporting, delivering, or receiving of bear viscera "or any product, item, or substance containing or labeled or advertised as containing, bear viscera." Violation carries a criminal penalty of up to one year in prison and fines, or a civil penalty of as much as $25,000 for each infraction.

Hunting Black Bears: Baiting and Dogs

Legal hunting of black bears usually occurs in the fall, during the months of September, October, and November (for general hunting laws, *see* chapter 5: *Recreational Hunting*). Five states, all in the west, have an additional spring hunt during April and May, among them Oregon, which also has the longest fall season, from August 1 to the New Year. About three-quarters of Alaska has no closed season on black bear at all, and each hunter may kill as many as three bears any time of year; in the remainder of the state the open season is September through June, with a bag limit of one.

The other states set the limit at one bruin per hunter, except for Washington, which allows one kill in the fall and another in the spring. Washington has the largest known black bear population, estimated at close to 30,000, although Alaska, Pennsylvania, and Maine have the highest average kill rate, more than 2,000 annually. Most states stipulate that cubs or females with cubs cannot be legally killed; a "cub" is sometimes defined as a bear less than one year old, sometimes as one weighing less than 100 pounds, and several states do not define the term.

Bears have traditionally been hunted with bait or with dogs. The use of bait for taking wildlife generally is perhaps the most divisive issue among hunters themselves, and the baiting of bears has been especially controversial. Some shooters reject bait for taking any animal (except fish, to which no one seems to object), while others hold that it depends on the species sought and the sort of lure employed, but there is no general concord on what the appropriately baitable species are or what is acceptable to use to attract them. First imposed in the early 1900s, legal restrictions on baiting were originally designed to prevent excessive killing of migratory birds, such as ducks and geese. Although the goal of these laws was mainly the conservation of wildlife, many hunters then and now also believe that the use of bait (for selected species) violates a standard of "fair chase" and is therefore "unethical" or "unsporting." This principle recommends the pursuit of animals with methods and devices that give them some chance to avoid being killed. Exactly what probability of escape is "sporting" for any given hunt is never specified, and perhaps cannot be, but presumably it is somewhere between certain success for the hunter and his returning home empty-handed.

Bear baiting becomes problematic under fair chase because it drastically lowers the probability that the prey will evade its destruction, and pushes the outcome for the hunter very close to the certain-kill end of the spectrum. The sense of smell in *U. americanus* is unimaginably acute. A bear can pick up the scent of rotting flesh or spoiled food, wafted on the wind for miles over hill and dale, then turn and make a beeline straight for the source. It is said that a bear's olfactory capacity is superior to a bloodhound's to the same degree that the dog's is superior to a human's. If there is a bear in the area and the wind is right, a dead and decaying animal or its body parts, or a mound of rotten fruit will attract it as inevitably as death itself. Typically elevated in a tree stand, a hunter concealed near the putrefaction has only to point his weapon and pull the trigger on a preoccupied animal engrossed in the free meal. There is here no real "chase" at all, let alone a "fair" one.

Along with this "ethical" problem, baiting can present ecological ones too. For example, baits draw carrion-eating animals that normally avoid one another, among them wolves, mountain lions, grizzly bears, and wolverines. These opportunistic meetings can lead to harmful encounters between the animals, and "inadvertent" shootings of protected species that would otherwise not have occurred. Visitations to "bait stations" desensitize bears to the scent of people, which can promote bear-human conflicts, both at the site and elsewhere. Moreover, unpleasant but nonlethal experiences in baited areas will cause the bears to avoid them, which reduces their available habitat. In any case, a baited area resplendent with the sight and smell of decomposing meat and littered with body parts is aesthetically offensive to most nonconsumptive users of the outdoors.

Despite these legitimate concerns, the current configuration of state laws indicates a lack of legal consensus on the issue of baiting black bears similar to that found among hunters. Of the twenty-eight states where *U. americanus* may be legally hunted, eighteen have banned the use of all lures or attractants to take the bear. The ten that allow them in 2000 are Alaska, Arizona, Idaho, Maine, Michigan, Minnesota, New Hampshire, Utah, Wisconsin, and Wyoming. This list was reduced by three in the 1990s, as voters in Colorado, Oregon, and Washington approved referenda prohibiting the practice (and the use of dogs).

Baiting regulations exhibit some common themes in the ten states that allow the practice. All require hunters to obtain baiting permits and post a sign at the baited area identifying themselves by name and address. Also, every state has restrictions on the placement of bait, though there are significant differences in the distances allowed. For example, in Maine bait must be placed at least 50 yards from any road and 500 yards from campgrounds or occupied dwellings, while in Idaho it is 200 yards from roads and half a mile from camps or homes; Alaska requires bait to be no closer than one-quarter mile from a road and one mile from a house.

The kind of bait placed and how it is packaged are also restricted. Most of the states have banned the use of game animals to attract bears, but only Wisconsin outlaws baiting with meat and parts of animal carcasses, as well as solid animal fat, bones, fish, and honey. Michigan bans plastic, wood, paper, glass, or metal, and the bait must be placed on the ground. Similarly, Idaho prohibits placing bait in paper, plastic, glass, metal, or wood containers, but allows the use of a single metal barrel of no more than 55 gallons capacity. On the other hand, Wyoming *requires* that all bait be placed in a 55-gallon or smaller container made of wood, metal, or plastic. In Arizona bait must be "biodegradable animal or vegetable matter contained within a single metal container not exceeding 10 gallons in volume." With one or two exceptions, all jurisdictions require that bait, containers, and other material be completely removed from the site within a week, or less, after the season closes.

Much of the bear baiting in these ten states is done in national forests, lands belonging to Americans generally and not only to the residents of that particular state. Since the early 1990s, the U.S. Forest Service (USFS) has been pressured by groups with a special interest in bear protection to prohibit baiting in these public lands, which the USFS is responsible for administering. Opponents of luring bears in these areas emphasize the adverse ecological impacts of baiting, many of which have been recognized by USFS officials themselves. Further, they argue that through several environmental statutes, Congress has given the USFS the authority to supersede state regulations and the responsibility to promote federal interests in ecological integrity by banning a destructive hunting practice in our national forests.

Unconvinced, in March 1995 the Forest Service issued its final policy on the use of bait in national forests. Commenting that "the use of bait in hunting is not contrary to Federal interests . . . [and] acknowledg[ing] the States' traditional role in managing wildlife," the USFS announced that "[w]here baiting is allowed by states, the practice will continue on National Forest System lands unless the authorized [USFS] officer determines on a site-specific basis that there is a need to prohibit or restrict the practice." To date, this policy remains in effect. The federal government has yet to close a national forest to bear baiting in any of the ten states.

Like baiting, hunting bears with dogs has also provoked a measure of controversy and for some of the same reasons. In this practice, packs of dogs are turned loose to locate a bear by scent. Once discovered by the frenzied canines, the animal almost invariably climbs a tree to elude them. The hunter eventually arrives on the scene and shoots the "treed" bear, which usually falls to the ground and is set upon by the dogs, if unrestrained. Many find that this procedure is no more "sporting" and provides no more of a "fair chase" than does baiting: shooting a bear out of a tree seems little different, to them, than shooting fish in a barrel. Others manifest a concern for the dogs, whose entanglements with cornered bears can lead to severe injuries, and there are those for whom packs of hunting dogs tearing through the woods is offensive to their environmental sensibilities.

Motivated by these and other considerations, currently Colorado, Massachusetts, Minnesota, Montana, New York, North Carolina, Oregon, and Washington have entirely banned the use of dogs for pursuing bears. Several states prohibit dogs at certain times or in certain areas, and a few have other dog restrictions. Michigan, Vermont, and Wisconsin, for example, limit the number of dogs used to hunt bears to six, while Maine sets the maximum at four.

Brown Bears
Taxonomists have divided the North American brown bear into three subspecies. *Ursus arctos arctos* is the Old World variety of the bear that is currently found throughout north Asia (Russia mostly) and was once widespread in Europe. *U. a. horribilis* is a predominantly lighter-colored bear commonly known as the grizzly, and *U. a. middendorfi* is an unusually large, salmon-fed incarnation found along the islands off the southern coast of Alaska, one often called the Kodiak bear. All three varieties inhabit Alaska, where the brown bear is alive and well, numbering perhaps 30,000 individuals. Estimates are that nearly as many live in Canada also.

The story is much different in the lower forty-eight states. Here, it is only the variety *horribilis* that clings to a tenuous existence after many decades of lethal persecution. The grizzly bear formerly inhabited all the Western states and most of the those in the Great Plains too, from the California coast across the Continental Divide and through the prairies. When the colonies won their independence from England, there were likely more than 50,000 grizzlies south of Canada. But the European-American settlers and ranchers loathed the bear, seeing in "Old Ephraim" predatory vermin bent on destroying their livestock herds and any person into which the beast could sink teeth and claws. Deprived of any legal protections, grizzlies everywhere were hounded by dogs, shot on sight, trapped with massive leghold devices, and poisoned with strychnine-laced carcasses. Within 200 years, the grizzly had been exterminated from all of its homelands in the conterminous United States except for a few isolated populations in the northern Rocky Mountains.

Today, approximately 1,100 grizzly bears occupy less than 2 percent of their historic range in the United States, excepting Alaska. Perhaps 1,000 of these are about evenly split between the Yellowstone Ecosystem—a vast area of some 14,000 square miles, centered on Yellowstone National Park in Wyoming but including parts of Montana and Idaho—and the Northern Continental Divide—a region of similar size in northern Montana, substantially constituted by Glacier National Park. Nearly all the remaining bears live in several national forests in the extreme north of the Idaho panhandle, and spilling over into Washington and Montana on the west and east, an area known as the Selkirk/Cabinet-Yaak Ecosystem. Totaling about 5,000 square miles, this is the southern tail end of a larger ecosystem that extends north into the Canadian Rocky Mountains of British Columbia, and abuts Banff National Park. In the United States the core of this grizzly country is the Cabinet Mountains and Yaak River watershed of northern Idaho and northwestern Montana.

The Cascade Mountains due east of Seattle may harbor half a dozen grizzlies. Although sightings of the bear in Idaho's Bitterroot Mountains are occasionally reported, these have not been confirmed by photograph, hair or scat samples, or by pawprints. As seen below, the Bitterroots have been targeted as prime habitat for reintroducing grizzlies to the wild.

Legal Protections for Grizzly Bears

After the total population had descended to an estimated 700 individuals, the FWS placed *Ursus arctos horribilis* on the list of threatened species in 1975, affording the bear the protections of the Endangered Species Act (ESA) (*see* this chapter: *Endangered Species Act*). A "threatened" species is one that is very likely to be in danger of extinction in the foreseeable future. This is a less urgent status than "endangered," which is attributed to species perilously close to becoming extinct at the present time. As with any threatened species, and endangered ones too, it is illegal to "take" grizzly bears, defined by the ESA as "to harass, harm, pursue, hunt, shoot, wound, kill, trap, capture, or collect, or to attempt to engage in any such conduct." Additionally, grizzly bears may not be imported, exported, possessed, sold, delivered, carried, or transported.

The legal status of the grizzly as threatened under the ESA has to be qualified in several respects. First, it does not apply to the species in Alaska, where about 1,100 brown bears, including *U. a. horribilis*, are killed by hunters every year. The ESA defines "species" to include both subspecies and distinct population segments, to account for situations where the same kind of animal is thriving in one location but imperiled in another. Such is the case with the North American brown bear. So in most of Alaska, a hunter is permitted to take one brown bear every four years, although other "Bear Management Areas" in the state allow "residents hunting . . . primarily for food" to take one animal every year. Neither bait nor dogs can be legally utilized to hunt brown bears in the Last Frontier, and cubs as well as females with cubs must be spared.

Further, the ESA provides a number of exceptions to the general prohibition on taking, most of which apply to the grizzly bear. For example,
the law allows the bears to be taken, even killed, in self-defense or in defense of other people. However, the Ninth Circuit Court of Appeals has
rejected the idea that grizzlies can be legally taken to protect property as
well. A rancher who had killed a grizzly preying upon his sheep was not
only denied compensation for the loss of the livestock, the court also upheld the fine levied against him for violating the ESA (*Christy v. Hodel*).

Permits may also be issued by the FWS to authorize taking of grizzlies
that is "incidental to, and not the purpose of, the carrying out of otherwise lawful activity." This is unintended and unplanned taking associated with customary human activities in nature, such as tree cutting, livestock raising, trail and road maintenance, the erection of structures,
commercial and sport fishing, and hunting of unprotected species. The
application for an incidental take permit must detail a "habitat conservation plan," explaining to the FWS how the applicant will minimize the
number of incidental takings that may occur. Permissible incidental taking must not "appreciably reduce the likelihood of the survival and recovery of the species in the wild." To date, no incidental take permits
have been issued for areas that grizzlies are known to inhabit in significant numbers.

Although the ESA protects all listed species from harm (notwithstanding the exceptions noted above), endangered wildlife have a more solid
shield than threatened ones, principally because it is nearly impossible to
secure incidental take permits for endangered species; the endangered
classification effectively shuts down most human activities in the species'
habitat. Recognizing this, in 1990 and 1991 a number of animal protection
organizations, lead by the Humane Society of the United States and the
Fund for Animals, and joined by several concerned citizens, submitted
petitions asking the FWS to reclassify the grizzly as endangered throughout the remnants of its range in the North Cascades, the Selkirk/Cabinet-
Yaak, the Northern Continental Divide, and the Yellowstone ecosystems.
By early 1993 the FWS had determined that reclassification was unjustified for the last two ecosystems, but agreed that the grizzlies in the North
Cascades and in the Cabinet-Yaak area should be upgraded to the endangered status. However, although the reclassification of these bears
was warranted, the FWS in 1998 still claimed that it was "precluded by
work on other species having a higher priority for listing." At seven years
and counting, as the work on higher-priority species apparently continues, both of these populations are still listed as threatened.

In its findings on the petitions, the FWS separated the Selkirk population from the Cabinet-Yaak one, a distinction the Service has since repu-
diated. The Service rejected the upgrade for the Selkirk bears because

"human-caused mortality is decreasing, reproduction and survivor rates are adequate . . . , and a proactive management program has been implemented." Unsatisfied with this decision, in 1993 the Biodiversity Legal Foundation and its director D. C. Carlton, along with several other environmental organizations and interested individuals filed suit in the federal District Court for the District of Columbia. They charged that the FWS decision not to reclassify the grizzlies in the Selkirk area was unjustified, arbitrary, and capricious.

Judge Paul Friedman agreed with the plaintiffs. In its findings, the FWS failed to adequately address some of the critical factors that must be considered when an ESA classification is determined. Notably, the Service maintained that the number of grizzly deaths caused by humans was decreasing in the Selkirk, and that the birth rate and survival of cubs were sufficient to sustain the population, but offered no evidence to support either conclusion. Judge Friedman also found suspect the FWS's reliance on the southward movement of Canadian bears to augment the U.S. population and establish its sustainability. The FWS was ordered to reconsider (*Carlton v. Babbitt*).

The FWS did so, and in March 1996 produced exactly the same decision on the status of the Selkirk bears, this time bolstered with additional information intended to justify the refusal to reclassify them. In 1998 the same plaintiffs hauled the Service before Judge Friedman once more, and again the court ruled that no credible argument had been provided for keeping the grizzlies on the threatened list.

Although the FWS now claimed that human-caused mortality of bears was stable, rather than declining, several grizzly deaths were not counted in the analysis. Furthermore, the contention that the Selkirk population could sustain an annual human-caused mortality rate of 4 percent had no scientific basis, the figure having been adopted from a study of a much larger population of bears. Friedman also found inexplicable how the FWS could agree that endangered status is warranted for the Cabinet-Yaak group, but not for the adjacent Selkirk bears, even though there is no great difference in their numbers and both groups face the same human threats to their habitat. Finally, addressing the appeal to an influx of Canadian bears to support the American population, the judge noted that "if FWS is going to rely on habitat north of the border to sustain the Selkirk population, it must evaluate whether those areas will continue to exist as grizzly bear habitat. . . . [FWS] did not make findings regarding the present or threatened destruction of the Canadian habitat" (*Carlton v. Babbitt*).

In May 1999 the FWS announced that the Selkirk grizzlies did warrant endangered status after all, but the reclassification was precluded by other listing actions.

Grizzly Bear Recovery

The biological and legal goal for any threatened or endangered species is rehabilitation from its imperiled condition and removal from the ESA list. Toward this end, the FWS is required to develop and implement recovery plans "for the conservation and survival" of listed species. Recovery plans are supposed to detail the measures necessary for halting or reversing the descent of species toward the oblivion of extinction. This is to be achieved with a description of "site-specific management actions" intended to promote the revival of the species, and "objective, measurable criteria" by which the progress of recovery can be monitored (*see also* this chapter: *Endangered Species Act of 1973: Recovery Plans*).

The first grizzly bear recovery plan was drafted in 1982. Its widely acknowledged inadequacies prompted the formation of the Interagency Grizzly Bear Committee (IGBC) the next year. Directed by the FWS and composed of representatives from the National Park Service, the U.S. Forest Service, and wildlife agencies in Idaho, Montana, Washington, Wyoming, and British Columbia, the IGBC is charged with coordinating the recovery of the bear. After nine years of work by the FWS and the IGBC, a revised draft of the grizzly bear recovery plan was made available for public review. Hundreds of comments from ordinary citizens and distinguished scientists flooded in, most highly critical of the plan, but in 1993 the FWS published a final version that was substantially the same as the draft.

Within a year, a total of forty-three environmental and animal protection organizations, lead by the Fund for Animals and the National Audubon Society, had filed two separate lawsuits against the FWS, both complaining that the recovery plan was completely unacceptable. The two suits were eventually consolidated. The legion of plaintiffs argued that the FWS had failed to produce either adequate site-specific management actions or objective, measurable criteria of recovery.

Once again, Judge Friedman was on the bench writing the opinion for the D.C. District Court. Although he found no fault in the FWS/IGBC treatment of the management measures to be taken for each of the ecosystems inhabited by the bears, Friedman rejected the notion that the plan contained satisfactory criteria of recovery. Three recovery criteria were offered by the FWS/IGBC: (1) annual sightings of females with cubs; (2) the distribution of females with cubs in the various ecosystems; and (3) the number of grizzlies killed by humans each year. The Fund for Animals and its allies maintained that adequate recovery criteria must speak to all five factors the ESA demands for listing a species in the first place, among them the incidence of disease or predation, any adverse impacts on habitat, and excessive use of the animals in commerce, recreation, science, or education. The FWS contended that this need not be done, only that the

plan's recovery criteria "should likely lead to a finding that the five statutory delisting factors are met."

"'Likely to lead,'" Friedman replied, "is not the language of the
ESA. . . . Since the same five statutory factors must be considered in
delisting . . . , in designing objective, measurable criteria, FWS must address each of the five statutory delisting factors." The three recovery criteria in the plan failed to do this. One of several problems was that they
said nothing about the effects of disease on the bears or the threat posed
to them by their predation on livestock. More importantly, the appeal to
the number of females with cubs and their distribution in a particular
ecosystem did not answer the question of how much habitat and of what
quality would be needed to produce a recovered grizzly population.
Counting bear sightings and gauging their occupancy of a certain area
provided no means "to assess present or threatened destruction, modification or curtailment of the grizzly bear's habitat." In any case, reliance
on observation of bears is a highly suspect methodology often criticized
as unreliable and subjective. What is most sorely lacking in the plan are
"habitat based recovery criteria . . . to measure the effect of habitat quality and quantity on grizzly recovery." Friedman ordered the FWS to re-
formulate the plan (*Fund for Animals v. Babbitt*).

In July 1999, nearly five years after Friedman's court order, the FWS
and the IGBC produced a draft of habitat-based recovery criteria, specifically tailored to the Yellowstone grizzly bears, and addressing the various other defects of the 1993 recovery plan. The draft discusses at great
length numerous indices of habitat quality, including the presence of
roads and trails, the amount of livestock grazing in the ecosystem, the
abundance of the four most important grizzly foods (whitebark pine
nuts, cutthroat trout, cutworm moths, and deer and elk carrion), and
commercial and residential development on public and private lands.
Additionally addressed are the key issues of disease, the relationship between encounters with livestock and bear mortality, and the reliability of
population monitoring methods.

The Yellowstone Ecosystem, located mostly in Wyoming, has become
the focus of grizzly management and recovery in the last several years.
The bear population there has nearly doubled since the original ESA listing in 1975, now standing at about 600. In 1999 thirty-three females with a
total of sixty-three cubs were counted, far exceeding the new recovery
plan goal of fifteen females with cubs. Also better than intended is human-
caused mortality, with nine bears killed in 1998 and 1999 combined, and
just two females. These numbers, as well as effective sanitation management, well-received grizzly information and education programs, stable
food supplies, and other factors have convinced the FWS and the IGBC
that *U. a. horribilis* is well along the road to recovery in Yellowstone—for

them, delisting is in the foreseeable future. Many critics of the way federal and state agencies have managed grizzlies contend that the major motivation behind delisting is not the recognition of a genuine recovery for the species, but a desire in Wyoming's Game and Fish Department to restore a grizzly bear hunt to the state. When, and if, the bears are removed from the ESA list, such a hunt will almost certainly be established. In March 2000 the FWS made available for public comment the "Conservation Strategy for the Grizzly Bear in the Yellowstone Area." This document details how the bear population will be managed after recovery has been achieved—presumably in a manner consistent with the 1999 Recovery Plan, once finalized—and the species is removed from the ESA list.

Reintroducing Grizzly Bears
A final aspect of species recovery is the reintroduction of individual animals into formerly occupied habitat. For grizzlies, the Bitterroot Ecosystem in central Idaho and western Montana has long been recognized as ideal country in which to establish a new population of bears. Totaling 26,000 square miles and including all or parts of ten different national forests, at the core of this ecosystem are three huge wilderness areas summing to over 6,000 square miles (about the size of Connecticut and Rhode Island combined), the largest continuous roadless area south of Canada. Historical records indicate that the grizzly was common in the Bitterroot during the 1800s, but there have been no confirmed sightings since the 1940s. Sheep ranchers are primarily responsible for the extermination of the bear in this region.

The effort to reintroduce the grizzly to the Bitterroot was spearheaded by an unusual coalition of wildlife protection and environmental use organizations: Defenders of Wildlife, the National Wildlife Federation, the Resource Organization on Timber Supply, and the Intermountain Forest Industry Association. During the mid-1990s this group, among other initiatives, lobbied for funding of the environmental impact statement (EIS) required for reintroductions, and hosted a series of public meetings in rural communities surrounding the Bitterroot region so local citizens could present their concerns. Most importantly, the coalition developed an innovative alternative for grizzly recovery in this ecosystem. This plan was submitted to the FWS in 1995, included in the draft EIS released by the Service for public comment in 1997, and emerged as the FWS's preferred alternative for the reintroduction of Bitterroot grizzlies in the final EIS published in March 2000.

The coalition's plan, and the one proposed by the FWS, calls for the release of at least twenty-five grizzlies into the wilderness areas of central Idaho. The release would follow a "phase-in" year during which special sanitation equipment would be installed at key locations, and information and education programs about the bears initiated. As provided by the ESA, these bears would be designated as an "experimental, non-essential population." An experimental population of an otherwise threatened species can be legally treated as "a species proposed to be listed." A nonessential population is one "whose loss is not likely to reduce the survival of the species in the wild." In essence, this means that the Bitterroot bears would have less protection than grizzlies in the other, established ecosystems. For example, federally funded mining operations or timber cutting could proceed in the recovery area without a formal FWS consultation or the agency's approval; these are required for such activities in the habitat of threatened or endangered species. Also, ranchers could obtain permits from the FWS to kill reintroduced grizzlies found molesting their livestock on private lands, provided wildlife agencies were unable to capture the depredating bears; the ESA does not allow such measures for listed species. The motivation for reducing safeguards for experimental populations is to promote the acceptance and cooperation of local people affected by wildlife reintroductions, citizens who tend to view ESA restrictions as unduly burdensome or costly.

Perhaps the most novel dimension of the preferred alternative is also intended to encourage the acquiescence and goodwill of the citizenry. This establishes a fifteen-member Citizen Management Committee charged with the responsibility to assist state and federal wildlife agencies in the implementation of the recovery of the Bitterroot grizzlies by making recommendations to promote that goal.

Thirteen of the committee members must reside in or around the recovery area, seven from Idaho, five from Montana, and one from the Nez Perce tribe, whose reservation is located in Idaho to the east of the area; the remaining members represent the U.S. Forest Service and the FWS. Those serving on the committee would represent "a cross-section of interests reflecting a balance of viewpoints, [individuals] selected for their diversity of knowledge and experience in natural resource issues, and for their commitment to collaborative decision making." The secretary of the interior would appoint two scientific advisors to attend committee meetings and supply technical expertise, but the scientists would not be allowed to vote on any recommendations.

At this writing, the public comments on the final EIS for grizzly recovery in the Bitterroots are still being analyzed by the FWS. It is very likely that the preferred alternative will prevail in the final decision.

NATIONAL WILDLIFE REFUGE SYSTEM IMPROVEMENT ACT OF 1997

The National Wildlife Refuge System Improvement Act (NWRSIA) is a substantial amendment to the National Wildlife Refuge Administration Act of 1966, which was itself originally sections 4 and 5 of the Endangered Species Preservation Act of 1966 (since repealed, the precursor to the Endangered Species Act of 1973; *see* this chapter: *Endangered Species Act*). Prior to the enactment of the NWRSIA, the statutory authorities for the administration of America's wildlife refuges derived piecemeal from three different federal laws: the 1966 Wildlife Refuge Administration Act, the Refuge Recreation Act of 1962, and the Refuge Revenue Sharing Act of 1964. Congress had considered and rejected a variety of bills in the early 1990s intended to unify the refuge system under its own "organic" act, most recently in 1996 when H.R. 511, though advocated by hunters' and anglers' lobbies, was staunchly opposed by the Clinton administration and many environmental groups. Finally, in 1997 Alaska Representative Don Young's bill garnered enough support to pass through Capitol Hill and receive the president's signature.

The 1966 act suffered from a major deficiency. Although it stated that the wildlife sanctuaries could be used in any way "compatible with the major purposes for which such areas were established," it did not explain what those purposes were, and so offered no notion of what compatible uses would be. The NWRSIA tries to remedy this defect with a mission statement, expressed in section 4: "administer a national network of lands and waters for the conservation, management, and where appropriate, restoration of the fish, wildlife, and plant resources and their habitats within the United States for the benefit of present and future generations of Americans." A "compatible use" of a wildlife refuge, according to the NWRSIA, is "a wildlife-dependent recreational use or any other use of a refuge that . . . will not materially interfere with or detract from the fulfillment of the mission of the system."

In 2000 there are 529 national wildlife refuges scattered throughout all fifty states, Puerto Rico, Guam, and the Johnson and Midway atolls. Total acreage of the system stands at more than 93 million, but 76 million of these are in Alaska alone, and a third of that total is the immense Arctic National Wildlife Refuge. Also part of the current system are more than 2,000 small wetlands and water-filled potholes called "Waterfowl Production Areas" (WPAs), set aside to promote the conservation of water birds. The system constitutes the largest and most diverse assortment of wildlife and their habitat in the world, containing over 200 species each of mammals and fish, another 200 of reptiles and amphibians, over 700 kinds of birds, and all 17 of the continent's major life zones, from desert scrub to alpine forest to treeless tundra.

Most of the refuges are administered exclusively by the Department of the Interior through the U.S. Fish and Wildlife Service (FWS). A number of units are "overlays" on regions managed by other agencies, such as the Army Corps of Engineers, the Bureau of Reclamation, the Department of Defense, and the Tennessee Valley Authority. In these areas, the administrating agency has primary jurisdiction, not the FWS, and refuges are managed according to the purposes for which the land was originally designated. For example, the air force conducts military exercises in over ninety refuge units, including low-level flights by supersonic aircraft, bombing practice, and missile firing.

The Origins of National Wildlife Refuges

During the late 1800s, feathered hats were all the rage in women's fashion. At that time there were no synthetic materials out of which to construct artificial feathers, so the only source for effecting this sartorial splendor was the real thing: birds. Egrets, flamingos, herons, ibises, swans, spoonbills, and many sorts of songbirds were slaughtered by the tens of thousands throughout the 1880s and 1890s for hats, mainly, but also for other trinkets and decorations like fans and boas. By the beginning of the twentieth century, wading birds had become so scarce in Florida (their prime habitat) that a plume of a few egret feathers cost $10 in Miami, equivalent to about $200 at the end of the century. Many of these birds were also taken for their meat, especially the passenger pigeon, a species that would eventually succumb entirely.

Nascent federal efforts to stop the carnage and save the birds came from President Theodore Roosevelt in 1903, when, by executive order, he created the Pelican Island Federal Bird Reservation off the east coast of Florida. All the wading birds inhabiting in the marshes and mangrove swamps of this five-acre reserve were protected from hunters. The establishment of this bird sanctuary is widely regarded as the advent of the wildlife refuge in America, a distinction probably owing largely to Roosevelt's reputation as a great conservationist, as well as his considerable charisma. In fact, the precedent is better placed with an eminently forgettable president, Benjamin Harrison, who in 1892 declared Afognak Island in Alaska a reserve for the protection and preservation of "salmon and other fish and sea animals, and other animals and birds."

Roosevelt issued fifty-one such executive orders founding similar wildlife reservations during his tenure in the White House, ending in 1909. Congress eventually followed T. R.'s initiative, forming the National Bison Range in Montana in 1908, and then took the lead in the process of building a mosaic of natural areas that would provide a safe haven for besieged wildlife. A major impetus in this endeavor, though not a proximate one, was the Migratory Bird Treaty Act of 1918 (*see* this chapter: *Migratory Bird Treaty Act*), which afforded protections for migrating flocks, but did nothing to preserve and augment their habitat, a legislative oversight that needed fixing. The Migratory Bird Conservation Act of 1929 supplied Congress with the authority to acquire land, including wetlands, and waters that could be set aside for wildlife, and remains to this day the primary legal device for ratifying the expansion of the refuge system.

Yet this new law had its own failing: It provided no permanent source of funding for purchasing and maintaining habitat. Land already in the public domain could be withdrawn and designated as a wildlife refuge, and of course citizens or corporations could donate natural areas for this purpose—both of these forms of acquisition have been important sources of expansion for the system. However, a more aggressive approach is to go out and buy land, or at least rent it. Where would the money come from? Strangely enough, the answer was supplied by a cartoonist. Jay "Ding" Darling had made a career of lampooning politicians with drawings appearing in the *Des Moines Register*. An avid hunter, he had particularly targeted what he saw as the excessive exploitation of waterfowl and the destruction of wetlands. In 1934 President Franklin D. Roosevelt appointed Darling chief of the Bureau of Biological Survey, what would later become the United States Fish and Wildlife Service. Within a few months, Darling had conceived and developed a novel idea: require all waterfowl hunters in the country to buy a stamp, and then allocate the revenue thereby generated for purchasing and leasing habitat for ducks and geese.

Congress bought the idea and passed the Migratory Bird Hunting Stamp Act of 1934. More commonly known as the "Duck Stamp Act," this law imposes the duty to buy a stamp upon every hunter over age sixteen who wishes to pursue waterfowl anywhere in the states or U.S. territories. In 1934 the cost was $1; in 2000 it is $15. During these sixty-six years, the Duck Stamp program has generated more than half a billion dollars that has been used to preserve over 4 million acres of waterfowl habitat. Darling himself designed the first stamp, and since 1949 there has been an annual competition for the best design. Typically, the competitors (and winners) are wildlife artists, but anyone can submit a drawing. The stamps are slightly larger than the average first-class postage stamp, and are much sought after by philatelic enthusiasts.

Another major source of revenue for acquiring refuge land is the Land and Water Conservation Fund, created by the Land and Water Conservation Fund Act of 1964. This fund receives money from fees paid by users of federal lands, a motorboat fuels tax, and a percentage of oil and gas lease payments made by operations on the outer continental shelf. Also, the North American Wetlands Conservation Act of 1989 is designed to facilitate public and private financial contributions to acquire, restore, and enhance wetlands and the waterfowl that depend upon them. All wetlands acquired under this act are added to the refuge system.

Not surprisingly, given both its origins in the conservation of wading birds and the Duck Stamp as its primary funding source for habitat acquisition, the wildlife refuge system has always been strongly geared toward the promotion of migratory waterfowl. Fully three-quarters of the refuges in the contiguous United States are centered on the two coasts, and on various lakes, rivers, wetlands, and the waterfowl migration routes called "flyways." Indeed the official FWS map of the nation's wildlife refuges designates each unit with the silhouette of what appears to be a goose in flight. Even though the Migratory Bird Conservation Act stipulated that any refuge acquired under its authority was to be an "inviolate sanctuary," it could not have been unexpected that by 1949 Congress had empowered the secretary of the interior to permit hunting on as much as 25 percent of any unit. In 1958 this proportion was increased to 40 percent. Today the NWRSIA allows this number to be exceeded if "the Secretary finds the taking of a species in more than forty percent of an area would benefit the species."

Hunting and Trapping in National Wildlife Refuges

The NWRSIA enjoins the secretary of the interior to administer the wildlife refuges in a manner fostering "wildlife-dependent recreation," defined as "a use of a refuge involving hunting, fishing, wildlife observation and photography, or environmental education and interpretation." Further, such activities are recognized as "priority general public uses of the System." These sorts of pastimes must be in harmony with the NWRSIA's statutory objective to conserve wild animals and their habitat for the enjoyment of people now and in the future: the concept of "compatible use."

Of these listed uses, only hunting has ignited any serious controversy, mainly generated by people appalled that a wildlife "refuge" system would allow the killing of animals for recreation (for more on hunting laws generally, *see* chapter 5: *Recreational Hunting*). Until 1984 many units had been closed to hunting for years. At that time, Secretary of the Interior William Clark opened most of them. In 2000 over 200 refuges allow hunting. Previously, refuge hunting regulations were reviewed each year, but this process was eliminated when Clark issued the new orders of 1984. Throughout the rest of the 1980s and into the early 1990s, animal welfare groups asked judges on several occasions to stop hunting in various units (for example, *Humane Society of the United States v. Lujan*). None granted the request.

Finally, in 1998, the federal District Court of the District of Columbia halted a government plan to allow buffalo hunting in northwestern Wyoming's National Elk Refuge. The FWS contended that a bison herd there had grown too large and needed thinning, this to be accomplished by permitting hunters to kill a specified number of the animals. The Fund for Animals charged that before the hunt could proceed, the FWS must perform compatibility studies, as required by the NWRSIA, to determine

if the hunt was consistent with the objective of the law, and an environmental assessment study, as demanded by the National Environmental
Policy Act (NEPA). Neither of these researches had been done and without them, the Fund concluded, any buffalo hunt on the refuge would be
illegal. Judge Ricardo Urbina ruled that the FWS had not violated the
NWRSIA—no compatibility study was needed in this situation—however, NEPA did indeed require an environmental assessment that had not
been produced (*Fund for Animals v. Clark*). The case is on appeal, but
meanwhile no buffalo have been taken by hunters in this sanctuary.

Refuge-specific regulations concerning the wildlife species that are
legal to take, bag limits, and methods of hunting often vary. Even so,
there are several general provisions that apply for any unit in the system.
Among these, each person must have a hunting license from the state in
which the refuge is located, waterfowl hunters over the age of sixteen
must have a Migratory Bird Hunting Stamp ("Duck Stamp"), neither al-
cohol- nor drug-tainted arrows can be used or possessed, and the use of
tree stands and artificial lighting to kill wildlife is prohibited, as is baiting
(except in Alaska). All units ban the use of lead-based shot, which is often
ingested by waterfowl and is poisonous to them (for more on both baiting and the toxic shot issue, *see* this chapter: *Migratory Bird Treaty Act of
1918: Baiting*; this chapter: *Migratory Bird Treaty Act of 1918: Subsistence
Hunting and Nontoxic Shot*).

For the most part, state hunting regulations are applied fairly uniformly to the national wildlife refuges found there. This is even more so
for trapping. A permit must be obtained from the FWS to set traps in a
refuge (though not in a WPA), but federal regulation of trapping is essentially exhausted by a statement in the Code of Federal Regulations
that trappers must have a state-issued license and comply with state
laws. Most state hunting and trapping regulations make no special mention of these refuges.

Trapping in the refuge system is also a concern for many (for trapping
laws generally, *see* chapter 4: *Commercial Trapping*). This occurs on at least
half of all units, despite not being included in the NWRSIA as a form of
"wildlife-dependent recreation." What is more, hunting and fishing in
the refuges are heavily regulated by the FWS. The *Code of Federal Regulations* contains nearly eighty pages of restrictions on these activities, listed
state by state for each refuge—but trapping has been virtually ignored by
the agency.

Congress had approved funding in 1997 for an FWS task force that
would study trapping in the system, especially the humaneness of trapping methods, but the agency successfully pleaded a dearth of time for
convening the study group. Instead, a survey was mailed to every refuge
manager in America asking for information on a number of different

items. Also disappointing to opponents of trapping was the outcome of voting in Congress on an amendment to the 1999 Interior Appropriations bill. The measure would have banned the use of steel-jaw leghold traps and neck snares, widely regarded as inhumane, in all national wildlife refuges. In July 2000 a solid majority of representatives approved the amendment, but in September the Senate voted to table it, squelching the proposal for at least another year.

The FWS survey revealed that steel-jaw leghold traps are used in half of refuges where trapping occurs, and snares in one quarter of them. Body-gripping traps and cages or other enclosures that capture and keep animals alive are utilized at a rate similar to that of the legholds. Raccoons are most often targeted by trappers in the refuges, followed by beavers, red foxes, striped skunk, and minks. The number of animals trapped in each unit was not addressed in the survey, and apparently no data is available on this statistic.

The most frequent purpose listed in the survey for trapping in the refuges is "recreation/commerce/subsistence." Next in regularity is "facilities protection" and predator control to protect migratory birds. About half the people engaged in trapping are refuge staff or volunteers, while only one quarter are private individuals. This ratio is surprising given that "recreation/commerce/subsistence" is the most common reason for trapping. In that case, private individuals would seem to be the predominant trappers, not staff or volunteers who presumably do the trapping for "facilities protection" and predator control.

There are very few regulations directly pertaining to any of the other aspects of "wildlife-dependent recreation" identified by the NWRSIA. These include the directive that motion picture photography in a wildlife refuge for commercial use must be officially approved by the FWS. Also, any "disturbing" of wildlife in the process of observing them "is prohibited except by special permit." The same goes for collecting, injuring, or destroying wild animals, or trying to, while engaged in environmental education or interpretation.

Otherwise, most federal regulations for national wildlife refuges apply in the same manner for anyone present there for just about any reason. For instance, unattended or unextinguished fires are not allowed, nor are dumping, gambling, begging, or stealing public or private property. Also, the use or distribution of controlled substances is prohibited, and no one may use alcohol "to a degree that may endanger oneself or other persons or property or unreasonably annoy persons in the vicinity."

Wildlife Refuges in Alaska
Alaska is the location of 82 percent of America's refuge acreage, and almost one-quarter of that is contained within a single unit, the vast Arctic

National Wildlife Refuge (ANWR). As residents of the Last Frontier rarely tire of asserting, Alaska is a special place.

One aspect of this distinction is that the state's sixteen units enjoy their own custom-made law, applicable nowhere else: the Alaska National Interest Lands Conservation Act of 1980 (ANILCA). Indeed, Part 36 of Title 50 of the *Code of Federal Regulations* is devoted entirely to the Alaskan refuge system, and Part 37 concerns only ANWR. At 181 pages total, ANILCA is as massive and labyrinthine as the state itself, containing dozens of provisions. Besides nearly tripling the size of the national refuge system, these include the creation of 56 million acres of wilderness areas, the designation of thirteen new wild or scenic rivers, the recognition of existing rights to mineral claims and access to enclosed private lands, and the establishment of timber harvest quotas on public lands.

Concerning Alaska's wildlife refuges specifically, ANILCA offers a mission statement for the system as a whole and for each individual unit. The overarching objective is conservation of wildlife populations and their habitats while also preserving water quality in the refuges and honoring international treaties, such as those concerning whales (*see* this chapter: *Legal Protections for Whales*), seals (*see* this chapter: *Fur Seal Act of 1966: The Fur Seal Treaty of 1911*), and polar bears (*see* this chapter: *Legal Protections for Bears: An International Agreement to Protect Polar Bears*). The law also stipulates that each unit of the state system must have a comprehensive land use plan, to be completed within a prescribed time period. In 1980 this planning requirement was unique to the Alaskan refuges.

Equally unprecedented in the regulation of the country's wildlife sanctuaries is Title VIII of ANILCA, which implements another purpose of Alaska's refuges: "to provide . . . the opportunity for continued subsistence uses by local residents." This title is essentially a remedy for a deficiency in the Alaska Native Claims Settlement Act of 1971. Although the primary purpose of the Settlement Act was to compensate native Alaskans for their claims to federal property, it also granted Indians and non-Indians alike the right to practice subsistence hunting and fishing on public lands. During the late 1970s, Congress became convinced that Alaskans who charged state and federal agencies with incompetence in protecting subsistence uses were correct, and specific provisions were added to ANILCA to improve the situation. "Subsistence use" is defined as "the customary and traditional uses by rural Alaskans of wild, renewable resources for direct personal or family consumption as food, shelter, fuel, clothing, tools, or transportation." ANILCA and federal regulations declare that "nonwasteful" subsistence uses have priority over all other consumptive uses of the natural resources in the refuge system. Further, the federal government must account for this sort of livelihood in drafting and implementing wildlife and land management policies, ensuring that such measures "cause the least adverse impact possible on local rural residents who depend upon subsistence uses." Nonetheless, this means of sustenance must be compatible with the effective conservation of natural resources, and is indeed subordinate to it when there is a conflict between the two. Refuge managers are empowered to close wildlife refuges when continued subsistence use will jeopardize the viability of a wildlife population.

(For more on the legal regulation of subsistence uses of wildlife, *see* this chapter: *Migratory Bird Treaty Act of 1918: Subsistence Hunting and Nontoxic Shot*; this chapter: *Legal Protections for Whales: Aboriginal Subsistence Whaling*; this chapter: *Fur Seal Act of 1966: The End of Commercial Sealing in the Pribilof Islands*; this chapter: *Legal Protections for Bears: An International Agreement to Protect Polar Bears*.)

The ANWR has been the subject of much acrimonious debate, beginning shortly after ANILCA was enacted. Called by some "America's Serengeti," wolves, wolverines, polar bears, grizzly bears, arctic foxes, musk oxen, moose, Dall sheep, and tens of thousands of caribou roam this 19-million-acre sanctuary in northeast Alaska, fronted by the Arctic Ocean. The coastal plain that sweeps to the sea is believed to overlie an oil and gas field valued in excess of $1 billion (though the figure is much disputed), and is immediately adjacent to Prudhoe Bay where the largest deposit of fossil fuels in the world was discovered in 1968. The plain is also the summer home and calving grounds for the Porcupine caribou herd, one of the few large migratory groups of the species left, numbering some 150,000 individuals.

At the insistence of Arizona's Representative Morris Udall, one of the drafters of the original legislation, ANILCA requires congressional approval before any industrial development of the ANWR or any Alaskan wildlife refuge may proceed. Republican lawmakers, especially Alaska's Congressman Don Young and Senator Frank Murkowski, have tried for years to secure that approbation. Steadfastly opposed by the Clinton administration and environmentalist groups, they have so far not met with success.

On the other hand, efforts to designate various regions of the ANWR as federal wilderness areas, within which such development is permanently prohibited, did succeed in 1996 when 8 million acres in the Brooks Range were declared the Mollie Beattie Wilderness Area. In March 1999 Congressman Bruce Vento of Minnesota introduced legislation that would baptize 1.5 million acres on the coastal plain as wilderness and thus legally immunize this coveted ecosystem from oil exploration or facilities construction forever. Still pending, Vento's bill honors the late Arizona congressman: it is called the Morris K. Udall Wilderness Act.

NONINDIGENOUS AQUATIC NUISANCE PREVENTION AND CONTROL ACT OF 1990

The Nonindigenous Aquatic Nuisance Prevention and Control Act (NANPCA) is designed to combat the havoc wreaked upon America's wildlife by hundreds of nonnative and transplanted animal species in U.S. waterways (some plants are included). Its major objectives are to prevent the unintentional introduction and dispersion of nonnative creatures into American waters, reduce the economic and environmental impact of established exotic species, and implement a program to assist the states in managing and removing nonnatives. The catastrophic effects of some introduced species have been known since at least 1929, when a massive onslaught of sea lamprey (*Lampreta* spp.) in the Great Lakes led to a major upheaval in the Lakes fisheries during the 1940s and 1950s. But an infestation of zebra mussels finally spurred the federal government to take action against the invaders.

Zebra Mussels

The zebra mussel (*Dreissena polymorpha*) was first discovered on the North American continent in 1988 at Lake St. Clair, a small body of water between Lakes Huron and Erie. Named for its striped shell, the native of central Asia had apparently been sucked into the ballast tanks of ocean-going ships, which take up and discharge water to aid in the trim and stability of the vessel. The ships then released the mollusk with ballast water as they traveled down the St. Lawrence River and through the Welland Canal connecting Lake Ontario with Erie. (Not coincidentally, the invasion of sea lamprey followed shortly after the Welland Canal was opened.)

Dreissena has proved amazingly adaptable to its new environment, spreading with incredible speed throughout the Great Lakes region and beyond. A dozen years after it was first observed, its dispersal has been slowed but a retreat is nowhere in sight. The zebra mussel is now also found throughout much of the Mississippi, Ohio, Arkansas, Tennessee, and Illinois rivers, in Lake Champlain and the Chesapeake Bay, and most recently seems to be encroaching up the Missouri River as well. In 1999 $4 billion dollars was spent on solving problems created by the mollusk, and the cost is rising.

Notorious for colonizing the water supply pipes of hydroelectric and nuclear power plants, public water supply plants, and industrial facilities, hordes of zebra mussels strangle water flow and severely reduce the capabilities of these installations. Their penchant for attaching to many types of objects in huge numbers has also hindered commercial and recreational boating. Perhaps worse, native species of mussel are no match for the more aggressive zebras (aggressive for mollusks, anyway), who often prefer attaching to the indigenous mussels themselves rather than to rocks or boats; the American mollusks are smothered.

The zebra mussel has probably received the greatest notoriety as a destructive nonnative species, but numerous other exotic creatures have been on a rampage too, from mitten and green crabs (*Eriocher sinensis* and *Carcinus maenas*) in San Francisco Bay and up the coast of Oregon, to ruffe fish (*Gymnocephalua cernuus*) in Lake Superior, to eastern lake trout (*Salvelinus namaycush*) in Yellowstone Lake, Wyoming. All these species have overwhelmed the native inhabitants of the environments they colonized. In the U.S. territory of Guam, the brown tree snake (*Boiga irregularis*) has been especially pernicious, devastating native bird populations, biting thousands of people, and causing hundreds of electric power outages. This ruinous serpent is poised to enter Hawaii, with the west coast of the American mainland the next step. More than $100 billion is spent every year in an attempt to control these and other invaders, and currently dozens of native wildlife species are engaged in a losing battle with them.

Even though the plague of zebra mussels was the major motivator behind the enactment of the NANPCA, the statute is written to include far more than this one bivalve species. The NANPCA expansively defines "nonindigenous species" as any species or "viable biological material" (which would include a virus) that has entered an ecosystem from beyond its historic range. This covers not only species brought to the United States from other nations but also those transported from one part of the country to another, such as the eastern trout stocked into Yellowstone. Federal regulation is activated once the immigrants become "aquatic nuisance species" in their new home. This phrase refers to organisms that "threaten the diversity or abundance of native species or the ecological stability of infested waters, or commercial, aquacultural or recreational activities dependent on such waters."

Aquatic Nuisance Species Task Force

Rather than issue specific prohibitions, the NANPCA created a "task force" that would provide various government entities with data concerning the influx of exotic species and advice on how best to cope with the problem. The members of the task force, as mandated by the NANPCA, are the director of the Fish and Wildlife Service, the undersecretary of commerce for oceans and atmosphere, the administrator of the Environmental Protection Agency, the commandant of the Coast Guard, the assistant secretary of the army for civil works, and, following 1996 amendments, the secretary of agriculture. The director and the undersecretary serve as cochairs and report to the secretaries of the interior and commerce. All these federal officials are expected to use the findings of the task force as the basis on which to issue the pertinent regulations.

The task force is also charged with providing technical assistance to individual states and to associations of states attempting to develop plans for battling troublesome, nonnative species, eventually reviewing and approving these state and interstate plans. At this writing, only New York, Michigan, and Ohio have received task force approval for their Aquatic Nuisance Species Management Plans. A dozen other states are in the process of elaborating their own strategies.

Several cooperative efforts between states are being developed, while currently two interstate programs are in operation. One of these, the Great Lakes Panel on Nonindigenous Species, was convened at the request of the task force as required by the NANPCA. It consists of representatives from federal, state, and local agencies as well as from the commercial sector. Their mission is to offer advice to anyone concerned about controlling aquatic nuisance species, make recommendations to the task force regarding zebra mussels, and submit annual reports to the task force detailing what has been done in the Great Lakes region to prevent and control harmful nonnative species. A final duty of the task force is to inform the secretary of state about nuisance species infesting waters shared with other nations, principally Canada, and suggest procedures for managing them.

The information and counsel provided to the federal government are contained in a comprehensive program that the task force is responsible for developing and implementing. This program is supposed to detail measures "to prevent the introduction and dispersal of aquatic nuisance species . . . to monitor, control and study such species, and disseminate related information." The first Aquatic Nuisance Species Program was submitted by the task force to Congress in December 1995, a report dominated by the zebra mussel and the ballast water problem.

Among other items concerning the zebra mussel, the program detailed the results of extensive research on the biology of the mollusk, the distribution of this information at various conferences and in numerous publications, and efforts to prevent the westward spread of zebra mussels beyond the Continental Divide and into the Rio Grande River. The program also noted the official designation of *Dreissena* in federal regulations as injurious wildlife. Further new regulations, issued by the Coast Guard and arising out of the work of the task force, include mandatory ballast water management requirements for ocean-going ships entering any of the Great Lakes or the Hudson River. The regulations direct all vessels sailing outside the "Exclusive Economic Zone" (EEZ; a band of ocean skirting the coasts to a width of 200 miles) to employ one of three practices: exchange ballast water before entering the EEZ, retain the ballast on board, or use some other "environmentally sound method of ballast water management" approved by the commandant of the Coast Guard.

Other issues on this topic addressed in the task force program included numerous studies and initiatives designed to understand ballast water as a vector for nonnative species generally, though focusing on the zebra mussel, and to halt the influence of this pathway.

1996 Amendments

Following the initial report of the task force, Congress made a series of changes to the NANPCA, amendments collectively labeled the National Invasive Species Act of 1996. Foremost among the revisions, the secretary of commerce, through the Coast Guard, must issue voluntary guidelines for preventing the introduction and spread of nonindigenous species in U.S. waters outside the Great Lakes (certain procedures with ballast water are already required by law).

The guidelines recommend that all vessels that operate in American waters and beyond the EEZ exchange ballast water where there is no threat of infesting U.S. waterways with nonnative species; such vessels are to keep records of their management of ballast water. Passenger vessels equipped with treatment systems that kill aquatic organisms in ballast water are exempt from these requirements. In 2000 the secretary's first report on the effectiveness of the guidelines is due in Congress, at which time a determination will be made on whether to retain these standards as purely voluntary or, if that is not adequately addressing the problem, convert them to mandatory regulations, provided with mechanisms of enforcement.

The secretary was further directed to create a "national ballast information clearinghouse," assisted in this endeavor by the task force and the Smithsonian Institution. This resource maintains information concerning ballasting practices, compliance with guidelines, the results of ballast water surveys, and other ecological data relevant to controlling aquatic nuisance species.

Another 1996 amendment called upon the task force to perform ecological studies and ballast water discharge surveys in the Chesapeake Bay, San Francisco Bay, Honolulu Harbor, the Columbia River, and any other location believed to be at risk from invasion by aquatic nuisance species. The task force was given the further duty of organizing a Western Regional Panel, modeled on the Great Lakes Panel, similarly comprised of federal, state, and local representatives from government and business. The duties of this panel are, among other things, to identify priorities for staving off invasions of harmful, nonnative species west of the 100th meridian, make recommendations regarding the zebra mussel in particular, develop an emergency response plan for confronting aquatic nuisance species, and report annually to the task force. The Western Panel conducted their first meetings in July 1997.

A final amendment requires the development and demonstration of a "Chicago Waterways Nonindigenous Species Dispersal Barrier." This obstruction is intended to prevent the movement of nonnative species from Lake Michigan through the Chicago Ship and Sanitary Canal to the Illinois River, and on to the Mississippi. It is believed that it was primarily this pathway that led to the infestation of the Mississippi River with zebra mussels, ruffe fish, and the round goby.

Executive Order 13112

The roots of the NANPCA can be traced to Executive Order 11987, issued by President Jimmy Carter in May 1977. Carter directed federal agencies to restrict the introduction of "exotic" species, referring to species not native to the United States. Unlike the Lacey Act (*see* this chapter: *Lacey Act*), which focuses on the deliberate *importation* of injurious wildlife for commercial purposes, EO 11987 concerns the unintentional introduction of such species: "the release, escape, or establishment of an exotic species into a natural ecosystem."

Carter's order, like much he tried to do during his term, was little heeded. Regulations implementing it were never produced. Then in February 1999 it was revoked entirely when President Bill Clinton issued Executive Order 13112, titled "Invasive Species."

An invasive species is a nonnative or "alien" species that causes or probably will cause "economic or environmental harm or harm to human health." With his directive, Clinton ordered all agencies to give due consideration to how federal programs will impact the status of invasive species by, among other things, preventing their introduction, monitoring their numbers, and controlling the interlopers through population management or eradication. The agencies are also called upon to make efforts to restore native species and their natural habitat, and to deny authorization or funding to projects that will likely result in the introduction of invasive species or enhance their welfare.

To assist federal agencies in meeting these objectives, an Invasive Species Council was created by EO 13112, composed of the Cabinet secretaries of state, treasury, defense, interior, agriculture, and commerce, and the administrator of the Environmental Protection Agency. The council's primary obligation is to "see that the federal agency activities concerning invasive species are coordinated, complimentary, cost-efficient, and effective." This duty is to be discharged by ensuring that agencies utilize the resources available to them from the Aquatic Nuisance Task Force, but more importantly by means of the Invasive Species Management Plan. This plan is supposed to be complete by September 2000 and will supply each federal agency with specific goals regarding invasive species, along with methods of achieving them. To be issued biennially, the first edition of the plan is also to include a review of current measures for preventing the introduction and spread of invasive species and the prospects for the future.

REFERENCES

Federal Laws

Airborne Hunting Act, 16 U.S.C. § 742j-l.

Alaska National Interest Lands Conservation Act of 1980, 16 U.S.C. §§ 410hh–410hh-5, 460mm–460mm-4, 539–539e, 3101–3233, and 43 U.S.C. §§ 1631–1642.

Bald Eagle Protection Act of 1940, 16 U.S.C. §§ 668–668d.

Dolphin Protection Consumer Information Act of 1990, 16 U.S.C. § 1385.

Endangered Species Act of 1973, 16 U.S.C. §§ 1531–1544.

Endangered Species Conservation Act of 1969, 83 Stat. 275 (repealed 1981).

Endangered Species Preservation Act of 1966, 80 Stat. 926 (repealed 1973).

Federal Land Policy and Management Act, 16 U.S.C. § 1338a.

Federal Law Enforcement Animal Protection Act of 2000, 18 U.S.C. § 1368.

Fishermen's Protective Act of 1967, 22 U.S.C. § 1978.

Fishery Conservation and Management Act, 16 U.S.C. § 1821(e)(2).

Fur Seal Act of 1966, 16 U.S.C. §§ 1151–1187.

International Dolphin Conservation Act of 1992, 16 U.S.C. §§ 1411–1418.

International Dolphin Conservation Program Act of 1997, 16 U.S.C. §§ 1361, 1385.

Lacey Act, 16 U.S.C. §§ 3371–3378.

Lacey Act of 1900, 18 U.S.C. § 42.

Land and Water Conservation Fund Act of 1964, 16 U.S.C. §§ 4601-4–4601-11.

Marine Mammal Protection Act of 1972, 16 U.S.C. §§ 1361–1421h.

Migratory Bird Conservation Act of 1929, 16 U.S.C. §§ 715–715r.

Migratory Bird Hunting Stamp Act of 1934, 16 U.S.C. §§ 718–718h.

Migratory Bird Treaty Act of 1918, 16 U.S.C. §§ 703–712.

National Environmental Policy Act of 1969, 42 U.S.C. §§ 4321–4347.

National Wildlife Refuge System Improvement Act of 1997, 16 U.S.C. §§ 668dd–668ee.

Nonindigenous Aquatic Nuisance Prevention and Control Act of 1990, 16 U.S.C. §§ 4701–4751.

North American Wetlands Act, 16 U.S.C. §§ 4401–4414.

Sentencing Reform Act of 1984, 18 U.S.C. §§ 3551–3626.

Whaling Convention Act of 1949, 16 U.S.C. §§ 916–916l.

Federal Regulations
Airborne Hunting, 50 C.F.R. Part 19.
Arctic National Wildlife Refuge, 50 C.F.R. Part 37.
Ballast Water Management for Control of Nonindigenous Species, 33 C.F.R. §§ 151.1500–1516.
Dolphin Safe Tuna Labeling, 50 C.F.R. §§ 216.90–95.
Eagle Permits, 50 C.F.R. Chapter 1, Part 22.
 Taking depredating eagles, § 22.23
 Taking for falconry purposes, § 22.24
 Taking for Indian religious purposes, § 22.22
 Taking for scientific or exhibition purposes, § 22.21
Endangered and Threatened Wildlife and Plants, 50 C.F.R. Part 17.
 Alaska natives exemption, § 17.5
 Critical habitat, wildlife, § 17.95
 Definitions, § 17.3
 Endangered Wildlife, Permits for taking, §§ 17.22–23
 Endangered Wildlife, Prohibitions, § 17.21
 Experimental Populations, §§ 17.80–84
 List, Endangered and threatened wildlife, § 17.11
 Threatened Wildlife, Permits for taking, § 17.32
 Threatened Wildlife, Prohibitions, § 17.31
Fur Seals: taking for subsistence purposes in the Pribilof Islands, 50 C.F.R. §§ 216.71–74.
Grizzly Bears, 50 C.F.R. § 17.40.
Injurious Wildlife, 50 C.F.R. Part 16.
Marine Mammals, Department of Commerce jurisdiction, 50 C.F.R. Parts 216–229.
 Authorization for commercial fisheries, Part 229
 Definitions, § 18.3
 Native American exemptions, §§ 18.23, 216.23
 Permits for scientific research and enhancement, §§ 18.31, 216.41
 Prohibitions, §§ 18.11–14
 Specifications for the humane handling, care, treatment, and transportation, 9 C.F.R. §§ 3.100–118
 Take reduction plan, §§ 229.31–32
 Taking incidental to commercial fishing, § 216.24
Marine Mammals, Department of Interior jurisdiction, 50 C.F.R. Part 18.
Migratory Bird Hunting, 50 C.F.R. Part 20.
 Baiting, § 20.21(i)
 Definitions, § 20.11
 Illegal hunting methods, § 20.21
 Nontoxic shot, § 20.134, §§ 20.140–143
National Wildlife Refuge System, 50 C.F.R. Subchapter C.
 Alaska, Part 36

Hunting and Fishing, Part 32
Hunting and Fishing, Areas closed to hunting, § 32.8
Hunting and Fishing, Refuge-Specific Regulations for Hunting, §§ 32.20–71
Prohibited Acts, Part 27
Subsistence use in Alaska, § 20.132
Subsistence uses, §§ 36.13–16
Trapping § 31.16
Whaling Provisions, 50 C.F.R. Part 230.
Aboriginal Subsistence Whaling, §§ 230.4–6, 8.

Federal Register
Finding on Petitions to Change Status of Grizzly Bear Populations, 63 Fed. Reg. 30,453–30,455 (June 4, 1998).
Import of Polar Bear Trophies from Canada, Final Rule, 64 Fed. Reg. 1529–1538 (January 11, 1999).
Marine Mammals: Incidental Take During Specified Activities, 65 Fed. Reg. 16828–16843 (March 30, 2000).
Migratory Bird Hunting: Regulations Regarding Baiting and Baited Areas, Final Rule, 64 Fed. Reg. 29,799–29,804 (June 3, 1999).
Migratory Bird Hunting: Seasons, Limits, and Shooting Hours, 64 Fed. Reg. 47,421–47,434 (August 31, 1999).
Notice of Updated Policy Regarding Harvest of Migratory Birds in Alaska Between March 10 and September 1, 64 Fed. Reg. 47,512–47,515 (August 31, 1999).
Taking of Marine Mammals Incidental to Commercial Fishing Operations, Finding, 64 Fed. Reg. 24,590–24,592 (May 7, 1999).
Use of Bait in Hunting, 60 Fed. Reg. 14,720–14,723 (March 20, 1995).

Executive Orders
Executive Order 13112, Invasive Species, President Bill Clinton, February 3, 1999.

Federal Cases
Supreme Court
Babbitt v. Sweet Home Chapter of Communities for a Great Oregon, 515 U.S. 100 (1995).
Baldwin v. Fish and Game Commission, 431 U.S. 288 (1978).
Bennet v. Spear, 520 U.S. 154 (1997).
Geer v. Connecticut, 161 U.S. 519 (1896).
Hunt v. United States, 278 U.S. 96 (1928).
Japan Whaling Association v. American Cetacean Society, 478 U.S. 221 (1986).
Kleppe v. New Mexico, 426 U.S. 529 (1976).
Missouri v. Holland, 252 U.S. 416 (1920).

Robertson v. Seattle Audubon Society, 503 U.S. 429 (1992).
TVA v. Hill, 437 U.S. 153 (1978).
United States v. The Abby Dodge, 223 U.S. 166 (1912).
United States v. Dion, 476 U.S. 734 (1986).

Circuit Courts of Appeals

Alaska Fish and Wildlife Federation and Outdoor Council v. Dunkle, 829
F.2d 933 (9th Cir. 1987), *cert. denied*, 485 U.S. 988 (1988).
American Bald Eagle v. Bhatti, 9 F.3d 163 (1st Cir. 1993).
Christy v. Hodel, 857 F.2d 1324 (9th Cir. 1988), *cert. denied*, 490 U.S.
1114 (1989).
Committee for Humane Legislation, Inc. v. Richardson, 540 F.2d 1141
(D.C. Cir. 1976).
Environmental Defense Fund v. TVA, 339 F. Supp. 806 (E.D. Tenn. 1971),
affirmed, 468 F.2d 1164 (6th Cir. 1972).
Metcalf v. Daley, 214 F.3d 1135 (9th Cir. 2000).
Palila v. Hawaii Department of Land and Natural Resources (Palila II), 852
F.2d 1106 (9th Cir. 1988).
United States v. Adams, 174 F.3d 571 (5th Cir. 1999).
United States v. Boynton, 63 F.3d 337 (4th Cir. 1995).
United States v. Delahoussaye, 573 F.2d 910 (5th Cir. 1978).
United States v. Fryberg, 622 F.2d 1010 (9th Cir. 1980).
United States v. Hayashi, 22 F.3d 859 (9th Cir. 1993).
United States v. Hugs, 109 F.3d 1375 (9th Cir. 1997).
United States v. Nuesca, 945 F.2d 254 (9th Cir. 1991).
United States v. Stenberg, 803 F.2d 422 (9th Cir. 1986).
United States v. Todd, 735 F.2d 146 (5th Cir. 1984).
United States v. White, 508 F.2d 453 (8th Cir. 1974).
United States v. Wulff, 758 F.2d 1121 (6th Cir. 1985).

District Courts

Brower v. Daley, 93 F. Supp. 2d 1071 (N.D. Cal. 2000).
Carlton v. Babbitt, 900 F. Supp. 526 (D. D.C. 1995) and 26 F. Supp. 2d
102 (D. D.C. 1998).
Fund for Animals v. Babbitt, 903 F. Supp. 96 (D.D.C. 1995).
Fund for Animals v. Clark, 27 F. Supp. 2d 8 (D. D.C. 1998).
Hill v. TVA, 419 F. Supp. 753 (E.D. Tenn. 1976), *rev'd*, 549 F. 2d 1064
(6th Cir. 1977).
Humane Society of the United States v. Lujan, 768 F. Supp. 360 (D. D.C.
1991).
National Rifle Association v. Kleppe, 425 F. Supp 1101 (D. D.C. 1976).
Northern Spotted Owl v. Hodel, 716 F. Supp. 479 (W.D. Wash. 1988).
Northern Spotted Owl v. Lujan, 758 F. Supp. 621 (W.D. Wash. 1991).

Oregon Natural Resource Council v. Turner, 863 F. Supp. 1277 (D. Or. 1994).

Palila v. Hawaii Department of Land and Natural Resources (Palila I), 471 F. Supp. 985 (D. Haw. 1979), *affirmed,* 639 F.2d 495 (9th Cir. 1981).

United States v. Abeyta, 632 F. Supp. 1301 (D. N.M. 1986).

United States v. McCullagh, 221 F. 288 (D. Kan. 1915).

United States v. Shauver, 214 F. 154 (E.D. Ark. 1914), *appeal dismissed,* 248 U.S. 594 (1919).

United States v. Thirty-Eight Golden Eagles, 649 F. Supp. 269 (D. Nev. 1986), *affirmed,* 829 F.2d 41 (9th Cir. 1987).

Books

Bean, Michael J., and Melanie J. Rowland. 1997. *The Evolution of National Wildlife Law.* 3d ed. Westport, CT: Praeger.

Busch, Briton. 1985. *The War against the Seals: A History of the North American Seal Fishery.* Kingston, OT: McGill-Queens University Press.

Donahue, Debra L. 1998. *Conservation and the Law.* Santa Barbara, CA: ABC-CLIO.

Garner, Robert. 1998. *Political Animals: Animal Protection Politics in Britain and the United States.* New York: St. Martin's.

Lopez, Barry. 1986. *Arctic Dreams.* New York: Scribners.

Lund, Thomas. 1980. *American Wildlife Law.* Berkeley and Los Angeles: University of California Press.

Lynch, Wayne. 1993. *Bears: Monarchs of the Northern Wilderness.* Seattle: The Mountaineers.

McNamee, Thomas. 1984. *The Grizzly Bear.* New York: McGraw-Hill.

Musgrave, Ruth, et al. 1998. *Federal Wildlife Laws Handbook.* Rockville, MD: Government Institutes.

Nilsson, Greta. 1990. "Birds." In *Animals and Their Legal Rights.* 4th ed. Washington, DC: Animal Welfare Institute.

Phelps, Norman. 2000. *Body Count: The Death Toll in America's War on Wildlife.* New York: The Fund for Animals.

Ransom, Jay Ellis. 1981. *Complete Field Guide to North American Wildlife.* New York: Harper & Row.

Servheen, Christopher, Stephen Herrero, and Bernard Peyton, comps. 1999. *Bears. Status Survey and Conservation Action Plan.* Gland, Switzerland: IUCN/SSC.

Sherry, Clifford. 1998. *Endangered Species.* Santa Barbara, CA: ABC-CLIO.

Stanfield, Leila. 1998. "Bear Baiting." In *Encyclopedia of Animal Rights and Animal Welfare.* Edited by Marc Bekoff. Westport, CT: Greenwood.

Stevens, Christine. 1990. "Marine Mammals." In *Animals and Their Legal Rights.* 4th ed. Washington, DC: Animal Welfare Institute.

Articles, Guidelines, and Reports

Bauer, Donald C. 1996. "Reconciling Polar Bear Protection under United States Laws and the International Agreement for the Conservation of Polar Bears." *Animal Law* 2: 9–100.

Eichstaedt, Richard Kirk. 1998. "'Save the Whales' v. 'Save the Makah': The Makah and the Struggle for Native Whaling." *Animal Law* 4: 145–172.

Fink, Richard J. 1994. "The National Wildlife Refuges: Theory, Practice, and Prospect." *Harvard Environmental Law Review* 18: 1–136.

Fox, Camilla. 1999. "Trapping on National Wildlife Refuges." Animal Protection Institute publication.

Glitzenstein, Eric, and John Fritschie. 1995. "The Forest Service's Bait and Switch: A Case Study on Bear Baiting and the Service's Struggle to Adopt a Reasoned Policy on a Controversial Hunting Practice within the National Forests." *Animal Law* 1: 45–77.

Markarian, Michael. 1997. "Migratory Massacre." *The Animals' Agenda* 17, no. 4 (July-August): 22–27.

Stewart, Kristin L. 1998. "Dolphin-Safe Tuna: The Tide is Changing." *Animal Law* 4: 111–137.

Weyhrauch, Bruce B. 1986. "Waterfowl and Lead Shot." *Environmental Law* 16: 883–934.

World Wide Web

Aquatic Nuisance Species Task Force, http://ANSTaskForce.gov.

Bureau of Land Management, National Wild Horse and Burro Program, http://www. wildhorseburro.blm.gov/.

Center for Wildlife Law, http://ipl.unm.edu/cwl.

Defenders of Wildlife, http://www.defenders.org/index.html.

Fund for Animals, http://www.fund.org.

International Whaling Commission, http://ourworld.compuserve.com/homepages/iwcoffice/iwc.htm.

Sea Shepherd Conservation Society, http://www.seashepherd.org.

U.S. Fish and Wildlife Service, http://www.fws.gov.

   Division of Endangered Species, http://endangered.fws.gov.

   Grizzly Bear Recovery, http://www.r6.fws.gov/endspp/grizzly/index.htm

   Grizzly Bear Recovery in the Bitterroot Ecosystem: Summary of the Final Environmental Impact Statement, http://www.r6.fws.gov/endspp/grizzly/press_release3102000.htm

   Migratory Bird Management, http://migratorybirds.fws.gov.

Wildlife Refuges, http://refuges.fws.gov.

Whaling and Fishing, Chapter 4, Hypertext book by Peter J. Bryant, http://darwin.bio.uci.edu/~sustain/bio65/lec04/b65lec04.htm.

Zebra Mussel, http://www.science.wayne.edu/~jram/zmussel.htm.

7. Laboratory Animals

HISTORY OF LAB ANIMAL USE AND ITS LEGAL REGULATION

Animals have been used in laboratories for research, testing, and experimentation for nearly 2,500 years, but only a little more than one century has elapsed since these procedures have been regulated by laws anywhere in the world. In America no laboratory animal received any legal protection until 1966, and then only dogs and cats were covered.

Antiquity

The first recorded use of an animal for experimentation occurred in about 450 B.C.E. when Alcmaeon of Croton severed the optic nerve of a dog, and noted that blindness resulted. Perhaps 150 years later in Athens, Hippocrates (or a student of his) induced a pig to drink colored water, and then cut the animal's throat to investigate swallowing. He also cut open the chest of another animal and studied the still beating heart, observing how the auricles and ventricles contracted alternately. During the third century B.C.E., Alexandria in north Egypt was a flourishing center of anatomical and physiological research conducted on living animals, led by Herophilos and Erasistratos.

In the second century C.E. Galen of Pergamon, physician to the Roman emperor Marcus Aurelius, dissected living pigs, goats, apes, and other animals in his search to understand respiration, nerve function, and heart action. He also probed the brains of conscious animals, a procedure he recommended not be done on apes because their expression during the operation was "unpleasant." The discovery of anesthetics, as well as any legal restrictions on such procedures, were still well over 2,000 years away. Since animals were regarded as lacking in both reason and a soul, neither Greek nor Roman law recognized them as anything other than objects—property to be used as their owners wished.

To these ancient scientists, it was clear that the best way to arrive at an understanding of bodily functions was to observe the internal workings of living organisms, accessed by cutting them open. This procedure came to be known as "vivisection." The roots of this word are from Rome and the two Latin terms, *vivus*, meaning "living," and *sectio*, "cutting." Literally, "vivisection" is the cutting of living bodies. The first known use of the concept comes from Celsus, a first century C.E. Roman chronicler of ancient medicine, who wrote of *incidere vivorum corpora:* "cutting the bodies of the living." By the 1500s, such terms as *vivorum sectio* and *viva sectio* had entered the parlance of Renaissance scientists. Within another 200 years the word "vivisection" was being used by English and German authors.

Meanwhile, the scientific method developed by Aristotle in Greece, and applied in animal experimentation by physicians like Galen, disappeared in Europe through the thousand years of the Dark and Middle Ages. Finally, vivisection was revived during the Italian Renaissance. In Padua and Bologna, Andreas Vesalius dissected living animals in public anatomy courses, demonstrating the functions of various parts of the body in much the same way as Galen had done. Throughout the 1500s, Vesalius was joined by several other Italian physicians, such as Jacob Berenger and Giambattista Canano, in performing experiments on live animals.

The Renaissance

In the 1600s animal use in early laboratories spread across Europe. In England William Harvey discovered the circulation of blood by vivisecting dogs, and Robert Boyle studied respiration by suffocating various animals in a pneumatic chamber. In Denmark Thomas Bartholinus conducted experiments on animals that led to a new theory of lymphatic resorption of food. In France Jean Pecquet cut open dogs and found the thoracic duct. And the work continued in Italy, where Gaspare Aselli dissected a dog and came upon what we now know as the lymphatic vessels of the mesentery.

All of these Enlightenment scientists shared an abhorrence of vivisecting humans, as it was said that some of the ancients like Herophilos and Erasistratos had done, designating it a crime and a sin. However, all agreed with the Greeks and Romans that, having neither rationality nor a soul, animals were of an entirely different order. For these investigators, and for the public generally, there were no discernible moral or religious impediments to using them in the lab, and consequently, there were no legal barriers either.

Reinforcing this license, the French philosopher Rene Descartes claimed that animals did not really suffer anyway. His highly influential arguments pointed out that animals did not have language because they had no minds, and if they had no minds, they were not conscious—certainly only a conscious being could feel pain. For Descartes, who himself participated in studies of blood circulation, animals were insensate machines, so any moral compunction or legal restriction on animal experimentation was groundless. Bolstered by this reasoning, a series of late seventeenth-century and early eighteenth-century physiologists such as Francois Bayle, Nicholas Malebranche, and Antoine Arnauld pursued vivisection zealously.

The 1700s wore on, and Descartes's influence seemed to wane—fewer scientists denied that the animals they used suffered. Even so, most believed that the pursuit of human knowledge justified the infliction of pain, though there was little appeal to any therapeutic value of the research. In any case, God had made the beasts expressly to serve man.

Then resistance to these beliefs began to build, especially in England.

There, such noteworthy scholars as Alexander Pope and Samuel Johnson vehemently rejected vivisection as barbarous and cruel, as inclining its practitioners to mistreating people, and as advancing knowledge very little while failing to provide a cure for anything. Perhaps most cogent of all was Jeremy Bentham, whose *Introduction to the Principles of Morals and Legislation* was widely read by the educated upper classes in the 1780s and 1790s. Bentham argued that laws should be designed to succor the well-being of everyone, measured essentially by the promotion of pleasure and the avoidance of pain. He speculated that, since animals had the capacity to experience pleasure and pain, "[t]he day may come when the rest of the animal creation may acquire those rights which never could have been withholden from them but by the hand of tyranny."

Cruelty Issues in England

As the nineteenth century dawned and brightened, many of England's gentry grew increasingly concerned with a variety of humanitarian causes, not the least of which was the treatment of animals, and instigated some major legal reforms. In 1807 slavery was abolished in Britain. By the middle of the century capital punishment had become rare, and the Factory Acts had provided relief for children working in the appalling conditions that followed the Industrial Revolution.

In 1822 Parliament passed the "Ill Treatment of Horses and Cattle Bill," popularly known as "Martin's Act" after its sponsor and main advocate, Richard Martin. The first significant animal protection law in the world, Martin's Act prohibited cruel mistreatment of various large farm animals, but made no mention of the smaller mammals and birds that populated the laboratories, or of vivisection in particular (*see also* chapter 3: *Anticruelty Laws: Early Anticruelty Laws and Their Origins*).

Just two years later, Arthur Broome founded the Society for the Prevention of Cruelty to Animals (SPCA), eventually endorsed by Queen Victoria who allowed the society the use of the prefix "Royal," beginning in 1840. Although the goal of the SPCA was to ensure that the new legislation was honored and enforced for all the animals covered, members of the society primarily focused on the treatment of cab and draft horses. This seems to be because there were so many horses and abuse of them was highly visible on nearly every urban thoroughfare.

At about the same time the SPCA was organizing, the leading French physiologist of the day and devotee of the Cartesian theory of the animal machine arrived in London: Francois Magendie. At public demonstrations, Magendie performed various experiments on animals, including a procedure using live puppies in which he severed the dorsal and ventral nerve bundles where they enter and exit the spinal cords of the dogs. Paralysis resulted.

Many Londoners were revolted and outraged at Magendie's exhibition, and some in Parliament began to draft legislation to regulate vivisection. Yet it would be another half century before these efforts came to fruition. During this time and in subsequent years, the meaning of "vivisection" broadened considerably. It came to include any kind of experiments on animals involving pain, such as the application of chemicals or other noxious physical stimuli, and not just the cutting of a partial dissection, or a surgery performed on a living animal.

Parliament passed new animal protection laws in 1835 and 1849 that broadened and strengthened the provisions of Martin's Act. Their language appeared to bring laboratory animals within the purview of these laws: the 1849 Cruelty to Animals Act made it illegal to "ill-treat, . . . abuse, or torture any animal." Even so, the first prosecution of vivisection under anticruelty legislation did not occur until 1874. Here, another French physiologist, Eugenne Mangan, had induced epilepsy in two dogs at the annual meeting of the British Medical Association. Mangan fled back across the Channel to France before he could be brought up on charges.

At Massachusetts General Hospital in Boston, the pain-relieving effects of ether were first demonstrated in 1846. Some began to use the substance on their laboratory animals, while most did not. In any case, the science of anesthesia was new and crude: ether, and later chloroform, were administered by a sponge soaked in the liquid and held at the nostrils of the animal. The anesthetic effects did not last long, and often wore off before the dissection or surgery could be completed. In that event, a reapplication might be made or neglected.

Despite the rustic state of anesthetic techniques, many scientists recognized its value as an essential aspect of the humane use of animals in research. By 1871 the British Association for the Advancement of Science had produced a set of guidelines for physiological experiments involving animals, the first such code of conduct on record, which give a prominent place to pain relief. Its first principle declared that "No experiment which can be performed under the influence of an anesthetic drug ought to be done without it."

Of course, this was simply a recommendation with no force of law behind it. Public dissatisfaction with this situation, along with a general sentiment against unregulated animal experimentation, continued to build in England during the 1870s. The heightened pitch corresponded to a move by British scientists to increase their use of animals to keep pace with their European colleagues, especially those in France.

There, Claude Bernard, a former student of Magendie, had established himself as the preeminent physiologist of his time. Bernard had been experimenting on animals for over twenty years, and in the process had made a number of foundational discoveries, including the revelation that digestion was completed in the intestine and not in the stomach, and that sympathetic nerves constrict blood vessels. His *Introduction to the Study of Experimental Medicine*, published in 1865, was widely regarded as the authoritative text in the field. In a chapter on vivisection, Bernard defended the practice on familiar grounds, though shorn of its theological trappings: "[I]t is essentially moral to make experiments on an animal, even though painful and dangerous to him, if they be useful to man."

Legal Regulation Begins in England

In early 1875 George Hoggan returned to London from Paris after spending several months with Bernard, working in his animal lab as a research assistant. Hoggan's disturbing account of the conditions he found there and the suffering inflicted by Bernard were widely publicized and discussed. Although Bernard's work was already notorious among those concerned with animal welfare, Hoggan's report seemed to instantly galvanize citizens and lawmakers alike.

Frustrated by what they saw as inertia at the RSPCA, Francis Power Cobbe and Lord Shaftesbury, along with Hoggan, founded the Victoria Street Society for the Protection of Animals from Vivisection. The new group immediately became a powerful lobbying force in Parliament. Even Queen Victoria got involved, prevailing upon Prime Minister Disraeli in 1875 to form the Royal Commission on Vivisection to study the matter. The commission interviewed numerous scientists, most notably Charles Darwin. Just four years earlier, Darwin had written in *The Descent of Man and Selection in Relation to Sex* that "[t]here is no fundamental difference between man and higher mammals in their mental faculties." He further asserted that "humanity to lower animals . . . [is] one of the noblest virtues with which man is endowed." Although supporting vivisection generally, Darwin testified that more protection for the animals was needed, and real benefits to humankind must be produced by the research to justify using them.

The Royal Commission on Vivisection submitted its report in January 1876. On the basis of ample public concern and powerful testimony such as Darwin's, the commission recommended legal restrictions on animal experimentation to prevent abuses and cruelty. This was seconded by the influential Victoria Street Society, and by other interested individuals. The Cruelty to Animals Act of 1876 was passed by both houses of Parliament, quickly receiving royal assent. It was the first law in the world to regulate the use of animals in scientific research.

The new law stipulated that anyone intending to perform experiments on living vertebrates—"vivisection" in the wider sense to include procedures that cause pain, even though no cutting is done—must apply to the home secretary for a license. The laboratory and the proposed procedures had to be registered with the government. To secure approval, the investigator must demonstrate that the research would result in an "advancement by new discovery of physiological knowledge or of knowledge which will be useful for saving or prolonging life or alleviating suffering."

America

These developments in England were observed with great interest by various individuals in America, where sentiment against animal experimentation had been brewing for the past decade. As early as 1867 Henry Bergh, the founder of the American Society for the Prevention of Cruelty to Animals, had attempted to include a ban on vivisection in an anticruelty bill considered by the New York state legislature. Although the bill was eventually signed into law and represented a significant strengthening of New York's original 1828 anticruelty statute, the prohibition on vivisection was vigorously opposed by prominent animal researchers and the state medical society. In the spirit of compromise, Bergh relented and the ban was dropped.

The passage of Britain's Cruelty to Animals Act reinvigorated the fledgling animal protection movement in the United States, and in 1880 a bill closely modeled on the new English law was introduced by U.S. Senator McMillan in the District of Columbia. Washington, D.C., was fast becoming a hotbed of experimental medicine at the time, but the medical community itself was divided over the efficacy of using animals in their research. Despite its having received unequivocal support from numerous leading judges, politicians, and scientists, the adversaries of the bill were too strong. The National Academy of Sciences and a committee formed by Johns Hopkins's William Welch and Harvard's Henry Bowditch, and consisting of prominent biomedical organizations, launched a withering attack on the proposed legislation. It was soundly defeated. Attempts to revive the bill in 1899, 1900, and 1902 were all futile. In 1919 another, more narrowly focused bill that would have banned only the use of dogs in D.C. labs was also defeated by Welch and his allies.

By the turn of the century, every state in America had passed an anticruelty law. Fourteen of these laws specifically exempted animal experimentation, but up through the Second World War there are no prosecutions of investigators on record from any of the states without this exemption. Legal regulation that might benefit laboratory animals entered a period of quiescence that lasted for nearly all of the first half of the 1900s. Perhaps surprisingly, when the drought finally ended in 1948, the new laws were not aimed at promoting the welfare of animals used in research; instead, their purpose was to ensure that laboratories were well supplied with animals.

Founded in Chicago in 1945, the National Society for Medical Research (NSMR) immediately began to work on what had become a chronic problem for the research community: obtaining sufficient numbers of research animals. The NSMR saw the millions of abandoned and unclaimed animals populating America's shelters and pounds as a ready resource going to waste, but the group lacked the legal authority to compel operators to surrender them. Success was not long in coming. In 1948 and 1949 the NSMR prevailed upon the legislatures of Minnesota, and then Wisconsin, to pass the country's first animal procurement laws. Similar city ordinances in Los Angeles and Baltimore followed quickly in 1950; in another two years, Illinois and New York had followed suit. These laws varied somewhat in their details but all shared a common requirement: pounds and shelters must surrender animals to research facilities upon demand. South Dakota, Oklahoma, Connecticut, Ohio, and Iowa also passed such procurement laws in the 1950s.

For the animal shelters in these localities, most of which were run by various humane organizations, the requirement to hand over animals for whom the shelter was supposed to provide a sanctuary from suffering was terribly demoralizing. In response to this distressing situation, several new humane organizations were formed in the 1950s, dedicated to battling the procurement laws and establishing legal controls over the care and use of research animals. Among the most effective of these new groups were the Animal Welfare Institute (AWI) with its lobbying arm, the Society for Animal Protective Legislation, founded by Robert Gesell, professor of physiology at the University of Michigan, and his daughter Christine Stevens; the Humane Society of the United States (HSUS), which, dissatisfied with its inaction, broke from the larger American Humane Association, rather like the Victoria Street Society had splintered off from the RSPCA eighty years earlier in England; Friends for Animals also dates its inception from this time.

Legal Regulation Begins in America

During the first half of the 1960s, AWI and HSUS influence provoked members of Congress to propose no less than six different bills regulating the use of animals in the laboratory. All of these proposals were patterned on Britain's 1876 Cruelty to Animals Act, emphasizing licensing, registration, and clear justification of procedures causing pain to animals. All the bills were staunchly opposed by the National Institutes of Health (NIH), the American Medical Association (AMA), the American Veterinary Medical Association, the NSMR, and the research community generally. All the bills failed.

Finally, in two separate events, the animal protection movement stumbled upon the strategy that would prove most effective for establishing the legal regulation of the care and use of research animals. The first began in July 1965 at a Pennsylvania hospital where Mr. Lakavage was recuperating from a heart attack. He happened to come across a newspaper article about William Miller, an animal dealer who had been arrested in Northampton County, Pennsylvania, for improperly loading animals to be sold to labs on his truck. Accompanying the article was a photograph of the seventeen dogs and two goats that had been removed from the truck while Miller obtained a more suitable vehicle. To his amazement, Lakavage recognized one of the dogs: it was Pepper, the Lakavage family Dalmatian, missing for several days. He immediately notified his wife who, along with their three young children, set out at once on a frantic search for Pepper.

Meanwhile, Miller had secured a larger truck and left for New York City. The Lakavages managed to trace their dog to a large animal dealer named Nersesian at his New York operation, but the distraught family was not allowed to enter the facility. As it turned out, Pepper was not at the Nersesian dog farm anyway—she had already been dropped at Montefiore Hospital in New York City and had died shortly thereafter on an operating table.

Just one week after Mr. Lakavage had seen Pepper in the photo, Congressman Joseph Resnick of New York introduced a bill to regulate the use of research animals. Notified of the Lakavage's plight, the AWI had contacted the office of Senator Joseph Clark of Pennsylvania, who had been a major sponsor and advocate of the unsuccessful laboratory animal protection bills of the early 1960s. Clark was out of town, but his office contacted Resnick, in whose district the Nersesian operation was located. Resnick's bill required that dog and cat dealers, and the research facilities that purchased them be licensed, inspected, and subject to humane standards established by the secretary of agriculture. In the other house of Congress, Senator Warren Magnuson and Senator Clark introduced companion bills.

Hearings began in September, continuing through the rest of the year and into 1966. Predictably, the bills were steadfastly resisted by the research community, lead by the NIH, the NSMR, and a host of state medical and veterinary schools and societies. The Department of Agriculture, with whom the legislation would lodge administrative, regulatory, and enforcement obligations, wanted no part of it. By early 1966, after a promising start, little progress had been made, but then another fortuitous event occurred. On February 4, *Life* magazine published an exposé titled "Concentration Camps for Dogs," complete with graphic photographs of the shocking conditions found at dog dealers' facilities: these were the animals destined for the laboratories.

The story instantly ignited public outrage, much as George Hoggan's description of Claude Bernard's lab had provoked widespread condemnation of animal experimentation in 1875 England. More than 80,000 letters expressing disgust and indignation flooded Congress, a deluge eclipsing that of any other issue, including civil rights and the Vietnam War. The HSUS reported that as many as half of all missing pets had been stolen and sold to research facilities, while articles in *Sports Illustrated* and *Reader's Digest* further detailed instances of pet theft for the labs. Major newspapers, too, jumped on the bandwagon, and the opponents of laboratory animal protection laws realized that their tactics had to change.

By early May, Senators Walter Mondale of Minnesota and Lister Hill of Alabama had introduced bills authored by the NSMR and the NIH, respectively. The main feature of both bills was that the research community would not be subject to federal regulation, but would effectively regulate itself through the application of the standards endorsed by the American Association for Accreditation of Laboratory Animal Care (*see* this chapter: *Public Health Service: Developing Standards for Laboratory Animals*). This maneuver failed, however, and the Resnick and Magnuson bills passed, unanimously in the Senate. The Laboratory Animal Welfare Act, later shortened to the Animal Welfare Act, was signed into law by President Lyndon Johnson in August 1966.

ANIMAL WELFARE ACT OF 1970

The Animal Welfare Act (AWA) is the first, and remains the only, major federal legislation in the United States governing the use of animals in research, testing, and education. (The AWA also applies to most animal exhibitions; *see* chapter 5: *Circuses and Zoos*.) In effect, the AWA is the national animal protection statute.

Laboratory Animal Welfare Act

The AWA began under another name, the Laboratory Animal Welfare Act of 1966 (LAWA), a statute inspired, not by concern for the treatment of laboratory animals generally, but by a rash of thefts of family pets for use in experimentation. Congressman Joseph Resnick of New York introduced the original bill in 1965 after becoming involved in an attempt to help a family recover a dog that had been stolen and then sold by a dealer to a hospital laboratory. Similar bills had been proposed several times in the early 1960s, but all had been effectively quashed by the research community, led principally by the National Institutes of Health (NIH), the American Medical Association (AMA), the American Veterinary Medical Association (AVMA), and the National Society for Medical Research (NSMR).

The tide turned in February 1966 when *Life* magazine published an exposé featuring disturbing photographs of the squalid conditions found at

dealers' operations, where dogs awaited shipment to the labs. After tor-
rents of public indignation greeted federal lawmakers, Congressman
Resnick's bill, along with a companion bill from Senator Warren Magnuson, passed through Congress in a few months. President Lyndon Johnson signed LAWA into law in August 1966 (for more detail on this sequence of events, *see* this chapter: *History of Lab Animal Use and Its Legal
Regulation: Legal Regulation Begins in America*).

Congress vested the administrative, regulatory, and enforcement responsibilities of LAWA with the U.S. Department of Agriculture (USDA),
reasoning that the agency's independence from the NIH, the AMA, and
the research community generally would prevent any improper compromises. In 1972 these responsibilities passed to a new office of the USDA,
the Animal and Plant Health Inspection Service (APHIS), which then
transferred enforcement and inspection duties in 1988 to a division called
Regulatory Enforcement and Animal Care (REAC). APHIS was reorganized in 1996, eliminating REAC and creating two new offices, the Animal Care Division, which inspects licensed dealers and registered facilities, and Investigative and Enforcement Services, charged with
investigating complaints of AWA violations.

Senator Robert Dole called LAWA "the dognapping bill of 1966," and
the preamble did explicitly state that its purpose was "to protect the owners of dogs and cats from theft of such pets, [and] to prevent the sale or
use of dogs and cats which have been stolen." This focus is clear in the
provisions of LAWA. Research facilities had to be registered with the
USDA, but only if they used dogs and cats, and they needed to keep
records only for these species. LAWA also required animal dealers to obtain licenses from the USDA, and to identify or mark all and only the
dogs and cats transported, purchased, or sold. Further, dealers were required to hold all dogs and cats for at least five business days before selling them. Researchers were prohibited from obtaining dogs and cats from
unlicensed dealers. LAWA did try to ensure that primates, guinea pigs,
hamsters, and rabbits were also treated humanely in research facilities,
but the statutory emphasis was obvious.

LAWA-imposed penalties for violation by a dealer included license
suspension or revocation, and imprisonment for up to one year and a
fine of up to $1,000. Research facilities could be fined $500 per day for
each violation.

LAWA directed the secretary of agriculture to "promulgate standards
to govern the humane handling, care, treatment, and transportation of
animals by dealers and research facilities." These standards, originating
at APHIS since 1972, were to include minimum requirements for feeding,
watering, shelter, sanitation of the facilities, and "adequate veterinary
care" (*see* this chapter: *Animal Welfare Act Regulations*). However, LAWA

did not authorize the secretary to make any rules of any sort for the treatment of animals in the course of the research "protocol," the experimental procedure itself: "Nothing in this Act . . . shall be construed as authorizing the Secretary to promulgate rules, regulations, or orders for the handling, care, treatment, or inspection of animals during actual research or experimentation."

Animal Welfare Act of 1970

Congress made a number of major changes to LAWA in 1970, starting with its name, and this is what we now know today as the Animal Welfare Act. The change reflects the broader scope of coverage the AWA now provides by adding animal exhibitors to the list of regulated entities, along with research facilities and animal dealers (*see* chapter 5: *Circuses and Zoos*).

The AWA defines a "research facility" as any individual, organization, or institution, including those of higher education (not elementary or secondary schools), using or intending to use animals for research, testing, or experimentation. A "dealer" is not only any operation buying, selling, or transporting animals, but also any that supplies animals for educational or exhibition purposes, or as pets. However, retail pet stores are not considered to be animal dealers, and are not regulated by the AWA or any federal law (for more on pet stores, *see* chapter 3: *Dog Law: Dog Breeding, "Puppy Mills," and Pet Stores*).

Enterprises that exhibit animals for money are under the control of the AWA and subject to USDA inspection. An "exhibitor" is any person displaying animals for compensation, such as in circuses, zoos, and carnivals. The AWA does not count livestock shows, dog and cat shows, or rodeos (*see* chapter 5: *Rodeos*) as exhibitions, and these events are not subject to any federal regulation.

The 1970 amendments expanded other definitions as well. "Animal" now includes not only those listed in LAWA, but also any "warm-blooded animal [that] the Secretary may determine is being used, or is intended for use, for research, testing, experimentation, or exhibition purposes, or as a pet." Record keeping is required for all covered animals, not just dogs and cats, and research facilities using any of these animals are subject to the law. Even so, rats, mice, and birds are specifically excluded, as are farm animals. The AWA also sharpens the idea of "adequate veterinary care," one left unexplained in LAWA, to make explicit reference to the use of anesthetic, analgesic, and tranquilizing drugs, although the decision of precisely when these drugs would be appropriate is left to the scientists. Finally, the 1970 amendments create penalties for those who interfere with USDA inspectors, and impose liability on the research facility, dealer, or exhibitor for acts of their agents or employees.

The AWA would be amended several times over the years, the first changes coming in 1976. The "intermediate handler" was added as an individual subject to the provisions of the AWA and its regulations. This is "any person . . . who is engaged in any business in which he receives custody of animals in connection with their transportation in commerce." Another new entity that must comply with the federal law is the "carrier," referring to airlines, railroads, and trucking and shipping operations that transport animals for a fee. These revisions came about as a result of documented abuses and mistreatment in the conveyance of animals from place to place, typically in the form of inadequate caging and crating that frequently caused injuries. Pursuant to these changes, in 1977 APHIS produced standards for the care and handling of animals in transit.

Another 1976 amendment prohibited "any person to knowingly sponsor or exhibit an animal in any animal fighting venture to which any animal was moved in interstate or foreign commerce" (see chapter 5: *Cockfighting and Dogfighting: Animal Welfare Act*).

Abuses of Research Monkeys and the AWA
The most significant modifications to the AWA came with the 1985 amendments. Officially called the Improved Standards for Laboratory Animals Act, these amendments were mainly instigated by two sordid events of the early 1980s involving monkeys. The first occurred in Silver Spring, Maryland, at the Institute for Behavioral Research (IBR).

Dr. Edward Taub, an IBR scientist, was experimenting with macaque monkeys to investigate how individuals who had lost the use of their limbs following a stroke might be trained to regain some capacity in the arms and legs. His research was funded by the NIH. Alex Pacheco, a representative of the fledgling People for the Ethical Treatment of Animals (PETA), posed as an aspiring researcher and obtained a technician job in Taub's lab. Over the course of several months, Pacheco documented the extraordinarily poor conditions in which the monkeys were housed, even though APHIS inspectors had found no AWA violations at the facility. In October 1981 Maryland police raided the IBR and seized seventeen monkeys, charging Taub with seventeen counts of animal cruelty for failing to provide adequate veterinary care.

Taub was eventually vindicated on all counts (for more on this case, see chapter 2: *Legal Standing under the Animal Welfare Act*). Even so, the incident attracted a great deal of media attention, and came just days before subcommittee chairman Doug Walgren of Pennsylvania held hearings on a number of bills introduced in the House of Representatives that proposed further regulations of research using animals. By August 1982 Walgren's Subcommittee on Science and Technology had crafted a composite bill based on the pending proposals. Nevertheless, Congress adjourned before any action was taken on it.

The issue was reinvigorated in 1983 when Senator Robert Dole sponsored a bill adapted from the Walgren draft. However, this one was written specifically as an amendment to the AWA. Adversaries of the Dole bill where formidable, notably the NIH, and the legislative wheels grind slowly in any case, so it was not until an incident in the spring of 1984 that real progress was made.

Individuals representing the Animal Liberation Front broke into the Head Injury Clinical Research Laboratory of the University of Pennsylvania and stole some sixty hours of videotape, shot by researchers during their NIH-funded study of head injuries. Among other abuses, the tapes revealed baboons in obvious pain and distress, lab personnel mocking and ridiculing them, and surgery being performed without anesthesia and under clearly nonsterile conditions, such as while the surgeons smoked cigarettes and pipes. PETA received copies of the tapes and produced an edited thirty-minute video called *Unnecessary Fuss*, a title inspired by the reaction to the affair of the lab's director, Dr. Thomas Gennarelli. PETA's videotape was widely distributed in the United States, Canada, and Europe (*see also* this chapter: *Animal Enterprise Protection Act: Animal Liberation Front*).

Over the next year the *New York Times,* the *Washington Post,* and many other newspapers across urban America editorialized in condemnatory terms on the treatment of research animals, specifically denouncing Gennarelli's research and demanding a halt to its funding by the NIH, while calling for serious reforms. When Senator Dole reintroduced his 1983 bill, and Congressman George Brown of California sponsored a similar house bill in the summer of 1984, the American media and much of public opinion was clearly in favor of making significant changes in the AWA. Nonetheless, the companion bills languished in subcommittees for another year, and legislative action was also substantially slowed by deliberation over the contemporaneous Health Research Extension Act. Finally in November 1985 Congress approved the Dole-Brown amendments under the name of the Improved Standards for Laboratory Animals Act, and President Ronald Reagan signed the new law two days before Christmas.

Improved Standards for Laboratory Animals Act
In the nearly twenty years that had elapsed since LAWA was enacted, the focus of Congress in regulating animal welfare had expanded dramatically. No longer was safeguarding the interests of pet owners in their dogs and cats the preoccupation. In section 1, the Improved Standards for Laboratory Animals Act observed that alternatives to research animals were being developed and that some of these were faster, cheaper, and

more accurate than methods using animals. Moreover, the unnecessary duplication of research using animals was a wasteful drain on resources that should be avoided, the amendment continued, and it was important to respond to the public concern for animal welfare.

Perhaps foremost among the 1985 changes to the AWA is that for the first time some minimal restrictions are placed on the way in which experimentation is conducted. As mentioned above, LAWA had explicitly denied the secretary of agriculture the authority to regulate the research protocol itself. Here, however, an amendment directs the secretary to develop standards that require investigators to "minimize pain and distress" during the research, as well as to consider alternatives to procedures that cause pain. Consultation with a veterinarian is now also necessary for designing research with painful procedures, and for supplying adequate pre- and postsurgical care. The withholding of anesthetics is permitted only when "scientifically necessary," but the scientists are left to determine when that necessity obtains. Finally, a single laboratory animal can no longer be used for more than one surgery, formerly a common practice, although again an exception to this rule is allowed in cases of "scientific necessity."

Another major change in the AWA is that all those involved with animals in the research facilities must be adequately trained. They must gain competence in methods of humane animal maintenance and experimentation, methods that will reduce the number of animals used and the pain caused to them, procedures for reporting failures in the animal care program, and how to take advantage of the information service provided by the National Agricultural Library (NAL). This service at NAL was also established by the 1985 amendments, one that, in cooperation with the National Library of Medicine, provides animal care personnel with facts about training, duplication, and how to reduce animal suffering and the numbers used.

To ensure compliance with these new rules, every research facility is required to establish an Institutional Animal Care and Use Committee (IACUC) (*see also* this chapter: *Animal Care Committees*). The chief executive officer of each facility appoints or approves the selection of the committee members. There must be at least three members, one of whom must be a veterinarian, another a person who represents "general community interests in the proper care and treatment of animals," and a third who is not affiliated in any way with the facility, nor is related to someone so affiliated. IACUC members are expected to be capable of evaluating the care and treatment afforded to the animals in light of the needs of the research facility. The votes of a majority of members are necessary to approve any committee actions or resolutions.

The IACUC is charged with the responsibility of reviewing all research proposals using animals, ensuring that, among other things, investigators will provide appropriate pain relief and euthanasia, have considered alternatives to using animals, are following standards for pre- and postsurgical care, and are properly trained in animal husbandry issues. Also, the IACUC is required to conduct semiannual inspections of all the areas of the facility where animals are used and housed, and then file a complete report of their findings with APHIS. This agency is also required to inspect each registered research facility at least once a year.

Another amendment requires the secretary—through APHIS—to issue "minimum standards . . . for the exercise of dogs, [and] a physical environment adequate to promote the well-being of primates" (for more on the AWA and dogs, *see* chapter 3: *Dog Law: Federal Dog Protection Law;* for primates, *see* this chapter: *Primates: Psychological Well-Being*).

Finally, the 1985 changes include an enhancement of the penalties for violating the AWA. Each violation is punishable by up to $2,500 in fines, and each day that the infraction continues is considered a separate offense. Ignoring orders from the secretary to stop violating any provision of the AWA or its regulations brings a $1,500 fine for each offense and for each day that the violation occurs. Animal dealers convicted of knowingly breaking the law can receive one year in prison or a fine of up to $2,500, or both.

Pet Protection Act

An amendment in 1990 brought the AWA back to concern for people's dogs and cats. Also known as the Pet Protection Act, legal duties are now imposed on research utilizing dogs and cats obtained at "random sources." These are more commonly known as pounds or shelters, and are generically labeled as Animal Control Facilities (ACF) (*see* chapter 3: *Animal Control Facilities*). The amendment demands that ACFs hold and care for these animals for at least five days before they can be legally sold to a licensed dealer.

The point of this restriction is to give the human owners some opportunity to recover their pets, or provide some time for adoption. Some states prohibit ACFs from supplying animals for research, and some shelters and pounds euthanize animals before the five-day period or have policies against supplying dealers. In these cases, this AWA amendment is superseded.

Before a dealer can sell a random-source dog or cat to a research facility (or anyone), he or she must provide the buyer with documentation containing information about the dealer, the animal, the pound or shelter from which the animal was obtained, a statement from that ACF affirming that the animal was held there for at least five days, and the date of acquisition. Both the research facility and the dealer must keep this documentation for at least one year, and it must contain an assurance that the person supplying the dog or cat was informed that the animal may be used for research purposes.

Legal Regulation of Laboratory Animals
Today, the AWA and its APHIS-issued regulations (*see* this chapter: *Animal Welfare Act Regulations*) govern virtually all research using laboratory animals (as the federal law defines the term "animal") in America. Additionally, all federally funded research must comply with the Public Health Service *Policy on Humane Care and Use of Laboratory Animals* and the NIH *Guide for the Care and Use of Laboratory Animals* (for an overview of both, *see* this chapter: *Public Health Service*). In 1998 APHIS's annual report listed a total of just over 1,200 research facilities in the United States, led by California at 171, with New York a distant second at 95. The total includes those facilities found at colleges and universities, those associated with one or more corporations or the federal government, as well as independent research institutions.

The regulations subsequently issued by APHIS under the authority of the AWA exclude mice, rats, and birds from the definition of "animal," so research facilities are not currently required to report on these species. The AWA itself does not contain this exclusion, and it has been challenged in federal courts several times, most recently in September 2000, apparently with success (*see* this chapter: *Animal Welfare Act Regulations: Laboratory Animals*). Since mice, rats, and birds are uncounted, no one knows exactly how many animals are used in America's labs. Estimates vary considerably depending on the source consulted, from as high as 70 million to as low as 10 million.

What is known are these figures compiled by APHIS for 1998 (rounded to the nearest thousand): 288,000 rabbits, 261,000 guinea pigs, 206,000 hamsters, 76,000 dogs, 57,000 primates, and 25,000 cats. Additionally, 27,000 sheep, 77,000 pigs, 54,000 other "farm animals" (mostly cows, goats, and horses in agricultural research and education), and 143,000 "other animals" (a variety of species, including gerbils, squirrels, otters, armadillos, and others). These figures yield a documented total of 1,210,000 in 1998, which is significantly lower than the 25-year average of 1,750,000 annually. Most informed sources guess that somewhere between 85 and 95 percent of all laboratory animals are mice and rats. Taking the higher number, this suggests a sum of approximately 24,000,000 animals.

These animals are subjected to countless scientific procedures in America's laboratories and educational institutions, protocols that can be grouped into one or another of three major categories: (1) testing the safety, effectiveness, and toxicity of innumerable drugs, chemicals, and other consumer products; (2) gathering medical, biological, and behavioral data; (3) serving as teaching tools in higher education, especially in medical and veterinary schools, but also including biology and psychology instruction in both secondary and postsecondary education (for more on this topic, *see* this chapter: *Dissection*).

APHIS does not keep statistics of animal use according to purpose, but the most recent estimates are that instruction in education accounts for about 15 percent of all animals, while perhaps 40 percent go for biomedical research. The remaining, largest percentage, and perhaps the most controversial use of animals in the lab, is for toxicity testing. Here, the dangers of many substances are established by harming animals, harms that are permitted by the AWA.

Toxicity Testing
Although scientists had begun studying the toxic effects of various drugs and poisons on animals at least as early as the 1850s, it was not until the 1920s that such researches were assiduously pursued, mainly in England. There, inspired by the work of two Japanese scientists, several investigators demonstrated that cancers and tumors could be induced in mice by painting parts of their shaved bodies with tars and chemicals.

In 1927 a British pharmacologist named J. W. Trevan devised what was to become the most widely applied—and most notorious—acute toxicity test in the world, the LD-50, or "lethal dose for 50 percent." Trevan was attempting to standardize the potency of some highly toxic drugs, notably digitalis, insulin, and diphtheria toxin. He decided to inject groups of rats and mice with various doses of these substances to see exactly how much would kill half of a test group; that lethal dose could then be precisely measured and designated as the level of acute toxicity. Over the next several decades, as an enormous array of chemicals came to permeate our industrialized society, the LD-50 test was adopted as the standard measure of acute toxicity.

The typical procedure for this test has as many as 100 or more animals exposed to the test substance by inhalation or oral ingestion. The most common method is oral ingestion, and rats are most often used as test subjects. Scientists make initial estimates of the toxicity range of the substance, and then varying doses are administered to groups of animals until 50 percent of one group dies. These dead animals are then autopsied to determine the precise cause of death. After two weeks, the surviving animals are killed and examined for further data on the effects of the test substance.

A second toxicity test, nearly as pervasive as the LD-50 and just as infamous, was developed in the 1940s from existing protocols written two decades earlier by British scientists. This test became standard procedure for evaluating most cosmetics—such as eye shadow, mascara, blush, nail polish, suntan lotion, deodorant, cologne, shaving cream, hairspray, and mouthwash—and numerous cleaning agents, including dish, laundry, and hand soap, glass, bathroom, countertop, and oven cleaners, toothpaste, shampoo, air freshener, and floor and furniture polish. John Draize, a scientist working for the Food and Drug Administration (FDA), refined two different tests for determining the poisonous properties of these and other substances.

In the Draize Eye Irritancy test, a liquid, flake, granule, or powdered substance is placed in a rabbit's eye (the eyelid is secured with clips) and its effects are observed and recorded at regular intervals, typically twenty-four, forty-eight, and seventy-two hours, and at four and seven days. The other eye serves as the control. The animals are usually restrained in stocks or boxes from which only their heads protrude, thus preventing them from scratching at their eyes. Rabbits are ideal subjects for the Draize test because they have no tear ducts from which tears would flow and dilute the substance, which would compromise the test.

Draize also developed a skin irritancy test, commonly administered to rabbits as well. In this procedure, the hair on the backs of the animals is shaved and the skin is slightly abraded. The substance to be tested is then put on a piece of gauze and taped in place on the abrasion. The entire trunk of the rabbit is then wrapped in some impermeable material, such as rubberized cloth. After a period of twenty-four hours, the wrapping is removed and lab technicians observe and record the effects of the substance on the rabbit's skin. The wrapping is then replaced and further observations made after two more days. Another round of testing will typically follow on previously unexposed areas of skin.

Toxicity Testing in the Public and Private Sectors

Today, the FDA does not demand the Draize test, the LD-50, or any particular form of toxicity testing. However, as authorized by the Food, Drug and Cosmetic Act of 1938, all pharmaceuticals must be analyzed with animal-based tests as part of the agency's approval process.

On the other hand, the FDA has no authority to require cosmetics manufacturers to test their products, either by using animals or any other method. However, if the safety of a cosmetic product has not been substantiated in some way, the manufacturer must label the item in this manner: "Warning—the safety of this product has not been determined." This labeling would undoubtedly discourage sales, and the failure to label accordingly would provoke costly lawsuits and federal regulatory action, so the FDA policy has the practical effect of ensuring exhaustive product testing in the cosmetic industry. Recognizing this, the FDA has explicitly disavowed the LD–50 test. At the same time, however, the agency has proclaimed that the Draize toxicity tests are preferable to methods that do not utilize animals.

Nonetheless, in the 1990s several leading firms in the cosmetics industry voluntarily halted animal testing on all or most of their products. The most recent addition came in July 1999 when Procter & Gamble announced it would no longer conduct animal tests on its "current beauty, fabric and home care, and paper products." P&G joins Mary Kay Cosmetics, which made a similar pledge in April of that year, and Gillette, which in 1997 became another giant of cosmetics and household products that has turned away from using animals in their toxicity investigations.

This trend actually began in the early 1980s when the Coalition to Abolish the Draize Test, led by legendary animal activist Henry Spira, managed to persuade Revlon to abandon animal testing, a move followed shortly thereafter by Avon. In 1991 the Cosmetics, Toiletry and Fragrance Association, the industry trade group, claimed that eye irritation testing had been reduced by 87 percent. Even so, in 2000 at least fifty major companies in the industry continue to test on animals, including Colgate-Palmolive, Johnson & Johnson, Dow, and Clorox.

In the public sector, the Consumer Product Safety Act of 1972 created an independent regulatory body, the Consumer Product Safety Commission (CPSC) with the power to issue standards, require warning labels, and ban dangerous merchandise entirely. Every consumer product is subject to regulation by the CPSC, with the exception of cars, food, liquor, tobacco, and firearms. Among other responsibilities, the commission actively studies consumer products for safety-related problems, research that involves some animal testing, although it is not clear how much. The Federal Hazardous Substances Act does not empower the CPSC (or any other federal entity) to require manufacturers to determine product safety by testing with animals. Even so, the commission identifies "highly toxic" substances exclusively on the basis of results from LD-50 and skin irritancy tests. At the same time, the official policy of the CPSC is that the number of animals subjected to testing should be reduced as far as possible, while urging the use of alternative methods.

President Richard Nixon created the Environmental Protection Agency (EPA) in 1970 to control and decrease air and water pollution, especially that produced by solid waste, radiation, and chemicals. Although the EPA legally cannot order animal testing, the agency does announce the sorts of tests that meet the restrictions of the Toxic Substances Control Act and the Federal Insecticide, Fungicide, and Rodenticide Act, and these have always heavily emphasized the use of animals. New EPA guidelines that took effect in 1997, however, do include statistical analyses and *in vitro* (literally, "in glass") studies of human cells and genes as acceptable alternatives for carcinogen risk assessment.

In October 1998, due largely to the persistence of Vice President Al Gore, the EPA announced a six-year program to test 2,800 high production volume (HPV) chemicals for their effects on the environment and human health. HPV chemicals are those that are produced at an annual rate of at least 1 million pounds each, substances that are found everywhere—in our homes, offices, stores, and on the streets. Despite the massive output, most of these chemicals have either never been tested for their toxicity or test results are not available to the public.

The HPV testing program is supposed to change that, at the expense of $700 million and the lives of an estimated 1.3 million lab animals. Spearheaded by People for the Ethical Treatment of Animals, the animal rights community vigorously attacked the program, focusing on Gore and derisively skewering his reputation as an "environmentalist." After nearly a year of unrelenting pressure, in October 1999 the EPA and the Clinton administration agreed to allow nonanimal alternatives, reducing the numbers needed by as much as 100,000 creatures, and to delay acute toxicity testing for two years so acceptable alternatives to the LD-50 test could be validated. The EPA and the Department of Health and Human Services also pledged to donate a total of $5 million to fund research into testing methods that do not use animals.

Validating Alternatives to Animals in Toxicity Testing

In the sense that is legally significant, the validation of alternatives to animal testing means winning the approval and endorsement of the FDA, CPSC, EPA, and other federal agencies. Given the decades-long emphasis on *in vivo* (in a live body) testing found in federal regulations, the development of alternatives has been stymied: regulated industries and progressive biotech companies must face laboring to develop *in vitro* and other options without an established method for gaining governmental acceptance.

This situation began to change in 1993 when Congress passed the NIH Revitalization Act. This law ordered the director of the NIH to prepare a plan to conduct or support research aimed at reducing the number of lab animals used, refining lab protocols to decrease pain and distress experienced by the animals, or replacing them entirely. The director must also validate these alternatives, promote their acceptance, and teach scientists to use them. The "three R's" of reduction, refinement, and replacement are borrowed from a text authored in 1959 by two British scientists, W. M. S. Russell and Rex Burch. Little noticed upon its publication, *The Principles of Humane Experimental Technique* was rediscovered in the early 1980s by animal activists and concerned scientists who saw therein a road map they could follow together to a destination harmonizing animal welfare and science. It was apparently through this route that members of Congress learned of the principles, embraced them, and wrote them into the NIH Revitalization Act.

To fulfill the congressional mandate, in 1994 a division of the NIH formed the *ad hoc* Interagency Coordinating Committee on the Validation of Alternative Methods (ICCVAM). Two years later the ICCVAM released their report, detailing the criteria that must be met to achieve regulatory acceptance of alternative methods. Among other items, the method must be "relatively insensitive to minor changes in protocol," cost effective, and one that can be conducted in an amount of time proportionate to the scope and significance of the results. Skeptics immediately complained that these requirements, and others, have never been demanded of animal tests, and were equally disturbed by the ICCVAM insistence that the new methods be accepted by the scientific community. It is precisely because scientists disagree about the validity of alternatives, the critics charged, that they have not been widely endorsed.

Despite such misgivings, in October 1999 Senator Mike DeWine of Ohio introduced the ICCVAM Authorization Act intending to make the *ad hoc* committee a permanent one. One year later the bill passed the House of Representatives, and as 2000 came to a close it seemed poised to win the approval of the Senate. If enacted, the law would establish a standing committee composed of the heads of at least sixteen federal agencies, including the NIH, FDA, CPSC, and EPA. The ICCVAM would be assisted by a scientific advisory committee with one member from the personal care, pharmaceutical, industrial chemicals, or agriculture industry; another from a university, state agency, or corporation that is developing alternative methods; and a third member from a nonprofit, national animal protection organization.

As with the *ad hoc* committee, the standing one would, among other duties, work on developing validation criteria, and "facilitate the acceptance of scientifically valid test methods" by federal agencies. This facilitation would be done by recommending testing methods that do not use animals to federal agencies. An ICCVAM recommendation must be accepted *unless* it is "not adequate in terms of biological relevance for the regulatory goal authorized by that agency," or it "does not generate data, in an amount and of scientific value that is at least equivalent to the data gathered prior to such recommendation," or it "is unacceptable for satisfactorily fulfilling the test needs for that particular agency." The bill leaves the determination of when any of these exceptions apply to the agency receiving the ICCVAM recommendation.

ANIMAL WELFARE ACT REGULATIONS

The Animal Welfare Act (AWA) (*see* this chapter: *Animal Welfare Act*) authorizes the secretary of agriculture to "promulgate standards to govern the humane handling, care, treatment, and transportation of animals by dealers and research facilities." Additionally, the secretary is empowered to issue licenses to animal dealers and to register research facilities "in accordance with such rules and regulations as he may prescribe." These standards and rules are published annually in the Code of Federal Regulations, and are commonly known as AWA regulations.

In practice, AWA regulations are issued by the Animal and Plant Health Inspection Service (APHIS), an agency of the U.S. Department of Agriculture (USDA). APHIS is also responsible for enforcing the regulations by licensing dealers and registering facilities, inspecting them through its Animal Care Division, and investigating complaints with its Division of Investigative and Enforcement Services.

In 1994 the Seventh Circuit Court of Appeals held that APHIS inspections and investigations can be conducted without a warrant or any form of prior notice given to dealers or (perhaps) research facilities. An animal dealer specializing in breeding and selling rabbits to research facilities claimed that warrantless inspections of his operation violated the Fourth Amendment protection against unreasonable searches and seizures. The court disagreed, finding that the APHIS inspections passed the test established by the Supreme Court for identifying exceptions to the warrant requirement.

First, government regulation of animal dealers is pervasive because they must obtain a license, maintain numerous records (*see* this chapter: *Animal Dealers*), and comply with various standards of care (*see* this chapter: *Veterinary Care; Animal Management*) to do business at all. Second, warrantless inspections are justified to achieve the goals of regulating animal dealers because many violations can be quickly corrected or hidden. Finally, the AWA clearly puts dealers on notice that they will be periodically inspected, informs them of who will make the inspections, and places limits on the time and scope of the scrutiny to which their operations will be subject. The court did not explicitly extend this holding to unannounced inspections of research facilities, and no other court has yet done so, but the same reasoning would seem to apply there (*Lesser v. Espy*).

The AWA and its regulations do *not* entitle the secretary or APHIS (or anyone else) to make rules governing the use of laboratory animals during experimental procedures: "Nothing in this Act . . . shall be construed as authorizing the Secretary to promulgate rules, regulations, or orders for the handling, care, treatment, or inspection of animals during actual research or experimentation." Even so, investigators are required to "minimize pain and distress" during their research, and consider alternatives to painful procedures. Further, they must consult with a veterinarian on proper pre- and postsurgical care, and when designing research with painful procedures. Anesthetics may be withheld only when "scientifically necessary," a determination to be made by the scientists themselves. Finally, no laboratory animal can be used for more than one surgery, although an exception to this rule can be made when scientists decide it is necessary.

There are two other sources of federal regulation of the treatment of laboratory animals. Research and experimentation using animals that is funded at least in part by the federal government, which accounts for nearly all that is conducted in the United States, must be done in accordance with the Public Health Service (PHS) *Policy on Humane Care and Use of Laboratory Animals*, and the *Guide for the Care and Use of Laboratory Animals* from the National Institutes of Health (NIH), a division of the PHS. The PHS *Policy* and the NIH *Guide* reinforce, elaborate, and supplement the AWA and its regulations in a number of different ways (for an overview of the PHS *Policy* and the NIH *Guide, see* this chapter: *Public Health Service*).

Laboratory Animals
The AWA defines "animal" to mean "any live or dead dog, cat, monkey (nonhuman primate mammal), guinea pig, hamster, rabbit, or such other warm-blooded mammal, as the Secretary may determine is being used, or is intended for use, for research, testing, [or] experimentation." In 1972 APHIS issued a regulatory definition of "animal" duplicating the AWA but further stipulating that "[t]his term excludes: Birds, rats of the genus *Rattus* and mice of the genus *Mus* bred for use in research." Most estimates are that the two rodent species alone account for around 90 percent of all laboratory animals, yet they are not protected by the AWA or its regulations.

Twenty years later, the Animal Legal Defense Fund (ALDF) and the Humane Society of the United States (HSUS) challenged the exclusion of rats, mice, and birds from AWA regulations. They argued that as animal welfare organizations their primary function is to provide information concerning the humane use of animals to their members and the public. This function could not be performed if research facilities are not required to report what they do with these species: the exemption constitutes an "informational injury" to the ALDF and the HSUS.

A federal district court accepted this argument and held that the exclusion was illegal, but on appeal the District of Columbia Circuit Court of Appeals vacated this decision in 1994. The appellate judge agreed with the defense offered by the USDA that because the two organizations had no right to this information, nor were they particularly well suited to contest federal agencies that withhold it, the ALDF and the HSUS had no standing to sue (*ALDF v. Espy*) (for details on this case and for discussion of legal standing, *see* chapter 2: *Do Animals Have Legal Rights?; Legal Standing under the Animal Welfare Act*).

In April 1997 the American Anti-Vivisection Society (AAVS) filed a petition asking APHIS to change the AWA regulations to include rats, mice, and birds within the category of protected animals. APHIS denied the request, pleading a lack of resources, just as it had against the ALDF and the HSUS. Undeterred, in January 1999 an organization affiliated with the AAVS called Alternatives Research and Development Foundation, along with In Vitro International and several individuals, again petitioned the agency to amend the definition of "animal."

The petitioners argued that Congress intended the AWA protections to cover all warm-blooded animals used in research—rats, mice, and birds, too—and the plain meaning of the statute indicates that these species are "animals" for AWA purposes. In the notice of the petition, APHIS pointed out that Congress could have amended the definition on numerous occasions but has not done so. Furthermore, if granted, the petition would instantly double the number of research facilities APHIS would be obligated to inspect, and appropriations are insufficient to fund that drastic increase in the workload. In any case, the agency believes these species are already adequately protected by the NIH *Guide for the Care and Use of Laboratory Animals,* which does require that federally funded research satisfy standards for the care and treatment of rats, mice, and birds.

Thousands of comments on the petition poured into APHIS. Meanwhile, impatient and pessimistic about the response, in March 1999 the petitioners filed suit in a federal district court, hoping to convince a judge to order the change. The USDA (the home agency of APHIS) asked the court to dismiss the case, arguing, as they had in 1992 against the ALDF and the HSUS, that the petitioners had no standing to sue. This time, however, the defense did not work. In June 2000 Judge Ellen Huvelle ruled that one of the plaintiffs, college student Kristine Gausz, had legal standing to file suit because she is "a researcher who witnesses the mistreatment of rats in her lab" (*Alternatives Research and Development Foundation v. Glickman*). Apparently believing its case was doomed, in September 2000 the USDA agreed to settle the issue out of court and amend the regulatory definition of "animal" to include mice, rats, and birds. The agency pledged to begin developing husbandry standards for these species, to be made available for public comment. Research facilities will also be required to report the numbers of these animals they use.

Even so, the battle is not yet over. Immediately after the USDA announcement, the National Association for Biomedical Research and the University of Mississippi, which has an animal care facility that would be subject to new regulations, moved to block the change. They managed to persuade Senator Thad Cochran of Mississippi, chairman of the Senate Appropriations Committee, to insert a rider into the 2001 agriculture appropriations bill preventing the USDA from using any funds allocated for the administration of the AWA to amend the definition of "animal" and develop the standards that the amendment requires. This means that nothing will change until at least 2002, and it is likely the research community will continue to pursue these and other methods of delay.

Animal Dealers

The use of animals in the laboratory starts when they are obtained from some provider. These animals can be legally obtained from virtually any source, so long as this is done without force or fraud. Even so, institutions usually acquire animals through dealers licensed by APHIS, which also has the power to deny, suspend, or revoke licenses.

"Class A" dealers are preferred by scientists because they breed animals in closed colonies specifically for the purpose of selling them to research facilities (among other customers). America's 2,900 class A dealers are thus breeders of "purpose-bred" species. Scientists believe that this sort of operation produces a higher-quality laboratory animal that will fulfill the goals of the research, whatever they are, but purpose-bred animals are also the most expensive. For example, Charles River Laboratories, the world's largest breeder and supplier of animals used in biomedical research—the biggest class A dealer—sells mice for $10 to $15 each, depending on size, age, sex, and variety; guinea pigs are $32 to $77 apiece, rabbits $58 to $126, and hamsters $8 to $19.50 (2000 prices).

Laboratory animals are much cheaper when they come from individuals or establishments that are not required to be federally licensed, most notably local animal shelters and pounds, known as "random sources." These animals—almost always dogs and cats—may even be free, especially in the five states that require pounds to surrender animals on demand, but quality control is nonexistent (*see* chapter 3: *Animal Control Facilities: Animal Seizure*). The AWA stipulates that animals acquired from random sources must be held at the research facility for five full days before they can be used in any research or experimentation, a provision that is thought to allow the owner of a lost animal sufficient time to reclaim it, and give the creature a better chance to be adopted. In England animals from random sources are not allowed in laboratories.

The AWA regulations also apply to the nearly 1,000 "class B" dealers currently operating in the United States. These are essentially middlemen, standing between research institutions and the class A dealers or random sources that supply the animals. The "B" type of animal dealer acts as a broker or auctioneer, negotiating or facilitating the sale of laboratory animals rather than breeding them. Over the years, class B dealers have become notorious for stealing pet dogs and cats, and combing classified ads for animals offered "Free to Good Home" and then acquiring them by posing as sincere adopters. The animals collected in this manner—these unscrupulous dealers are sometimes called "bunchers"—are then sold at considerable profit to research facilities, or to other dealers who do business with the facilities. The federal Pet Safety and Protection Act, first proposed as an amendment to the AWA in 1996 and presently still held up in congressional committees, would end this practice by prohibiting class B dealers from selling any dogs or cats to research facilities.

The legal regulation of laboratory animals begins with these dealers. An animal dealer is defined as "any person" (with certain exceptions; *see* below) who transports, delivers for transportation, buys, sells, or negotiates the purchase of "[a]ny dog or other animal [as defined by the AWA] whether alive or dead." As noted above, class A dealers also breed animals, while those of class B do not. Dealers of either type must obtain a license from APHIS. This requires proving that their operations are in compliance with AWA regulations, both in the initial application and during any subsequent inspection. In a curious contrast, research facilities (*see* this chapter: *Research Facilities*) are not required to demonstrate compliance before they receive their registration from APHIS. Annual license fees are calculated according to the gross income the dealer receives from selling animals, with a maximum charge of $750 (in 2000). To be granted a license renewal, dealers have to file a report with APHIS every year, detailing, among other things, how much money was made selling animals, and how many were sold and held.

The AWA was originally written to protect the interests of pet owners primarily, some of whose dogs and cats were turning up in laboratories. This emphasis manifests itself in the regulations with a strict requirement that dealers keep detailed records concerning every dog and cat they trade in. For each animal processed, a dealer must record a number of items: the name and address of the person from whom the dog or cat was acquired (for class B dealers), and to whom the animal was sold or given; the USDA license or registration number, or the driver's license number of these people; the dates the animal was obtained and subsequently relinquished or disposed of; the required USDA tag number or tattoo; a description of the animal, including breed, sex, date of birth or approximate age, and distinctive markings; and the name of the person who transported the dog or cat as well as the method of transportation.

The "bunchers" mentioned above falsify these records. For example, in a well-publicized case that saw the largest fine ever levied against an animal dealer ($200,000), Julian and Anita Toney were found, among other things, to have falsely identified the source of many of the dogs they obtained and subsequently sold to research facilities, used forged certificates in these sales, and failed to properly identify sixty dogs by omitting certain items and fabricating others (*Toney v. Glickman*).

Not everyone who trades in animals qualifies as a dealer. Those who do not qualify are exempt from both the federal licensing requirement and AWA regulations, and the animals they trade in are not protected by this federal law. Retail pet stores are not considered dealers (for more on pet stores, *see* chapter 3: *Dog Law: Dog Breeding, "Puppy Mills," and Pet Stores*), nor are private individuals who breed and sell fewer than twenty-five dogs or cats per year, or who make less than $500 annually doing so. Thus, animals found in pet stores and in hobby breeding operations are not protected by the AWA, nor are household pets generally.

Also not considered dealers are farmers and ranchers who raise livestock to be sold as food, or those who raise furbearing animals to sell their pelts. So, the AWA does not cover "any domestic species of cattle, sheep, swine, goats, llamas, or horses . . . kept and raised on farms, and used or intended for use as food or fiber, or for improving animal nutrition, breeding management, or production efficiency, or for improving the quality of food or fiber." Further excluded are mink, fox, rabbits, and chinchilla raised for meat or fur, and horses and llamas used as work or pack animals. Although the killing of animals for food is regulated by the federal Humane Methods of Slaughter Act, and state anticruelty laws typically govern the treatment of many of these animals, they are nonetheless placed out of bounds from the safeguards afforded by AWA regulations (*see* chapter 3: *Anticruelty Laws;* chapter 4: *Humane Methods of Slaughter Act;* chapter 4: *Fur Farming*).

Research Facilities

A research facility is defined as "any school (except an elementary or secondary school), institution, organization, or person that uses or intends to use animals in research, tests, or experiments." Any such facility is subject to AWA regulations when either one of two circumstances applies to it. First, live animals are purchased or transported "in commerce." This refers to any interstate trade involving animals, or any trade that has interstate effects. Second, the research facility receives federal funds by grant, award, loan, or contract for the purpose of conducting research using animals.

Legally then, a research facility could avoid AWA regulation only if it has not obtained any federal funding whatever, and has acquired animals (again, not counting mice, rats, and birds) without affecting interstate commerce in any way. Such a case would be one in which animals are purchased and transported exclusively in the same state as that in which the facility is located, and they are paid for entirely with cash to an animal provider with no out-of-state transactions. This situation would appear to be extremely rare, but there are no statistics available for verification.

Research facilities are required to file a registration form with APHIS; the registration must be updated every three years by submitting a new form. These forms are supplied by APHIS and include a copy of AWA regulations and standards. As of 2000, there are just over 1,200 registered research facilities in the United States. Each registrant must file an annual report with APHIS, assuring the federal government that "professionally accepted standards governing the care, treatment, and use of animals . . . were followed by the research facility." Scientists are required to further attest that they considered alternatives to painful procedures in designing their experiments, known as the "research protocol."

Also to be included in the report are what sort of animals and how many of them were used in the laboratories, which species and how many received appropriate pain relief, and the species and numbers of those for whom pain relief was withheld, along with the reasons why. In 1998, 111,000 animals were not given any pain relief during or after some research protocol, including 2,000 dogs and 785 primates. The almost invariable justification, allowed by the AWA, is some version of the appeal to "scientific reasons."

All facilities with laboratory animals (except those using only mice, rats, and birds) must have both an attending veterinarian, and an Institutional Animal Care and Use Committee (IACUC)(*see also* this chapter: *Animal Care Committees: Institutional Animal Care and Use Committee*). Appointed or approved by the chief executive officer of the facility, the IACUC needs to have at least three members, one of whom must be a veterinarian (usually the one attending), and another a person not affiliated in any way with the facility who "will provide representation for general community interests in the proper care and treatment of animals." This committee has two major responsibilities: first, to evaluate all proposed research projects using animals, as well as proposed changes in ongoing projects; second, to review the entire animal care program of the facility at least twice a year, and file reports of its findings with the appropriate institutional official. The IACUC is essentially an oversight group, intended to ensure that the institution is in compliance with all applicable federal laws.

The AWA regulations require extensive record keeping, beginning with all IACUC materials, including minutes of meetings, records of proposed activities (whether approved or not), and semiannual program reviews. As with dealers, and again reflecting the household pet focus of the AWA, the requirements here for dogs and cats are especially stringent. Research facilities must have the following records for each dog and each cat on the premises: the name and address of the person from whom the animal was acquired; the USDA license or registration number, or the driver's license number of this person; the date the animal was obtained; the required USDA tag number or tattoo for each dog and cat, and any identification number assigned by the facility; a description of the animal, including breed, sex, date of birth or approximate age, and distinctive markings; and the date of euthanasia, or the name and address of any person to whom a dog or cat is sold, or who otherwise transports or disposes of the animal. All these records are to be kept for at least three years.

Standards directly related to the care and treatment of laboratory animals can be grouped under three general headings: (1) veterinary care; (2) animal management (husbandry); and (3) personnel qualifications and training.

Veterinary Care

The major facets of veterinary care covered by AWA regulations are pain management, surgery, euthanasia, and health maintenance.

"Investigators" (persons designing and conducting the research protocol) are expected to construct protocols that minimize pain, distress, and discomfort or avoid them entirely. Alternative procedures that would not cause pain should be considered and the investigator must justify the claim that there are no such alternatives. In that case, the analgesics or anesthetics used to alleviate pain, along with the dosages, need to be specified. Even so, investigators are permitted to withhold all pain relief during any procedure, so long as the "scientific reasons" offered for doing so are sufficient. The use of paralytics, which paralyze skeletal muscles, without anesthesia is prohibited. It is essential for providing appropriate pain relief that research personnel have the ability to recognize indicators of its occurrence. Although these indicators tend to vary with species, the general rule is that unless there is good reason to believe otherwise, procedures that would cause pain in humans should be assumed to cause pain in animals.

Aseptic surgical facilities must be provided for all procedures involving animals: surgical gloves, masks, and an operating room used only for that purpose. Appropriate aseptic techniques must be used to prepare the animals for surgery, and to sterilize the surgical instruments and supplies. Minor surgery, a procedure that does not invade a body cavity or cause permanent impairment, need not be performed in a fully aseptic facility. Also, surgery on rodents does not have to be done in a separate operating room. AWA regulations prohibit using an animal for more than one major operation, but there are exceptions to this rule. Just as investigators can cite "scientific reasons" to justify withholding pain relief, the same sort of appeal can be offered for performing multiple surgical procedures on the same animal. APHIS does not keep data on the incidence of this circumstance. Finally, personnel slated to participate in surgical procedures must be "appropriately qualified" to do so, although those qualifications are not specified.

AWA regulations define "euthanasia" as "the humane destruction of an animal accomplished by a method that produces rapid unconsciousness and subsequent death without evidence of pain or distress, or a method that utilizes anesthesia produced by an agent that causes painless loss of consciousness and subsequent death." In the research protocol, it is often called "sacrificing" the animal. Euthanasia must proceed in a manner consistent with this definition, although AWA regulations do not demand any particular method. As before, any method inconsistent with this definition is allowed so long as it is "justified by scientific reasons." There is no point in any research protocol at which investigators are required to euthanize research animals.

Maintaining research animals in a healthy condition is the responsibility of the attending veterinarian, assisted by a properly trained staff. Emergency, weekend, and holiday care must be provided, and the animals are to be observed daily to assess their health and well-being. Adequate veterinary care includes providing suitable facilities, equipment, and service, and appropriate methods to prevent, control, diagnose, and treat diseases and injuries. The veterinarian determines the suitability of analgesics and anesthetics, ensures that surgical procedures are properly performed, and that postoperative care is satisfactory. Typically, the veterinarian also participates in the training of personnel in the care and handling of the animals.

Animal Management
Fully two-thirds of AWA regulations are devoted to the details of animal management or husbandry. The Code of Federal Regulations contains over seventy pages of "Specifications for the Humane Handling, Care, Treatment and Transportation" of animals covered by the federal law. The specifications are divided into six general categories or "subparts": (1) dogs and cats; (2) guinea pigs and hamsters; (3) rabbits; (4) nonhuman primates; (5) marine mammals; and (6) all other "warm-blooded" animals.

In each of these categories, standards are prescribed for both indoor and outdoor housing facilities, for feeding, watering, and sanitation, and for transporting the animals. These standards are often very precise and species specific, while others are more general. This section surveys those categories and standards most germane to regulating the husbandry of laboratory animals: the handling, care, and treatment of dogs, cats, guinea pigs, hamsters, rabbits, and primates.

Standards for marine mammals are most applicable to zoos, aquariums, and other animal exhibitions, while those for other "warm-blooded" animals are generic versions of those for the named species, so these will be neglected here (for marine mammals, see chapter 5: *Circuses and Zoos: AWA Regulations for the Exhibition of Marine Mammals*). Also, transportation regulations are pertinent for carriers, intermediate handlers, and other operations that transport animals, not research facilities (for transportation standards, *see* this chapter: *Primates: Transportation;* chapter 3: *Dog Law: Federal Dog Protection Law*).

The specifications for dogs and cats, and those for primates are identical in many instances, or nearly so (for more detail, *see* this chapter: *Primates: The Animal Welfare Act and Its Regulations;* chapter 3: *Dog Law; Federal Dog Protection Law*). General housing standards are the same for these three species: well constructed and regularly maintained, readily cleaned and sanitized, effective in preventing escape, access by other animals, or injury. Housing facilities must be equipped with heating, cooling, ventilation, lighting, running potable water, and "disposal and drainage systems that are constructed and operated so that animal wastes are eliminated and the animals stay dry."

More precise housing specifications include preventing temperatures from falling below 45 degrees Fahrenheit or rising above 85 degrees Fahrenheit for more than four consecutive hours, and providing a diurnal lighting cycle uniformly diffused throughout the facility. Outdoor housing is permitted only for dogs, cats, and primates that are adapted to the climate conditions found at the facility, and this must include shelters to escape the weather. Dog and cat shelters must be large enough to allow each animal to stand, sit, and lie down normally. Primate shelters must be heated if the outside temperature falls below 45 degrees Fahrenheit. Additionally, exterior housing for primates must be enclosed by a fence, typically 6 feet tall, or more.

AWA regulations also detail the specifications for the "primary enclosure" of these animals: the construction and dimensions of their cages or pens. As with the general housing standards, the cages should be safe, structurally sound, clean, and provide protection from the elements. Water and food should be readily accessible. Floors are to be constructed of solid materials that do not injure the animals' feet. Perhaps most importantly, these regulations stipulate exacting "minimum space requirements" for the enclosures. Besides requiring that they have "sufficient space . . . to make normal postural adjustments with freedom of movement," the regulations specify precise dimensions in feet, inches, meters, and centimeters, depending on the weight of the animal. For example, a primate weighing between 33 and 55 pounds must be housed in a pen at least 3 feet tall with 8 square feet of floor space. Cats over 8.8 pounds require a cage of at least 3 square feet and 2 feet in height. For dogs it's a little more complicated; required canine floor space is calculated by taking the measurement of the dog in inches from the tip of the nose to the base of the tail, adding 6, squaring the sum, and then dividing by 144.

Groups of as many as twelve dogs or cats may be housed together in the same primary enclosure, but they must be compatible; aggressive animals are to be isolated. Puppies or kittens of less than four months old may not be housed with adult animals. One of the most recent additions to AWA regulations is that research facilities must exercise their dogs on a regular basis by providing them with enough space to move about; forced exercise devices like treadmills and carousels are not acceptable means of meeting this requirement. Further, any dog that is kept "without sensory contact with another dog, must be provided with positive physical contact with humans at least daily." The phrase "positive physical contact" is not further explained.

Another recent addition to the standards is that primates must be supplied with "environmental enhancements to promote their psychological well-being" (*see* this chapter: *Primates: Psychological Well-Being*). These include allowances for the social-grouping needs of primates, so long as the species can coexist harmoniously. Primates kept individually in cages are supposed to be able to see and hear other primates of compatible species. Also called for here are devices for enriching their enclosures by means of such items as perches, swings, mirrors, and other objects to manipulate. Such enrichment also includes allowing primates the opportunity to forage for food, and giving unspecified "special attention" to infants, primates housed alone, and great apes. Primates are never to be maintained in restraint devices unless this is necessary for "health reasons." Such reasons are not specified.

Dogs, cats, and primates must be fed at least once every day with "clean, wholesome, and palatable" food, appropriate to the species and in quantities sufficient for the age and size of the animal. Food receptacles must be cleaned and sanitized at least once every two weeks, while the primary enclosures must be cleaned daily of excrement and food particles and sanitized in the prescribed way twice a month. Water is to be made available either continuously, or for at least one hour twice a day.

Housing for guinea pigs, hamsters, and rodents, like those for all AWA-protected animals, is to be safe, structurally sound, maintained in good condition, and adequately ventilated, while providing effective confinement. Indoor temperatures must not exceed 85 degrees Fahrenheit, and, for guinea pigs and hamsters, must not dip below 60 degrees Fahrenheit; no heating is required for rabbits. "Ample light . . . of good quality and well distributed" should be provided, but there is no diurnal lighting requirement here as there is for dogs, cats, and primates. AWA regulations prohibit housing hamsters outdoors, and guinea pigs may be confined outside only in an "appropriate climate," though it is not stated what that climate is. Outdoor housing is permitted for rabbits, but only if it contains shelter from the weather and protection from predators.

The cages for guinea pigs, hamsters, and rabbits, again as for all AWA-protected animals, are to be well built, repaired when necessary, allow easy access to food and water, and be without sharp edges or protrusions that could cause harm to the animal. Floors may be constructed of wire or mesh, provided that "such floors . . . protect the animal's legs and feet from injury." Solid floors must be covered with litter. Space requirements for these enclosures are just as specific here as they are for dogs, cats, and primates, again depending on the species and weight of the individual animal. For example, guinea pigs must have a cage at least 6.5 inches tall; each one weighing more than 350 grams requires 101 square inches of floor space. Hamsters at 100 grams or more get 5.5 inches of height, and 19 square inches of floor space. A rabbit weighing 12 pounds or more must be provided with 5 square feet of floor area and a 14-inch-tall cage. Females with litters for all these species are to be given more space.

Guinea pigs, hamsters, and rabbits must be fed at least once every day with tasty, uncontaminated food, in an amount appropriate for the size of the animal. Food and water receptacles must be sanitized at least once every two weeks. The litter in primary enclosures with solid floors has to be replaced each week, as do the pans under wire or mesh floors. AWA regulations stipulate that guinea pig and hamster enclosures are to be sanitized with hot water and detergent at least once every two weeks. Rabbit enclosures need similar cleaning not less than once a month.

Personnel Qualifications and Training

Training and instruction in animal care and use for scientists, technicians, and any other person involved with the animals is required at all research facilities. The content of the training program is also mandated, covering several different areas. Foremost is instruction on humane methods of animal maintenance and experimentation, attending especially to the basic needs of each species, proper handling and care of them, appropriate care prior to and after the research procedure, and aseptic surgical methods. The education program must also include details of protocols that minimize the use of animals or reduce their levels of distress, the proper use of analgesics and anesthetics, and procedures for reporting violations of regulations or standards. Finally, research personnel must be instructed on where they can find documentation on all these matters, such as the National Agricultural Library.

ANIMAL CARE COMMITTEES

American scientists first utilized animals extensively for experimentation, testing, and teaching during the 1870s and 1880s. At that time, there were no laws regulating the care and treatment of laboratory animals, and no legal restrictions on what could be done to them in the labs. Many state anticruelty laws specifically exempted the use of animals in science, and those jurisdictions without the exemption never prosecuted the scientists (*see* chapter 3: *Anticruelty Laws*). Nor were there any generally accepted standards of animal husbandry for the laboratories—these matters were determined entirely by the scientists themselves, assisted by unskilled custodial staff.

Newly formed animal welfare groups in the urban centers of the east coast, especially the American Society for the Prevention of Cruelty to Animals (ASPCA) and local SPCAs, accused the researchers of various forms of animal abuse, and lobbied for protective legislation. Several bills of this nature were introduced on Capitol Hill in the late 1890s and into the new century, but none ever passed either house of Congress. Even so, about this time scientists and physicians started to form special committees focused on animal care to address some of the issues raised by the ASPCA and other organizations. More importantly for the researchers, the committees were intended to demonstrate that the sort of government regulation that the animal welfare groups sought to impose was not needed.

Early Animal Care Committees
One of the first attempts at such self-regulation by the research community was a committee formed at Harvard University in 1907. The members were all scientists actively engaged in research using animals, and although their main concern was to solve the growing problem of a shortage of laboratory animals, they also claimed the authority to stop what they believed to be improper or unnecessary experiments. The committee did develop general guidelines for the humane care of animals at Harvard labs, yet these were directed primarily at caging, feeding, and sanitation matters arising before and after the animals were actually used in some experimental procedure. The guidelines did not address causing and relieving pain during the procedure itself. An Animal Care Committee was formed at the University of Michigan at about the same time, also composed of scientists using animals, and one with similar husbandry concerns.

In 1915, the Mayo Clinic in Rochester, Minnesota, hired a veterinarian, Simon Brimhall, to apply the principles and practices of veterinary medicine to provide for the clinic's laboratory animals. This is the first time an individual not directly engaged in research, yet one with expertise in animal medicine, was made responsible for overseeing the care and use of laboratory animals, in consultation with researchers. In the years to come, federal law would require similar credentials for those charged with such oversight duties. Dr. Brimhall is generally recognized as the founder of a distinct discipline of veterinary science: medical care for laboratory animals. Moreover, he was the first person other than the research personnel themselves to establish policies concerning the welfare of these creatures, and to monitor how well the policies were put into practice.

Federal guidelines for the treatment of laboratory animals did not become available until 1939. Then, the National Institutes of Health (NIH) began issuing "Rules Regarding Animals" to institutions receiving money from the government that had also established some type of Animal Care Committee. Among other rules, dogs and cats obtained from local pounds had to be held at the research facility for at least as long as the pound would have retained them, and the animals had to be returned to their owners if claimed. Also, the director of the research facility was required to approve any surgery before it could be performed, and if a procedure caused discomfort, the animal was to be anesthetized. The NIH further required that animals no longer useful for research purposes be painlessly killed. The NIH expected the committees to ensure that the rules were followed, but the institutions were not required to form committees. There were no federal enforcement mechanisms, no assurance of compliance with the rules was demanded nor inspections performed, and the only penalty for noncompliance was withdrawal of funding. There is no record of the NIH ever having revoked funding from a facility for failing to follow these rules.

After the Second World War the federal government started spending rapidly increasing sums of money on basic research in science and medicine. The budget of the NIH skyrocketed, rising from $185,000 in 1945 to $8 million in 1947. Corresponding with the accelerated cash flow were burgeoning numbers of animals used in this research.

Following the by now well-established lead of the Mayo Clinic, institutions with large research programs, especially public universities, began to employ veterinarians to supervise the handling of the animals and concentrate on their health, even though there were still no legal requirements to do so. This practice tended to produce conflicts between the investigators conducting the research and the veterinarians concerned with animal welfare. Researchers saw the veterinarians as interfering rather than helping, especially when they demanded expenditures on disease control. To those doing the research, it was cheaper just to euthanize the sickly and get another healthy animal. Animal Care Committees, which typically included the veterinarian and research scientists, became a device for settling these sorts of conflicts.

Developing Standards for Animal Care

This particular advantage of such committees, and a slowly growing public concern for laboratory animal welfare, started to gain some political influence and affect legislation. In 1947 the Michigan legislature became the first lawmaking body to mandate the creation of an Animal Care Committee. The state statute established a committee in the Michigan Department of Public Health with the authority to regulate the use of animals in research facilities. The members of the committee were representatives of local humane societies and deans from universities that used animals in their laboratories. The committees were responsible for drafting and issuing rules that promoted the humane treatment of these animals. Although the Michigan law stood alone for years, the drive to formally codify and oversee such standards was gaining momentum.

In 1950 a number of veterinarians tending to laboratory animals organized into a group focused on medical care in the institutional setting. Initially called the Animal Care Panel, the organization was later renamed the American Association for Laboratory Animal Science (AALAS). In 1965 AALAS created a standard-setting body independent of the federal government, one still in operation today, the American Association for the Accreditation of Laboratory Animal Care (AAALAC). Its stated mission was to formulate principles that "promote high-quality animal care, use, and well-being," which included forming an Animal Care Committee. Even so, the AAALAC has never had the authority to legally enforce their standards—compliance is voluntary. Then as now, research facilities may choose to pursue certification by the AAALAC or ignore the association entirely. Once accreditation is secured, as much as three years might elapse before any effort is made to review the institution's subsequent performance (*see also* this chapter: *Public Health Service: Developing Standards for Laboratory Animals*).

Similarly, the Institute of Laboratory Animal Resources (ILAR), formed in 1952 under the auspices of the National Research Council and amply assisted by a special committee of AALAS, developed guidelines on laboratory animal facilities, space, equipment, and personnel. The first edition of the *Guide for Laboratory Animal Facilities and Care* appeared in 1963, but because these were merely guidelines and not laws, compliance was still entirely voluntary, and no institution was required to form an Animal Care Committee as an overseeing body.

A survey conducted by ILAR in 1961 revealed that only 30 percent of research facilities had Animal Care Committees, and another survey seven years later indicated that the total was still only 40 percent. In those institutions with committees, there was little consistency on their oversight duties: some reviewed proposed research projects, some simply allocated space for the animal programs, others served a general advisory capacity. By the late 1960s, it was clear that voluntary, self-regulation had been very slow to catch on.

Mandating Animal Care
In 1970 the Animal Welfare Act (AWA) (*see* this chapter: *Animal Welfare Act*) demanded verification that federal standards for the use and care of

laboratory animals were being met. For the first time, monitoring requirements were backed by the force of law, introducing legal accountability into research facilities. The AWA was a renaming of the Laboratory Animal Welfare Act of 1966, and included a significant amendment to the earlier statute.

Originally, the 1966 act directed the secretary of agriculture to promulgate regulations for the "humane handling, care, treatment, and transportation of animals by dealers and research facilities," but did not establish any mechanism for the government to confirm that institutions were complying with the regulations. The AWA sought to fill this gap in 1970 by requiring each research facility using animals to file an annual report with the U.S. Department of Agriculture (USDA) demonstrating that it had achieved the standards issued by the secretary. This was the first attempt in America at explicit government regulation of animal experimentation that included a corroboration device. (In 1972 the USDA established the Animal and Plant Health Inspection Service [APHIS], charged it with the administration and enforcement of the AWA, and directed that the annual reports be sent to APHIS.)

At last, institutions using animals in research were legally required to meet certain standards and prove that they had done so. Yet problems persisted. The reporting requirement was supposed to encourage, and not compel, institutions to form Animal Care Committees. However, another ILAR survey in 1978 found that the percentage of institutions with such committees was virtually unchanged since the 1968 study. Moreover, two organizations that had traditionally been supportive of animal research done with compassion and mercy, the Humane Society of the United States (HSUS) and the Animal Welfare Institute (AWI), each issued a scathing critique of the USDA reporting requirements. The HSUS filed a petition in 1982 charging that the reporting system guidelines were vague, inconsistently applied, and too lenient, especially concerning what constituted pain and distress or "appropriate" pain relief. The AWI conducted a 1984 study of the annual reports of 214 research facilities and found that over one-quarter of these operations had significant and persistent violations of USDA standards, yet virtually no enforcement action had been taken against them. Indeed, most had received increases in federal money for experimentation. Perhaps worse, many of the offenders had received accreditation from the AAALAC.

Spurred by these and other sources of dissatisfaction, public pressure began to build on Congress to push through federal legislation mandating structured Animal Care Committees with specific authority and clear guidelines. The lawmakers responded. Bills proposed on Capitol Hill in the early 1980s advanced the idea of a standardized and structured review of research activities—known as "protocols"—by a committee composed of individuals from the institution itself and from the community. This was an attempt to find a middle ground between unadulterated self-regulation—where government has little or no role, essentially the situation that had prevailed until this time—and pervasive government regulation—which the research community had always vigorously opposed. In this compromise position, government would establish fairly broad guidelines and each institution would craft its own research program according to its particular goals, while an oversight group associated with both the institution and the community would ensure consistency between them.

The most influential model for this type of council was the Animal Ethics Review Committee at the University of Southern California (USC). At USC research protocols were scrutinized by a bioethicist, a "humanist," a surgeon, a veterinarian, a lawyer, a biomedical scientist, a historian, and a person unaffiliated with the university. The committee members closely followed the *Guide for the Care and Use of Experimental Animals* that had been developed by the Canadian Council on Animal Care. Of primary importance was the demand that researchers make some determination of how much pain the protocol would cause and how long the discomfort would have to be endured. Additionally, some justification was required for using procedures that caused pain and distress. Those that involved fighting, and burn or freeze injuries received special attention, and the use of paralyzing drugs without anesthesia during surgery was prohibited.

Institutional Animal Care and Use Committee
With these sources of inspiration and guidance, the AWA was substantially amended in 1985. Section 13b requires that every research facility either purchasing animals in interstate commerce or receiving federal funding form and maintain an Institutional Animal Care and Use Committee (IACUC) to review proposed research projects and scrutinize the facility's animal program. Further, the Health Research Extension Act, passed at the same time, directed the Public Health Service (PHS) to include the IACUC requirement in its *Policy on Humane Care and Use of Laboratory Animals*, and in the National Institutes of Health (NIH, a division of PHS) *Guide for the Care and Use of Laboratory Animals* (for an overview of the PHS *Policy* and the NIH *Guide, see* this chapter: *Public Health Service*). This brought to a close the era of self-regulation by discretionary Animal Care Committees and opened up a new age of government regulation of the care and use of laboratory animals.

Members of each IACUC are appointed by the chief executive officer of the institution. AWA and federal regulations require that the committee have at least three members, while the PHS *Policy* says there must be five.

In either case, an IACUC must include a veterinarian, a scientist with experience in using laboratory animals, a nonscientist, and someone not affiliated with the institution. One person can fulfill two of these roles.

The committee has two main functions: (1) to review all research proposals that are seeking federal government funding; and (2) to oversee ongoing projects with an evaluation of the entire research program every six months. The IACUC has the authority to require modifications before a proposal can be approved, and it can demand changes in continuing protocols or the program as a whole. A proposal may be rejected entirely: no activity involving animals can begin unless it is first approved by the IACUC. Similarly, committee members can suspend ongoing projects if, in their judgment, the research activities are not in compliance with the law.

Despite this broad authority, it should be emphasized here that, according to AWA and federal regulations, an IACUC is not permitted to mandate a particular plan of research or its implementation. The AWA explicitly asserts that "Nothing in this Act . . . shall be construed as authorizing the Secretary to promulgate rules, regulations, or orders with regard to design, outlines, guidelines, or performance of actual research or experimentation by a research facility." In other words, IACUC control is confined to how animals are treated before and after the experimental procedures, and how they are used by investigators—the committee has no control over what is done with them in the research protocol. As one commentator has described the situation, IACUCs can peer through the window of the laboratory door, but the scientist still holds the key to the lock.

Protocol Review

When a new research project using animals is proposed, the "investigators" (those conducting the research) must fill out an application form and submit it to the IACUC. The application is evaluated by the committee, and the results of this appraisal are reported in writing to the administrative officer responsible for programs utilizing animals. This report attests that either the project is in compliance with the AWA and its regulations, the PHS *Policy*, and the NIH *Guide*, or that it is not (federally funded proposals using only rats, mice, or birds must meet the requirements of just the *Policy* and the *Guide*; AWA regulations do not cover these species). If it is not in compliance, the investigator can modify the proposal and resubmit it. Whether approved or not, the investigator is entitled to hear both the majority and minority opinions if the committee's judgment is not unanimous.

The application for the use of animals must address a number of issues that the IACUC is charged with scrutinizing. A written narrative of the methods to be employed in the protocol is expected, along with a concise statement of what the project is intended to accomplish and how this would advance human knowledge or promote social good. The species to be used in the protocol must be identified and the number of animals needed specified; applicants are required to state why they have selected the species and why that particular number is called for. IACUCs must also make sure that applicants have considered alternatives to using animals or at least less invasive procedures, and explained why these have been rejected. Investigators also need to address whether the proposal duplicates previous research projects and, if so, why a replay is necessary.

There must be a description of exactly what the investigators intend to do with the research animals, especially any surgical procedures and physical restraints. In this context, the application must realistically assess the degree of pain and discomfort that various procedures will cause and how long the distress will last, from the low-level sort momentarily induced by needle punctures, to the chronic pain produced by toxicity testing or carcinogenic studies that either cannot or will not be relieved by analgesic or anesthetic drugs. The type of pain-relieving drugs to be used must be specified, including the dose and frequency with which they will be administered. Although it is the stated aim of the AWA, federal regulations, and PHS *Policy* to minimize pain and discomfort, investigators are permitted to maintain animals in continuous states of severe discomfort so long as they provide a written justification, appealing to "scientific necessity," for doing so.

A description of postprocedure care is also to be given to the IACUC. The individuals who provide this care should be identified, and its frequency and duration, along with analgesic and antibiotic data, specified. Finally, the application needs to state the circumstances or criteria by which the research animals will be humanely killed: euthanasia. A description of how this will be done must be included. If euthanasia will not be performed, investigators should indicate what the final disposition of the research animals will be.

Program Review
The IACUC is required to inspect all institutional animal facilities at least twice a year to ensure that the animal care program is in compliance with the relevant standards. These inspections may or may not be announced, at the discretion of the committee. A formal report is prepared on the findings, and the report must be approved by a majority of the committee; dissenting views should also be included in the final report. Problems identified during the evaluation of the facility are noted as either significant—a serious threat to animal health—or minor. The report should include directions for correcting these problems and a timetable for doing so. If the facility cannot make the required corrections, the IACUC must inform APHIS and the funding agency of this determination.

During these semiannual inspections, the committee is to be especially attentive to a number of different features of the animal facilities and the program itself. Animal housing must be provided that is appropriately sized for the species, provides adequate ventilation, and allows easy access to food and water. The IACUC should verify that cages and other confinement devices are cleaned and sanitized regularly, and that waste collection and disposal is frequent. Since the animals must be monitored every day, provisions must be made for emergency, weekend, and holiday care. Dogs must be given the opportunity to exercise and measures taken to promote the psychological well-being of primates (*see* this chapter: *Primates: Psychological Well-Being*).

Research facilities are responsible for adequately training their personnel in humane methods of animal maintenance and experimentation, from the scientists themselves and the lab technicians and students who assist them, to the individuals responsible for the husbandry of the animals. As part of every six-month review, the IACUC ensures that such training has been supplied. Further, the committee checks on the occupational health program required of all research facilities. In particular, the members look for medical evaluations of personnel before they assumed their positions, with subsequent periodic medical evaluations, while supplying personnel with information both concerning health risks and professional treatment should injury or illness occur.

IACUCs and State "Sunshine Laws"

Every state code in America contains a statute permitting citizens to attend meetings convened by employees of agencies and institutions funded by public money. Interested individuals legally cannot be denied access to these assemblies. Additionally, most states also allow the public to peruse certain documents, such as minutes taken at meetings, transcripts, and financial records. These statutes are known as "Sunshine Laws," and they are founded on the principle that citizens have a right to know how their tax dollars are being spent and what decisions these public entities are making. The laws are intended to bring these matters into bright daylight, and prevent them from being concealed in dark, cloudy boardrooms.

Since the early 1980s, animal protection organizations have tried to wield sunshine laws as wedges to pry open the doors of the conference rooms where IACUCs gather to discuss research protocols using animals and the status of their institutions' animal care programs. This tactic has distinct advantages over recourse to the federal Freedom of Information Act (FOIA), another kind of sunshine law. Under FOIA, any person is entitled to be provided with unclassified information from government agencies upon request. For example, when asked to do so, the NIH must disclose certain information about research using animals that it has funded, including the nature of the protocol, the justification for relying on animal models, how many and what species of animal, and how much funding has been granted. Similarly, the USDA is required to produce copies of inspection reports, applications for licenses and registrations, reporting forms and other information. The problem is that a FOIA request can only provide data *after* the fact—after a protocol has been funded and the research conducted, after an inspection has been done and violations noted. Sunshine laws can allow access *before* a protocol or an animal care program is approved by an IACUC, during deliberations, when there may be an opportunity to influence the process in favor of the animals.

The appeal to sunshine laws to access IACUC proceedings has met with mixed results for those concerned with laboratory animal welfare. Currently, none of these state laws explicitly address whether or not they apply to animal care committees. The issue of when, or if, public access may be denied has been left to the courts to decide, through judicial interpretation of the statute. Courts in at least five states have ruled that IACUC meetings are closed to the general public: California, Massachusetts, New York, Oregon, and Virginia. The legal basis for these rulings has differed to some degree but generally looks for and does not find that IACUCs function in the public interest.

For example, in 1992 the New York Court of Appeals, the state's highest court, decided that the American Society for the Prevention of Cruelty to Animals was not entitled to monitor IACUC meetings at the Stony Brook campus of the state university system. Reasoning that the only bodies subject to the sunshine of popular scrutiny are those discussing and making decisions on matters of policy affecting citizens of New York, the court found that the IACUC was merely an "advisory body" serving the federal government, not the state (*ASPCA v. Board of Trustees*).

On the other hand, the Oregon Supreme Court settled on another legal theory to deny access. Here, members of People for the Ethical Treatment of Animals (PETA) wanted to attend IACUC meetings at the University of Oregon when experiments with barn owls were discussed, but the school prohibited attendance by the public. The court held that the ban did not invade any legally protected interest of PETA, so the group had no standing—no right to sue—to challenge the rule closing IACUC meetings (*PETA v. IACUC;* for more on the issue of legal standing to sue on behalf of animals, *see* chapter 2: *Legal Standing under the Animal Welfare Act*).

In six other states, IACUC proceedings must be open, to varying degrees, to the public: Florida, Kentucky, North Carolina, Texas, Vermont, and Washington. Perhaps appropriately for the Sunshine State, the application of Florida's sunshine law to animal care committees has never been denied or challenged. IACUC meetings at the University of Florida in Gainesville have been open to the public since 1985. They are advertised in a local newspaper and are usually attended by a few animal rights activists and members of the press.

It is not known how many institutions in the United States have voluntarily opened their meetings without a legal struggle. Students for the Ethical Treatment of Animals won such a battle in North Carolina when the group demanded copies of four research proposals using animals from the IACUC at Chapel Hill. The state court of appeals held that this information must be made available, though the university could remove personal information about the scientists submitting the proposals (*Students for the Ethical Treatment of Animals v. Huffines*). Similarly, finding in favor of the Animal Legal Defense Fund (ALDF), the Vermont Supreme Court upheld a lower court injunction ordering the University of Vermont IACUC to make its records available to the public; furthermore, citizens have the right to attend its meetings (*ALDF v. IACUC*).

PUBLIC HEALTH SERVICE (PHS)

The United States Public Health Service (PHS) is an umbrella term for eight federal agencies dedicated to promoting and safeguarding human health. Housed in the Department of Health and Human Services, the PHS agencies are the Centers for Disease Control and Prevention, the Agency for Health Care Policy, the Agency for Toxic Substances and Disease Registry, the Indian Health Service, the Substance Abuse and Mental Health Services Administration, the Food and Drug Administration, and the National Institutes of Health. Most of these agencies are further subdivided into various centers, institutes, and bureaus, and all of them either conduct research with animals, fund it, or utilize the results of such research.

The National Institutes of Health (NIH) is the preeminent force in America behind the use of animals in research, experimentation, and testing. Exact figures are unknown but recent estimates indicate that at least nine out of every ten laboratory animals are the subjects of scientific investigations funded wholly or in part by NIH, or those carried out at NIH facilities. In 1999 NIH provided almost $13 billion for "extramural" research conducted at hundreds of nongovernmental institutions. All of this research must be done according to the NIH *Guide for the Care and Use of Laboratory Animals* as well as the PHS *Policy on Humane Care and Use of Laboratory Animals*. The *Guide* and the *Policy* reinforce, elaborate, and supplement many of the provisions of the Animal Welfare Act (AWA) and its regulations (*see* this chapter: *Animal Welfare Act*; this chapter: *Animal Welfare Act Regulations*). AWA regulations are the major other source of legal restrictions on the treatment of laboratory animals.

The Marine Hospital Service

The PHS began in 1798 when the Fifth Congress of the new nation enacted legislation to establish a Marine Hospital Service, ensconced in the Treasury Department. The law was intended to encourage the expansion of the small merchant marine, and to provide health care for seamen. A single clerk in the Treasury Department collected twenty cents every month from the wages of each sailor to help pay for the construction of hospitals. Over the next seventy years numerous marine hospitals were constructed on the east coast and along the Mississippi River and its major tributaries; a hospital was also opened in San Francisco. The service reorganized in 1870, with a central administration headed by the first surgeon general, Dr. John Woodworth. As epidemics of small pox, yellow fever, cholera, typhus fever, and bubonic plague waxed and waned across the country, the service began to evolve from a medical program for sailors into a national health force.

As its range of influence expanded and the focus shifted to fighting and treating these contagious diseases, biomedical research blossomed at the service. A bacteriological laboratory was opened at the Staten Island Marine Hospital in 1887 and then moved four years later to Washington, D.C., where it was named the Hygienic Laboratory. By the 1890s the nation's capital had become a center of biomedical research, mainly focused on the study of various diseases. Most of these investigations used animals. The basic procedure was to infect the lab animals with a virus, and introduce various substances into their bodies, checking to see if the illness then abated. Although the government had been funding such research at various east coast medical schools for several years, the work at the Hygienic Laboratory inaugurated direct federal participation in experimentation with these creatures.

At the time there were no federal laws regulating the use of animals in laboratories, and many state anticruelty laws provided specific exceptions for scientists and their experiments with animals. Humane societies in and around Washington, with the backing of the American Society for the Prevention of Cruelty to Animals, were especially outraged by the proliferation of animal research in their area, so they lobbied in Congress in 1896 and 1900 for protective legislation. Meeting with staunch resistance led by the federal government, especially the Marine Hospital Service, and the research community, both attempts failed.

In 1902 the Biologic Control Act led to a further increase in the use of animals at the federal research lab. The act required the Hygienic Laboratory to create standards for the regulation of vaccines and antitoxins, substances that could be deadly if contaminated or administered improperly. Vaccines and antitoxins are produced by using animals. For example, diphtheria antitoxin is made by injecting horses with increasingly potent doses of the diphtheria bacteria; blood is then taken from the animals and the blood serum extracted. When injected into a person with diphtheria, antibodies in the "horse serum" neutralized the toxins causing the patient's symptoms. Of course the horses died of the disease.

Between 1903 and 1907 the Hygienic Laboratory ran numerous experiments on horses, pigs, and goats in the process of establishing standards for the manufacture of smallpox and rabies vaccines and various antibacterial serums. The lab was also authorized by the Biologic Control Act to issue licenses to pharmaceutical companies wishing to produce vaccines and serums. These businesses also used animals, mostly livestock, in much the same way.

The Marine Hospital Service was reorganized and its authority expanded in 1912 at the behest of Congress, and its name was changed to the Public Health Service (PHS). The First World War followed within a few years, and the pace of research quickened again, motivated mainly by the incidence of injury and disease in American soldiers and sailors. Much of this research, too, used animals. For example, the cause of anthrax outbreaks among the troops was traced to contaminated shaving brushes, discovered by infecting animals. Similarly, bunion pads widely used to cover smallpox vaccinations were applied to animals, who then became infected with tetanus. Scourges of venereal disease and the influenza epidemic of 1918 instigated further research, again by producing these afflictions in animals.

Shortly after the war, the government realized that military personnel needed a health agency of their own, so fifty PHS hospitals were designated for this purpose and transferred to the newly formed Veterans' Administration.

The National Institutes of Health
The Ransdell Act of 1930 changed the name of the Hygienic Laboratory to the National Institute of Health (NIH; notice the singular). A number of chemists had appealed to Senator Joseph Ransdell of Louisiana for help in 1926. The scientists had been trying, without success, to find philanthropic backing for a private-sector institute devoted to applying chemistry to medical problems. With Ransdell's sponsorship, a publicly funded institute focused on human health received the blessing of the American medical community, representing the dawn of a new era of cooperation and coordination between physicians, scientists, and the federal government.

The 1930s saw yet another acceleration of biomedical research. In no small measure due to the efforts of what had become the PHS, life expectancy had increased significantly since the days of its inception as the Marine Hospital Service, and this resulted in a higher incidence of degenerative diseases of the aged, such as arthritis, cancer, and heart disease. Many drug therapies and surgical techniques to treat these problems were first tested on animals with the ailments induced in the laboratory. In 1937 the National Cancer Institute was created, marking the beginning of the partitioning of NIH into various institutes, according to the medical condition focused upon. For the first time, NIH, through the Cancer Institute, was authorized to award grants to scientists who were not employed by the federal government, as well as provide stipends for researchers to come to Washington and pursue their investigations at government facilities.

This also marks the beginning of federal guidelines—not yet laws—for the treatment of laboratory animals. In 1939 NIH started to distribute "Rules Regarding Animals" to grant recipients with committees devoted to establishing standards for the care of animals used in research (*see* this chapter: *Animal Care Committees*). Among other rules, NIH required research facilities to hold dogs and cats obtained from local pounds for at least as long as the pound would have kept them, and if claimed by their owners, the animals had to be returned. All surgeries had to be approved by the director of the facility, and anesthesia provided for any procedure causing discomfort. Also, a painless death was required for animals no longer useful for research purposes. Grants were not conditional upon forming such a committee, but when one was in place, NIH demanded that the members verify compliance with the rules. Even so, the committees were not expected to provide NIH with an assurance of compliance (as they must today) (*see* this chapter: *PHS Policy on Humane Care and Use of Laboratory Animals*), no inspections were required, and violation of the rules could be punished only by withdrawing the funding. Evidently, NIH never resorted to this penalty.

In 1939, after 141 years there, the PHS was transferred from the Treasury Department to the newly created Federal Security Agency, which became the Department of Health, Education and Welfare (HEW) fourteen years later. HEW was itself renamed the Department of Health and Human Services in 1979. During the Second World War, numerous research opportunities presented themselves, and NIH became the major research arm of the PHS. It studied the effects of high-altitude flying, developed a vaccine for typhus, improved vaccines for plague and yellow fever, and developed drugs to combat malaria. As always, animals were the primary subjects in these studies, mostly rodents but also dogs, pigs, and goats.

Government funding of biomedical research accelerated during the Second World War, as did the use of animals in the experiments. Although NIH naturally concentrated on the welfare of American military personnel, it was also particularly concerned with protecting the health of workers employed in the defense industries. Among other investigations, the scientists developed methods to determine the amount of lead or TNT in urine so that workers could be tested for excessive exposure, demonstrated how lead is attracted to bone tissue, discovered that sodium deficiency was the key factor that resulted in death after burn injuries, and learned that methyl, ethyl propyl, isopropyl, and butyl ether vapors were extremely toxic for workers. All of these findings were revealed through the use of animal models: dogs, cats, rats, guinea pigs. Animals also figured prominently in other researches not directly related to the war effort: x-ray treatments for cancer were first tested on mice in NIH labs.

Then in 1944 Congress passed the Public Health Service Act, the first law to profoundly affect the course of research utilizing laboratory animals, as well as NIH and the scientific research community. The act allowed NIH to expand the grants program initiated with the Cancer Institute to include the entire agency, igniting an explosion of public money awarded for biomedical research. In the ten-year period from 1947 to 1957, NIH funding grew from $4 million to over $100 million, and the use of animals multiplied exponentially.

The postwar flood of money allowed for the proliferation of new institutes, arranged in categories specializing in various medical areas. By 1949 the National Cancer Institute had been joined by the National Heart Institute, the National Microbiological Institute (absorbed into the National Institute of Allergy and Infectious Diseases in 1955), the Experimental Biology and Medicine Institute (absorbed into the National Institute of Arthritis and Metabolic Diseases in 1950), the National Institute of Dental Research, and the National Institute of Mental Health. By 1960 four more institutes had been added to these six. In 2000 there were twenty-five institutes and centers, eighteen of them using animals in NIH facilities or providing funding for extramural research with animals in private-sector facilities.

Developing Standards for Laboratory Animals

During the late 1940s, the steady flow of money to U.S. laboratories produced a critical shortage of animals. The supply of experimental subjects could not keep pace with burgeoning research demands purchased with federal funding. To solve the problem, scientists in the midwest and northeast increasingly turned to local pounds and shelters to procure dogs and cats for their investigations. Various humane societies in these localities, lead by their national federation, the American Humane Association (AHA), objected vehemently to this pillaging of what were supposed to be sanctuaries for animals (for more on this episode, *see* chapter 3: *Animal Control Facilities: Animal Seizure*).

The tumult was especially intense in the Chicago area, where several major research institutions were lobbying for legislation that would require pounds and shelters to surrender animals to them on demand. The local chapters of the AHA, with the backing of the Chicago newspapers and much of public opinion, fought them hard, alleging that the labs were places of abuse and cruelty. When the Illinois legislature rejected an animal procurement law (neighboring Minnesota and Wisconsin both passed such laws), veterinarians from these institutions in the Chicago area organized to address the moral and medical issues raised in the battle over the pound animals and by animal research generally. This event in the private sector would one day pervasively impact federal regulation of laboratory animals.

The Animal Care Panel (ACP), headed by Bennett Cohen of Northwestern University and Robert Flynn of the Argonne National Laboratory, held its first annual meeting in Chicago in 1950. After several years of discussion and planning, and a false start in 1957, by 1960 the ACP had a productive committee in place focused on developing standards for laboratory animal care and use. The Animal Facilities Certification Committee, chaired by Dr. Cohen and including Dr. Flynn, also worked on establishing an accreditation program to implement the standards.

The work of this committee soon drew the attention of NIH, which had begun dueling with animal protection groups over the regulation of laboratory animals. Against several initiatives and bills proposed in Congress, NIH argued for self-regulation by the research community, rather than the government control favored by the Humane Society of the United States, the Animal Welfare Institute, and others. Unfortunately for NIH, at the time there were no widely recognized standards for the care and use of laboratory animals, and no independent, generally accepted authority that would facilitate self-regulation—a mechanism to make the argument practical was missing. The new standard-setting and accreditation program of the ACP committee looked like the answer.

Developing an NIH-Approved Accreditation Program

In 1961 the NIH contracted with the ACP to "determine and establish professional standards for laboratory animal care and facilities." Financial assistance to the ACP committee was also provided by several state and national medical associations. Their efforts ultimately produced in 1963 the *Guide for Laboratory Animal Facilities and Care,* published by an office of the PHS but substantially written by the veterinarians, physicians, and other scientists on the ACP committee. This document was intended as a set of recommendations for all research facilities and as presenting conditions of funding for those that received federal money, but it had no force of law. This status was to change twenty-two years later.

Soon after the 1963 edition of the *Guide* appeared, the now highly influential ACP committee concentrated its energies on constructing an accreditation program by which research facilities across the country could voluntarily evaluate their animal management systems. Naturally enough, the accreditation program was based upon the standards contained in the *Guide*.

In 1964 NIH and the ACP board of directors agreed that a privately operated, voluntary program of accreditation of animal care programs was feasible, could function nationally, and was greatly preferable to government regulation. The ACP committee was charged with initiating a new nonprofit corporation to administer the accreditation program: the American Association for the Accreditation of Laboratory Animal Care (AAALAC). Articles of incorporation were filed in April 1965, and the fourteen charter members of AAALAC, mostly national medical associations—including the American Medical Association and the American Veterinary Medical Association—held their first meeting shortly thereafter in the Chicago area.

In less than a year, a Council of Accreditation had been created and given the responsibility of reviewing the applications filed by institutions seeking accreditation and the forms submitted by consultants who participated in on-site visits of such institutions. The first two institutions were accredited in 1967: the Howard University College of Medicine in Washington, D.C., and the University of Louisville in Kentucky. Although the fledgling organization was now incorporated with a formal administrative structure for implementing the standards contained in the *Guide* and had validated it first applicants, financing became an immediate problem, one that persisted for some time. In the first few years, institutions were merely asked to contribute $100 as an annual accreditation fee, but this proved insufficient, so in 1971 a mandatory fee structure was implemented. Also intensifying the need for money was that, after an initial surge of interest, by 1970 the number of applicants had begun to decline.

The Ascendancy of the *Guide for the Care and Use of Laboratory Animals*

The turning point for the role of AAALAC and its *Guide* in shaping the treatment of laboratory animals came in 1971. That year NIH announced that it would accept accreditation by AAALAC as proof that an institution requesting federal funding was in compliance with government policy on the care of laboratory animals. The position of the federal government on this matter and that of the private association were now officially identical, and the *Guide* was the definitive statement of that view.

Moreover, since NIH was, and still is, the major source of federal money for all research, including that using animals, this provided a powerful incentive for institutions to seek AAALAC accreditation. This development, and other promotional efforts, appeared to work: applications doubled between 1970 and 1972, and by 1975 a total of more than 280 institutions housing nearly half the laboratory animals in the country had received the AAALAC imprimatur. In four more years, the number stood at 378. As of 1999, 612 research facilities are accredited by AAALAC in the United States and nine other countries: Austria, Belgium, Canada, Egypt, England, France, Indonesia, Peru, and the Philippines. The organization's name was changed in 1996 to reflect this global status: the Association for Assessment and Accreditation of Laboratory Animal Care International (AAALAC International).

By the start of the 1980s, AAALAC and NIH had been opposing animal welfare legislation for the more than twenty years that had passed since the inception of the ACP certification committee. The ACP, out of which AAALAC had developed, was primarily motivated to form in the first place as a reaction to public concern about the treatment of laboratory animals (which was itself a response to the grab for pound and shelter animals), and as an alternative to government regulation. The thinking at NIH and the ACP had always been that with an effective, responsible program of self-regulation in the form of voluntary accreditation, no legal constraints were needed. The self-regulation provided by the AAALAC program and based on the *Guide*, they had happily claimed, served much the same function as law without that onerous government coercion: Animal welfare was significantly enhanced; the evaluation was done by individuals outside of the institution, which eliminated bias and conflicts of interest; and personnel of the facility and prospective investigators, grantors, and clients could be assured that the animals were receiving high-quality care.

Ironically, government regulation could not be stopped, but AAALAC and NIH won anyway: the federal laws eventually adopted were substantially the same as the standards the association had already developed and NIH had approved.

In 1966 Congress passed the Laboratory Animal Welfare Act (LAWA), amended in 1970 to include animals in exhibitions and so renamed the Animal Welfare Act (AWA) (*see* this chapter: *Animal Welfare Act*). This law directed the secretary of agriculture to issue regulations for the care, handling, treatment, and transportation of animals used in research, experimentation, and testing. These regulations are largely based upon and in many instances are the same as those found in the *Guide for the Care and Use of Laboratory Animals*. Recall that the ACP committee that evolved into the AAALAC substantially wrote the *Guide* and received ample support from NIH throughout the process. Furthermore, amendments to the

AWA in 1985, and provisions of the companion Health Research Extension Act, in effect bestowed legal authority on the guidelines for the care and use of lab animals that the ACP committee had originally established in the 1960s. Since 1985 all NIH-funded animal research must comply with the standards set forth in the *Guide*.

Today, this critical resource is in its seventh edition, the latest published in 1996. Both the AAALAC accreditation program and the federal government view the *Guide* as the canonical source of standards for research animals. Additionally, the Public Health Service *Policy on Humane Care and Use of Laboratory Animals* (*see* this chapter: *PHS Policy on Humane Care and Use of Laboratory Animals*) accepts accreditation by the AAALAC as fulfilling a government requirement for institutions to provide assurance that the appropriate standards have been met. The *Policy* relies upon the *Guide* as the basis for evaluation.

In short, over the past forty years the federal government has followed the lead of AAALAC and its *Guide* in establishing the legal regulation of the care and use of research animals. With the possible exception of the Animal Welfare Act itself, no single document has had a greater influence on the way the research community conducts their work with animals.

Accordingly, we now turn to an overview of the *Guide*. It is divided into four main sections: (1) Institutional Policies and Responsibilities; (2) Animal Environment, Housing, Management; (3) Veterinary Medical Care; and (4) Physical Plant.

Institutional Policies and Responsibilities

The *Guide* lists four principal areas of concern in monitoring the care and use of animals. First, and most importantly, is the Institutional Animal Care and Use Committee (IACUC)(*see also* this chapter: *Animal Care Committees*).

This committee is charged with the responsibilities of oversight and evaluation, ensuring that the institution's research program using animals complies with the standards found in the *Guide*, as well as in the Animal Welfare Act, federal regulations, and PHS *Policy*. The IACUC must be established by the administrative official responsible for the research facility by appointing at least three persons to serve. One committee member must be a veterinarian, one a scientist actively engaged in research using animals, and another a "public member to represent general community interests in the proper care and use of animals." This person from the general public should not be affiliated with the institution or be involved with research using animals. In the course of fulfilling its responsibilities, the IACUC has several major functions, including semiannual inspection of the facilities and evaluation of the program, review of research projects planning to use animals, meeting at least twice a year, and filing reports on its findings.

A second major aspect of overseeing an institution's animal program, and of particular interest for the IACUC, is a description of the animal care and use protocol. This form, submitted by researchers to the IACUC, details the proposed activities that involve animals—how they are to be handled and what exactly is to be done with them, before, during, and after the experimental procedure. A number of specific topics must be addressed here: the reasons why animals are to be used; the justification for the particular species intended and the number of animals to be used; the availability or appropriateness of alternatives to using animals; methods of pain relief and euthanasia; whether or not the proposal duplicates previous research; and the training and safety of the personnel working with the animals.

The *Guide* also addresses the issue of physical restraint, which is defined as "the use of manual or mechanical means to limit some or all of the animal's normal movement." Such restraints are to be used as "little as possible" and only as necessary to fulfill particular research goals, not as a convenience for animal handlers or as a standard means of confining the animal. Multiple major survival surgeries are "discouraged": these are surgical procedures that expose a body cavity or produce physical dysfunction. IACUC approval permits such surgeries, but these must be justified by "scientific reasons" and not by appeal to cost cutting that results from reusing an animal. Such scientific justification is also needed for restricting food and fluid consumption, and animals so deprived should be closely monitored.

Personnel qualifications and training, as well as their safety and health on the job are discussed in the institutional policies and responsibilities. The people caring for and using animals are expected to be qualified to do so, and the institution has the obligation to make sure that this is the case, either by providing formal instruction or on-the-job training. An occupational health and safety program is required for all research facilities using animals. This program must address several pertinent items: the identification of potential hazards to personnel, procedures for controlling and minimizing them, and a determination of the risks of encountering such dangers; training to inform workers of the hazards and how to deal with them; the importance of personal hygiene, including making available washing and showering facilities; providing personal protection equipment, such as clothing and gloves; and the development and implementation of a program of medical evaluation and preventative medicine, including a regular schedule of immunization.

Animal Environment, Housing, and Management

The physical environment in which research animals live begins with their "primary enclosure": the cage. These enclosures should be maintained in good condition and allow animals to satisfy their normal physical and behavioral needs, such as the elimination of bodily waste, typical movements and changes in posture, social interactions with others of the same species, remaining clean and dry, accessing food and water, and avoiding injury. The construction of primary enclosures should thus provide for these basic needs while proving durable and readily cleaned. Some research animals are housed outdoors in pens, barns, corrals, or pastures, usually in groups. In these situations, the animals must be provided with some protection from weather extremes by means of shelters, shaded areas, fans, or heating elements. These forms of refuge must be available to all the animals located in the outdoor enclosure.

The *Guide* provides precise space recommendations for the most commonly used laboratory animals. Unlike the AWA regulations (*see* this chapter: *Animal Welfare Act*), farm animals, mice, rats, and birds are also listed. These space allocations are a function of the particular species to be housed and the weight of the individual animal. For example, a rat weighing less than 100 grams should be enclosed in a cage that supplies 17 square inches of floor space and 7 inches in height while a 25-gram mouse should have 1 square foot on the cage bottom and 5 inches to the top. A dog weighing over 30 pounds gets at least 24 square feet, while the recommended height here is supposed to be sufficient to allow it to stand in a "comfortable position." Space recommendations for primates are further broken down according to the genera to be confined. Macaque monkeys, for example, weighing between 3 and 10 pounds are to be provided with 4.3 square feet of floor space and 30 inches of cage height. A 30-pound chimpanzee requires 15 square feet of floor area in an enclosure 5 feet tall.

Temperature and humidity control are also addressed. The *Guide* recommends various acceptable temperature ranges for laboratory animals, from 64 to 79 degrees Fahrenheit for rodents to between 64 and 84 degrees Fahrenheit for dogs, cats, and primates. Humidity should be maintained between 30 and 70 percent. Ventilation requirements should be determined by calculating the heat generated by the animals housed, the amount of heat transfer through room surfaces, and that from any other heat sources. Odor, allergen, and particle control should also be accounted for in establishing ventilation systems. Recycled air can be used for ventilation, but needs to be adequately filtered to remove any pathogens.

The illumination of the animal housing areas is to promote the wellbeing of the animals, as well as allow adequate inspection of their enclosures and safe working conditions. A timer system is recommended to provide regular diurnal lighting patterns. Finally, extraneous noise should be kept to a minimum; noisy animals need to be housed well away from quieter ones. In general, facilities should be designed to accommodate boisterous animals, rather than resorting to methods of noise reduction.

According to the *Guide*, the behavioral management of research animals includes three components: the structural environment, the social environment, and animal activity. The structural environment refers to various objects and devices placed in the animal enclosures: "cage furniture, equipment for environmental enrichment, objects for manipulation by the animals, and cage complexities." Recommended items include resting boards, shelves, perches, foraging devices, nesting materials, tunnels, and swings. The social environment includes the opportunities animals have for contact and communication with each other. Obviously, this feature requires an understanding of the social needs of the particular species; compatibility and safety are especially important. This sort of social interaction is a component of animal activity, which also includes simply moving about as well as exercising cognitive skills: "animals should have opportunities to exhibit species-typical activity patterns."

The management of research animals concerns not only their behaviors, but more crucially a host of husbandry issues. "Husbandry" refers to those aspects of management that are perhaps most commonly thought of as constituting animal care: food, water, bedding, and sanitation. Animals are to be fed nutritious, palatable, unadulterated food every day, although the *Guide* allows that research protocols may be approved that call for less frequent feeding. Clean water should also be available to animals "according to their particular requirements." Feeders and watering devices should be readily accessible, and the latter need to be checked daily to make sure they are working properly and have not become contaminated. No recommendations are given by the *Guide* for cleaning feeders. Nor are any specific guidelines given for the type of bedding to be used: "No bedding is ideal for any given species under all management and experimental conditions, and none is ideal for all species."

The major sanitation problems addressed are bedding change, cleaning and disinfection, waste disposal, and pest control. Bedding is to be replaced as frequently as needed to keep the animals clean and dry. The *Guide* does not say how often this might be, simply noting that it is a matter of "professional judgment." Sanitation frequency is also not precisely indicated, but a general rule is provided that larger enclosures and accessories should be cleaned twice a month, while cages are typically sanitized weekly. Disinfection is to be accomplished with hot water (143 to 180 degrees Fahrenheit), chemicals, or both.

Storage areas, washing rooms, procedure areas, and corridors in the animal facility must also be "cleaned regularly and disinfected as appropriate to the circumstances." The *Guide* recommends that waste disposal, including that of animal bodies, be accomplished by contracting with a commercial waste-disposal company or by on-site incineration. Hazardous wastes must be contained or sterilized before they can be removed from the facility. Pest prevention, control, and eradication are required, preferably by employing nontoxic methods and substances.

Animal care should be provided every day, including holidays and weekends; emergency veterinary care must also be available at any time.

Veterinary Medical Care

The major items of veterinary care treated in the *Guide* are animal procurement, preventative medicine, surgery, pain management, and euthanasia. Research facilities must acquire animals legally, preferably from USDA-licensed "class A" dealers. These are operations that breed and raise animals specifically for use in laboratories, what are known as "purpose-bred" vendors. These vendors are desirable because they usually have precise genetic and pathogen data on their animal colonies, which provides buyers with valuable information on which to base the purchasing decision (*see also* this chapter: *Animal Welfare Act Regulations: Animal Dealers*).

Preventative medicine begins with the separation of newly acquired animals from the rest of the population of the research facility. Quarantine of incoming animals is urged, at least until their health status can be ascertained, although this might not be needed for rodents supplied by dealers who provide complete information on animal fitness. In any case, research facilities should have sufficient information from the vendor to determine the appropriate length of the quarantine, the potential risks presented by the new animals to personnel and other research animals, and any treatment procedures required. No matter the necessity or length of quarantine, the *Guide* recommends that all incoming animals be stabilized physiologically and psychologically before they are used in a protocol. The duration of the stabilization period is a function of the species, its intended use, and how it was transported to the facility.

Preventative medicine also includes at least daily observations of the animals, looking for sickness, injury, or abnormal behavior. Any such observations are to be reported immediately, and a diagnosis made promptly by laboratory services designed for that purpose. The attending veterinarian must then prescribe a "therapeutically sound" course of treatment or therapy that does not introduce a variable that compromises research goals.

Surgery on animals is classified as major or minor. Major surgery "penetrates and exposes a body cavity or produces substantial impairment of physical or physiologic functions." Minor surgery does not expose a body cavity nor result in any physical dysfunction. Aseptic surgical facilities must be provided for all procedures involving mammals, except for rodents: this means an operating room used only for that purpose, an animal preparation room, and a surgeons' preparation room. Appropriate aseptic techniques must be used to prepare the animals for surgery, and to sterilize the surgical instruments and supplies. Surgery on rodents does not need to be performed in a separate operating room, and with the approval of the IACUC, minor surgery on rodents does not need to be performed in a fully aseptic facility.

The *Guide* stresses the importance of presurgical planning: identifying necessary equipment and supplies and delineating the roles of personnel to participate in surgery on animals, the location and nature of the facilities, an evaluation of animal health prior to surgery, and an appropriate course of postoperative care. After surgery, incisions, physiological functioning, and body temperature should be closely monitored, looking as well for signs of pain and distress. Also stressed is ensuring that the personnel to perform the various functions throughout the surgical event are properly trained. The IACUC is responsible for verifying that the individuals involved in surgery are sufficiently qualified to fulfill their respective roles.

Perhaps the most crucial component of veterinary care is the prevention and alleviation of pain. The *Guide* states emphatically that the appropriate application of anesthetics and analgesics is both morally required and essential for sound experimental design. Pain management cannot be effectively accomplished without the ability to recognize the occurrence of suffering and discomfort in research animals. This recognition results from observing the manifestation of pain in animal vocalization, abnormal posture, immobility, and other behavioral indicators. As a rule of thumb, the *Guide* offers a basic assumption for identifying pain and discomfort in animals: "[P]rocedures that cause pain in humans also cause pain in animals." We also find a caution here about using neuromuscular blocking drugs—these paralyze skeletal muscles but do not relieve pain—since they tend to cause acute distress when administered to conscious animals and humans alike.

Euthanasia

Euthanasia is defined as "the act of killing animals by methods that induce rapid unconsciousness and death without pain and distress." The *Guide* cites the *Report of the American Veterinary Medical Association (AVMA) Panel on Euthanasia* (1993) as providing standards for euthanizing research animals, and is the authoritative reference source for the federal government on this issue (*see also* chapter 3: *Animal Control Facilities: Euthanasia*). Because of its commanding status, and since euthanasia of the research animals is the culmination of almost every protocol, a closer look at the AVMA *Report* is worth our time here, even though the *Guide* itself offers few specifics.

The AVMA *Report* lists three basic procedures for euthanizing animals, depending on the species and the type of data sought: inhalants, intravenous injection of drugs, and physical methods. General concerns about the use of inhalants—or, put less kindly, gassing—begins with the need to rapidly expose the animals to the gas or "agent" with properly functioning equipment. The longer it takes to inhale a sufficient quantity to cause death, the less humane the animals' demise is likely to be, producing convulsions or extreme distress. Very young animals are resistant to the suffocation induced by these agents, so it takes them significantly longer to die by this means than it does adults; the *Report* recommends that inhalants not be used on them.

Inhalants typically employed as anesthetics may be used for euthanasia—ether, halothane, isoflurane, and enflurane, for example—but these gases emit irritating vapors that tend to cause struggling and anxiety, and they are hazardous to human personnel, especially pregnant women. Carbon dioxide and carbon monoxide are the preferable inhalants, particularly for rodents and birds, but CO_2 is not recommended for larger animals, such as dogs, cats, and rabbits. CO presents a significant health hazard to humans because it is difficult to detect, highly toxic, and quite explosive at higher concentrations. The *Report* recommends that only compressed CO, sold commercially, be employed (rather than mixing sodium formate and sulfuric acid or introducing exhaust fumes from gas engines), and that the chamber used for euthanizing be located outdoors.

Barbiturates are the preferred drugs for intravenous injection. Overdoses of barbiturates produce almost immediate unconsciousness, followed quickly by anesthesia and cardiac arrest. The drug of choice here is sodium pentobarbital, because it is potent, long acting, stable, and inexpensive. It is recommended for dogs, cats, and "other small animals." Sometimes sodium pentobarbital is combined with other drugs, such as lidocaine and phenytoin. A concoction with chloral hydrate and magnesium sulfate is acceptable for euthanizing large animals. The AVMA panel expressly condemns the use of certain injectable drugs, including strychnine, nicotine, caffeine, and potassium chloride.

A wide variety of physical methods of euthanasia are considered and approved in the *Report*. Although acknowledging that some people regard these physical methods as "aesthetically displeasing," the AVMA panel points out that sometimes these procedures are more humane and practical than either the use of inhalants or drugs. These circumstances include euthanasia for small, easily handled animals, for large animals, and when other methods might invalidate experimental results. The penetrating captive bolt pistol is recommended for cattle, horses, and pigs. With this device, either gunpowder or compressed air drives a piston or "bolt" into the brain of the animal. The *Report* cautions that since "[i]t is imperative that a cerebral hemisphere and the brainstem are sufficiently disrupted by the projectile . . . , correct placement of the captive bolt on the animal's head is critical." Similarly crucial is the placement of a bullet from a firearm, an acceptable method of euthanasia when other procedures cannot be used.

Cervical dislocation is acceptable for mice, birds, and young rats and rabbits. This procedure is better known as breaking the neck, and is accomplished by gripping the base of the skull with one hand and forcefully pulling on the tail or the hind legs of the animal with the other; this separates the cervical vertebrae from the skull. However, this method may also be "aesthetically displeasing," and there is evidence to suggest that consciousness may persist for several seconds after the technique is applied. Therefore, the *Report* observes, cervical dislocation should only be used for valid "scientific reasons" and approved by the IACUC. Due to the same concerns, decapitation also calls for a special justification. Decapitation is often chosen over lethal injection or inhalation in order to analyze body tissues and fluids without chemical contamination. Manually operated guillotines for rodents are commercially manufactured and widely available.

The AVMA panel rejects electrocution, stunning, and exsanguination (bleeding to death) as the sole means of euthanasia. All these must be done in conjunction with other methods that ensure a painless death. Although electrocution does typically kill an animal by causing a cardiac arrest, consciousness persists for as much as half a minute after the current is applied. Bleeding tends to cause extreme distress in the animal and should be deployed only on unconscious animals. Stunning may be accomplished with an unspecified object that delivers a "single, sharp blow . . . to the central skull bones" of mice or rats; stunning can also be done with a nonpenetrating captive bolt or electric shock.

Finally, the *Report* approves the use of microwave irradiation, which at this time is available only in units designed for mice and rats. This instrument is not at all like the household microwave oven, which is strongly condemned for euthanasia. Instead, the microwave energy of the laboratory apparatus is directed entirely at the head of the animal, causing instantaneous unconsciousness, followed by death a split second later. These devices are expensive and still rather rare, and are typically employed by neurobiologists who want to fix brain metabolites without damaging the brain.

Physical Plant

This last category of the *Guide* contains recommendations for the construction of the research facility itself. The details of the structure depend a great deal upon the nature and scope of the research conducted at the facility.

Minimally, separate spaces are needed for animal housing, care, and sanitation, for receipt and quarantine of incoming animals, and for storage. More elaborate research facilities also need special areas for surgery, intensive care, necropsy, and radiography, for waste storage and the containment of hazardous materials, as well as for receiving supplies. Sanitation space for cleaning and sterilizing equipment and enclosure paraphernalia, along with cold storage space for animal carcasses may also be necessary. In addition, the most sophisticated laboratories with the most extensive animal programs typically have office space and other rooms for supervisors, administrative staff, and animal technicians, including lounges and fully equipped locker rooms and lavatories. Finally, the *Guide* recommends security systems with card-keys, electronic surveillance, and alarms (for the motivations of security concerns, *see* this chapter: *Animal Enterprise Protection Act*).

The corridors in a research facility should be 6 to 8 feet wide. Doors should be 42 by 84 inches, opening into animal rooms, and preferably equipped with windows. The *Guide* notes that exterior windows can constitute a source of "enrichment" for certain animals, such as primates and dogs, but the effects on temperature, light control, and security should be assessed and accounted for.

Floors should be resistant to moisture, chemicals, and impacts; floor drains may also be needed, especially in dog kennels and primate rooms, and these should be properly graded. Walls and ceilings, too, should be impervious to moisture, chemical cleaners, and impact. Ceilings with exposed ductwork, plumbing, and lighting fixtures are to be avoided unless they can be readily cleaned, and all lighting needs to be equipped with protective covers. Electric outlets and switches should be available in sufficient numbers and also designed for moisture resistance. Finally, noise control is mentioned as an important consideration: masonry walls are preferable to metal or plaster for noise abatement, and routine chores that are noisy need to be performed in areas separate from animal housing.

PHS *Policy on Humane Care and Use of Laboratory Animals*

Soon after President Lyndon Johnson signed LAWA into law in August 1966, the PHS made it official policy that any research using animals funded by one of its agencies, principally NIH, must comply with the provisions of the new federal statute. The policy was strengthened in 1973, when the PHS required additional compliance with the standards delineated in the *Guide for the Care and Use of Laboratory Animals*.

A third PHS policy was developed in 1979 through the NIH Office for Protection from Research Risks (OPRR). This one covered research using any vertebrate animal and gave institutions two main options for securing federal approval of their animal care and use program: (1) accreditation by AAALAC, or (2) a guarantee that the institution's own animal care committee had determined that the program was in compliance with the *Guide.* The OPRR was dissolved in 2000, with the duties relating to laboratory animals elevated to its own office, the Office of Laboratory Animal Welfare (OLAW).

Finally, hot on the heels of the major amendments to the AWA in late 1985, and as directed by the Health Research Extension Act, the PHS issued its own statement on animal research, the *Policy on Humane Care and Use of Laboratory Animals.* All research and testing that is funded at least in part by any agency of the PHS must comply with the rules found in the *Policy,* and the OLAW is responsible for ensuring compliance. The *Policy* is presented as the implementation of the "U.S. Government Principles for the Utilization and Care of Vertebrate Animals Used in Testing, Research, and Training."

There are nine principles, summarized as follows: (1) transportation, care, and use should comply with the provisions of the AWA; (2) research should be relevant to human or animal health, the good of society, or the advancement of knowledge; (3) alternatives to animals should be explored; (4) avoiding and minimizing animal pain is imperative; (5) appropriate pain relief should be provided; (6) animals facing severe or chronic pain should be euthanized; (7) veterinary care must be provided along with appropriate husbandry; (8) personnel should be adequately trained; and (9) exceptions to the principles should not be made by the investigators, but by the institution's animal care committee.

As with previous PHS policies, the 1985 *Policy* stipulates that research facilities receiving federal funding must structure their animal care and use program in accordance with the *Guide.* But now there is a new requirement, inspired by an amendment to the AWA: these facilities must have an Institutional Animal Care and Use Committee (IACUC). The IACUC must have at least five members (the AWA amendment and federal regulations require three), and these must include a veterinarian, a practicing scientist experienced in animal research, a person who is not a scientist (the *Policy* lists an ethicist, a lawyer, and a member of the clergy as examples), and a person having no affiliation with the institution and who is not related to someone with such an affiliation.

The IACUC has two basic functions: program review and protocol review. The committee must study the entire animal care and use program and inspect the entire facility at least once every six months; its appraisal is again based upon the *Guide,* and a report of its findings is submitted to the institutional official responsible for the program. Proposed research projects are scrutinized by the IACUC in order to determine their consistency with the AWA, federal regulations, and the *Guide.* Areas of prime concern are procedures to minimize pain and distress, the use of appropriate pain relief, timely euthanasia, the provision of medical care, the proper training of personnel, and appropriate husbandry techniques. The

Policy gives the IACUC the authority to deny approval to proposed projects, and suspend approval of ongoing research. The IACUC also must file an annual report with the OLAW, describing any changes that have occurred in its membership, the facility, or its animal care and use program. Finally, the committee must inform the OLAW of any serious violations of the *Policy*, or deviations from the *Guide*, or any research projects that were suspended.

No federally funded research can proceed until the PHS—through the OLAW—has been provided with an Animal Welfare Assurance: "Without an applicable PHS-approved Assurance no PHS-conducted or supported activity involving animals at the institution will be permitted to continue." The Assurance contains a complete description of the animal care and use program at the facility including: who is responsible for administering the program and ensuring compliance with the *Policy;* the credentials and responsibilities of the veterinarian participating in the program; and a synopsis of the training provided to personnel in the humane practice of animal care, methods for reducing the numbers of animals used, and for minimizing the distress they experience. Further, the Assurance must verify that the institution has either been accredited by the AAALAC, or has been successfully evaluated by its IACUC.

The *Policy* also stipulates the sort of information concerning animals that applicants must provide when seeking PHS funding, including the species and numbers of animals, why animals are necessary in the protocol, what is proposed to be done with them, how any pain is to be minimized, and what methods of euthanasia will be employed. Record keeping requirements are listed as well.

PRIMATES

The primates are an order of mammals distinguished mainly by their highly social nature, large complex brains, correspondingly elevated intelligence, excellent hearing and acute binocular vision, but only a mediocre sense of smell. Perhaps most distinctive of the order is that their hands and feet are nicely adapted for grasping, with most species having opposable thumbs and all but one species opposable big toes. That one primate species is *Homo sapiens,* the human beings. Humans also have far less body hair than other primates, a much higher forehead, and an S-shaped rather than straight spine. The nonhuman primates (henceforth simply "primates," our topic here) are native to tropical and subtropical climates—none are indigenous to the United States. Mainly herbivorous and tree dwelling, they are active during the day while resting in the hours of darkness.

Primates are taxonomically classified into three families. The *Pongidae,* or "apes," are represented by chimpanzees (*Pan troglodytes*), gorillas

(*Gorilla gorilla*), orangutans (*Pongo pygmaeus*), and gibbons (*Hylobaltes* spp.). The *Cercopithecidae* are the "Old World" monkeys of Africa and south and east Asia, such as baboons (*Papio* spp. mainly), macaques (*Macaca* spp.), and langurs (*Presbytis* spp.). Third are the *Cebidae* or "New World" monkeys found in Central and South America, for example the spider monkey (*Ateles* and *Brachyteles* spp.) and the marmoset (*Callithrix* spp. mostly). There are some 240 primate species in all, ranging from the diminutive marmoset, weighing about 8 ounces and standing 12 inches tall, to the hulking, 6-foot, 500-pound lowland gorilla.

Monkeys and apes have entertained humans in various forms of animal exhibition for centuries, from the city zoo to the traveling circus to the organ grinder on the corner. But it is as laboratory animals that primates figure most prominently in America today, as the subjects of animal protection law, in terms of their impact on human well-being, and in sheer numbers. Much more common in times past, by the late 1990s perhaps a dozen monkeys—apparently none of them gorillas or chimpanzees—performed in American circuses; the exact number is not known. American zoos currently hold about 2,000 primates. At least ten times that total are housed in dozens of research institutions, some privately owned and others operated by the federal government. Accordingly, we discuss primates in this chapter, and begin with their disposition as laboratory animals.

Laboratory Animals
The first documented occasion on which a primate served as an experimental subject comes from the second century C.E. Galen of Pergamon, physician to the Roman emperor Marcus Aurelius, dissected living "apes," probably chimpanzees, hoping to understand respiration, nerve function, and heart action in both the primates and, by extrapolation, in humans. He also opened the brains of conscious chimps, though after a few trials he recommended that apes not be used for the procedure because their expression during the operation was "unpleasant."

Although primates have been used in the laboratories of the Western world for research and experimentation for hundreds of years, it has only been within the last century and a quarter that scientists have pressed their endeavors with these species in earnest. Many point to David Ferrier as the first of a still swelling wave of researchers to focus on primates as the experimental models that would best enlighten us about human physiology and neurology. Working at King's College Hospital in London during the 1870s, Dr. Ferrier, rather like Galen over 2,000 years earlier, was fascinated by the simian brain. Ferrier supposed that probing the gray matter of macaques and orangutans would ultimately reveal the mysteries of the human brain.

The hypothesis caught on and gained powerful support in 1908 Vienna when Karl Landsteiner took a solution made from bits of the ground-up spinal cord of a boy killed by polio and injected it between the vertebrae of two monkeys. Both animals died. Further confirmations that the nonhuman primate was the archetype for the science of the human body came rapidly: In 1911 it was found that monkeys could be infected with measles, in 1914 it was mumps, and in 1928 yellow fever. Indeed, it was Landsteiner whose research with rhesus macaques in 1940 led to the discovery of the "Rh factor"—knots of protein that dot the surface of red blood cells—in both simian and human blood. "Rh" is from rhesus.

By the time the Second World War ignited Europe, the nascent biomedical research community in England and America was clamoring for primates to use as lab animals, especially rhesus macaques. The trouble was that the animals were notoriously difficult to transport out of Africa and Asia to the laboratories of the Western world. Wild monkeys are quite hard to handle: they can fly into an uncontrollable frenzy with little provocation, and they have very sharp teeth that they are always ready to use. Methods of restraint and confinement to manage the simian furies, as well as the generally unhealthy environment of the cargo hold on interminable sea voyages, caused many fatalities before the intended destination could be reached. After the war ended, the modern airline industry began to develop and American pharmaceutical companies developed powerful and safe sedatives—safe for primates anyway. One such wonder drug created in 1956—marketed by the trade name "Sernalyn"— proved so effective for monkeys that tests began on humans for commercial approval by the U.S. Food and Drug Administration. It didn't make it. Sernalyn is more commonly known as "PCP" or "angel dust."

Today, the barbiturate of choice for primates is Ketamine, concocted in the early 1970s as a replacement for Sernalyn, ubiquitously administered both for shipping the animals and for mood control at the research facility. As Sernalyn (and later Ketamine) made the monkeys tractable, and jet transportation drastically shortened the travel time, scientists and handlers learned how to keep the animals alive for the duration of the trip.

Postwar prosperity also found the federal government investing hundreds of million of dollars in biomedical research. Suddenly, almost overnight, a flood of monkeys was streaming into America's laboratories, peaking at nearly 2 million total from 1956 to 1965. Most of these were rhesus macaques, with about half of them killed in the search for a polio vaccine. In 2000, various macaque species—crab-eating, stumptail, pigtail, along with the rhesus—remain by far the most commonly used lab primates, followed by squirrel monkeys and baboons. These species are obtained from animal dealers, and they are not cheap: $1,000 to $2,000 each, the larger individuals usually more expensive. The dealers typically import primates from South Asia, Africa, and South America, although a few of the biggest ones have begun their own captive-breeding programs. Among the major suppliers of primates today are Charles River Laboratories, Hazelton Research, Worldwide Primates, and Primate Products.

After 1966, when Congress passed the Laboratory Animal Welfare Act (*see* this chapter: *Animal Welfare Act: Laboratory Animal Welfare Act*) imposing standards for the treatment of primates (and other species) in research facilities, the numbers declined precipitously, cut almost in half. Still, since the mid-1960s another 1.7 million primates have gone through America's laboratories, over 57,000 in 1998, the most recent year for which statistics are available, and close to the yearly average over the last two decades. About 90 percent of the documented primates in the United States (the total kept as pets is unknown) are held by public and private research institutions, led by the approximately 17,000 animals housed at the eight Regional Primate Research Centers (RPRCs).

Seven of the RPRCs are operated by major universities and all are primarily funded by the National Institutes of Health (NIH)(*see* this chapter: *Public Health Service*): the University of California at Davis; the New England RPRC at Harvard University; the Oregon Health Sciences University at Beaverton; Tulane University in New Orleans; the University of Washington in Seattle; the University of Wisconsin at Madison; and the Yerkes RPRC, run by Emory University in Atlanta. The eighth RPRC—Southwestern, located in San Antonio, Texas—is the newest and the only one affiliated with a private institution, the Southwest Foundation for Biomedical Research. Among the other top private facilities using primates are the Laboratory for Experimental Medicine and Surgery in Primates in New York, and Syntex, a major pharmaceutical company near San Francisco.

Over the past half century, many of the primates in these and numerous other facilities lived, suffered, and died as subjects of scientific research that has produced advancements so stunning that the list reads like a miracles-of-modern-medicine roll call: vaccines against polio, rubella, and hepatitis B; perfecting techniques for organ transplants, and the development of the antirejection drugs essential for them; other drugs that have proved extremely effective for treating mental illness and in chemotherapy; and the progress that has been made so far in combating AIDS has been achieved by using primates in the lab. Almost certainly, when the HIV virus is defeated, the victory will come as the result of experiments done on these animals.

Providing for "Retired" Chimpanzees

To date, New Zealand is the only country in the world that will not allow some primate species to serve as lab animals. In October 1999 the New

Zealand Parliament amended the nation's Animal Welfare Act to prohibit the use of chimpanzees, gorillas, and orangutans for protocols in research, testing, and education "unless such use is in the best interests of the [animal]" or its species.

Although the United States has no law even approximating this degree of protection for apes, in October 2000 the House of Representatives passed the cleverly titled Chimpanzee Health Improvement, Maintenance, and Protection Act (CHIMP Act); the Senate will almost certainly approve the measure as well. The bill authorizes the secretary of health and human services to establish and operate a sanctuary system "to provide for the lifetime care of chimpanzees that have been used, or were bred or purchased for use, in research conducted or supported by the National Institutes of Health, the Food and Drug Administration, or other agencies of the federal government, and with respect to which it has been determined by the Secretary that the chimpanzees are not needed for such research."

A surfeit of chimps arose at American research installations during the late 1990s, mainly due to the National Chimpanzee Breeding Plan instituted in 1985 as a response to the rapidly escalating threat of AIDS. Reasoning that a species sharing 98 percent of its genetic material with *Homo sapiens* would be the ideal model to develop a vaccine for HIV, and recognizing that the deadly virus likely originated in the same equatorial haunts frequented by the animals, much money and effort was expended to stock up on chimps. Government and private research facilities now hold approximately 1,000 chimps, an excess that features many of the animals languishing in cages. According to the CHIMP Act, primates accepted into the sanctuary system could not be used for any further research, but there are several exceptions to this ban, all identifying situations in which chimps may be needed again. So, far from a complete proscription, the CHIMP Act provides a refuge just as long as the appropriate research circumstances do not arise.

First, chimps may be used for "noninvasive behavioral or medical studies based on information collected during the course of normal veterinary care that is provided for the[ir] benefit." Also, chimps that are needed for research because of their unique "prior medical history [or] prior research protocols" can be returned to the labs, as can those sent to the sanctuary before "technological or medical advancements" made them indispensable as experimental subjects. Finally, research that is "essential to address an important public health need" can be conducted on chimps already placed in the sanctuary. Research protocols using these formerly protected chimps must cause no more than "minimal" pain, distress, and physical and mental harm.

Animal Exhibitions

Primates have been held in captivity and placed on display for human observation and entertainment since at least 2500 B.C.E. (*see* chapter 5: *Circuses and Zoos: A Brief History of Zoos;* and chapter 5: *Circuses and Zoos: A Brief History of Circuses*). Pictures and hieroglyphics discovered at Sakkarah in Egypt show that the Old Kingdom pharaohs kept monkeys in the world's first zoos. King Solomon's royal palace in 1000 B.C.E. Palestine contained a collection of animals that featured chimpanzees, along with many other species. When the Greeks founded the great zoo of Alexandria in the third century B.C.E., primates were among its denizens.

In Europe, the emperor Charlemagne set up animal displays during the seventh century C.E. that included monkeys. Throughout the Renaissance, the major urban centers of the Continent established zoos, and most of them had some primates captured in Africa and South Asia. The same can be said of the new American zoos, although these were started later, after the Civil War had ended. Then, and now, the "Monkey House" has always been one of the most frequented zoo exhibits. The showing of primates was not unique to the West or the Old World. In the late 1200s, Marco Polo reported that the Mongol Emperor Kublai Khan had stocked his personal zoo in China with monkeys, and just over two centuries later Hernan Cortes said the same of Moctezuma's gardens in central Mexico.

In American circuses, the use of exotic animals developed from the merger of mobile zoos with traveling shows that featured juggling, tightrope walking, clowns, and trained horses and dogs. In the 1800s everybody loved the "menagerie," an outfit usually consisting of two or three large cages confining wild animals from Africa, mounted on wagons rolling from town to town, presenting the creatures to the public for a fee. As early as the 1850s, many of these menageries displayed monkeys that had been taught some tricks, and this never ceased to delight the crowds. By the turn of the century, nearly all of the menageries had been absorbed into circuses, and during their heyday in the 1930s and 1940s most had trained primates, usually chimpanzees or macaque monkeys, riding bicycles or horses, performing acrobatics, and doing other stunts that made them seem eerily human. Today, primates have all but disappeared from the circuses. Evidently, no primate protection or animal welfare organization has investigated the matter, and the federal government does not keep this statistic, but people knowledgeable about circus animals estimate that ten or twelve monkeys, probably macaques, still perform under the Big Top.

One of the most famous animals in American history was a circus gorilla, a primate whose celebrity in the United States has never been equaled by another conspecific—Washoe does not even come close. Variously called "Buddha" and "Buddy," the ape was best known as "Gargantua," named for the giant king in Rabelais's poem *Gargantua and Pantagruel*. Gargantua acquired such a fearsome reputation for viciousness (a disposition provoked mainly by abusive treatment) that he was billed by the Ringling Brothers, with standard circus hyperbole, as the "Most fiendishly ferocious brute that breathes!" His exhibit was enormously popular, drawing throngs of people to the show just to see him. During the 1930s and 1940s, at a time when the gorilla species was still little understood, *everybody* knew who Gargantua was. So great was his fame that, like another acclaimed circus animal, Jumbo the elephant, Gargantua's name entered the English language to signify any very large thing: "gargantuan" (*see also* chapter 5: *Circuses and Zoos: Elephants*).

The Animal Welfare Act and its Regulations

For nearly one hundred years after David Ferrier burrowed into the simian brain, and even longer since menageries first started carting monkeys around the country, primates had no legal protections whatever in America. There were no required standards for transporting, handling, or caring for these species in either animal exhibitions or in research facilities. Since the early years of the twentieth century, every state has had an anticruelty law in their code books, and many of these statutes are written to protect "any animal." Even so, most of these also contain an express exception for wild animals, and in any case there is no record of a cruelty to animals conviction under a state law that involved abuse of a primate.

Finally, in 1966 the Laboratory Animal Welfare Act directed the secretary of the U.S. Department of Agriculture (USDA) to "promulgate standards to govern the humane handling, care, treatment, and transportation of animals by dealers and research facilities." "Animal" is defined to include any "nonhuman primate mammal." These standards were to specify minimum requirements for housing, sanitation, feeding, and watering the animals, as well as "adequate veterinary care." Among other things, amendments in 1970 expanded the scope of the entities regulated by the law beyond the laboratory to include circuses and zoos, or "any person (public or private) exhibiting any animals . . . to the public for compensation." Regulations issued in 1972 added "animal acts" as regulated forms of exhibition. Appropriately, the expansion called for a name change, and the federal statute has since been known as the Animal Welfare Act (AWA). Today, the AWA and its regulations, issued by the Animal and Plant Health Inspection Service (APHIS; an office of the USDA), comprise the overwhelmingly dominant source of legal restrictions on the treatment of primates in the United States (*see also* this chapter: *Animal Welfare Act Regulations*).

AWA regulations for the care of primates in research facilities, zoos, circuses, and other exhibitions address three main areas. The majority of the standards concern housing, the manner in which the animals are confined. Also covered are husbandry issues (nutrition, hydration, and general health), and the transportation of primates from place to place.

General housing standards require that the animals be provided with dwellings that are well constructed and regularly maintained, while effectively preventing escape, access by other animals, and injury. Housing facilities should be kept neat and orderly, avoiding the accumulation of garbage or unused equipment, fixtures, or furniture. All surfaces in the primate house must be readily cleaned and sanitized—including dirt, sand, or gravel floors—and kept free of excessive rust. Spot-cleaning and sanitization must be done every day. All primate housing facilities are required to have electricity to power ventilation, lighting, running potable water, and "disposal and drainage systems that are constructed and operated so that animal wastes are eliminated and the animals stay dry." A diurnal lighting cycle, uniformly diffused throughout the facility, is required.

Captive primates must not be exposed to temperatures below 45 or above 85 degrees Fahrenheit for more than four consecutive hours, no matter if they are housed indoors or out. If the time and temperatures fall outside of this range, heating or cooling must be provided. Whether inside or out, appropriate ventilation is required at all times with windows, vents, fans, or air conditioning. Outdoor housing is permitted only for primates that are adapted to the climate conditions found at the facility, and in any case has to be equipped with continuously available shelter from sun, wind, and weather.

A new rule issued in 1994 mandates that outdoor enclosures be surrounded with a perimeter fence high enough to keep other, undesirable animals (dogs, skunks, raccoons) from getting in, and positioned far enough away to prevent any physical contact between the primates and the undesirables. Fences less than 6 feet tall are allowed only with the approval of APHIS. A fence is not required if a wall has already been constructed around the grounds, so long as it is sufficiently sturdy and tall enough. Zoos must place a barrier between primate enclosures and any public viewing areas. Primates used in circuses, whether merely uncaged or allowed physical contact with the audience, must be controlled and supervised at all times by an experienced handler or trainer. These same temperature, ventilation, and lighting requirements also apply to mobile or traveling housing facilities; a public barrier to separate the animals from people is stipulated here as well.

AWA regulations detail further specifications for the "primary enclosure," the cage, pen, or other confinement area where the animals spend most or all of their lives. As with the general housing standards, these enclosures should be safe, structurally sound, clean, dry, and provide protection from the elements. Water and food should be readily accessible.

Floors are to be constructed of solid materials that do not injure the animals' feet. After another new rule was issued in 1994, these regulations have also stipulated precise "minimum space requirements" for primates' primary enclosures.

Formerly, for over a quarter century, the floor space of a primate's enclosure was calculated at three times the area occupied by the animal while standing on four feet. Now, the dimensions are a function of each animal's weight, intended to afford "sufficient space . . . to make normal postural and social adjustments with adequate freedom of movement." For example, a primate weighing between 6.6 and 22 pounds (3 to 10 kilograms)—a typical macaque—must be confined in a cage with at least 3 square feet of floor space and 1.5 feet of head room. Another species, such as a baboon, at 33 to 55 pounds (15 to 25 kilograms) requires a space no less than 3 feet tall with 8 square feet of floor area, while one over 55 pounds, a chimpanzee for example, gets 25 square feet of floor area and 84 inches in height. The regulations also direct that great apes weighing more than 110 pounds be given "an additional volume of space in excess of that required for [primates over 55 pounds] . . . to allow for normal postural adjustments." The "additional volume" is not specified.

Primate husbandry begins with feeding the animals. They must be fed at least once every day with "clean, wholesome, and palatable" food, appropriate to the species and in quantities sufficient for the age and size of the animal. Drinking water is to be made available either continuously, or "provided as often as necessary for the health and comfort of the animal," but at least twice a day for an hour at the minimum. Cleaning and sanitization of food receptacles is required at least once every two weeks.

Primary enclosures must be cleaned of excrement and food particles every day, and sanitized in the prescribed way twice a month. Materials that cannot be cleaned with steam, hot water, or detergents—such as dirt, sand, or grass—have to be removed when they become contaminated. Finally, research facilities and exhibitors "must have enough employees to carry out the level of husbandry practices and care required. . . . The employees . . . must be trained and supervised by an individual who has the knowledge, background, and experience in proper husbandry and care of nonhuman primates to supervise others."

Veterinary care is not demanded by the AWA regulations for primates specifically, however, all research facilities, as well as circuses and zoos, must have an attending veterinarian, and establish and maintain programs of "adequate veterinary care" for the animals in their charge. This phrase is not explained, but various elements of such a program are mentioned, including making available the facilities, personnel, equipment, and services needed to comply with the law, and treating diseases and injuries with "appropriate methods." Attending vets are also supposed to provide "guidance" for the people who handle and care for the animals, and provisions must be made to observe all the animals every day, though this need not be done by the vet himself or herself.

The regulations also empower veterinarians to make exceptions to several of the rules governing the treatment of primates. For example, with a vet's approval the 45-to-85-degree-Fahrenheit temperature range can be exceeded for sheltered and outdoor housing, though, curiously, no such discretion is mentioned when confining primates indoors. Animal doctors can also authorize an exemption from the minimum space requirements for individual animals.

One other veterinarian-authorized exemption has proved very controversial—appropriately enough it seems, since the regulation to which a doctor of veterinary medicine can make an exception here has been itself much disputed. APHIS produced additions to the housing standards in 1991, directing researchers and exhibitors to "develop, document, and follow an appropriate plan for environmental enhancement to promote psychological well-being" of primates. The attending vet can order that a primate be denied any "environmental enhancement" on the basis of its health or physical condition.

Psychological Well-Being

These new regulations came about in large part as the result of two sordid incidents involving research monkeys that occurred in the early 1980s. In the first, a scientist conducting federally funded research was arrested in 1981 and charged with seventeen counts of cruelty to animals in violation of the Maryland state law, one count for each of the macaque monkeys he was keeping in the utterly deplorable conditions of his lab. The animals, most of them having had one arm surgically paralyzed and several suffering from untreated wounds, lived in filth-encrusted cages stacked in a vermin-infested facility. Although, incredibly to many, the researcher was eventually vindicated in a federal appellate court on all counts, the incident attracted a great deal of media attention, and for years the press followed the fate of the "Silver Spring monkeys," named for the Maryland community in which the research facility was located (for more on this incident, *see* chapter 2: *Legal Standing under the Animal Welfare Act*).

The second incident occurred in 1984 at the Head Injury Clinical Research Laboratory of the University of Pennsylvania, and also involved federally funded research activity. Here, the Animal Liberation Front stole some videotape shot by researchers during their study of head injuries, and portions of the film were subsequently widely distributed in the United States, Canada, and Europe. Among other abuses, the tapes revealed baboons in obvious pain and distress, lab personnel mocking and ridiculing them, and surgery being performed without anesthesia and under clearly nonsterile conditions, such as while surgeons smoked cigarettes and pipes. These two affairs shocked the national consciousness, the reverberations shaking the halls of the Capitol (*see also* this chapter: *Animal Enterprise Protection Act: Animal Liberation Front*).

In 1985 Congress responded to the public clamor, in part, by amending the AWA. The lawmakers directed the secretary of the USDA, through APHIS, to issue "minimum requirements . . . for a physical environment adequate to promote the psychological well-being of primates." The phrase "psychological well-being of primates" was not, and has never been defined by Congress or the USDA, and its meaning has been hotly debated ever since it appeared in the AWA and, later, in the agency's regulations. This later appearance took some time. After six years and a lawsuit accusing the USDA of serious foot dragging in producing the regulations ordered by Congress, APHIS finally delivered in 1991.

The agency delivered requirements that are generally known as "performance standards," this in contrast to "engineering standards." An engineering standard is one that demands a specific construction or action to fulfill a certain purpose, for example mandating cage size to provide adequate space: if a 20-pound rhesus monkey is to be kept in a cage, it must be one built to provide a least 6 square feet of floor area and 32 inches of headroom. Performance standards do not offer this sort of precise guidance to reaching a goal, instead they give a particular outcome—like "promoting psychological well-being"—and suggest various methods that might achieve this result.

Such is the case here. The 1991 regulations require very few specific items. No particular toys or activities are demanded, just the provision of some "means of expressing noninjurious species-typical activities." Nothing definite needs to be done for special categories of primates—infants, the emotionally troubled, closely confined research animals, those that are completely isolated from conspecifics, or great apes—they must simply be given "special attention." Group housing is not required for these highly gregarious species, just a plan that must "address the social needs" of primates.

Exceptions are also readily available in the regulations. For one, social grouping may be withheld entirely from animals that are "vicious," "debilitated as a result of age or other conditions," or incompatible with others. Even the two items that do clearly provide engineering standards are immediately qualified with exemptions: animals housed alone must be able to hear and see other primates "unless the attending veterinarian determines that it would endanger their health, safety, or well-being." And although in general primates must not be confined in restraint devices, they can be so restricted if approved by the vet or if restraint is required by an approved research procedure. Also, as mentioned above, the attending vet is authorized to exempt any individual primate from the benefits of the environmental enhancement plan.

Courts Assess Primate Psychological Well-Being

The Animal Legal Defense Fund (ALDF) and several other plaintiffs filed suit against the USDA shortly after these regulations were published, complaining that in producing performance rather than engineering standards the agency had failed to act as directed by Congress (for details on this case and others, sketched below, that followed in its wake, *see* chapter 2: *Legal Standing under the Animal Welfare Act*). The district court agreed with the ALDF and ordered the USDA to write new regulations. However, the District of Columbia Circuit Court of Appeals reversed that decision, ruling in 1994 that the plaintiffs had no standing to sue as injured parties because the regulations did not harm them in any direct or immediate way (*ALDF v. Espy II*).

Undeterred, the ALDF sued again in 1996, this time attempting to establish the standing of four individuals who had observed monkeys in several different zoos. The animals' living conditions were in compliance with the regulations for promoting the psychological well-being of the primates, yet the sight of them nonetheless caused the plaintiffs "aesthetic injury." In 1998 the D.C. Circuit Court of Appeals found for the ALDF and one of the four, Marc Jurnove, ruling that he did indeed have standing to sue the USDA for injuring him in this way. Among other disturbing observations, Jurnove had witnessed a chimpanzee confined in complete isolation, squirrel monkeys housed next to bears, and a solitary macaque provided with nothing more than an unused swing (*ALDF v. Glickman I*). Having settled the matter of standing, the legal issue then passed to the regulations themselves: Were the performance standards contrary to the mandate Congress had dispensed back in 1985?

In February 2000 Judge Williams of the D.C. Circuit answered "no." Indeed, Williams found that the 1991 regulations were not really performance standards at all, but in fact they were just the sort of engineering standards that satisfy the congressional command for "minimum requirements." In support of this startling conclusion, the judge pointed out that the rules for cage size, which determine appropriate space according to the weight of each animal, did state exact engineering standards. Moreover, he wrote, "the regulations on environmental enrichment, special consideration of certain primates . . . , and restraint devices all plainly provide engineering standards."

Judge Williams seems to have missed the point here. The cage size requirements—located in another section of the regulations and having been issued three years later—are not part of the "psychological well-being" regulations being contested by Jurnove, and they are indisputably engineering standards. Similarly for the restrictions on restraint devices: they are undeniably engineering standards and are not being challenged here. On the other hand, it is difficult to see how telling regulated entities to provide some "means of expressing noninjurious species-typical activities" and to give "special consideration" to some animals qualifies as a minimum requirement that demands specific actions to achieve the desired result.

Jurnove also maintained that the social grouping rule originally proposed by APHIS in 1989 did offer an acceptable engineering standard consistent with the intentions of Congress. According to that rule, "primates must be grouped . . . with compatible members of their species or with other[s]." This requirement was dropped in the final version in favor of a plan that "address[es] the social needs" of primates, a performance standard that, Jurnove claimed, could not be a reasonable interpretation of the 1985 amendment to the AWA.

Judge Williams ruled that it was reasonable. This is because comments from opponents of the 1989 version pointed out that social grouping in primates can spread disease, and lead to "threatening, chasing, fighting, wounding, hair-pulling," and competition for food, water, and shelter. Moreover, Williams averred, the listing of exceptions to social grouping in the final rule indicates that housing primates together is presupposed as the "norm" (*ALDF v. Glickman II*). Once again, the judge's reasoning is hard to understand. It does not follow from the fact that an objection was raised to the idea of required social grouping that Congress was not ordering social grouping. Moreover, although putting forward exceptions does suggest that group housing is standard or normal, this does not state or imply that such housing is *required*, nor does it indicate that Congress did not intend to impose such a requirement. That is precisely Jurnove's point.

A New Policy for the Psychological Well-Being of Primates?

After the decision in *ALDF v. Glickman I*, finding that Jurnove did have standing to sue, APHIS perhaps anticipated another setback when the legality of the regulations concerning primate psychological well-being was eventually considered. As we have seen in *ALDF v. Glickman II*, the D.C. Circuit's February 2000 ruling held that there was nothing wrong with the regulations. Meanwhile, however, in July 1999 APHIS had already published a "Draft Policy on Environmental Enhancement for Nonhuman Primates" and invited comments.

According to APHIS, the new policy was crafted because research facilities, exhibitors, and dealers "did not necessarily understand" what the government expected of them when developing their environmental enhancement plans. Also, APHIS continued, "there has been considerable disagreement in various sectors of the public over the adequacy of the performance standards." The lawsuits were not mentioned.

The Draft Policy may represent a degree of improvement over the 1991 regulations. It claims to provide "what must be included" in the plan of each regulated entity to promote the psychological well-being of primates, which suggests engineering standards. Other items mentioned in the draft need only be "considered." On the contentious social grouping issue, rather than simply "address social needs," the Draft Policy states a clear, substantive requirement: "the plan must provide for each primate of a species known to be social in nature to be housed with other primates whenever possible." Even so, a couple of new exemptions from group housing are added to those already given in the current regulation: "documented unavailability of compatible individuals," and, in research facilities, as required by an approved experimental procedure.

Unlike the existing regulation, the new policy explains in more depth what the "special attention" for primate infants needs to be. For instance, babies should not be taken from their parents before they would naturally separate in the wild, and the attending veterinarian should supervise the procedure. Yet no further details are offered on special considerations for emotionally disturbed primates, closely confined research animals, those that are completely isolated, or great apes. On the other hand, much more detail is provided for the structure of primate enclosures, going beyond mere cage size. Among other things, the Draft Policy mentions elevated resting surfaces, nest boxes for species that sleep in cavities, sufficient vertical space for primates with long tails, and scent-retaining surfaces for species that routinely scent-mark.

Additionally, "the plan should provide each primate to have, on a daily basis, some type of time-consuming foraging opportunity . . . , [and] a variety of portable or movable items for manipulation." The language of this last stipulation is representative of the Draft Policy: with the exception of the one concerning group housing, none of its provisions are stated in the strong sense of *required* that is captured by the use of the term "must." Instead, they are all couched in the weaker sense of the merely *recommended*, things that "should" be done. The legal significance of this distinction is that a failure to comply with what "must" be done is clearly a violation, while it is much more arguable that neglecting to do what "should" be done is worthy of citation. In practice, this means that an APHIS inspector would be reluctant to fault a plan guilty of such neglect.

Under the Draft Policy, as with the current regulation, research facilities, exhibitors, and dealers are not required to submit their environmental enhancement plan to APHIS for approval, although they must make it available to the agency upon request. To date, few if any such plans have been requested, although APHIS inspectors are supposed to verify that each regulated entity holding primates has a plan. If a plan to promote the psychological well-being of primates is not officially requested, it remains the property of the facility, exhibitor, or dealer, and the general public has no right to see it. On the other hand, once a plan is obtained by APHIS, it becomes a government document that any citizen is entitled to peruse under the Freedom of Information Act.

Transportation
About 25,000 primates are brought into the United States annually by importers, most of these going to animal dealers, but some directly to zoos. From the dealers, thousands are regularly moved each year to research facilities, and sometimes zoos transfer or exchange primates with one another. Animals also often flow into and out of the Regional Primate Research Centers, though their well-established breeding colonies make the RPRCs virtually self-sufficient, and they can ignore the importers.

Primates are transported by a variety of carriers—from airlines to railroads to trucking firms—but any operation that ships the animals for a fee comes under the purview of AWA regulations. So, too, does the "intermediate handler," defined as any business that "receives animals in connection with their transportation in commerce." These businesses typically accept the animals from importers or dealers, holding them at some facility until the carrier picks them up for delivery.

Carriers and intermediate handlers are required by law to refuse to carry or hold any primate unless it has been certified in writing that the animal was offered food and water within the last four hours, and they must reject any animal delivered to them more than four hours before departure time. Their holding facilities must be maintained at a temperature between 45 and 85 degrees Fahrenheit, unless a veterinarian says otherwise, and are required to be clean and sanitary, with shade and shelter from rain or snow. After a primate has arrived at a holding area, the carriers and intermediate handlers are required to notify immediately the "consignee" (the person taking possession of the animal) of the arrival. If unable to reach the consignee, they have to keep trying, at least once every six hours for up to twenty-four hours. After one day without success, the animal has to go back to the "consignor" (the person who handed over the animal for delivery or holding). In the meantime, the primate must be properly cared for, fed and housed "in accordance with generally accepted professional and husbandry standards."

Primates confined in improper primary enclosures must also be refused by carriers and intermediate handlers. The cages, crates, or cartons containing the animals must be secure and strong, with locks that cannot be accidentally opened or opened by the primates, and without any sharp points or edges that could injure them. Enclosures must be constructed with solid, leak-proof bottoms or removable wire mesh floors, and they must prevent primates from putting any part of their bodies outside the enclosures. Ventilation openings are required, and they must cover at least 32 percent of the total wall area; measures need to be taken to ensure that the openings cannot be obstructed.

The size requirements for the cages or cartons used in transportation are not nearly so precise here as they are for research facilities, exhibitors, and dealers. The regulations here stipulate only that each animal be given enough space to turn around and sit upright, allowing clearance between the head and the top of the enclosure. Unless a mother and infant or a male and female that are pair bonded are being transported, primates must be moved singly, one for each enclosure. Primates can be shipped with other animals, but if these other species are predators or enemies, they have to be kept out of their sight lines.

AWA regulations state that primates over one year old must be offered food at least once every twenty-four hours, under one year every twelve hours; those of any age are to be given water every twelve hours. Research facilities, exhibitors, and dealers are required to attach written feeding and watering instructions to the outside of each primate enclosure shipped. Food and water receptacles must be located inside the enclosure but designed so that they can be filled from the outside.

The motor vehicle, rail car, aircraft, or marine vessel that transports primates must provide the animals with a sufficient supply of air for normal breathing. For surface transportation, the temperature of the cargo space has to be kept between 45 and 85 degrees Fahrenheit, but for air transport the temperature has to be "maintained at a level that ensures the health and well-being of the species." To verify that the animals are alright, the operator of the conveyance, or some other person on board, is required to observe them at least once every four hours; aircraft with cargo holds that are inaccessible during flight are exempted from this requirement. Any primate that is "obviously" sick or injured cannot be transported unless it is moved to receive veterinary attention.

State Laws

Most states codes make no mention of primates. Those that do offer a mixed bag of legal restrictions. Currently, only California, Colorado, New Hampshire, and Rhode Island prohibit the possession of all species of primates as pets, with exceptions made for research facilities and exhibitions. Some local governments have banned pet primates as well, for example, New York City and St. Louis (although neither the states of New York or Missouri have any laws regulating primate ownership); Seattle, Spokane, Des Moines, and King County, Washington (Seattle and Spokane ban "inherently dangerous animals," and classify monkeys and apes as dangerous; the state of Washington does not have any primate laws); and Fairfax County, Virginia.

Several other states allow private ownership of primates generally or some species in particular according to a state-issued permit. Unlike the permit (or "license") system for dogs, primate permits rarely require shots, checkups, or health requirements of any kind. Florida does not issue pet permits for chimpanzees, gorillas, gibbons, and baboons, but other primates can be kept following payment of a $100 permit fee. Texas requires a permit for only the same species that Florida has prohibited; all other species are unregulated in the Lone Star State. Georgia has a general primate permit at more than double the Florida rate. Hawaii allows pet primates but the would-be owner must secure a $1,000 bond, and the state Board of Agriculture must approve the importation of any monkeys. Kentucky specifically states that no permit is required to buy, sell, exhibit, or own a primate. In Nevada, a permit is required only in the city of Las Vegas.

In 2000 Mississippi is the only state that has adopted regulations designed for keeping primates, specifically gorillas, chimps, orangutans, gibbons, macaques, baboons, and mandrills. To acquire a permit—$150 annually for each animal—primate owners must be at least twenty-one years old, have two years' experience in the care and handling of the species, and carry $100,000 in liability insurance for each animal in the event it causes injuries. Health records must be maintained and each primate must have an "injectable microchip transponder" implanted in its body.

Any permanent housing facility for primates in Mississippi, including a personal residence, is required to have a surrounding fence no less than 8 feet tall, and any cages must have double, locking doors and an attached secondary enclosure to seal off the animal while the cage is cleaned. Outdoor enclosures must provide "adequate shelter from inclement weather," and all confinement areas must have "adequate drainage of surface water" while being cleaned of fecal matter every day. Minimum cage sizes are specified according to species, with dimensions much more generous than those found in the AWA regulations—for example, the minimum cage height for any primate is 8 feet. All enclosures must have elevated perching areas and "horizontal climbing structures." No provisions are included to address the social needs of these animals. Primates cannot be restrained with tethers or chains, and owners are required to give them drinking water "in clean containers" daily. Frequency of feeding is not specified in the Mississippi regulations, just unspoiled food of the sort appropriate for the animal.

ANIMAL ENTERPRISE PROTECTION ACT OF 1992 (AEPA)

Sometime in the small hours of a Sunday morning in late May 1984, five men and one woman broke into the Head Trauma Research Center at the University of Pennsylvania. Once inside, the vandals destroyed a computer, damaged other laboratory equipment, and stole a number of videotapes. They also left their calling card: spray-painted on a wall were the initials ALF. This springtime raid brought national recognition to the Animal Liberation Front and its mission, an endeavor that came to be known as "animal enterprise terrorism."

The Animal Liberation Front

The ALF is a shadowy, underground group, spawned during the 1960s and early 1970s from a constellation of activist enclaves operating in England, especially the Hunt Saboteurs Association (HSA). Beginning in 1962 and still active today, the HSA focused on disrupting fox hunts by harassing hunters and distracting the hounds. After ten years of these tactics, two members of the HSA decided an escalation of action was in order.

Inspired by a nineteenth-century antivivisection group of the same name, Ronald Lee and Cliff Goodman founded the "Band of Mercy" in 1972, and began devoting themselves to slashing the tires and smashing the windows of hunters' vehicles (*see also* chapter 5: *Recreational Hunting Safety & Preservation Act of 1994: Hunt Sabotage*). Soon, Lee and Goodman expanded their operations to include all forms of animal exploitation. In 1975 Lee was apprehended while attempting to firebomb a British research facility. He was convicted of arson and served three years in prison. Upon his release in 1978, along with a number of cohorts, Lee formed the Animal Liberation Front.

The first known ALF raid in the United States occurred in March 1979 at New York Medical Center, where five animals were taken. However, the real tune-up for the raid at the Head Trauma Research Center came on a cold night in December 1982 in Washington, D.C. The next morning, officials at Howard University Medical School were confronted with $2,600 in property damage and thirty-five missing cats. Two years later, Dr. Thomas Gennarelli's head injury lab at the University of Pennsylvania was hit.

Gennarelli's research, funded by the National Institutes of Health (NIH)(*see* this chapter: *Public Health Service: National Institutes of Health*) and ongoing for fifteen years, studied the anatomical effects of blunt-force head injuries such as those occurring in car accidents, in football games, and boxing contests. There is no penetrating wound with this sort of injury, instead the damage results when the soft cerebral tissue is violently wrenched within the hard, bony skull. To gather data on this damage, Gennarelli used a number of baboons, cementing the head of each in a special helmet and then driving a piston into the helmet, forcing the head into a brutal backward lurch. The videotapes the ALF had stolen depicted many hours of this procedure, typically administered with insufficient anesthesia, or none at all. What was worse, researchers and technicians were filmed jeering at and joking about the helpless, writhing animals.

The tapes were given to People for the Ethical Treatment of Animals (PETA), which produced a thirty-minute, edited version called *Unnecessary Fuss,* a title inspired by Gennarelli's statement to the press that he would "not discuss the laboratory studies because it has the potential to stir up all sorts of unnecessary fuss." The video was shown throughout the United States, and excerpts were broadcast on NBC *News* and CNN. The furor resulting from this publicity reverberated all the way to Capitol Hill. Within eighteen months of the May 1984 raid, the Animal Welfare Act had been substantially amended to include (among other things) requirements that research facilities pursue means for promoting the psychological welfare of primates, minimize pain and distress, consult with a veterinarian, and form animal care committees to approve and oversee experiments involving animals (*see also* this chapter: *Primates: Psychological Well-Being;* this chapter: *Animal Welfare Act: Improved Standards for Laboratory Animals Act;* this chapter: *Animal Care Committees: Institutional Animal Care and Use Committee*).

Emboldened by the positive exposure to animal suffering that the Penn action had brought, as well as by the subsequent congressional response, the ALF escalated its activities throughout the remainder of the 1980s, grabbing more headlines and public attention. Highlights of these actions include an April 1985 raid at the University of California, Riverside, where nearly 1,000 laboratory animals were stolen and $600,000 in damage done, and in October 1986, the University of Oregon was plundered to the tune of $120,000 in damage and 264 animals confiscated. At the University of California, Davis, the construction of the Veterinary Diagnostic Laboratory was halted in April 1987 when the ALF burned the uncompleted structure to the ground, resulting in a $4.5 million loss. More arson followed in April 1989, this time in Tucson at the University of Arizona, along with extensive vandalism totaling half a million dollars, and over 1,200 animals stolen. And on the Fourth of July 1989 a physiology professor's lab at Texas Tech University in Lubbock was forcibly entered, five cats were removed, research data was destroyed, and nearly $70,000 worth of equipment was wrecked.

By 1990 the proliferation of destructive events in California—nearly half of all those documented in America—had earned the ALF an official designation in that state as a terrorist group. Moreover, the last two incidents mentioned above, and the UC-Davis fire, were listed in the FBI publication *Terrorism in the United States* (1990), and brought the ALF the Bureau classification of "domestic terrorist organization." That same year, the Association of American Medical Colleges reported that attacks on labs alone had cost $3.5 million (not counting the UC-Davis arson) and 15,000 staff hours in damages and lost data, and an additional $5.5 million spent on the installation and maintenance of security systems to prevent further sabotage.

The Justice Department released the *Report to Congress on the Extent and Effects of Domestic and International Terrorism on Animal Enterprises* in 1993. The *Report* stated that since 1979 there had been 313 documented cases of property damage and theft, mainly at university research facilities, but also at fur farms and retailers, and at meat-processing and packing plants; 53 of these incidents occurred in 1987 alone. At least 60 percent of the attacks could be definitively attributed to members of the ALF, who usually take credit for raids by leaving their acronym at the ravaged site and by issuing press releases immediately afterward.

Yet this is not always the case. Sometimes the only clues to the identity of the perpetrators are spray-painted slogans such as "We Shall Return," "Vivisection Will End," and "Stop the Torture," often accompanied by the signature of some other band. After observing that twenty-three separate named groups had claimed responsibility for "acts of animal rights extremism" in America—the Animal Avengers, Earth First!, Farm Sanctuary, the Urban Gorillas, among others—the *Report* noted that "individuals or groups that operate under other names are believed to be associated by membership or leadership with the Animal Liberation Front." The Justice Department guessed that about 100 people were so associated.

Very few people know who these members and leaders are. Because their activities are illegal, the identities of those involved with the ALF are unknown to the general public and law enforcement personnel. Moreover, most ALF members are unknown to each other. There is no central organization or membership list, instead there are individuals and small groups of varying sizes called "cells" working independently. Becoming part of one of these cells is simply a matter of participating in an appropriate action: "Any group of people who are vegetarians or vegans and who carry out actions according to ALF guidelines have the right to regard themselves as part of ALF." These guidelines include "to liberate animals from places of abuse and place them in good homes . . . to inflict economic damage upon those who profit from the misery and exploitation of animals; and to reveal the horrors and atrocities committed against animals" (ALF website).

Although forced entry, firebombing, and vandalizing buildings are not easily understood as nonviolent activities, the ALF does not regard property damage as a form of violence, and has explicitly disavowed physical harm perpetrated against other humans. At this writing, no ALF action in the United States has ever resulted in bodily injury or death to any person. To date only a handful of self-proclaimed ALF members have ever been apprehended, tried, and convicted in America for damages wrought at a research facility or other operation using animals.

Lawmakers React

Breaking into any public or private structure or taking or destroying the property of another person have of course been illegal for a long time. Even so, in September 1989 Representative Charles Stenholm of Texas, particularly incensed by the Independence Day destruction at Texas Tech (his alma mater), introduced the "Farm Animals and Research Facilities Protection Act" to the House of Representatives.

Unlike in 1985, when the ALF assault at Penn's Head Trauma Research Center was the major motivating force behind legislation on behalf of animals, this time federal lawmakers were going after the lab saboteurs. Cosponsored in the Senate by Howell Heflin of Alabama, Stenholm's bill made it illegal to release any lab animal without authorization, to forcibly enter a research facility, or to receive, conceal, or retain material taken during a raid. The bill was enthusiastically supported by the research community and by food animal lobbyists, led by the American Veterinary Medical Association, the National Association for Biomedical Research, and the American Meat Institute.

Opposition to the bill focused on two issues. First, critics noted, the legislation is redundant, since theft, arson, and vandalism are already illegal. Moreover, by the late 1980s twenty-four states had already passed their own laws criminalizing such sabotage when directed at research facilities, as well as outlawing the release of animals and the disruption of experiments (in 2000 thirty-two states have such laws). The second line of resistance came from those, especially the American Civil Liberties Union, who worried that as written the bill would stifle the attempts of both lab employees and the media to expose abuses in the use of research animals.

As debate on the Stenholm-Heflin bill ground on, the ALF expanded their activities, specifically targeting the commercial fur industry (*see* also chapter 4: *Fur Farming*). Notably, two installations operated by the U.S. Department of Agriculture were hit in August 1991, the Fur Animal Research Farm at Washington State University and the Experimental Furbearer Research Station in Oregon, resulting in the release of mink and coyote into the surrounding countryside. Also, a February 1992 fire at a Michigan State University lab conducting toxicology and nutrition research on minks produced a $75,000 loss.

Federal Protection for Animal Enterprises

These and other raids in late 1991 and early 1992 finally clinched the matter for Congress. Compromises were made, wording was changed, and in August 1992, President George Bush signed the Animal Enterprise Protection Act (AEPA).

Under the AEPA "animal enterprise terrorism" is a federal offense, so investigations of suspected incidents are handled by the FBI. An animal enterprise is defined as any "commercial or academic enterprise that uses animals for food or fiber production, agriculture, research, or testing." Also included are ventures that utilize animals for entertainment and education: circuses, zoos, aquariums, rodeo (*see* chapter 5: *Circuses and Zoos;* chapter 5: *Rodeos*), and agricultural fairs and expositions.

Interestingly, this definition of covered entities is broader than that found in the Animal Welfare Act (AWA)(*see* this chapter: *Animal Welfare Act*), the federal animal protection law. The AWA specifically excludes animals used in rodeos and on farms and fairs from its protections, yet the AEPA criminalizes attempts to free the animals confined in these substantially unregulated enterprises. Similarly, while the AEPA does not limit the reference of the term "animal" by defining it, AWA regulations do offer a definition, but it is one that leaves out mice, rats, birds, and all invertebrates (though this may change; *see* this chapter: *Animal Welfare Act Regulations: Laboratory Animals*). Thus, the user of virtually any animal is covered by the AEPA even though many creatures are not protected by the AWA.

The AEPA outlaws any activities, including using the United States mail, that cause or are intended to cause "physical disruption to the functioning of an animal enterprise" resulting in economic damage exceeding $10,000. Explicitly banned are damaging, destroying, or removing property belonging to the animal enterprise, including any records and the animals themselves. Also included as economic damage are the cost of repeating an experiment when data are obliterated, or any loss of profits that might result from vandalizing the facility, so long as these are at least $10,000. Losses of less than this figure do not activate the AEPA, though state laws are typically applicable, and more than two-thirds of the states have them.

A special provision exempts the disclosure of improprieties at an animal enterprise from qualifying as an illegal "physical disruption." Thus, a whistleblower employed by the enterprise, or any other person, whose revelations undoubtedly hamper its operation to a greater or lesser extent would not be considered a "terrorist" under this act, so long as the disclosure is done lawfully.

Punishment for violation of the AEPA consists of a fine and one year in prison or both. The act also allows for aggravating circumstances that enhance the penalty and permits restitution. If a person is seriously injured as a result of the disruption of an animal enterprise, the prison sentence may be increased to as many as ten years; should the disruption cause the death of a person, the offender may be imprisoned for life or "for any term of years." Moreover, an offender may have to pay the costs of repeating an experiment that he or she disrupted or invalidated, and provide restitution for any economic loss suffered to food production or farm income.

After the AEPA

Through 1999 there had yet to be any prosecutions under the AEPA. Nonetheless, incidents of vandalism at research facilities steadily declined during the 1990s as institutions have spent millions of dollars on security systems, evidently presenting an effective deterrent. These incidents have declined, but not disappeared.

At this writing, the most recent major raid on a lab took place at the University of Minnesota in April 1999. ALF members reportedly caused $3.5 million in damage to computers and research equipment, while absconding with more than 100 mice, rats, pigeons, and salamanders. As they have done many times in the past, the vandals videotaped themselves in the course of the destruction, dressed in black from head to toe; the tape was then released to the press. Also in accord with their *modus operandi*, slogans were spray-painted on the walls of the lab, including "Stop Killing Animals . . . or else." At a press conference following the raid, an individual claiming to speak for the ALF was accused of condoning terrorism. In response, the spokesperson pointed out that during the 1800s those who engaged in unlawful activities on behalf of slaves were also regarded as terrorists.

During the 1990s, ALF members shifted their attention away from the labs, stealthily treading a path of less resistance. In a campaign dubbed "Operation Bite Back," the focus increasingly turned to fur farming, beginning with the 1991 raids on the government fur operations mentioned above. The attacks escalated during the last quarter of 1995, with raids on two ranches in British Columbia and the release of over 7,000 mink. The ALF hit two U.S. farms shortly thereafter, the Jordan Mink Farm in Olympia, Washington, which lost 400 animals, and the McEllis Fur Farm, where 30 foxes were turned loose into the Tennessee hills. The ALF contends that "liberated" mink and fox are not domesticated, so they are typically released into the wild rather than placed in the homes of supporters, as is done with stolen rats, mice, dogs, cats, and other laboratory animals.

In January 1996 another 400 mink were set free, this time from the Zimbal Minkery of Sheboygan, Wisconsin. Over the next several months, the ALF claimed responsibility for no less than a dozen raids on fur farms in eight different states and in British Columbia again, actions that culminated in November 1996 when the Alaska Fur Company in Minnesota was set ablaze, and nearly $2 million in furs were incinerated. Assaults on fur farms continued through the remainder of the 1990s. Highlights included a May 1997 raid in Oregon that saw 10,000 mink freed, a ten-day spree in August 1998 at farms in Minnesota, Iowa, and Wisconsin, where a total of over 12,000 mink left their opened cages, an August 1999 attack on Krieger's Fur Farm in Bristol, Wisconsin, which lost 3,000 mink, and the next month 100 foxes released from a Chandler, Minnesota, fur farm. September 2000 saw the largest raid yet, when 14,000 mink were turned out of their cages at the Earl Drewelow & Sons Fur Farm in New Hampton, Iowa.

Among this series of raids in the late 1990s were the activities of Justin Samuel and Peter Young, two ALF soldiers who released hundreds of mink from several farms in Wisconsin and South Dakota during October 1997. Young remains a fugitive at this writing, but Samuel has achieved the dubious distinction of being the first individual tried and convicted under the AEPA. Apprehended in Belgium and extradited to the United States, Samuel pled guilty in exchange for the dropping of felony charges, and received the maximum misdemeanor sentence of two years in a federal penitentiary. As an aggravating circumstance to justify enhancing the penalty, the district court magistrate cited dozens of letters received from fur farmers describing how they live in fear of being "victimized" by the ALF. In addition, Samuel must pay $364,106 in restitution to the owners of the farms he and Young raided.

DISSECTION

The word "dissection" derives from the Latin verb *dissecare*, meaning to cut apart or to cut up. The dissection of vertebrate and invertebrate organisms has been a standard exercise in the biology classes of American colleges since at least the 1920s, and seems to have begun in the 1880s. By the 1950s most high school biology classes also featured units on dissection, and today junior high school and even elementary school students routinely cut up dead animals as part of their education. Recent polls indicate that as many as three out of every four Americans under retirement age participated in this exercise at some point during their schooling. The main educational goal of dissection is to have students acquire knowledge about the anatomy and physiology of certain species, and animals generally, in a very immediate and real way, a "hands-on" learning experience that many believe is superior to reading written descriptions or looking at drawings or photographs.

The number of animal corpses dissected in U.S. classrooms each year is not known. No state or federal law requires schools or suppliers to report how many dead creatures they use or sell. Few estimates have been offered, but probably one of the most credible puts the total at about 6 million vertebrates in secondary education, and perhaps 4 million in college, with frogs (*Rana* spp.) accounting for better than half of the 10 million. The remainder includes fetal pigs, dogs, cats, minks, rabbits, rats, mice, pigeons, salamanders, snakes, turtles, lampreys, and several kinds of fish. At least as many invertebrates are dissected, principally crayfish, locusts, clams, starfish, and various species of worm. Parts of animals are also cut up in lab classes, mainly the eyes, hearts, and lungs of cattle, and the brains and other internal organs of sheep.

The animal bodies are purchased by American schools from biological supply companies such as WARD'S, Nasco, Fisher Scientific, Nebraska Scientific, and the Carolina Biological Supply Company. The suppliers obtain the animals from a number of different sources. Frogs, the most common dissection subject, are almost invariably captured in the wild, mostly from areas along the west coast of Mexico. They may be killed by the supplier and preserved on the premises or shipped alive in barrels to the schools, were the teachers or students kill them. Most often, the corpses of dogs and cats are purchased from animal control facilities—pounds primarily, and a few shelters—where they have been euthanized as unwanted pets (*see* chapter 3: *Animal Control Facilities*). Skinned mink and rabbit carcasses usually originate on fur farms, sometimes with other animal breeders who provide them along with the rodent species. Fetal pigs, as well as the body parts from cows and sheep, come from slaughterhouses.

Legal Regulation of Suppliers and Schools
Neither federal nor state laws have a significant impact on the biological supply companies that provide animals for dissection or on the schools that use them in their classes.

Animal dealers are subject to the legal requirements of the federal Animal Welfare Act and its implementing regulations (AWA)(*see* this chapter: *Animal Welfare Act;* this chapter: *Animal Welfare Act Regulations: Animal Dealers*). The AWA defines a "dealer" as "any person who in commerce, for compensation or profit, . . . buys, or sells, or negotiates the purchase or sale of: Any dog or other animal whether alive or dead (including unborn animals, organs, limbs, . . . or other parts) for research [or] teaching." According to the AWA, biological supply companies are animal dealers and must be licensed as such (a "class B" license). Nonetheless, this law barely touches these firms.

First, the "other animal" mentioned in the definition of dealer refers to the meaning of "animal" as given in AWA regulations, not any ordinary meaning of the term. Federal regulations stipulate that this word specifically *excludes* rats, mice, birds, reptiles, amphibians, fish, and all invertebrates (*see* this chapter: *Animal Welfare Act Regulations: Laboratory Animals*). These species account for at least 90 percent of the animals sold in the United States for dissection.

Furthermore, even though the definition of dealer does include those who trade in dead animals, and not just live ones, the predominant focus of AWA restrictions is to provide for the humane treatment of the animals used in laboratories, whether in a research facility or a school (the standards also apply to most animal exhibitions, but not rodeos; *see* chapter 5: *Circuses and Zoos;* chapter 5: *Rodeos*). Humane care is obviously not relevant to the handling of a corpse. Therefore, only supply companies holding *live* dogs, cats, and rabbits are subject to the standards for humane treatment that the AWA imposes on regulated entities. Applicable state laws have the same narrow scope.

Accurate information on the company procedures of these operations is very difficult to come by, but it appears that few if any of the firms supplying specimens for dissection keep or sell living animals on the premises—that is, "animals" as defined by the AWA. In 1991 Carolina Biological Supply Company (CBSC), the largest one of its kind in the United States today, was charged with ten violations of the AWA, with most of the counts related to the treatment of live cats. Although the company was eventually fined for committing some of the infractions, they mainly concerned record-keeping requirements—the primary AWA duties for dealers in dead animals—not the handling of the cats. Today at their Burlington, North Carolina, facilities CBSC does not house, take possession of, or offer for sale living animals that are protected by AWA regulations. This seems to be the prevailing if not exclusive practice of these businesses.

For their part, the AWA and similar state laws specifically exempt all elementary and secondary schools from any of their requirements and restrictions on the use of animals, alive or dead. As originally written, the AWA also exempted the care and handling of animals in postsecondary education, but a rule issued in 1989 brought colleges and universities under the purview of the law. Even so, once again, legal standards for humane treatment are not applicable to dead animals, in whatever institutional setting this may occur.

Legal Rights of Students

For better than sixty years, with little if any protest, generations of students more or less willingly cut up millions of dead vertebrate and invertebrate animals. Certainly, squeamishness of varying degrees led an unknown number of pupils, and perhaps some of their parents, to discussions with science teachers on the need for the exercise, but no one ever took the matter to court.

No one until Jenifer Graham came along in the spring of 1987. At that time, Jenifer was a fifteen-year-old high school sophomore in Victorville, California, a medium-sized city about an hour northeast of Los Angeles. She was confronted there with a biology class requirement that demanded the dissection of a frog. Already a vegetarian who would not wear leather or use consumer products tested on animals, Jenifer decided that on moral grounds she must decline to participate in a procedure that involved the harming and death of a sentient creature. The school rejected her suggestion that she perform some alternative study that did not involve killing an animal, and awarded her a "D" for the class, even though all her other coursework was of "A" caliber. The grade was later grudgingly changed to a "C," but, aided by the Humane Society of the United States, Jenifer had already decided to sue.

In her lawsuit, filed in the federal district court in Los Angeles, Jenifer argued that her moral objections to dissection are tantamount to religious beliefs, so requiring her to cut up a frog violated her right to the free exercise of religion, as guaranteed by the First Amendment (for more on freedom of religion and the use of animals, *see* chapter 4: *Legal Challenges to Ritual Slaughter*). The high school countered that California colleges and universities required dissection for admission. In August 1988, after announcing that dissection was not required by the state education system, the court dismissed the case and ordered the school to provide Jenifer with a frog that had died of natural causes to complete the dissection portion of the course, and to award her an "A" grade. This attempt at compromise—which upholds both Jenifer's right to refuse dissection and the school's insistence on the necessity of using real frogs rather than models—ultimately failed. By the time Jenifer graduated in 1989, predictably, the school had not found a naturally deceased frog.

Meanwhile, animal protection organizations were instrumental in drafting a bill for consideration by the California state legislature that would entitle students to refuse to participate in dissections. Jenifer Graham's testimony in favor of the bill proved critical to its passage, and in March 1988 Governor George Deukmejian signed the Student's Rights Bill into law.

Effective the following January, the new law applies to public education in kindergarten through the twelfth grade, and entitles "any pupil with a moral objection to dissecting . . . animals, or any parts thereof, . . . [to] choose to refrain from participation in an education project involving harmful or destructive use of animals." A parent or guardian of the student must substantiate the protest, and any teacher requiring dissection in a course must inform his or her students of their rights under this law. However, California also gives its teachers the discretion to reject the student's objection: "if the teacher believes that an adequate alternative education project is possible, the teacher may work with the pupil to develop and agree upon an alternative." Presumably, if the instructor does not believe that there is an acceptable alternative, the student will not be excused from the dissection exercise. If another course of study is settled upon, it cannot be more difficult than the dissection or wielded as a form of punishment for the dissident student, nor does California allow discrimination against those who object.

Jenifer Graham's protest generated quite a bit of notoriety—every major media outlet in the country reported it, Jenifer appeared in a commercial for Apple computers inspired by the controversy, and a made-for-TV movie depicting her story aired within two years. Perhaps for this reason, it is widely believed that California's was the first "choice-in-dissection" law enacted by a state legislature. In fact, Florida had passed a similar, though far less focused and detailed law three years earlier in 1985. Only two sentences in the Florida statute address the issue, providing that with the written request of a parent or guardian, students "may be excused" from dissections and experiments on "non-living mammals or birds . . . or on non-living non-mammalian vertebrates." No alternative projects, moral objections or their substantiation, or protections against penalization are mentioned. Teacher discretion is suggested by the phrasing that a pupil "may be excused," instead of the standard language of legal duty demanding that something "shall be" done.

By 2000 five other states had enacted right-to-choose laws, bringing the total to seven: Louisiana, Pennsylvania, New York, Rhode Island, and Illinois, along with Florida and California. An eighth state, Maine, was unable to gather enough votes in the legislature to pass a bill of this nature, but in 1989 the Maine Department of Education made it their official policy to excuse students from dissection who do not wish to participate and to provide for an alternative project. New Jersey may become the ninth state: a bill requiring schools to provide alternative projects for students who choose not to dissect was introduced in July 2000. A similar bill proposed about the same time in the state of Washington legislature died in committee. Although there is as yet no legal requirement throughout the two jurisdictions, numerous elementary and secondary schools in Massachusetts and Connecticut have already adopted policies that give their students a choice. Chicago public schools had done the same before the Illinois state law was passed in late 1999.

To date, Pennsylvania's Right of Refusal law is the most rigorous, requiring both public and private schools to notify students and their parents or guardian before classes begin of the "right to decline to participate in an education project [or test] involving harmful or destructive use of animals." Further, students who do refuse must be offered an alternative course of study or examination, which includes videotapes, models, films, books, and computers. Such students cannot be disadvantaged or punished in any manner as a result of exercising their right to choose, and Pennsylvania teachers have no discretion to overrule a pupil's objections. Despite this stringency, Pennsylvania's law provides the right to refuse dissections only of vertebrate animals and not those involving invertebrates; grasshopper dissections, for example, cannot be evaded there. Rhode Island and Maine are the only states whose laws apply to the cutting apart of species from both phyla of the animal kingdom.

Currently, there is no federal right-to-choose law, and none has ever been introduced in Congress.

Alternatives to Dissection

Maryland does not at this writing legally entitle students to opt out of dissection procedures, however the Old Line state does require school boards to educate their pupils about alternatives to dissection, and how they can avail themselves of these opportunities. In the absence of an express right to choose without penalty such options over dissection, this requirement seems toothless, but its emphasis on alternatives can powerfully undermine the notion that nothing but the slicing of real "live," dead animals will serve the pedagogical goals of science. None of the current state laws demand that any particular alternative be utilized, but there are hundreds of them to choose from, mostly computer-based programs available on CD-ROM.

For example, the *DissectionWorks* program from ScienceWorks, Pierian Spring Software's *BioLab* series, and Tangent Scientific's *DryLab* series display the dissection of "virtual" pigs, cats, frogs, fish, and other species, including invertebrates, with the student using the computer mouse to control simulated cutting. *Digital Frog* and *CatLab* offer similar capabilities in programs focused entirely on these two species. Additionally, several companies offer amazingly elaborate and "lifelike" three-dimensional models in molded plastic of many of the commonly dissected species, as well as various internal organs. Numerous series of videotaped dissections are also available, showing in graphic detail the procedure done on cats, rats, fetal pigs, pigeons, frogs, crayfish, perch, earthworms, and pig hearts and sheep brains.

Comparative analyses that focused on the respective pedagogical effectiveness and cost of dissections and alternatives have revealed that the nondestructive options stand up very well. During the 1990s, a dozen different studies of students in secondary and postsecondary education in the United States and the United Kingdom indicated no significant differences in test scores or lab performances between those who participated in dissections and those who used computers, videos, models, or simply listened to lectures. In a few cases the pupils who did not dissect performed better than their cutting classmates.

Moreover, in at least some circumstances, the alternatives appear to be the more cost-effective option as well. For example, Carolina Biological Supply Company currently sells dead frogs at $8 each. Assuming one frog for every two students, and an average class size of thirty, this represents an investment of $120 for each class. A *Digital Frog* CD-ROM now costs $150, and perhaps five or six of them would be needed to serve a class of the same size, totaling, say, $900. But, of course, the computer program represents a long-term investment in material that will be used over and over again in many classes for years, while the dead frogs will be a continuing cost, one that will exceed the price of the CD-ROMs after just eight classes. The savings are even more pronounced when the *Cat-Lab* CD-ROM—at $50 each—is compared to the CBSC price for dead cats—$35 each. Using the same assumptions, the initial expenditure for *CatLab* is cheaper than buying the cat carcasses for our hypothetical science class.

REFERENCES

Federal Laws
Animal Enterprise Protection Act of 1992, 18 U.S.C. § 43.
Animal Welfare Act of 1970, 7 U.S.C. §§ 2131–2157.
Consumer Product Safety Act of 1972, 15 U.S.C. § 2051.
Federal Hazardous Substances Act, 15 U.S.C. § 1261.
Food, Drug, and Cosmetic Act of 1938, 21 U.S.C. §§ 301–392.
Freedom of Information Act, 5 U.S.C. § 552.
NIH Revitalization Act of 1993, 42 U.S.C. § 283e.

Federal Regulations
Animal Welfare, 9 C.F.R. Chapter 1, Subchapter A.
Definitions, §1.1
Environmental enhancement to promote psychological well-being of primates, § 3.81
Exercise for dogs, § 3.8
Handling of animals, § 2.131.
Institutional Animal Care and Use Committee, § 2.31
Research facilities, §§ 2.30–38
Standards for humane handling, care, treatment, and transportation, §§ 3.1–42 (Part 3)
Dogs, §§ 3.1–19
Marine mammals, §§ 3.100–118
Nonhuman primates, §§ 3.75–92
Warmblooded animals other than dogs, cats . . . , §§ 3.125
Veterinary care, § 2.40

Federal Register
Draft Policy on Environmental Enhancement for Nonhuman Primates, 64 Fed. Reg. 38,145–38,150 (July 15, 1999).
Licensing Requirement for Dogs and Cats, Decision and Policy Statement, 64 Fed. Reg. 137: 38,546–38,548 (July 19, 1999).
Notice of Petition for Rulemaking to Amend the Definition of 'Animal' in 9 C.F.R. § 1.1, Animal Welfare, 64 Fed. Reg. 18: 4356–4367 (Jan. 28, 1999).
Solid Resting Surfaces for Dogs and Cats, Final Rule, 64 Fed. Reg. 75: 19,251–19,254 (April 20, 1999).

State Laws
California, Pupil with moral objection to dissection, Cal. Educ. Code § 32255.
Florida, Education, Biological experiments on living subjects, Fla. Stat. Ann. § 233.0674.
Illinois, Dissection Alternative Act, 105 Ill. Comp. Stat. 112/1.
Mississippi, Mississippi Department of Wildlife, Fisheries and Parks, Regulations for inherently dangerous animals, Public Notice 3523.002.
New York, Education, Dissection of animals, N.Y. Educ. Law § 17 S 809.4.
Pennsylvania, Pupil's right of refusal; animal dissection, Pa. Cons. Stat. § 15-1523.
Rhode Island, Animal dissection and vivisection, right to refuse, R.I. Gen. Laws § 16-22-20.

Federal Cases
Circuit Courts of Appeals
  Animal Legal Defense Fund v. Espy (ALDF v. Espy I), 23 F.3rd 496 (D.C. Cir. 1994).
  Animal Legal Defense Fund v. Espy (ALDF v. Espy II), 29 F.3d 720 (D.C. Cir. 1994).
  Animal Legal Defense Fund v. Glickman (ALDF v. Glickman I), 154 F.3d 426 (D.C. Cir. 1998).
  Animal Legal Defense Fund v. Glickman (ALDF v. Glickman II), 204 F.3d 229 (D.C. Cir. 2000)(unreported case at press time).
  International Primate Protection League v. Institute for Behavioral Research, Inc., 799 F.2d 934 (4th Cir. 1986), *cert. denied*, 481 U.S. 1004 (1987).
  International Primate Protection League v. Administrators of the Tulane Educational Fund, 895 F.2d 1056 (5th Cir. 1990), *reversed*, 500 U.S. 72 (1991).
  Lesser v. Espy, 34 F.3d 1301 (7th Cir. 1994).
  Toney v. Glickman, 101 F.3d 1236 (8th Cir. 1996).

District Courts
Alternatives Research & Development Foundation v. Glickman, 101 F.
Supp. 2d 7 (D. D.C. 2000).
Animal Legal Defense Fund v. Glickman, 943 F. Supp 54 (D. D.C. 1996).

State Cases
New York
*American Society for the Prevention of Cruelty to Animals v. Board of
Trustees*, 591 N.E.2d 1169 (N.Y. 1992).

North Carolina
Students for the Ethical Treatment of Animals v. Huffines, 420 S.E.2d 674
(N.C. Ct. App. 1992).

Oregon
*People for the Ethical Treatment of Animals v. Institutional Animal Care
and Use Committee*, 817 P.2d 1299 (1991).

Vermont
*Animal Legal Defense Fund v. Institutional Animal Care and Use
Committee*, 616 A.2d 224 (Vt. 1992).

Books
Balcombe, Jonathan. 2000. *The Use of Animals in Higher Education.* Wash-
ington, DC: Humane Society Press.
Bentham, Jeremy. [1780] 1996. *Introduction to the Principles of Morals and
Legislation.* New York: Oxford University Press.
Bernard, Claude. [1865] 1980. *An Introduction to the Study of Experimental
Medicine.* Translated by Henry Copley Green. Birmingham, AL: Clas-
sics of Medicine Library.
Blum, Deborah. 1994. *The Monkey Wars.* New York: Oxford University
Press.
Branigan, Cynthia A. 1997. *The Reign of the Greyhound.* New York: Howell
Book House.
Brooman, Simon, and Debbie Legge. 1997. *Law Relating to Animals.* Lon-
don: Cavendish.
Darwin, Charles. [1871] 1950. *The Descent of Man and Selection in Relation
to Sex.* New York: P. F. Collier.
Fano, Alix. 1997. *Lethal Laws.* New York: Zed Books.
Finsen, Lawrence, and Susan Finsen. 1994. *The Animal Rights Movement in
America: From Compassion to Respect.* New York: Twayne.
Francione, Gary L. 1995. *Animals, Property, and the Law.* Philadelphia:
Temple University Press.

Frasch, Pamela D., et al. 2000. *Animal Law.* Durham, NC: Carolina Academic Press.

Garner, Robert. 1998. *Political Animals: Animal Protection Politics in Britain and the United States.* New York: St. Martin's.

Ogden, Tom. 1993. *Two Hundred Years of the American Circus.* New York: Facts On File.

Orlans, F. Barbara. 1993. *In the Name of Science.* New York: Oxford University Press.

Orlans, F. Barbara, et al. 1998. *The Human Use of Animals.* New York: Oxford University Press.

Pacheco, Alex, and Anna Francione. 1985. "The Silver Spring Monkeys." In *In Defense of Animals.* Edited by Peter Singer. New York: Blackwell.

Rudacille, Deborah. 2000. *The Scalpel and the Butterfly: The War between Animal Research and Animal Protection.* New York: Farrar, Straus and Giroux.

Rupke, Nicolaas A., ed. 1987. *Vivisection in Historical Perspective.* London: Routledge.

Stevens, Christine. 1990. "Laboratory Animals." In *Animals and Their Legal Rights.* 4th ed. Washington, DC: Animal Welfare Institute.

Welsh, Heidi J. 1990. *Animal Testing and Consumer Products.* Washington, DC: Investor Responsibility Research Center.

Articles, Guidelines, and Reports

"ALF Action." *The Animals' Agenda,* bimonthly continuing feature.

American Veterinary Medical Association. 1993. "1993 Report of the AVMA Panel on Euthanasia." *Journal of the American Veterinary Medical Association* 202: 229–249.

Church, Jill Howard. 1997. "The Business of Animal Research" *The Animals' Agenda* 17, no. 4 (July/August): 30–32.

Cohen, Henry. 1987. "The Legality of the Agriculture Department's Exclusion of Rats and Mice from Coverage under the Animal Welfare Act." *St. Louis University Law Journal* 31: 543–549.

Department of Justice, Criminal Division. 1993. *Report to Congress on the Extent and Effects of Domestic and International Terrorism on Animal Enterprises.*

Detweiler, Rachelle. 2000. "Animals Spared by HPV Concession." *The Animals' Agenda* 20, no. 1 (January/February): 11–12.

Kniaz, Laura G. 1995. "Animal Liberation and the Law: Animals Board the Underground Railroad." *Buffalo Law Review* 43: 765–834.

National Institutes of Health. 1992. *Institutional Animal Care and Use Committee Guidebook.* NIH publication no. 92–3415.

National Research Council. 1996. *Guide for the Care and Use of Laboratory Animals.* National Academy Press.

Rowan, Andrew. 1990. "Ethical Review and the Animal Care and Use Committee." *Hasting Center Report* Special Supplement (May/June): 19–24.

Steneck, Nicholas H. 1997. "Role of Institutional Animal Care and Use Committees in Monitoring Research." *Ethics & Behavior* 7: 173–184.

Weiss, Rick. 2000. "Animal Regulations to Expand." *The Washington Post,* 3 October, at A23.

———. 2000. "Bill Rider Would Nullify Animal Rights Legal Victory." *The Washington Post,* 11 October, at A29.

World Wide Web

Animal and Plant Health Inspection Service (APHIS), USDA, http://www.aphis.gov.

Animal Care, http://www.aphis.gov/ac/.

Animal Extremist/Ecoterror Crimes, http://www.furcommission.com/attack.

Animal Liberation Front, http://www.animalliberationfront.com/.

Charles River Laboratories, http://www.criver.com.

Humane Society of the United States, http://www.hsus.org.

National Institutes of Health, http://www.nih.gov.

Office of Laboratory Animal Welfare, http://grants.nih.gov/grants/olaw/olaw.htm.

Policy on Humane Care and Use of Laboratory Animals, http://grants.nih.gov/grants/olaw/references/phspol.htm.

Public Health Service, http://www.dhhs.gov/phs.

State Primate Regulations, http://www.monkeyzone.com/regulati.htm.

Appendix 1:
Animal Organizations

There are thousands of "animal organizations" in America, when this phrase is taken to refer widely to collections of people who have formed groups focusing on issues pertaining to nonhumans. A large majority of these organizations, including hundreds of "Societies for the Prevention of Cruelty to Animals," operate within a particular geographical region of the country, usually a city, county, or state. Only a tiny percentage of them are directly involved with legal issues, either as litigants in court or through active lobbying of legislators. Overwhelmingly, animal organizations are locally oriented, with an immediate emphasis on influencing the attitudes and actions of the general public, not those of lawmakers and judges. They are parochial activists and educators, not players in the nation's legal arena.

This appendix alphabetically lists only the major animal organizations that are actively engaged in legal matters at the national level. Due to this focus, some groups that are importantly involved in some dimensions of animal law are excluded here. For example, Farm Sanctuary has been very active in courts and legislatures, but this has been mainly at the state level, such as pressing for the enforcement of anticruelty laws in stockyards and sponsoring a California law protecting downed livestock. Similarly, the American Feed Industry Association (AFIA) has a powerful lobbying force in Washington, D.C., influencing such items as taxation on livestock feed ingredients and FDA approval of drug additives, but the AFIA is not strictly speaking an "animal organization" and does not operate within the legal system on issues related to animal welfare.

Most of the national organizations working in animal law concentrate on protecting animals, with some going so far as to advocate abolishing the use of animals for many or for all human purposes; a minority are dedicated to promoting human interests in using animals, and resisting legal efforts to restrict those uses.

The following organizations are listed alphabetically, and include a brief description of the orientation of each and a few representative legal accomplishments. Contact information is also provided. All website

URLs are prefixed by http://www. All quotations are taken from organizational mission statements or other promotional material.

American Anti-Vivisection Society (AAVS)
Founded in 1883 by Caroline Earle White (who had cofounded the first American animal shelter in Philadelphia a decade earlier), the AAVS initially attempted to establish legal regulations on the use of animals in laboratories. Within a few years, the organization hardened their stance and since that time the AAVS has advocated the legal abolition of all research, testing, and experimentation using animals. The AAVS was a powerful lobbying force behind the enactment of both the Animal Welfare Act and amendments to this law establishing increased protections for primates. More recently, through its scientific branch, the Alternatives Research and Development Foundation, the organization has been deeply involved in legal efforts to change the regulatory definition of "animal" under the Animal Welfare Act to include mice, rats, and birds. In 1997, AAVS petitioned the U.S. Department of Agriculture to prohibit the production of monoclonal antibodies (MAbs) in all U.S. laboratories; MAbs are produced by creating tumors in mice. The AAVS also petitioned the National Institutes of Health (NIH) to end such production and use in all NIH-funded experiments. In 1999 the agency announced that all NIH-funded researchers will be directed to consider in vitro methods as the default method when producing MAbs.
 Address 801 Old York Rd., Suite 204, Jenkintown, PA 19046
 Phone 215-887-0816
 Web aavs.org

American Humane Association (AHA)
The AHA is a network of humane societies, animal shelters, and animal control offices "working to prevent cruelty, abuse, neglect and exploitation of animals, and to ensure that their interests and well-being are fully, effectively, and humanely guaranteed." Among other campaigns, the AHA strives to provide alternatives to animal testing and participated in the drafting of legislation to create the Inter-Agency Coordinating Committee for the Validation of Alternative Methods, a vehicle to encourage the use of alternative testing among federal agencies. Along with Defenders of Wildlife, the AHA has sued the Department of Commerce to prevent the weakening of regulations for dolphin-safe tuna. The organization has also worked to protect downed livestock and amend the Animal Welfare Act to prohibit the interstate transportation of fighting roosters. Further, the AHA has lobbied for bills that have yet to be approved by Congress, such as those establishing protections for veal calves, providing for the humane slaughter of chickens, and prohibiting the steel-jaw leghold trap.

Address 63 Inverness Dr. East, Englewood, CO 80112-5117
Phone 800-227-4645
Web americanhumane.org

American Meat Institute (AMI)

"Dedicated to increasing the efficiency, profitability and safety of meat and poultry trade worldwide," the AMI was founded in 1906 in Chicago, Illinois, mainly as a response to the passage of the Federal Meat Inspection Act. The organization was originally called the American Meat Packers Association but this was changed in 1940 to the AMI. In 1979 the AMI moved its headquarters from Chicago to Washington, D.C., as legislative affairs and concerns became its top priority. The trade organization represents almost three-quarters of the processors in America's $100-billion meat and poultry industry. In legal affairs, the mission of the AMI is to resist government regulation that its constituent corporations believe to be unduly burdensome. In the domain of animal law, this resistance has included opposition both to the Humane Slaughter Act in 1958 and to amendments to the law proposed in 1978, a decades-long rejection of a federal humane slaughter law for poultry, and opposition to bills designed to protect downed livestock and veal calves. The AMI has also opposed efforts to outlaw the slaughter of downed animals for human consumption. The AMI was a major supporter of the Animal Enterprise Protection Act, which makes property damage at facilities using animals a federal offense.

Address 1700 North Moore St., Suite 1600, Arlington, VA 22209
Phone 703-841-2400
Web meatami.org

American Medical Association (AMA)

The AMA was formed in 1847 at the Academy of Natural Sciences in Philadelphia to act as a unified voice for physicians across the country striving to advance the "art and science of medicine." Today the AMA has over 250,000 members. Although the AMA is not an "animal organization" and has no wide interests in the domain of animal law, it has been a powerful force for ensuring that animals remain available for use in the laboratories of scientists, physicians, and educators with as little government regulation as possible. As long ago as the 1890s, the AMA adamantly opposed the first bills introduced into Congress to restrict the use of animals in laboratories, and in 1908 it established the Council for the Defense of Medical Research specifically to answer opponents of lab animal use. This resistance continued into the 1960s against the proposals on Capitol Hill that would become the Animal Welfare Act (AWA). The AMA also resisted amendments in the 1980s to strengthen the AWA, in particular requirements to provide for the psychological well-being of primates. Over the course of more than a century, perhaps no group has been more effective in limiting legal protections for laboratory animals than the AMA.

Address   515 N. State St., Chicago, IL 60610
Phone   312-464-4394
Web   ama-assn.org

American Society for the Prevention of Cruelty to Animals (ASPCA)
The ASPCA began in 1866, when Henry Bergh, inspired by the model of the Royal Society for the Prevention of Cruelty to Animals, received a charter of incorporation from the New York State legislature. Since that time, the mission of the ASPCA has remained essentially unchanged: Through its Government Affairs Department, the ASPCA works on "the need for laws regarding animal cruelty, the necessity for stronger penalties for existing laws, and the need to license and regulate certain industries and businesses that use animals." The ASPCA is not an abolitionist organization. It drafts and obtains sponsors for the introduction of federal, state, and municipal legislation; petitions legislators and government officials for their support; and assists other animal welfare organizations in the passage of legislation. The department also runs a legislative alert program, informing members of the public about issues affecting animals in their states and about how they can urge their representatives to take appropriate action. The ASPCA has aided in the strengthening of basic anticruelty laws in many states; helped ban or restrict forms of hunting and trapping; limited the use of animals for experimentation by elementary school students; and promoted the humane use of animals in food production, including a federal ban on the marketing of downed animals.

Address   424 E. 92nd St., New York, NY 10128
Phone   212-876-7700
Web   aspca.org

Animal Legal Defense Fund (ALDF)
Founded in 1979, the ALDF has established a network of over 700 attorneys fighting to protect and promote animal interests through legal action. The ALDF is the preeminent animal organization working in federal courts all over the country to protect nonhumans in every dimension of animal use. Among many other cases, the organization has directed a 1991 lawsuit demanding that the USDA write rules to safeguard the psychological well-being of primates used in research and ensure exercise for dogs confined in labs; a landmark victory in 1999 over "legal standing," giving animal rights advocates the right to challenge federal agencies

over treatment of animals under the Animal Welfare Act; and, in 2000, legal challenges to the roundup of wild horses by the Bureau of Land Management in Wyoming and Utah. The ALDF has also written model laws for state or city ordinances banning the sale of fur, state anticruelty statutes, state endangered species acts, state leghold trap restrictions, state marine mammal captivity standards, and pet protection ordinances. The organization publishes the *Attorney Update*, a regular bulletin of animal law cases brought by its attorney members around the country and other newsworthy and precedent-setting litigation.

Address   127 Fourth St., Petaluma, CA 94952
Phone   707-769-7771
Web   aldf.org

Animal Protection Institute (API)

The Animal Protection Institute was founded in 1968 and is dedicated to informing, educating, and advocating the humane treatment of all animals. API has over 82,000 members. Specific areas of concern to the organization include companion animals, wildlife, animal protection legislation, food and fiber animals, animals used in entertainment, animals used in laboratory research, and humane education in schools. API has been very active in promoting the end of the trade in bear parts throughout the country and the world by supporting the Bear Protection Act, a bill pending in Congress that would prohibit all forms of bear-part trade, importation, and exportation. In 1997, API, joined by the Fund for Animals, successfully sued the Bureau of Land Management, forcing the agency to reform its requirements for adopting wild horses to prevent them from being sold into slaughter for pet food or meat by those who adopt them.

Address   P.O. Box 22505, Sacramento, CA 95822
Phone   916-731-5521
Web   api4animals.org

Animal Welfare Institute (AWI)

Christine Stevens and her father, Robert Gesell, founded the AWI in 1951, primarily out of their dissatisfaction with the established animal protection community of the time. The AWI works specifically for the humane treatment of laboratory animals, a ban on steel-jaw leghold traps, the prevention of trade in wild-caught exotic birds, the preservation of species threatened by extinction, the reform of cruel treatment of farm animals (such as intensive confinement in factory farms), and the encouragement of humane science teaching and prevention of painful experiments on animals in schools. The Society for Animal Protective Legislation (SAPL) is the companion organization to the AWI and performs its legal tasks. Among its many accomplishments, the SAPL played an essential role both in winning congressional approval of the Humane Slaughter Act in 1958 and in strengthening the law with amendments in 1978; worked for the passage of the Marine Mammal Protection Act in 1972; and in 1991 joined other litigants in demanding that the USDA write rules to safeguard the psychological well-being of primates used in research and ensure exercise for dogs confined in labs. In 2000, SAPL helped to pass legislation banning the production of videos depicting animal cruelty. Currently, the Society is working for legislation to prohibit the importation, exportation, and trade of all bear parts, and to ban the use of steel-jaw leghold traps in the United States.

Address   P.O. Box 3650, Georgetown Station, Washington, DC 20007
Phone   202-337-2334
Web   awionline.org

Defenders of Wildlife (DOW)

Founded in 1947, DOW currently has over 140,000 members and supporters. The organization has a staff of forty-six wildlife biologists, attorneys, ecologists, research analysts, educators, and other conservationists. DOW "utilizes litigation, education and research to defend wildlife by forming interdisciplinary teams within its staff to promote multifaceted solutions to wildlife programs." In 1973 the Defenders aided in the passage of the Endangered Species Act (ESA), and has served as a successful plaintiff on behalf of endangered species to enforce the ESA; DOW has also developed and proposed legislation to eliminate threats to the ESA. Although the organization focuses on the ESA, DOW has also effectively promoted legal protections for dolphins, and a requirement to use "dolphin-safe" labeling on tuna containers. DOW and several other animal welfare organizations successfully sued the Fish and Wildlife Service (FWS) and Interior secretary Bruce Babbitt to help protect the Florida manatee from extinction. The FWS was charged with failing to implement and enforce existing laws, which resulted in increasing and dangerous numbers of manatee deaths and the loss and degradation of manatee habitat. The FWS is now designating extensive new manatee refuges and sanctuaries throughout Florida and adopting new regulations under the Marine Mammal Protection Act. DOW has also spearheaded efforts to reintroduce the endangered gray wolf in Yellowstone National Park and in Arizona and New Mexico.

Address   1101 14th St. NW, #1400, Washington, DC 20005
Phone   202-682-9400
Web   defenders.org

Doris Day Animal League (DDAL)

The DDAL was founded in 1987 by actress Doris Day, whose long history of working with and for animals began in the early 1970s when she cofounded Actors and Others for Animals. She also established the Doris Day Pet Foundation in 1977 to provide homes for unwanted animals, organize free spaying and neutering programs, and provide medical attention to pets whose families needed financial aid. The DDAL is a lobbying organization devoted to enforcing existing laws, promoting new legislation, and encouraging the public to get involved in the legal process. The legislation recently passed to establish the Inter-Agency Coordinating Committee for the Validation for Alternative Methods was largely supported and promoted by the DDAL. California representative Elton Gallegly, the major sponsor of successful legislation outlawing depictions of animal cruelty, became aware of "crush videos" when the DDAL informed him about these depictions.

Address 227 Massachusetts Ave. NE, Suite 100, Washington, DC 20002
Phone 202-546-1761
Web ddal.org

Fund for Animals
Cleveland Amory founded the Fund for Animals in 1967, serving as the Fund's president without pay for eleven years. In 1974 Amory wrote *Man Kind? Our Incredible War on Wildlife*, which has been widely credited with launching the antihunting movement in the United States. While the Fund for Animals strives to protect every animal species through education, litigation, and animal care, its major legal victories have involved protections for wildlife, including support for the Airborne Hunting Act, the Marine Mammal Protection Act, and the Endangered Species Act; successful petitions to add dozens of animals to the list of threatened and endangered species; a 1985 lawsuit blocking the federal government and state of Minnesota from instituting a sport hunting and commercial trapping season on wolves; drafting and promoting a 1992 ballot initiative in Colorado that banned hunting of black bears with dogs or bait; backing of another successful initiative in 1994 that halted trapping on public lands in Arizona; and reaching a legal settlement with the Bureau of Land Management in 1997 to prevent the agency from adopting wild horses to people who plan to sell the horses to slaughter. The Black Beauty Ranch in Texas is the Fund's sanctuary for hundreds of abused and abandoned animals, a refuge established originally to house hundreds of feral burros that the Fund, after winning a court order, had prevented the National Park Service from killing. The ranch provides a home for over 900 animals on its 1,300 acres of hills in eastern Texas. The Fund also runs a Wildlife Rehabilitation Center, a Spay and Neuter Clinic, and a Rabbit Sanctuary.

Address 200 W. 57th St., New York, NY 10019
Phone 212-246-2096
Web fund.org

Humane Society of the United States (HSUS)

The Humane Society of the United States was founded in 1954 to help ensure that "the physical needs of domestic animals are met, wild animals and their environments are protected, and to aid in the treatment of animals overall from exploitation to respect and compassion." The HSUS works through legal, educational, legislative, and investigative means to promote the humane treatment and protection of all animals. During the last forty-seven years, the HSUS has emerged as the world's largest animal protection organization, encompassing nine regional offices, five affiliates, an international arm, 250 staff members—including veterinarians, wildlife biologists, lawyers, animal behaviorists, and other professionals—and seven million members and constituents. The HSUS spends over $1 million each year for lobbying on Capitol Hill. Among its many legal victories on behalf of animals, the HSUS was a major supporter of the Animal Welfare Act, the Humane Methods of Slaughter Act, the Horse Protection Act, and the Marine Mammal Protection Act; worked with legislators in twenty-seven states to establish the mandatory spaying and neutering of animals adopted from shelters; successfully urged four states to pass bans on cockfighting since 1978; initiated a lawsuit in 1985 that halted the commercial slaughter of North Pacific fur seals for their fur; spearheaded the effort to upgrade penalties for animal cruelty, resulting in eighteen states enacting felony-level penalties for animal cruelty since 1986; and in 1999 secured a prohibition of canned hunting in Oregon.

Address   2100 L Street NW, Washington, DC 20037
Phone   202-452-1100
Web   hsus.org

Humane USA PAC

The newest animal organization, established in 2000, Humane USA PAC was formed to promote and elect officials supportive of the humane treatment of animals. This political action committee provides information about state and federal lawmakers regarding their positions on the welfare and treatment of animals as well as house and senate legislation regarding animal protection. This organization also stresses the importance of devoting financial resources to electoral activity in an attempt to ensure the election of animal protection advocates and to influence the composition of federal and state governments. Although it is too new to have recorded any victories in animal law, Humane USA PAC emphasizes legal activity and legislation as the source for animal protection and welfare: "Laws reflect the ethical values of a culture. Lasting change for animals will occur only by creating a body of law that shapes the way people interact with and treat animals."

Address P.O. Box 19224, Washington, DC 20036
Web humaneusa.org

National Association for Biomedical Research (NABR)

The roots of the NABR are found in the Association for Biomedical Research (ABR), set up in 1979 for the purpose of lobbying to promote the interests of researchers using animals. The ABR was established by employees of Charles River Laboratories, the world's largest supplier of lab animals, in response to a New York statute repealing the state's pound seizure law. In the mid 1980s, the ABR changed its name to the NABR. The membership of the organization includes over 350 public and private universities, medical and veterinary schools, teaching hospitals, voluntary health agencies, professional societies, pharmaceutical companies, and other animal research–related firms, among them Putting People First and Americans for Medical Progress. Through its public relations arm, the Foundation for Biomedical Research, the NABR asserts the "vital role of humane animal use in biomedical research, higher education and product safety testing, and strives to ensure that animals used in laboratory research are treated humanely and experience the least amount of pain possible." The NABR has fought attempts in other states to scrap pound seizure laws, and has consistently opposed amendments to strengthen the federal Animal Welfare Act (AWA), including those imposing stricter record-keeping requirements on the sellers of lab animals, extending protections to mice and rats, and providing for the psychological well-being of primates. Most recently, the NABR has in federal court resisted attempts by animal advocates to establish their standing on behalf of lab animals under the AWA.

Address 818 Connecticut Avenue NW, Suite 200,
            Washington, DC 20006
Phone 202-857-0540
Web nabr.org

National Rifle Association (NRA)

The NRA was formed in 1871 by Union Army veterans Colonel William C. Church and General George Wingate to "promote and encourage rifle shooting on a scientific basis." Today, with over two million members and an operating budget of about $100 million, the NRA is among the most politically influential organizations affecting animal law. The NRA has taken an active role in the lives of hunters through its publication of *The American Hunter,* launched in 1973, and its various programs to educate hunters and promote safety. One such program is the Youth Hunter Education Challenge, which continues education with young adults after basic hunter education courses. Through its lobbying arm, the Institute for Legislative Action (ILA), the NRA is the most powerful political force for limiting government regulation of hunting and the use of firearms and for promoting the freedoms of hunters and gun owners. For example, in the domain of animal law, the NRA has supported increased hunting in National Wildlife Refuges; backed an amendment to the Marine Mammal Protection Act to permit sport hunters to import polar bear parts from Canada; and vigorously opposed bans on toxic shot, steel-jaw leghold traps, "canned hunts," and pigeon shoots. The NRA has also supported "Hunters' Rights" amendments in Minnesota, North Dakota, and Virginia, which make any legal prohibition of hunting unconstitutional.

ILA *Address*   1250 Waples Mill Rd., Fairfax, VA 22030-7400
ILA *Phone*   800-392-8683
ILA *Web*   nraila.org

National Trappers Association (NTA)

The NTA is a single-issue organization with a mission "to promote sound conservation, legislation and administrative procedures; to save and faithfully defend from waste the natural resources of the United States; to promote sound environmental education programs; and to promote a continued annual fur harvest using the best tools presently available for that purpose." The NTA was formed in 1959 by small group of Michigan trappers alarmed about a bill proposed in the state legislature that would eliminate the trapping of certain fur-bearing animals. Since that time, the group has consistently opposed all bills introduced in Congress that would ban the steel-jaw leghold trap, as well as numerous restrictions on trapping introduced into many state legislatures. Having suffered few political defeats, the NTA is the strongest protrapping force in American law, and can be credited with almost singlehandly maintaining the lawful use of the leghold trap in most of America.

Address   Membership Secretary, P.O. Box 3667,
            Bloomington, IL 61702
Phone   309-829-2422
Web   nationaltrappers.com

National Wildlife Federation (NWF)

"The mission of the National Wildlife Federation is to educate, inspire, and assist individuals and organizations of diverse cultures to conserve wildlife and other natural resources and to protect the Earth's environment in order to achieve a peaceful, equitable and sustainable future." The NWF was created in 1936 by editorial cartoonist J. N. "Ding" Darling when President Franklin D. Roosevelt convened the first North American Wildlife Conference to stimulate public interest in the management and development of America's natural resources. Founded with the sole purpose of educating the public about the importance of conserving wildlife, the NWF is not opposed to hunting animals, only to eliminating them or depleting their numbers. Its Office of Federal and International Affairs, in Washington, D.C., carries conservation concerns to Congress, government agencies, and the courts to help ensure the development and enforcement of effective conservation policies and laws that protect the conservation of wild species and their habitats. For example, in 1997 a U.S. district court ruling in a case brought by the NWF forced the release of documents proving that the slaughter of wild bison by Montana state officials was illegal; in 2000 the NWF joined Defenders of Wildlife and the Sierra Club in a lawsuit charging several federal agencies with failing to protect panther habitat in Florida; and most recently, the NWF has opposed downgrading the gray wolf from endangered to threatened under the Endangered Species Act.

Address   8925 Leesburg Pike, Vienna, VA 22184
Phone   800-822-9919
Web   nwf.org

People for the Ethical Treatment of Animals (PETA)

PETA was formed in 1981 by Alex Pacheco and current president Ingrid Newkirk. With over 700,000 members and offices in three countries, PETA is one of the largest animal protection organizations in the world. The group focuses its attention on factory farms, laboratory animals, the fur trade, and the entertainment industry, and advocates a clear abolitionist message that animals are not to be "eaten, worn, experimented on, or used for entertainment." The majority of PETA's efforts have always been directed toward activism, education, and public protest, rather than the courts or legislatures. Its primary impact on animal law has been as a watchdog and whistleblower, alerting state and federal authorities to alleged violations of animal protection laws. To take a few of many examples, PETA uncovered abuse of lab animals, resulting in the first arrest and conviction of an animal experimenter on charges of cruelty to animals and the first confiscation of abused lab animals; distributed an undercover video showing a Las Vegas entertainer beating orangutans, resulting in the U.S. Department of the Interior revoking his captive-bred wildlife permit; and conducted an undercover investigation of scabies experiments on dogs and rabbits at Ohio's Wright State University, which led to charges of eighteen violations of the Animal Welfare Act, halting the research. Less active on the legal front, PETA did support both the ICCVAM Authorization Act, which will permanently establish a government committee to review alternatives to animal tests and recommend changes in testing procedures, and the Chimpanzee Health Improvement, Maintenance, and Protection Act, which will establish a system of sanctuaries for government-owned chimpanzees no longer needed in federally funded research protocols. PETA has also sued the University of Oregon to gain access to the proceedings of the University's Animal Care Committee.

Address   501 Front Street, Norfolk, VA 23510
Phone   757-622-7382
Web   peta-online.org

Wildlife Legislative Fund of America (WLFA)
The Wildlife Legislative Fund of America provides direct lobbying and litigation support to protect and advance the interests of hunters, fishermen, trappers, and scientific wildlife management professionals in the courts and in federal and state legislatures. This is accomplished through coalition building, ballot issue campaigning, and legislative and government relations. The WLFA was formed in 1978 in response to an Ohio ballot issue proposing an end to trapping throughout the state. Within the WLFA is the Sportsmen's Legal Defense Fund (SLDF), which provides legal representation for sportsmen involved in lawsuits dealing with outdoor sports. For example, in 1999 the SLDF successfully defended a New Mexico hunter against charges that he violated the state anticruelty law by using a snare to take two deer. The SLDF has also confronted several legal challenges to state "hunter harassment" laws, which make it illegal to disrupt a lawful hunt. Indeed, the WLFA was the prime mover in the late 1980s behind a series of bills that eventually became the Recreational Hunting Safety and Preservation Act, a federal law banning "hunter harassment."

Address   801 Kingsmill Parkway, Columbus, OH 43229
Phone   614-888-4868
Web   wlfa.org

Appendix 2:
Tables of Authorities: Cases

Page numbers on which cases are discussed in this book follow each citation.

FEDERAL CASES

Supreme Court

Babbitt v. Sweet Home Chapter of Communities for a Great Oregon, 515 U.S. 100 (1995); **375–378**, 380.

Baldwin v. Fish and Game Commission, 431 U.S. 288 (1978); 295, 307.

Bennett v. Spear, 520 U.S. 154 (1997); 390.

Church of Lukumi Babalu Aye v. City of Hialeah, 508 U.S. 520 (1993); 186, **187–190**.

[Dred] Scott v. Sanford, 60 U.S. 393 (1857); 23.

Employment Division v. Smith, 494 U.S. 872 (1990); 189.

Geer v. Connecticut, 161 U.S. 519 (1896); 318, 320, 328, 329.

Hunt v. United States, 278 U.S. 96 (1928); 320, 322.

Japan Whaling Association v. American Cetacean Society, 478 U.S. 221 (1986); 45, 61, 353.

Kleppe v. New Mexico, 426 U.S. 529 (1976); 144, 321–323.

Lujan v. Defenders of Wildlife, 504 U.S. 555 (1992); 24, 25, 36, **46–49,** 58, 61.

Marbury v. Madison, 5 U.S. 137 (1803); 10.

Miller v. California, 413 U.S. 15 (1973); 95.

Missouri v. Holland, 252 U.S. 416 (1920); 329.

Robertson v. Seattle Audubon Society, 503 U.S. 429 (1992); 382.

Sentell v. New Orleans & Carroliton Railroad Co., 166 U.S. 698 (1897); 115.

Sierra Club v. Morton, 405 U.S. 727 (1972); **40–45,** 48, 54, 56, 61.

Texas v. Johnson, 491 U.S. 397 (1989); 305.

TVA v. Hill, 437 U.S. 153 (1978); **385–386**.

United States v. The Abby Dodge, 223 U.S. 166 (1912); 328.

United States v. Dion, 476 U.S. 734 (1986); 342, 379.

United States v. Eichmann, 496 U.S. 310 (1990); 305.

Circuit Courts of Appeals

Jones v. Butz, 374 F. Supp. 1284 (S.D.N.Y. 1974), *aff'd*, 419 U.S. 806 (1974); 184, 185.

National Rifle Association v. Kleppe, 425 F. Supp. 1101 (D. D.C. 1976); 334.

Northern Spotted Owl v. Hodel, 716 F. Supp. 479 (W.D. Wash. 1988); 35, 382.

Northern Spotted Owl v. Lujan, 758 F. Supp. 621 (W.D. Wash. 1991); 383.

Oregon Natural Resource Council v. Turner, 863 F. Supp. 1277 (D. Or. 1994); 389.

Palila v. Hawaii Department of Land and Natural Resources (Palila I), 471 F. Supp. 985 (D. Haw. 1979), *aff'd*, 639 F.2d 495 (9th Cir. 1981); 374–376.

Texas Beef Group v. Winfrey, 11 F. Supp. 2d 858 (N.D. Tex. 1998); 201.

United States v. Abeyta, 632 F. Supp. 1301 (D. N.M. 1986); 342.

United States v. McCullagh, 221 F. 288 (D. Kan. 1915); 328.

United States v. Shauver, 214 F. 154 (E.D. Ark. 1914), *appeal dismissed*, 248 U.S. 594 (1919); 328.

United States v. Thirty-Eight Golden Eagles, 649 F. Supp. 269 (D. Nev. 1986), *aff'd*, 829 F.2d 41 (9th Cir. 1987); 342.

FOREIGN CASES

McDonald's Corporation v. Steel, English High Court of Justice, Queen's Bench Division (Q.B. Div'l Ct. 1997); 164.

STATE CASES

Alabama
Jones v. State, 473 So. 2d 1197 (Ala. Crim. App. 1985); 288.

Arizona
State v. Stockton, 333 P.2d 735 (Ariz. 1958); 281.

California
Farm Sanctuary v. Department of Food and Agriculture, 74 Cal. App. 4th 495 (Cal. Ct. App. 1998); 190, 191.

People v. Baniqued, 101 Cal. Rptr. 2d 835 (Cal. Ct. App. 2000); 281.

People v. Speegle, 62 Cal. Rptr. 2d 384 (Cal. Ct. App. 1997); 86–88.

Colorado
People v. Bergen, 883 P.2d 532 (Colo. Ct. App. 1994); 288.

Georgia
Brackett v. State, 236 S.E.2d 689 (Ga. Ct. App. 1977); 281.

Hargrove v. State, 321 S.E.2d 104 (Ga. 1984); 287.

Hawaii
State v. Kaneakua, 597 P.2d 590 (Haw. 1979); 281.

Indiana
Lykins v. State, 726 N.E.2d 1265 (Ind. Ct. App. 2000); 76, 77.

Kansas
Hearn v. City of Overland Park, 772 P.2d 758 (Kan.), *cert. denied,* 493 U.S. 976 (1989); 286.
State v. Claiborne, 505 P.2d 732 (Kan. 1973); 281.
State v. Rodriguez, 8 P.3d 712 (Kan. 2000); 79.

Maryland
State v. Taub, No. 11848–81 (1981), Maryland District Court (unreported case); 52.
Taub v. State, 43 A.2d 819 (Md. 1983); 52.

Massachusetts
Commonwealth v. Higgins, 178 N.E. 536 (Mass. 1931); 29.

Michigan
People v. Cumper, 268 N.W.2d 696 (Mich. Ct. App. 1978); 288.

Minnesota
State v. Miner, 556 N.W.2d 578 (Minn. Ct. App. 1996); 304.

Mississippi
Stephens v. State, 3 So. 458 (Miss. 1888); 29.

Missouri
Missouri v. Stout, 958 S.W.2d 32 (Mo. Ct. App. 1997); 30, 75.
State v. Young, 695 S.W.2d 882 (Mo. 1985); 280.
United Gamefowl Breeders Association v. Nixon, 19 S.W.3d 137 (Mo. 2000); 280, 283.

Nebraska
State v. Schott, 384 N.W.2d 620 (Neb. 1986); 76, 164.

New Mexico
New Mexico v. Cleve, 980 P.2d 23 (N.M. 1999); 81.
State v. Buford, 331 P.2d 1110 (N.M. 1958); 280, 281.

New York
American Society for the Prevention of Cruelty to Animals v. Board of Trustees, 591 N.E.2d 1169 (N.Y. 1992); 474.

North Carolina

State v. Fowler, 205 S.E.2d 740 (N.C. Ct. App. 1974); 75.

Students for the Ethical Treatment of Animals v. Huffines, 399 S.E.2d 340 (N.C. Ct. App. 1991); 475.

Ohio

State v. Anderson, 566 N.E.2d 1224 (Ohio), *cert. denied,* 501 U.S. (1991); 286.

State v. Bryson, 605 N.E.2d 1284 (Ohio Ct. App. 1992); 283.

State v. Gaines, 580 N.E.2d 1158 (Ohio 1990); 288.

State v. Longhorn World Championship Rodeo, Inc., 483 N.E.2d 196 (Ohio Ct. App. 1985); 272.

Oklahoma

In re Initiative Petition No. 365, 9 P.3d 78 (Okla. 2000); 280.

Oregon

People for the Ethical Treatment of Animals v. Institutional Animal Care and Use Committee, 817 P.2d 1299 (Or. 1991); 474.

State v. Albee, 847 P.2d 858 (Or. Ct. App. 1993); 282, 283.

State v. Kittles, No. 93–6346 (1995) (unreported case), *cert. denied,* 936 P.2d 363 (Or. 1997); 85.

Pennsylvania

Commonwealth v. Barnes, 629 A.2d 123 (Pa. 1993); 164.

Commonwealth v. Tapper, 675 A.2d 740 (Pa. Super. Ct. 1996); 30.

Hulsizer v. Labor Day Committee, 718 A.2d 865 (Pa. 1999); 81.

Tennessee

State v. Tabor, 678 S.W.2d 45 (Tenn. 1984); 282.

Texas

Celinski v. State, 911 S.W.2d 177 (Tex. Crim. App. 1995); 30.

Vermont

Animal Legal Defense Fund v. Institutional Animal Care and Use Committee, 616 A.2d 224 (Vt. 1992); 475.

CASES, ALPHABETICAL LISTING

Alaska Fish and Wildlife Federation v. Dunkle, 829 F.2d 933 (9th Cir. 1987), *cert. denied,* 485 U.S. 988 (1988); 333.

Alternatives Research & Development Foundation v. Glickman, 101 F. Supp. 2d 7 (D. D.C. 2000); 456.

United States v. Thirty-Eight Golden Eagles, 649 F. Supp. 269 (D. Nev. 1986), *aff'd*, 829 F.2d 41 (9th Cir. 1987); 342.
United States v. Thomas, 74 F.3d 701 (6th Cir. 1996); 95.
United States v. Todd, 735 F.2d 146 (5th Cir. 1984); 326, 327.
United States v. White, 508 F.2d 453 (8th Cir. 1974); 341.
United States v. Wulff, 758 F.2d 1121 (6th Cir. 1985); 330.

Appendix 3:
Tables of Authorities:
Statutes and Regulations

Page numbers on which statutes and regulations are discussed in this book follow each citation.

FEDERAL LAWS

Administrative Procedure Act, 5 U.S.C. §§ 551–559, 701–706, 801–808; 8.

Airborne Hunting Act, 16 U.S.C. § 742j-l; 290, 340.

Alaska National Interest Lands Conservation Act of 1980, 16 U.S.C. §§ 410hh–410hh-5, 460mm–460mm-4, 539–539e, 3101–3233, and 43 U.S.C. §§ 1631–1642; 418.

Animal Enterprise Protection Act of 1992, 18 U.S.C. § 43; 514–516.

Animal Welfare Act of 1970, 7 U.S.C. §§ 2131–2157; 3, 31, 33, 34, 38, 49, 50, 52, 57–60, 62, 103, 120, 122, 127, 207, 229, 230, 236, 247, 270, 272, 288–290, **441–453,** 454, 455, 468–472, 475, 482, 483, 485, 492, 499, 503, 505, 511–514, 517, 518.

Bald Eagle Protection Act of 1940, 16 U.S.C. §§ 668–668d; 36, 211, 290, **338–343,** 378, 379.

Civil Rights Act of 1964, 45 U.S.C. § 2000e; 19.

Consumer Product Safety Act of 1972, 15 U.S.C. § 2051; 451.

Dolphin Protection Consumer Information Act of 1990, 16 U.S.C. § 1385; 361, 365.

Endangered Species Act of 1973, 16 U.S.C. §§ 1531–1544; 35–37, 46, 211, 212, 290, 341, 348, 358, 362, **369–390,** 399, 405, 406, 408–411.

Endangered Species Conservation Act of 1969, 83 Stat. 275 (repealed 1981); 357, 371.

Endangered Species Preservation Act of 1966, 80 Stat. 926 (repealed 1973); 357, 370, 412.

Executive Order 13112, Invasive Species, President Bill Cinton, February 3, 1999; 424, 425.

FEDERAL REGULATIONS

FEDERAL REGISTER

Animal Welfare; Marine Mammals, 64 Fed. Reg. 35: 8735–8755 (Feb. 23, 1999); 238–240.

Draft Policy on Environmental Enhancement for Nonhuman Primates, 64 Fed. Reg. 38,145–38,150 (July 15, 1999); 63, 243, 505, 506.

Finding on Petitions to Change Status of Grizzly Bear Populations, 63 Fed. Reg. 30,453–30,455 (June 4, 1998); 406.

Import of Polar Bear Trophies from Canada, Final Rule, 64 Fed. Reg. 1529–1538 (Jan. 11, 1999); 396.

Marine Mammals: Incidental Take during Specified Activities, 65 Fed. Reg. 16,828–16,843 (March 30, 2000); 394.

Marine Mammals and Certain Other Regulated Animals; Perimeter Fence Requirements, Final Rule, 64 Fed. Reg. 200: 56,142–56,148 (Oct. 18, 1999); 245.

Migratory Bird Hunting: Regulations Regarding Baiting and Baited Areas, Final Rule, 64 Fed. Reg. 29,799–29,804 (June 3, 1999); 337, 338.

Migratory Bird Hunting: Seasons, Limits, and Shooting Hours, 64 Fed. Reg. 47,421–47,434 (Aug. 31, 1999); 331–333.

Notice of Petition for Rulemaking to Amend the Definition of "Animal" in 9 C.F.R. 1.1, Animal Welfare, 64 Fed. Reg. 18: 4356–4367 (Jan. 28, 1999); 456.

Notice of Updated Policy Regarding Harvest of Migratory Birds in Alaska between March 10 and September 1, 64 Fed. Reg. 47,512–47,515 (Aug. 31, 1999); 333.

Solid Resting Surfaces for Dogs and Cats, Final Rule, 64 Fed. Reg. 75: 19,251–19,254 (April 20, 1999); 122.

Taking of Marine Mammals Incidental to Commercial Fishing Operations, Finding, 64 Fed. Reg. 24,590–24,592 (May 7, 1999); 367.

Use of Bait in Hunting, 60 Fed. Reg. 14,720–14,723 (March 20, 1995); 403.

STATE STATUTES

Anticruelty Laws (complete)

Alabama, Ala. Code § 13A-11-14; 73, 74.

Alaska, Alaska Stat. § 11.61.140; 308.

Arizona, Ariz. Rev. Stat. § 13-2910; 272.

Arkansas, Ark. Code Ann. § 5-62-101; 73, 74.

California, Cal. Penal Code § 1-14-597; 75, 76, 79, 281.

Colorado, Colo. Rev. Stat. § 18-9-201; 75, 79, 272.

Connecticut, Conn. Gen. Stat. § 53-247; 72, 75, 208.

Delaware, Del. Code Ann. tit. 11 § 1325; 74, 75.

Florida, Fla. Stat. Ann. § 46-828.12; 73, 253.

Georgia, Ga. Code Ann. § 16-12-4; 78, 208.
Hawaii, Haw. Rev. Stat. § 37-711-1109; 73, 74, 208.
Idaho, Idaho Code § 25-35-14; 208, 272.
Illinois, 510 Ill. Comp. Stat. 70/3; 75, 79.
Indiana, Ind. Code § 35-46-3.
Iowa, Iowa Code § 717B.2; 74, 75, 208.
Kansas, Kan. Stat. Ann. § 21-4310; 75, 272, 281.
Kentucky, Ky. Rev. Stat. Ann. § 50-525.125.
Louisiana, La. Rev. Stat. Ann. § 14:102.
Maine, Me. Rev. Stat. Ann. tit. 7-739-4011; 72, 73, 75, 253.
Maryland, Md. Code Ann. § 27-59; 75.
Massachusetts, Mass. Gen. Laws § 4-272-77.
Michigan, Mich. Comp. Laws § 28.245; 75, 77, 79, 261.
Minnesota, Minn. Stat. § 343.21; 72, 75, 77, 78, 253.
Mississippi, Miss. Code § 97-41-1; 77.
Missouri, § 578.012; 74, 77, 272.
Montana, Mont. Code Ann. § 45-8-211; 73, 75, 272.
Nebraska, Neb. Rev. Stat. § 28-1001; 261, 272.
Nevada, Nev. Rev. Stat. 574.101; 75, 79.
New Hampshire, N.H. Rev. Stat. Ann. § 644:8; 77.
New Jersey, N.J. Stat. Ann. § 4-22-17; 73.
New Mexico, N.M. Stat. Ann. § 3-18-1; 79, 272.
New York, N.Y. Agriculture and Markets Law § 350; 72, 73, 272.
North Carolina, N.C. Gen. Stat. § 14-360.
North Dakota, N.D. Cent. Code § 36-21-1; 75, 77.
Ohio, Ohio Rev. Code Ann. § 959.13; 75.
Oklahoma, Okla. Stat. tit. 21-1685; 77, 253.
Oregon, Or. Rev. Stat. § 167.315; 78, 272.
Pennsylvania, Pa. Cons. Stat. § 18-511; 75.
Rhode Island, R.I. Gen. Laws § 4-1-2.
South Carolina, S.C. Code Ann. § 47-1-40.
South Dakota, S.D. Codified Laws § 40-1-2.
Tennessee, Tenn. Code Ann. § 39-14-202.
Texas, Tex. Penal Code Ann. § 9-42.09; 75.
Utah, Utah Code Ann. § 76-9-301; 272.
Vermont, Vt. Stat. Ann. tit. 13-352; 72, 253.
Virginia, Va. Code Ann. § 3.1-796.122; 75.
Washington, Wash. Rev. Code § 16.52.205; 75, 272.
West Virginia, W. Va. Code § 61-8-19a; 78, 79.
Wisconsin, Wis. Stat. § 951.02; 75, 78.
Wyoming, Wyo. Stat. Ann. § 6-3-203; 272.

Cockfighting

Alaska, Alaska Stat. § 11.65.145 (animal fighting); 282.

Arizona, Ariz. Rev. Stat. § 13-2910.03–.04; 282.

Colorado, Colo. Rev. Stat. § 18-9-204 (animal fighting); 282.

Delaware, Del. Code Ann. tit. 11-1326 (animal fighting); 279, 282.

Florida, Fla. Stat. Ann. § 828.12 (animal fighting); 282.

Hawaii, Haw. Rev. Stat. § 711-1109(1)(c) (animal fighting); 281, 282.

Idaho, Idaho Code § 25-3506; 282.

Indiana, Ind. Code §§ 35-46-3-8 to 35-46-3-10 (animal fighting); 282.

Iowa, Iowa Code § 725.11 (animal fighting); 282.

Maine, Me. Rev. Stat. Ann. tit. 17-1033 (animal fighting); 282.

Maryland, Md. Code Ann. § 27-59; 282.

Michigan, Mich. Comp. Laws § 28.244 (animal fighting); 282.

Minnesota, Minn. Stat. § 343.31; 282.

Nevada, Nev. Rev. Stat. 574.070 (animal fighting); 282.

New Jersey, N.J. Stat. Ann. § 4.22-24 (animal fighting); 282.

New York, N.Y. Agriculture and Markets Law § 351; 282.

North Carolina, N.C. Gen. Stat. § 14-362; 282.

North Dakota, N.D. Cent. Code § 36-21.1-07; 282.

Pennsylvania, Pa. Cons. Stat. § 18-5511-H.1 (animal fighting); 282.

Rhode Island, R.I. Gen. Laws § 4-1-9; 282.

South Carolina, S.C. Code Ann. § 16-17-650; 282.

Texas, Tex. Penal Code Ann. § 42.09 (animal fighting); 282.

Vermont, Vt. Stat. Ann. tit. 13-352 (animal fighting); 279.

Wisconsin, Wis. Stat. § 951.08; 282.

Wyoming, Wyo. Stat. Ann. § 6-3-203(c)(ii)(iv); 282.

Dissection

California, Cal. Educ. Code § 32255 (pupil with moral objection to dissection); 519, 520.

Florida, Fla. Stat. Ann. § 233.0674 (education, biological experiments on living subjects); 520.

Illinois, 105 Ill. Comp. Stat. 112/1 (Dissection Alternative Act); 520.

New York, N.Y. Educ. Law § 17 S 809.4 (dissection of animals); 520.

Pennsylvania, Pa. Cons. Stat. § 15-1523 (pupil's right of refusal; animal dissection); 520, 521.

Rhode Island, R.I. Gen. Laws § 16-22-20 (animal dissection and vivisection, right to refuse); 520.

Dogfighting

Alabama, Ala. Code § 3-1-29; 286.

Alaska, Alaska Stat. § 11.65.145 (animal fighting); 286, 287.

Arizona, Ariz. Rev. Stat. § 13-2910.01, 02; 286.

Colorado, Colo. Rev. Stat. § 18-9-204 (animal fighting); 286, 287.

Connecticut, Conn. Gen. Stat. § 53-247; 287.

Florida, Fla. Stat. Ann. § 828.12 (animal fighting); 287.

Georgia, Ga. Code Ann. § 16-12-37; 287.

Hawaii, Haw. Rev. Stat. § 711-1109.3; 286.

Iowa, Iowa Code § 725.11; 286.

Idaho, Idaho Code § 25-3507; 286.

Kentucky, Ky. Rev. Stat. Ann. § 525.125, 130 (animal fighting); 287.

Louisiana, La. Rev. Stat. Ann. § 14:102.5; 287.

Maine, Me. Rev. Stat. Ann. tit. 17-1033 (animal fighting); 287.

Massachusetts, Mass. Gen. Laws ch. 272-88; 279, 287.

Michigan, Mich. Comp. Laws § 28.244 (animal fighting); ; 287.

Minnesota, Minn. Stat. § 343.31; 287.

Mississippi, Miss. Code Ann. § 97-41-19; 286.

Montana, Mont. Code Ann. § 45-8-210 (animal fighting); 282, 286, 287.

Nevada, Nev. Rev. Stat. 574.070; 287.

New Hampshire, § 644: 8-9; 287.

New Jersey, N.J. Stat. Ann. § 4.22-24 (animal fighting); 287.

New Mexico, N.M. Stat. Ann. § 30-18-9; 286.

New York, N.Y. Agriculture and Markets Law § 351; 287.

North Dakota, N.D. Cent. Code § 36-21.1-07; 287.

Oklahoma, Okla. Stat. tit. 21-1696; 286.

Pennsylvania, Pa. Cons. Stat. § 18-5511-H.1 (animal fighting); 287.

Rhode Island, R.I. Gen. Laws § 4-1-9; 287.

Vermont, Vt. Stat. Ann. tit. 13-352 (animal fighting); 286.

Virginia, Va. Code Ann. § 3.1-796.125; 286, 287.

West Virginia, W. Va. Code § 61-8-19a (animal fighting); 286.

Wisconsin, Wis. Stat. § 951.08; 286, 287.

Wyoming, Wyo. Stat. Ann. §§ 6-3-203(c)(ii)(iv); 287.

Euthanasia in Animal Control Facilities

Arizona, Ariz. Rev. Stat. § 11-1021; 108.

Delaware, Del. Code Ann. tit. 3-8001; 109.

Florida, Fla. Stat. Ann. § 46-828.058; 108.

Georgia, Ga. Code Ann. § 4-11-5.1; 108.

Kansas, Kan. Stat. Ann. § 47-1718; 109.

Louisiana, La. Rev. Stat. Ann. § 40-1041; 110.

Maine, Me. Rev. Stat. Ann. § 17-1042; 108.

Maryland, Md. Code Ann. § 27-59A; 108.

Massachusetts, Mass. Gen. Laws ch. 20-151A; 108.

New Jersey, N.J. Stat. Ann. § 4:22-19; 109.

Ohio, Ohio Rev. Code § 4729.532; 109.

Oklahoma, Okla. Stat. tit. 4-502; 109.

Oregon, Or. Rev. Stat. § 48-609.405; 108.
Rhode Island, R.I. Gen. Laws § 4-19-11.1.
South Carolina, S.C. Code Ann. § 47-3-420; 108, 109.
Tennessee, Tenn. Code Ann. § 44-17-303; 109.
West Virginia, W. Va. Code § 30-10A-7; 110.

Police Dog Laws
Alabama, Ala. Code § 13A-5-6; 13A-11-15; 124, 125.
Arizona, Ariz. Rev. Stat. § 13-707;
Connecticut, Conn. Gen. Stat. § 53-247; 124.
Delaware, Del. Code Ann. tit. 11, 4206; 125.
Massachusetts, Mass. Gen. Laws. ch. 272, 77A; 124.
Michigan, Mich. Comp. Laws § 750.50c; 125.
New Hampshire, N.H. Rev. Stat. Ann. § 625:9; 125.
North Carolina, N.C. Gen. Stat. § 15A-1340.17; 125.
Ohio, Ohio Rev. Code Ann. § 2921.321; 125.
Oklahoma, Okla. Stat. tit. 21, 649.2; 125.
Rhode Island, R.I. Gen. Laws § 4-1-30; 124.
Tennessee, Tenn. Code Ann. § 39-14-105; 124.
Utah, Utah Code Ann. § 76-3-204.
Virginia, Va. Code Ann. § 18.2-144.1; 125.

Sexual Contact with Animals
Arkansas, Ark. Code Ann. § 5-14-122; 93.
Delaware, Del. Code Ann. tit. 11 § 777; 92, 94.
Georgia, Ga. Code Ann. § 16-6-6; 93.
Idaho, Idaho Code § 18-6605; 93.
Kansas, Kan. Stat. Ann. § 21-3505; 93, 94.
Louisiana, La. Rev. Stat. Ann. § 89; 93.
Maryland, Md. Code Ann. art. 27 § 554; 93.
Massachusetts, Mass. Gen. Laws ch. 272-34; 92, 93.
Michigan, Mich. Comp. Laws § 750.158; 92, 93.
Minnesota, Minn. Stat. § 609.294; 93.
Mississippi, Miss. Code Ann. § 97-29-59; 93.
Montana, Mont. Code Ann. § 45-5-505; 92, 93, 94.
Nebraska, Neb. Rev. Stat. § 28-1010; 93.
New York, N.Y. Penal Law § 130.20; 93.
North Carolina, N.C. Gen. Stat. § 14-177; 92.
North Dakota, N.D. Cent. Code § 12.1-20-12; 93.
Oklahoma, Okla. Stat. tit. 21 § 886; 92, 93.
Pennsylvania, Pa. Cons. Stat. § 18.3129; 93.
Rhode Island, R.I. Gen. Laws § 11-10-1; 92, 93.
South Carolina, S.C. Code Ann. § 16-15-120; 92, 93.

Miscellaneous

Alabama, Ala. Code § 2-15-110 (handling of livestock); 275.

Maine, Me. Rev. Stat. Ann. tit. 7-3972.1(F) (unlawful use of animals), § 7-3981 (transportation of animals); 130, 131, 275.

Michigan, Mich. Comp. Laws § 28.246 (animal confined on railroad cars); 275.

Minnesota, Minn. Stat. § 343.24 (cruelty in transportation); 275.

Ohio, Ohio Rev. Code Ann. tit. 23 § 2307.81 (disparagement of perishable agricultural or aquacultural food products); 201.

Ohio, Ohio Rev. Code Ann. § 959.20 (ban on certain devices to stimulate animals); 272.

Rhode Island, R.I. Gen. Laws § 4-20-1 (rodeo animals and livestock); 271, 272.

Wisconsin, Wis. Stat. § 29.879 (humane, adequate and sanitary care of wild animals); 208.

STATE REGULATIONS

Carriage Rides

Atlanta, Georgia, Code of Ordinances, Animal-Drawn Vehicles, § 162-151; 133.

Massachusetts, Department of Public Safety, Regulations for the Operation of Horse Drawn Carriages, 520 C.M.R. 13.00; 133, 134.

San Antonio, Texas, Code of Ordinances, Horse-Drawn Carriages, § 33-462; 133.

Hunting and Trapping Regulations

See World Wide Web, State Wildlife Agencies.
http://www.wildlife.state.co.us/about/StateAgencyWebSites.htm

Racing Commission Rules

See the states' Racing Commission Rule Books.

Alabama, Greyhound Care, § 2-2, 4; 255.

Arizona, Greyhound Care, §§ R19-2-324–331; 255–258.

California, Use of Whips, § 1688; Racing Soundness Examination, § 1846; 260, 261.

Colorado, Veterinary Practice, § 5.208; Use of Whips, § 7.740; 261, 262.

Florida, Veterinarians Inspect Stables, § 61D-6.009(h); 262.

Idaho, Safety, § 060.06; 261.

Iowa, Facilities Responsibilities, Stalls, § 491-10.2(1); Jockey, Conduct, § 491-10.5(2)j(4); 261, 262.

Kansas, Post to Finish, Disabled Horse, § 112-7-22(n); 260.

Standards in Animal Control Facilities and Pet Stores

Miscellaneous

Bibliography

BOOKS

American Law Institute. 1985. *Model Penal Code*. Philadelphia, PA: American Law Institute.

American Meat Institute. 2000. *Meat and Poultry Facts*. Washington, DC: AMI Publications.

Animal Welfare Institute. 1990. *Animals and Their Legal Rights*. 4th ed. Washington, DC: Animal Welfare Institute.

Balcombe, Jonathan. 2000. *The Use of Animals in Higher Education*. Washington, DC: Humane Society Press.

Bean, Michael J., and Melanie J. Rowland. 1997. *The Evolution of National Wildlife Law*. 3d ed. Westport, CT: Praeger.

Beirne, Piers. 1998. "Bestiality." In *Encyclopedia of Animal Rights and Animal Welfare*. Edited by Marc Bekoff. Westport, CT: Greenwood Press.

Bekoff, Marc, ed. 1998. *Encyclopedia of Animal Rights and Animal Welfare*. Westport, CT: Greenwood Press.

Bentham, Jeremy. [1780] 1963. *Introduction to the Principles of Morals and Legislation*. New York: Oxford University Press.

Bernard, Claude. [1865] 1980. *An Introduction to the Study of Experimental Medicine*. Translated by Henry Copley Green. Birmingham, AL: Classics of Medicine Library.

Bestrup, Craig. 1997. *Disposable Animals: Ending the Tragedy of Throwaway Pets*. Leander, TX: Camino Bay Books.

Blackstone, William. 2001. *Commentaries on the Laws of England*. London: Cavendish (London: Callaghan & Co., 1872).

Blum, Deborah. 1994. *The Monkey Wars*. New York: Oxford University Press.

Branigan, Cynthia A. 1997. *The Reign of the Greyhound*. New York: Howell Book House.

Brooman, Simon, and Debbie Legge. 1997. *Law Relating to Animals*. London: Cavendish.

Budiansky, Stephen. 1997. *The Nature of Horses*. London: Weidenfeld and Nicolson.

565

Bunting, Greta. 1997. *The Horse: The Most Abused Domestic Animal.* Toronto: University of Toronto Press.

Busch, Briton. 1985. *The War Against the Seals: A History of the North American Seal Fishery.* Kingston, OT: McGill-Queens University Press.

Caras, Roger A. 1985. *Harper's Illustrated Handbook of Dogs.* New York: HarperPerrenial.

Clemen, Rudolf Alexander. 1966. *The American Livestock and Meat Industry.* New York: Johnson Reprint Corporation (New York: Ronald Press, 1923).

Croke, Vicki. 1997. *The Modern Ark: The Story of Zoos.* New York: Scribner.

Curtis, Patricia. 1984. *The Animal Shelter.* New York: E. P. Dutton.

Dale, Edward E. 1960. *The Range Cattle Industry.* Norman: University of Oklahoma Press.

Darwin, Charles. [1871] 1950. *The Descent of Man and Selection in Relation to Sex.* New York: P. F. Collier.

Donahue, Debra L. 1998. *Conservation and the Law.* Santa Barbara, CA: ABC-CLIO.

Eisnitz, Gail. 1997. *Slaughterhouse.* Amherst, NY: Prometheus Books.

Fano, Alix. 1997. *Lethal Laws.* New York: Zed Books.

Favre, David S., and Murray Loring. 1983. *Animal Law.* Westport, CT: Quorum Books.

Feinberg, Joel. 1973. *Social Philosophy.* Englewood Cliffs, NJ: Prentice-Hall.

Fekety, Sally. 1998. "Shelters." Pp. 315–317 in *Encyclopedia of Animal Rights and Animal Welfare.* Edited by Marc Bekoff. Westport, CT: Greenwood Press.

Finsen, Lawrence, and Susan Finsen. 1994. *The Animal Rights Movement in America: From Compassion to Respect.* New York: Twayne.

Fisher, James. 1967. *Zoos of the World.* New York: Natural History Press.

Fleig, Dieter. 1996. *The History of the Fighting Dogs.* Translated by William Charlton. Neptune City, NJ: T. F. H. Publications.

Francione, Gary L. 1995. *Animals, Property, and the Law.* Philadelphia: Temple University Press.

Frasch, Pamela D., et al. 2000. *Animal Law.* Durham, NC: Carolina Academic Press.

Friend, Ted. 1998. "Circuses and Circus Elephants." In *Encyclopedia of Animal Rights and Animal Welfare.* Edited by Marc Bekoff. Westport, CT: Greenwood Press.

Garner, Robert. 1998. *Political Animals: Animal Protection Politics in Britain and the United States.* New York: St. Martin's.

Gewirth, Alan. 1992. "Rights." Pp. 1103–1107 in *Encyclopedia of Ethics.* Vol. 2. Edited by Lawrence Becker. New York: Garland.

Gillespie, James R. 1995. *Modern Livestock & Poultry Production.* 5th ed. Albany, NY: Delmar.

Grandin, Temple. 2000. "Handling and Welfare of Livestock in Slaughter Plants." Pp. 409–439 in *Livestock Handling and Transport*. 2d ed. Edited by Temple Grandin. New York: CABI.

Hodgson, Robert G. 1945. *The Mink Book*. 2d ed. Toronto: Fur Trade Journal of Canada.

Hohfeld, Wesley. 1920. *Fundamental Legal Conceptions as Applied in Judicial Reasoning*. New Haven, CT: Yale University Press.

Johnson, William M. 1990. *The Rose-Tinted Menagerie*. London: Heretic Books.

Kent, James. 1894. *Commentaries on American Law*. St. Paul, MN: West.

Krause, Tom. 1984. *National Trapping Association Trapping Handbook*. Bloomington, IL: National Trappers Association.

Kreger, Michael D. 1998. "Zoos, History of Zoos" Pp. 369–371 in *Encyclopedia of Animal Rights and Animal Welfare*. Edited by Marc Bekoff. Westport, CT: Greenwood Press.

Lawrence, Elizabeth Atwood. 1982. *Rodeo: An Anthropologist Looks at the Wild and the Tame*. Knoxville: University of Tennessee Press.

Leavitt, Emily Stewart, and Diane Halverson. 1990. "The Evolution of Anti-Cruelty Laws in the United States." In *Animals and Their Legal Rights*. 4th ed. Washington, DC: Animal Welfare Institute, 1990.

———. 1990. "Humane Slaughter Laws." In *Animals and Their Legal Rights*. 4th ed. Washington, DC: Animal Welfare Institute.

Liss, Cathy. 1998. "Trapping." Pp. 338–340 in *Encyclopedia of Animal Rights and Animal Welfare*. Edited by Marc Bekoff. Westport, CT: Greenwood Press.

Lopez, Barry. 1986. *Arctic Dreams*. New York: Scribner.

Lund, Thomas. 1980. *American Wildlife Law*. Berkeley and Los Angeles: University of California Press.

Lyman, Howard. 1998. *Mad Cowboy: Plain Truth from the Rancher Who Won't Eat Meat*. New York: Simon & Schuster.

Lynch, Wayne. 1993. *Bears: Monarchs of the Northern Wilderness*. Seattle: The Mountaineers.

Mason, Jim, and Peter Singer. 1990. *Animal Factories*. New York: Harmony Books.

McCrea, Roswell C. 1969. *The Humane Movement*. New York: McGrath (New York: Columbia University Press, 1910).

McNamee, Thomas. 1984. *The Grizzly Bear*. New York: McGraw-Hill.

Mench, Joy A. 1998. "Chickens." Pp. 101–105 in *Encyclopedia of Animal Rights and Animal Welfare*. Edited by Marc Bekoff. Westport, CT: Greenwood Press.

Mullan, Bob, and Gary Marvin. 1999. *Zoo Culture*. 2d ed. Urbana: University of Illinois Press.

Musgrave, Ruth, and Mary Anne Stein. 1993. *State Wildlife Laws Handbook*. Rockeville, MD: Government Institutes.

Musgrave, Ruth, et al. 1998. *Federal Wildlife Laws Handbook*. Rockeville, MD: Government Institutes.

National Research Council. 1996. *Guide for the Care and Use of Laboratory Animals*. Washington, DC: National Academy Press.

Nilsson, Greta. 1990. "Birds." In *Animals and Their Legal Rights*. 4th ed. Washington, DC: Animal Welfare Institute.

Ogden, Tom. 1993. *Two Hundred Years of the American Circus*. New York: Facts On File.

Olsen, Stanley J. 1985. *Origins of the Domestic Dog*. Tucson: University of Arizona Press.

Orlans, F. Barbara. 1993. *In the Name of Science*. New York: Oxford University Press.

Orlans, F. Barbara, et al. 1998. *The Human Use of Animals*. New York: Oxford University Press.

Pacheco, Alex, and Anna Francione. 1985. "The Silver Spring Monkeys." In *In Defense of Animals*. Edited by Peter Singer. New York: Blackwell.

Phelps, Norman. 2000. *Body Count: The Death Toll in America's War on Wildlife*. New York: The Fund for Animals.

Randolph, Mary. 1995. *Dog Law*. 2d ed. Berkeley, CA: Nolo Press.

Ransom, Jay Ellis. 1981. *Complete Field Guide to North American Wildlife*. New York: Harper & Row.

Rhodes, Richard. 1997. *Deadly Feasts: Tracking the Secrets of a Terrifying New Plague*. New York: Simon & Schuster.

Rollin, Bernard. 1995. *Farm Animal Welfare*. Ames: University of Iowa Press.

Romans, John R., et al. 1994. *The Meat We Eat*. 13th ed. Danville, IL: Interstate.

Rudacille, Deborah. 2000. *The Scalpel and the Butterfly: The War between Animal Research and Animal Protection*. New York: Farrar, Straus and Giroux.

Rupke, Nicolaas A., ed. 1987. *Vivisection in Historical Perspective*. London: Routledge.

Scott, George Ryley. 1983. *The History of Cockfighting*. London: Triplegate.

Servheen, Christopher, Stephen Herrero, and Bernard Peyton, comps. 1999. *Bears. Status Survey and Conservation Action Plan*. Gland, Switzerland: IUCN/SSC.

Sherry, Clifford. 1998. *Endangered Species*. Santa Barbara, CA: ABC-CLIO.

Sinclair, Upton. 1988. *The Jungle*. Urbana: University of Illinois Press (New York: Doubleday, 1906).

Smith, Bruce W. 1981. *Nature's Jewels: A History of Mink Farming in the United States*. Brookfield, WI: National Board of Fur Farm Organizations.

Stanfield, Leila. 1998. "Bear Baiting." Pp. 86–88 in *Encyclopedia of Animal*

Rights and Animal Welfare. Edited by Marc Bekoff. Westport, CT: Greenwood Press.

Stevens, Christine. 1990. "Dogs." In *Animals and Their Legal Rights.* 4th ed. Washington, DC: Animal Welfare Institute.

———. 1990. "Laboratory Animals." In *Animals and Their Legal Rights.* 4th ed. Washington, DC: Animal Welfare Institute.

———. 1990. "Marine Mammals." In *Animals and Their Legal Rights.* 4th ed. Washington, DC: Animal Welfare Institute.

Stone, Christopher. 1974. *Should Trees Have Standing?* Los Altos, CA: William Kaufman.

Toby, Milton C., and Karen L. Perch. 1999. *Understanding Equine Law.* Lexington, KY: The Blood-Horse.

Twyne, Pearl, and Valerie Stanley. 1990. "Horses." In *Animals and Their Legal Rights.* 4th ed. Washington, DC: Animal Welfare Institute.

Vialles, Noel. 1994. *Animal to Edible.* Translated by J. A. Underwood. London: Cambridge University Press, 1994.

Wellman, Carl. 1992. "Concepts of Rights." Pp. 1100–1103 in *Encyclopedia of Ethics.* Vol. 2. Edited by Lawrence Becker. New York: Garland.

Welsh, Heidi J. 1990. *Animal Testing and Consumer Products.* Washington, DC: Investor Responsibility Research Center.

White, Richard. 1994. "Animals and Enterprise." In *The Oxford History of the American West.* New York: Oxford University Press.

Wise, Stephen. 2000. *Rattling the Cage: Towards Legal Rights for Animals.* Cambridge, MA: Perseus Books.

Wolfson, David J. 1999. *Beyond the Law: Agribusiness and the Systematic Abuse of Animals Raised for Food or Food Production.* Watkins Glen, NY: Farm Sanctuary.

Wooden, Wayne S., and Gavin Ehringer. 1996. *Rodeo in America.* Lawrence: University Press of Kansas.

ARTICLES, GUIDELINES, AND REPORTS

"ALF Action." *The Animals' Agenda,* bimonthly continuing feature.

American Veterinary Medical Association. "1993 Report of the AVMA Panel on Euthanasia." *Journal of the American Veterinary Medical Association* 202 (1993): 229–249.

Animal Welfare Committee, Fur Commission USA. *Standard Guidelines for the Operation of Mink and Fox Farms.* September 1997.

Aulrich, Richard J. "Michigan's Fur Bearing Industry." *Michigan State University Extension Special Report,* SR 499201, 28 July 1998.

Bauer, Donald C. "Reconciling Polar Bear Protection under United States Laws and the International Agreement for the Conservation of Polar Bears." *Animal Law* 2 (1996): 9–100.

Bilger, Burkhard. "Enter the Chicken: On the Bayou, Cockfighting Remains Undefeated." *Harper's Magazine* 298, no. 1786 (March 1999): 48–57.

"BSE Watch." *The Animals' Agenda,* bimonthly continuing feature.

Carmel, Krystyna M. "The Equine Liability Acts: A Discussion of Those in Existence and Suggestions for a Model Act." *Kentucky Law Journal* 83 (1994): 157–196.

Church, Ann. "Legislative Progress for Animals." *The Animals' Agenda* 17, no. 2 (March/April 1997): 22–26.

Church, Jill Howard. "The Business of Animal Research." *The Animals' Agenda* 17, no. 4 (July/August 1997): 30–32.

Cohen, Henry. "The Legality of the Agriculture Department's Exclusion of Rats and Mice from Coverage under the Animal Welfare Act." *St. Louis University Law Journal* 31 (1987): 543–549.

Collins, Earl K. "The History of Fur Farming." *The Black Fox Magazine* (January 1937): 31–33, 66–67.

Crecente, Brian D. "Fashionable Brutality: Dogfighting on the Rise." *APBnews.com,* 17 July 2000.

Department of Justice, Criminal Division. *Report to Congress on the Extent and Effects of Domestic and International Terrorism on Animal Enterprises.* 1993.

Detweiler, Rachelle. "Animals Spared by HPV Concession." *The Animals' Agenda* 20, no. 1 (January/February 2000): 11–12.

Donald, Rhonda Lucas. "The No-Kill Controversy." *Shelter Sense* (September 1991): 3–6.

Eichstaedt, Richard Kirk. "'Save the Whales' v. 'Save the Makah': The Makah and the Struggle for Native Whaling." *Animal Law* 4 (1998): 145–172.

Eidinger, Joan. "Nowhere to Run: Dog Racing in Decline." *The Animals' Agenda* 20, no. 5 (September/October 2000): 30–35.

Favre, David, and Vivien Tsang. "The Development of Anti-Cruelty Laws During the 1800's." *Detroit College of Law Review* 1 (1993): 1–35.

Fink, Richard J. "The National Wildlife Refuges: Theory, Practice, and Prospect." *The Harvard Environmental Law Review* 18 (1994): 1–136.

Fox, Camilla. "Trapping on National Wildlife Refuges." Animal Protection Institute publication, 1999.

Frasch, Pamela D., et al. "State Animal Anti-Cruelty Statutes: An Overview." *Animal Law* 5 (1999): 69–80.

Glitzenstein, Eric, and John Fritschie. "The Forest Service's Bait and Switch: A Case Study on Bear Baiting and the Service's Struggle to Adopt a Reasoned Policy on a Controversial Hunting Practice within the National Forests." *Animal Law* 1 (1995): 45–77.

Goodwin, J. P. "Opening the Cages: Freedom from Fur Farms." *The Animals' Agenda* 17, no. 1 (January/February 1997): 22–23.

Grandin, Temple, and Joe Regenstein. "Religious Slaughter and Animal Welfare." *Meat Focus International* (March 1994): 115–123.

Handy, Geoffrey L. "Local Animal Control Management." *MIS Report* 25, no. 9 (September 1993): 1–20.

———. "Handling Animal Collectors." *Shelter Sense* (May–June 1994): 3–10.

Hessler, Katherine. "Where Do We Draw the Line between Harassment and Free Speech?: An Analysis of Hunter Harassment Law." *Animal Law* 3 (1997): 129–162.

Holzer, Henry Mark. "Contradictions Will Out: Animal Rights vs. Animal Sacrifice in the Supreme Court." *Animal Law* 1 (1995): 83–108.

Hubert, Cynthia. "Seven-Year Term for Dog Fighting." *Sacramento Bee*, 26 July 1999.

Katme, A. M. "An Up-To-Date Assessment of the Muslim Method of Slaughter." *Humane Slaughter of Animals for Food*, Universities Federation for Animal Welfare (1987): 37–46.

Kaufman, Marc. "Cracks in the Egg Industry." *Washington Post*, 4 April 2000, at A1.

Kelch, Thomas G. "Toward A Non-Property Status for Animals." *New York University Environmental Law Journal* 6 (1998): 531–585.

Kniaz, Laura G. "Animal Liberation and the Law: Animals Board the Underground Railroad." *Buffalo Law Review* 43 (1995): 765–834.

Lake, Aaron. "1998 Legislative Review." *Animal Law* 5 (1999): 89–112.

———. "1999 Legislative Review." *Animal Law* 6 (2000): 151–178.

Larson, Peggy W. "Rodeo Is Cruel Entertainment." *Pace University Environmental Law Review* 16 (1998): 115–123.

Lockwood, Randall. "The Psychology of Animal Collectors." *Trends* 9, no. 6 (1993/1994): 18–21.

Maggitti, Phil. "Reining in the Carriage Trade." *The Animals' Agenda* 15, no. 4 (July/August 1995): 16–19.

Markarian, Michael. "Migratory Massacre." *The Animals' Agenda* 17, no. 4 (July/August 1997): 22–27.

Marquis, Joshua. "The *Kittles* Case and Its Aftermath." *Animal Law* 2 (1996): 197–201.

Mendelson, Joseph. "Should Animals Have Standing? A Review of Standing under the Animal Welfare Act." *Boston College Environmental Affairs Law Review* 24 (1997): 795–820.

Moretti, Laura A. "The Struggle to Save the Last of America's Misfits." *The Animals' Agenda* 18, no. 6 (November/December 1998): 22–27.

National Greyhound Association Board of Directors. "NGA Inspection Guidelines." National Greyhound Association, 1993, amended 2000.

National Institutes of Health. *Institutional Animal Care and Use Committee Guidebook.* NIH publication no. 92–3415, 1992.

National Research Council. *Guide for the Care and Use of Laboratory Animals.* National Academy Press, 1996.

NOVA, "The Brain Eater." Production of WGBH Boston, PBS affiliate. Broadcast transcript, February 1998.

Patronek, Gary J. "Hoarding of Animals: An Under-Recognized Public Health Problem in a Difficult-to-Study Population." *Public Health Reports* 114 (1999): 81–87.

Pitt, Kenneth P. "The Wild Free-Roaming Horses and Burros Act: A Western Melodrama." *Environmental Law* 15 (1984): 504–531.

Professional Rodeo Cowboys Association. "Official Rodeo Rules." November 1998.

Provance, Jim. "Drugs: Racing's Dark Horse." *Toledo Blade,* 28 January 2001.

Rowan, Andrew. "Ethical Review and the Animal Care and Use Committee." *Hasting Center Report* Special Supplement (May/June 1990): 19–24.

Samuels, David. "Going to the Dogs." *Harper's Magazine* 298, no. 1785 (February 1999): 52–63.

Scheiner, Craig Ian. "Statutes with Four Legs to Stand On?: An Examination of 'Cruelty to Police Dog' Laws." *Animal Law* 5 (1999): 177–225.

Steneck, Nicholas H. "Role of Institutional Animal Care and Use Committees in Monitoring Research." *Ethics & Behavior* 7 (1997): 173–184.

Stewart, Kristin L. "Dolphin-Safe Tuna: The Tide is Changing." *Animal Law* 4 (1998): 111–137.

Sturla Kim. "The Role of Animal Shelters." *The Animals' Agenda* 17, no. 2 (March/April 1997): 40–46.

———. "Fixing the Feline." *The Animals' Agenda* 17, no. 5 (September/October 1997): 33–36.

Sunstein, Cass. "Standing for Animals (with Notes on Animal Rights)." *UCLA Law Review* 47 (2000): 1333–1368.

Weisberg, Lisa. "Legislative Proposals Protecting Animals in Entertainment." *Pace University Environmental Law Review* 16 (1998): 125–132.

Weiss, Rick. "Animal Regulations to Expand." *Washington Post,* 3 October 2000, at A23.

———. "Bill Rider Would Nullify Animal Rights Legal Victory." *Washington Post,* 11 October 2000, at A29.

Weyhrauch, Bruce B. "Waterfowl and Lead Shot." *Environmental Law* 16 (1986): 883–934.

Wise, Steven. "The Legal Thinghood of Nonhuman Animals." *Boston College Environmental Affairs Law Review* 23 (1996): 471–546.

Wolfson, David J. "McLibel." *Animal Law* 5 (1999): 21–60.

WORLD WIDE WEB

American Association for Horsemanship Safety,
   http://www.law.utexas.edu/dawson/index.htm.
American Greyhound Council, http://www.agcouncil.com.
Animal and Plant Health Inspection Service, USDA, http://www.
   aphis.usda.gov.
   Animal Care, http://www.aphis.gov/ac/
   Horse Protection Act, www.aphis.usda.gov/oa/pubs/fshpa.html
   Horse Protection Strategic Plan, http://www. aphis.usda.gov/oa/
   pubs/hpa.html.
Animal Extremist/Ecoterror Crimes, http://www.furcommission.com/
   attack.
Animal Liberation Front, http://www.animalliberationfront.com/
Animal Protection Institute, http://www.api4animals.org.
   Circus Campaign, http://www.api4animals.org/doc.asp?ID/61.
Aquatic Nuisance Species Task Force, http://ANSTaskForce.gov.
Bans on Animal Acts in the United States, http://circuses.com.
Bureau of Land Management, National Wild Horse and Burro Program,
   http://wildhorseandburro.blm.gov/.
Center for Wildlife Law, http://ipl.unm.edu/cwl.
Charles River Laboratories, http://www.criver.com.
Coalition to Abolish the Fur Trade, http://www.banfur.com.
Cockfighting in Oklahoma, http://www.tulsaworld.com/archive.
Complete Guide to Horse Racing,
   http://www.equineinfo.com/horseracing.htm.
Defenders of Wildlife, http://www.defenders.org/index.html.
Dog Owner's Guide, Dogs and the Law, http://www.canismajor.
   com/dog/laws1.html.
Doris Day Animal League, http://www.ddal.org/index.html.
Federal Register, http://access.gpo.gov/su_docs.
Findlaw, State Resources, http://www.findlaw.com/11stategov.
Food and Drug Administration, http://www.fda.gov.
Food Safety and Inspection Service, http://www.fsis.usda.gov.
Fund for Animals, http://www.fund.org.
Fur Commission USA, http://www.furcommission.com.
Fur Information Council of America, http://www.fur.org.
The Fur Trade, http://www.worldanimal.net/fur-trade.html.
Government Printing Office homepage, http://www.access.gpo.gov/
   su_docs.
Greyhound Network News, http://www.greyhounds.org/gnn.
Greyhound Protection League, http://www.greyhounds.org.
Humane Farming Association, http://www.hfa.org.

Humane Society of the United States, http://www.hsus.org.
  Animal Fighting, http://www.hsus.org/current/
  Animal Sheltering, http://www.hsus.org/programs/companion/
    animal_shelters.html
  Circuses and the Law, http://www.hsus.org/current/circus_law.
    html
  Facts about Greyhound Racing, http://www.hsus.org/whatnew/
    sadog_facts.html
  Tennessee Walking Horse Abuse, http://www.hsus.org/info/
    twhfacts.html.
Hunt Saboteurs, http://www.enviroweb.org/HSA.
International Species Information System, http://www.worldzoo.org.
International Whaling Commission, http://ourworld.compuserve.com/
  homepages/iwcoffice/iwc.htm.
The Jockey Club, http://home.jockeyclub.com.
KBR's World of Wild Horses and Burros, http://www.kbrhorse.
  net/whb/blmhorse.html.
Kosher Slaughter, http://www.whit.org/shofar/html/kosher.html.
Lexis-Nexis Academic Universe, Legal Research, http://web.
  lexis-nexis.com/universe.
Mad Cow Disease Homepage, http://mad-cow.org/.
National Agricultural Statistics Service, http://www.usda.gov/nass.
National Greyhound Association, http://nga.jc.net.
National Institutes of Health, http://www.nih.gov.
  Office of Laboratory Animal Welfare, http://grants.nih.gov/grants/
    olaw/olaw.htm.
National Trappers Association, http://www.nationaltrappers.com.
People for the Ethical Treatment of Animals, Media Center—Factsheets,
  Animals in Entertainment, http://www.peta.org/mc/facts.
Professional Rodeo Cowboys Association, http://www.prorodeo.com.
Public Health Service, http://www.dhhs.gov/phs.
  Policy on Humane Care and Use of Laboratory Animals, http://grants.
    nih.gov/grants/olaw/references/phspol.htm.
Puppy Mills, http://www.puppymills.com.
Santería, http://religioustolerance.org/santeri.htm.
Sea Shepherd Conservation Society, http://www.seashepherd.org.
State Anticruelty Laws, http://www.law.utexas.edu/dawson/cruelty/
  cruelty.htm.
State Primate Regulations, http://www.monkeyzone.com/regulati.htm.
State Wildlife Agencies, http://wildlife.state.co.us/about/StateAgency
  WebSites.htm.
Thomas Legislative Information, http://thomas.loc.gov.
United Poultry Concerns, http://www.upc-online.org/.

U.S. Fish and Wildlife Service, http://www.fws.gov.
  Division of Endangered Species, http://endangered.fws.gov
  Grizzly Bear Recovery, http://www.r6.fws.gov/endspp/grizzly/
  index.htm
  Grizzly Bear Recovery in the Bitterroot Ecosystem: Summary of the
  Final Environmental Impact Statement, http://www.r6.fws.
  gov/endspp/grizzly/press_release3102000.htm
  Migratory Bird Management, http://migratorybirds.fws.gov
  Wildlife Refuges, http://refuges.fws.gov.
Whaling and Fishing, Chapter 4, Hypertext book by Peter J. Bryant,
  http://darwin.bio.uci.edu/~sustain/bio65/lec04/b65lec04.htm.
World Animal Net, International Animal Protection Laws,
  http://www.worldanimal.net/legislinks.html.
Zebra Mussel, http://www.science.wayne.edu/~jram/zmussel.htm.

Index

About the Author

Jordan Curnutt is associate professor of Philosophy and director of Religious Studies at St. Cloud State University in St. Cloud, Minnesota. Professor Curnutt teaches courses in social and moral philosophy and in religion, including introductory and advanced ethics, philosophy of law, multicultural philosophy, world religions, and the religions of Asia. He has also taught courses in the Honors program studying Eastern philosophy and Native American and African traditional religions. Additionally, he has been engaged in Interactive Television teaching and has taught courses at the Minnesota Correctional Facility–St. Cloud.

Professor Curnutt's current research interests concern animal ethics and law, and the philosophy and study of religion, especially religious epistemology and religious pluralism. His publications include papers on the morality of hunting, the moral basis for vegetarianism, the justification of religious belief, and the book *Business Ethics* (ABC-CLIO, 1999), coauthored with John Dienhart. Professor Curnutt is a member of the Institutional Animal Care and Use Committee at SCSU.